ACT ASSESSMENT® for BRAINIACS

Mark Alan Stewart

THOMSON
PETERSON'S™

Australia • Canada • Mexico • Singapore • Spain • United Kingdom • United States

About The Thomson Corporation and Peterson's

The Thomson Corporation, with 2002 revenues of US$7.8 billion, is a global leader in providing integrated information solutions to business and professional customers. The Corporation's common shares are listed on the Toronto and New York stock exchanges (TSX: TOC; NYSE: TOC). Its learning businesses and brands serve the needs of individuals, learning institutions, corporations, and government agencies with products and services for both traditional and distributed learning. Peterson's (www.petersons.com) is a leading provider of education information and advice, with books and online resources focusing on education search, test preparation, and financial aid. Its Web site offers searchable databases and interactive tools for contacting educational institutions, online practice tests and instruction, and planning tools for securing financial aid. Peterson's serves 110 million education consumers annually.

For more information, contact Peterson's, 2000 Lenox Drive, Lawrenceville, NJ 08648; 800-338-3282; or find us on the World Wide Web at www.petersons.com/about.

Credits:
"'I Am Christina Rossetti,'" by Anthony H. Harrison, *Humanities*, Vol. 14, No. 4 (July/August 1993), pp. 33–37. Published by The National Endowment for the Humanities.

"The American Renaissance," by James S. Turner, *Humanities*, Vol. 13, No. 2 (March/April 1992). Published by The National Endowment for the Humanities.

"The Artful Encounter," by Richard Wendorf, *Humanities*, Vol. 14, No. 4 (July/August 1993), pp. 9–12. Published by The National Endowment for the Humanities.

ISBN 0-7689-1344-6

Printed in the United States of America

10 9 8 7 6 5 4 3 2 1 05 04 03

First Edition

CONTENTS

PART V: THE ACT SCIENCE REASONING TEST

PART VI: THE BRAiNiAC CHALLENGE

Every year, more than 2 million high-school students take the ACT Assessment. But only a small percentage have what it takes to get the scores needed for admission to America's top colleges and universities. This book is for any student who wants to join their ranks and has the raw brainpower needed for the task.

"ACT Assessment" is the official name of the exam, but we're going to refer to it simply as ACT from now on.

WHAT IS AN ACT BRAiNiAC?

There's no single litmus test for an ACT Brainiac. But you can probably count yourself among the Brainiac brotherhood or sisterhood if any of the following describes you:

- You're a curve-raiser in school and know you don't need much instruction and guidance on basics.
- You get As and Bs in school (gym class doesn't count), and you scored high on the PSAT.
- You've already worked your way through one of those big, thick ACT books that covers everything, and you want to supplement your study and practice with more advanced materials in order to gain an additional edge on your ACT competition.
- You're a repeat ACT test-taker whose scores were okay the first time around, but you need even higher scores to get into your top-choice schools or to win that scholarship you need.

WHAT MAKES *ACT FOR BRAiNiACS* SPECIAL?

Simple: It's designed for the brainiest students—the ones just described. Sure, *ACT for Brainiacs* briefly covers all the ACT basics, just to make sure you're up to speed. But the book doesn't dwell on basics. Instead, it cuts to the chase, moving quickly ahead to more advanced concepts and to the toughest and most complex types of questions that the test-makers might throw at you.

Part I gives you an overview of the Brainiac approach. Lesson 1 covers principles of ACT preparation, unveils selected pacing plans for achieving ACT scores worthy of a Brainiac, and highlights eight broad test-taking strategies. Lesson 2 briefly covers the format of the ACT and what each of the four tests covers and then, begins to distinguish the tough questions from the average ones that you've already mastered.

Parts II–V are where the challenge begins. You'll focus on each of the four ACT tests—English, Mathematics, Reading, and Science Reasoning—one per part. For each test, you'll learn how to tackle the most complex and advanced questions and how to apply the most advanced strategies. Following each lesson is a Brain Teaser, where you'll apply what you just learned to some really tough practice questions.

Part VI contains more ACT-style questions for you to practice what you learned in Parts I–V. Just as with the practice questions in Parts II–V, you'll find nothing but toughies in Part VI—the kinds of questions that only the top test-takers can handle and that set them apart from all the rest.

Finally, this book assumes that you weren't looking for a comprehensive ACT review when you bought it—you were looking for advanced preparation for every last point you could score. But, just in case you have a momentary lapse in braininess or need a gentle reminder, visit www.petersons.com or www.act.org for the basics, like registration information. You probably know about these procedures already—after all, you're a Brainiac—but they're there if you need them.

ABOUT THE ICONS IN THIS BOOK

You'll see five icons throughout *The Brainiac Series.* These symbols serve as guideposts for the student:

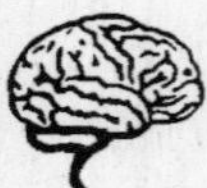

The SUPER-BRAINIAC icon
Signals a particularly sophisticated strategy or concept.

The STRATEGY icon
Signals a *general* procedural tip or strategy.

The BTW icon
"BTW" stands for *by the way.* This icon signals related information Brainiacs would probably want to know to broaden their knowledge of a particular topic.

The HEADS UP icon
Alerts Brainiacs to a common blunder, testing trap, or trick that might trip up even the brainiest Brainiac.

X-REF

The CROSS-REFERENCE icon
Signals a reference to a concept or other information located elsewhere in the book.

PART I

BRAINSTORMING THE ACT

LESSON 1
How Do Brainiacs Gear Up for the ACT?

This lesson lays the groundwork for your approach to the ACT. Here, you'll learn about:

- Critical principles of preparation for the test
- Pacing strategies that match your personal goals and abilities
- When to use (and not to use) a calculator during the Mathematics Test
- Eight general strategies you need to know up front

BRAiNiACS KNOW WHERE TO FOCUS

The ACT actually consists of four tests:

1. An *English* Test
2. A *Mathematics* Test
3. A *Reading* Test
4. A *Science Reasoning* Test

Brainiacs don't spin their ACT-prep wheels by spending more time than they need to on each of the ACT tests or by rehashing what they already know. And they know to focus on simulated testing without being fixated on practice test scores.

EMPHASIZE CERTAIN TESTING AREAS

In gearing up for the ACT, the non-Brainiac tends to focus on strengths while neglecting weaknesses. He tells himself: "I can't handle this tough stuff right now; so I'll either face it later or skip it altogether and hope to make some lucky guesses on the exam." Brainiacs know that they can't hide any of their ACT scores from college admissions officials and are disciplined enough to devote more time to remedying their weaknesses than to basking in their strengths.

KEEP PRACTICE SCORES IN PERSPECTIVE

If you're like most Brainiacs, you've set your sights on one or two particular colleges or universities, and you have a good idea what ACT scores you'll need for admission. However, don't psyche yourself out by obsessing over your

practice-test scores. Gloating over high scores can lead to complacency and overconfidence, while brooding over low scores can result in discouragement and self-doubt. Either way, you're sabotaging yourself. The bottom line: Try not to concern yourself with the test scores themselves, but rather with the constructive steps you can take between now and exam day to improve these scores.

BRAiNiACS KEEP THEIR ATTITUDE AND EGO IN CHECK

If you're like most Brainiacs, you've always been a curve-raiser, and you've probably got a sizable ego (okay, let's call it "healthy.") But if you're not careful, your ego could easily come between you and your highest possible ACT scores. You are only human, and a healthy dose of humility will serve you well during the days and weeks before the ACT.

OVERCONFIDENCE ABOUT YOUR ACT PROWESS

Okay, so in school, you score nothing but straight As, you make the honor roll every term, and your classmates just voted you "Biggest Brainiac." Think you can just "wing it" on the ACT and still manage to crush the competition? Think again. You might be the brainiest fish in your little pond, but there are thousands of other Brainiacs out there who are taking the ACT very, very seriously and who would be more than happy to bump you down the ACT-scoring curve. Enough said?

YOUR EXPECTATIONS FOR YOURSELF

You'd love perfect ACT scores, wouldn't you? Each time the test is administered, a few Brainiacs do score a "straight 36" across all four tests. Will you be next to do so? Probably not. Your innate fallibility, not to mention the statistical odds, are stacked heavily against your fulfilling this ACT fantasy. So relax, follow a sensible study and practice schedule, and have faith that on exam day you'll perform as well as you can reasonably expect. Surrender whatever stubborn insistence on ACT perfection you're harboring, and, paradoxically, you'll probably score higher as a result.

YOUR EXPECTATIONS FOR ACT EXPERTS AND OTHERS

Even some of the best test-takers invite disappointing ACT scores by relying entirely on the "sage" advice of experts. Be realistic about the benefits you can garner from this book—or from any ACT product or service. It's ultimately up to you to make the ACT-prep effort you need to perform your personal best on exam day.

A more common mistake among Brainiacs is wrongly assuming that they already know it all and should just ignore any advice from others. When it comes to the ACT, foolish pride has been the undoing of many a Brainiac! Don't tune others out. Remember: Fresh ideas and valuable insights can come from any source—not just from experts, but also from your "less intelligent" friends and classmates.

BRAiNiACS KNOW HOW TO BEAT ACT ANXIETY

You may have never had a serious problem with test anxiety. But this doesn't mean you're immune, especially considering the importance of the ACT. In fact, you're probably under a lot more pressure than the non-Brainiac to "ace" the ACT. You may even be feeling pressure to excel. With expectations so high, don't be surprised if you start feeling anxious during your practice tests and as exam day draws near.

Test anxiety, whether experienced before or during a test, can hinder your performance. So, it's a good idea to try to keep a lid on it (without expecting to eliminate it entirely). If you're starting to feel the heat, try the following anxiety-busting techniques:

- After taking one or two timed practice tests, if the running clock still interferes with your concentration or makes you anxious, condition yourself by practicing individual questions under a strict 1-minute limit per question. Don't spend any more or less than 1 minute on any question. Use a minute-timer with an alarm. Spend 20 minutes each day (20 questions) for a week on this exercise.

- Join (or form) a group of test-takers to openly discuss your anxieties. Invite suggestions from your peers about how to reduce your fears. Try taking practice questions in front of the group; your peers may recognize some manifestations of your anxiety—a certain posture, a nervous habit, or tension in specific muscles—that you didn't notice. Then, make a conscious effort to eliminate those symptoms. You might discover that if you eliminate a key symptom, the underlying test anxiety will subside.
- Before taking practice tests, try simple relaxation techniques: stretching, quieting your thoughts, breathing deeply, or whatever else works for you. Some people find a quick burst of vigorous exercise to be highly effective.
- Reward yourself for good behavior. For example, if you're easily distracted during your practice tests, promise yourself a pizza if you can get through an entire test section without looking up from the paper.
- You'll be anxious about the ACT only if you're actually thinking about it. So, during the weeks that you're gearing up for the test, keep yourself busy with your regular activities. Try not to discuss the ACT with others except during planned study sessions or classes.

BRAiNiACS KNOW WHEN THEY'VE PEAKED

Preparing for the ACT is a bit like training for an athletic event. You need to familiarize yourself with the event, learn to be comfortable with it, and build up your skill and endurance. At some point—hopefully around exam day—your motivation, interest, and performance will peak. Sure, it takes some time and effort to get comfortable with the exam; to correct poor test-taking habits; to bone up on whatever math, grammar, and science you may have forgotten; to develop an instinct for recognizing wrong-answer choices; and to find your optimal pace. But there's a point beyond which additional study and practice confer little or no additional benefit. Don't drag out the process by starting several months in advance or by postponing the ACT to give yourself more time than you really need for preparation.

BRAiNiACS KNOW THEIR OPTIMAL PACE

Each of your four ACT test scores—English, Math Reasoning, Reading, and Science Reasoning—will be based on the number of questions you answer correctly. While the brainiest of Brainiacs might be capable of tackling nearly every available question within a test's time limit, a borderline Brainiac may need to make random guesses on some of the tougher questions.

The following tables will help you determine your optimal strategy, which depends on your aptitude or ambition for each ACT test. Referring to each table, determine the percentage of all other test-takers you hope to beat, (your "percentile rank"), and then, note the approximate number of questions you need to answer correctly to attain your goal. As a rule of thumb, you should plan to randomly answer about *half* the number of questions that you cannot answer correctly and still attain your percentile goal. Keep in mind: Your goal might be higher for one test than for another, depending on where your natural abilities lie.

English Test (75 Questions, 45 minutes):

To rank in the 99th percentile, you need 72 correct answers.

To rank in the 90th percentile, you need 64 correct answers.

To rank in the 80th percentile, you need 59 correct answers.

To rank in the 70th percentile, you need 54 correct answers.

Mathematics Test (60 Questions, 60 minutes):

To rank in the 99th percentile, you need 57 correct answers.

To rank in the 90th percentile, you need 50 correct answers.

To rank in the 80th percentile, you need 44 correct answers.

To rank in the 70th percentile, you need 40 correct answers.

Reading Test (40 Questions, 35 minutes):

To rank in the 99th percentile, you need 38 correct answers.

To rank in the 90th percentile, you need 34 correct answers.

To rank in the 80th percentile, you need 31 correct answers.

To rank in the 70th percentile, you need 29 correct answers.

Science Reasoning Test (40 Questions, 35 minutes):

To rank in the 99th percentile, you need 38 correct answers.

To rank in the 90th percentile, you need 34 correct answers.

To rank in the 80th percentile, you need 31 correct answers.

To rank in the 70th percentile, you need 29 correct answers.

X-REF **You'll examine the ACT scoring system in detail during lesson 2.**

BRAiNiACS USE A CALCULATOR SPARINGLY DURING THE MATH TEST

According to the testing service, ACT test-takers who use a calculator during the test score slightly higher as a group than those who don't. This fact should not surprise you. After all, using a calculator can help ensure the accuracy of any calculation. In fact, using a calculator is arguably more important for Brainiacs than for other test-takers. Why? The average test-taker will miss many math questions due to errors in *reasoning* (or lack of reasoning). But Brainiacs won't, by virtue of their superior reasoning powers. The kinds of errors Brainiacs are most likely to make are careless computational mistakes—and no Brainiac wants that to happen.

To make sure that your calculator turns out to be your ACT ally rather than your nemesis, follow these points of advice:

1. Use your calculator as a tool to check your work, not as a crutch. No ACT math question *requires* the use of a calculator. (The ACT is designed as a *reasoning* test, not as a number-crunching drill.) So, try to perform every computation using your brain. Then, use your calculator to verify the answers you're not 100 percent comfortable with.
2. Use a calculator during practice testing. Get a feel for the calculations you're comfortable performing without it and the ones you think you'd better check with the calculator—just to be safe.

BRAiNiACS UNDERSTAND ACT STRATEGIES

Here are some basic test-taking strategies that apply to all four ACT tests. What you'll find here is common-sense advice for guessing, pacing yourself, and tracking your answers during the tests. Even if you've read these strategies elsewhere, it's a good idea to reinforce them in your mind. Besides, even Brainiacs should expect to pick up at least a few fresh insights and ideas here.

EIGHT GENERAL STRATEGIES

1. "Educated" guesswork can boost your score.

The ACT scoring system won't penalize you for incorrect responses. If you can eliminate just *one* incorrect choice, you're better off when making a random guess among the remaining choices. Of course, the more choices you can eliminate, the better your odds. But the point is that you should always try to eliminate at least one choice before answering each question.

On the SAT (the other standardized test for college admission), a fractional point is deducted for each incorrect response. The purpose of the penalty is to eliminate the statistical advantage of random guesswork. But the ACT doesn't follow suit, although neither scoring system is inherently fairer than the other.

2. If you're not sure what the correct answer choice is, don't dwell on it . . . move on.

If you can't figure out the correct answer, don't obsess over it. People under pressure are especially prone to this tendency. Your time is better spent on questions you haven't considered yet. Even if you've answered every other question, get away from the one that's stumping you and check your work on others you weren't sure about—or, if you are taking the Math test, go back and check your calculations.

3. Start with the types of questions you can answer most quickly.

It makes sense to attack the easier questions first, just in case you run out of time. After all, every question is worth the same: one point. Since easier questions require less time than tougher ones, try to identify and answer the easier questions first (without sacrificing accuracy) before handling the tougher ones.

4. Use a watch to keep yourself on track.

To make sure you stay at your proper pace, keep track of the time. There will probably be a clock in the testing room, but bring a watch anyway.

Try using a watch with hands. At the start of each timed section, set the minute hand to either "3" (for the 45-minute English Test) or "5" (for the 35-minute Reading or Science Reasoning Test). During any test, you will know your time has elapsed when the hands reach 12. A quick glance at your watch will tell you if you need to pick up the pace.

5. Mark your answers in groups.

It's both time-consuming and easy to lose your place when you move back and forth between test booklet and answer sheet. Instead, try marking answers in groups. For example, if you're working with a set of 10 reading questions, all based on the same passage, attempt to answer each question in the group, and circle your answer choices in the test booklet. Then, after you've finished all 10 questions, transfer your 10 answers to the answer sheet. This way you're making only one trip to the answer sheet to fill in those ovals.

The Math Test is the only one in which questions don't come in groups. But does this mean you should abandon this strategy for the Math Test? No. Just answer a certain number of math questions at a time (perhaps five) before transcribing your answers to the answer sheet.

6. Circle your answers in your test booklet.

Always circle your answer choice in your test booklet as well as fill it in on your answer sheet (but don't circle any other choice). Why? What if you skip a certain question but forget to skip it on your answer sheet? Or, what if you select choice (B) but inadvertently fill in choice (C) on your answer sheet? (Either could happen to an absent-minded Brainiac.) Circling answers in your test booklet will ensure that you can track the error and make changes, if needed.

7. Mark questions you want to come back to.

On any test section, there are bound to be at least a few questions of which you're not 100 percent sure. Mark these questions (for example, with a large question mark) so you can return to them later if you have time. You might even make shorthand notes to remind yourself later why you're unsure of your answer and why another answer choice might be the correct one.

8. Don't leave any question unanswered on your answer sheet.

Remember, you are not penalized for incorrect responses on the ACT. So if you must make a random guess, be sure to bubble-in one of the answer choices for that question. You've got nothing to lose, and your odds of earning credit for the question will improve infinitely—from 0 to either 20 or 25 percent.

Each English, Reading, and Science Reasoning question includes four answer choices—so your odds of making a correct random guess are 25 percent. Each Math question includes five answer choices—so your odds of making a correct random guess are 20 percent in the Math section.

LESSON 2
What to Expect of the ACT

This lesson will give you a brief overview of the test itself. Here, you'll learn about:

- The abilities measured by the ACT
- The structure of each of the four tests
- The scoring of the tests
- The types of questions

Most of what you'll find in Lesson 2 is basic information, not strictly for Brainiacs. But all of it is "need-to-know" information, so pay close attention anyway.

ABILITIES MEASURED BY THE ACT

The ACT consists of *four distinct tests*, each with its own focus. The order in which the four tests are presented is always the same:

1. *English* Test (75 questions, 45 minutes)
2. *Mathematics* Test (60 questions, 60 minutes)
3. *Reading* Test (40 questions, 35 minutes)
4. *Science Reasoning* Test (40 questions, 35 minutes)

The total testing time for the entire ACT is 2 hours, 55 minutes—not counting brief breaks between sections. But, as you can see, the total number of questions per test, as well as time limit, varies among the four tests.

THE ENGLISH TEST (75 QUESTIONS, 45 MINUTES)

The *English Test* is designed to measure your ability to recognize effective and ineffective writing and to remedy specific writing problems. For this test, you'll need a firm grasp of the conventions of standard written English and of so-called "rhetorical" skills (the appropriate and effective expression and organization of ideas). The number of questions covering each of the various writing skills, or elements, is always about the same. Here's the breakdown, with a brief description of each element (numbers are approximate):

Elements of usage and mechanics

- Punctuation (10 questions)
- Grammar and Usage (12 questions)
- Sentence Structure (18 questions)

Elements relating to rhetorical skills

- Strategy (12 questions)
- Organization (11 questions)
- Style (12 questions)

There are five writing passages, each accompanied by 15 questions that test the various elements. (All of the elements are tested within each passage.)

THE MATHEMATICS TEST (60 QUESTIONS, 60 MINUTES)

The *Mathematics Test* is designed to measure your understanding of basic math concepts typically covered through the beginning of twelfth grade. These include the six areas listed below. The number of questions covered in each area is always about the same. Here's the breakdown, along with a brief description of each area (numbers are approximate):

Pre-Algebra (14 questions)

- Applying the four basic arithmetic operations
- Fractions, percent, ratio, and proportions
- Decimal numbers, place value, and scientific notation
- Integers, number signs, and ordering numbers by value
- Prime numbers, factors, and divisibility
- Basic descriptive statistics (mean, median, and mode)
- Counting techniques (permutations and combinations) and basic probability
- Interpretation of graphical data (charts and graphs)
- Matrices

Elementary Algebra (10 questions)

- Solving systems of linear equations by substitution
- Simplifying and factoring algebraic expressions
- Properties of exponents and roots
- Solving factorable quadratic equations

Intermediate Algebra (9 questions)

- Applying the quadratic formula
- Complex numbers
- Algebraic problems involving inequalities and absolute value
- Functions, including inverse and logarithmic functions
- Progressions and patterns (of a series of numbers or other terms)

Coordinate Geometry (9 questions)

- Defining and graphing points and lines on the coordinate plane
- The distance and midpoint formulas
- Equations of curved figures ("conic sections") and their graphs

Plane Geometry (14 questions)

- Properties and relationships involving parallel and perpendicular lines
- Properties of triangles, quadrilaterals, and other polygons
- The Pythagorean theorem and special properties of right, isosceles, and equilateral triangles
- Properties of a circle
- Applications involving three-dimensional figures (including cubes, other rectangular solids, and right cylinders)

Trigonometry (4 questions)

- Definitions and properties of trigonometric functions
- Trigonometric identities
- Solving trigonometric equations
- Applying trigonometric functions to right triangles
- Graphing trigonometric functions

THE READING TEST (40 QUESTIONS, 35 MINUTES)

The *Reading Test* is designed to measure your ability to understand a reading passage and to draw reasonable inferences from it. You will see four reading passages on the test, each one accompanied by 10 questions. Each passage is drawn from one of the four broad categories listed below.

- One *Prose Fiction* passage (10 questions)
- One *Social Studies* passage (10 questions)
- One *Humanities* passage (10 questions)
- One *Natural Sciences* passage (10 questions)

What you'll encounter in ACT reading passages is similar to what college freshmen find in their texts—in terms of both subject matter and reading level. Here are just some of the academic areas that are fair game for an ACT reading passage based on the four categories above (these are not comprehensive lists):

- *Prose Fiction:* short stories and excerpts from short stories and novels
- *Social Studies:* history, economics, sociology, political science, psychology
- *Humanities:* art, film, language, literary criticism, philosophy
- *Natural Sciences:* astronomy, biology, geology, physics, technology

The test-makers don't specify particular question types for the Reading Test. However, based on analysis of previously administered Reading Tests, the following types of questions are the most common:

- *Simple detail questions*—Can you understand detail in the context of the passage?
- *Recap questions*—Do you understand a large portion of the passage or the passage as a whole?
- *Restatement questions*—Do you understand specific ideas the author is trying to convey?
- *Inference questions*—Do you recognize what the passage implies, or infers, but does not state explicitly?

X-REF

These four aren't the only question types you might encounter on the Reading Test. Later in this book, we'll examine not only the common types listed above, but also less common, more advanced question types.

THE SCIENCE REASONING TEST (40 QUESTIONS, 35 MINUTES)

The *Science Reasoning Test* is designed to measure your ability to interpret, analyze, and evaluate scientific information from various fields, such as biology, chemistry, the earth and space sciences, and physics. You don't need advanced knowledge of any specific field to handle science reasoning questions. However, you *might* need knowledge of the basics you learned in introductory high-school course work to handle a few of the questions.

The Science Reasoning test is organized into seven sets of scientific information, each one accompanied by several questions. Each of the seven sets is cast in one of three formats, listed here along with the approximate number of questions in each format:

- *Data Representation (15 questions).* This format presents scientific information in textual as well as visual forms, such as graphs, scatter plots, and tables. Data representation questions gauge your ability to read, interpret, and draw conclusions from the graphical data.
- *Research Summaries (18 questions).* This format provides an account of one or more scientific experiments. Research summary questions test your ability to understand or critique the design of the experiment(s) and to interpret their results.
- *Conflicting Viewpoints (7 questions).* This format presents two or more conflicting hypotheses or viewpoints, each based on the same premises or data. Conflicting viewpoints questions measure your ability to understand, compare, and evaluate the hypotheses or viewpoints.

Here's the breakdown of a typical Science Reasoning Test. Keep in mind: We've only presented you with one possibility; the sequence of sets by format and the number of questions per set can vary. Notice that the Research Summary format can also accommodate graphical data and questions about interpreting that data:

- *Set 1 (5 questions):* Data Representation
- *Set 2 (6 questions):* Research Summaries
- *Set 3 (6 questions):* Research Summaries
- *Set 4 (5 questions):* Data Representation
- *Set 5 (7 questions):* Conflicting Viewpoints
- *Set 6 (6 questions):* Research Summaries
- *Set 7 (5 questions):* Data Representation

YOUR ACT SCORES AND SUBSCORES

The ACT testing service produces a dizzying array of scores for each ACT test taken—well over a dozen altogether—that can hurt even a Brainiac's brain! How can this be, given that the ACT contains only four tests? In this section, you'll learn the answer to this question.

YOUR SCORES FOR EACH TEST AND YOUR "COMPOSITE" SCORE

For each of your four ACT tests—English, Math Reasoning, Reading, and Science Reasoning—the testing service will generate three scores for the test *as a whole*:

1. **Raw Score.** This score is simply the number of questions you answer correctly (1 point for each correct answer).
2. **Scale score.** The scoring system converts each raw score to a scale score from 1-36, which are the scores that are reported to you and the schools you've designated. (Converting raw scores to scale scores adjusts for slight variations in overall difficulty level from test to test, in case you were wondering why they're used.) Scale scores compare your performance with everybody who has taken the test—whether this year, last year, or ten years ago. In theory, the skill level required to score, for example, a 30 today, is the same as it was, and will remain the same.
3. **Percentile score ("rank").** Based on your scale score, the scoring system then determines your percentile score (or rank). Percentile scores range from 0-99 and tell you how your ACT performance compares to all other test-takers. A percentile score of 60, for example, means that out of every 100 test-takers, you performed better than 60. You will see your percentile scores on your score report, but they're not sent to your designated schools. (All the schools will see are your scale scores.)

The testing system will also generate your *composite* scale score and, based on it, your percentile rank. Your composite score is simply the average of your four scale scores.

The five scale scores just described are the ones in which schools are most interested; they'll use these scores to compare you with other applicants.

BENCHMARK ACT SCORES FOR BRAiNiACS

During lesson 1, you examined various pacing plans for different percentile-rank goals. Here's a table that includes some of the data from lesson 1 and shows you how percentile benchmarks correspond to scale scores. The table includes benchmarks only for the 50th percentile rank and higher, with the assumption that your Brainiac brain will score at least as high as the "perfectly average" test-taker.

In this table, score conversions are approximate, based on several previously administered ACT tests. Conversions for your particular test might differ slightly. So, use this table to get a feel for how raw scores translate to scale and percentile scores.

English Test

Raw Score (out of 75)	*Scale Score (1–36)*	*Percentile Rank*
72	33	99
64	28	90
59	25	80
54	23	70
49	21	60
46	20	50

Mathematics Test

Raw Score (out of 60)	*Scale Score (1–36)*	*Percentile Rank*
57	32	99
50	28	90
44	25	80
40	23	70
36	21	60
31	19	50

Reading Test

Raw Score (out of 40)	*Scale Score (1–36)*	*Percentile Rank*
38	35	99
34	30	90
31	26	80
29	24	70
26	22	60
24	21	50

Science Reasoning

Raw Score (out of 40)	*Scale Score (1–36)*	*Percentile Rank*
38	32	99
34	27	90
31	25	80
29	23	70
25	21	60
23	20	50

Did you notice that, for the Mathematics Test, raw scores as a percentage of the total number of questions convert to higher scale scores than they do for the other three tests? That's because math questions each include five answer choices, compared to four for the other tests. Simply put, more choices result in more incorrect answers.

YOUR ACT "SUBSCORES"

As if you haven't looked at enough scores already, for specific areas covered by the English, Mathematics, and Reading Tests, the scoring system will also generate raw, scale, and percentile *subscores* (each scale subscore ranges from 1–18). Here are the various subscore areas for these three tests (there are no subscore areas for the Science Reasoning Test):

Test	*Subscore Areas*
English	Usage/Mechanics Rhetorical Skills
Mathematics	Pre-Algebra/Elementary Algebra Intermediate Algebra/Coordinate Geometry Plane Geometry/Trigonometry
Reading	Social Studies/Sciences Arts/Literature
Science Reasoning	(No Subscore Areas)

Subscores are also reported to the schools. So, if you're a trigonometry dunce, you can't hide this fact behind your brilliant performance in the other sub-areas of the Math Reasoning Test. The moral is clear: You'd better be prepared in every area; otherwise, be prepared for a demotion from Brainiac!

TEST DIRECTIONS AND EXAMPLE QUESTIONS

In this final section of lesson 2, take a quick glance at the directions for each of the four tests along with typical questions for each test (with explanatory answers)—one easier than average, the other tougher than average.

THE ENGLISH TEST

Here are test directions that are similar to what you will see at the beginning of the English Test:

> **Directions:** This test consists of six passages in which particular words or phrases are underlined and numbered. Alongside the passage, you will see alternative words and phrases that could be substituted for the underlined part. Select the alternative that expresses the idea most clearly and correctly or that best fits the style and tone of the entire passage. If the original version is best, select "No Change."
>
> The test also includes questions about entire paragraphs and the passage as a whole. A boxed number identifies these questions.
>
> After you select the correct answer for each question, mark the oval corresponding to the correct answer on your answer sheet.

Here's a brief excerpt from a sample English passage (and believe us, it's *much* shorter than the ones on the exam).

Regeneration: A Natural Miracle

Urodeles, a kind of vertebrate that <u>include</u> (1) such small, lizard-like creatures as newts and salamanders, have an enviable ability few other animals enjoy. They can regenerate arms, legs, and other body parts injured or destroyed by accidents or <u>by those who prey on them.</u> (2)

Now, look at two ACT-style questions (along with explanations) about this passage. As with every ACT English question, you are asked here to choose the correct answer from the four choices—labeled either (A), (B), (C), and (D) or (F), (G), (H), and (J). This first question is pretty easy; the featured rule of grammar is a simple one, and the best answer choice is easy to distinguish from the others. Only a small percentage of test-takers would answer this question incorrectly.

Q **1.** (A) NO CHANGE
(B) includes
(C) comprise
(D) numbers

A **The correct answer is (B).** The only reasonable choices are (A) and (B). Neither choice (C) nor choice (D) makes any sense in context. The subject of the verb *include* is the pronoun *that*, which can be either singular or plural. To tell which it is, refer to its antecedent, *kind*. Since *kind* is singular, so is *that*. Hence, the singular verb *includes* is needed.

Now, here's a more difficult English question. To analyze it, you need to make a judgment call between the best choice and the "runner up" choice. What's more, this question involves not only a rule of grammar but also two separate rhetorical issues. A higher percentage of test-takers would respond incorrectly to this question.

Q **2.** (F) NO CHANGE
(G) by animals who prey on them
(H) predatory animals
(J) these vertebrates' predators

A **The correct answer is (H).** The original version includes one minor problem: It isn't clear to which noun the indefinite pronoun "those" refers. The three alternatives, choices (G), (H), and (J), each remedy this problem. Of these three choices, choice (J) is easiest to eliminate because it is awkward and confusing. Choices (G) and (H) are both clear in meaning and grammatically correct. (The preposition "by" is optional; you can achieve proper parallelism between the two phrases separated by the word "or" either with or without this word.) Of these two remaining choices, choice (H) is more concise and is therefore preferable to choice (G).

THE MATHEMATICS TEST

Here are test directions that are similar to what you will see at the beginning of the Mathematics Test:

Directions: Solve each problem; then, on your answer sheet, mark the oval corresponding to the correct answer.

Be careful not to spend too much time on any one question. Instead, solve as many problems as possible, and then use the remaining time to return to those questions you were unable to answer the first time around.

You may use a calculator on any problem in this test. However, some problems can best be solved without the use of a calculator.

Note: Unless otherwise stated, you can assume that:

1. Diagrams that accompany problems are not necessarily drawn to scale.
2. All figures lie in the same plane.
3. The word "line" refers to a straight line (and lines that appear straight are straight).
4. The word "average" refers to arithmetic mean.

Every ACT math question will ask you to solve a mathematical problem, choosing the correct answer from the five choices—labeled either (A), (B), (C), (D), and (E) or (F), (G), (H), (J), and (K). Here are two sample questions, along with explanations. This first problem is easy to understand—no formulas or tricky math is needed. Most test-takers would answer this question correctly.

Q **1.** Village A's population, which is currently 6,800, is decreasing at a rate of 120 each year. Village B's population, which is currently 4,200, is increasing at a rate of 80 each year. At these rates, in how many years will the population of the two villages be equal?

(A) 9
(B) 11
(C) 13
(D) 14
(E) 16

A **The correct answer is (C).** One way to solve this problem is to subtract 120 from A's population while adding 80 to B's population—again and again until the two are equal—keeping track of the number of times you perform these simultaneous operations. (You'll find that number to be 13.) But there's a faster way to solve the problem that also helps you avoid computation errors. The difference between the two populations is currently 2,600 (6,800 − 4,200). Each year, that gap closes by 200 (120 + 80). So, you can simply divide 2,600 by 200 to determine the number of years it would take for the gap to close completely. That's easy math for you, Brainiac: 2,600 ÷ 200 = 13.

Now, here's a more difficult math question. You need to analyze each of three statements (numbered with Roman numerals), which makes the question more time consuming. It's also relatively complex. You need to understand rules involving algebraic inequalities and negative numbers and apply these rules repeatedly to different scenarios. What's more, the best approach to solving the problem is anything but obvious. Most test-takers would respond incorrectly to this question.

Q **2.** If $p > q$ and $rs < 0$, which of the following is (are) true for all non-zero integers p and q?

I. $\frac{ps}{r} > \frac{qr}{s}$

II. $p - \frac{r}{s} > q + \frac{r}{s}$

III. $prs < qrs$

(F) I only
(G) II only
(H) I and II only
(J) II and III only
(K) I, II, and III

A **The correct answer is (J).** First, look at the two statements (II and III) that are always true:

II. Given $rs < 0$, either r or s (but not both) is negative. Hence, the fraction $\frac{r}{s}$ must have a negative value. So, subtracting $\frac{r}{s}$ from another number will yield a greater number, while adding $\frac{r}{s}$ to another number will yield a smaller number. Since $p > q$, $p - \frac{r}{s}$ must be even greater than $q + \frac{r}{s}$.

III. Multiplying two unequal numbers by the same negative number reverses the original inequality. Since $p > q$ and rs is a negative number ($rs < 0$), p multiplied by rs must be less than q multiplied by rs.

Now, look at statement I.

I. Statement I is true in some cases but not in others. You know that the values of both $\frac{s}{r}$ and $\frac{r}{s}$ are negative (less than 0). But, whether $p \times \frac{s}{r}$ is less than $q \times \frac{r}{s}$ depends on the values used. For example, assume $p = 2$ and $q = 1$. Then, assume that $r = 5$ and $s = -1$. In this case, statement I is true:

$$\frac{(2)(-1)}{5} > \frac{(1)(5)}{-1}$$

$$-\frac{2}{5} > -5$$

Now, assume $p = 2$ and $q = 1$, just as before, but that $r = -1$ and $s = 5$. In this case, statement I is false (the inequality should be reversed, as shown here):

$$\frac{(2)(5)}{-1} < \frac{(1)(-1)}{5}$$

Since you've discovered one conflicting result, that's enough to eliminate I.

THE READING TEST

Here are test directions that are similar to what you will see at the beginning of the Reasoning Test:

> **Directions:** This test consists of four passages, each followed by several questions. Read each passage and select the best answer for each question following the passage. Then, on your answer sheet, mark the oval corresponding to the best answer.

Here's a sample reading passage, which is typical of an ACT passage, except that it is much shorter than the ones you will find on the test.

> **On the test, the general subject category and passage number will immediately precede each reading passage, like the one below.**

Passage I—Social Science

A legendary island in the Atlantic Ocean beyond the Pillars of Hercules was first mentioned by Plato in the *Timaeus*. Atlantis was a fabulously beautiful and prosperous land, the seat of an empire nine thousand years before Solon. Its inhabitants overran part of Europe and Africa, Athens alone being able to defy them. Because of the impiety of its people, the island was destroyed by an earthquake and inundation. The legend may have existed before Plato and may have sprung from the concept of Homer's Elysium. Much speculation that such an island once actually existed has spawned various historical theories, one of which is that pre-Columbian civilizations in America were established by colonists from the lost island.

Now, look at two ACT-style questions and explanations about this passage. Just like every ACT reading question, these ask you to choose the correct answer from the four choices—labeled either (A), (B), (C), and (D) or (F), (G), (H), and (J). This first one is relatively simple; the best answer choice is easy to distinguish from the others. Most test-takers would answer this question correctly.

1. The main purpose of the passage is to

(A) discuss the legend of Atlantis and its possible origins.
(B) make the point that enduring legends are often rooted in classical literature.
(C) refute the claim that Atlantis actually existed.
(D) compare Plato's description of Atlantis with Homer's.

A **The correct answer is (A).** The passage's main purpose must encompass all of the ideas presented in the passage without referring to ideas outside the passage. Choice (A) fits the bill, since the passage describes Atlantis and its inhabitants, explains its demise, and then discusses the possibility that Atlantis either originated in Homer's Elysium or that it actually existed. Choice (B) generalizes from the passage information, which provides no support for the point in choice (B). Choice (C) is incorrect because it is too narrow and because the passage makes no attempt to refute the claim to which choice (C) refers. Choice (D) is incorrect because the passage makes no such comparison—nor does it indicate how either Plato or Homer described Atlantis.

Now here's a more difficult reading question. To analyze it, you need to recall different bits of information scattered throughout the passage and infer what the passage does not explicitly state. A high percentage of test-takers would respond incorrectly to this question.

Q **2.** Which of the following statements finds the LEAST support from the passage?

(F) The people of Atlantis were imperialistic and warring.
(G) Resistance by the Athenians contributed to the demise of Atlantis.
(H) Solon eventually replaced Atlantis as the seat of Atlantis' former empire.
(J) The inhabitants of Atlantis were disrespectful of their gods.

A **The correct answer is (G).** Although the passage does indicate that Athens successfully resisted incursions by the people of Atlantis, nothing in the passage supports the claim that this resistance helped cause the demise of Atlantis. Choices (F) and (J) both find strong, explicit support in the passage, which states that Atlantis' inhabitants overran other countries and that they were an "impious" people. Choice (H) is not supported as strongly by the passage as the other wrong answer choices. However, it is reasonable to infer choice (H) from the statement that Atlantis was "the seat of an empire nine thousand years before Solon."

THE SCIENCE REASONING TEST

Here are test directions that are similar to what you will see at the beginning of the Science Reasoning Test:

> **Directions:** This test consists of seven passages, each followed by several questions. Read each passage and select the best answer for each question following the passage. Then, on your answer sheet, mark the oval corresponding to the best answer. You may NOT use a calculator on this test.

Here's a sample Science Reasoning passage (along with two graphs), which is typical of an ACT passage.

In small communities, infectious organisms such as Varicella-zoster virus, which causes chicken pox, occasionally become extinct. The threshold at which such extinctions occur is known as the *critical community size*. Extinctions are followed by a period in which there are no infections until the virus is reintroduced from an outside source.

Researchers collected data on these extinctions, or *fadeouts*, in various communities before a fadeout was defined as a period of three or more weeks in which there were no new reported cases of the infection. They then attempted to develop computer models of the patterns of fadeouts seen, using information about the dynamics of the infection. The first of the following two figures shows the real data on chickenpox versus the data generated by two different computer models. The second figure demonstrates the different assumptions made by the two models concerning the duration of the *infectious period* (the period in which an individual can transmit the infection to another individual). This was the only difference between the two models.

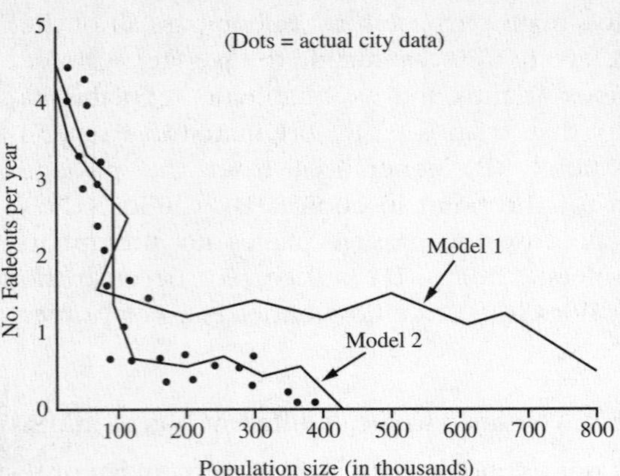

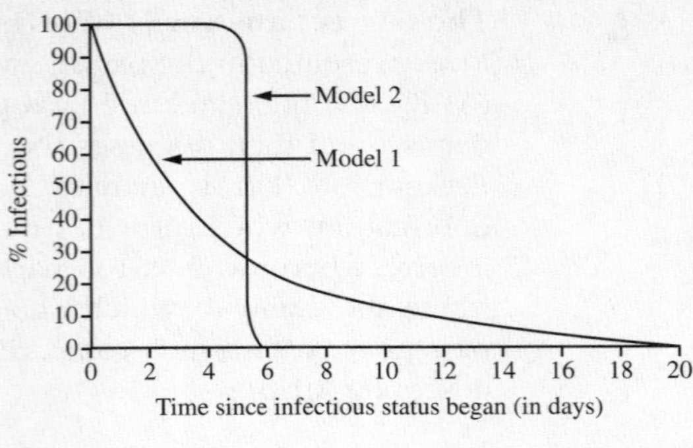

Now, look at two ACT-style questions (along with explanations) based on the passage and the two graphs. Just like every ACT Science Reasoning question, these ask you to choose the correct answer from the four choices—labeled either (A), (B), (C), and (D) or (F), (G), (H), and (J). This first one is relatively easy. To answer it, you need to analyze only one of the two graphs. What's more, the analysis involves little more than a cursory visual inspection of the two curves as compared to the scatter plot (the pattern of dots). Most test-takers would answer this question correctly.

Q 1. Which of the following statements is best supported by the first figure?

(A) As the number of viruses increases toward one million, the number of fadeouts per year declines.
(B) Model 2 predicts the number of fadeouts per year better than Model 1 for populations over 150,000.
(C) Model 1 is a better predictor of fadeouts for communities under 300,000, while Model 2 is a better predictor of annual fadeouts for communities over 300,000.
(D) Both models overestimate the number of annual fadeouts for chicken pox.

A **The correct answer is (B).** In the figure, notice that at community sizes under 100,000 (the left end of the graph), the two curves of Model 1 and Model 2 track each other closely. Also, notice that the two Models are both quite accurate in tracing the "dots," which indicate actual fadeouts. Beyond the 100,000 population level, however, the curves gradually diverge—with Model 2 tracking actual fadeouts more closely than Model 1.

Now, here's another question based on the same passage and graphs. This one requires you to analyze both graphs, and the answer choices are more difficult to understand. These two features make this question more complex and challenging than the preceding one. A much lower percentage of test-takers would answer this question correctly.

Q 2. Which of the following statements might explain the difference in the abilities of Models 1 and 2 to predict the actual number of annual fadeouts of chicken pox?

(F) Model 2 predicts that there will be more individuals spreading infection in the early infectious period, resulting in a lower number of predicted fadeouts, compared with Model 1.
(G) Model 1 predicts that there will be some individuals spreading infection in the late infectious period, reducing the number of predicted fadeouts, compared with Model 2.
(H) Model 2 predicts that there will be a longer infectious period in larger communities, increasing the number of predicted fadeouts, compared with Model 1.
(J) Model 2 predicts a more constant rate of movement from an infectious to a noninfectious status.

A **The correct answer is (F).** To answer this question, you need to consider data from both graphs. Only choice (F) fits the information in both graphs: Model 2 does, in fact, predict a greater number of people spreading infection early in the infectious period, and it also predicts a smaller number of fadeouts than does Model 1.

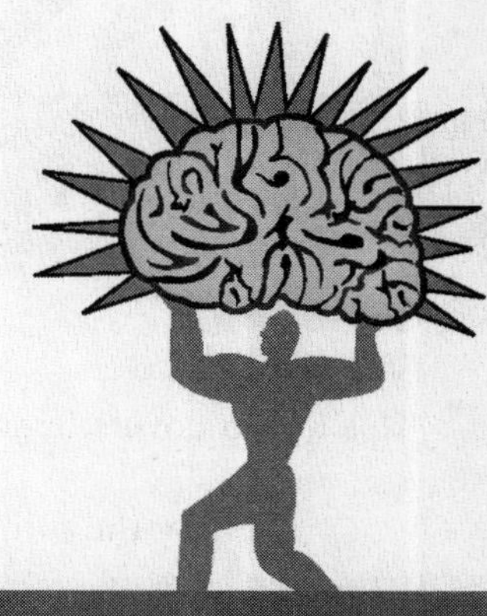

PART II

THE ACT ENGLISH TEST

LESSON 3
English Test Strategies

This lesson covers Brainiac strategies for the ACT English Test. In this lesson, you'll:

- Review the format and test directions for the English Test
- Learn how Brainiacs figure out the most common English questions using special insights and other tools at their cognitive disposal. (Six sample questions will serve as illustrations.)
- Apply Brainiac insights to 15 tough questions based on an ACT-style passage

THE ENGLISH TEST DIRECTIONS REVISITED

During Lesson 2, you took a first glance at the features of the ACT English Test. To refresh your memory, here are directions similar to the ones you'll see on the test:

> **Directions:** This test consists of five passages in which particular words or phrases are underlined and numbered. Alongside each passage you will see alternative words and phrases that could be substituted for the underlined portion. Select the alternative that expresses the idea most clearly and correctly or that best fits the style and tone of the entire passage. If the original version is best, select "No Change."
>
> The test also includes questions about entire paragraphs and the passage as a whole. These questions are identified by a number in a box.
>
> After you select the correct answer for each question, mark the oval on your answer sheet that corresponds to the correct answer.

Here are three additional features of the ACT English Test format you should know:

- Each passage will be titled to help you get an idea about the topic of the passage; however, you don't need to have specific knowledge of a topic to handle the questions for the passage.
- If a question involves the sequence of paragraphs in a passage, then the paragraphs will be numbered. The same is true if a question refers to one or more paragraphs by number (for example, "In paragraph 3, . . ."); otherwise, the paragraphs won't be numbered.

- Each passage appears in the left-hand column of your test booklet, while the questions corresponding to the passage appear next to it, in the right-hand column. This feature makes it easier to glance back and forth between a question and the relevant portion of the passage.

THE ENGLISH TEST IS REALLY AN "EDITING" TEST

The English test is essentially an editing exercise. You're given a passage that contains a number of grammatical mistakes, stylistic weaknesses, errors in punctuation, lapses in logic, and other writing flaws. Your job is to detect those flaws and pick alternative ways of writing and organizing the passage—correcting the flaws without introducing new ones.

Most questions in each set are based on underlined portions of the passage. The questions based on underlined words generally cover usage and mechanics—the rules of grammar, usage, and "mechanical" details like punctuation. A few questions in each set are *not* based on underlined portions of the passage. Instead, they're marked by boxed item numbers appearing in various places in the passage—between sentences, at the end of paragraphs, or at the end of the entire passage. The boxed items are generally Rhetorical Skills items, which deal with larger questions of writing strategy, overall organization, content choice, and style.

No question type is inherently easier than another. Whatever the skill, the test-makers can devise no-brainers as well as mind-benders.

WHAT THE ENGLISH TEST COVERS—THE NUTS AND BOLTS

In Lesson 2, you reviewed a breakdown of the areas covered on the English Test. You saw that the test questions fall into two broad categories: "Usage/Mechanics" and "Rhetorical Skills." Let's look at the breakdown again, along with detailed lists of what the different areas encompass. (The number of questions indicated for each category are approximate.)

USAGE/MECHANICS

Usage/Mechanics refers to the degree to which a sentence obeys the rules of English grammar and usage. Forty of the 75 questions cover Usage/Mechanics, and one of your two subscores for the test will be based on your responses to these 40 questions, which cover the three broad categories described below.

Punctuation (10 questions)

A question in this category might test you on the placement of a punctuation mark, either within a sentence or at the end. Fair game includes the use of the period, comma, colon, semi-colon, and the "em" dash. The test's emphasis is on the use of these marks to achieve sentence sense and clarity. Also tested is the use of apostrophes (to indicate either the possessive case or a contraction). The test does *not* cover the use of quotation marks.

Grammar and Usage (12 questions)

This category covers a lot of ground, including: (1) *agreement* between two different grammatical elements of a sentence, such as subject and verb, a pronoun and its antecedent (the noun to which it refers), or a modifying phrase (such as a prepositional phrase or a so-called "appositive") and whatever it modifies; (2) *forms and cases* of particular parts of speech, including verbs, pronouns, adjectives, and adverbs; and (3) *idioms*—words and phrases that are proper and acceptable simply due to their widespread use.

Sentence Structure (18 questions)

These questions test you on the relationships between different parts of a sentence and on how to arrange the grammatical elements of a sentence so that the meaning is clear and unambiguous. Specific issues covered include *parallelism* between elements that are grammatically equivalent, *placement of modifiers* vis-a-vis the words they modify, and *shifts* in voice (passive or active) and tense (present, past, etc.).

RHETORICAL SKILLS

Rhetorical Skills covers the overall organization of the passage (which topic logically belongs first? which belongs last?), transitions from topic to topic, decisions about what to include and what to omit from the passage, and stylistic choices. Thirty-five of the 75 questions cover Rhetorical Skills, and one of your two subscores for the test will be based on your responses to these 35 questions. The test-makers list three broad categories under the "Rhetorical Skills" rubric, as listed and described below.

Strategy (12 questions)

A *strategy* question might involve adding or deleting a sentence that provides a *transition* from one sentence (or paragraph) to another or that provides support for certain ideas in the passage. In handling any strategy question, your job is to evaluate a proposed addition, deletion, or revision (typically choosing the best among four options) in terms of its effect on the purpose of the passage or on how well it serves to communicate the ideas of the passage.

Organization (11 questions)

A question of this type deals with the *sequence of ideas* in the passage. These questions typically take one of two forms. In one form, you're asked to select the best sequence of sentences within a paragraph. In the other, you must select the best sequence of paragraphs for the passage as a whole. For either type, your job is to determine the sequence that makes for the most logical and cohesive passage.

Style (12 questions)

This is a catch-all category that embraces stylistic problems such as wordiness, awkwardness, ambiguity, and redundancy, as well as the "appropriate" tone and choice of words for the passage.

WHAT'S NOT COVERED

Very subtle stylistic or esthetic considerations are not tested on the ACT, nor are rules of grammar and usage that are disputed or changing. Also excluded are slang, colloquialisms, technical jargon, geographic or ethnic dialects, archaic language (like Shakespeare's), and creative or experimental language (like James Joyce's).

SAMPLE PASSAGE AND QUESTIONS (1-10)

Before learning the Brainiac strategies for handling ACT English Test questions, read the following passage and answer the 10 questions based on it. (While some questions are average in difficulty, and some are tougher than average, there are no easy questions in the bunch.) In the next section, we'll analyze each of these 10 questions.

This passage is somewhat shorter than the typical ACT passage, and the 10 questions based on it are fewer in number than on the actual test, which includes 15 questions per passage. In this lesson's Brain Teaser and in Part VI you'll tackle full-length passages accompanied by 15 questions each, as they appear on the actual test.

The Viking Mission—In Search of Life

[1]

A major goal of the Viking spacecraft missions of the late 1980s were to determine whether [1] the soil of Mars is dead, like the soil of the moon, or teeming with microscopic life, like the soils of Earth. Soil samples brought into the Viking lander were sent to three separate biological laboratories to be tested in different ways for indications of the presence of living things. [2]

[2]

[3] First, it was assumed that life on Mars would be like life on Earth; which is [4] based on the element carbon thriving by chemically transforming carbon compounds. Second, on Earth, where there are large life-forms (like human beings and pine trees), there are also small ones (like bacteria), and the small ones are far more abundant, thousands or millions of them being [5] in every gram of soil. To have the best possible chance of detecting life, an instrument should look for the most abundant kind of life. The lander's laboratories, therefore, were designed to detect carbon-based Martian microbes living in the soil—more specifically, to nourish any life in the Martian soil and to detect with sensitive instruments the chemical activity of the organisms. [6]

[3]

One characteristic of earthly plants is to transform [7] carbon dioxide in the air into the compounds that make them up. Accordingly, one Viking experiment, called the carbon assimilation test, added radioactive carbon dioxide to the atmosphere above the soil sample, then flooded the sample [8] with simulated Martian sunlight.

[4]

(1) Unfortunately, neither this one nor [9] the other Viking experiment uncovered clear indications of Martian life-forms. (2) Living organisms on Earth give off gases. (3) The gas exchange test, another experiment on each lander, was designed to detect this kind of activity. (4) Plants give off oxygen, animals give off carbon dioxide, and water is exhaled by both. (5) Nutrients and water were added to the soil, and the chemical composition of the gas above the soil was continuously analyzed for changes that might indicate life. [10]

Q 1. (A) NO CHANGE
(B) was the determination of whether
(C) was to determine whether
(D) was determining if

A **The correct answer is (C).** The subject of the verb is "goal," so the verb should be singular—"was" rather than "were." Eliminate the original version, choice (A). Notice that the sentence intends to provide two alternatives ("whether . . . or . . ."). The word "whether" conveys this intent more clearly than the word "if." Eliminate choice (D). That leaves choices (B) and (C). Although "the determination of" and "to determine" in this context are both acceptable, the former is wordier and is a bit awkward. Hence, (C) is the best choice.

Q 2. (F) NO CHANGE
(G) the existence of life.
(H) indications that living things exist there.
(J) the presence of living things indicating life.

A **The correct answer is (F).** The original version is fine. Although it's possible to create a more concise and less awkward version (e.g., "indications of life on Mars"), none of the alternatives listed provide such a version. Choice (G) results in the idiomatically improper "tested . . . for the existence of life," which is also a bit nonsensical. Choice (H) is the runner-up choice; it is grammatically correct, and contains no idiom or usage problems. However, choice (H) suffers from a so-called *vague pronoun reference*. Given the structure of the sentence, it isn't clear what the pronoun "there" refers to. In all likelihood, it refers to Mars. But since Mars had not been mentioned since early in the previous sentence, the writer should either clarify the reference by replacing "there" with its antecedent "on Mars" or simply omit the pronoun, as in the original, and best, version. Choice (J) is redundant; the writer should choose either "the presence of living things" or "indications of life," but not both, since they say essentially the same thing.

Q 3. Which of the following sentences, if added to the beginning of paragraph 2, would most smoothly and logically lead into the paragraph?

(A) This was a challenging scientific assignment in two respects.
(B) The tests were based on two underlying ideas.
(C) For two reasons, the Viking scientists were uncertain how to proceed.
(D) There were two main objectives being pursued in these experiments.

A **The correct answer is (B).** The paragraph is devoted to explaining the two underlying assumptions, or "ideas," that guided the scientists who designed the Viking experiments and those ideas that influenced the laboratories' design. Choice (B) sets this up accurately and clearly. In contrast, each of the three other options would only mislead the reader as to what's coming in paragraph 2.

Q 4. (F) NO CHANGE
(G) Earth, that is
(H) Earth—
(J) Earth, which is

A **The correct answer is (H).** The semicolon in the original version is wrong, since what follows the semicolon can't stand alone as a sentence. Fixing this problem requires changing the punctuation mark. If the word "thriving" (later in the sentence) was replaced by either "which thrives" or "thrives," then (J) would be the best choice. But you're stuck with "thriving," which is a *gerund* (a verb transformed into a noun by adding "ing"). Mixing a gerund with a regular verb within the same grammatical construct (in this case, mixing "which is based" and "which is . . . thriving") is considered improper, *and it sounds wrong*. Choice (H) fixes this problem by omitting "which is." Read the original sentence aloud, then read it aloud using choice (H) instead. Notice that choice (H) *sounds* better. Notice also that it uses an *em* dash (—), a mark used to signal a phrase that elucidates or describes what precedes it. Since the second part of the sentence describes "life on Earth," the use of the *em* dash here is appropriate and effective. Hence, choice (H) provides the best alternative to the original version.

X-REF

In question 4, notice that choices (G) and (J) differ in only one respect: "that" versus "which." Although both choices were incorrect because of a punctuation problem, the test-makers could have designed question 4 to test you instead on word usage—specifically, when to use "that" or "which" in a particular sentence. You'll learn the rule, along with other frequently tested *usage* rules, during Lesson 5.

Q 5. (A) NO CHANGE
(B) containing thousands or millions of them
(C) with thousands or millions of them
(D) numbering in the thousands or millions

A **The correct answer is (D).** The underlined portion contains the superfluous word "being," which can and should be omitted. Although deleting "being" is the only revision needed, none of the answer choices provides this option. Of the three alternatives, choice (D) is the clearest and most idiomatic—that is, the most normal-sounding to a person with a well-developed "ear" for the language. Given the phrase that choice (D) provides, an even more effective sentence might also replace "in every gram" with "per gram," in order to avoid the successive use of the preposition "in." But this would be a subtle refinement in style only, and question 5 doesn't provide this option anyway. Besides, your job is not to look for the *ideal* version but rather to choose the best among four. Choice (B) is wrong because it's unclear who or what "contains" the thousands or millions of life-forms mentioned. Similarly, choice (C) is wrong because it's unclear who or what the preposition "with" describes, or *modifies*.

Q **6.** (F) NO CHANGE
(G) and to detect the chemical activity of the organisms with sensitive instruments.
(H) and, using sensitive instruments, to detect the chemical activity of the organisms.
(J) as well as to, with sensitive instruments, detect the organisms' chemical activity.

A **The correct answer is (H).** This underlined portion is about as lengthy as you'll find on the ACT English Test. Although it's grammatically correct and contains no idiom or usage errors, notice that the modifying phrase "with sensitive instruments" separates the verb "detect" from its direct object "chemical activity." While there's nothing wrong with doing this, you can make the sentence a bit clearer by joining these two elements, which calls for restructuring (rearranging) the underlined portion. Choice (H) provides an effective way to do this. This choice not only joins the verb and its direct object, but it also sets apart the modifying phrase with commas. This additional technique makes for an even clearer sentence. Choice (G) also fixes the problem in the original version but in the process places "with sensitive instruments" at the end so that it's unclear what or whom the phrase describes. Choice (J) separates, or splits, the infinitive "to detect." The result is not only grammatically incorrect but also clumsy in the way it sounds, or "reads" (a huge clue that it's not the best version).

Whenever you see a lengthy underlined portion, chances are that, like Question 6, the question at hand will focus on the structure of that part. In other words, your job will be to determine the most effective arrangement of elements within the underlined portion.

Q **7.** (A) NO CHANGE
(B) the transformation of
(C) that of transforming
(D) that they transform

A **The correct answer is (D).** In the sentence, the verb "is" anticipates what's called a *subject complement*—something that complements or completes the meaning of the sentence's subject. Since the sentence is telling you about what the subject ("characteristic") *is* rather than what it *does*, the infinitive "to transform" clearly does not match the subject. Hence, the original version cannot be the best of the four options. Each of the three alternatives, choices (B), (C), and (D), fixes this problem. Choice (B) provides a noun, while choices (C) and (D) each provide a *noun clause*; all three indicate what the subject "is." Among the three, however, choice (D) is the most idiomatic (normal-sounding).

Q **8.** (F) NO CHANGE
(G) flooded it
(H) had it flooded
(J) had the sample flooded

A **The correct answer is (F).** The underlined phrase is parallel in construction to "added radioactive carbon dioxide." Repeating "the sample" here is necessary to make clear that it is the soil sample, rather than the atmosphere, that was flooded. Choice (H) is more concise than the original version; it contains no parallelism problem either. However, the use of the pronoun "it" in place of "soil sample" leaves it unclear what "it" refers to. (Is "it" the soil sample or the atmosphere?) As for choices (H) and (J), neither one is parallel in its construction to "added radioactive carbon dioxide."

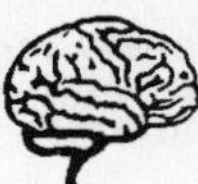

Both choice (H) and choice (J) employ what's called the *passive voice*—in which the subject is *acted upon.* Although the passive voice is acceptable in standard written English, the writer should not mix it with the active voice, especially in the same sentence.

Q **9.** (A) NO CHANGE
(B) neither this or
(C) neither this experiment nor
(D) neither this nor

A **The correct answer is (D).** The correlative "neither . . . nor . . ." is the correct idiom. However, the word "one" has no clear antecedent, and it can be safely omitted, as in choice (D), without the need to replace it with "experiment," as in choice (C). As for choice (B), "neither . . . or . . ." is an improper idiom.

Q **10.** Which of the following provides the most logical ordering of the sentences in paragraph 4?

(F) NO CHANGE
(G) 3, 5, 2, 4, 1
(H) 5, 2, 1, 3, 4
(J) 3, 2, 4, 5, 1

A **The correct answer is (G).** The preceding paragraph 3 discussed one experiment, while paragraph 4 clearly discusses another. Of the five sentences, (3) offers the smoothest, most logical transition from paragraph 3 to 4. The viable options are thus narrowed to choices (G) and (J). Immediately following sentence (3) (which should come first in the paragraph), it is logical to expect a description of the experiment, *then* perhaps an explanation of its rationale. Sentence (5) provides the description, while sentences (2) and (4) provide the rationale. This sequence, (5),(2),(4), is precisely what choice (G) indicates.

TOP 10 BRAiNiAC STRATEGIES FOR ANSWERING ENGLISH TEST QUESTIONS

If you read the explanations for the preceding 10 questions, you already picked up some strategies Brainiacs know to use when answering English Test questions. You'll review them here and learn about some others.

X-REF

Specific strategies for grammar, punctuation, usage, and rhetorical skills questions will be covered in the lessons to follow. The tips here are more general.

1. BRAINIACS START BY SPENDING 30-40 SECONDS READING THE ENTIRE PASSAGE STRAIGHT THROUGH.

When you tackle the English Test, pretend you're a writer about to revise the rough draft of a piece of work you're writing. In order to do this, it helps to have a general sense of the overall meaning and purpose of the passage before you begin. It's especially important because, as you'll see, some of the test items turn on the *meaning* of a given sentence or paragraph as well as its grammatical form. So, begin work on a particular passage by reading it quickly from beginning to end, looking for its general theme, its style and tone, and the basic sequence of ideas. The passages are generally short (300 to 400 words), so 30–40 seconds should be ample time for this task.

2. BRAINIACS TACKLE "ORGANIZATION" QUESTIONS OUT OF SEQUENCE.

For each passage, at least 2 or 3 of the 15 questions will be marked by boxed numbers appearing somewhere in the passage. These "box" questions generally deal with rhetorical skills. Expect at least one box question to involve the overall *organization* of a specific paragraph or of the passage as a whole.

Organization questions can be especially time-consuming if you need to *re*-read the entire passage to answer the question. Yet that's exactly what many test-takers end up doing when facing a "whole passage" question. It's more efficient to take a different approach: After you read the entire passage through (see Strategy 1 on page 31), check for an Organization question involving the whole passage. If you see one, handle it *immediately*—before going back to tackle questions dealing with specific parts of the passage. In other words, answer the Organization question while you're focusing on the big picture (i.e., the whole passage). That way, you won't need to re-read the entire passage again just to answer this one question.

There is a different approach to use for Organization questions involving specific paragraphs. Save these questions for *last*—after you've handled all questions dealing with underlined portions. Why? The second time you read the passage, you should be in a Usage/Mechanics mode of thinking—which means you're single-mindedly focused on the underlined portions and the kinds of errors you'll find there. To handle an Organization question along the way, you'll need to interrupt that mode, backtrack to re-read a paragraph, then resume Usage/Mechanics mode. This can be distracting. (Try it and you'll probably agree.) Furthermore, Usage/Mechanics questions are the least time-consuming, so you'll want to get them out of the way.

Question 3:

This organization question deals with one entire paragraph. Save it for last, after you've answered questions 4–10.

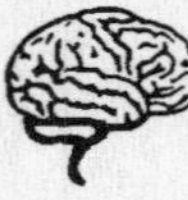

Brainiacs answer "whole-passage" Organization questions *first* but "whole-paragraph" Organization questions *last.* When in Usage/Mechanics mode, Brainiacs stay there until they've answered all questions involving underlined portions.

3. BRAINIACS USE THEIR ENGLISH INSTINCTS TO "LISTEN" FOR SENTENCES THAT DON'T "SOUND" RIGHT.

Most questions on the ACT English Test involve underlined phrases and test your ability to apply the rules of English grammar and usage correctly to those phrases. However, these questions will also reward the writer who's developed a good "feel" or "instinct" for the language. So, when you read a sentence containing underlining, *listen*—as if you were reading aloud—for anything that sounds awkward, confusing, odd, or just plain weird. If you're certain that something sounds wrong, but you're not sure why, don't worry about it. Eliminate the first answer choice ("No Change") and look for a better alternative. In short, trust your instincts and your ear.

Question 4:

As you read the underlined portion for the first time, you probably guessed that what was needed was a comma instead of a semicolon. Since choice (G) fixed that error, you might have selected it as the correct choice. If you did, you were wrong! To catch the error in choice (G), you needed to read the entire sentence with the alternative that choice (G) provides, *listening* carefully for anything awkward. Assuming you have good English instincts, the phrase that choice (G) provides, together with the word "thriving," should have *sounded* wrong to you.

4. BRAINIACS DON'T RELY EXCLUSIVELY ON THEIR EAR; THEY APPLY THE RULES OF STANDARD WRITTEN ENGLISH TO CHECK THEIR INSTINCTS.

On the English Test, you won't need to explain grammatical errors, and you won't need to know grammar terminology. In other words, you won't score any points for knowing exactly *why* a wrong answer choice is wrong, technically speaking. But does this mean that it's pointless to study (or review) the rules of grammar, and that you should rely exclusively on your ear for English? Not at all. Regardless of what your ego might tell you, your ear for correct English is by no means infallible. It might suffice for easier questions, but not for the trickier ones—when your ear might tell you that a certain wrong answer sounds right.

Question 5:

In handling this question, perhaps your ear betrayed you, and choice (C) sounded more "correct" than choice (D). If so, you're not alone, even among ACT Brainiacs. Question 5 would fall squarely into the "tough" category because many test-takers commit just the kind of error that choice (C) exemplifies. It's for questions like this one that a solid knowledge of the rules and conventions of standard written English can save your ACT hide!

X-REF

Your English language instincts, and hence your ACT English Test scores, can be greatly enhanced by knowing the specific rules that linguists and grammarians have devised to explain how sentences are normally constructed. In the lessons ahead, you'll review the rules that are tested most frequently on the ACT.

5. BRAINIACS KNOW THE FOUR BASIC PRINCIPLES FOR ERROR-SPOTTING IN ACT SENTENCES.

These four basic principles can help you zero in on the grammatical and stylistic errors that most often appear in ACT passages—a useful supplement to your instinctive "ear" for what's right and wrong in English. When in doubt about where the error is located in a sentence containing an underlined word or phrase, follow these four steps in the sequence indicated. If there is an error, you'll probably uncover it through this process.

- **Find the verb, then its subject. Check subject-verb agreement, correct tense, and proper verb formation.**

  Question 1:

  The underlined portion creates a subject-verb agreement error.

- **Examine all pronouns. Make sure each has a clear antecedent with which it agrees in person and number.**

  Question 8:

  In choice (G), the antecedent of the pronoun "it" is unclear.

- **Look for wobbling of the sentence structure. Make sure modifiers are attached to what they modify, parallel ideas are grammatically parallel, and comparisons are clear and logical.**

  Question 4:

  Choice (J) corrected a punctuation problem but failed to correct the improper grammatical parallel between "which is based . . ." and "[which is] thriving. . . ."

  Question 6:

  The underlined portion "detaches" a verb from its direct object, so you should look for a better option among the choices.

Question 7:

The verb "is" sets up a subject complement, which must logically match the sentence's subject. (In the original version, it does not.)

Question 8:

Choices (H) and (J) mix the passive and active voices.

- **Listen for awkwardness, wordiness, and incorrect use of idioms.**

Question 5:

The underlined portion contains the superfluous word "being," which can and should be omitted.

Question 7:

Although grammatically correct, neither choice (B) nor choice (C) is idiomatic.

Question 9:

Choice (C) is too wordy to be a viable option, even though it is grammatically and idiomatically correct.

X-REF **If any of the rules mentioned here, or the terms used, seem unfamiliar, don't worry—they're all clearly explained in the lessons that follow.**

6. BRAINIACS "PREDICT" WHAT THE CORRECT ANSWER WILL LOOK LIKE *BEFORE* SCANNING THE CHOICES.

Assume you've "heard" an error in an underlined phrase. To tackle the question about that phrase, first consider how you'd correct the error ***if you had written the sentence***. Do this before looking at any of the answer choices. Try rephrasing the faulty part of the sentence in your mind, figuring out what word or punctuation mark you'd eliminate, change, move, or add, and imagine how the improved phrase or clause would read. You should have no trouble doing this; after all, you are a Brainiac and know how to write well.

This step is an important one—but one that average test-takers skip. By correcting the error before checking the answer choices, you'll zero in on the correct choice more quickly and be far less tempted by wrong answer choices.

Questions 1–10

You can apply this strategy to any of the questions in the previous set. If you didn't, go back now and reconsider each item in turn, without looking at the answer choices. You'll see that, in every case, you can predict, or pre-phrase, how the best version might "read."

7. BRAINIACS NEVER SELECT AN ANSWER CHOICE MERELY BECAUSE IT CORRECTS ALL ERRORS IN AN UNDERLINED PORTION.

Scanning the answer choices to eliminate those that fail to correct the error in an underlined portion might leave you with more than one possible option. If this happens, read the remaining answer choices carefully. Although each corrects the original error, you'll find that incorrect options introduce new errors, whereas the correct answer does not. Be sure to "listen" for these new errors so you can zero in on the best answer choice.

Question 1:

Choice (D) corrects the subject-verb agreement error but creates a new problem with the word "if" instead of "whether."

Question 5:

Choices (B) and (C) both fix the problem with the underlined portion, but both also introduce a new problem—the modifying phrase that the choice provides lacks a clear antecedent.

Question 6:

Choices (G) and (J) both restructure the underlined portion to fix the problem with it, but each also introduces a new and similar problem.

Introducing a new problem in an answer choice is probably the test-makers' favorite wrong-answer ploy, as you saw through many examples in the previous section.

8. BRAINIACS ARE CAREFUL TO NEITHER "OVER-CORRECT" NOR "UNDER-CORRECT."

On each of the four ACT tests (including the English Test), the test-makers will give you *roughly* equal numbers of each correct answer choice. What this means is that for the questions that include "No Change" as the first answer choice, the correct answer will in fact be "No Change"—the first choice, either choice (A) or choice (F), in about *1 out of 4* questions. Of course, this choice usually means that the original sentence contains no errors or other problems—that it's perfectly correct as written and in no need of revision.

Of the ten sample questions in the preceding set, eight included "No Change" as a first choice, either choice (A) or choice (F). "No Change" was the correct answer to exactly 2 of these 8 questions—just the percentage you might expect from a typical set of ACT English Test questions.

Despite this simple statistical fact, most test-takers tend to "over-correct"—to find errors where none exist. To avoid this tendency, keep in mind that *if you read a sentence that sounds perfectly okay, it probably is*. This doesn't mean you shouldn't look at the three alternative options for a better one—especially one that's more concise. But be careful not to violate your initial instinct that the original version was perfectly fine. Also, be careful not to err on the flip side and "under-correct." In roughly three out four cases, "No Change" is an incorrect answer.

Question 2:

The original underlined portion could probably stand improvement, as the analysis indicates. But that doesn't mean that "No Change," choice (F), is an incorrect answer. As it turns out, the original version, imperfect as it may be, is nevertheless the best of the four choices listed. Test-takers who tend to over-correct would probably reject choice (F), and they'd be wrong.

A good way to make sure you don't "over-correct" or "under-correct" is to keep count of the number of choice (A) and choice (F) answers, and adjust if the count is too high or too low. For example, when you've completed the first passage with its 15 test items, check how many (A)s and (F)s you've picked. If you've found no (A) or (F) items, you may be overanalyzing the sentences, finding "errors" where none actually exist. If you've found too many—say, six or more—you may be overlooking errors. Adjust accordingly.

9. BRAINIACS LOOK AROUND THE UNDERLINING FOR IMPORTANT CLUES.

Most of the questions in each set will involve underlined portions and deal with Usage/Mechanics issues. The average test-taker assumes that focusing just on the underlined portion will suffice. But as the preceding set illustrates, to handle nearly any of these questions, you also need to look at what precedes and follows the underlined portion.

Question 1:

Questions like this one, which cover subject-verb agreement problems, generally turn on a single word appearing somewhere before or after the underlined portion. (In this case, that word is the singular subject, "goal," near the beginning of the sentence.)

Question 4:

To get this question correct, you needed to notice not just the punctuation problem but also the single word "thriving" (later in the sentence), which was the key to homing in on the correct choice.

10. BRAINIACS CHOOSE THE SHORTEST ANSWER—BUT ONLY IF ALL ELSE IS EQUAL!

Occasionally, you'll find that eliminating all the answers that contain errors does not narrow your options to a single choice. You may find that two (or rarely three) answer choices all appear correct and equally clear, graceful, and unambiguous.

When this happens, choose whichever answer is shortest. Generally speaking, the test-makers regard a concise, tightly worded sentence as more stylistically effective than a wordy, loosely structured one. Therefore, when all other factors appear equal, the shortest sentence is the one that the test-makers are most likely to consider correct.

Question 1:

Choices (B) and (C) are both grammatically and idiomatically correct. But choice (C) has a "tighter" structure and is more concise than choice (B) and is, therefore, the better choice.

Question 8:

Choices (F) and (G) are both grammatically and idiomatically correct. Although choice (G) is more concise, it suffers from a pronoun reference problem. Hence, in this case, "all else" is *not* equal!

BRAIN TEASER

In this quiz, you'll read one ACT-length passage and answer 15 tough questions based on it. For each of the 15 questions, you'll see a hint to help you handle it.

The questions in this set cover all six official testing categories: punctuation, grammar and usage, sentence structure, strategy, organization, and style—just like each set you'll encounter on the actual test. The big difference is that, in this quiz, you find any no-brainers or "gimmees" among the questions.

Attempt all 15 questions, but don't put yourself under a time limit. Focus instead on applying the strategies you have learned in this lesson. Then be sure to read the explanations that follow the quiz. They're just as important as the questions, because they explain how to apply the strategies to the questions.

QUIZ

The following paragraphs may or may not be arranged in the best possible order. The last item will ask you to choose the most effective order for the paragraphs as numbered.

Movies: Economics and Artistry

[1]

The strength of film as an art form has always derived (1) from cinema's role of entertaining a large and avid public. During the silent movie era of the 1920s, there grew up a generation of filmmakers whose essential vision belonged to no other medium than that of (2) the cinema, and whose public was a universal audience who watched their movies worldwide. Just as (3) the first dramas of Shakespeare, their art was not a product of the *salon*, but of the common playhouse. This is what gave such great moviemakers as D. W. Griffith and Sergei Eisenstein [4] their strength and freshness.

[2]

However, there has always been a price to be paid for the popular appeal of movies. The salon artist has only a known patron, or group of patrons, to satisfy, if he is (5) strong enough he can, like the painters of the Renaissance, mold their taste to match his own. (6) This may also be true of the greatest artists of the movies, from Chaplin in the twenties to Bergman or Antonioni in the sixties. Furthermore, (7) the larger and more numerous the public audience and the more costly the movies to produce, equally great are (8) the pressures brought to bear on the less conventional creators to make their work conform to the pattern of the more conventional artist. Today, the most expensive and popular movies, however skillfully crafted they may be (9)—think of any film by Steven Speilberg as an example—are also the most thoroughly conventional.

[3]

(1) The worldwide popularity of film and its power to transmit culture and values are unprecedented in the history of art. (2) As the twenty-first century begins the emergence of movies (10) in the last century can clearly be seen as its (11) most important artistic development. (3) But what make (12) the movies truly unique is the special relationship between moviemaker and audience. (13) [14] [15]

1. (A) NO CHANGE
   (B) always derived
   (C) has always been derived
   (D) derived

   Hint: For the correct choice of verb tense, think about the time frame to which the passage applies the idea that the first sentence conveys. Consider not just the first sentence or even the first paragraph, but also the passage as a whole.

2. (F) NO CHANGE
   (G) medium other than
   (H) medium besides that of
   (J) other medium besides

   Hint: Always check for clear antecedents when it comes to all pronouns. Also, to be rhetorically effective, a sentence must be free of redundancy.

3. (A) NO CHANGE
(B) Compared to
(C) Similar to
(D) As were

Hint: Listen to the entire sentence with each option for anything that sounds wobbly, awkward, or just plain weird to your ear.

4. The writer is considering adding the following phrase at this point in the passage:

(1920s movie geniuses from America and Europe, respectively)

Would this phrase be a relevant and appropriate addition to the passage, and why?

(F) Yes, because it helps to clarify the role played by these two moviemakers in the development of the art of filmmaking.
(G) Yes, because it provides interesting details about the background of the two moviemakers mentioned.
(H) No, because the only information it adds is irrelevant to the theme of the passage.
(J) No, because it singles out these two moviemakers as though they were the only significant film artists of their era.

Hint: Consider the proposed clause in light of the ideas that the paragraph already conveys.

5. (A) NO CHANGE
(B) satisfy—if
(C) satisfy, and if
(D) satisfy. For if

Hint: Answer choices that fix one problem sometimes create a new one.

6. (F) NO CHANGE
(G) enough, like the painters of the Renaissance, he can mold their taste to match his own.
(H) enough he can mold their taste to match his own tastes and those of the painters of the Renaissance.
(J) enough he can mold their taste to, like the painters of the Renaissance, match his own.

Hint: Don't expect the best choice to always provide an ideal, or "perfect," sentence.

7. (A) NO CHANGE
(B) However,
(C) Therefore,
(D) OMIT this underlined portion (and begin the sentence with "The").

Hint: Sometimes you need to read the entire paragraph to handle a question involving only a brief underlined portion.

Hint: Words that provide transitions between sentences are sometimes needed for a writer to make a rhetorical point.

8. (F) NO CHANGE
(G) the greater
(H) the greater are
(J) similarly large are

Hint: There's an idiom here that you may or may not know. If you don't know it, try looking for a match in grammatical structure between to parallel clauses.

9. Which of the following proposals for the underlined phrase would make for the clearest sentence, disregarding the possible need to revise the punctuation?

(A) NO CHANGE
(B) Move it to the beginning of the sentence
(C) Move it so that it immediately follows "Today" (the first word in the sentence)
(D) Move it to the end of the sentence

Hint: Pronouns should not always be placed as near as possible to the noun to which they refer, especially if another noun lurks nearby.

Hint: Be sure to listen to each version of the entire sentence; use your English instinct and your ear to narrow down the choices.

10. (F) NO CHANGE
(G) begins, the emergence of movies
(H) begins, movies which emerged
(J) begins; the emergence of movies

Hint: Whenever you need to re-read a sentence to try and make sense of it, take that as you cue to eliminate the original version as the best of the four choices.

11. (A) NO CHANGE
(B) that century's
(C) the last century's
(D) what turned out to be its

Hint: A more concise, and less repetitive, choice is a better one—all else being equal. But "all else" is not always equal.

12. (F) NO CHANGE
(G) what it takes to make
(H) what makes
(J) making

Hint: When you see an underlined verb, you should think not only about its tense but also about whether it agrees with its subject in terms of number—singular versus plural.

Hint: Never assume that an answer choice is the best one merely because it corrects the original version's problems and is free of grammatical errors.

13. (A) NO CHANGE
(B) moviemaker and his audience
(C) a moviemaker and an audience
(D) moviemakers and their audiences

Hint: In phrases such as "either . . . or . . ." and "between . . . and . . . ," the two elements should be parallel in grammatical structure.

14. Which of the following provides the most logical ordering of the sentences in paragraph 3?

(F) NO CHANGE
(G) 3, 2, 1
(H) 2, 1, 3
(J) 1, 3, 2

Hint: Transition words, which indicate the flow of ideas from one sentence to another, provide useful clues for Organization questions.

Item 15 poses a question about the passage as a whole.

15. For the sake of the unity and coherence of this passage, which of the following provides the most effective ordering of the paragraphs?

(A) NO CHANGE
(B) 1, 3, 2
(C) 2, 3, 1
(D) 3, 1, 2

Hint: In organizing a passage's ideas, it makes sense for supporting material to follow the idea that the material supports.

ANSWERS AND EXPLANATIONS

1. **The correct answer is (A).** The present perfect tense ("has always derived") is appropriate to describe the past up to and including the present. The passage discusses the role of cinema from its inception to the present time. Hence, the original version is perfectly fine. Choice (B) and (D) both employ the past tense. Choice (C) uses the unnecessary word "been."

2. **The correct answer is (G).** In the original version, the relative pronoun "that" has no antecedent (in other words, there's no noun to which it refers). Accordingly, "that of" should be omitted. Choice (G) fixes the problem. (The word "other" is proper either preceding or following "medium.") Choice (H) fails to fix the original version's pronoun-reference problem. Choice (J) fixes the problem but creates a new one: the use of both "other" and "besides" is redundant. One or the other should be used—but not both.

Redundancies can easily slip past the average ACT test-taker. Be sure to scrutinize every word in and around the underlined portion for two words or phrases that say essentially the same thing.

3. **The correct answer is (C).** The passage seeks here to point out a similarity between Shakespeare's first dramas and the early filmmakers' art. To accomplish this with "Just as," the two clauses should be grammatically parallel, but they're not. ("Just as" Shakespeare's first plays *were or did what?*) Given the sentence's structure, choice (C) provides the proper idiom to make the point. Choice (B) distorts the intended meaning by suggesting a distinction or difference rather than a similarity. Choice (D) should sound awkward to you, because it supplies an improper idiom.

4. **The correct answer is (H).** The paragraph already infers that these two people were geniuses of the silent movie era of the 1920s. Eliminate choice (F). What's more, information about where they came from is irrelevant, since the passage doesn't discuss national differences in cinema. Eliminate choice (G). Choice (H) provides both of these reasons for not adding the phrase, and is therefore the correct answer. You can eliminate choice (J) because the reason it provides is unsupported by the information in the paragraph.

5. **The correct answer is (C).** The original wording creates a run-on sentence. Choice (C) fixes the problem. So does choice (D), but "For" doesn't connect the two ideas logically. The dash in choice (B) leaves the relationship between the two ideas vague and confusing.

6. **The correct answer is (F).** The sentence intends to convey the idea that the salon artist was like the Renaissance painters in that he could mold his patrons' tastes. The structure of the original version clearly conveys this idea. The structure in choice (G) distorts this message, suggesting that the salon artist is like the Renaissance painters only in that he is strong enough. Choice (H) completely distorts the sentence's intended meaning, inferring that the salon artist's tastes are similar to those of the Renaissance artists. Choice (J) splits the infinitive "to match"; the result is a wobbly, awkward sentence.

The perfect, or ideal, sentence is partly in the ear of the beholder. In Question 7, perhaps the original version didn't strike you as the best possible way to express the idea at hand. Or, perhaps it did. The point is that the ACT English Test is not a quest for perfection but rather an exercise in comparing the quality of alternatives.

7. **The correct answer is (B).** The idea in this sentence is in contrast to the idea of the previous sentence; hence, "However" is a more logical word with which to start the sentence. Choice (C) suggests wrongly that the sentence is a conclusion based on the information in the previous sentence; in other words, choice (C) misleads the reader as to the relationship between the two sentences. Following choice (D)'s suggestion would undermine the rhetorical effectiveness of the paragraph. Without an appropriate word or phrase to signal that a contrasting idea is ahead, the paragraph fails to make its point.

8. **The correct answer is (G).** The idiomatic construction in English runs, "the larger . . . the greater." Once you've used the first half of a pair of phrases like these, you're committed to using the second half as well. Choices (H) and (J) undermine the parallel construction between the two phrases by adding the word "are." Choice (J) is also very awkward.

9. **The correct answer is (D).** The original sentence presents its ideas in an awkward and confusing

sequence. Particularly, notice the great separation between the subject complement "are also the most thoroughly conventional" and the subject that it complements. Choice (D) eliminates the gap, helping to clarify the relationship between the two elements. Using either choice (B) or choice (C) would result in a pronoun-reference problem. (Read the sentence under either proposal, and you'll "hear" that the pronoun "They" seems to refer to "today.")

10. **The correct answer is (G).** Without a comma between "begins" and "the," the sentence nonsensically suggests that it is the twenty-first century that begins, or initiates, an emergence. Choices (G) and (H) both add the comma needed to set off the modifying phrase "As the twenty-first century begins" from the sentence's subject ("The emergence"). Choice (H), however, creates a new problem. It changes the sentence's subject from "the emergence" to "movies." But it is the *emergence* of movies, not movies themselves, that is an "artistic development." So, choice (H) creates disagreement between the subject and subject complement. Choice (J), which inserts a semicolon (instead of a comma), is incorrect because "As the twenty-first century begins" is not an independent clause (one that can stand on its own as a sentence).

11. **The correct answer is (B).** With the original version, the pronoun reference (what "its" refers to) is a bit unclear, even though the first noun preceding "its" is the intended antecedent ("the last century"). Choices (B) and (C) both solve this stylistic problem by replacing the pronoun with its antecedent. Of the two choices, choice (B) sounds less repetitive and therefore is the better choice. Choice (D) provides a phrase that is both idiomatically and grammatically proper in context, but it is wordier than choice (B) and hence is not as good a choice.

12. **The correct answer is (H).** In the original version, the plural verb "make" doesn't agree in number with its singular subject "relationship" or with the singular verb "is." Choice (H) fixes the problem by changing "make" to the singular form "makes." Choice (G) is idiomatically and grammatically correct, but it distorts the sentence's intended meaning by suggesting that the special relationship described *is the only way* to make movies unique. Choice (J) is the runner-up, but it is not as rhetorically effective as choice (H). Read both versions again, and you'll see that choice (H) makes the point more clearly and effectively.

13. **The correct answer is (A).** The underlined portion is concise, idiomatic, and grammatically correct. One equally acceptable alternative is "a moviemaker and his audience." But none of the listed options provide this alternative. Choice (B) undermines the structural parallelism between "moviemaker" and "audience" by adding an article ("his") to one but not to the other. Choice (C) does not suffer from the same problem as choice (B). But in choice (C), the article "an" is too vague. (What audience? Any kind at all?) Choice (D) is the runner-up. As in the original version, choice (D) provides parallel grammatical structure. The problem with choice (D) is the word "audiences." Although this plural form is grammatically correct, so is the singular "audience." In context, the singular form more appropriatly conveys the point of the sentence.

14. **The correct answer is (H).** Neither sentence (1) nor sentence (2) say anything about the "special relationship" to which sentence (3) refers. Hence, it wouldn't make logical sentence for either (1) or (2) to follow (3). Eliminate choices (G) and (J). Also, notice the word "But" at the beginning of sentence (3). This keyword signals that what immediately precedes it is in opposition to what follows. Sentence (1) provides the appropriate opposition: The universal power of film may seem unique, sentence (1), *but* not compared with the "truly" unique relationship between moviemaker and audience, sentence (3).

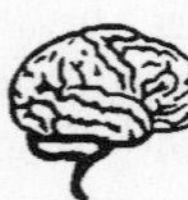

In the preceding question, the rhetorical impact of juxtaposing sentences (1) and (3) is subtle—just the kind of nuance you'll need to recognize the very toughest ACT English questions. Kudos if you got this question right—and for the right reason!

15. **The correct answer is (D).** The third paragraph should come first; it introduces the topic and places the movies in their context as the leading twentieth-century artistic innovation. The other two paragraphs, which discuss some specifics about the development of movies as an art form, logically follow.

LESSON 4

Punctuation

Thirteen percent of the total number of questions on the ACT English Test are questions about punctuation. In this lesson, you'll systematically review the punctuation issues covered on the test, and you'll find out how the test-makers design questions about punctuation that trick all but the brainiest test-takers. Here's what you'll need to know about:

- Comma splices and run-on sentences
- Sentence fragments (incomplete sentences)
- Uses and misuses of commas
- The colon and the semicolon
- The "em dash"
- The apostrophe (for possessives and contractions)

After reviewing these topics, you'll apply what you've reviewed to 15 tough ACT-style questions.

COMMA SPLICES AND RUN-ON SENTENCES

There's nothing wrong with combining two main clauses (clauses that can each stand alone as a complete sentence) into one sentence, as long as the clauses are properly connected. Be on the lookout for the following two flaws: (1) a comma splice and (2) a run-on sentence.

A *comma splice* occurs where a comma appears between two main clauses but without any connecting word such as *and*, *or*, *but*, *yet*, *for*, and *so*. To fix this grammatical error, you can always replace the comma with either a period or a semicolon. But in most cases, adding an appropriate connector word is rhetorically more effective.

A *run-on sentence* occurs where there is no punctuation between main clauses. To fix this grammatical error, you can always insert a period or a semicolon between the two main clauses. But in most cases, just as with comma splices, adding an appropriate connecting word is rhetorically more effective. Look at the following examples:

Comma splice: Dan ran out of luck, Mike continued to win.

Run-on: Dan ran out of luck Mike continued to win.

Correct, but ineffective: Dan ran out of luck. Mike continued to win.

Correct and effective: Dan ran out of luck, *but* Mike continued to win.

On the ACT English Test, you'll probably encounter one example of each of these two flaws. Don't expect to have difficulty recognizing either flaw. As long as you read the entire "sentence" carefully, the error should jump out at you. To trick up a comma splice or run-on question, the test-makers typically resort to one or more of three answer-choice ploys:

- Obscuring the problem with a smooth and logical transition from one clause to the other
- Fixing the grammatical error, but creating a new problem
- Offering a choice between two different connecting words, both of which fix the grammatical error

Here's an example that incorporates the first two ploys:

Q The Aleutian Islands of Alaska include many islands near the populated mainland, the majority of them are uninhabited by humans.

(A) NO CHANGE
(B) mainland but
(C) mainland, yet
(D) mainland; the

A **The correct answer is (C).** In the original sentence, notice that as you read *the majority of them*, there's still no hint of the comma-splice problem. The transition from one clause to the other seems smooth and logical. It isn't until you get to the next word (*are*) that the splice becomes apparent. (In fact, without *are*, the sentence would be perfectly fine.) Notice also that choice (C) adds the connecting word yet, which gives the sentence a reasonable meaning by underscoring the contrast between the mainland (which is populated) and the unpopulated nearby islands. Choice (B) also adds an appropriate connecting word. But choice (B) creates a new problem by omitting the comma, which should remain here to make clear that the writer is conveying two distinct ideas. Although choice (D) solves the comma-splice problem by replacing the comma with a semicolon, the resulting sentence is rhetorically ineffective.

If you correct a comma splice or run-on sentence by inserting a connecting word such as *and*, *but*, or *yet* without any punctuation, you might end up with a confusing sentence. In most cases, the best solution to either problem is to use a comma followed by a rhetorically appropriate connector. (By the way, the first sentence of this paragraph provides a perfect example: a comma followed by the conjunction *and*.)

SENTENCE FRAGMENTS (INCOMPLETE SENTENCES)

It was probably your fifth- or sixth-grade teacher who first informed you that a sentence must include both a subject and a predicate. Well, your teacher was right, and the ACT is here to remind you. Grammarians call incomplete sentences "sentence fragments." A sentence fragment, although punctuated as a sentence, cannot properly stand alone as a sentence. Some sentence fragments lack either a subject or a verb—two basic elements every sentence must have. Any average test-taker can easily recognize this type of fragment:

Fragment: Expensive private colleges, generally out of financial reach for most families with college-aged children.

Fragment: Without question, responsibility for building and maintaining safe bridges.

In other cases, the sentence fragment has both a subject and a verb, but the verb appears in a clause that begins either with a subordinating conjunction (e.g., *since*, *although*, *while*) or with a relative pronoun (e.g., *which*, *that*, *who*) that makes the clause dependent on another clause. Here's an example:

Fragment: Carbon dating, *which* can be used in estimating the age of materials that are of organic origin only, *since* the method is based on the predictable decay of carbon-based organic compounds.

Although this collection of words is pretty long (31 words), it is a sentence fragment rather than a true sentence. Why? Not because it lacks a subject and a verb; actually, it contains three verbs, each with its own subject. But each of these clauses is a dependent rather than an independent clause, so none is enough to make a free-standing sentence.

Subordination of a dependent clause to a main clause can be achieved through the use of:

- **Words modifying relative pronouns: _which, who, that_**
- **Words establishing time relationship: _before, after, as, since_**
- **Words establishing a causal relationship: _because, since_**
- **Words of admission or concession: _although, though, despite_**
- **Words indicating place: _where, wherever_**
- **Words of condition: _if, unless_**

Brainiacs generally don't have any trouble recognizing sentence fragments, even ones like the preceding one, when they see them on the ACT. However, an especially long fragment containing a string of subordinate clauses might escape your detection if you're not paying close attention. Here's an example of the sort of long fragment that might trip you up if you're not careful.

One cannot deny that, even after the initial flurry of the feminist movement subsided, Congresswoman Bella Abzug, undeniably her female constituency's truest voice, as well as its most public advocate.

(A) NO CHANGE
(B) who was her constituency's
(C) and also its
(D) was also its

A **The correct answer is (D).** With the phrase that choice (D) provides, the sentence can be distilled down to this: *One cannot deny that Bella Abzug was its [the feminist movement's] most public advocate*. Adding the verb was is the key to transforming the original fragment into a complete sentence. None of the other options provides the necessary verb to establish a predicate for the would-be sentence.

If you're not sure whether a sentence is complete, ask yourself two questions: What's the subject? Where's the verb that establishes a predicate?

USES AND MISUSES OF COMMAS

A comma indicates a pause that should correspond to a pause in the logic of the sentence. Commas make it clear to the reader that the logic of the sentence is being (temporarily) interrupted. The ACT tests four different uses (and misuses) of the comma. Pay particular attention to the last one listed below, which generally makes for more challenging test questions than the others:

- Overuse of the comma, resulting in the splitting of a grammatical unit
- Too few commas, resulting in a confusing sentence
- Commas used to separate a list of three or more items
- Commas used in pairs to set appositives (parenthetical phrases)

COMMAS THAT SPLIT A GRAMMATICAL UNIT

Commas should not needlessly separate parts of the sentence that "want" to be together, such as the subject and verb:

Incorrect: Former Secretary of State Henry Kissinger, is the author of several books on the history of diplomacy.

The verb *is* should not be separated by a comma from its subject *Henry Kissinger* (unless a parenthetical phrase intervenes between them—not the case here).

Similarly, no comma should come between the verb and a subject complement that may follow it:

Incorrect: The nineteenth-century explorers Lewis and Clark may be, two of America's most-admired historical figures.

In the same way, a preposition should not be separated from its object by a comma:

Incorrect: As the storm continued, pieces of driftwood as well as, large quantities of sand were blown up onto the front porch.

The preposition *as well as* needs to remain connected to its object, the phrase *large quantities of sand*.

When commas are overused on the ACT, it will usually be in sentences where the commas jarringly separate parts of the sentence that seem to "want" to be together. These abuses are easy enough for any Brainiac to spot.

COMMAS FOR SENTENCE SENSE

A tougher task is deciding whether a sentence uses too *few* commas, a problem that can easily confuse the reader. Here's the guideline: A sentence should use the minimum number of commas needed for a reader to understand the intended meaning of the sentence.

Too few commas: Enzyme catalysis takes place in living systems and as it is not a laboratory procedure is therefore subject to cellular controls.

Better: Enzyme catalysis takes place in living systems, and as it is not a laboratory procedure is therefore subject to cellular controls.

Also acceptable: Enzyme catalysis takes place in living systems, and, as it is not a laboratory procedure, is therefore subject to cellular controls.

There are two special situations that you should look for in ACT sentences: commas used to separate items in a list, and commas used to set off parenthetical phrases. You'll look at both types of situations immediately ahead.

COMMAS FOR LISTS OF THREE OR MORE ITEMS

When three or more words, phrases, or clauses are presented in sequence, they should be separated by commas. Here are examples of each:

Commas separating a list of words: The Galapagos Islands boast some of the world's most unusual plants, birds, mammals, reptiles, and fish.

Commas separating a list of phrases: We looked for the missing gloves under the sofa, in the closet, and behind the dresser, but we never found them.

Commas separating a list of clauses: The plot of the movie was a familiar one: boy meets girl, boy loses girl, mutant from outer space devours both.

Notice two things about how these lists are crafted. First, you normally insert the word "and" before the final item in the series ("plants, birds, mammals, reptiles, and fish"). Second, the last comma (the one after reptiles in this example) is optional. Sometimes called the *serial comma*, it may be included or omitted according to taste. (The ACT test-makers have no special preference, and there's no "right" or "wrong" about it on the exam.) The other commas, however, are not optional; they must be used.

COMMAS FOR SETTING OFF APPOSITIVES (PARENTHETICAL PHRASES)

Wherever a commonly used parenthetical phrase such as *for example*, *that is*, or *first of all* appears, it should be separated from the rest of the sentence by commas (or, if the phrase appears at the beginning of a sentence, by one comma). These phrases are easy enough for any test-taker to spot.

Another type of parenthetical phrase is an *appositive*, which names or describes a noun. It, too, should be set off by commas. In the next example, "the great left-handed Dodger pitcher" is an appositive:

Sandy Koufax, the great left-handed Dodger pitcher, was the guest of honor at this year's sports club banquet.

Sometimes a parenthetical phrase may be quite long:

> I was surprised to learn that Paula, my cousin Frank's former girlfriend and a well-known local artist, had decided to move to Santa Fe.

You can probably see how the ten words enclosed by commas interrupt the main flow of the sentence. If you're unsure, try this test: Read the sentence without the phrase. If it still makes grammatical sense and the meaning is basically the same, then the phrase is parenthetical and should be set off by commas. This example passes the test—the interrupting words (*my cousin Frank's former girlfriend and a well-known local artist*) should be surrounded by commas.

Now try applying the test you just learned about to an ACT-style sentence, which actually involves two separate appositive issues.

The following example incorporates two similar issues into the same paragraph in order to help illustrate the concept you just learned. On the actual test, don't expect one paragraph to test you twice on the same concept.

During the 1980s when their funds dried up[1] the Girls Choir of Harlem temporarily disbanded. However, in 1989, the choir reassembled and,[2] in November of 1997, made their debut at Lincoln Center's Alice Tully Hall.

Q 1. (A) NO CHANGE
(B) Place a comma before and after the underlined portion
(C) Place a comma before, but not after, the underlined portion
(D) Place a comma after, but not before, the underlined portion

A **The correct answer is (B).** The sentence makes perfect grammatical and logical sense without the underlined portion. This is a good indication that the portion is an appositive, which should be set off by a pair of commas. Without a comma after *dried up*, the sentence nonsensically suggests that the Girls Choir became *dried up!* Thus, neither choice (A) nor choice (C) can be correct. A comma is also needed immediately after *1980s* for clarity.

Q 2. (A) NO CHANGE
(B) reassembled
(C) reassembled; and
(D) reassembled, and

A **The correct answer is (A).** If you omit the appositive in November of 1997, the clause makes perfect grammatical and logical sense: . . . *the choir reassembled and made their debut* . . . . No punctuation mark is needed immediately after *reassembled*.

X-REF **As for choice (C) in the preceding question, you'll examine the proper uses of the semicolon just ahead in this lesson.**

THE COLON AND THE SEMICOLON

Many ACT test-takers are uncertain about how the proper uses of the colon (:) and the semicolon (;) differ. To ensure that you're not among those test-takers, keep in mind the following guidelines and examples.

Use the colon to introduce either a *list* or a *restatement*.

Here's an example of a colon used to introduce a list:

For my term paper, I decided to write about the Beatles' last three albums: *The White Album*, *Abbey Road*, and *Let It Be*.

Notice that the colon alerts the reader that a list specifying whatever has just been referred to is immediately ahead.

Usually, if an introductory word precedes the list and leads directly into it, you should omit the colon. Thus, if the sentence reads like the following, you do not need a colon: For my term paper, I decided to write about several of the Beatles' albums, including *The White Album*, *Abbey Road*, and *Let It Be*.

Here's an example of using a colon to introduce a restatement:

Barbara was named valedictorian for one reason: her exceptional academic achievement.

What follows the colon "restates" what precedes it; the words "her exceptional academic achievement" name the "one reason" mentioned before the colon.

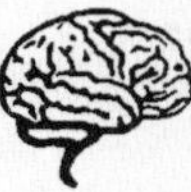

Here's a handy rule of thumb for testing whether a colon is appropriate in a given sentence. If either the phrase *that is* or the word *namely* could be inserted at the same spot as the colon, instead of it, then a colon is probably correct.

Use a semicolon to connect two independent clauses.

You've already learned that you can use one of the connecting words to connect two independent clauses; another proper way to connect two independent clauses is with a semicolon (;). By the way, in the sentence you just read, a semicolon was used properly.

Now look at an ACT-style example that tests you on both the colon and semicolon:

Adams was initially drawn into the slavery question not by the controversy over slavery itself; but by the so-called "gag rule" used by the South to stifle debates in the Senate concerning slavery.

(A) NO CHANGE
(B) itself. Instead,
(C) itself, but
(D) itself: but

A **The correct answer is (C).** The semicolon in the middle of this sentence is used incorrectly because it doesn't connect two independent clauses. The first part of the sentence (from *Adams* through *itself*) is an independent clause—it could stand alone as a sentence. However, the rest of the sentence couldn't stand alone as a sentence; it lacks a subject and verb (and therefore isn't even a proper clause). Therefore, the semicolon should be replaced by a comma. The result of choice (B) is a sentence fragment following the period. As for choice (D), a semicolon is improper because what follows is neither a list nor a restatement.

In the preceding example, what if you were to omit a punctuation mark altogether between *itself* and *but*? For the purpose of conveying the sentence's ideas, this option would not be as effective as inserting a comma. But it would come very close—too close for the ACT. That's why it's not listed as an answer choice.

THE "EM DASH"

The em dash (—), which we'll simply call a *dash* from now on, is the punctuation mark that looks like a long hyphen. The ACT covers this mark less frequently than the others you've examined in this lesson. But the mark is fair game on the ACT, so it's best to be ready for it—just in case.

A pair of dashes can be used in the middle of a sentence—instead of commas or parentheses—to set off particularly important parenthetical material (just like in this sentence). Also, a single dash can be used instead of a comma before a concluding phrase—to help set off and emphasize what follows (just like in this sentence).

But, the dash should *never* be used as a substitute for the colon, or vice versa. (Remember: The colon is used to introduce either a list or a restatement.) This distinction is a likely focus of an ACT question involving the dash. Here's a typical example:

Q In the business of high technology, company leaders sometimes stumble by waiting too long to see what new technologies develop: trading time for the prospect of more information and less uncertainty.

(A) NO CHANGE
(B) develop. They trade
(C) develop—trading
(D) develop while they trade

A **The correct answer is (C).** In the original version, what follows the colon is obviously not a list—nor is it a restatement of what precedes it. (Replacing the colon with *namely* or *that is* wouldn't make much sense, would it?) Hence, the colon is inappropriate here. On the other hand, a dash, choice (C), works quite nicely to emphasize the rationale behind the poor decisions that company leaders sometimes make. Choices (B) and (D) are rhetorically ineffective alternatives. (Notice how each one essentially severs the logical connection between the idea of the first clause and that of the second clause.)

The "em" in "em dash" refers to the width of an upper-case "M." It's a term used by typographers. Go ahead and compare this em dash (—) to this "M"; they're almost equal in width, aren't they? That's no coincidence.

THE APOSTROPHE (FOR POSSESSIVES AND CONTRACTIONS)

The apostrophe is used for two purposes in English, both frequently tested on the ACT. The rules for both are pretty simple, so our review will be brief. Don't expect any brain strain—either here or in handling apostrophes on the test.

A *possessive* is used to indicate ownership or some other close connection between a noun or pronoun and what follows it ("Susan's car," "the company's employees"). Form the possessive as follows:

- For a singular noun, add *'s*—as in *the dog's paw* or *James's necktie*.
- For a plural noun ending in *s*, just add an apostrophe—as in *the Wangs' apartment* or *the birds' feathers*.
- For a plural noun that does not end in *s*, add *'s*, as in *the children's teacher or the cattle's hooves*.
- The possessive pronouns *his, hers, its, ours, yours,* and *theirs* contain no apostrophes.

The other use of an apostrophe is in a *contraction*, a word made up of two or more words from which letters have been omitted for easier pronunciation.

Contractions are *not* generally considered "incorrect" or "slangy"; they're perfectly acceptable in all but the most formal writing.

The apostrophe is usually (but not always!) inserted in place of the letters omitted. If in doubt, mentally "expand" the contraction to determine which letters have been left out; this is often a useful guide to determining where the apostrophe belongs.

- we've got to go = we have got to go
- I'd rather not = I would rather not
- she won't mind = she will not mind
- it's your turn = it is your turn
- you're welcome = you are welcome

Proper use of the apostrophe in a contraction is basically a matter of correct spelling—no biggee for a Brainiac.

BRAIN TEASER

In this quiz, you'll tackle 15 ACT-style questions focused primarily on punctuation—tougher than the average ACT punctuation question. Keep in mind: You won't encounter ACT-length passages in this quiz. Instead, you'll examine an eclectic series of discrete sentences, along with 1-3 questions based on each one.

Many questions in this quiz also involve some of the other official testing areas—namely, grammar, sentence structure, idiom, and style. Therefore, these questions serve as not only a *review*, but also as a *preview* of what is to come in Part II.

Attempt all 15 questions, but don't put yourself under a time limit. Focus instead on applying the rules and guidelines you have learned in this lesson. Then be sure to read the explanations that follow the quiz. They're just as important as the questions, because they explain how to apply the rules and guidelines to the questions.

QUIZ

Engineering teams monitor over a hundred former nuclear test sites for radiation levels, the civilian populace is banned from any area with sufficiently high levels.

1. (A) NO CHANGE
   (B) levels in which the
   (C) levels, and the
   (D) levels because the

2. (F) NO CHANGE
   (G) will be banned
   (H) are banned
   (J) is prohibited

The need to foster allegiances among all the United States, a need recognized by Madison and Hamilton, among others, during their burgeoning independence from England.

3. (A) NO CHANGE
   (B) What was needed
   (C) There was a need
   (D) It was necessary

4. (F) NO CHANGE
   (G) others during
   (H) others—during
   (J) other states, during

5. (A) NO CHANGE
   (B) its
   (C) the state's
   (D) the states'

The practice of drawing voting district boundaries, on the basis of how people are likely to vote, is known as "gerrymandering."

6. (F) NO CHANGE
   (G) OMIT both commas
   (H) OMIT only the first comma
   (J) OMIT only the second comma

The former Princess Alix of Hesse-Darmstadt and one of Queen Victoria's numerous grandchildren, the Tsarina (called Alexandra once she became married to Tsar Nicholas), giving birth to four daughters—Olga, Tatiana, Marie, and Anastasia—before producing a male child, who would eventually succeed the Tsar.

7. (A) NO CHANGE
   (B) having given
   (C) gave
   (D) had given

8. (F) NO CHANGE
   (G) daughters—namely, Olga
   (H) daughters: Olga
   (J) daughters, who included Olga

It was the publication of the short story *The Strand*, and the series of books which followed, that the public finally took an interest in Arthur Conan Doyle's Sherlock Holmes character, enabling him to give up his practice and turn to writing full time.

9. (F) NO CHANGE
   (G) It was with
   (H) As a result of
   (J) OMIT the underlined portion.

10. (A) NO CHANGE
    (B) character, which enabled
    (C) character; enabling
    (D) character. This enabled

Special effects <u>are</u> a <u>movie makers'</u> tool for communicating a unique imaginative experience. <u>And after all—that's</u> one of the reasons we all go to the movies.
(11: "are"; 12: "movie makers'"; 13: "And after all—that's")

11. (A) NO CHANGE
(B) is
(C) are one of
(D) could be

12. (A) NO CHANGE
(B) movie makers
(C) movie maker's
(D) OMIT the underlined portion

13. (F) NO CHANGE
(G) And—after all, that's
(H) And, after all, that's
(J) And that after all is

Ignorance of the law does not preclude <u>one's being arrested</u> for <u>a violation of it.</u>
(14: "one's being arrested"; 15: "a violation of it.")

14. (F) NO CHANGE
(G) one from being arrested
(H) ones' being arrested
(J) one's arrest

15. (A) NO CHANGE
(B) violating it.
(C) violating the law.
(D) its violations.

ANSWERS AND EXPLANATIONS

1. **The correct answer is (C).** In the original sentence, two main clauses are improperly separated by only a comma, without an appropriate connecting word. Choice (C) inserts an appropriate word (*and*), resulting in a sentence that makes its point clearly. Choices (B) and (D) each seem to fix the comma splice by transforming the second main clause into a subordinate clause. But with choice (B), the result is a confusing string of subordinate clauses, while with choice (D), the result is an illogical idea. (It makes sense that civilians are banned from these areas because the teams are monitoring for radiation—not the other way around.)

In question 1, *and* is not the only connecting word that fixes the comma splice and makes sense. So do the words *yet* or *but* (although either one would give the sentence a somewhat different meaning). Therefore, remember that in most cases, there's more than one effective way to revise an underlined portion. But don't' worry—the answer choices will only list *one* such way.

2. **The correct answer is (F).** The present-tense *is banned* is consistent with the present-tense *monitor*. Choice (G) provides for an unwarranted shift in tense from present to future. Choice (H) results in subject-verb disagreement—between the plural *are* and the singular *populace*. Choice (J) results in the non-idiomatic phrase *prohibited from any area*. (It would be idiomatic to say that the populace is prohibited from *entering* any area, for example.)

3. **The correct answer is (C).** With the underlined portion, the would-be sentence is actually a sentence fragment. Choice (B) fails to correct this problem. Choices (C) and (D) each provide the subject and verb needed to transform the fragment into a complete sentence. Notice "a need," which begins the second clause. In context, what precedes this clause should identify the particular need to which the clause refers. Choice (C) more explicitly and clearly identifies that "need" than choice (D) does.

4. **The correct answer is (F).** In context, the phrase *among others* is a parenthetical thought and thus is properly set off by commas—one preceding it and one following it. Choice (G) improperly omits the second comma, creating ambiguity as to what "others" refer—people like Madison and Hamilton or states. Choice (H) improperly combines the use of a comma and a dash for this purpose. Choice (J) is nonsensical; in context, *others* is clearly not intended to refer to states but rather to people (like Madison and Hamilton).

5. **The correct answer is (D).** The original version correctly uses the plural possessive *their* to refer to its intended antecedent *all the United States*. But the intervening clause obscures this reference. Choices (C) and (D) both solve this problem by replacing the pronoun with its antecedent. However, choice (C) uses the singular contraction *state's* where the plural form *states'* is needed.

6. **The correct answer is (G).** Without the clause that is surrounded by commas, the sentence fails to adequately define *gerrymandering*. Both commas should be omitted to make clear that the clause is an essential part of the definition.

7. **The correct answer is (D).** The last phrase of the sentence (who would eventually succeed the Tsar) makes clear that all events described in the sentence occurred in the past, and that the birth of the four daughters preceded the events described after it. Accordingly, the past perfect *had given*, choice (D), is appropriate here. By the same token, neither the present tense, choice (A), nor the present perfect tense, choice (B), nor the simple past tense, choice (C), reflect the logical sequence of events.

X-REF **During Lesson 6, we'll examine problems in tense shift in greater detail.**

8. **The correct answer is (F).** The pair of dashes appropriately sets off the list of four daughters as an appositive. (Remove the list along with the dashes, and the sentence makes perfect sense.) The word *namely*, choice (G), is superfluous and redundant; the sentence is already clear that these are the daughter's names. Choice (H) would be correct if the sentences ended with the list of daughters. But since the sentence continues, beginning with a dash, a dash preceding the list is needed for a proper appositive. In choice (J), *who included* obscures the sentence's meaning by implying that Alexandra might have given birth to more than four daughters.

9. **The correct answer is (B).** As it stands, the original version is actually a sentence fragment. Try replacing what follows the underlined portion up to the first comma (*the publication . . . which followed*) with simply *The Strand*. Here's the result: *It was* The Strand *that the public finally took an interest in Arthur Conan Doyle's. . . .* As you can see, something's missing. Choice (B) supplies the missing piece (*with*) that makes for a complete and logical sentence. Neither choice (C) not choice (D) solves the problem.

10. **The correct answer is (F).** A comma is the appropriate punctuation mark here—it separates the main clause from a dependent one. Choice (H) is wrong because the final part of the sentence (beginning with *enabling*) is not an independent clause. Choice (J) is grammatically correct, but one of the results is an unclear pronoun reference. (What does *This* refer to—the public's interest or Doyle's Sherlock Holmes character?)

11. **The correct answer is (A).** The term "special effects" is used here in the singular sense—hence, the singular subject complements *tool*. Nevertheless, it is idiomatic to say that *special effects are a tool* rather than *special effects is a tool*. (The word *are* should sound more correct to you.) Here's a similar idiom that might hit closer to home for you: *My parents are the reason I'm leaving home after graduation*.

12. **The correct answer is (H).** The word *maker's* is a possessive; the sentence refers to something (the *tool* of special effects) that belongs to the movie makers. Therefore, it should be spelled with an apostrophe *s*, as possessives generally are. As for choice (J), simply omitting the reference to movie makers obscures the rhetorical and logical connection between the ideas of the two sentences.

13. **The correct answer is (C).** The parenthetical phrase *after all* should be surrounded by commas to set it off from the rest of the sentence. None of the three other options sets off the phrase.

14. **The correct answer is (J).** In the original version, the noun clause *one's being arrested*, which includes the possessive pronoun *one's*, is grammatically correct. (Noun clauses take the possessive verb form.) However, choice (J) is more succinct and graceful. Choice (G) is also grammatically correct, but, again, choice (J) is better. In choice (H), the apostrophe after the *s* is incorrect because *one* is a singular pronoun.

15. **The correct answer is (B).** The pronoun *it* would more clearly refer to its antecedent *the law* if it were positioned closer to the antecedent. But since this solution is not listed as an option, another solution to the confusing reference is to replace *it* with the antecedent. Also, *a violation* sounds a bit awkward in context; *violating* is more graceful. Choice (B) solves both problems. Choice (C) solves only the latter problem. Choice (D) results in ambiguity as to whether *one* or *the law* is committing a violation. The intended antecedent of *its* is *one*, of course, but the grammatical construction is confusing.

X-REF

During Lesson 7, you'll take a closer look at *ambiguous pronoun references*—a different sort of problem than the pronoun-antecedent agreement problems you examined here in Lesson 4. Also, both of the preceding questions involved writing *style* issues—conciseness, awkwardness, clarity, and idiom. Throughout Part II, you'll encounter many more examples of these issues.

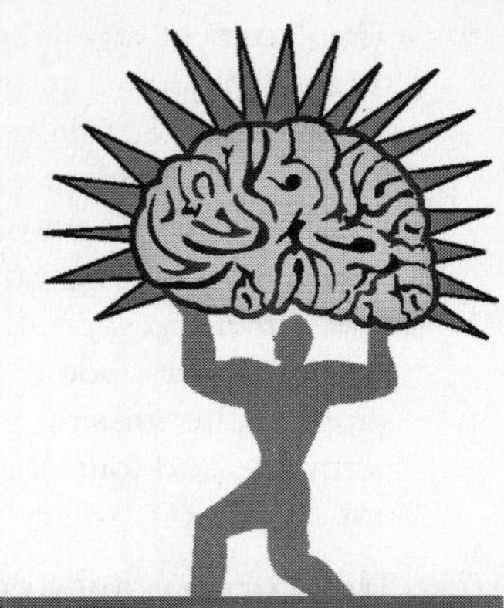

LESSON 5
Parts of Speech

In this lesson, you'll grapple with grammar issues involving adjectives, adverbs, pronouns, and verbs. The seven general issues covered here and listed below are the ones that appear most frequently on the ACT English Test—with the single exception noted (see **X-REF**):

- Choice between adjective and adverb
- Choice of adjective for comparisons
- Choice of personal pronoun
- Choice of relative pronoun
- Pronoun-antecedent agreement
- Subject-verb agreement
- Forms of irregular verbs

In addition to learning how to fix errors involving these issues, you'll look at how each error might appear in a tougher-than-typical ACT question. Then, you'll apply what you've reviewed to 15 tough ACT-style questions.

X-REF **One frequently tested topic involving a part of speech *not* covered in this lesson is the topic of *verb tense*. Don't worry: You'll learn all you need to know about this tricky area in Lesson 6.**

CHOICE BETWEEN ADJECTIVE AND ADVERB

Adjectives describe nouns, while *adverbs* describe verbs, adjectives and other adverbs. Adverbs generally end with *-ly*, while adjectives don't. Look for adjectives incorrectly used as adverbs (and vice versa).

Incorrect: The movie ended *sudden*.

Correct: The movie ended *suddenly*.

(The adverb *suddenly* describes the verb *ended*.)

Although adverbs generally end with *-ly*, some adverbs don't. Also, if you're dealing with two adverbs in a row, sometimes the *-ly* is dropped from the second adverb. There are no hard-and-fast rules here. Trust your ear as to what sounds correct.

Incorrect: Risk-takers drive fastly, play hardly, and arrive lately for their appointments.

Correct: Risk-takers drive *fast*, play *hard*, and arrive *late* for their appointments.

Incorrect: The Canadian skater jumps *particularly highly*.

Correct: The Canadian skater jumps *particularly high*.

Also keep in mind that adjectives, not adverbs, should be used to describe verbs involving the senses (sight, taste, smell, hearing, touch).

Incorrect: Dinner tasted *awful* delicious.

Correct: Dinner tasted *awfully* delicious.

(The adjective *delicious* is used to describe the verb *tasted*, while the adverb *awfully* is used to describe *delicious*.)

Word choices that violate these rules are generally easy to spot because the words simply sound wrong. Even so, the test-makers do have their ways of desigining tough questions involving these issues. In the following sentence, for instance, all four options conform to the rules, so you need to make some close judgment calls.

A recent report from the Department of Energy suggests that over the next two decades demand for crude oil will increase <u>at an alarming and quick rate.</u>

(A) NO CHANGE
(B) at a rate that is alarming and quick.
(C) at an alarmingly quick rate.
(D) alarmingly quickly.

The correct answer is (C). In the original version, the adjectives *alarming* and *quick* both describe *rate* (a noun). Hence, this version is grammatically correct. But it would make more sense for *alarming* to describe the adjective *quick*, as choices (C) and (D) provide. So, you can eliminate choices (A) and (B). This is where the question becomes tricky. In choice (D), the use of two adverbs in the phrase *increase alarmingly quickly* is technically correct—but doesn't choice (D) sound a bit awkward, especially compared with choice (C)? Even though choice (D) is more concise, choice (C) supplies a clearer, more graceful expression of the idea.

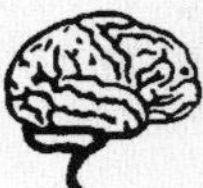

Brainiacs know that the most concise answer choice is not necessarily the best one. It might obscure the meaning of a sentence or make for a clumsy phrase.

CHOICE OF ADJECTIVE FOR COMPARISONS

As you read an ACT sentence, pay close attention to any adjective ending in *-er*, *-ier*, *-est*, and *-iest*. Adjectives ending in *-er* and *-ier* should be used to compare *two* things, while adjectives ending in *-est* and *-iest* should be used in dealing with three or more things.

Comparative Form (two things)	***Superlative Form (three or more things)***
brighter	brightest
greater	greatest
fewer	fewest
lesser	least
more	most
better	best

Incorrect: Frank is less intelligent than the other four students.

Correct: Frank is the *least* intelligent among the *five* students.

Correct: Frank is *less* intelligent than *any* of the other four students (The word *any* is singular, so the comparative form is proper.)

Another way of making a comparison is to precede the adjective with a word such as *more*, *less*, *most*, or *least*. But if both methods are used together, the sentence is incorrect.

Incorrect: Francis is *more healthier* than Greg.

Correct: Francis is *healthier* than Greg.

Correct: Francis is *more healthy* than Greg.

Let's look at an example of a tough ACT-style sentence the test-makers might design on these grammar issues.

Q The more busy the trading floor at the stock exchange, the less likely that large institutional investors can influence the direction of price by initiating large leveraged transactions.

(A) NO CHANGE
(B) The busier is the
(C) As a result of a busier
(D) The busiest the

A **The correct answer is (A).** The original version correctly uses *more* preceding the adjective *busy*. It is idiomatic to say *The more . . ., the less . . . .* (Although replacing the underlined portion with *The busier the* would also be grammatically correct and idiomatic, this option is not available among the answer choices.) Choice (B) is wrong because *The busier is the* is not idiomatic. Choice (C) is wrong because the result, while it might look like a complete sentence, is actually not. Choice (D) is wrong because it uses the superlative *busiest* where the comparative *busier* is appropriate.

When the ACT tests you on an idiomatic phrase that is unfamiliar to you, use the process of elimination to determine whether or not the phrase is proper. In the preceding question, for example, you can rule out choices (C) and (D) because they result in grammatical errors.

ERROR IN CHOICE OF PERSONAL PRONOUN

Personal pronouns are words such as *they*, *me*, *his*, and *itself*—words that refer to specific people, places, and things. Pronouns take different forms depending on how they're used in a sentence. Just for the record, you'll find all the various forms in the following table.

	Subjective Case	***Possessive Case***	***Objective Case***	***Objective Case—Reflexive***
first-person singular	I	my, mine	me	myself
first-person plural	we	our, ours	us	ourselves
second-person singular	you	your, yours	you	yourself
second-person plural	you	your, yours	you	yourselves
third-person singular	he, she, it	his, her, hers, its	him, her, it	himself, herself, itself
third-person plural	they	their, theirs	them	themselves

In ACT sentences, you'll find very few (if any) first-person or second-person personal pronouns. Why do the test-makers shun pronouns such as *we*, *you*, and *our*? Because ACT sentences are academic in nature, not conversational or informal. (But you probably already noticed that, didn't you?)

You can generally trust your ear when it comes to detecting personal-pronoun errors. In some cases, however, even a Brainiac's ear can falter—so make sure you're "tuned in" to the following uses of pronouns.

Incorrect: Either him or Trevor *would be* the best spokesman for our group.

Incorrect: The best spokesperson for our group *would be* either him or Trevor.

Correct: Either Trevor or *he would be* the best spokesperson for our group.

Correct: The best spokesperson for our group *would be* either *he* or Trevor.

(Any form of the verb *to be* is followed by a subject pronoun, such as *he*.)

Incorrect: One can't help admiring *them* cooperating with one another.

Correct: One can't help admiring *their cooperating* with one another.

(The *possessive* form is used when the pronoun is part of a "noun clause," such as *their cooperating*.)

Incorrect: In striving to understand others, we also learn more about *us*.

Correct: In striving to understand others, *we* also learn more about *ourselves*.

(A *reflexive* pronoun is used to refer to the sentence's subject.)

What appears to be a reflexive pronoun may not even be a real word! Here's a list of "non-words," any of which might masquerade as a reflexive pronoun in a ACT sentence: *ourself, our own selves, theirselves, theirself, themself, their own self, their own selves.*

Now, look at *two* ways in which one of these tricky pronoun-case issues might rear its ugly head in an ACT sentence:

> Despite his admiring of (1) the great jazz musicians that preceded himself, Art Blakey opposed them trivializing (2) the popular genre.

Q **1.** (A) NO CHANGE
(B) him admiring
(C) that he admired
(D) his admiration of

A **The correct answer is (D).** Although the noun clause *his admiring* is perfectly acceptable here, the word *of* should be omitted. (*His admiring of* is not idiomatic.) None of the alternative choices provides *his admiring*. However, choice (D) provides an an appropriate, idiomatic substitute. Choice (B) is wrong because it improperly uses the object-case *him* in a noun clause. Choice (C) is not idiomatic. (A proper idiom here would be *Despite the fact that he admired.*)

Q **2.** (A) NO CHANGE
(B) their trivializing
(C) these musicians trivializing
(D) trivializing

A **The correct answer is (B).** Choice (B) corrects the improper use of "them," replacing it with the possessive "their," which properly precedes the gerund "trivializing." Choice (C) fails to correct the problem; instead, it simply substitutes the noun for the object-case pronoun. Choice (D) omits any reference to the musicians who preceded Blakey, leaving you with no idea as to who was trivializing.

In the preceding example, the sentence contained two underlined portions involving *the same kind* of grammar issue. But don't expect this to happen on the actual test.

ERROR IN CHOICE OF RELATIVE PRONOUN

The English language includes only a handful of *relative pronouns*. Here they are:

which

who

that

whose

whichever

whoever

whomever

Don't worry about what the term "relative pronoun" means. Instead, just remember the following rules about when to use each one.

1. Use *which* to refer to things.

2. Use either *who* or *that* to refer to people.

   Incorrect: Amanda, *which* was the third performer, was the best of the group.

   Correct: Amanda, *who* was the third performer, was the best of the group.

   Correct: The first employee *that* fails to meet his or her sales quota will be fired.

   Correct: The first employee *who* fails to meet his or her sales quota will be fired.

3. Whether you should use *which* or *that* depends on what the sentence is supposed to mean.

   One meaning: The third page, *which* had been earmarked, contained several typographical errors.

   Different meaning: The third page *that* had been earmarked contained several typographical errors.

   (The first sentence merely describes the third page as earmarked. The second sentence also suggests that the page containing the errors was the third earmarked page.)

Now look at how the test-makers might design a tough question involving the *that*-versus-*which* issue. Since all four options might sound okay to your ear, you'll need to fall back on the rules we just reviewed.

Q An art critic's primary task is elucidation, which is not easily separable from a second task: evaluation.

(A) NO CHANGE
(B) a task which is
(C) that is
(D) OMIT the underlined portion.

A **The correct answer is (A).** The relative prounoun *which* clearly describes elucidation, as opposed to describing a certain type or form of elucidation. Hence, choice (A) is correct, and choice (C) is incorrect. Choice (B) commits the reverse error: It uses *which* where *that* is called for—to describe a specific type of task. Choice (D) leaves it a bit unclear as to what is "not easily seperable." Hence, although choice (D) makes for the most concise version, the original version is preferable.

First use you ear to ferret out correct answers and rule out incorrect ones. But if more than one option *sounds* okay, compare those choices first for clarity and conformance with the rules of English grammar, *then* for conciseness.

4. Whether you should use *who* (*whoever*) or *whom* (*whomever*) depends on the grammatical function of the person (or people) being referred to. Confused? Don't worry; just take a look at the sample sentences here, and you shouldn't have any trouble deciding between *who* and *whom* on the ACT.

   Incorrect: It was the chairman *whom* initiated the bill.

   Correct: It was the chairman *who* initiated the bill.

   Incorrect: First aid will be available to *whomever* requires it.

   Correct: First aid will be available to *whoever* requires it.

Incorrect: The team members from East High, *who* the judges were highly impressed with, won the debate.

Correct: The team members from East High, with *whom* the judges were highly impressed, won the debate.

On the ACT, to make sure that *who (whoever)* and *whom (whomever)* are being used correctly, try substituting a regular pronoun, then rearrange the clause (if necessary) to form a simple sentence. If a subject-case pronoun works, then *who (whoever)* is the right choice. On the other hand, if an object-case pronoun works, then *whom (whomever)* is the right choice. Here's how it works with the foregoing sentences:

It was the chairman *whom* initiated the bill.

He initiated the bill.

He is a subject-case pronoun, so *whom* should be replaced with *who*.

First aid will be available to *whomever* requires it.

She requires it.

She is a subject-case pronoun, so *whomever* should be replaced with *whoever*.

The team members from East High, *who* the judges were highly impressed with, won the debate.

The judges were impressed with *them*.

Them is an object-case pronoun, so *who* should be replaced by *whom*.

For some sentences, it's easy to tell which is correct—*who* or *whom*—just based on how they sound in the sentence. But for other sentences, your ear might betray you. Here's a good example, which would clearly rank in the tough ACT category.

General Grant, whom Lincoln greatly respected for his ability to lead his troops, was nevertheless defeated in many a battle.

(A) NO CHANGE
(B) who
(C) with respect to whom
(D) a man who

The correct answer is (A). Transform the phrase *whom Lincoln respected* into a sentence with a simple pronoun: *Lincoln respected him*. Hence, the original version is correct, and choices (B) and (D) are incorrect. Choice (C) uses the correct relative pronoun (whom), but it results in the very awkward, and wordy, phrase "with respect to whom Lincoln greatly respected. . . ."

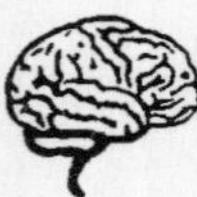

The *who*-versus-*whom* rules reside in the inner sanctum of English grammar—definitely Brainiac territory and not for the faint of heart.

PRONOUN-ANTECEDENT AGREEMENT

An *antecedent* is simply the noun to which a pronoun refers. In ACT sentences, make sure that pronouns agree in *number* (singular or plural) with their antecedents.

Singular: Studying other artists actually helps a young *painter* develop *his* or *her* own style.

Plural: Studying other artists actually helps young *painters* develop *their* own style.

But what's the rule for pronouns that refer to nouns describing a group of people or things (called *collective nouns*)? The pronoun can either be singular or plural, depending on whether the collective noun is used in a singular or plural sense.

Correct: The legislature hesitates to punish *its* own members for ethics violations. (*legislature* used in the singular sense)

Correct: The planning *committee* recessed, but Jack continued to work without *them*. (*committee* used in the plural sense)

Since the rule for collective nouns depends on the context, this area makes for a tougher test question—one that many test-takers will get wrong. Here's an ACT-style example:

Q Since it is our legislature that is to blame for this country's increasing dependency on oil, it is up to them to reverse this trend.

(A) NO CHANGE
(B) it
(C) our legislators
(D) the legislature

A **The correct answer is (D).** The antecedent of *them* (a plural pronoun) is *legislature* (a singular noun). One way to remedy the disagreement is to replace *them* with *it*, as in choice (B). But the intervening prepositional phrases obscure the pronoun reference. What's more, the phrase *it is up to it* sounds a bit odd, doesn't it? A better solution is to replace the underlined pronoun *them* with its antecedent, as in choice (D). Choice (C) leaves you wondering whether *our legislators* and *the legislature* are one and the same. Since choice (D) makes the sentence's meaning clearer, it is a better choice than (C).

Singular pronouns are generally used in referring to antecedents such as *each*, *every*, *either*, *neither*, and *one*.

Correct: *Neither* of the two countries imposes an income tax on *its* citizens.

Correct: *One* cannot be too kind to *oneself*.

When it comes to antecedents such as *anyone, anybody, everybody, everyone,* or *a person,* the rules of English grammar get a bit fuzzy. For instance, any grammarian would agree that the first sentence below is correct, but whether the second one is correct is hotly debated among grammarians.

Correct: **If *anyone* offends you, please don't confront *him* or *her*.**

Proper? **If *anyone* offends you, please don't confront *them*.**

Because the rule of grammar here is unsettled, rest assured that you will not encounter these words as pronoun antecedents on the ACT.

SUBJECT-VERB AGREEMENT (WHEN A VERB AND SUBJECT ARE SEPARATED)

A verb should always "agree" in number—either singular or plural—with its subject. Don't be fooled by any words or phrases that might separate the verb from its subject. In each sentence below, the singular verb *was* agrees with its subject, the singular noun *parade*:

Correct: The *parade was* spectacular.

Correct: The *parade* of cars *was* spectacular.

Correct: The *parade* of cars and horses *was* spectacular.

An intervening clause set off by commas can serve as an especially effective "smokescreen" for a subject-verb agreement error. Pay careful attention to what comes immediately before and after the intervening clause. Reading the sentence without the clause often reveals a subject-verb agreement error.

Incorrect: John, as well as his sister, *were* absent from school yesterday.

Correct: *John*, as well as his sister, *was* absent from school yesterday.

Here's how this type of subject-verb agreement error might show up in an especially tricky ACT sentence. What makes this one difficult is the use of not just one, but *two* intervening prepositional phrases, both of which have plural objects.

Q Grade-school instruction in ethical and social values, particularly the values of respect and tolerance, are required for any democracy to thrive.

(A) NO CHANGE
(B) values of respect and of tolerance, are
(C) value of respect, together with tolerance, is
(D) values of respect and tolerance, is

A **The correct answer is (D).** In the original sentence, the subject of the plural verb *are* is the singular noun *instruction*. The correct answer choice must resolve this subject-verb agreement problem. Also, the second *of* in the underlined phrase should be deleted because its use results in an awkward and nonsensical clause, which seems to suggest that *of tolerance* is a value. Choice (B) fails to correct the problem. Choices (C) and (D) both correct the problem by changing *are* to *is*. However, choice (C) creates two new problems. First, using the word *value* instead of *values* distorts the meaning of the underlined phrase. Respect and tolerance are not referred to in choice (B) as values. However, the original sentence, considered as a whole, clearly intends to refer to respect and tolerance as examples of ethical and social *values*. Secondly, the phrase *together with tolerance* (set off by commas), adds an unnecessary clause and results in a sentence that is wordy and awkward. Choice (D) is clearer and more concise.

Keep a keen eye out for ACT sentences that separate verbs from their subjects. If part of the sentence is underlined, it's a good bet that you're being tested on subject-verb agreement.

SUBJECT-VERB AGREEMENT (PRONOUN AND COMPOUND SUBJECTS)

The average test-taker can easily determine whether a personal pronoun such as *he*, *they*, or *its* is singular or plural. But other pronouns are not so easily identified as either singular or plural. Here are two lists, along with some sample sentences, to help you keep these pronouns straight in your mind:

Singular pronouns:

anyone, anything, anybody
each
either, neither
every, everyone, everything, everybody
nobody, no one, nothing
what, whatever
who, whom, whoever, whomever

Correct: *Every* possible cause *has* been investigated.

Correct: *Each* one of the children here *speaks* fluent French.

Correct: *Neither* of the pens *has* any ink remaining in *it*.

Correct: *Whatever* he's doing is very effective.

Correct: *Everything* she touches *turns* to gold.

Even when they refer to a "compound" subject joined by *and*, the pronouns listed above remain *singular*.

Correct: *Each adult and child* here *speaks* fluent French.

Correct: *Every* possible *cause and suspect was* investigated.

Plural pronouns:

both
few
many
several
some
others

Correct: *Few* would *argue* with that line of reasoning.

Correct: *Many claim* to have encountered alien beings.

Correct: *Some thrive* on commotion, while *others need* quiet.

It's especially easy to overlook a subject-verb agreement problem in a sentence involving a compound subject (multiple subjects joined by connectors such as the word *and* or the word *or*). If joined by *and*, a compound subject is usually plural (and takes a plural verb). But if joined by *or*, *either . . . or*, or *neither . . . nor*, compound subjects are usually singular.

Plural: The chorus *and* the introduction *need* improvement.

Singular: *Either* the chorus *or* the introduction *needs* improvement.

Singular: *Neither* the chorus *nor* the introduction *needs* improvement.

But what if one subject is singular and another one is plural? Which form should the verb take? Now you're entering Brainiac territory. Here's the rule: Look to see which subject is *closer* to the verb; the verb should agree with that subject.

Plural: Either the rhythm or the *lyrics need* improvement.

Singular: Either the lyrics or the *rhythm needs* improvement.

In some cases, you can't tell whether a subject is singular or plural without looking at how it's used in the sentence. This is true of so-called *collective* nouns and nouns of *quantity*. These special animals might call for either a singular verb or a plural verb, depending on whether the noun is used in a singular or plural sense. (Now you're even deeper into Brainiac territory!)

Correct: Four years *is* too long to wait. (*four years* used in singular sense)

Correct: Four years can *pass* by quickly. (*four years* used in plural sense)

Correct: The majority *favors* the Republican candidate. (*majority* used in singular sense)

Correct: The majority of the voters here *favor* the Republican candidate. (*majority* used in plural sense)

Here's an ACT-style sentence involving a "compound" subject. What makes this one tricky is that even a Brainiac with an ear for English might be mislead to an incorrect answer choice.

Q Neither the result of the first experiment nor that of the second were what the researchers had expected.

(A) NO CHANGE
(B) was what
(C) was that which
(D) resulted in what

A **The correct answer is (B).** In the original version, the plural verb *were* does not agree in number with its singular subject *neither result*. Choice (B) remedies this problem. So does choice (C); but the phrase that choice (C) supplies is not idiomatic. Choice (D) creates a redundancy ("the result . . . resulted in").

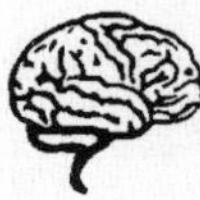

Brainiacs use their ear for English as their first weapon against the ACT English Test—but just to be safe, they use their knowledge of English grammar as a backup.

FORMS OF IRREGULAR VERBS

With most verbs, the same form is used for all tenses except that *-ed* is added for the past tenses—as in *walk* (present tense), *walked* (past tense), and *have walked* (present perfect tense). Verbs such as these are called *regular* verbs. Forming regular verbs is an extreme no-brainer, so the ACT won't test you directly on this. (What test-taker wouldn't recognize the problem with a sentence like *He walk to the store*?)

Some verbs, however, use distinctive forms for different tenses—as in *see*, *saw*, and *have seen*. These kinds of verbs are called *irregular* verbs. An ACT sentence that incorporates an irregular-verb issue will typically involve a tense-shift issue as well. In Lesson 6, you'll examine shifts in verb tense in greater detail. The following example, which tests you on irregular verb forms, also provides a good preview on the topic of verb tense.

Q By the time Lindbergh's little plane landed on an airfield outside Paris, the exhausted pilot had flew single-handedly for over 30 hours without a break.

(A) NO CHANGE
(B) had flown
(C) flew
(D) had flied

A **The correct answer is (B).** In the original version, the use of the past perfect tense (with the helping verb *had*) is entirely appropriate in context. (Lindbergh's flying occurred prior to his landing, and both events occurred in the past.) But in the past perfect tense, *flown*, not *flew*, is the incorrect form of the irregular verb *fly*. Choice (C) uses the simple past tense, which fails to establish the sequence of events. Choice (D) uses the improper verb form *flied*.

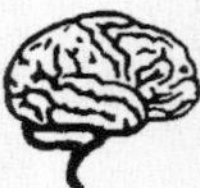

The English language contains more irregular verbs than this lesson can possibly cover. Although the average test-taker might benefit from a review of the most common irregular verbs, Brainiacs don't need the refresher course—they know incorrect verb forms when they hear them—simply because these forms sound wrong.

BRAIN TEASER

In this quiz, you'll tackle 15 ACT-style questions focused primarily on parts of speech— tougher than most ACT part-of-speech questions. Keep in mind: You won't encounter ACT-length passages in this quiz. Instead, you'll examine an eclectic series of discrete sentences, along with 1–3 questions based on each one.

X-REF

Many questions in this quiz also involve some of the other official testing areas—such as sentence structure, idiom, and style. Therefore, these questions serve as not only a *review* but also as a *preview* of what's ahead in Part II.

Attempt all 15 questions, but don't put yourself under a time limit. Focus instead on applying the rules and guidelines you have learned in this lesson. Then be sure to read the explanations that follow the quiz. They're just as important as the questions, because they explain how to apply the rules and guidelines to the questions.

QUIZ

Avoiding unnecessarily incurred (1) expenses should be a fundamentally (2) budgetary objective for every individual, business, and government.

1. (A) NO CHANGE
   (B) unnecessary
   (C) incurring unnecessary
   (D) unnecessary incurred

2. (F) NO CHANGE
   (G) fundamental
   (H) most fundamental
   (J) fundamentally important

Analysts are uncertain as to who (3) the proposed Social Security reforms would harm the most (4)—the baby boomers or their children.

3. (A) NO CHANGE
   (B) as to whom
   (C) who
   (D) which

4. (F) NO CHANGE
   (G) most
   (H) more
   (J) more so

The Republican and Democratic parties each seems to prefer criticizing the other's (5) policies over making constructive proposals themselves. (6)

5. (A) NO CHANGE
   (B) one another's
   (C) each other's
   (D) the other one's

6. (F) NO CHANGE
   (G) itself.
   (H) theirselves.
   (J) OMIT the underlined portion.

Vast differences among the ways children learn are often disregarded by schools who administer (7) the same curriculum to each and every student.

7. (A) NO CHANGE
   (B) whom administer
   (C) that administer
   (D) administering

Who the terrorists are, as well as at whom (8) their recent terrorist activities were aimed, are (9) currently under investigation by the bureau.

8. (F) NO CHANGE
   (G) whom
   (H) at who
   (J) who

9. (A) NO CHANGE
   (B) is
   (C) are each
   (D) are both

Had each of the nations had their (10) own way during the negotiations, international relations might have degenerated into chaos.

10. (F) NO CHANGE
    (G) Had all the nations had their
    (H) Had every nation had its
    (J) Had differing nations had their

Raising a child alone and holding down a full-time job requires (11) strong organization skills. (12)

11. (A) NO CHANGE
    (B) require
    (C) each require
    (D) need

12. (F) NO CHANGE
    (G) skills of organization.
    (H) organizational skills.
    (J) skills in organizing.

Four days are generally the longest humans can go without water, although evidence in the form of second-hand, anecdotal reports suggest that some have actually gone as long as two weeks.

13. (A) NO CHANGE
(B) would be
(C) are considered
(D) is

14. (F) NO CHANGE
(G) suggests
(H) would suggest
(J) suggested

By having had concealed its weapons of mass destruction, the regime breeded deep distrust among the international community.

15.
(A) NO CHANGE
(B) bred
(C) breed
(D) breeds

ANSWERS AND EXPLANATIONS

1. **The correct answer is (B).** In the underlined portion, the adverb *unnecessarily* describes the adjective *incurred*—and there's nothing wrong with the form of either one. But, the word *incurred* in the original version is not needed. (*Avoiding a necessary* expense implies that the expense is incurred.) Hence, you can replace the underlined portion with the single word *unnecessary*. Choice (C) strings together two gerunds (*avoiding incurring*), resulting an a confusing and awkward phrase. Choice (D) incorrectly uses an adjective (*unnecessary*) to describe another adjective (*incurred*).

X-REF **The underlined portion for question 1 provides an example of receptiveness, or redundancy. We'll take a detailed look at the problem of redundancy in Lesson 6.**

2. **The correct answer is (G).** For the sentence to make sense, the adjective *fundamental* should be used instead of the adverb *fundamentally* to describe the noun *objective*—as in choice (G). Choice (H) misuses the superlative *most*. (It would be correct to say *the most* instead of *a most*.) As for choice (J), *fundamentally* and *important* mean essentially the thing. (To fix this redundancy, you could use either *important* or *fundamental*.)

3. **The correct answer is (B).** The phrase *as to*, although it can be omitted, is idiomatic. However, *who* should be replaced with *whom* because the pronoun is being used in the *objective* (as opposed to *subjective*) sense (as in: The reforms would harm *it*). Choice (B) corrects this error, while choice (C) does not. As for choice (D), it would be correct to say *which group*; but the relative pronoun *whom* is more appropriate than *which* in reference to people—in this case, baby boomers and children.

4. **The correct answer is (H).** A comparison is being made here between two groups, so the comparative form (*more*) should be used instead of the superlative form (*the most* or *most*).

5. **The correct answer is (A).** The phrase *each seems* is key here because it establishes a singular subject (and corresponding verb). The relative pronouns in choices (B) and (C) are appropriate for referring to a *plural* noun, so you can eliminate both of those choices. Choice (D) is grammatically correct but not as concise as the original version.

6. **The correct answer choice is (G).** The phrase *each seems* establishes a singular subject (and corresponding verb). Accordingly, the reflexive pronoun should be singular (*itself*), not plural (*themselves*). As for choice (H), *theirselves* is not a word. Choice (J) is the runner-up because it contains no grammatical error. However, the reflexive pronoun is needed here to clarify who would make the proposal and to help get the point across (as in: Do it yourself.).

7. **The correct answer is (C).** The underlined portion presents a *who*-versus-*that* issue, not a *who*-versus-*whom* issue. Since *schools* are things—not persons—the relative pronoun *that* should be used, as in choice (C). Choice (D), the runner-up, is grammatically correct but not as clear in meaning as choice (C).

8. **The correct answer is (F).** The original sentence properly uses *whom* to refer to the object of the terrorists' attacks. Choice (G) omits the necessary preposition *at*. Choices (H) and (J) both use the subjective *who*, which is incorrect in context. Choice (J) also omits the necessary preposition *at*.

9. **The correct answer is (B).** The original version results in a subject-verb agreement error. The noun clause *Who the terrorists are* is the sentence's subject and is considered singular. Hence, the verb *is*, not *are*, should be used. Choices (C) and (D) are wrong because both use the plural verb *are*.

10. **The correct answer is (H).** Removing the prepositional phrase *of the nations* reveals a pronoun-antecedent disagreement—between *each*, which is singular, and *their*, which is plural. Choice (H) remedies the problem with the singular *every* and *its*. Choice (G) also fixes the problem, but in each case the use of the plural form confuses the sentence's meaning, by implying that the nations share the same *way*.

X-REF **In the underlined portion, did *had . . . had* sound repetitive and therefore wrong to you? It shouldn't have; *had had* is the proper past-perfect form of the verb *to have*. You'll examine the past perfect tense, as well as all the other tenses, in the following lesson.**

11. **The correct answer is (B).** The original version contains a subject-verb agreement error. The subject (*raising . . . and . . . holding*) is considered plural, so the plural form *require* should be used instead of the singular *requires*. Choice (C) mixes the singular *each* with the plural verb form *require*. (The alternative phrase *each requires* would have been correct.) Choice (D) replaces *requires* with *need*. Although *need* is correct insofar as it is a plural verb form, it is a poor choice of words because it fails to convey the sentence's intended meaning.

12. **The correct answer is (H).** The adjective *organizational* should be used instead of the noun *organization*, since the word is intended to modify (describe) a noun (*skills*). Choice (H) corrects the errors. Choice (G) is not idiomatic. (It sounds clumsy, doesn't it?) As for choice (J), it's idiomatic to refer to either one's *skill in organizing* or one's *organizational skills.* However, mixing the two, as in choice (J), is not idiomatic.

13. **The correct answer is (D).** The noun *four days* is used in the singular sense here, so the plural verb form *are* should be replaced with the singular form *is*. Choice (B) results in an awkward and nonsensical sentence. Choice (C) fails to correct the subject-verb agreement problem.

14. **The correct answer is (G).** The verb *suggest* does not agree with its singular subject *evidence*. Choice (G) provides the correct, singular form (*evidence suggests*). As for choice (H), adding *would* is an alternative way to solve the subject-verb agreement problem. (It is correct to say *evidence would suggest.*) But the resulting sentence provides an incomplete thought (the evidence would suggest . . . *if what*?). Choice (J) attempts to solve the subject-verb agreement problem by supplying the past-tense verb form (*suggested*); but the result is a confusing shift in tense, and hence in time frame, from one part of the sentence to another.

15. **The correct answer is (B).** The correct past-tense form of the irregular verb *breed* is *bred*, not *breeded*. Choice (C) provides the plural verb form, which disagrees with the singular subject *regime*. Choice (D) is wrong because it provides the *present* verb form, which results in an improper shift in tense from the past perfect (*having had concealed*) to the present tense (*breeds*).

X-REF

Don't worry if you don't understand why the tense shift in choice (D) is wrong. You'll learn why in the next lesson. Besides, tense shifting, especially where one of the perfect tenses is involved, is one of the trickiest topics in all of English grammar—even for many Brainiacs.

LESSON 6

Construction Shifts, Wordiness, Awkwardness, and Omissions

During this lesson, you'll focus first on three of the most nebulous, and tricky, aspects of standard written English:

- Verb *tense* (simple and perfect forms of the present, past, and future tenses)
- The passive and active *voices*
- The so-called "subjunctive" *mood*

Just like on the ACT, you'll cover these three areas primarily through sentences involving *construction shifts*—that is, where tenses, voices, or moods are mixed, or when the sentence shifts from one tense, voice, or mood to another.

Then, you'll review four types of "style" issues the ACT covers—all of which involve overuse or under-use of words:

- Redundancy (repetitiveness)
- Superfluous (unnecessary) words
- General wordiness and awkwardness
- Omission of necessary words

In addition to learning how to identify and correct problems involving these issues, you'll see how each problem might arise in a tougher-than-typical ACT question. Then, you'll apply what you've learned to 15 tough ACT-style questions.

Construction shifts fall into the Sentence Structure category of the test-makers' "Usage/Mechanics" subscore area, while the style issues listed above all fall into the "Style" category of the "Rhetorical Skills" subscore area.

MIXING AND SHIFTING VERB TENSES

Tense refers to how a verb's form indicates the *time frame* (past, present, or future) of the sentence's action. There are six different tenses. Verb forms for the simple past, present, and future tenses are the easiest to form:

Simple present: I *save* enough money each month to pay for my car.

Simple past: I *saved* enough money to buy my car.

Simple future: I *will save* enough money to buy a new car.

The so-called *perfect* tenses are the tricky ones; they describe events occurring *prior to* other events. An event described in the *past perfect* tense is one that happened prior to another past event:

Past perfect: I *had saved* enough money to buy a car, but I lost the money while gambling.

Past perfect: He *had had* enough food but had kept eating anyway.

An event described in the *present perfect* tense is one that happens prior to and up to the present:

Present perfect: I *have saved* enough money to buy a car, but now I need the money to pay my medical bills.

Present perfect: He *has had* enough food but is continuing to eat anyway.

An event described in the *future perfect* tense is one that happens prior to some anticipated future event:

Future perfect: By next month I *will have saved* enough money to buy a car, but I might need the money to pay my medical bills.

Future perfect: He *will have had* enough food once he has finished eating the dessert.

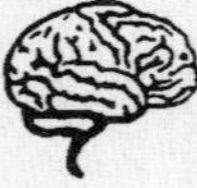

Notice just above that, for each perfect tense, the second sample sentence uses a form of the confusing verb *to have.* This verb is one of the test-makers' favorites for testing you on perfect tenses. To the non-Brainiac, it looks like it might be redundant (for example, *had had*)—but it's not!

If you needlessly mix tenses or shift tense from one time frame to another, the result might be confusing and perhaps even illogical. In other words, verb tenses must reflect the sequence of events clearly, accurately, and logically. Here are a few simple examples:

Incorrect: If it rains tomorrow, we cancel our plans.

Correct: If it rains tomorrow, we *will cancel* our plans.

Incorrect: When Bill arrived, Sal still did not begin to unload the truck.

Correct: When Bill arrived, Sal still had not begun to unload the truck.

The warning about mixing and shifting tenses also applies to the sentences like these, which are especially likely to trip up the average test-taker:

> **Incorrect:** *To go* to war is *to have traveled* to hell.
>
> **Correct:** *To go* to war is *to go* to hell.
>
> **Correct:** *To have gone* to war is *to have traveled* to hell.
>
> **Incorrect:** *Seeing* the obstacle *would have allowed* him to alter his course.
>
> **Correct:** *Having seen* the obstacle *would have allowed* him to alter his course.
>
> **Correct:** *Seeing* the obstacle *would allow* him to alter his course.

On the ACT, a typical tense mixing or shifting problem might be obvious: The sentence will sound wrong and won't make much sense without the phrase that the correct choice provides. However, since there are no hard-and-fast rules for which tenses can and cannot mix, the test-makers are happy to exploit this fact in designing trickier sentences and questions. Here's a good example:

Q Companies that have failed to make cost-of-living adjustments in their workers' salaries <u>cannot</u> attract or retain competent employees.

(A) NO CHANGE
(B) were not able to
(C) will be unable to
(D) could not

A **The correct answer is (C).** The original sentence mixes the past perfect tense (*have failed*) with the present tense (*cannot*). Compare this sentence with one that uses *fails* instead of *have failed*. The revised version makes more sense, doesn't it? Of course, you're stuck with *have failed* for this question. And, matching tenses by changing *cannot* to either *have been unable to* or *have not* is not among the listed options. But choice (C), which provides a shift to future tense, also makes sense: The first clause describes an event occurring in the past up to the present, while the second clause anticipates future events. This forward movement in time is understandable and logical in context. Choices (B) and (D) each provide a past tense verb form, which illogically reverses the time frame—back to the past from the present perfect.

Here's an even more challenging question, which involves a shift from the past to the past perfect tense. The original sentence will probably sound perfectly fine, and it might seem to make sense—if you're not paying close attention:

Q Lincoln promulgated his controversial Emancipation Proclamation, <u>which had declared</u> all slaves held in rebel territory free, only after the North had won a significant military victory.

(A) NO CHANGE
(B) declaring
(C) which declared
(D) a document that had declared

A **The correct answer is (C).** This sentence shifts from past tense (*promulgated*) to past perfect (*which had*, then *had won*). The shift seems to make sense, since the sentence describes a past event (Lincoln's promulgation) followed by an even earlier one (the North's victory). But the past perfect *had declared* implies nonsensically that, at some point in the past, the Proclamation no longer declared that the slaves were free. The simple past tense, which choice (C) provides, makes sense. Choice (B) is ambiguous; it's unclear whether it was Lincoln or the Proclamation that *declared*. Choice (D) suffers from the same problem as the original version.

THE PASSIVE AND ACTIVE VOICES

In a sentence expressed in the *active voice*, the subject "acts upon" an object. Conversely, in a sentence expressed in the *passive voice*, the subject "is acted upon" by an object. Either voice is grammatically acceptable. However, one may be clearer and less awkward than the other, depending on the particular sentence. In this next sentence, for example, the passive voice is needed for emphasis and clarity.

Active (acceptable): Only the sun itself *surpasses* the Tetons in beauty.

Passive (more effective): Sunrise over the Tetons *is surpassed* in beauty only *by* the sun itself.

In any event, a sentence should not mix the two voices. Also, in most cases, the voice should not *shift* from one sentence to the next. Here's a sentence where the active voice is better:

Passive (acceptable): While repetitive tasks are not generally performed reliably by humans for prolonged time periods, such tasks can be performed reliably by computers almost endlessly.

Active (better): While most humans cannot perform repetitive tasks reliably for a prolonged time period, computers can perform such tasks endlessly and reliably.

Mixed (awkward): While humans generally cannot perform repetitive tasks reliably for a prolonged time period, repetitive tasks can be performed endlessly by computers in a reliable manner.

Typically, to avoid an awkward shift in voice, what's needed is to restructure an entire sentence. So on the ACT, if you see an entire sentence underlined, be sure to check for a needless voice shift (either in the original version or among the alternatives), as in the following example:

Q The recent increase in the number of fish caught by commercial vessels can be explained largely by improved sonar technology. Less stringent quotas have also contributed to the trend.

(A) NO CHANGE
(B) Largely explaining the recent increase in the number of fish caught by commercial vessels is improved sonar technology.
(C) Improved sonar technology largely explains the recent increase in the number of fish caught by commercial vessels.
(D) Largely, improved sonar technology explains the recent increase in the number of fish that commercial vessels catch.

A **The correct answer is (A).** The original version is cast entirely in the passive voice (*caught by* and *explained largely by*). Although in the next sentence there is a shift to the active voice, the shift is not awkward, and it does not obscure the idea that the writer seeks to convey. The sentence that choice (B) provides mixes voices and is a bit confusing. The sentence in choice (C) is a bit clearer than the one in choice (B), but it also mixes voices. As for choice (D), the position of *largely* is awkward an confusing. What's more, because of sentence's structure, the reader expects the writer to list something else that improved sonar technology explains—rather than something else that explains the increase in the number of fish caught.

Keep in mind that both the active and passive voices are grammatically proper; therefore, don't eliminate an answer choice merely because it uses the passive voice. Check the answer choices for consistency in voice.

THE SUBJUNCTIVE MOOD

When grammarians talk about the so-called *subjunctive mood*, they're delving deep into Brainiac territory. Nevertheless, the test-makers consider this strange and menacing animal fair game for the ACT English Test, so make sure you understand its uses and misuses.

The subjunctive mood should be used to express a *wish* or a *contrary-to-fact* condition. These sentences should include words such as *if, had, were*, and *should*.

Incorrect: I wish it *was* earlier.

Correct: I wish it *were* earlier.

Incorrect: Suppose he speeds up suddenly.

Correct: Suppose he *were* to speed up suddenly.

Incorrect: If the college lowers its tuition, I would probably enroll.

Correct: *Should* the college lower its tuition, I *would* probably enroll.

Correct: *If* the college *were* to lower its tuition, I *would* probably enroll.

Incorrect: *Had* he driven slower, he will recognize the landmarks from now on.

Correct: *Had* he driven slower, he *would* recognize the landmarks from now on.

Correct: *If* he *had* driven slower, he *would* recognize the landmarks from now on.

The subjunctive mood can be tricky because it uses its own idiomatic verb forms and because you can't always trust your ear when it comes to catching an error. Just remember: If the sentence uses a regular verb tense (past, present, future, etc.) to express a wish or contrary-to-fact condition, then it is grammatically incorrect, even if the subjunctive verb form is also used. Look again, for example, at the *incorrect* sample sentences from the preceding page.

- **I wish it *was* earlier. (It *was* earlier uses past tense.)**
- **Suppose he speeds up suddenly. (*He speeds up suddenly* uses present tense.)**
- **If the college lowers its tuition, I would probably enroll. (First clause uses present tense, second clause uses subjunctive form)**
- **Had he driven slower, he will recognize the landmarks from now on. (First clause uses subjunctive form, second clause uses future tense)**

The subjunctive mood is also used in clauses of recommendation, request, suggestion, or demand. These clauses should include the word *that*:

Incorrect: Ann suggested we should go to the Chinese restaurant.

Correct: Ann *suggested that* we go to the Chinese restaurant.

Incorrect: I insist you be quiet.

Correct: I *insist that* you be quiet.

Incorrect: The supervisor preferred all workers wear uniforms from now on.

Correct: The supervisor *preferred* that all workers wear uniforms from now on.

Now look at an ACT-style sentence that tests on subjunctive mood. You'll no doubt agree that, unless you're really tuned in to this tricky concept, it's easy to get this question wrong:

The Environmental Protection Agency would be overburdened by its detection and enforcement duties <u>if it fully implemented</u> all of its own regulations.

(A) NO CHANGE
(B) if it was to implement
(C) were it to fully implement
(D) if it implements fully

The correct answer is (C). The sentence clearly intends to express a hypothetical or contrary-to-fact situation; yet the underlined phrase does not use the subjunctive *were*. Choice (C) corrects the problem. Choice (B) incorrectly uses *was* instead of the subjunctive *were*. Choice (D) incorrectly uses the present tense.

REDUNDANT WORDS AND PHRASES

On the ACT, look for words and phrases that express the same essential idea twice. This syndrome is known as "redundancy." In many cases, correcting the problem is as simple as omitting one of the redundant phrases.

Redundant: *The reason that* we stopped for the night was *because* we were sleepy.

Redundant: *Because* we were sleepy, we *therefore* stopped for the night.

Better: We stopped for the night because we were sleepy.

redundant: The *underlying* motive *behind* his seemingly generous offer was old-fashioned greed.

Better: The motive behind his seemingly generous offer was old-fashioned greed.

Better: The underlying motive for his seemingly generous offer was old-fashioned greed.

Redundant: One of the fossils is twenty thousand years old *in age*.

Better: One of the fossils is twenty thousand years old.

Redundant: The German Oktoberfest takes place *each October of every year*.

Better: The German Oktoberfest takes place *every October*.

Redundant: *At the same time* that lightning struck, we *simultaneously* lost our electric power.

Better: At the same time that lightning struck, we lost our electric power.

Redundant: *Both* unemployment levels *as well as* interest rates can affect stock prices.

Better: Both unemployment levels and interest rates can affect stock prices.

Better: Unemployment levels as well as interest rates can affect stock prices.

Redundant: Not only does dinner smell good, but it *also* tastes good *too*.

Better: Not only does dinner smell good, but it tastes good too.

On the ACT, be on the lookout for sentences that have the following "themes" and keywords. Redundancies are most likely to spring up in these kinds of sentences:

- **Words establishing cause-and-effect (because, since, if, then, therefore)**
- **References to time (age, years, hours, days)**
- **Words used in conjunctions (both, as well, too, also)**

ACT questions involving redundancy are inherently more difficult than average—simply because it's so easy to overlook this problem. To make these questions even tougher, the test-makers might place considerable distance between the two words or phrases that create the redundancy. Here's a perfect example:

Q Due to a negligible difference in Phase III results as between patients using the drug and those using a placebo, the Food and Drug Administration refused to approve the drug on this basis.

(A) NO CHANGE
(B) based on this difference.
(C) for this reason.
(D) OMIT the underlined portion

A **The correct answer is (D).** In the original sentence, *due to* and *on this basis* serve the same function—to express that the FDA's refusal was based on the Phase III results. (The redundancy is easy to miss since one phrase begins the sentence while the other phrase ends it.) Of the three alternatives, only choice (D) corrects the problem, simply by omitting *on this basis*.

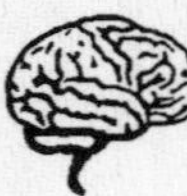

The answer choice "OMIT the underlined portion" is often the correct choice for a question that tests you on redundancy. Therefore, when you see this option—usually choice (D)—be sure to look around the sentence for an idea that expresses the same idea as the underlined portion.

SUPERFLUOUS (UNNECESSARY) WORDS

You just took a look at one variety of unnecessary verbiage: redundancy. Now look at some other kinds of sentences in which certain words can simply be omitted without affecting the meaning or effectiveness of the original sentence. Remember: Briefer is better!

Each sentence in the first group below contains an *ellipsis*: a word or phrase that can be omitted because it is clearly implied. (In the incorrect version, the ellipsis is italicized.)

Superfluous: The warmer the weather *is*, the more crowded the beach *is*.

Concise: The warmer the weather, the more crowded the beach.

Superfluous: He looks exactly like Francis *looks*.

Concise: He looks exactly like Francis.

Superfluous: That shirt is the ugliest *shirt that* I have ever seen.

Concise: That shirt is the ugliest I have ever seen.

Each sentence in the next group includes a superfluous preposition. (In the incorrect version, the preposition is italicized.)

Superfluous: The other children couldn't help *from* laughing at the girl with mismatched shoes.

Concise: The other children couldn't help laughing at the girl with mismatched shoes.

Superfluous: One prominent futurist predicts a nuclear holocaust by the year *of* 2020.

Concise: One prominent futurist predicts a nuclear holocaust by the year 2020.

Superfluous: They made the discovery *in* around December of last year.

Concise: They made the discovery around December of last year.

Superfluous: The waiter brought half *of* a loaf of bread to the table.

Concise: The waiter brought half a loaf of bread to the table.

Superfluous words can also appear in a series of parallel clauses. Both versions of the next sentence use proper parallelism, but briefer is better—as long as the meaning of the sentence is clear.

Superfluous: My three goals in life are to be healthy, *to be* wealthy, and *to be* wise.

Concise: My three goals in life are to be healthy, wealthy, and wise.

How might the test-makers devise a tougher-than-average question involving superfluous words? One way is by tempting you with a more concise choice that turns out too concise—as in the following example:

Q

Some varieties of parrots live as long as one hundred years.

(A) NO CHANGE
(B) one hundred years.
(C) to be one hundred years old in age.
(D) as long as the age of one hundred years.

A

The correct answer is (A). Choice (B) is obviously more concise, but it creates problems. First, it is not idiomatic. (It would be idiomatic to say that some varieties of parrots lived *for* one hundred years.) Second, omitting *as long as* unfairly implies that the varieties to which the writer refers never live less than one hundred years. Choice (C) suffers from this problem as well; what's more, it creates a redundancy—the word *old* expresses the same idea as *in age*. (One or the other, but not both, should be used.) Choice (D) provides an illogical phrase—it's grammatical construction implies that *one hundred years* is an *age*.

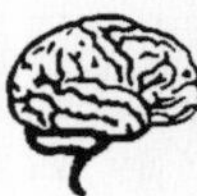

Brainiacs know that if an underlined portion contains a word or phrase that is clearly implied by the sentence, it's safe to omit that word or phrase. But Brainiacs also recognize that, in certain instances, briefer is not always better!

GENERAL WORDINESS AND AWKWARDNESS

You've just learned that unnecessary words can sometimes be omitted from an ACT sentence, thereby improving it. Here, we'll focus on phrases that can be *replaced* with more concise or graceful ones.

At this point in Part II, you've seen many examples of wordy and awkward phrases in ACT-style sentences and answer choices. In fact, the wordy and awkward phrases on the ACT are limited in variety only by the collective imagination of the test-makers. Nevertheless, a few such phrases show up on the exam more often than others, so you should be especially alert for these.

Wordy: Failure can, *some of the time*, serve as a prelude to success.

Concise: Failure can *sometimes* serve as a prelude to success.

Wordy: *As a result of Greg's being* a compulsive overeater, *it is not likely that he will* live past the age of fifty.

Concise: *Because Greg* is a compulsive overeater, *he is unlikely to* live past the age of fifty.

Wordy: Before the mother eats, she feeds *each and every one* of her offspring.

Concise: Before the mother eats, she feeds each of her offspring.

Wordy: There are fewer buffalo on the plains today than *there ever were* before.

Concise: There are fewer buffalo on the plains today than ever before.

Wordy: Discipline is crucial to *the attainment of* one's objectives.

Concise: Discipline is crucial to *attaining* one's objectives.

Wordy: Her husband was waiting for her on the platform *at the time of the train's arrival*.

Concise: Her husband was waiting for her on the platform *when the train arrived*.

Awkward: Calcification *is when* (or *is where*) calcium deposits form around a bone.

Concise: Calcification *occurs when* calcium deposits form around a bone.

Awkward: *There are* eight cats in the house, *of which* only two have been fed.

Concise: Of the eight cats in the house, only two have been fed.

Awkward: The wind poses a serious threat to the old tree, and *so does* the snow.

Concise: The wind and snow both pose a serious threat to the old tree.

OMISSION OF NECESSARY WORDS

On the flip side of redundancy and wordiness is the error of *omission*. Excluding a necessary word can obscure or confuse the meaning of the sentence, or perhaps even result in a sentence that is downright illogical. Check especially for the omission of important "little" words—prepositions, pronouns, conjunctives, and especially the word *that*.

Omission: The newscaster announced the voting results were incorrect. (What did the newscaster announce: the results or the fact that the results were incorrect?)

Clearer: The newscaster announced *that* the voting results were incorrect.

Omission: The color of the blouse is different from the skirt.

Clearer: The color of the blouse is different from *that* of the skirt.

Omission: The lost hiker went without food, water, or shelter two days.

Clearer: The lost hiker went without food, water, or shelter *for* two days.

Omission: Missing the deadline would be a disaster the first order.

Clearer: Missing the deadline would be a disaster *of* the first order.

As you've just seen, one "little" word can make all the difference! Your mind can easily trick you by filling in a key word that is not actually there. The moral is: Read every ACT sentence that contains an underlined portion slowly and carefully!

Now look at a sentence that actually involves *two* omission issues. And they're both especially tough, for two reasons. First, many people commit these particular omission errors—so both "sound" okay to most test-takers. Second, neither omission results in patent nonsense or il-logic. With each one, the problem is a bit more subtle.

This example involves two similar issues for the purpose of illustration. On the actual test, don't expect to see the same issue covered twice in one sentence.

Some evolutionary theorists <u>believe the</u> [1] main reason humans began to walk in an upright posture <u>is they</u> [2] needed to reach tree branches to obtain food.

Q **1.** (A) NO CHANGE
(B) believe that the
(C) hold the belief that
(D) believe in

A **The correct answer is (B).** Inserting the word *that* between *believe* and *the* makes it clearer as to what the theorists believe. Choice (C) accomplishes the same thing as choice (B), but choice (C) is awkward and unnecessarily wordy. Choice (D) is wrong because, in this context, it is not idiomatic to say that one believes *in* a reason.

Q 2. (A) NO CHANGE
(B) is because they
(C) is that they
(D) is: they

A **The correct answer is (C).** The phrase *is they* sounds wrong, doesn't it? And, it's a bit confusing. It is idiomatic to say that the reason for something is *that* . . . , as in choice (C). Choice (B) results in a redundancy: *the reason* and *because* convey essentially the same idea. The colon that choice (D) adds needlessly interrupts the flow of the sentence.

BRAIN TEASER

In this quiz, you'll tackle 15 ACT-style questions that focus primarily on the topics you reviewed in this lesson. These questions are tougher than average ACT questions on the same topics. Keep in mind: You won't encounter ACT-length passages in this quiz. Instead, you'll examine an eclectic series of discrete sentences, along with 1-3 questions based on each one.

X-REF **Many questions in this Brain Teaser also involve some of the other official testing areas—such as grammar, idiom, and style. Therefore, these questions serve as a *review* of what Part II has already covered as well as a *preview* of what's still ahead.**

Attempt all 15 questions, but don't put yourself under a time limit. Focus instead on applying the rules and guidelines you learned about in this lesson. Be sure to read the explanations that follow the quiz. They're just as important as the questions themselves, because they explain how to apply the rules and guidelines to the questions.

QUIZ

Having signed the NATO defense treaty, NATO members each agreed that any attack on a member nation is to be considered an attack on all.

1 = "Having signed"; 2 = "is to be"

1. (A) NO CHANGE
   (B) Having had signed
   (C) Signing
   (D) After the signing of

2. (F) NO CHANGE
   (G) was to
   (H) would
   (J) will

As the anthropologists expect, the technologies available to the ancient culture being currently scrutinized was more advanced than that of other cultures of its time.

3 = "expect"; 4 = "being currently scrutinized"

3. (A) NO CHANGE
   (B) might have expected
   (C) have expected
   (D) had expected

4. (F) NO CHANGE
   (G) currently scrutinized
   (H) being scrutinized currently
   (J) under current scrutiny

The sensation of having eaten enough is actually created by a chemical in the brain; a chemical that consuming simple sugars depletes.

5 = "having eaten"; 6 = "brain; a"; 7 = "consuming simple sugars depletes."

5. (A) NO CHANGE
   (B) eating
   (C) eaten
   (D) one's having eaten

6. (F) NO CHANGE
   (G) brain, a
   (H) brain a
   (J) brain: a

7. (A) NO CHANGE
   (B) is depleted by consuming simple sugars.
   (C) the consumption of simple sugars depletes.
   (D) is depleted as simple sugars are consumed.

Contrary to popular myth, war heroes rarely earn their status by acting as if they themselves are invincible.

8 = "themselves are"

8. (F) NO CHANGE
   (G) are
   (H) were
   (J) themselves were

If empty space was nothing real, then any two atoms located in this "nothingness" would contact each other since nothing would be between them.

9 = "If empty space was"

9. (A) NO CHANGE
   (B) In the event that empty space is
   (C) If empty space is
   (D) Were empty space

As many as 125 years ago, the science fiction writer Jules Verne wrote predictions that foretold the future existence of such modern mechanical devices as the airplane, the submarine, and even the fax machine.

10 = "that foretold the future existence"

10. (F) NO CHANGE
    (G) that foretold
    (H) of the existence
    (J) OMIT the underlined portion

Only through a comprehensive, federally funded vaccination program can a new epidemic of tuberculosis be curbed, just like the spread of both cholera as well as the spread of typhoid were curbed.
11 12

11. (A) NO CHANGE
(B) and the spread of
(C) as well as
(D) and

12. (F) NO CHANGE
(G) was curbed.
(H) had been curbed.
(J) OMIT the underlined portion

To avoid confusion between oral medications, pills for different medications should differ from one another in terms of their color, shape, and size.
13 14 15

13. (A) NO CHANGE
(B) confusing
(C) confusion in
(D) being confused by

14. (F) NO CHANGE
(G) different pills
(H) they
(J) pills

15. (A) NO CHANGE
(B) in
(C) in terms of their
(D) from one another in

ANSWERS AND EXPLANATIONS

1. **The correct answer is (A).** *Having signed* is a present perfect verb form, while *agreed* is a past-tense verb form. Shifting from one tense to the other is proper here to convey the shift in time frame. As for choice (B), the past perfect forms *Having had signed* together with *had agreed* (not *agreed*) would be acceptable as well here. Choices (C) and (D) each leave the purpose and meaning of the first clause vague. (The connection between the signing and the agreement is unclear.)

2. **The correct answer is (H).** The context makes clear that *an attack* is a possible future event. Neither the present tense, choice (F), nor the past tense, choice (G), make sense in this context. Choice (H) implies mere possibility, while choice (J) implies certainty. Hence, choice (H) makes more sense than choice (J).

3. **The correct answer is (D).** The past perfect *had expected* makes sense in context because the expectations occurred prior to the current scrutiny. Choices (A), (B), and (C) all use a present tense verb form, which fails to establish the appropriate chronological sequence.

4. **The correct answer is (J).** The original version awkwardly splits the grammatical element *being scrutinized*. Although *currently being scrutinized* would be a good alternative, this phrase is not among the listed choices. Besides, choice (J) reworks the phrase into an even clearer, more graceful idiom. Choice (H) corrects the problem with the original version, but it is very awkward.

X-REF

In Lesson 7, we'll examine more about splitting grammatical units—when it's acceptable and when it's not.

5. **The correct answer is (A).** The present perfect verb form is appropriate here, since eating occurs prior to and up to the time of the sensation. The word *eaten* is the correct past participle form of the verb *to eat*. Neither the present tense, choice (B), nor the past tense, choice (C), is as effective in conveying the proper sequence of events. Choice (D) is unnecessarily wordy. (The possessive *one's* is superfluous and confusing.)

6. **The correct answer is (G).** A semicolon is inappropriate here because the clause that follows cannot stand alone as a complete sentence. Either a dash or a comma, as in choice (G), is appropriate because the clause describes what precedes the mark. Simply omitting any punctuation mark, choice (H), makes for a confusing, even nonsensical, sentence. As for choice (J), what follows the punctuation mark is neither a list nor a restatement, and so a colon is not appropriate.

7. **The correct answer is (B).** Notice that the first clause uses the passive voice (*created by* . . .), while the underlined portion shifts to the active voice. Choice (B) avoids the shift by transforming the phrase into its passive-voice equivalent. The passive voice is needed here for emphasis and clarity. Choice (C) fails to correct the shift in voice. Choice (D) corrects the shift in voice; however, by using the preposition *as*, choice (D) obscures the cause-and-effect relationship between the consumption of simple sugars and the depletion of the chemical.

8. **The correct answer is (H).** The original version intends to express a contrary-to-fact situation, so the subjunctive *were* (instead of *are*) is appropriate here. Also, the reflexive pronoun *themselves* is improper here. (Compare to *consider themselves invincible*, which uses the reflexive pronoun properly.)

9. **The correct answer is (D).** The subjunctive mood is appropriate here because this sentence involves a contrary-to-fact situation. However, the underlined part incorrectly uses the past-tense *was*. To correct this problem, the underlined phrase should be replaced with either *If empty space were* or *Were empty space*, as in choice (D). Both choice (B) and choice (C) incorrectly use the present-tense *is* instead of a subjunctive form. Choice (B) is also wordy.

10. **The correct answer is (J).** This sentence tells you that Jules Verne wrote "predictions that foretold" something—a clear example of redundancy, since a prediction *by definition* foretells something. Then it tells you that his predictions foretold "the future existence" of certain things. Obviously, if Verne was foretelling something, what he was foretelling *had to be* in the future. Each of these redundancies should be eliminated, saving words and making the revised sentence much crisper in style.

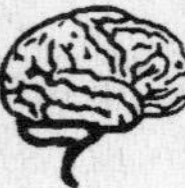

In the preceding example, a Brainiac also would have noticed how to make the original sentence even more concise and graceful: by replacing *wrote predictions of* with the single word *predicted*. (". . . Jules Verne *predicted* such devices as the airplane, the submarine, and even the fax machine.")

11. **The correct answer is (D).** In the original version, the idiom *both . . . as well as* is redundant (and improper). Since *both* is not underlined, as well as should be replaced with *and*. Also, the second occurrence of *the spread of* can be omitted because it is implied through a parallel construction. Choice (D) pares down the underlined phrase to its most concise form.

X-REF

You'll explore much more about the concept of grammatical parallelism in Lesson 7.

12. **The correct answer is (J).** Because the preposition *like* sets up an ellipsis, *were curbed* is implied and can be omitted. Choices (G) and (H) fail to omit superfluous words. Also, choice (G) poses a subject-verb agreement problem, while choice (H) employs the past perfect tense, which is improper in context.

13. **The correct answer is (A).** The original version is the most effective of the four choices in identifying the problem to which the writer's suggestions relate. Choice (B) results in a clause that makes no sense. (A medication is not in itself either confusing or confused.) Choice (C) makes for a clause that is vague and confusing. (What is *confusion in oral medications* supposed to mean?) As for choice (D), the use of the passive voice in this context suggests, nonsensically, that it is *pills* that are confused.

14. **The correct answer is (F).** Many test-takers who notice the words *different* and *differ* would assume that there is a problem with repetitiveness that should be fixed. But to get the point across, the sentence needs both words—at least within its grammatical structure. Choices (G) and (J) are wrong because they obscure the point that pills *for different medications* should look different from one another. Choice (H) is even worse—the pronoun *they* has no antecedent whatsoever (at least within the sentence).

15. **The correct answer is (B).** The phrase *from one another* is clearly implied, and so it can be omitted. The phrase *in terms of* is superfluous, and so it can also be omitted. Finally, it is clear from the context that *their* refers to pills, and so this word can be omitted.

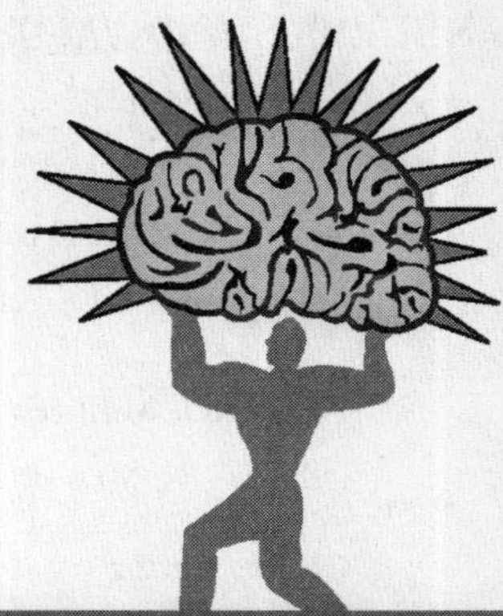

LESSON 7

Sentence Structure and Sense

During this lesson, you'll turn your focus from word choice to overall sentence structure; specifically, you'll examine whether the parts of a sentence relate to each other in a way that makes the meaning of the sentence clear, unambiguous, logical, and rhetorically effective. Here are the general issues you'll cover in this lesson (and the ACT English Test *will* cover each and every one of these):

- Placement of pronouns relative to their antecedents
- Placement of modifying words and phrases relative to the nouns they modify
- Splitting of a grammatical unit—when it's okay and when it's not
- Occurences of "dangling" modifiers—when dangling modifiers are acceptable and when they're not
- Occurences of strings of subordinate clauses
- Achievement of rhetorical balance through structural balance
- Parallelism between items in a list
- Parallelism between the two parts of a so-called "correlative"

In addition to learning how to recognize and fix problems involving these issues, you'll look at how the test-makers might incorporate each issue into a tougher-than-average test question. Then, you'll apply what you've reviewed to 15 tough ACT-style questions.

Most of the topics in this lesson fall into the Sentence Structure category of the test-makers' "Usage/Mechanics" subscore area. Other topics in this lesson fall into the "Rhetorical Skills" subscore area (which includes three subcategories: Strategy, Organization, and Style).

AMBIGUOUS AND VAGUE PRONOUN REFERENCES

As you learned in Lesson 5, every pronoun must agree with its antecedent noun in number—either singular or plural. However, the fact that a pronoun and its antecedent are in accord doesn't preclude a problem with pronoun reference. You need to also make sure the intended antecedent of the pronoun is clear and unambiguous. Here's a simple example of an ambiguous pronoun reference, along with suggestions of how to correct it:

Unclear: Minutes before Kevin's meeting with Paul, *his* wife called with the bad news. (Whose wife called—Kevin's or Paul's?)

Clear: *Kevin's* wife called with the bad news minutes before *his* meeting with Paul.

Clear: Minutes before Kevin's meeting with Paul, *Kevin's* wife called with the bad news.

Ambiguous pronoun reference errors are usually clarified in one of two ways:

- By placing the noun and pronoun as near as possible to each other, without other nouns coming between them (as in the second sentence above)
- By replacing the pronoun with its antecedent (as in the third sentence above)

Here's an ACT-style sentence that illustrates the latter solution. This sentence involving pronoun reference is trickier than average because you can easily figure out what the writer intended as the pronoun's antecedent; therefore, it's tempting to think that there's nothing wrong with the sentence.

Q E-mail accounts administered by employers belong to them, and they can be seized and used as evidence against employees.

(A) NO CHANGE
(B) so they
(C) and so e-mails
(D) but

A **The correct answer is (C).** In the original version, the antecedent of *they* is separated from its intended antecedent *accounts* by two other nouns (*them* and *employer*). Choice (C) makes the reference as unambiguous as possible by replacing the pronoun *they* with its antecedent. Also, adding the word *so* enhances the sentence's rhetorical effectiveness—by making it clearer that e-mails can be used as evidence *because* they belong to the employer. Choice (B) fails to correct the ambiguous pronoun reference. Choice (D) is wrong for two reasons. First, the connecting word *but* misleads the reader into thinking that an opposing idea is ahead. Second, by omitting the pronoun *they*, choice (D) creates a dependent clause that need not be preceded by a comma.

On the ACT, also check for the *vague* use of such pronouns as *it*, *you*, *that*, or *one*—without clear reference to any particular antecedent. Here are some simple examples:

Vague: When one dives in without looking ahead, *you* never know what will happen. (Does *you* refer to the diver or to the broader *one*?)

Clear: *One* never knows what will happen when *one* dives in without looking ahead.

Clear: When *you* dive in without looking ahead, *you* never know what will happen.

Vague: When the planets are out of alignment, *it* can be disastrous. (*It* does not refer to any noun.)

Clear: Disaster can occur when the planets are out of alignment.

Clear: When the planets are out of alignment, disaster can strike.

When you see a pronoun in an ACT sentence, ask yourself: "To what noun does this pronoun refer?" If the answer is the least bit unclear, you can be certain that the sentence (or answer choice) is wrong.

PLACEMENT OF MODIFIERS

A *modifier* is a word or phrase that describes, restricts, or qualifies another word or phrase. Modifying phrases are typically set off with commas, and many such phrases begin with a relative pronoun (*which*, *who*, *that*, *whose*, *whom*). Modifiers should generally be placed as close as possible to the word(s) they modify. Positioning a modifier in the wrong place can result in a confusing or even nonsensical sentence.

Misplaced: His death shocked the entire family, which occurred quite suddenly.

Better: His death, which occurred quite suddenly, shocked the entire family.

Misplaced: *Nearly dead*, the police finally found the victim.

Better: The police finally found *the victim*, *who was nearly dead*.

Unclear: Bill punched Carl while wearing a mouth protector.

Clear: While wearing a mouth protector, Bill punched Carl.

Modifiers such as *almost*, *nearly*, *hardly*, *just*, and *only* should immediately precede the word(s) they modify, even if the sentence sounds correct with the parts separated. For example:

Misplaced: Their one-year-old child *almost* weighs *forty pounds*.

Better: Their one-year-old child weighs *almost forty pounds.*

Note the position of *only* in the following sentences:

Clear: *Only the assistant* was able to detect obvious errors.

Unclear: The assistant was *only* able to detect obvious errors.

Unclear: The assistant was able to *only* detect *obvious errors.*

Clear: The assistant was able to detect *only obvious errors*.

You just saw how shifting the position of a modifier even slightly can radically change or distort a sentence's meaning. Yet the impact of such shifts escapes most test-takers—a fact that the test-makers are all too willing to exploit, as in the following ACT-style example:

Q Exercising contributes frequently to a sense of well being as well as to longevity.

(A) NO CHANGE
(B) Exercising frequently contributes
(C) Frequently exercising contributes
(D) Frequent exercise contributes

A **The correct answer is (D).** In the original sentence, *frequently* is probably intended to describe (modify) *exercising* (frequent exercise). But separating these words makes it appear that *frequently* describes *contributing*, which doesn't make sense in the overall context of the sentence. Choice (D) corrects the problems. With this choice, it is clear that what is frequent is *exercise* (rather than *contributing*). Choice (C) also clears up the confusion as to whether *frequently* describes *exercising* or *contributes*. But in this choice, an adverb is used incorrectly to describe a gerund (*exercising*). Adverbs must be used to describe only verbs, adjectives, and other adverbs.

The general rule about placing modifiers near the words they modify applies *most* of the time. In some cases, however, trying to place a modifier near the words it modifies actually confuses the meaning of the sentence, as with the modifier *without his glasses* in the sentences below.

Unclear: Nathan can read the newspaper and shave *without his glasses*. (It is unclear whether *without his glasses* refers only to *shave* or to both *shave* and *read the newspaper*)

Unclear: *Without his glasses, Nathan* can read the newspaper and shave. (This sentence implies that these are the only two tasks Nathan can perform without his glasses.)

Clear: *Even without his glasses*, Nathan can read the newspaper and shave.

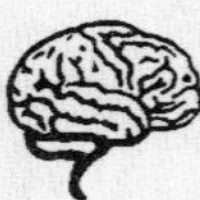

Brainiacs don't apply the rule about placement of modifiers mechanically. Instead, they check to see whether the sentence as a whole makes sense.

SPLITTING A GRAMMATICAL UNIT

Splitting apart clauses or phrases (by inserting another clause between them) often results in an awkward and confusing sentence.

Split: The value of the dollar *is not*, relative to other currencies, *rising* universally.

Better: The value of the dollar *is not rising* universally relative to other currencies.

Split: The government's goal this year *is to provide* for its poorest residents *an economic safety net.*

Split: *The government's goal* is to provide an economic safety net *this year* for its poorest residents.

Better: The government's goal this year is to provide an economic safety net for its poorest residents.

In ACT sentences, look especially for *split infinitives*. An infinitive is the plural form of an "action" verb, preceded by the word "to." If *to* is separated from its corresponding verb, then you're dealing with a "split infinitive" and a grammatically incorrect sentence.

Improper (split): The executive was compelled *to*, by greed and ambition, *work* more and more hours each day.

Correct: The executive was compelled by greed and ambition *to work* more and more hours each day.

Improper (split): Meteorologists have been known *to* inaccurately *predict* snowstorms.

Correct: Meteorologists have been known *to predict* snowstorms inaccurately.

In some cases, the splitting of a grammatical unit is jarring and obvious. But in other cases, it can go unnoticed by all but the most alert test-takers. For example, most test-takers—including many Brainiacs—would find no fault with the original version of the following sentence, at least upon first reading.

Q Typographer Lucian Bernhard was influenced, perhaps to a greater extent than any of his contemporaries, by Toulouse-Lautrec's emphasis on large, unharmonious lettering.

Which of the following is the best editorial proposal for the preceding sentence, disregarding punctuation and capitalization?

(A) NO CHANGE
(B) MOVE the underlined portion to the beginning of the sentence
(C) MOVE the underlined portion to the end of the sentence
(D) OMIT the underlined portion

A **The correct answer is (B).** The original sentence awkwardly splits the main clause with an intervening subordinate one (set off by commas). Choice (B) keeps the main clause intact. Choice (C) creates a pronoun reference problem: It is not clear whether the pronoun *his* refers to Bernhard or Toulouse-Lautrec.

Whenever you see a clause set off by commas in the middle of the sentence, check the words immediately before and after the clause. If keeping those words together would sound better to your ear or would more effectively convey the main point of the sentence, then you can safely eliminate any answer choice that separates those words.

DANGLING MODIFIERS

A *dangling modifier* is a modifier that doesn't refer to any particular word(s) in the sentence. The best way to correct a dangling-modifier problem is to reconstruct the sentence.

Dangling: *Set by an arsonist*, firefighters were unable to save the burning building. (This sentence makes no reference to whatever was set by an arsonist.)

Better: Firefighters were unable to save the burning building from *the fire set by an arsonist*.

In the preceding example, the dangling modifier problem was pretty obvious. But this isn't always the case. Sentences with dangling modifier problems often "sound" perfectly fine. And the ACT test-makers have their ways of masking these problems with smooth sounding sentences. Here's a good example:

By imposing price restrictions on oil suppliers, these suppliers will be forced to lower production costs.

(A) NO CHANGE
(B) Imposing price restrictions
(C) If price restrictions are imposed
(D) In the event of price restrictions

The correct answer is (C). The original sentence includes a dangling modifier. The sentence makes no reference to whomever (or whatever) is imposing the price restrictions. Choice (C) corrects the problem by reconstructing the underlined portion using the passive voice. (Also notice the consistency in voice between the two clauses (*are imposed* and *will be forced*). Choice (B) lacks the preposition needed for the original version to make grammatical sense as a complete sentence. (An additional revision would be needed as well: *Imposing price restrictions on oil suppliers would force these suppliers. . . .*) Choice (D) corrects the dangling modifier problem, but it lacks a verb and is unnecessarily wordy—especially compared to choice (C).

Suppose the original sentence above was preceded by this one: *Powerful oil cartels often impose artificial constraints on oil prices.* This additional sentence would solve the dangling-modifier problem, because you'd know who (or what) is doing the imposing. But with the addition, the second clause of the original sentence would need restructuring—for example, *they will force these suppliers to lower production costs.*

Whenever you see a possible dangling modifier, be sure to check the preceding sentence for the modifier's antecedent.

Despite the rule against dangling modifiers, certain dangling modifiers are idiomatically acceptable.

Acceptable: *Judging* from the number of violent crimes committed every year, our nation is doomed. (The sentence makes no reference to whomever is judging; however, it is acceptable anyway.)

Acceptable: *Considering* the star's great distance from Earth, its brightness is amazing. (Although this sentence does not reveal who is doing the considering, it is acceptable anyway.)

If you encounter a dangling modifier in an ACT sentence that you've heard before from well-educated people, it's probably one of those idiomatic exceptions to the prohibition against dangling modifiers.

STRINGS OF SUBORDINATE CLAUSES

A *subordinate clause* is one that does not stand on its own as a complete sentence. Stringing together two or more subordinate clauses can result in an awkward and confusing sentence.

Awkward: Barbara's academic major is history, *which* is a very popular course of study among liberal arts students, *who* are also contributing to the popularity of political science as a major.

Better: Barbara's academic major is history, which, along with political science, is a very popular course of study among liberal arts students.

Keep in mind that juxtaposing subordinate clauses is not necessarily wrong. In some cases, stringing subordinate clauses together is preferable to other means of structuring a sentence. It all depends on the particular sentence. Here's an ACT-style sentence that illustrates this point.

Q By relying unduly on anecdotal evidence, which often conflicts with more reliable data, including data from direct observation and measurement, <u>scientists risk losing credibility among their peers</u>.

Which of the following is the best suggestion for the underlined portion, disregarding changes in punctuation and capitalization?

(A) NO CHANGE
(B) Move the underlined portion to the beginning of the sentence
(C) Reposition the underlined portion between *evidence* and *which* (immediately following the first comma)
(D) Reposition the underlined portion between *data* and *including* (immediately following the second comma)

A **The correct answer is (B).** The original sentence strings together three dependent clauses—all of which precede the main clause, which is underlined. Since only the first clause modifies the main clause, it makes sense to move the main clause to the beginning of the sentence. Although choices (C) and (D) break the long string of dependent clauses, each proposal results in a more serious problem. Choice (C) makes it appear that the antecedent of *which* is *peers*. (But the intended antecedent of *which* is *anecdotal evidence*.) Similarly, choice (D) makes it appear that *data* is a type of *peer*, which makes no sense.

RHETORICAL BALANCE BETWEEN PARTS OF A SENTENCE

An effective sentence gets its point across by placing appropriate emphasis on its different parts. If you're dealing with two equally important ideas, they should be separated as two distinct "main clauses," and they should be similar in length (to suggest equal importance).

Unbalanced: Julie and Sandy were the first two volunteers for the fund-raising drive, *and* they are twins.

Balanced: Julie and Sandy, *who* are twins, were the first two volunteers for the fund-raising drive.

Commingled (confusing): Julie and Sandy, *who* are twins, are volunteers.

Separated (balanced): Julie and Sandy are twins, *and* they are volunteers.

On the other hand, if you're dealing with only one main idea, it should receive greater emphasis (as a main clause) than the other ideas in the sentence.

Equal emphasis (confusing): Jose and Victor were identical twins, *and* they had completely different ambitions.

Emphasis on second clause (better): *Although* Jose and Victor were identical twins, they had completely different ambitions.

To know whether a sentence strikes the most appropriate rhetorical balance, you need to understand the point that the writer is trying to convey. And to handle a tough ACT question involving this concept, you'll also need to recognize subtle distinctions between answer choices—distinctions that would slip past average test-takers. Here's a good example:

Q Treating bodily disorders by non-invasive methods is generally painless, and these methods are less likely than those of conventional Western medicine to result in permanent healing.

(A) NO CHANGE
(B) although these methods
(C) even though these methods
(D) methods which

A **The correct answer is (B).** Notice that the original sentence contains two main clauses, connected by *and*. Two problems should have occurred to you as you read the sentence: (1) the connector *and* is inappropriate to contrast differing methods of treatment (it fails to get the point across), and (2) the second clause expresses the more important point but does not receive greater emphasis than the first clause. Choice (B) corrects both problems by transforming the second clause into a subordinate one—by replacing *and* with *although*. Choice (C) corrects the first problem, but it places the rhetorical emphasis on the wrong clause (the first one). Choice (D) results in a confusing, even nonsensical, sentence.

X-REF **In the preceding example, another way to achieve appropriate rhetorical balance would be to begin the sentence with a word such as *although* and to omit *and*. This revision transforms the independent clause that begins the sentence into a dependent one. Recall from Lesson 4 that you can fix comma splices in the same way.**

PARALLELISM (LISTS)

Sentence elements that are grammatically equal—such as a list, or "string," of items—should be constructed similarly; otherwise, the result will be what is referred to as *faulty parallelism*. Whenever you see a string of items, look for inconsistent or mixed use of:

- Prepositions (such as *in*, *with,* or *on*)
- Gerunds (verbs with an *-ing* added to the end)
- Infinitives (plural verbs preceded by *to*)
- Articles (such as *a* and *the*)

Faulty: Flight 82 travels first to Boise, then to Denver, then Salt Lake City. (The word *to* precedes only the first two of the three cities in this list.)

Parallel: Flight 82 travels first to Boise, then Denver, then Salt Lake City.

Parallel: Flight 82 travels first to Boise, then to Denver, then to Salt Lake City.

Faulty: Being understaffed, lack of funding, and being outpaced by competitors soon resulted in the fledgling company's going out of business. (Only two of the three listed items begin with the gerund *being*.)

Parallel: Understaffed, underfunded, and outpaced by competitors, the fledgling company soon went out of business.

Parallel: As a result of understaffing, insufficient funding, and outpacing on the part of its competitors, the fledgling company soon went out of business.

Faulty: Among *the* mountains, *the* sea, and desert, we humans have yet to fully explore only the sea.

Parallel: Among *the* mountains, sea, and desert, we humans have yet to fully explore only the sea.

Parallel: Among *the* mountains, *the* sea, and *the* desert, we humans have yet to fully explore only the sea.

As you can see, this type of parallelism problem isn't difficult to recognize or fix. The best ploy the test-makers have to trip you up is to drop the article or preposition before the second item, hoping that by the time you read the third list item, you might not "hear" the faulty parallelism. Here's an ACT-style illustration:

Q Long before the abolition of slavery, many freed indentured servants were able to acquire property, interact with people of other races, and to maintain their freedom.

(A) NO CHANGE
(B) as well as to
(C) and maintain
(D) as well as maintaining

A **The correct answer is (C).** In the original version, the second item does *not* repeat the preposition *to*, but the third (underlined) item does. Choice (C) corrects this faulty parallelism, while choice (B) does not. Choice (D) improperly mixes the use of a prepositional phrase (beginning with *to*) with a construction that instead uses a gerund (*maintaining*).

Just because all items in a string are parallel, don't assume that the string is problem-free! Repeating the same preposition, article, or other modifier before each item in a string can sometimes result in an awkward and unnecessarily wordy sentence. In other instances, repeating the modifier may be necessary to achieve clarity.

Awkward: Some pachyderms can go for days at a time without water or without food or without sleep.

Better: Some pachyderms can go for days at a time without water, food, or sleep.

Unclear: Going for broke and broke usually carry identical consequences.

Clear: Going for broke and going broke usually carry identical consequences.

PARALLELISM (CORRELATIVES)

You just saw how items in a list can suffer from faulty parallelism. Now look at how this grammatical error shows up in what are called *correlatives*. Here are the most commonly used correlatives:

- either . . . or . . .
- neither . . . nor . . .
- both . . . and . . .
- not only . . . but also . . .

Whenever you spot a correlative in a sentence, make sure that the element immediately following the first correlative term is parallel in construction to the element following the second term.

Faulty: Those wishing to participate should *either* contact us by telephone *or* should send e-mail to us.

Parallel (but repetitive): Those wishing to participate *either should* contact us by telephone *or should* send e-mail to us.

Parallel: Those wishing to participate should *either* contact us by telephone *or* send e-mail to us.

ACT parallelism questions involving correlatives are generally tougher than those involving lists, for two reasons:

- Correlatives are idiomatic, so if you're unfamiliar with the idiom, you might not know whether there's a problem.
- Unlike items in a list, the two parts of a correlative can be separated by one or more intervening clauses, which can make faulty parallelism easy to miss.

Here's a tough ACT-style question that illustrates both features:

Q Species diversity in the Amazon basin results not from climate stability, as once believed, but rather climate disturbances.

(A) NO CHANGE
(B) also from
(C) instead
(D) rather from

A **The correct answer is (D).** The idiomatic correlative in this sentence is *not . . . but rather. . . .* In the original sentence, *from* follows the first correlative term, but not the second. Choice (D) corrects the faulty parallelism (*from* appears in each correlative term). Although choice (B) also corrects the faulty parallelism, it uses the nonsensical (and improper) correlative *not . . . but also*. (The idiom is *not only . . . but also*, which in any event would completely alter the sentence's meaning.)

X-REF **You just read that correlatives are idiomatic. We'll review other frequently tested idioms in Lesson 8.**

BRAIN TEASER

In this quiz, you'll tackle 15 ACT-style questions that focus primarily on sentence structure. These questions are tougher than average ACT questions in this category. Keep in mind: You won't encounter ACT-length passages in this quiz. Instead, you'll examine an eclectic series of discrete sentences, along with 1–3 questions based on each one.

X-REF **Many questions in this quiz also involve other official testing areas already covered in Part II. Therefore, these questions serve as a *review* of this lesson and previous ones.**

Attempt all 15 questions, but don't put yourself under a time limit. Focus instead on applying the rules and guidelines you learned about in this lesson. Then be sure to read the explanations that follow the quiz. They're just as important as the questions themselves, because they explain how to apply the rules and guidelines to the questions.

QUIZ

Although the hospital administrators interviewed many staff members about the repeated cases of staph infections, they had no [1] explanation for the puzzling pattern of outbreaks.

1. (A) NO CHANGE
   (B) no staff member had an
   (C) the staff had no
   (D) they have had no

Corporate financial statements for the first three quarters of the year showed that the sales increases they had [2] enjoyed each year of the previous decade had slowed considerably.

2. (F) NO CHANGE
   (G) that they
   (H) the companies had
   (J) OMIT the underlined portion

A fabled center of monastic life during the Middle Ages, thousands of visitors each summer travel to the island of Iona. [3]

3. (A) NO CHANGE
   (B) each summer thousands of visitors travel to the island of Iona.
   (C) visitors travel to the island of Iona by the thousands each summer.
   (D) the island of Iona is visited by thousands of visitors each summer.

Dismayed by [4] the news that one of the firm's top executives had suddenly decided to [5] accept a job with a rival company, the price of the company's stock fell sharply the following day.

4. (F) NO CHANGE
   (G) Due to dismay over
   (H) Dismayed about
   (J) As a result of being dismayed by

5. (A) NO CHANGE
   (B) decided to suddenly
   (C) suddenly decided to
   (D) had decided suddenly to

[6] Considered to be the most unforgiving course in the world, cyclists must train especially hard in order to meet the challenge posed by it. [7]

6. The writer is considering adding a phrase to the beginning of this sentence. Which of the following would be most effective?
   (F) NO CHANGE (Do not add any phrase.)
   (G) ADD *Since it's*
   (H) ADD *Because the course is*, and OMIT *course* (later in the sentence)
   (J) ADD *Although it is*

7. (A) NO CHANGE
   (B) that is posed.
   (C) it poses.
   (D) OMIT the underlined portion

Humans naturally crave to do good, act reasonably, <u>and to think</u> [8] <u>decently, these</u> [9] urges must have a global purpose in order to have meaning.

8. (F) NO CHANGE
(G) and think
(H) think
(J) as well as to think

9. (A) NO CHANGE
(B) decently, although these
(C) decent, but these
(D) decently, and these

<u>Not only smoking cigarettes but also cigar smoking has been banned now</u> [10] from many public places.

10. (F) NO CHANGE
(G) Cigarette smoking and cigar smoking are both banned now
(H) Not only has smoking cigarettes been banned but so has cigar smoking
(J) Smoking cigarettes along with cigars is now banned

A well-trained operatic voice <u>cannot only be</u> [11] as sweet, but also <u>as priceless as, the</u> [12] mellifluous tones of a well-tuned Stradivarius violin <u>can be.</u> [13]

11. (A) NO CHANGE
(B) can be not only
(C) can be
(D) not only can be

12. (F) NO CHANGE
(G) priceless, like
(H) as priceless as the
(J) as priceless, as the

13. (A) NO CHANGE
(B) can.
(C) are.
(D) OMIT the underlined portion

(1) The California gold rush, (2) the historical development instilling the greatest sense of manifest destiny in the populace, (3) <u>wore not</u> [14] the clothing of political ideology but rather a suit spun of gold and greed. [15]

14. (F) NO CHANGE
(G) did not wear
(H) wore not just
(J) weared not

15. Which of the following is the most effective sequence for the sentence's three numbered clauses?
(A) 1, 2, 3
(B) 2, 1, 3
(C) 1, 3, 2
(D) 2, 3, 1

ANSWERS AND EXPLANATIONS

1. **The correct answer is (B).** You can't tell from the context who *they* are—the hospital administrators, the staff members, or both. Choice (B) clears up the ambiguity by supplying the antecedent in place of the pronoun. So does choice (C), but its use of the singular *staff* instead of the plural *staff members* makes for a reference that is less clear than the one that choice (B) provides. Choice (D) fails to clear up the ambiguity; what's more, it improperly shifts tense from past to present perfect.

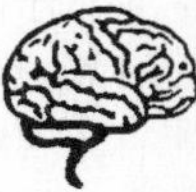

If two answers are both grammatically correct and equally effective in all other respects, then the more concise phrase is better. But Brainiacs keep in mind that briefer is not always better. For example, notice that the correct answer to question 1 was actually the lengthiest of all four options!

2. **The correct answer is (H).** Who is the *they* referred to in the second half of the sentence? Presumably, it is the corporation being discussed; yet, the words *the corporation* or their equivalent (*the company*, *the firm*) don't appear anywhere in the sentence. Choice (H) clears up the vague reference by replacing the pronoun with its intended antecedent noun. Choice (G) fails to resolve the problem, and it provides an unwarranted shift to the simple past tense. Choice (J) solves the pronoun-reference problem, but it still leaves unclear who or what enjoyed the sales increases.

3. **The correct answer is (D).** The first clause is supposed to modify *the island of Iona*. But it's next to *thousands of visitors*, resulting in the absurd suggestion that visitors were *a fabled center*. Among the alternatives, only choice (D) positions the modifier next to what it should modify. Admittedly, the passive-voice construction is a bit awkward, and, ideally, the entire sentence should be restructured. But choice (D) is the best of the listed options.

As you read the preceding analysis, did you think of an even better way to restructure the sentence—one that was not listed among the answer choices? Here's one possibility (perhaps this revised version came to your mind): *Each summer, thousands of visitors travel to the island of Iona, a fabled center of monastic life during the Middle Ages.* Remember: Although the correct answer choice will be the best among the four listed alternatives, it won't necessarily result in the best possible sentence.

4. **The correct answer is (G).** The original sentence contains a dangling modifier—and a long one at that. The entire opening clause, ending in the word *company*, is designed to modify, or provide more information about, *whom*? Who, exactly, was *dismayed by the news*? One way to fix the error is to rewrite the second clause (following the comma) to name the person or people who were dismayed—for example: . . . *company, Wall Street traders drove the price of the company's stock down sharply the following day*. But none of the answer choices provide this sort of solution. However, choice (G) supplies another good solution: With the noun *dismay* in place of the verb *dismayed*, the opening clause is no longer a modifying phrase! Neither choice (H) nor choice (J) corrects the problem; in each case, you're still left with the unanswered question as to whom is dismayed.

5. **The correct answer is (A).** The adverb *suddenly* describes the verb *decided*, and so it is correctly positioned immediately preceding that verb. Inserting an adverb between the two component verbs of a participle verb form (*had decided*) is perfectly acceptable. Choice (B) repositions *suddenly* so that it appears to describe *accept*, but the context makes clear that it was *deciding*, not *accepting*, that occurred *suddenly*. Choice (C) omits *had*, shifting the tense from past perfect to simple past. But the past perfect tense is more appropriate here, since the decision occurred prior to another past event: The fall in the company's stock price. Choice (D) splits *decided to*. Although this phrase is not a grammatical unit, the split is awkward. The original version is clearer and more graceful.

6. **The correct answer is (H).** The entire first half of the sentence (ending in the word *world*) is a dependent clause that appears to modify, or describe, *cyclists*. Obviously, this relationship makes no sense in context. Neither choice (G) nor choice (J) is any better. However, choice (H) makes clear that what is considered unforgiving is not cyclists but rather the course: *Because the course is considered to be the most unforgiving in the world, . . .*

7. **The correct answer is (C).** The passive voice sounds awkward in this context. Choice (C) provides the active-voice equivalent, which sound more graceful here. Choice (B) is even worse than the original version—it's awkward and vague (posed by *what*?). Simply omitting the underlined portion leaves it unclear as to exactly what challenge the writer is referring.

8. **The correct answer is (G).** The underlined portion lacks proper parallelism; *to* should simply be omitted, as in choice (G). Neither choice (H) nor choice (J) correct the problem.

9. **The correct answer is (B).** The original "sentence" is comprised of two main clauses (each of which could stand on its own as a complete sentence) separated only by a comma. This comma splice can be corrected by an appropriate connecting word, such as *but*, *yet*, or *although*, as in choice (B). Choice (C) does not employ proper parallelism. (The adverb *decently* should be used instead of the adjective *decent*). As for choice (D), the connector *and* places equal rhetorical emphasis on the two clauses. However, the second clause should receive greater emphasis.

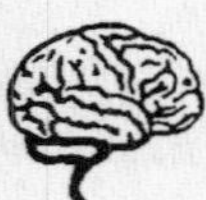

For question 9, try reversing the two clauses, using *and* to connect them. The point of the sentence is a bit unclear, isn't it. That's a good clue that the two clauses should *not* receive equal emphasis—and that a word such as *but*, *yet*, or *although* would work better rhetorically.

10. **The correct answer is (G).** In the original version, the terms following each part of the correlative pair *not only . . . but also* are not grammatically parallel. The sentence is also awkward. Choice (G) reconstructs the sentence so that it is clear and concise. Choice (H) is awkward and confusing, especially in its use of the correlative *not only . . . but so*, which is not idiomatic. Choice (J) distorts the meaning of the original sentence by suggesting, rather nonsensically, that what is banned is smoking both cigarettes and cigars *at the same time*.

11. **The correct answer is (B).** The underlined portion is awkward and fails to establish proper parallelism between the phrases following the two parts of the correlative *not only . . . but also*. The underlined portion should be replaced with *can be not only*. Choice (C) omits the second, and essential, part of the correlative pair *not only . . . but also*. Choice (D) fails to correct the faulty parallelism.

12. **The correct answer is (J).** If you remove the appositive *but also as priceless as*, you're left with *as sweet the mellifluous tones*. . . . As you can see, the second *as* is missing from the idiomatic word pair *as . . . as*. Choice (J) corrects the problem by placing a comma before *as* instead of after it. (Without the appositive, the sentence now sounds correct: *as sweet as the mellifluous tones . . .* .) Choice (G) omits the second, and essential, part of the idiomatic word pair *as . . . as*. Choice (H) omits one of the two commas that should surround the appositive.

13. **The correct answer is (D).** The idiom *as . . . as . . .* sets up an *ellipsis*—a phrase that is clearly implied and can therefore be omitted. The underlined phrase *can be* is implied; hence, simply omitting it results in a crisper, more concise, sentence.

X-REF

In the sentence on which question 13 is based, nothing is lost (and no grammatical errors are created) by simply omitting the underlined portion. In Lesson 6, you examined other examples of unnecessary, or superfluous, words and phrases—examples that appear frequently on the ACT.

14. **The correct answer is (F).** The correlative pair *not . . . but rather* is idiomatic. Notice that what follows the correlative's first part (*not*) is grammatically parallel to what follows the second part (*but rather*). Also, *wore* is the correct past-tense form of the verb *to wear*. Choice (G) lacks proper parallelism. Choice (H) results in the illogical correlative pair *not just . . . but rather*. Choice (J) uses an improper form of the verb *to wear*.

15. **The correct answer is (B).** The subject of the verb *wore* is *gold rush*, but the intervening clause obscures this subject-verb relationship. Switching clause (1) with clause (2) solves the problem.

LESSON 8
Usage and Idioms for Brainiacs

The ACT English Test also covers *word usage* and *idioms*. In this lesson, you'll examine the following:

- Usage errors—using the wrong word to express the intended idea
- Idioms—phrases that are either proper or improper simply based upon whether they have become acceptable over time through repeated and common use

In many instances, you'll recognize improper word usage or a phrase that is "not idiomatic" simply because the word or phrase doesn't *sound* right. But that doesn't mean you should rely solely on your ear when it comes to the ACT. Although it's impossible to predict what specific usage and idiom issues will pop up on the test, it is still wise to prepare for the most difficult and most frequently used ones.

After you review the lists in this lesson, you'll tackle 15 tough ACT-style questions involving word usage and idioms. Most (but not all) of the questions test you on words and phrases covered in this lesson.

The English language contains more idioms and usage issues than you can shake a thesaurus at. So, don't expect the words and phrases covered in this lesson to be the only ones you'll encounter in ACT idiom and usage questions. The test-makers don't design the ACT to be that predictable.

DISTINGUISH GERUNDS FROM INFINITIVES

A *gerund* is a noun formed by adding *-ing* to a verb. It looks the same as the present participle form of the verb—swimming, working, enjoying—but it's used in all the ways a noun is used: as the subject or object of a verb, as the object of a preposition, and so on. For example, in the sentence, "Swimming is my favorite exercise," *Swimming* is the subject of the verb.

An *infinitive* is the basic form of a verb, usually with *to* in front of it: to swim, to work, to enjoy. Like a gerund, it can also be used as a noun, either by itself or in a phrase called an infinitive phrase. For example, in the sentence, "To know him is to love him," the infinitive phrase *To know him* is the subject of the sentence (and *to love him* is the subject complement).

But just knowing the difference between a gerund and an infinitive won't help you much on the ACT. You also need to be sensitive to which one "sounds" right in a particular sentence. Unfortunately, there are no logical rules to

follow (as is usually true with idioms). Similar meanings sometimes require opposite structures: A person promises *to do* something, but she is committed *to doing* it; she may hesitate *to do* something, but she objects *to doing* it, and so on.

On the ACT, an easier question will involve a phrase that not only sounds wrong, but is also confusing—as in the following sentence:

> The sensitive nature of the negotiations required the company president's traveling halfway around the globe to participate personally in the final phase of the discussion.

According to idiomatic usage, the word *required* should be followed by an infinitive rather than a gerund, so the sentence should say, "required the company president *to travel* halfway around the globe . . . "

By contrast, a tougher question in a non-idiomatic phrase might sound acceptable, and it might very well make sense. To make things even trickier, the test-makers might incorporate an infinitive or gerund form of a word that isn't frequently used. Take a look at the following sentences:

more
greater
fewer
less

Words describing and comparing size, number, and quantity are often misused. Distinguish words used to describe *degree* or *amount* (weight, size, etc.) from those used to describe *number* (quantity).

- *More* salt is used in the stew recipe than in the soup recipe.
- The *amount* of salt used in the stew recipe is *greater* (not *more*) than that used in the soup recipe.
- The *number* (not *amount*) of people in Smallville is *smaller* (not *fewer*) than the number of people in Bigville.
- *Fewer* (not *less*) people reside in Smallville than in Bigville.

such

The word *such* can be used as an alternative to *of these* or *of those*, but using it this way can sometimes sound awkward.

Proper: Good liars may appear successful, but most *such* people are usually miserable inside.

Awkward: A good liar may appear successful, but *such a person* is usually miserable inside.

to be
as being
as

Neither *as* or *as being* is a proper substitute for the infinitive *to be*.

Proper (but confusing): Many people consider Lincoln America's greatest president.

Proper (and clearer): Many people consider Lincoln *to be* America's greatest president.

Improper: Many people consider Lincoln *as* America's greatest president.

Improper: Many people consider Lincoln *as being* America's greatest president.

former
latter

Use *former* to refer to the first of two items in a sequence, and use *latter* to refer to the second of the two items. Do not use either term, however, to compare *three or more* items.

Improper: Graphic arts, music theory, and literature all interested Gwen, but among these course, of study only the *latter* was offered at the local college.

Proper: Graphic arts and music theory both interested Gwen, but the latter course of study was not offered at the local college.

because
since
as a result of
as
so
being that (awkward)

All of these terms can be used to express a cause-and-effect relationship. But they are not interchangeable.

Unclear: *Since* the prankster set off the alarm, the school has been evacuated. (Does *since* mean "because" or "after"?)

Clear (but wordy): *As a result of* the prankster's setting off the alarm, the school has been evacuated.

Clear: *Because* the prankster set off the alarm, the school has been evacuated.

Unclear: The prankster has been expelled from school *since* he set off the alarm. (Does *since* mean "because" or "after"?)

Unclear: *Since* the prankster set off the alarm, he has been expelled from school. (Does *since* mean "because" or "after"?)

Clear: The prankster was expelled from school *since* (or *because*) he refused to stop setting off the alarm.

Unclear: The school was evacuated, *as* the prankster set off the alarm. (Does *as* mean "because" or "at the same time that"?)

Acceptable: The prankster was expelled from school, *as* (or *since*) he could not resist setting off the alarm.

Proper (but awkward): *Being that* the prankster is about to set off the alarm, the school will probably be evacuated.

Better: The prankster is about to set off the alarm, *so* the school will probably be evacuated.

although
despite (the fact that)
in spite of (the fact that)

All of these terms can be used to express the same idea, but only the last two are interchangeable.

Improper: *Despite* (or *in spite of*) *the fact of* her parents' financial assistance, she was unable to pay her credit card bill.

Proper (but wordy): *Despite* (or *in spite of*) *the fact that* her parents assisted her financially, she was unable to pay her credit card bill.

Proper (concise): *Despite* (or *in spite of*) her parents' financial assistance, she was unable to pay her credit card bill.

Proper (concise): *Although* her parents assisted her financially, she was unable to pay her credit card bill.

to do so

The word *so*, like the word *such*, can serve as shorthand for a word (or words) appearing earlier in the sentence (an antecedent). But it should be used in this way only as the past of the idiom *to do so*.

Awkward and unclear: The House of Representatives quickly passed the bill, but the Senate failed *to so pass it*.

Proper: The House of Representatives quickly passed the bill, but the Senate failed *to do so*.

nevertheless
nonetheless
anyway

Nevertheless and *nonetheless* have the same meaning, but they differ in terms of where they are placed for greatest impact. *Anyway* is a more concise alternative to both.

- Stan suffered a painful injury when he fell off his horse, but he *nevertheless* kept riding.
- Stan suffered a painful injury when he fell off his horse, but he kept riding *nonetheless*.
- Stan suffered a painful injury when he fell off his horse, but he kept riding *anyway*.

alike
whether . . . or

Either of these terms can be used to place two items on equal footing.

- Humans should dignify all living things, flora and fauna *alike*.
- Humans should dignify each living thing, *whether it be* flora *or* fauna.
- *Whether* flora *or* fauna, any living thing should be accorded dignity as such.

even

Besides its more obvious meaning ("equal" or "tied"), *even* can be used as a modifier for rhetorical emphasis. But its placement can be crucial to the meaning of the sentence.

- Canada is *even* larger than the United States. (Canada is being compared to other countries).
- *Even* Canada is larger than the United States.(The United States is being compared to other countries).

if
whether
whether or not

The words *if* and *whether* can be used interchangeably; *whether or not* carries a distinct meaning.

Proper: Nobody knows if (or whether) Kurt survived the war.

Improper: Nobody knows whether Kurt survived the war or not.

Proper: Nobody knows whether or not Kurt survived the war.

Proper: Whether or not Kurt survived the war, his family will continue to celebrate his birthday.

as of
as for
as with
as in

Each of these idiomatic phrases carries its own distinct meaning.

- *As of* yesterday, the leader still had not transmitted any news about his expedition.
- *As for* the youngest climber, he quit about halfway up.
- *As with* mountain climbers, some politicians don't quit until they reach the summit.

As in mountain climbing, in politics only the fittest reach the summit.

as opposed to

Use *as opposed to* when expressing a preference, but don't use *prefer* in the same sentence.

- The chef decided to fry the fish *as opposed to* broiling it.
- I like fried fish *as opposed to* broiled fish.
- The chef preferred frying the fish *to* (not *as opposed to*) broiling it.

regarding
in regard to
as regards
with respect to
respecting
concerning
as to
about

All of these terms are proper and have essentially the same meaning. In the first sentence below, any of the terms could be used. In the second sentence, any of the terms except *as to* and *about* would be appropriate.

- Richard consulted his accountant *as to* the income-tax consequences of the sale.
- *In regard to* (not *as to* or *about*) the first issue, neither candidate is in favor of a tax increase for the middle class.
- Do not confuse the proper idioms to the left with the following improper ones:

 in regards to
 with regards to
 as regarding
 as respecting
 in respect of

while
although

While or *although* can both be used to subordinate one idea to another. However, *while* is appropriate only when describing concurrent events or conditions (occurring at the same time).

- *Although* (or *while*) the mortality rate from car accidents last year was high, the death rate from cancer was much higher.
- *Although* (not *while*) last year's mortality rates appear very high, one must keep in mind that the rates have decreased steadily over the last decade.

such as
like

Use *such as* to give examples. Use *like* to express similarity between two things.

- Mold can grow in many places, *such as* (not *like*) bathrooms, forests, and petri dishes.
- The mold growing in the bathroom looked very much *like* the mold I've seen in the forest.

which
under which
in which
by which
of which

The proper phrase depends on the point you wish to make.

- Einstein originated the theory of relativity, *which* holds that time is a relative concept.
- Einstein originated the theory of relativity, *under which* time is a relative concept.
- Einstein's theories emerged during the same century *in which* his theories were first confirmed empirically.
- Most people have heard of Einstein's theory of relativity, *by which* the time between two events depends on the observer.
- Einstein's theory of relativity fascinates today's scientists, only a few *of which* ever met Einstein personally.

based on
based upon
on the basis of

All three phrases are proper idioms, but only the first two are interchangeable in all instances.

- *Based upon* (or *based on* or *on the basis of*) the stock's past performance, I don't think I should sell it.
- My opinion about this stock is *based upon/on* (not *on the basis of*) its past performance.

by
by way of
by means of

Which phrase is proper depends on how it is used in the sentence.

- The hikers reached the valley *by* taking the main trail.
- The hikers reached the valley *by way of* the main trail.
- The hikers reached the valley *by means of* horseback.

account for
on account of
take into account

Which phrase is proper depends on how it is used in the sentence.

- *The scout leader could not account for* the missing child.
- *The scout leader was reprimanded on account of* his losing the child.
- *The results of the scout leader's roll call failed to take into account* the missing child.

among
between

Use *among* for three or more items. Use *between* for two items.

- *Among* the many celebrities at the gala, she was dressed most flamboyantly.
- He was *between* a rock and a hard place.

like
as
as if
as though

Use *as though* or *as if* (not *like*) for the subjunctive mood. Use *as* (not *like*) for a simile. Use *like* to make an analogy between two different things.

Improper: He looked *like* he was about to cry.
Proper: He looked *as though* he were about to cry.
Proper: He looked *as if* he were about to cry.

Improper: The television news reporter spoke about the election *like* a non-partisan journalist should.
Proper: The television news reporter spoke about the election *as* a non-partisan journalist should.

Improper: The prisoner behaved *as* a caged animal.
Proper: The prisoner behaved *like* a caged animal.

differ
different

The proper preposition to use with each of these words depends on the context.

Improper: Smith and Adams *differ about* their positions on the issues.
Improper: Smith and Adams *differ from each other on* their positions on the issues.
Proper: Smith and Adams *differ on* their positions on the issues.

Proper: The positions of Smith and Adams *differ from* those of all other candidates.
Proper: Smith and Adams *differ with* each other as to who is the better candidate.
Proper: The candidates *differ in* party membership but not in ideology.

Improper: Smith's position on the issue is *different than* that of Adams.
Proper: Smith's position on the issue is *different from* that of Adams.
Proper: The candidates are *different in* party membership but not in ideology.

In each of the following sentence groups, the proper preposition depends on the context.

It is not always easy to *distinguish* good art *from* (not *with* or *and*) bad art.
The university *distinguished* the alumnus *with* an honorary doctoral degree.
Fluffy the cat can be *distinguished by* her unique markings.

The two analysts *agreed with* each other.
The two analysts *agreed to* examine the numbers further.
The two analysts *agreed on* (not *about*) only one conclusion.

No reasonable jury could *concur in* (not *about*) finding the defendant guilty.
The jury members have decided to *concur with* one another regarding the defendant's guilt.

Susan's former boyfriend plans to *interfere with* (not *in*) the wedding reception.

Susan's former boyfriend *interfered in* (not *by*) spiking the punch at the wedding reception.

The Cougars will *prevail over* (not *against*) the Panthers in the upcoming game.

The Cougars' coach must *prevail on* his team to play more aggressively during the second half of the game.

The contract *provides for* mandatory arbitration in the event of a dispute.

The contract *provides that* the parties must arbitrate any dispute.

The cave *provided* shelter for the bears.

The mother bear *provided for* her cubs.

Gary was *disappointed in* his son.

Gary was *disappointed with* (not *in* or *by*) his son's test results.

The runner grew *impatient with* (not *about* or *at*) the slow pace of the race.

Sprinters are often *impatient in* (not *with* or *about*) waiting for the final lap of longer races.

Doug will surely *die from* excessive smoking.

Doug will surely *die of* pneumonia.

John *confided in* his older brother.

John *confided to* his older brother that he stole the bicycle.

Each of the following phrases illustrates the proper (and improper) use of particular prepositions.

acquiesce *in* (not *to*) illegal activity
alarmed *at* (not *about*) the news
apologize *for* (not *about*) a mistake
ignorant *of* (not *about*) the facts
independent *of* (not *from*) parental assistance
insist *on* (not *in*) a course of action
oblivious *of* (not *about* or *to*) the time
preferable *to* (not *than* or *over*) the other choice
required *of* (not *from*) all students
rich *in* (not *with*) resources
short *of* (not *on*) cash
succeed *in* (not *with*) an attempt
superior *to* (not *over*) the alternatives
aside from (not *outside of*) one particular instance
within (not *inside of*) a few minutes
price/cost *of* (not *for*) a shirt
could *have* (not *of*) won the game

BRAIN TEASER

In this quiz, you'll tackle 15 ACT-style questions that focus on word usage and idioms. These questions are tougher than average ACT questions in this category. Keep in mind: You won't encounter ACT-length passages in this quiz. Instead, you'll examine an eclectic series of discrete sentences, along with 2 or 3 questions based on each one.

Attempt all 15 questions, but don't put yourself under a time limit. Focus instead on applying the rules and guidelines you have learned about in this lesson. Then be sure to read the explanations that follow the quiz. They're just as important as the questions themselves, because they explain how to apply the rules and guidelines to the questions.

QUIZ

Cambodia **remains being** [1] a **largely** [2] underdeveloped country because virtually all educated citizens were slaughtered during the regime of Pol Pot.

1. (A) NO CHANGE
   (B) still is
   (C) remains as
   (D) remains

2. (F) NO CHANGE
   (G) primarily
   (H) mostly
   (J) large

The sheer **amount** [3] of information in the world seems to explode as faster and faster **means of access are** [4] devised.

3. (A) NO CHANGE
   (B) number of pieces
   (C) quantity
   (D) quantities

4. (F) NO CHANGE
   (G) access is
   (H) means to access it are
   (J) ways of accessing it are

Despite the fact of a jury's verdict, [5] the judge can rule **in favor of** [6] the other party, overriding the jury's decision.

5. (A) NO CHANGE
   (B) In spite of the verdict of a jury,
   (C) Whatever the verdict,
   (D) Despite a jury's verdict,

6. (F) NO CHANGE
   (G) otherwise, favoring
   (H) for
   (J) favoring

In regard to [7] the third and final trimester of human gestation, there remains considerable disagreement **in** [8] how the mother's rights should be weighed against those of the unborn child.

7. (A) NO CHANGE
   (B) As respecting
   (C) About
   (D) Regards to

8. (F) NO CHANGE
   (G) on the issue of
   (H) as to
   (J) OMIT the underlined portion

Irregardless of [9] the historical, and adverse, social consequences of constraints on free speech and expression, some political leaders seem never to learn **the lessons of such consequences.** [10]

9. (A) NO CHANGE
   (B) Regardless of
   (C) Due to
   (D) Unaware of

10. (F) NO CHANGE
    (G) their lessons.
    (H) from these consequences.
    (J) these historical lessons.

Any music instructor would without a doubt agree that a student of music performance should practice the applying of tonal as well as rhythmic principles on a weekly or daily basis.

(underlined portions: 11 "without a doubt agree"; 12 "the applying of"; 13 "weekly or daily basis.")

11. (A) NO CHANGE
(B) not disagree
(C) agree with certainty
(D) no doubt agree

12. (F) NO CHANGE
(G) the application of
(H) his or her applying
(J) OMIT the underlined portion

13. (A) NO CHANGE
(B) basis that is either daily or weekly.
(C) weekly, or even daily, basis.
(D) daily to weekly basis.

The president assured the senator that his administration had no intention to encroach on congressional prerogatives in this matter.

(underlined portions: 14 "to encroach"; 15 "on")

14. (F) NO CHANGE
(G) of encroaching
(H) about encroaching
(J) of encroachment

15. (A) NO CHANGE
(B) against
(C) the
(D) OMIT the underlined portion

ANSWERS AND EXPLANATIONS

1. **The correct answer is (D).** The original version uses the awkward and non-idiomatic *remains being*. Either *is still* or *remains* should be used instead. Choice (B) reverses the words in one of the two suggested idioms, distorting the sentence's meaning. Choice (C) is wrong because *as* serves to transform *Cambodia remains* into a main clause that receives more rhetorical emphasis than it should.

2. **The correct answer is (F).** The phrase *largely underdeveloped* is an idiomatic way of expressing the idea that Cambodia is, to a great extent, underdeveloped. Choices (G) and (H) are not idiomatic. Choice (J), which replaces the adverb *largely* with the adjective *large*, results in a nonsensical assertion: The reason Cambodia is large is that its educated citizens were slaughtered.

3. **The correct answer is (A).** The word *amount* is used properly here to describe "information" in a non-quantifiable sense. Choice (B) is wrong because it is not idiomatic to refer to a *sheer number* (in the singular). Choices (C) and (D) are wrong because "information" is not used here as a quantity of anything in particular.

4. **The correct answer is (J).** The phrase *means of access* is idiomatic. However, the sentence is unclear as to what is being accessed. Presumably, it is information; but the sentence would be improved by at least providing a pronoun reference, as in choice (J). (The word *ways* is a perfectly fine substitute for *means*.) Choice (G) is wrong because it is *means* of access (or *ways* of accessing), not *access* itself, that are "devised." Choice (H) is wrong because *means to access* is not idiomatic. (The gerund *accessing* is idiomatic here, but the infinitive *to access* isn't.)

5. **The correct answer is (D).** In the original version, *the fact of* is superfluous and idiomatically improper. Choice (D) corrects this problem by simply omitting the phrase. Choice (B) is grammatically correct, however, although *In spite of* is an idiomatic alternative to *Despite*, choice (B) is not as concise as choice (D). Choice (C) is concise and idiomatic but is unclear as to whose or what verdict is under discussion. In contrast, choice (D) is explicit that it is the jury's verdict that is under discussion.

6. **The correct answer is (F).** The original version is idiomatic and clear in meaning. Choice (G) provides an idiomatic use of otherwise; however, *otherwise* and *favoring the other party* both express the same basic idea, creating a redundancy. What's more, choice (G) sets up an awkward string of subordinate clauses. As for choice (H), although *for* is an idiomatic alternative to *in favor of* , its use here creates ambiguity: One possible meaning is that the judge can rule *in place of* (or *by proxy for*) the other party. Since choice (F) is less ambiguous, it is a better choice. As for choice (J), the phrase *rule favoring* is confusing.

7. **The correct answer is (A).** *In regard to* is idiomatic. *Respecting* and *Regarding* would also be idiomatic and appropriate here, however, *As respecting,* choice (B), and *Regards to,* choice (D), are not. As for choice (C), it's awkward and confusing to begin this sentence with *About.*

8. **The correct answer is (H).** It is idiomatic to say that you disagree *over*, *about*, or *as to* something, but not *in* something. Choice (G) is wordy and awkward. (The phrase *the issue of* is clearly implied and hence redundant as well.) Choice (J) omits the preposition altogether; the result is confusing and idiomatically improper.

9. **The correct answer is (B).** *Irregardless* is not a word and should be replaced by *regardless*, which is idiomatic in context. Choice (C) nonsensically suggests that the social consequences being discussed are *the cause of* some leaders' failure to learn the lessons of these consequences. Choice (D) is grammatically correct and idiomatic. But *Unaware of* is rhetorically ineffective in conveying the point of the sentence.

10. **The correct answer is (H).** As used here, the word *such* is idiomatic but awkward. (The word *these* would be more graceful.) Choice (G) creates an ambiguous pronoun reference. (Does *their* refer to *consequences*, *free speech and expression*, or *political leaders*?) Choice (J) refers to *these* historical lessons, which are not mentioned anywhere in the sentence. Choice (H) is the best of the four options. It is idiomatic to say that one *learns from* something.

11. **The correct answer is (D).** The phrase *without a doubt* is idiomatic, but the sentence would be clearer and more effective if this phrase were set off by commas. Choice (D) is also idiomatic, and it is crisper and more concise than the original version. Choice (B) is wrong because the double negative *not disagree* is awkward and confusing. Choice (C) provides an idiomatically questionable phrase.

12. **The correct answer is (G).** The phrase *applying of* is not idiomatic and should be replaced with either *applying* or *application of,* as in choice (G). Choice (H) is wrong because *his or her* is clearly implied and should therefore be omitted. As for choice (J), it is idiomatic to say that you *put into practice* a principle or that you *practice applying* a principle. However, it is not idiomatic to say that you *practice a principle*.

English language idioms are, in a word, idiosyncratic. And question 12 provides a perfect example of just how idiosyncratic they can be. Although you practice *applying* a principle, you don't practice *playing* a scale. Instead, you simply *practice a scale.* (Go figure!)

13. **The correct answer is (C).** The underlined portion is rhetorically ineffective. (Which schedule is the writer suggesting: a weekly one or a daily one?) In choice (C), the idiom *or even* is properly, and effectively, used as a rhetorical device: to make the point that it is a good idea to practice applying these principles at least every week, and possibly as often as every day. Choice (B) is wordy, and it unfairly implies that a student should have only two choices in practice schedule: daily or weekly. Choice (D) is awkward and confusing.

14. **The correct answer is (G).** The word *encroach* means "intrude." Here, the infinitive *to encroach* might sound okay, but it's not. It is idiomatic to use a gerund following *no intention*. Therefore, the sentence should read, "the administration had no intention *of encroaching* on congressional prerogatives. . . ." Neither choice (H) nor choice (J) is idiomatic.

15. **The correct answer is (A).** It is idiomatic to say that something "encroaches on" another thing. None of the three alternatives is idiomatic.

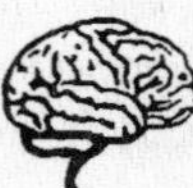

Although the ACT English Test isn't designed to directly measure your vocabulary, expect at least a few questions to involve words that many test-takers won't know. The well-read Brainiac definitely holds an advantage when it comes to these questions—as you can see from the preceding example.

PART III

THE ACT MATHEMATICS TEST

LESSON 9

Math Strategies

This lesson covers general strategies for the ACT Mathematics Test. In this lesson, you'll:

- Review the test directions and clarify the notes
- Learn how Brainiacs breeze through even the toughest math questions by using special insights, shortcuts, and other tools at their cognitive disposal
- Apply the Brainiac's math tool set to 10 tough ACT-style math questions

THE MATH DIRECTIONS REVISITED

In Lesson 2, you glanced at test directions that were essentially the same as the ones for the official ACT Mathematics Test. To refresh your memory, here they are again:

> **Directions:** Solve each problem; then, on your answer sheet, mark the oval corresponding to the correct answer.
>
> Be careful not to spend too much time on any one question. Instead, solve as many problems as possible, and then use the remaining time to return to those questions you were unable to answer at first.
>
> You may use a calculator on any problem in this test. However, some problems can best be solved without the use of a calculator.
>
> *Note:* Unless otherwise stated, you can assume that:
>
> 1. Diagrams that accompany problems are not necessarily drawn to scale.
> 2. All figures lie in the same plane.
> 3. The word "line" refers to a straight line (and lines that appear straight are straight).
> 4. The word "average" refers to arithmetic mean.

Although the basic directions don't need clarification, the notes call for some explanation. Here's what they're really saying:

1. The purpose of figures is to convey information to help you understand the problem and answer the question, not to "give away" the correct answer with a picture. So, the test-makers distort certain diagrams a bit. The bottom line: Do not assume that any figure is drawn to scale (unless you see a note below the diagram stating that it is "drawn to scale").

Why don't the test-makers always draw their figures to scale? Well, if you could use your eye to measure lengths, angles, and so forth, you might be able to answer certain questions (especially geometry questions) without any knowledge of mathematical concepts—which would defeat the purpose of the math test.

2. Don't second-guess whether geometry figures such as triangles, quadrilaterals, and circles are actually two-dimensional. You can safely assume they are, so you can rule out that one of these types of figures might be warped or twisted away from a flat plane.
3. Technically, a line can be either straight or curved. But on the ACT, whenever you see the word "line," you can assume the question refers to a straight line.
4. The term *arithmetic mean* refers to the simple average of a series of numbers or other terms, as opposed to a median, mode, weighted average, or other method of describing the central tendency of the set.

SAMPLE MATH QUESTIONS

We're going to show you some strategies that Brainiacs use to get a leg up on the competition when it comes to math questions. But before we do that, you should attempt each of the following three sample questions. The explanations that follow provide conventional methods of solving the problems. The strategies you'll learn afterward show how true Brainiacs apply non-conventional methods to handle these and other types of math questions more insightfully, efficiently, and accurately than other test-takers.

These questions are moderate in difficulty level. The ones you'll tackle in this lesson's Brain Teaser are more difficult.

1. If Susan drinks 10% of the juice from a 16-ounce bottle immediately before lunch and 20% of the remaining amount with lunch, approximately how many ounces of juice are left to drink after lunch?

(A) 4.8
(B) 5.5
(C) 11.2
(D) 11.5
(E) 13.0

A **The correct answer is (D).** First, determine 10% of 16, and then subtract that number from 16:

$$16 \times .1 = 1.6$$
$$16 - 1.6 = 14.4$$

Susan now has 14.4 ounces of juice. Next, determine 20% of 14.4, and then subtract that number from 14.4:

$$14.4 \times .2 = 2.88$$

Round off 2.88 to the nearest tenth: 2.9

$$14.4 - 2.9 = 11.5$$

Q **2.** The average of six numbers is 19. When one of those numbers is taken away, the average of the remaining five numbers is 21. What number was taken away?

(A) 2
(B) 8
(C) 9
(D) 11
(E) 20

A **The correct answer is (C).** You can use the formula for arithmetic mean (below) to solve this problem algebraically:

$$AM = \frac{\text{sum of terms in the set}}{\text{number of terms in the set}}$$

In the question, you started with six terms. Let a through f equal those six terms:

$$19 = \frac{a + b + c + d + e + f}{6}$$
$$114 = a + b + c + d + e + f$$
$$f = 114 - (a + b + c + d + e)$$

Letting f = the number taken away, here's the arithmetic-mean formula, applied to the remaining five numbers:

$$21 = \frac{a + b + c + d + e}{5}$$
$$105 = a + b + c + d + e$$

Substitute 105 for $(a + b + c + d + e)$ in the first equation:

$$f = 114 - 105$$
$$f = 9$$

Q 3. If p pencils cost $2q$ dollars, how many pencils can you buy for c cents? [1 dollar = 100 cents]

(A) $\frac{pc}{2q}$

(B) $\frac{pc}{200q}$

(C) $\frac{50pc}{q}$

(D) $\frac{2pq}{c}$

(E) $200pcq$

A **The correct answer is (B).** Here's how you'd solve this problem conventionally:

1. Express $2q$ dollars as $200q$ cents (1 dollar = 100 cents).
2. Let x equal the number of pencils you can buy for c cents.
3. Think about the problem "verbally"; then, set up an equation and solve for x

- "p pencils is to $200q$ cents as x pencils is to c cents"
- "The ratio of p to $200q$ is the same as the ratio of x to c" (in other words, the two ratios are proportionate)

$$\frac{p}{200q} = \frac{x}{c}$$

$$\frac{pc}{200q} = x$$

TOP 10 MATH STRATEGIES FOR BRAiNiACS

We've shown you how to solve the preceding questions using conventional methods. But those methods are often time-consuming and involve a lot of calculations, which adds to the possibility of error. Here, you'll learn some strategies for handling these math questions more efficiently. We'll use the three sample questions you just looked at as examples of these strategies.

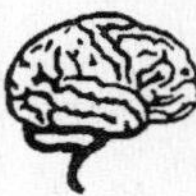

True Brainiacs bring to bear their insight, intuition, and creativity to ACT math questions. That's how they raise the curve and distinguish themselves from other test-takers.

1. BRAINIACS NARROW DOWN ANSWER CHOICES UP FRONT BY SIZING UP THE QUESTION.

If the question asks for a number value, you can probably narrow down the answer choices by estimating the size and type of number you're looking for. Use your common sense and real-world experience to formulate a "ballpark" estimate for word problems.

Question 1:

You can narrow down answer choices by looking at the problem from a "common sense" viewpoint. The five answer choices in this question provide some useful clues. Notice that they range in value from 4.8 to 13.0. That's a wide spectrum, isn't it? But what general size number should you look for? Without crunching any numbers, it's clear that most of the juice will still remain in the bottle, even after lunch. So, you're looking for a value much closer to 13 than to 4. You can safely eliminate (A) and (B).

2. BRAINIACS KNOW THAT COMMON SENSE CAN SOMETIMES REVEAL THE RIGHT ANSWER.

In many questions, you can eliminate all but the correct answer without resorting to precise calculations.

Question 1:

Look at the question from a broader perspective. If you subtract 10% from a number, then 20% from the result, that adds up to slightly less than a 30% decrease from the original number. 30% of 16 ounces is 4.8 ounces. Therefore, the solution must be a number a bit larger than 11.2 (16 − 4.8). Answer choice (D), 11.5, is the only choice that fits the bill!

Question 3:

In a general sense, the question is asking: "If you can by an item for a dollar, how many can you buy for one cent?" Since one cent is $\frac{1}{100}$ dollar, you can buy $\frac{1}{100}$ of one item for a cent. Therefore, you're probably looking for a fractional answer with a great number in the denominator—something on the order of 100 (as opposed to a number such as 2, 3 or 6). Choice (B) is the only choice that appears to be in the right ballpark. As it turns out, (B) is, indeed, the correct answer.

3. BRAINIACS SCAN ANSWER CHOICES FOR CLUES TO SOLVING THE PROBLEM.

Scan the answer choices to see what all or most of them have in common, such as radical signs, exponents, factorable expressions, or fractions. Then, try to formulate a solution that looks like the answer choices.

Question 3:

Notice that each answer choice includes all three letters (p, q, and c); therefore, the solution you're shooting for must also include all three letters. Also, notice that every choice but (E) is a fraction. So, anticipate building a fraction to solve the problem.

4. BRAINIACS WON'T BE REELED IN BY TOO-OBVIOUS, "SUCKER-BAIT" CHOICES.

The test-makers will intentionally "bait" you with wrong-answer choices that result from common errors in calculation and setting up and solving equations. Don't assume that your response is correct just because your solution appears among the five answer choices! Rely instead on whether you understood what the question called for and performed the calculations and other steps carefully and accurately.

Question 1:

In this question, the four incorrect answer choices are "sucker bait":

- (A) 4.8 — You performed the wrong calculation: 30% of 16 ounces = 4.8 ounces
- (B) 5.5 — This is the number of ounces Susan drank. (The question asks for the amount remaining.)
- (C) 11.2 — You performed the wrong calculation: 30% of 16 ounces = 4.8 ounces
  16 − 4.8 = 11.2
- (D) 11.5 — This is the correct answer.
- (E) 13.0 — You confused percentages with raw numbers, erroneously converting 30% (10% + 20%) to 3.0: 16 − 3.0 = 13.0

Question 2:

This question contains two "sucker-bait" answer choices:

(A) 2 This would be the correct answer to the question: "What is the difference between 19 and 21?" But, this question is asking something entirely different.

(E) 20 20 is simply 19 + 21 divided by 2. If this solution strikes you as too simple, you've got good instincts!

5. **BRAINIACS DON'T DO MORE WORK THAN NEEDED TO GET TO THE ANSWER.**

If the question asks for an approximation, it's a clue that precise calculations may be unnecessary.

Question 1:

Notice that each answer choice is carried to exactly one decimal place and that the question asks for an approximate value. These two features are clues that you can probably round off your calculations to the nearest "tenth" as you go.

6. **BRAINIACS LOOK FOR SHORTCUTS TO CONVENTIONAL WAYS OF SOLVING PROBLEMS.**

The adage "There's more than one way to skin a cat" applies to many ACT math questions.

Question 2:

You can solve this problem quickly by simply comparing the two sums. Before the sixth number is taken away, the sum of the numbers is 114 (6×19). After taking away the sixth number, the sum of the remaining numbers is 105 (5×21). The difference between the two sums is 9, which must be the value of the number taken away.

7. **BRAINIACS KNOW WHEN TO PLUG IN NUMBERS FOR VARIABLES.**

If the answer choices contain variables (like x and y), the question might be a good candidate for the "plug-in" strategy. Pick simple numbers (so the math is easy), and substitute them for the variables. You'll definitely need your pencil for this strategy.

Question 3:

This question is a perfect candidate for the plug-in strategy. Instead of trying to set up and solve an algebraic equation, use easy numbers for the three variables. For example: $p = 2$, $q = 1$, and $c = 100$. These simple numbers make the question easy to work with: "If 2 pencils cost 2 dollars, how many pencils can you buy for 100 cents?"

Obviously, the answer to this question is 1. Plug the numbers into each answer choice to see which choice equals 1. Only (B) fits the bill:

$$\frac{(2)(100)}{(200)(1)} = 1.$$

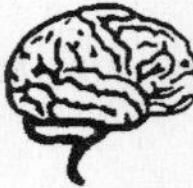

Plugging numbers into all five answer choices takes time, and calculation errors are always possible. Brainiacs can cut down the time and risk by scanning the choices for ones that are most likely to work. In question 3, notice that c is a much greater number than either p or q. Only a fraction with c in the numerator and a great number in the denominator (or vice versa) is likely to yield a quotient you're looking for. With this in mind, (B) jumps off the page as the likely choice!

8. **BRAINIACS KNOW WHEN TO WORK BACKWARD FROM NUMERICAL ANSWER CHOICES.**

If a question asks for a number value, and you draw a blank about how to set up and solve the problem, don't panic. You might be able to work backward by testing each answer choice. Although this might take a bit of time, if you test the answer choices in random order, the statistical odds are that you'll only need to test three choices to find the correct one.

Question 2:

You've already learned that comparing the two sums is the quickest shortcut to the answer. But if this strategy didn't occur to you, working backward from the answer choices would be the next quickest method. After the sixth number is taken away, the sum of the five remaining numbers is $21 \times 5 = 105$. To test an answer choice, add this sum to the number provided in the choice, dividing the new sum by 6. If the result is 19, you've found the correct choice. Here's how to do the math for (C), the correct answer choice:

$$\frac{105 + 9}{6} = \frac{114}{6} = 19$$

ACT math questions list numerical answer choices in either ascending or descending order of value. Therefore, if you use the strategy of working backward, start with the median value: (C). For example, if (C) turns out too large and the choices are in ascending order, then the only two viable choices are the two that are smaller than (C)—either (A) and (B). Of course, you might also be able to eliminate an answer choice right away by sizing up the questions (a previous strategy). Doing so would make your job even quicker!

9. **BRAINIACS ALWAYS CHECK THEIR WORK.**

Always check your work. Here are three suggestions for doing it:

1. Do a reality check. Ask yourself whether your solution makes sense based on what the question asks. (This check is especially appropriate for word problems.)
2. For questions where you solve algebraic equations, plug your solution into the equation(s) to make sure it works.
3. Confirm your calculations (except for the simplest no-brainers) with your calculator. It's easy to accidentally push the wrong number on the keypad. And what they say is true: "Garbage in, garbage out!"

Checking your calculations is especially crucial for questions asking for an approximation. Why? If your solution doesn't precisely match one of the five answer choices, you might conclude that you should just pick the choice that's closest to your solution—a big mistake if you miscalculated!

Question 1:

A reality check on this question will tell you that (C), 11.5, seems about right, and most of the other choices don't.

10. BRAINIACS READ THE QUESTION ONE LAST TIME BEFORE MOVING ON.

Among ACT Brainiacs, carelessness in reading a math question is by far the most common cause of error. Even if your solution is among the choices and you're confident your calculations are accurate, don't move on quite yet. Read the question again and make sure you've answered the precise question asked. For example, does the question ask for:

- Arithmetic mean or median?
- A circumference or an area?
- A sum or a difference?
- A perimeter or a length of one side only?
- An aggregate rate or a single rate?
- Total time or average time?

Also check to make sure you:

- Used the same numbers provided in the question
- Didn't inadvertently switch any numbers or other expressions
- Didn't use raw numbers where percentages were provided, or vice-versa

Question 1:
The question asked for the amount of juice remaining, not the amount she drank. Also, a careless test-taker might subtract 10 ounces instead of 10%.

Question 2:
A careless test-taker might inadvertently switch the numbers 19 and 21.

Question 3:
The question asks for an answer in cents, not dollars.

NUMBER FORMS AND RELATIONSHIPS—A QUICK REVIEW

Before you tackle this lesson's Brain Teaser and forge ahead in Part III, briefly review ten basic rules for expressing and combining numbers in different forms—fractions, ratios, percents, and decimal numbers (including scientific notation). These ten rules are building blocks for the more complex concepts and questions you'll encounter in the lessons ahead. Even though these basics shouldn't be a stretch, you should still make sure you understand them (and the examples of each one) before you move on.

1. RENAMING A PERCENT AS A DECIMAL NUMBER (AND VICE VERSA)

For percent-to-decimal rewriting, move the decimal point two places to the *left* (and drop the percent sign). For decimal-to-percent rewriting, move the decimal point two places to the *right* (and add the percent sign).

$9.5\% = .095$

$.004 = .4\%$

2. RENAMING A PERCENT AS A FRACTION (AND VICE VERSA)

For percent-to-fraction rewriting, *divide* by 100 (and drop the percent sign). For fraction-to-percent rewriting, *multiply* by 100 (and add the percent sign). Percents greater than 100 are rewritten as numbers greater than 1.

$$810\% = \frac{810}{100} = \frac{81}{10} = 8\frac{1}{10}$$

$$\frac{3}{8} = \frac{300}{8}\% = \frac{75}{2}\% = 37\frac{1}{2}\%$$

3. COMBINING FRACTIONS BY ADDITION OR SUBTRACTION

To combine fractions by addition or subtraction, the fractions *must* have a common denominator. If they already do, simply add (or subtract) numerators. If they don't, you can multiply all of the denominators together to find a common denominator, or you can try and find the *least common denominator* (LCD), by working your way up in multiples of the greatest of the denominators given.

$$\frac{1}{6} + \frac{1}{3} + \frac{2}{5} = \frac{5}{30} + \frac{10}{30} + \frac{12}{30} = \frac{5 + 10 + 12}{30} = \frac{27}{30}$$

(For denominators of 6, 3, and 5, try out successive multiples of 6 (12, 18, 24 . . .), and you'll hit the LCD when you get to 30.)

4. COMBINING FRACTIONS BY MULTIPLICATION OR DIVISION

To multiply fractions, multiply the numerators, and multiply the denominators. (The denominators need not be the same.) To divide fractions, multiply the reciprocal of the divisor (the number after the division sign). To simplify the multiplication or division, divide factors common to a numerator and a denominator before combining fractions. It's okay to divide across fractions.

$$\frac{\frac{9}{2}}{\frac{9}{8}} = \left(\frac{9}{2}\right)\left(\frac{8}{9}\right) = \frac{8}{2} = 4$$

5. COMBINING DECIMAL NUMBERS BY MULTIPLICATION

The number of decimal places (digits to the right of the decimal point) in a product should be the same as the total number of decimal places in the numbers you multiply.

(23.6)(.07) = 1.652 (3 decimal places altogether)

(.01)(.02)(.03) = .000006 (6 decimal places altogether)

6. COMBINING DECIMAL NUMBERS BY DIVISION

When you divide one decimal number by another (or compute a fraction), you can move the decimal point in both numbers by the same number of places either to the left or right without altering the quotient (value of the fraction).

$$11.4 \div 3 = \frac{11.4}{.3} = \frac{114}{3} = 38$$

$$1.14 \div 3 = \frac{1.14}{3} = \frac{114}{300} = .38$$

$$114 \div .03 = \frac{114}{.03} = \frac{11{,}400}{3} = 3{,}800$$

7. EXPRESSING DECIMAL NUMBERS IN SCIENTIFIC NOTATION

To express a decimal number in *scientific notation*, place the decimal point after the number's first digit, and then multiply that number by 10 raised to the number (power) of places you shifted the point. A negative exponent signifies a fractional number x ($-1 < x < 1$).

$837{,}000 = 8.37 \times 10^5$ (decimal point shifts 5 places to the left)

$8{,}370 = 8.37 \times 10^3$ (decimal point shifts 3 places to the left)

$8.37 = 8.37 \times 10^0$ (decimal point unchanged in position)

$.0837 = 8.37 \times 10^{-2}$ (decimal point shifts 2 places to the right)

$.000837 = 8.37 \times 10^{-4}$ (decimal point shifts 4 places to the right)

To multiply two numbers that are expressed in scientific notation, apply *addition* to the exponents. Conversely, to divide one scientifically notated number by another, subtract the exponent of the latter from that of the former.

$(5 \times 10^5)\ (4 \times 10^4) = 20 \times 10^{(5+4)} = 20 \times 10^9 = 2 \times 10^8$, or 200,000,000

$(5 \times 10^{-5})\ (4 \times 10^4) = 20 \times 10^{(-5+4)} = 20 \times 10^{-1} = 2 \times 10^0$, or 2

$(5 \times 10^5) \div (4 \times 10^4) = 1.25 \times 10^{(5-4)} = 1.25 \times 10^1 = 12.5$

$(5 \times 10^{-5}) \div (4 \times 10^4) = 1.25 \times 10^{(-5-[-4])} = 1.25 \times 10^{-1} = .125$

8. COMPUTING PERCENT CHANGES

To determine a percent change from one number to another, always compute the percent change based on the value *before* the change.

10 increased by 2 is a 20% increase. (Compare the change to the original number: 10. The change in percent is $\frac{2}{10}$, or 20%.) But 12 decreased by 2 is a $16\frac{2}{3}$% decrease. (Compare the change to the original number: 12. The change in percent is $\frac{2}{12}$, or $\frac{1}{6}$, which equals $16\frac{2}{3}$%.)

9. SETTING UP EQUIVALENT PROPORTIONS (RATIOS OR FRACTIONS)

You can express any ratio as a fraction. Hence, you can set two equivalent ratios equal to each other, as fractions. If one of the four terms is missing from the equation, you can solve for the missing term using algebra. As with fractions, you can simplify ratios to simplest form by dividing common factors.

If 3 miles is equivalent to 4.83 kilometers, to find the mile-equivalent to 11.27 kilometers, set up a proportion, and then use the *cross-product method* (multiplying numerator by denominator across the equality sign, equating the two products) to solve for x:

$$\frac{3}{4.83} = \frac{x}{11.27}$$

$$(4.83)(x) = (3)(11.27)$$

$$4.83x = 33.81$$

$$x = \frac{33.81}{4.83}$$

$$x = 7$$

10. ALTERING A PROPORTION (RATIO OR FRACTION)

Adding the same quantity to both terms of a ratio (or to both the numerator and denominator of a fraction) alters the ratio (or the value of the fraction)—unless the original ratio was 1:1—in which case, the ratio goes unchanged. If the original numerator is greater than (or less than) the original denominator, then adding the same number to both decreases (or increases) the fraction's value.

$$\frac{5}{3} > \frac{5+1}{3+1}, \text{ but } \frac{3}{5} < \frac{3+1}{5+1}$$

BRAIN TEASER

During this quiz, you'll try your hand at ten math questions that illustrate the top ten math strategies you learned in this lesson. For each question, you'll see at least one hint to help you focus on those strategies. Generally, the questions get tougher as you go along. (All but the first two are tougher than average.)

Attempt all ten questions, but don't put yourself under a time limit. Focus instead on applying the strategies. Then, be sure to read the explanations that follow the quiz. They're just as important as the questions because they explain how to apply the strategies to the questions.

QUIZ

1. Jill is now 20 years old, and her brother Gary is now 14 years old. How many years ago was Jill's age three times Gary's age at that time?

(A) 3
(B) 8
(C) 9
(D) 11
(E) 13

Hint: Try working backward from the answer choices.

Hint: Don't be lured by "sucker bait."

2. If $2x + 1$ is a multiple of 5, and if $2x + 1 < 100$, how many possible values of x are prime numbers?

(F) Five
(G) Six
(H) Seven
(J) Eight
(K) Nine

Hint: Try using the plug-in strategy.

Hint: Don't do more work than needed to get to the answer.

3. At ABC Corporation, five executives earn \$150,000 each per year, three executives earn \$170,000 each per year, and one executive earns \$180,000 per year. What is the average salary of these executives?

(A) \$156,250
(B) \$160,000
(C) \$164,480
(D) \$166,670
(E) \$170,000

Hint: Don't fall for too-obvious choices; complex questions call for complex solutions.

Hint: Narrow down the answer choices by making a common-sense estimate.

4.

In the figure above, what is the length of *DB*?

(F) $3\sqrt{21} - 8$
(G) 8
(H) $5\sqrt{7} - 8$
(J) $5\sqrt{5}$
(K) $18 - 5\sqrt{6}$

Hint: Check the answer choices for clues to solving the problem.

5. If a train travels $r + 2$ miles in h hours, which of the following represents the number of miles the train travels in one hour and 30 minutes?

(A) $\frac{3r + 6}{2h}$
(B) $\frac{3r}{h + 2}$
(C) $\frac{r + 2}{h + 3}$
(D) $\frac{r}{h + 6}$
(E) $\frac{3}{2}(r + 2)$

Hint: Try the plug-in strategy, using easy numbers.

6. A spinner containing seven equal regions numbered 1 through 7 is spun two times in a row. What is the probability that the first spin yields an odd number and the second spin yields an even number?

(F) $\frac{2}{7}$
(G) $\frac{12}{49}$
(H) $\frac{24}{49}$
(J) $\frac{1}{2}$
(K) $\frac{4}{7}$

Hint: Know the limits of sizing up the question to estimate the solution.

Hint: Look out for too-obvious, "sucker-bait" answer choices.

7.

If O is the center of the circle in the figure above, what is the area of the shaded region?

(A) $\frac{3}{2}\pi$

(B) 2π

(C) $\frac{5}{2}\pi$

(D) $\frac{8}{3}\pi$

(E) 3π

Hint: Your solution must include what the answer choices all have in common.

Hint: A dose of intuition can shortcut the conventional route to solving the problem.

8.

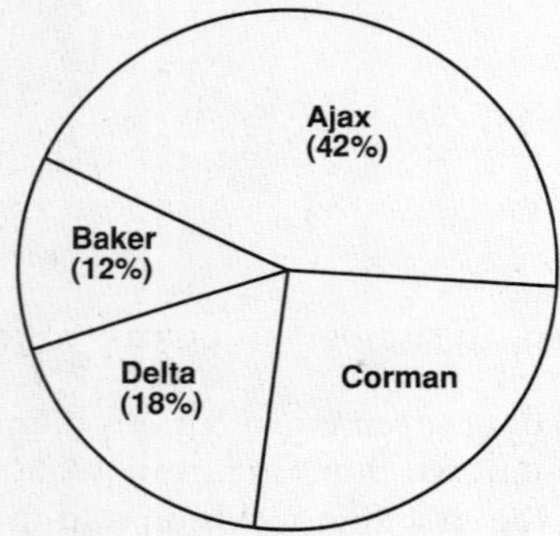

The pie chart above compares payments made last month by XYZ Corporation to four different suppliers. If XYZ paid Ajax \$17,700 during the month, then how much did XYZ pay Corman during the month?

(F) \$14,000

(G) \$12,400

(H) \$11,800

(J) \$11,250

(K) \$10,800

Hint: Check your work to be sure you didn't confuse one number with another and didn't confuse percentages with raw numbers.

Hint: Don't rely on visual measurements to answer questions that are accompanied by figures.

9. If $a > 0$, which of the following must be true?

I. $\left(\sqrt{a}\right)^3 + \left(\sqrt{a}\right)^3 = \left(\sqrt{2a}\right)^3$

II. $\left(\sqrt{a}\right)^3 \times \left(\sqrt{a}\right)^3 = a^3$

III. $\left(\sqrt{a}\right)^3 - \sqrt{a^3} = 0$

(A) I only

(B) II only

(C) I and III only

(D) II and III only

(E) I, II, and III

Hint: Confirm your understanding of the rules for roots and exponents by plugging in a few "easy" numbers.

Hint: In handling Roman-numeral questions, eliminating one numbered statement—I, II, or III—might tell you that another statement must be true.

10. A container holds 10 liters of a solution that is 20% acid. If 6 liters of pure acid are added to the container, what percent of the resulting mixture is acid?

(F) 8

(G) 20

(H) $33\frac{1}{3}$

(J) 40

(K) 50

Hint: Estimate the size of the answer you're looking for in order to narrow down the answer choices and check your work.

ANSWERS AND EXPLANATIONS

1. **The correct answer is (D).** This problem involves setting up and solving a linear equation. (You'll tackle other word problems requiring this type of task during Lesson 11.) There are two ways to solve this problem: (1) the conventional way, and (2) by working backwards from the answer choices.

The conventional way: Set up and solve an equation. Jill's age x years ago can be expressed as $20 - x$. At that time, Gary's age was $14 - x$. The following equation emerges:

$$20 - x = 3(14 - x)$$
$$20 - x = 42 - 3x$$
$$2x = 22$$
$$x = 11$$

Jill was three times as old as Gary 11 years ago. (Jill was 9 and Gary was 3.)

Working backward from the answer choices: Try each answer choice, one at a time. Start with (A):

$$20 - 3 = 17$$
$$14 - 3 = 11$$

Is 17 three times greater than 11? No.

Go on to answer choice (B).

Eventually, you'll get to the correct answer (D):

$$20 - 11 = 9$$
$$14 - 11 = 3$$

Is 9 three times greater than 3? Yes!

By the way, did you notice the "sucker bait" answer choice here? 11 years ago, Jill was 9 years old. A test-taker who forgets exactly what the questions asks for might look for Jill's age among the answer choices, and choose (C).

2. **The correct answer is (F).** This problem involves integers, factors, and prime numbers. (You'll review these concepts during Lesson 10.) Don't waste time trying to reason through this problem in a purely abstract manner. Instead, start plugging in numbers for x, and keep going until you see a pattern that allows you to get to the answer as quickly as possible. And use your pencil! Here's how to do it. A prime number is a positive integer greater than 1 that is not divisible by any integer other than itself and 1. The least prime number is 2. Since the question asks for prime numbers, x must be positive. To check for a pattern (read: shortcut), start scratching out some equations, working your way up from the least possible value for x:

$$2(2) + 1 = 5$$
$$2(4.5) + 1 = 10$$
$$2(7) + 1 = 15$$
$$2(9.5) + 1 = 20$$
$$2(12) + 1 = 25$$

Notice that as the sum increases by multiples of 5, the value of x in every other equation is an integer that also increases by multiples of 5, and that ends with either 2 or 7. This makes the rest of your job much easier. No integer ending in 2 (other than the integer 2) is a prime number. So, you know that, in addition to the integer 2, you need only consider values for x ending in 7 that are less than 49 (because $2x + 1 < 100$):

$$\{2, 7, 17, 27, 37, 47\}$$

Five of these integers—2, 7, 17, 37, and 47—are prime numbers.

3. **The correct answer is (B).** This question covers the concept of weighted average. (You'll examine this concept in more detail during Lesson 11.) The salaries range from \$150,000 to \$180,000. Since five of the eight executives earn the lowest salary in the range, common sense should tell you that the average salary is not between these figures (the mid point is near \$166,000), but rather closer to \$150,000. The problem is too complex to solve by calculating a simple average of three numbers. Therefore, eliminate choices (D) and (E). Now, here's how to solve the problem. Assign a "weight" to each of the three salary figures (to save time, express all numbers in thousands):

$$5(150) = 750$$
$$3(170) = 510$$
$$1(180) = 180$$

Then, determine the weighted average of the nine salaries:

$$750 + 510 + 180 = 1{,}440$$
$$\frac{1{,}440}{9} = 160$$

4. **The correct answer is (H).** This problem involves the Pythagorean theorem, which applies to all right triangles—triangles with one 90° angle. (You'll learn more about the theorem, and how to apply it, in Lesson 12.) Notice that all but one of the answer choices includes a square root, and that three of them indicate a difference (one term is

subtracted from another). These features provide a clue that you need to find the difference between two lengths ($CB - CD$), and that you'll probably be using the Pythagorean theorem to do it.

To find DB, you subtract CD from CB. Thus, you need to find those two lengths first. ΔACD is a right triangle with sides 8, 15, and 17 (one of the Pythagorean triplets). Thus, $CD = 8$. CB is one of the legs of ΔABC. Determine CB by applying the theorem:

$$15^2 + (CB)^2 = 20^2$$
$$225 + (CB)^2 = 400$$
$$(CB)^2 = 175$$
$$CB = \sqrt{(25)(7)}, \text{ or } 5\sqrt{7}$$

Accordingly, $CD = 5\sqrt{7} - 8$

If you tried to answer the question simply by comparing the length of *DB* to the other lengths in the figure, and then estimated the numerical values of the answer choices, you might have chosen the wrong answer. *DB* appears to be the same length as *AD* (17), yet its actual length (based on the numbers provided) is just over 5! The moral: Never answer a geometry question by measuring, or "eyeballing," any geometry figure that might accompany it.

5. **The correct answer is (A).** This is an algebraic word problem involving rate of motion (speed). (You'll examine complex word problems involving rate of motion in Lesson 11.) You can solve this problem either conventionally or by using the plug-in strategy.

The conventional way: Notice that all of the answer choices contain fractions. This is a clue that you should try to create a fraction as you solve the problem. Here's how to do it. Given that the train travels $r + 2$ miles in h hours, you can express its rate in miles per hour as $\frac{r+2}{h}$. In $\frac{3}{2}$ hours, the train would travel $\frac{3}{2}$ this distance:

$$\left(\frac{3}{2}\right)\left(\frac{r+2}{h}\right) = \frac{3r+6}{2h}$$

Using the plug-in strategy, let $r = 8$ and $h = 1$. Given these values, the train travels 10 miles (8 + 2) in 1 hour. So, obviously, in $1\frac{1}{2}$ hours the train will travel 15 miles. Start plugging these r and h values into the answer choices. You won't need to go any further than choice (A):

$$\frac{3r+6}{2h} = \frac{3(8)+6}{2(1)} = \frac{30}{2}, \text{ or } 15$$

Even if you had no clue about how to handle this question, you could at least eliminate choice (E) out of hand. It omits *h*! Common sense should tell you that the correct answer must include both *r* and *h*.

6. **The correct answer is (G).** This problem involves the concept of probability. (You'll examine this concept in more detail in Lesson 15.) There are four odd numbers (1, 3, 5, and 7) and three even numbers (2, 4, and 6) on the spinner. So, the probability of yielding an odd number with the first spin are 4 in 7, or $\frac{4}{7}$. The probability of yielding an even number with the second spin are 3 in 7, or $\frac{3}{7}$. To determine the probability of both events occurring, combine the two individual probabilities by multiplication:

$$\frac{4}{7} \times \frac{3}{7} = \frac{12}{49}$$

You can try to estimate the solution in order to eliminate certain answer choices. But for certain types of problems, including those involving probability, the size of the correct answer can be surprising. You'd be on the right track by "intuiting" that the solution is less than 50%—and eliminating choices (J) and (K)— but you might be surprised that the solution is even less than 25%. So, be sure to know the limits of this strategy.

Notice the "sucker-bait" answer choice in this question: Choice (J) provides the simple average of the two individual probabilities: $\frac{4}{7}$ and $\frac{3}{7}$. This should strike you as too easy a solution to what appears to be a complex problem.

7. **The correct answer is (E).** This problem involves arcs and circles, which you'll examine in great detail in Lesson 13. To solve this problem, you need to understand equilateral triangles as well as how to compute the area of a circle. The starting point is the 60° angle in the figure. Given this angle, all three interior angles of both triangles

must measure 60°, and, therefore, all sides of both triangles are the same length: 3 (as provided in the figure). Notice that this length (3) is also the circle's radius (the distance from its center to its circumference).

Next, determine the circle's area. The area of any circle is πr^2, where r is the circle's radius. Thus, the area of the circle is 9π.

Finally, you need to determine what portion of the circle's area is shaded. The four angles formed at the circle's center (O) total 360°. You know that two of these angles account for 120°, or $\frac{1}{3}$ of those 360°. Your intuition should tell you that each of the two larger angles also accounts for 120° ($\frac{1}{3}$ of 360°) and, accordingly, that the shaded portion accounts for $\frac{1}{3}$ the circle's area, or 3π.

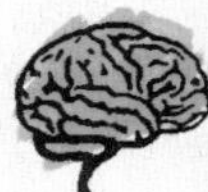

True Brainiacs won't need to plod through each of the preceding, conventional steps. Instead, they will look at the 60° angle in the figure and recognize right away that both triangles are equilateral and, extended out to their arcs, form two pie slices, each one $\frac{1}{6}$ the size of the whole pie (the circle). What's left are two big slices, each of which is twice the size of a small slice. So, the shaded area must account for $\frac{1}{3}$ the circle's area. (With this intuition, the problem is reduced to calculating the simple mechanics of calculating the circle's area, then dividing it by 3.)

8. **The correct answer is (H).** This problem involves percents as well as the concept of proportion (both of which you reviewed in this lesson). First, determine Corman's payments as a percentage of all payments: 100% − (42% + 12% + 18%) = 28%. Since the ratio of Ajax payments to Corman payments is the same on a percent basis as it is on a dollar basis, you can equate the two ratios, expressing each one as a fraction. Let x equal the amount paid to Corman, then solve for x (the third step below illustrates so-called "cross-multiplication"):

$$\frac{28}{44} = \frac{x}{17{,}700}$$

$$\frac{2}{3} = \frac{x}{17{,}700}$$

$$3x = (2)(17{,}700)$$

$$3x = 35{,}400$$

$$x = 11{,}800$$

Expect 1 to 2 of your 60 ACT math questions to involve data presented in graphical form such as a table, bar chart, line graph, or pie chart. Questions like these almost always test you on percent, proportion, or arithmetic mean (simple average).

9. **The correct answer is (D).** This question tests you directly on certain rules for combining exponents and radicals. (You'll review all those rules in Lesson 10.) Here's the analysis of each equation:

(I) $(\sqrt{a})^3 + (\sqrt{a})^3 = 2(\sqrt{a})^3$, not $(\sqrt{2a})^3$.

(II) This equation is true for all positive values of a. The term $(\sqrt{a})^3$ is equal to $(\sqrt{a})(\sqrt{a})^2$, and $(\sqrt{a})^2 = a$. Accordingly:

$$(\sqrt{a})^3 \times (\sqrt{a})^3 = (\sqrt{a})$$
$$(\sqrt{a})^2 \times (\sqrt{a})$$
$$(\sqrt{a})^2 = (\sqrt{a})^2(\sqrt{a})^2(\sqrt{a})^2 = a^3$$

(III) This equation is true for all positive values of a. Another way of expressing this equation is:

$$(\sqrt{a})^3 = \sqrt{a^3}$$

Try plugging in a few test numbers for a. Use "easy" numbers—ones for which $\sqrt{a}$ is an integer. For example, let $a = 4$, then let $a = 16$:

$$(\sqrt{4})^3 = 2^3 = 8 \qquad (\sqrt{16})^3 = 4^3 = 64$$

$$\sqrt{4^3} = \sqrt{64} = 8 \qquad \sqrt{16^3} = \sqrt{4{,}096} = 64$$

To test equation (III) using the number 16, you don't need to find $\sqrt{4{,}096}$. Instead, you can work backward from your other numerical answer, and calculate 64^2 to see if it equals 4,096.

Assuming you start with equation (I) and determine that (I) need not be true, you can eliminate choices (A), (C), and (E). That leaves only choices (B) and (D), both of which include (II). So, you don't need to analyze equation (II); you know it must be true. Your only remaining task is to analyze equation (III).

10. **The correct answer is (K).** This is an algebraic word problem involving the concept of mixture. (You'll apply this concept to other word problems in Lesson 11.) Common sense should tell you that when you add more acid to the solution, the percent of the solution that is acid increases. So, you're looking for an answer that's greater than 20—either choices (H), (J), or (K). If you need to guess at this point, your odds are 1 in 3. Here's how to solve the problem. The original amount of acid is (10)(20%) = 2 liters. After adding 6 liters of pure acid, the amount of acid increases to 8 liters, while the amount of total solution increases from 10 to 16 liters. The new solution is $\frac{8}{16}$ (or 50%) acid.

Notice the "sucker bait": choice (F). 8 liters is the amount of acid in the resulting mixture.

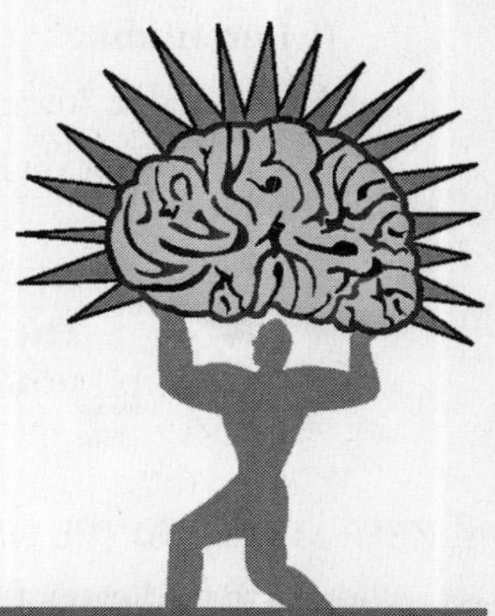

LESSON 10

Number Properties, Exponents, Roots, and Functions

In this lesson, you'll broaden your mathematical horizons by dealing with numbers in more abstract, theoretical settings. You'll examine a variety of relationships and patterns among numbers—drawing on the skills that separate Brainiacs from all the rest! In this lesson, you'll learn:

- The results of applying the four basic operations to number signs and integers
- The rules for factors, multiples, divisibility, prime numbers, and the *prime factorization* method
- The impact of exponents and radicals on the size and sign of numbers
- The rules for combining exponential numbers and terms under radical signs using the four basic operations
- The rules for simplifying terms containing radical signs
- Functions and the relationship between inverse functions, especially between exponential and logarithmic functions

BASIC PROPERTIES OF NUMBERS

You'll begin this lesson with a cut-to-the-chase review of the basics about integers, number signs (positive and negative), and prime numbers. First, let's make sure you're up to speed on the following definitions. You'll need to know these for this lesson as well as the test:

Absolute value (of a real number)

The number's distance from zero (the origin) on the real-number line. The absolute value of x is indicated as $|x|$. (The absolute value of a negative number can be less than, equal to, or greater than that of a positive number.)

Integer

Any non-fraction number on the number line: $\{\ldots, -3, -2, -1, 0, 1, 2, 3, \ldots\}$. Except for the number zero (0), every integer is either positive or negative and either even or odd.

Factor (of an integer *n*)

Any integer that you can multiply by another integer for a product of n.

Prime number

Any positive integer that has exactly two positive factors: 1 and the number itself. In other words, a prime number is not divisible by (a multiple of) any positive integer other than itself and 1.

The factors of any integer *n* include 1 as well as *n* itself. Zero (0) and 1 are not considered prime numbers; 2 is the first prime number.

NUMBER SIGNS AND THE FOUR BASIC OPERATIONS

Note: A "?" indicates that the sign depends on which number is greater.

Addition	Subtraction	Multiplication	Division
$(+) + (+) = +$	$(+) - (-) = (+)$	$(+) \times (+) = +$	$(+) \div (+) = +$
$(-) + (-) = -$	$(-) - (+) = (-)$	$(+) \times (-) = -$	$(+) \div (-) = -$
$(+) + (-) = ?$	$(+) - (+) = ?$	$(-) \times (-) = +$	$(-) \div (+) = -$
$(-) + (+) = ?$	$(-) - (-) = ?$		$(-) \div (-) = +$

Because multiplication (or division) involving two negative terms always results in a positive number: (1) Multiplication or division involving any *even* number of negative terms gives you a positive number; (2) Multiplication or division involving any *odd* number of negative terms gives you a negative number.

INTEGERS AND THE FOUR BASIC OPERATIONS

Addition and Subtraction

integer ± integer = integer

even integer ± even integer = even integer

even integer ± odd integer = odd integer

odd integer ± odd integer = even integer

Multiplication and Division

integer × integer = integer

integer ÷ non-zero integer = integer, but only if the numerator is divisible by the denominator (if the result is a quotient with no remainder)

odd integer × odd integer = odd integer

even integer × non-zero integer = even integer

even integer ÷ 2 = integer

odd integer ÷ 2 = non-integer

PRIME NUMBERS LESS THAN 100

2 3 5 7	31 37	61 67
11 13 17 19	41 43 47	71 73 79
23 29	53 59	83 89 97

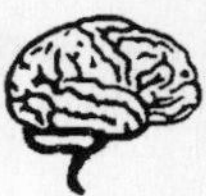

True Brainiacs know all the prime numbers between 0 and 100 without having to think about them.

FACTORS AND DIVISIBILITY

Figuring out whether one number (f) is a factor of another (n) is no big deal: If $\frac{n}{f}$ is an integer, then f is a factor of n (and n is divisible by f). Almost any test-taker can figure this out using a calculator. However, determining all the factors of great integers can be tricky; it's easy to overlook some factors. Remember the following basic rules, which are based on the definition of the term *factor*:

1. Any integer is a factor of itself.
2. 1 and −1 are factors of all integers (except 0).
3. The integer zero has every number as a factor but is not a factor of any integer.
4. A positive integer's greatest factor (other than itself) will never be greater than one half the value of the integer.

PRIME FACTORIZATION

To find all factors of a great number, use a method called *prime factorization*. Divide the number by each prime number in turn, starting with 2 and working up from there (2, 3, 5, 7, 11 . . .). Then, using the same method, try to find factors for the quotients as well. Test prime numbers up to the point where your quotient is no greater than the greatest factor you've already found. For example, here's how you apply prime factorization to the number 110 (prime-number quotients are shown in italics):

$110 \div 2 = 55$, and $55 = \mathit{5} \times \mathit{11}$
$110 \div 3 =$ non-integer
$110 \div 5 = 22$, and $22 = \mathit{2} \times \mathit{11}$
$110 \div 7 =$ non-integer
$110 \div 11$ (already covered)

The prime factor quotients are 2, 5, and 11, and their product is 110. That's no coincidence. *The product of all prime-number quotients will equal your original number.* To find all other *positive* factors of 110 (aside from 1 and 110), combine any two or more prime factors by multiplication:

$2 \times 5 = 10$
$2 \times 11 = 22$
$5 \times 11 = 55$

Here's the complete set of positive factors of 110:

{1, 2, 5, 10, 11, 22, 55, 110}

On the ACT, a difficult factoring question will involve more than simply finding the factors of an integer. Look at the following question, for example, which also requires you to compare factors of two numbers and distinguish between prime and other factors:

Q What is the difference between the sum of all positive factors of 48, excluding its prime factors, and the sum of all positive factors of 36, excluding its prime factors?

(A) 12
(B) 20
(C) 27
(D) 33
(E) 42

A **The correct answer is (D).** The positive factors of 48 are: {1, 2, 3, 4, 6, 8, 12, 16, 24, 48}. The positive factors of 36 are: {1, 2, 3, 4, 6, 9, 12, 18, 36}. The two sets have in common the numbers 1, 2, 3, 4, 6, and 12 and share the same prime numbers: 2 and 3. Thus, all you need to compare are these two sums:

$$8 + 16 + 24 + 48 = 96$$

$$9 + 18 + 36 = 63$$

The difference between the two sums = 96 − 63 = 33.

SHORTCUTS FOR FINDING FACTORS

To help you ferret out factors, apply the following shortcuts for divisibility:

If the integer has this feature:	*Then it is divisible by:*
The last digit is 0, 2, 4, 6 or 8	2
The sum of the digits is divisible by 3	3
The number formed by the last 2 digits is divisible by 4	4
The number ends in 5 or 0	5
The number meets the tests for divisibility by 2 and 3	6
The number formed by the last 3 digits is divisible by 8	8
The sum of the digits is divisible by 9	9

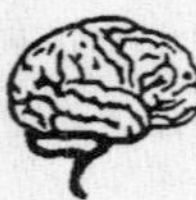

Brainiacs memorize these shortcuts by applying them to the numbers between 0 and 100 that are *not* included in the list of prime numbers given earlier in this lesson.

EXPONENTS (POWERS)

An *exponent* or *power* refers, of course, to the number of times a number (known as the *base* number) is multiplied by itself. On the ACT, easier exponent questions require little more than calculating an exponential number (or comparing two such numbers). A tougher exponent question will focus on one or both of the following:

- The impact of exponents on the *size* and *sign* of a number
- The rules for *combining* terms that contain exponents

EXPONENTS AND THE REAL NUMBER LINE

Raising base numbers to powers can have surprising effects on the size and/or sign (negative vs. positive) of the base number. You must consider four separate regions of the real-number line:

1. Values greater than 1 (to the right of 1 on the number line)
2. Values less than -1 (to the left of -1 on the number line)
3. Fractional values between 0 and 1
4. Fractional values between -1 and 0

The following table indicates the impact of positive-integer exponent (x) on base number (n) for each region:

$n > 1$:	n raised to any power: $n^x > 1$ (the greater the exponent, the greater the value of n^x)
$n < -1$:	n raised to even power: $n^x > 1$ (the greater the exponent, the greater the value of n^x)
	n raised to odd power: $n^x < 1$ (the greater the exponent, the lesser the value of n^x)
$0 < n < 1$:	n raised to any power: $0 < n^x < n < 1$ (the greater the exponent, the lesser the value of n^x)
$-1 < n < 0$:	n raised to even power: $0 < n^x < 1$ (the greater the exponent, the lesser the value of n^x, approaching 0 on the number line)
	n raised to odd power: $-1 < n^x < 0$ (the greater the exponent, the greater the value of n^x, approaching 0 on the number line)

The preceding rules are easy enough for Brainiacs to understand. But when you apply these rules to an ACT question, it can be confusing, especially since some of the ACT questions are designed specifically to create confusion. Here's an illustration:

If $-1 < x < 0$, which of the following must be true?

I. $x^2 < -x$
II. $x^3 > x$
III. $\frac{1}{x^3} < -\frac{1}{x^2}$

(A) I only
(B) II only
(C) I and II only
(D) II and III only
(E) I, II, and III

A **The correct answer is (E).** The key to analyzing each equation is that raising x to successively higher powers moves the value of x closer to zero (0) on the number line.

(I) Both x^2 and $-x$ are positive fractions between 0 and 1, but x^2 is closer to zero (0) on the number line—that is, less than x.

(II) Both x^3 and x are negative fractions between 0 and -1, but x^3 is closer to zero (0) on the number line—that is, greater than x.

(III) Both $\frac{1}{x^3}$ and $\frac{-1}{x^2}$ are negative numbers less than -1 (to the left of -1 on the number line). But $x^3 > -x^2$ because x^3 is closer to zero on the number line. Accordingly, taking the reciprocal of each value (that is, dividing 1 by each value) reverses the inequality. For example, let $x = -\frac{1}{2}$:

$$x^3 = -\frac{1}{8}, \text{ and } \frac{1}{x^3} = (1)(-8) = -8$$

$$x^2 = \frac{1}{4}, \text{ and } -\frac{1}{x^2} = (-1)(4) = -4$$

COMBINING BASE NUMBERS AND EXPONENTS

Can you *combine* base numbers using addition, subtraction, multiplication, or division *before* applying exponents to the numbers? The answer depends on which operation you're performing.

Addition and Subtraction

When you add or subtract terms, you cannot combine base numbers or exponents. It's as simple as that.

$$a^x + b^x \neq (a + b)^x$$
$$a^x - b^x \neq (a - b)^x$$

If you don't believe it, try plugging in a few easy numbers. Notice that you'll get a different result depending upon what you do first: combine base numbers or apply each exponent to its base number.

$$(3 + 4)^2 = 7^2 = 49$$
$$3^2 + 4^2 = 9 + 16 = 25$$

Multiplication and Division

It's a whole different story for multiplication and division. First, remember these two simple rules:

1. You can combine base numbers first, but only if the exponents are the same:

$$a^x \times b^x = (ab)^x$$

$$\frac{a^x}{b^x} = \left(\frac{a}{b}\right)^x$$

2. You can combine exponents first, but only if the base numbers are the same. When multiplying these terms, add the exponents. When dividing them, subtract the denominator exponent from the numerator exponent:

$$a^x \times a^y = a^{(x+y)}$$

$$\frac{a^x}{a^y} = a^{(x-y)}$$

To cover all bases, also keep in mind these additional rules for exponents:

$(a^x)^y = a^{xy}$

$a^0 = 1\ [a \neq 0]$

$a^{\frac{x}{y}} = \sqrt[y]{a^x}$

$a^{-x} = \frac{1}{a^x}$

On the ACT, a tricky exponent question might use the same number for the base of one term as for the exponent of another. Here's an example:

Q $\frac{9^{11} \times 11^9}{11^{11} \times 9^9} = ?$

(A) $\frac{1}{9}$

(B) $\frac{9}{11}$

(C) $\frac{81}{121}$

(D) 1

(E) 9

A **The correct answer is (C).** The key to this question is to recognize that since the base numbers 9 and 11 appear in both the numerator and denominator, you can factor out 9^9 and 11^{11}:

$$\frac{9^{11} \times 11^9}{11^{11} \times 9^9} = \frac{9^2}{11^2} = \frac{81}{121}$$

EXPONENTS YOU SHOULD KNOW

For the ACT, memorize the exponential values in the following table. You'll be glad you did, since these are the ones you're most likely to see on the test.

	Power & Corresponding Value						
Base	2	3	4	5	6	7	8
2	4	8	16	32	64	128	256
3	9	27	81	243			
4	16	64	256				
5	25	125	625				
6	36	216					

ROOTS AND RADICALS

On the flip side of exponents and powers are *roots* and *radicals*. On the ACT, square roots and cube roots are the two most common root varieties. A tough root question will focus on one or both of the following:

- The effect of roots on the *size* and *sign* of the quantity inside the radical
- The rules for *combining* terms that contain radical signs

ROOTS AND THE REAL NUMBER LINE

As with exponents, the root of a number can bear a surprising relationship to the size and/or sign (negative vs. positive) of the number (another of the test-makers' favorite areas). Here are four rules you should remember:

1. If $n > 1$, then $1 < \sqrt[3]{n} < \sqrt{n} < n$ (the greater the root, the lesser the value). However, if n lies between 0 and 1, then $n < \sqrt{n} < \sqrt[3]{n} < 1$ (the greater the root, the greater the value).

   $n = 64$ $\qquad$ $n = \frac{1}{64}$

   $1 < \sqrt[3]{64} < \sqrt{64} < 64$ $\qquad$ $\frac{1}{64} < \sqrt{\frac{1}{64}} < \sqrt[3]{\frac{1}{64}} < 1$

   $1 < 4 < 8 < 64$ $\qquad$ $\frac{1}{64} < \frac{1}{8} < \frac{1}{4} < 1$

2. Every negative number has exactly one cube root, and that root is a negative number. The same holds true for all other odd-numbered roots of negative numbers.

   $\sqrt[3]{-27} = -3$ $\qquad$ $\sqrt[5]{-32} = -2$

   $(-3)(-3)(-3) = -27$ $\qquad$ $(-2)(-2)(-2)(-2)(-2) = -32$

3. Every positive number has two square roots: a negative number and a positive number (with the same absolute value). The same holds true for all other even-numbered roots of positive numbers.

   $\sqrt{16} = \pm 4$

   $\sqrt[4]{81} = \pm 3$

4. Every positive number has only one *cube* root, and that root is always a positive number. The same holds true for all other odd-numbered roots of positive numbers.

The square root (or other even-number root) of any negative number is an imaginary number, not a real number. That's why the preceding rules don't cover those roots.

On the ACT, tough questions involving roots and the number line often involve exponents as well, as in the following question:

For a non-zero number x such that $-1 < x < 1$, which of the following inequalities must be true?

I. $x^{-2} > x^2$

II. $\sqrt[3]{x} > \sqrt[5]{x}$

III. $\sqrt[3]{x^2} > \left(\sqrt[3]{x}\right)^2$

(A) I only
(B) II only
(C) I and III only
(D) II and III only
(E) I, II, and II

A **The correct answer is (A).** Here's the analysis of each inequality:

(I) $x^{-2} = \frac{1}{x^2}$. Since x^2 is a fraction between 0 and 1, its reciprocal $\frac{1}{x^2}$ must be a number greater than 1.

(II) If $-1 < x < 0$, then applying a higher root yields a *greater negative* value—approaching 0 on the real number line. However, if $0 < x < 1$, then applying a higher root yields a lower *positive value*—approaching 0 on the real number line. Hence, whether (II) is true depends on the sign of x.

(III) The inequality $\sqrt[3]{x^2} > \left(\sqrt[3]{x}\right)^2$ is equivalent to $\left(x^2\right)^{\frac{1}{3}} > \left(x^{\frac{1}{3}}\right)^2$. Applying the laws of exponents, the inequality becomes $x^{\frac{2}{3}} > x^{\frac{2}{3}}$, which is obviously false.

COMBINING RADICALS

The rules for combining terms that include radicals are quite similar to those for exponents. Keep the following two rules in mind (one applies to addition and subtraction, while the other applies to multiplication and division).

Addition and Subtraction

If a term under a radical is being added to or subtracted from a term under a different radical, you cannot combine the two terms under the same radical.

$$\sqrt{x} + \sqrt{y} \neq \sqrt{x + y}$$

$$\sqrt{x} - \sqrt{y} \neq \sqrt{x - y}$$

$$\sqrt{x} + \sqrt{x} = 2\sqrt{x}, \text{ not } \sqrt{2}$$

Multiplication and Division

Terms under different radicals can be combined under a common radical if one term is multiplied or divided by the other, but only if the radical is the same.

$$\sqrt{x}\sqrt{x} = \left(\sqrt{x}\right)^2, \text{ or } x$$

$$\sqrt{x}\sqrt{y} = \sqrt{xy}$$

$$\frac{\sqrt{x}}{\sqrt{y}} = \sqrt{\frac{x}{y}}$$

$\sqrt[3]{x}\sqrt{y} = ?$ (you cannot combine different bases and different exponents)

SIMPLIFYING RADICALS

On the ACT, always look for the possibility of *simplifying radicals* by moving what's inside the radical to the outside. Check inside your square-root radicals for *perfect squares*: factors that are squares of tidy numbers, especially integers, or other terms. The same advice applies to *perfect cubes*, and so on. Here are two examples:

$$\sqrt{\frac{20x}{x^3}} = \sqrt{\frac{(4)(5)}{x^2}} = \frac{2\sqrt{5}}{x}$$

$$\sqrt[3]{\frac{3}{8}} = \sqrt[3]{\frac{3}{2^3}} = \frac{1}{2}\sqrt[3]{3}$$

If you can't remove all or part of what is below a radical sign, you might still be able to push the radical around a bit. On the ACT, the correct answer *won't* include a denominator with a radical. So, to match your solution to the correct choices, you'll need to remove all radicals from any denominator by multiplying both numerator and denominator by the radical value (called *rationalizing the denominator*). Here's an example:

$$\frac{3}{\sqrt{15}} = \frac{3\sqrt{15}}{\sqrt{15}\sqrt{15}} = \frac{3\sqrt{15}}{15}, \text{ or } \frac{1}{5}\sqrt{15}$$

On the ACT, a tough root question might involve combining radicals by addition (or subtraction) *and* by multiplication (or division), as well as simplifying radical expressions along the way. Here's an example:

Q $\sqrt{\frac{x^2}{36} + \frac{x^2}{25}} = ?$

(A) $\frac{x^2}{11}$

(B) $\frac{x^2\sqrt{61}}{61}$

(C) $\frac{11x}{30}$

(D) $\frac{x^2}{15}\sqrt{\frac{x}{2}}$

(E) $\frac{x}{30}\sqrt{61}$

A **The correct answer is (E).** You cannot move either term out of the radical without first combining them, using a common denominator:

$$\sqrt{\frac{x^2}{36} + \frac{x^2}{25}} \sqrt{\frac{25x^2 + 36x^2}{(36)(25)}} = \sqrt{\frac{61x^2}{(36)(25)}} = \frac{x}{(6)(5)}\sqrt{\frac{61}{1}} = \frac{x}{30}\sqrt{61}$$

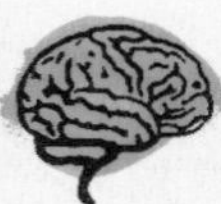

On the ACT, if you can simplify an expression under a radical sign by removing perfect squares, cubes, etc., do it! Also, eliminate radicals from denominators. More than likely, these steps will be necessary to solve the problem at hand.

ROOTS YOU SHOULD KNOW

Memorize the roots in the following table. If you encounter one of these radical terms on the exam, chances are you'll need to know its equivalent integer to answer the question.

Square roots of positive numbers:	**Cube roots of positive (and negative) integers:**
$\sqrt{121} = \pm 11$	$\sqrt[3]{(-)8} = (-)2$
$\sqrt{144} = \pm 12$	$\sqrt[3]{(-)27} = (-)3$
$\sqrt{169} = \pm 13$	$\sqrt[3]{(-)64} = (-)4$
$\sqrt{196} = \pm 14$	$\sqrt[3]{(-)125} = (-)5$
$\sqrt{225} = \pm 15$	$\sqrt[3]{(-)216} = (-)6$
$\sqrt{625} = \pm 16$	$\sqrt[3]{(-)343} = (-)7$
	$\sqrt[3]{(-)512} = (-)8$
	$\sqrt[3]{(-)729} = (-)9$
	$\sqrt[3]{(-)1{,}000} = (-)10$

FUNCTIONS

In a *function* (or *functional relationship*), the value of one variable depends upon (or is *a function of*) the value of another variable. In mathematics, the relationship is expressed in the form of $y = f(x)$, where y is a *function* of x. To find the value of the function for any value x, simply substitute the x-value for x wherever it appears in the function. For instance, suppose that $f(x) = x^2 + 3x + 4$. Here's how you'd find $f(2 + a)$:

$$\begin{aligned} f(2 + a) &= (2 + a)^2 + 3(2 + a) - 4 \\ &= 4 + 4a + a^2 + 6 + 3a - 4 \\ &= a^2 + 7a + 6 \end{aligned}$$

On the ACT, it's unlikely that you'll encounter a function question as simple as the preceding example. On the simplest function questions, your task will probably be one of the following two:

1. Apply the same function twice. For example:

   If $f(x) = x + 1$, then $\frac{1}{f(x)} \times f\left(\frac{1}{x}\right) = \left(\frac{1}{x + 1}\right)\left(\frac{1 + x}{x}\right) = \frac{1}{x}$

2. Apply two different functions, where one function is a function of the other. For example:

   If $f(x) = x^2$ and $g(x) = x + 3$, then to find $g(f(x))$, substitute $f(x)$ for x in the function $g(x) = x + 3$: $g(f(x)) = f(x) + 3$. Then, substitute x^2 for $f(x)$: $g(f(x)) = x^2 + 3$.

As you can see, easier function questions amount to little more than an exercise in substitution.

In mathematical terms, a function g that is a function of f can be written either as $(f \bullet g)(x)$ or as $f(g(x))$.

A more challenging function question might involve an *inverse function* in which $f(g(x)) = g(f(x)) = x$. Inverse functions are so named because they "undo" each other. That is, for any value x, calculating $f(x)$ and substituting the result into $g(x)$ brings you back to the value of x, where you started. Given a function $f(x)$, determine its inverse function $g(x)$, as in this example:

Q Which of the following is the inverse function $g(x)$ for $f(x) = \frac{2x}{x + 4}$?

(A) $g(x) = \frac{4x}{x - 2}$

(B) $g(x) = \frac{4x}{2 - x}$

(C) $g(x) = \frac{x + 4}{2x}$

(D) $g(x) = \frac{-2x}{x + 4}$

(E) $g(x) = \frac{4x}{x + 2}$

A **The correct answer is (A).** To find the inverse function, write y for $f(x)$, then, interchange x and y in the original equation: $y = \frac{2x}{x - 4}$ becomes $x = \frac{2y}{y - 4}$

$$x = \frac{2y}{y - 4}$$

$$(y - 4)x = 2y$$

Then, solve for y in terms of x:

$$xy - 4x - 2y = 0$$

$$y(x - 2) = 4x$$

$$y = \frac{4x}{x - 2}$$

In another challenging type of function question, your job is to determine a certain function that is expressed in terms of another function. As in easier questions involving two functions, where one is a function of the other, substitute the *dependent* function for the variable in the *independent* function. Here's an example:

Q If $f(x) = x^2$ and $f(g(x)) = \frac{1}{x^2 + 1}$, then $g(x)$ could be which of the following?

(A) $\frac{1}{x + 1}$

(B) $\sqrt{x} + 1$

(C) $\frac{1}{\sqrt{x^2 + 1}}$

(D) $\frac{1}{x}$

(E) $\frac{1}{x^2}$

A **The correct answer is (C).** In $f(x) = x^2$, substitute $g(x)$ for x: $f(g(x)) = [g(x)]^2 = \frac{1}{x^2 + 1}$. Accordingly, $g(x) = \pm\frac{1}{\sqrt{x^2 + 1}}$. The positive value is the one that's listed as choice (C).

EXPONENTIAL AND LOGARITHMIC FUNCTIONS

Among the most important and test-worthy examples of two inverse functions is the relationship between an *exponential* and a *logarithmic* function. By definition, each one is the inverse of the other. Stated in mathematical terms, for any constant $b > 0$ and $\neq 1$:

The exponential function $f(x) = b^x$ is the inverse of the logarithmic function $g(x) = \log_b x$ in other words:

$y = b^x$ is equivalent to $x = \log_b y$

For example, $125 = 5^3$ is equivalent to $3 = \log_5 125$.

In the logarithmic function $g(x) = \log_b x$, the variable x is the logarithm, and b is the base of the algorithm.

If no base number is given, then the base number is understood to be 10.

An easier ACT question might provide a logarithmic function, and then ask for its equivalent exponential function, as in these two simple examples (answer choices are omitted):

Q If $\log_x 125 = 3$, then $x = ?$

A The function $\log_x 125 = 3$ is equivalent to $x^3 = 125$. Hence, $x = \sqrt[3]{125} = 5$

Q If $\log_x y = z$, then in terms of x and z, $y = ?$

A The function $\log_x y = z$ is equivalent to $y = x^z$.

To make no-brainer questions like these harder, test-makers might resort to negative or fractional exponents, as in these two examples (again, answer choices are omitted):

Q If $\log_{\frac{1}{2}} x = -4$, then $x =$?

A The answer is 16. Given $\log_{\frac{1}{2}} x = -4$, $x = \left(\frac{1}{2}\right)^{-4} = 2^4 = 16$

Q If $x = \log^4 \sqrt{64}$, then what is the value of x ?

A The answer is $\frac{3}{2}$. The function $x = \log_4 \sqrt{64}$ is equivalent to $4^x = \sqrt{64} = \sqrt{4^3} = 4^{\frac{3}{2}}$.

A more challenging ACT question might require you to apply one or more of the following basic properties of algorithms. Notice that each one follows from (or, is equivalent to) one of the laws of exponents:

Logarithm property	***Equivalent law of exponents***
1. $\log_b xy = \log_b x + \log_b y$	1. $b^x b^y = b^{(x+y)}$
2. $\log_b\left(\frac{x}{y}\right) = \log_b x - \log_b y$	2. $\frac{b^x}{b^y} = b^{(x-y)}$
3. $\log_b x = -\log_b\left(\frac{x}{y}\right)$	3. $b^{-x} = \frac{1}{b^x}$
4. $y\log_b x = \log_b x^y$	4. $(b^x)^y = b^{xy}$
5. $\log_b 1 = 0$, b ≠ 0	5. $b^0 = 1$, $b \neq 0$

To separate Brainiacs from the rest, the test-makers might require you to perform *both* of the following tasks:

1. Express an exponential function as its equivalent logarithmic function (or vice versa)
2. Apply one or more of the properties of logarithms

Here's a question that involves both these tasks (this question is as complex as any algorithm question you'll find on the ACT):

Q If $b^x = 5$ and $b^y = 2$, then $\log_b 20 = ?$

(A) $x + 2y$
(B) $x - 2y$
(C) $xy + 10$
(D) $5x + 2y$
(E) $2x + 5y$

A **The correct answer is (A).** First, express $b^x = 5$ and $b^y = 2$ in their equivalent logarithmic form: $\log_b 5 = x$ and $\log_b 2 = y$. You can express $\log_b 20$ as $\log_b(2^2)(5)$, which in turn can be expressed as $\log_b 2^2 + \log_b 5$, applying algorithm property 2. Now apply property 4: $\log_b 2^2 = 2\log_b 2$. Substituting x for $\log_b 5$ and y for $\log_b 2$ gives you $x + 2y$, choice (A).

Test-makers aren't interested in your ability to look up information in logarithm tables. So, you won't find any logarithm tables on the ACT, or in this book. They *are* interested in your understanding of the relationships between exponential and logarithmic functions and the properties of logarithms.

BRAIN TEASER

In this quiz, you'll attempt ten tough ACT-style questions covering the topics from this lesson. Focus on applying the concepts and techniques you learned in this lesson, *not* on answering the questions as quickly as possible. Then, read the explanations that follow the quiz, even for the questions you answered correctly.

QUIZ

1. If x, y, and z are consecutive negative integers, and if $x > y > z$, which of the following must be a positive odd integer?

   (A) $(x - y)(y - z)$
   (B) xyz
   (C) $x - yz$
   (D) $x(y + z)$
   (E) $x + y + z$

2. If integer $x \geq 1$, which of the following statements, if true, establishes that x is an even number?

   I. $x^3 - x^2 - x$ is an even integer.

   II. $\frac{x}{2} - \frac{x}{3} - x$ is an integer.

   III. $3x + 2x + x$ is an even integer.

   (F) I only
   (G) II only
   (H) 1 and II only
   (J) I and III only
   (K) I, II, and II

3. If n is the first of two consecutive odd integers, and if the difference of their squares is 120, which of the following equations can be used to find their values?

   (A) $(n + 1)^2 - n^2 = 120$
   (B) $n^2 - (n+2)^2 = 120$
   (C) $[(n + 2) - n]^2 = 120$
   (D) $n^2 - (n + 1)^2 = 120$
   (E) $(n + 2)^2 - n^2 = 120$

4. If $x = -1$, then $x^{-3} + x^{-2} + x^2 + x^3 = ?$

   (F) -2
   (G) -1
   (H) 0
   (J) 1
   (K) 2

5. $\frac{\sqrt[3]{81x^7}}{\sqrt{9x^4}} - \frac{\sqrt{162x^5}}{\sqrt[3]{729x^6}} =$

   (A) $3x^3 - \frac{1}{3}$
   (B) $\sqrt[3]{2x} - 3$
   (C) $\sqrt[3]{3x} - \sqrt{2x}$
   (D) $3x^2 - \sqrt{2}$
   (E) $9x - \sqrt{3}$

6. Code letters X, Y, and Z each represent one digit in the three-digit prime number XYZ. If neither X nor Y is an odd integer, and if the sum of the three digits is 7, how many different numbers might XYZ represent?

   (F) 1
   (G) 2
   (H) 3
   (J) 4
   (K) 5

7. $(x - 1)$ is a prime number between 40 and 50. What is the sum of all the possible unique prime factors of x?

   (A) 12
   (B) 15
   (C) 19
   (D) 21
   (E) 23

8. What is the greatest value of a positive integer n such that 3^n is a factor of 18^{15}?

   (F) 45
   (G) 33
   (H) 30
   (J) 18
   (K) 15

9. If $f(x) = 3x + 2$, then for which of the following functions $g(x)$ does $g(f(x))$ equal $f(g(x))$?

   (A) $-3x + 2$
   (B) $\frac{x - 2}{3}$
   (C) $\frac{1}{3x + 2}$
   (D) $\frac{1}{3x} + 2$
   (E) $\frac{x}{3} + \frac{1}{2}$

10. If $x = \log 2$ and $y = \log 5$, then $2y - 3x = ?$

   (F) $\log \frac{8}{25}$
   (G) $\log \frac{25}{8}$
   (H) $\log \frac{25}{4}$
   (J) $\log 25$
   (K) $\log 200$

ANSWERS AND EXPLANATIONS

1. **The correct answer is (A).** Given that x, y, and z are consecutive negative integers, either one integer is odd or two integers are odd. In addition, a negative number multiplied by a negative number yields a positive number. With this in mind, consider each answer choice in turn:

   (A) $(x - y)$ must be odd and positive because $x > y$. Similarly, $(y - z)$ must be odd and positive because $y > z$. The product of the terms must, therefore, be odd and positive.

   (B) xyz must be negative and even

   (C) $x - yz$ must be negative (because yz, a positive number, is subtracted from the negative number x). Whether choice (C) is odd or even depends on whether one or two of the three integers are odd. yz must be even; however, x could either be even or odd.

   (D) $(y + z)$ must be negative and odd. Thus, the product of x and $(y + z)$ must be positive (either odd or even).

   (E) $x + y + z$ must be negative. Whether choice (E) is odd or even depends on whether one or two of the three integers are odd.

2. **The correct answer is (H).** Here's the analysis for each statement:

   (I) For any integer x, odd or even, the expression represents an even integer. If x is an even integer, all three terms are even, and combining them by subtracting always yields an even integer. If x is an odd integer, x^3, and x are all odd and combining them by subtraction always yields an odd integer.

   (II) $\frac{x}{2}$ and $\frac{x}{3}$ must both be integers in order for the expression to represent an integer. Accordingly, x must be a multiple of 6 (and can be any such multiple) for the expression to be an integer. All multiples of 6 are, of course, even integers.

   (III) $3x + 2x + x = 6x$, which is an even integer regardless of whether x is even or odd.

3. **The correct answer is (E).** The other integer is $n + 2$. The difference between n and $(n + 2)$ must be positive, so the term $(n + 2)$ must appear first in the equation.

4. **The correct answer is (H).** Any term to a negative power is the same as "the reciprocal of" the term, but raised to the *positive* power. In addition, a negative number raised to a power is *negative* if the exponent is *odd*, yet *positive* if the exponent is *even*:

$$-1^{(-3)} + [-1^{(-2)}] + [-1^2] + [-1^3]$$
$$= \frac{-1}{1} + \frac{1}{1} + 1 - 1 = 0$$

5. **The correct answer is (C).** Simplify all four terms by removing perfect squares. Then, for each fraction, divide common factors:

$$\frac{\sqrt[3]{81x^7}}{\sqrt{9x^4}} - \frac{\sqrt{162x^5}}{\sqrt[3]{729x^6}} = \frac{(3x^2)\sqrt[3]{3x}}{3x^2} - \frac{(9x^2)\sqrt{2x}}{9x^2}$$
$$= \sqrt[3]{3x} - \sqrt{2x}$$

6. **The correct answer is (J).** Any multiple-digit prime number must end in an odd digit other than 5 (1, 3, 7, or 9). Since the sum of the three digits is 7, Z must be either 1 or 3, and four possibilities emerge: 601, 421, 241, and 223.

7. **The correct answer is (E).** The quantity $(x - 1)$ could be 41, 43, or 47 (all different prime numbers between 40 and 50). Accordingly, the integer x could be 42, 44, or 48. Applying prime factorization, determine the prime factors of each of these three numbers:

$$42 = 2 \times 3 \times 7$$
$$44 = 2 \times 2 \times 11$$
$$48 = 2 \times 2 \times 2 \times 2 \times 3$$

   Determine the sum of the different prime factors: $2 + 3 + 7 + 11 = 23$.

8. **The correct answer is (H).** You can express the base number 18 as the product of its prime factors:

$$18^{15} = 3^{15} \times 3^{15} \times 2^{15} = 3^{30} \times 2^{15}$$

   Thus, the greatest possible value of n is 30.

9. **The correct answer is (B).** The question describes inverse functions, in which the correct choice for $g(x)$ will yield $f(g(x)) = x$. Substitute each answer choice in turn for $g(x)$ in the function $f(g(x)) = 3[(g(x)] + 2$. You'll see that only choice (B) results in $g(f(x)) = x$:

$$f(g(x)) = 3\left(\frac{x-2}{3}\right) + 2 = x - 2 + 2 = x$$

10. **The correct answer is (G).** Since no base numbers are given, both bases are understood to be 10. Substitute the expressions given for x and y as follows: $2y - 3x = 2\log 5 - 3\log 2$. To combine the two terms, apply the properties of logarithms: $2\log 5 - 3\log 2 = \log 5^2 - \log 2^3 = \log 25 - \log 8 = \log\frac{25}{8}$.

LESSON 11
Advanced Algebra Concepts and Applications

You've already performed a lot of algebra in Part III of this book. You've combined and simplified algebraic expressions, solved linear equations in one variable, and solved systems of two equations in two variables. In this lesson, you'll move ahead to the skills needed for more complex ACT algebra—the skills that separate Brainiacs from all the rest. These skills include:

- Factoring quadratic expressions
- Finding the roots of quadratic equations by factoring
- Finding the roots of quadratic equations by applying the quadratic formula
- Recognizing unsolvable equations when you see them
- Handling algebraic inequalities

Then, you'll learn to set up and solve algebraic equations for ACT word problems involving:

- Weighted averages
- Direct and inverse variation
- Speed (rate of motion)
- Mixtures
- Interest on investment

FACTORABLE QUADRATIC EQUATIONS

A *quadratic equation* includes a "squared" variable, such as x^2. An equation is quadratic if you can express it in this standard form: $ax^2 + bx + c = 0$, where:

x is the variable

a, b, and c are constants (numbers)

$a \neq 0$

b can equal 0

c can equal 0

Here are four examples (notice that the b-term and c-term are not essential; in other words, either b or c, or both, can equal zero):

Quadratic equation	***Same equation, but in the form: $ax^2 + bx + c = 0$***
$2w^2 = 16$	$2w^2 - 16 = 0$ (no b-term)
$x^2 = 3x$	$x^2 - 3x = 0$ (no c-term)
$3y = 4 - y^2$	$y^2 + 3y - 4 = 0$
$7z = 2z^2 - 15$	$2z^2 - 7z - 15 = 0$

Every quadratic equation has exactly two solutions, called *roots*. (The two roots might be the same.) On the ACT, you'll always be able to find the two roots by *factoring*. To solve any factorable quadratic equation, follow these three steps:

1. Put the equation into the standard form: $ax^2 + bx + c = 0$.
2. Factor the terms on the left side of the equation into two linear expressions (with no exponents).
3. Set each linear expression (root) equal to zero and solve for the variable in each one.

Some quadratic expressions are easier to factor than others. If either of the two constants b or c is zero, factoring is no sweat. In fact, in some cases, as in the following right-hand equation, no factoring is needed:

A quadratic with no c term:	***A quadratic with no b term:***
$2x^2 = x$	$2x^2 - 4 = 0$
$2x^2 - x = 0$	$2(x^2 - 2) = 0$
$x(2x - 1) = 0$	$x^2 - 2 = 0$
$x = 0, 2x - 1 = 0$	$x^2 = 2$
$x = 0, \frac{1}{2}$	$x = \sqrt{2}, -\sqrt{2}$

Otherwise, factoring is a bit trickier. You need to apply the FOIL method, in which you add together these terms:

(F) The product of the **F**irst terms of the two binomials

(O) The product of the **O**uter terms of the two binomials

(I) The product of the **I**nner terms of the two binomials

(L) The product of the **L**ast (second) terms of the two binomials

Note the following relationships:

(F) is the first term (ax^2) of the quadratic expression

(O + I) is the second term (bx) of the quadratic expression

(L) is the third term (c) of the quadratic expression

On the ACT, tougher quadratic equations come with coefficients that make it more difficult to factor. Here's a typical example (answer choices are omitted):

Q If $7z = 2z^2 - 15$, what is one possible value for z?

A **The correct answer could be either $-\frac{3}{5}$ or 5.** First put the equation into standard form: $2z^2 - 7z - 15 = 0$. Notice that z^2 has a coefficient of 2. This complicates the process of factoring into two binomials. A bit of trial and error may be required to determine all coefficients in both binomials. Set up two binomial shells: $(2z \quad)(z \quad) = 0$. One of the two missing constants must be negative, since their product (the "L" term under the FOIL method) is -15. The possible integral pairs for these constants are: $(1,-15)$, $(-1,15)$, $(3,-5)$, and $(-3,5)$. Substituting each value pair for the two missing terms in the shell equation reveals that 3 and -5 are the missing constants (remember to take into account that the first x-term includes a coefficient of 2): $(2z + 3)(z - 5) = 0$

You can check your work by reversing the process:

$$(F) + (O) + (I) + (L) = 0$$

$$2z^2 - 10z + 3z - 15 = 0$$

$$2z^2 - 7z - 15 = 0$$

Now, solve for z:

$$(2z + 3)(z - 5) = 0$$

$$2z + 3 = 0, z - 5 = 0$$

$$z = -\frac{3}{2}, 5$$

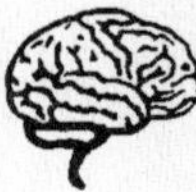

When dealing with a quadratic equation, your first step is usually to put it into the standard form $ax^2 + bx + c = 0$. But keep in mind: the only essential term is ax^2.

THE QUADRATIC FORMULA AND COMPLEX NUMBERS

Rational roots exist, but they are difficult to find for some quadratic equations. For example, $12x^2 + x - 6 = 0$ can be solved by factoring, but the factors are not easy to see:

$$12x^2 + x - 6 = (3x - 2)(4x + 3)$$

Faced with a quadratic equation that's difficult to factor, you can always use the quadratic formula, which states that, for any equation of the form $ax^2 + bx + c = 0$:

$$x = \frac{-b \pm \sqrt{b^2 - 4ac}}{2a}$$

In the equation $12x^2 + x - 6 = 0$, for example, $a = 12$, $b = 1$, and $c = -6$. Plugging these values into the quadratic formula, you'll find that the two roots are $\frac{2}{3}$ and $-\frac{3}{4}$.

Some quadratic equations have no rational roots (solutions). These are the quadratics that separate ACT Brainiacs from all the rest. Referring to the quadratic formula, if $b^2 - 4ac$ turns out to be a negative number, then its square root will be *imaginary*, and hence so will the roots of the quadratic equation at hand. In general, if N is a positive number, then $\sqrt{-N}$ is written as $i\sqrt{N}$, where i is the square root of -1. For example, $\sqrt{-4} = i\sqrt{4} = 2i$ and $\sqrt{-3} = i\sqrt{3}$. So if the ACT asks you to find the root of a quadratic equation, and some of the answer choices are expressed in terms of i, it's a clue that the equation's roots might very well include an imaginary number. Here's a typical example:

Q Which of the following is a root of the equation $x^2 = 4x - 5$?

(A) $4 - i$
(B) $2 - i$
(C) $2 + 2i$
(D) $3i$
(E) $2 - 2i$

A **The correct answer is (B).** First, express the equation in the quadratic form $ax^2 + bx + c = 0$, which is $x^2 - 4x + 5 = 0$.

In this equation, $a = 1$, $b = -4$, and $c = 5$. Apply the quadratic formula, using these values:

$$x = \frac{-(-4) \pm \sqrt{(-4)^2 - 4(1)(5)}}{2(1)} = \frac{4 \pm \sqrt{16 - 20}}{2} = \frac{4 \pm \sqrt{-4}}{2} = \frac{4 \pm 2i}{2} = 2 \pm i$$

The two roots are $2 + i$ and $2 - i$ (B).

Numbers of the form $a + bi$, where a and b are both real numbers and $i = \sqrt{-1}$, are called *complex numbers*—hence, the heading for this section. Whenever you perform arithmetic with complex numbers, treat i as any other variable, unless i is raised to an even power, in which case replace the term with a real number. For example, replace i^2 with -1 and i^4 with 1.

NON-LINEAR EQUATIONS WITH TWO VARIABLES

In the world of math, solving non-linear equations in two or more variables can be *very* complicated, even for bona-fide mathematicians. But on the ACT, all you need to remember are these three general forms:

Sum of two variables, squared: $(x + y)^2 = x^2 + 2xy + y^2$
Difference of two variables, squared: $(x - y)^2 = x^2 - 2xy + y^2$
Difference of two squares: $x^2 - y^2 = (x + y)(x - y)$

You can verify these equations using the FOIL method:

$$(x + y)^2 = (x + y)(x + y) = x^2 + xy + xy + y^2 = x^2 + 2xy + y^2$$

$$(x - y)^2 = (x - y)(x - y) = x^2 - xy - xy + y^2 = x^2 - 2xy + y^2$$

$$(x + y)(x - y) = x^2 + xy - xy - y^2 = x^2 - y^2$$

For the ACT, memorize the three equations listed on the previous page. When you see one form on the exam, it's a sure bet that your task is to rewrite it as the other form, as in the following example:

Q If $x^2 - y^2 = 100$, and if $x + y = 2$, then $x - y =$

(A) -2
(B) 10
(C) 20
(D) 50
(E) 200

A **The correct answer is (D).** If you're on the lookout for the difference of two squares, you can easily handle this question. Use the third equation you just learned, substituting 2 for $(x + y)$, then solving for $(x - y)$:

$$x^2 - y^2 = (x + y)(x - y)$$
$$100 = (x + y)(x - y)$$
$$100 = (2)(x - y)$$
$$50 = (x - y)$$

Can you work backward from the answer choices to solve this problem? Try it, but you won't get very far. There are two lessons here: (1) You usually can't solve quadratics using a shortcut, and (2) Always look for one of the three common quadratic forms; if you see it, rewrite it as its equivalent form to answer the question as quickly and easily as possible.

EQUATIONS THAT CAN'T BE SOLVED

One equation in one variable is not necessarily solvable. For example, $3x - 3 - 4x = x - 7 - 2x + 4$ simplifies to $0 = 0$, and thus x could equal any real number. Similarly, a system of two equations in two variables is not necessarily solvable. What appears to be a system of two equations in two variables might actually be the same equation expressed in two different ways. For example, the equation $2b = 60 - 2a$ is identical to the equation $a + b = 30$:

$$2b = 60 - 2a$$
$$2b = 2(30 - a)$$
$$b = 30 - a$$
$$a + b = 30$$

Thus, either a and b could each be any real number.

When you encounter a question in which one of the answer choices is "any real number," keep in mind that the question might be testing you on whether you recognize one of the two identities discussed above.

SOLVING ALGEBRAIC INEQUALITIES

You can solve algebraic inequalities in the same manner as equations. Isolate the variable on one side of the equation, factoring and "canceling" wherever possible. However, one important rule distinguishes inequalities from equations: Whenever you multiply or divide by a negative number, you must reverse the inequality symbol. Simply put: If $a > b$, then $-a < -b$.

Here are some general rules for algebraic inequalities. Study them until they're second nature to you; you'll put them to good use on the ACT.

1. Adding or subtracting unequal quantities to (or from) equal quantities:

   If $a > b$, then $c + a > c + b$

   If $a > b$, then $c - a < c - b$

2. Adding unequal quantities to unequal quantities:

   If $a > b$, and if $c > d$, then $a + c > b + d$

3. Comparing three unequal quantities:

   If $a > b$, and if $b > c$, then $a > c$

4. Combining the same *positive* quantity with unequal quantities by multiplication or division:

   If $a > b$, and if $x > 0$, then $xa > xb$

   If $a > b$, and if $x > 0$, then $\frac{a}{x} > \frac{b}{x}$

   If $a > b$, and if $x > 0$, then $\frac{x}{a} < \frac{x}{b}$

5. Combining the same *negative* quantity with unequal quantities by multiplication or division:

   If $a > b$, and if $x < 0$, then $xa < xb$

   If $a > b$, and if $x < 0$, then $\frac{a}{x} < \frac{b}{x}$

   If $a > b$, and if $x < 0$, then $\frac{x}{a} > \frac{x}{b}$

Even though there's nothing austere about the inequality concept and the preceding rules, ACT inequality questions can be a bit confusing, as this brain-bending example demonstrates:

Q For any negative number x, if $a > x > b$ and $x > c > d$, then which of the following must also be true?

I. $a + b + x > x + c + d$

II. $\frac{ax}{b} > \frac{cd}{b}$

III. $\frac{a-d}{x} < \frac{c+b}{x}$

(A) II only
(B) III only
(C) I and II only
(D) II and III only
(E) I, II, and III

A **The correct answer is (D).** Look at an analysis of each statement:

(I) You can subtract x from both sides of the inequality, leaving $a + b > c + d$. (The inequality is true depending on how a and b compare in value to c and d.) For example, $1 + (-3) > -1 + (-4)$, but $1 + (-3) < -1 + (-2)$.

(II) Since a and x are both greater than c and d, and since c and d are both negative, $ax < cd$, regardless of whether ax is positive or negative. Dividing both products by b, a negative number, reverses the inequality, and statement (II) must be true.

(III) First, compare the two numerators. Since d is negative, $(a - d) > a$. Since c and b are both less than a, and since all three terms are negative, $(c + b) < a$. Therefore, $(a - d) > (c + b)$. Dividing both expressions by b, a negative number, reverses the inequality, and statement (III) must be true.

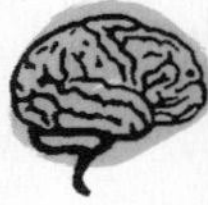

True Brainiacs avoid the plug-in strategy for making comparisons that involve variables with a range of possible values. Instead, Brainiacs try to identify the general dynamic between the two quantities, as in the preceding analysis.

COMPLEX "FORMULA" AND OTHER WORD PROBLEMS

Certain types of word problems call for distinct formulas. Here are the types of formulas you need to know for the ACT:

- Weighted averages
- Direct and inverse variation
- Speed (rate of motion)

Most other types, however, don't require special formulas. Instead, simply set up a system of two equations, then solve for the unknown by algebraic substitution. Here are the two types that appear most frequently on the ACT:

- Mixtures (of two substances)
- Interest (on a monetary investment)

In this section, you'll learn how to handle the five types listed above.

Remember: For any type of word problem, including these five, instead of setting up and solving a system of equations, you might be able to work backward from the answer choices. If not, you can almost always narrow down your choices by estimating the size of the answer.

WEIGHTED AVERAGE PROBLEMS

Solve *weighted average* problems using the arithmetic mean (simple average) formula, except give the set's terms different weights. For example, if a final exam score of 90 receives *twice* the weight of each of two mid-term exam scores of 75 and 85, think of the final-exam score as *two* scores of 90—and the total number of scores as 4 rather than 3:

$$WA = \frac{75 + 85 + (2)(90)}{4} = \frac{340}{4} = 85$$

A more complex weighted-average problem might provide the weighted average and ask for one of the terms. Or it might require conversions from one unit of measure to another. Here's an example that would rank among the most challenging ACT word problems. It incorporates both features, and actually requires conversions for two different units of measure!

Q A certain olive orchard produces 315 gallons of oil annually, on average, during four consecutive years. How many gallons of oil must the orchard produce annually, on average, during the next six years, if oil production for the entire ten-year-period is to meet the goal of one barrel per month? [1 barrel = 31.5 gallons]

(A) 240
(B) 285
(C) 396
(D) 420
(E) 468

A **The correct answer is (D).** This problem requires two types of unit conversions: barrels to gallons and months to years. Express the weighted-average goal in gallons per year: 1 barrel per month = (12)(31.5) gallons per year. In the weighted-average formula, 315 annual gallons receives a weight of 4, while the average annual number of gallons for the next six years (x) receives a weight of 6:

$$(12)(31.5) = \frac{(4)(315) + 6x}{10}$$
$$378 = \frac{1260 + 6x}{10}$$
$$3780 = 1260 + 6x$$
$$3780 - 1260 = 6x$$
$$420 = x$$

This solution (420) is the average number of gallons needed per *year* over the next six years.

Check your answer by sizing up the question to avoid calculation errors. What size number are you looking for? Notice that the stated goal is a bit greater than the annual average production over the first four years, so you're looking for an answer that is greater than the goal—a number greater than 378 gallons per year.

DIRECT AND INVERSE VARIATION (PROPORTION)

Two quantities are said to vary *directly* if they change in the same direction; as one increases, the other increases. Conversely, two quantities vary *inversely* if they change in opposite directions; as one increases, the other decreases. Variation problems on the ACT always assume *proportionate* changes. In any ACT variation problem—direct or inverse—you can find a missing term by setting up an algebraic equation that expresses two proportions as equal. The way you go about this, however, is different for direct variation than for inverse variation.

Easier variation questions involve direct variation and use numbers. These questions are essentially the same as the proportion problems—where you ask, for example: "a is to b as c is to what?" Tougher variation questions will involve one or more of these features:

- Literal expressions, in which letters are used to signify numbers
- Conversions from one unit of measurement to another
- Inverse variation (which can be more confusing than direct variation)

The next example incorporates the first two features, while the one that follows involves inverse variation:

Q If a truck can carry m pounds of coal, how many trucks are needed to carry p tons of coal? [1 ton = 2,000 pounds.]

(A) $\frac{p}{2000m}$

(B) $\frac{m}{2000p}$

(C) $\frac{2000}{p+m}$

(D) $\frac{2000p}{m}$

(E) $2000m(p - m)$

A **The correct answer is (D).** You're comparing trucks with pounds. This is a direct variation, because the number of trucks increases as the number of pounds increases. The question asks: "1 is to m as what is to p?" First, set up a proportion (equate two ratios, or fractions). Then convert either pounds to tons (divide m by 2,000) or tons to pounds (multiply p by 2,000). We'll use the second conversion method. Cross-multiply to solve for x:

$$\frac{1}{m} = \frac{x}{2000p}$$

$$mx = 2000p$$

$$x = \frac{2000p}{m}$$

Q If a bag of cat food can feed 5 cats for four days, then how long could it feed 8 cats, if all cats eat the same amount each day?

(A) $2\frac{1}{2}$ days
(B) 3 days
(C) 5 days
(D) $6\frac{2}{5}$ days
(E) 10 days

A **The correct answer is (A).** This problem involves *inverse* variation because the more cats, the fewer days. Instead of equating two ratios (fractions) with inverse variation, it's easier to equate two products. In this problem, multiply the number of cats by the number of days in each instance and set them equal; then solve for x:

$$(5)(4) = (8)(x)$$
$$20 = 8x$$
$$\frac{20}{8} = x$$

5 bags of food can feed 8 cats for $\frac{5}{2}$, or $2\frac{1}{2}$, days.

When tackling inverse variation, be careful setting up your equation. An unwary test-taker would translate the preceding verbal question as follows: "5 is to 4 as what is to 8?" Wrong! If you're not 100% certain you've set up the problem correctly, think about the general size of the numerical answer you are looking for. In this question, you're looking for a number that's "not quite half of 4," aren't you? This reality check will help you avoid setting up the wrong proportion.

SPEED (RATE OF MOTION) PROBLEMS

ACT speed problems are a bit overrated in terms of their difficulty. They all involve the same familiar formula:

distance = rate × time

An easier speed problem will involve a *single* distance, rate, and time. A more difficult speed problem might involve different rates; for example, either:

- Two different times over the same distance

or

- Two different distances covered in the same time

In either type, apply the basic speed formula to each of the two events. Then solve for the missing information by algebraic substitution. Use the same approach for any of the following scenarios:

- One object making two separate "legs" of a trip—either in the same direction or as a round trip
- Two objects moving in the same direction
- Two objects moving in opposite directions

Here are two examples, each involving one of the first two scenarios (you'll encounter the third scenario during the Brain Teaser in this lesson):

Q Janice left her home at 11:00 a.m., traveling along Route 1 at 30 mph. At 1:00 p.m., her brother Richard left home and started after her on the same road at 45 mph. At what time did Richard catch up to Janice?

(A) 2:45 p.m.
(B) 3:00 p.m.
(C) 3:30 p.m.
(D) 4:15 p.m.
(E) 5:00 p.m.

A **The correct answer is (E).** Notice that the distance Janice covered is equal to that of Richard's—that is, distance is constant. Letting x equal Janice's time, you can express Richard's time as $x - 2$. Substitute these values for time and the values for rate given in the problem into the speed formula for Richard and Janice:

Formula: rate $\times$ time = distance
Janice: $(30)(x) = 30x$
Richard: $(45)(x - 2) = 45x - 90$

Because the distance is constant, you can equate Janice's distance to Richard's, then solve for x:

$$30x = 45x - 90$$
$$15x = 90$$
$$x = 6$$

Janice had traveled six hours when Richard caught up with her. Because Janice left at 11:00 a.m., Richard caught up with her at 5:00 p.m.

Q How far in kilometers can Scott drive into the country if he drives out at 40 kilometers per hour (kph), returns over the same road at 30 kph, and spends eight hours away from home, including a one-hour stop for lunch?

(A) 105
(B) 120
(C) 145
(D) 180
(E) 210

A **The correct answer is (B).** Scott's actual driving time is 7 hours, which you must divide into two parts: his time spent driving into the country and his time spent returning. Letting the first part equal x, the return time is what remains of the 7 hours, or $7 - x$. Substitute these expressions into the motion formula for each of the two parts of Scott's journey:

Formula: rate $\times$ time = distance
Going: $(40)(x) = 40x$
Returning: $(30)(7 - x) = 210 - 30x$

Because the journey is round trip, the distance going equals the distance returning. Simply equate the two algebraic expressions, then solve for x:

$$40x = 210 - 30x$$
$$70x = 210$$
$$x = 3$$

Scott traveled 40 mph for 3 hours, so he traveled 120 miles.

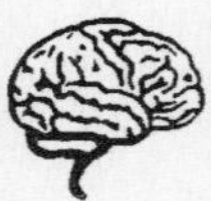

Regardless of the type of speed problem you're solving, always start with the same task: set up *two* distinct equations patterned after the simple motion formula ($r \times t = d$).

MIXTURE PROBLEMS

In ACT mixture problems, you combine substances with different characteristics, resulting in a particular mixture or proportion, usually expressed as percentages. Substances are measured and mixed by either volume or weight—but not by number (quantity).

How many quarts of pure alcohol must you add to 15 quarts of a solution that is 40% alcohol to strengthen it to a solution that is 50% alcohol?

(A) 4.0
(B) 3.5
(C) 3.25
(D) 3.0
(E) 2.5

The correct answer is (D). The original amount of alcohol is 40% of 15. Letting x equal the number of quarts of alcohol that you must add to achieve a 50% alcohol solution, $.4(15) + x$ equals the amount of alcohol in the solution after adding more alcohol. You can express this amount as 50% of $(15 + x)$. Thus, you can express the mixture algebraically as follows:

$$(.4)(15) + x = (.5)(15 + x)$$
$$6 + x = 7.5 + .5x$$
$$.5x = 1.5$$
$$x = 3$$

You must add 3 quarts of alcohol to obtain a 50% alcohol solution.

INVESTMENT PROBLEMS

More challenging ACT investment problems usually involve interest and require more than simply calculating interest earned on a given principal amount at a given rate. They usually call for you to set up and solve an algebraic equation. When handling these problems, it's best to eliminate percent signs (or multiply by 100 to eliminate decimals).

Dr. Kramer plans to invest $20,000 in an account paying 6% interest annually. How much more must she invest at the same time at 3% so that her total annual income during the first year is 4% of her entire investment?

(A) $32,000
(B) $36,000
(C) $40,000
(D) $47,000
(E) $49,000

A

The correct answer is (C). Letting x equal the amount invested at 3%, you can express Dr. Kramer's total investment as $20{,}000 + x$. The interest on $20,000 plus the interest on the additional investment equals the total interest from both investments. You can state this algebraically as follows:

$$.06(20{,}000) + .03x = .04(20{,}000 + x)$$

Multiply all terms by 100 to eliminate decimals, then solve for x:

$$\begin{aligned} 6(20{,}000) + 3x &= 4(20{,}000 + x) \\ 120{,}000 + 3x &= 80{,}000 + 4x \\ 40{,}000 &= x \end{aligned}$$

She must invest $40,000 at 3% for her total annual income to be 4% of her total investment ($60,000).

For investment problems, you can size up the question to see if your calculated answer appears to be in the right ballpark. But don't rely on your intuition to derive a *precise* solution. Interest problems can be misleading on the surface. For instance, you might have guessed that Dr. Kramer would need to invest more than *twice* as much at 3% than at 6% to lower the overall interest rate to 4%. Not true!

BRAIN TEASER

In this quiz, you'll attempt 10 tough ACT-style questions covering the topics from this lesson. Focus on applying the concepts and techniques you learned in this lesson, *not* on answering the questions as quickly as possible. Then read the explanations that follow the quiz, even for the questions you answered correctly.

QUIZ

1. If $\frac{9b^3 - 15b^2 - 6b}{18b^2 + 6b} = 13b - 17$, then $b =$

(A) $3\frac{1}{2}$

(B) 3

(C) $1\frac{7}{25}$

(D) $\frac{5}{16}$

(E) $-\frac{14}{5}$

2. If $a > b$, then which of the following statements must also be true?

I. If $x < 0$, then $\frac{a}{x} < \frac{b}{x}$.
II. If $c > d$, then $b - d < a + c$.
III. If $x < 0$, then $\frac{x}{a} < \frac{x}{b}$.

(F) I only
(G) III only
(H) II and III only
(J) I and III only
(K) I, II, and III

3. It takes Paul m minutes to mow the lawn. Assuming he mows at a constant rate, after Paul mows for k minutes, what part of the lawn remains to be mowed?

(A) $\frac{m-k}{m}$

(B) $\frac{m}{k}$

(C) $1 - \frac{k}{m}$

(D) $\frac{k-m}{k}$

(E) $\frac{k}{m}$

4. How many ounces of soy sauce must be added to an 18-ounce mixture of peanut sauce and soy sauce consisting of 32% peanut sauce in order to create a mixture that is 12% peanut sauce?

(F) 21

(G) $24\frac{3}{4}$

(H) $26\frac{2}{3}$

(J) 30

(K) $38\frac{2}{5}$

5. Barbara invests \$2,400 in the National Bank at 5%. How much additional money must she invest at 8% so that the total annual income will be equal to 6% of her entire investment?

(A) \$1,200
(B) \$3,000
(C) \$1,000
(D) \$3,600
(E) \$2,400

6. Under which of the following conditions must $a^2 - b^2$ be greater than $(3a + 3b)(2a - 2b)$?

(F) $b < a < -1$
(G) $b < 0 < a$
(H) $a < 0 < b$
(J) $a < b < 0$
(K) $a < b < -1$

7. Which of the following is one root of the equation $5x^2 + 8 = 4x$?

(A) $\frac{5-6i}{4}$

(B) $\frac{-2+6i}{5}$

(C) $\frac{2+6i}{5}$

(D) $\frac{1+3i}{10}$

(E) $\frac{5-4i}{8}$

8. David averaged 70 on his first m exams. After taking n more exams, his overall average increased to 75. In terms of n and m, his average for his last n exams was

(F) $\frac{5m + 75}{n}$
(G) $\frac{5m}{n} + 75$
(H) $\frac{5n}{m} + 75$
(J) $m + 15n$
(K) $\frac{70m + 75n}{m + n}$

9. How many pounds of nuts selling for 70 cents per pound must be mixed with 30 pounds of nuts selling at 90 cents per pound to make a mixture that sells for 85 cents per pound?

(A) 24
(B) 20
(C) 15
(D) 12
(E) 10

10. A passenger train and a freight train leave at 10:30 a.m. from stations that are 405 miles apart. The trains travel toward each other at a constant speed, the passenger train traveling 45 mph faster than the freight train. If they pass each other at 1:30 p.m., how fast is the passenger train traveling, in miles per hour?

(F) 75
(G) 82.5
(H) 90
(J) 95
(K) 105

ANSWERS AND EXPLANATIONS

1. **The correct answer is (C).** On the left side of the equation, factor the numerator and denominator. (There's a factorable quadratic expression in the numerator.) Then divide common terms and solve for b:

$$\frac{3b(3b^2 - 5b - 2)}{6b(3b + 1)} = 13b - 17$$

$$\frac{(3b + 1)(b - 2)}{2(3b + 1)} = 13b - 17$$

$$\frac{b - 2}{2} = 13b - 17$$

$$b - 2 = 26b - 34$$

$$-25b = -32$$

$$b = \frac{32}{25}$$

2. **The correct answer is (J).** (I) is always true. Dividing each of two unequal numbers by the same negative number reverses the inequality. (II) could be either true or false, depending on the difference between a and b compared to the difference between c and d. (III) is always true. Multiplying each of two unequal numbers by the same negative number reverses the inequality.

Be sure to plug in easy, valid numbers for variables when you check your analysis.

3. **The correct answer is (A).** The longer Paul mows, the more lawn is mowed, so the variation is direct. Let x equal the portion of the lawn Paul has mowed after k minutes, set up the proportion, and solve for x:

$$\frac{m}{1} = \frac{k}{x}$$

$$mx = k$$

$$x = \frac{k}{m}$$

Paul has mowed $\frac{k}{m}$ of the lawn in k minutes. Still not mowed, then, is $1 - \frac{k}{m}$, or $\frac{m - k}{m}$.

4. **The correct answer is (J).** Letting x equal the number of ounces of soy sauce added to the mixture, $18 + x$ equals the total amount of the mixture after the soy sauce is added. The amount of peanut sauce (5.76 ounces) must equal 12% of the new total amount of the mixture, which is $18 + x$. You can express this as an algebraic equation and solve for x:

$$5.76 = .12(x + 18)$$

$$576 = 12(x + 18)$$

$$576 = 12x + 216$$

$$360 = 12x$$

$$30 = x$$

30 ounces of soy sauce must be added to achieve a mixture that includes 12% peanut sauce.

5. **The correct answer choice is (A).** If Barbara invests x additional dollars at 8%, her total investment will amount to $(2{,}400 + x)$ dollars.

$$.05(2400) + .08x = .06(2400 + x)$$

$$5(2400) + 8x = 6(2400 + x)$$

$$12000 + 8x = 14400 + 6x$$

$$2x = 2400$$

$$x = 1200$$

6. **The correct answer is (F).** $a^2 - b^2$ can be expressed in its factored form: $(a + b)(a - b)$. Notice the similarity between this expression and the other one. Factor out the constants (numbers) in $(3a + 3b)(2a - 2b)$ so that it more closely resembles $a^2 - b^2$:

$$(3a + 3b)(2a - 2b) = 6(a + b)(a - b)$$
$$= 6(a^2 - b^2)$$

Given $b < a < -1$, choice (F), $(a^2 - b^2)$ must be a negative number. Multiplying this negative number by 6 yields an even lesser number (to the left on the real number line). Therefore, if $b < a < -1$, then $a^2 - b^2 > (3a + 3b)(2a - 2b)$.

7. **The correct answer is (C).** First, express the equation in the standard form: $5x^2 - 4x + 8 = 0$ $[a = 5, b = -4, c = 8]$. Then, apply the quadratic formula:

$$x = \frac{-(-4) \pm \sqrt{(-4)^2 - 4(5)(8)}}{2(5)}$$

$$= \frac{4 \pm \sqrt{16 - 160}}{10}$$

$$= \frac{4 \pm \sqrt{-144}}{10}$$

$$= \frac{4 \pm 12i}{10}$$

$$= \frac{2 \pm 6i}{5}$$

The two roots are $\frac{2 + 6i}{5}$, choice (C), and $\frac{2 - 6i}{5}$.

8. **The correct answer is (G).** Since David's overall average was 75, his exam scores for $(m + n)$ exams totaled $75(m + n)$, or $75m + 75n$. Since he averaged 70 on his first m exams, his aggregate score for those exams was $70m$. Hence, his total on the last n exams was $(75m + 75n) - (70m) = 5m + 75n$. Accordingly, his average for his last n exams was $\frac{5m + 75n}{n} = \frac{5m}{n} + \frac{75n}{n} = \frac{5m}{n} + 75$.

9. **The correct answer is (E).** The cost (in cents) of the nuts selling for 70 cents per pound can be expressed as $70x$, letting x equal the number that you're asked to determine. You then add this cost to the cost of the more expensive nuts ($30 \times 90 = 2{,}700$) to obtain the total cost of the mixture, which you can express as $85(x + 30)$. You can state this algebraically and solve for x as follows:

$$70x + 2700 = 85(x + 30)$$
$$70x + 2700 = 85x + 2550$$
$$150 = 15x$$
$$10 = x$$

10 pounds of 70-cent-per-pound nuts must be added in order to make a mixture that sells for 85 cents per pound.

10. **The correct answer is (H).** Notice that each train traveled for exactly 3 hours; in other words, time is constant. Let x equal the rate (speed) of the freight train. You can express the rate of the passenger train as $x + 45$. Substitute these values for time and rate into the speed formula for each train:

Formula: rate $\times$ time = distance
Passenger: $(x + 45)(3) = 3x + 135$
Freight: $(x)(3) = 3x$

The total distance the two trains cover is given as 405 miles. Express this algebraically and solve for x:

$$(3x + 135) + 3x = 405$$
$$6x = 270$$
$$x = 45$$

Accordingly, the rate of the passenger train was 45 + 45, or 90 mph.

LESSON 12

Plane Geometry and Right-Triangle Trigonometry

In this lesson, you'll learn how the test-makers design tough questions covering:

- Relationships among angles formed by intersecting lines
- Characteristics of any triangle, and of right, isosceles, and equilateral triangles
- Trigonometric functions involving the sides and angles of right triangles
- Characteristics of squares, rectangles, trapezoids, parallelograms, and rhombuses

X-REF **This lesson doesn't deal with other polygons, circles, three-dimensional figures, or coordinate geometry. You'll explore those topics in the next two lessons.**

LINES AND ANGLES

Lines and line segments are the basic building blocks for most ACT geometry problems. If a problem involves nothing more than intersecting lines and the angles they form, then the question will probably be pretty easy. To handle it, just remember four basic rules about angles formed by intersecting lines:

1. Vertical angles are equal in degree measure, or *congruent* ($\cong$).
2. If adjacent angles combine to form a straight line, their degree measures total 180. In fact, a straight line is actually a 180° angle.
3. If two lines are perpendicular ($\perp$) to each other, they intersect at right (90°) angles.
4. The sum of the measures of all angles where two or more lines intersect at the same point is 360° (regardless of how many angles are involved).

The term *congruent* and its symbol (≅) are used in mathematics to indicate that two geometric features are identical (the same size, length, shape, etc.). From now on, we'll use the "equality" sign (=) instead. Keep in mind that wherever it's indicated that two angles, lines segments, or triangles are *equal*, it means that they're *congruent*.

On the ACT, line-angle questions almost always involve either a "wheel spoke" or parallel lines with a transversal.

ANGLES FORMED BY INTERSECTING LINES

When two or more lines intersect at the same point, they form a "wheel-spoke" pattern with a "hub." On the ACT, wheel-spoke questions require you to apply one or more of the preceding four rules to figures like the following.

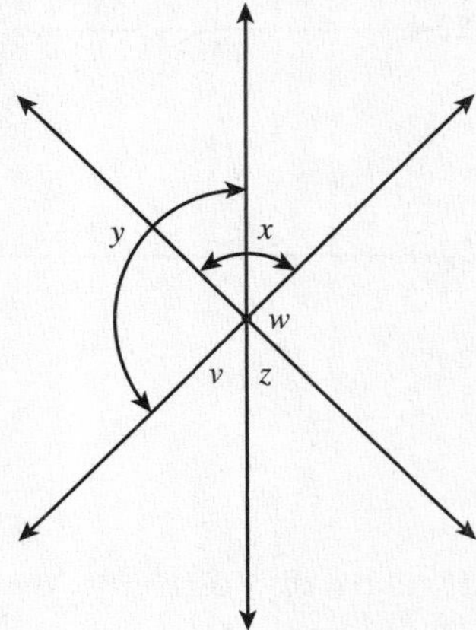

More challenging wheel-spoke questions focus on overlapping angles, and require you to apply rule 1 (about vertical angles) to determine the amount of the overlap. For instance, a question about the preceding figure might test your ability to recognize one of the following relationships:

$x + y - z = 180$	$x + y$ exceeds 180 by the amount of the overlap, which equals z, the angle vertical to the overlapping angle.
$x + y + v + w = 360$	The sum of the measures of all angles, excluding z, is 360°; z is excluded because it is already accounted for by the overlap of x and y.
$y - w = z$	w is congruent to its vertical angle, so $y - w$ equals the portion of y vertical to angle z.

You'll get to try a relatively difficult wheel-spoke question during this lesson's Brain Teaser.

PARALLEL LINES AND TRANSVERSALS

ACT problems involving parallel lines also involve at least one *transversal*, which is a line that intersects each of two (or more) lines. In the figure below, because $l_1 \parallel l_2$ and $l_3 \parallel l_4$, the upper-left "cluster" of angles 1, 2, 3, and 4 matches each of the three other clusters. In other words:

All the odd-numbered angles are congruent to one another.

All the even-numbered angles are congruent to one another.

If you know the measure of just one angle, you can determine the measure of all 16 angles!

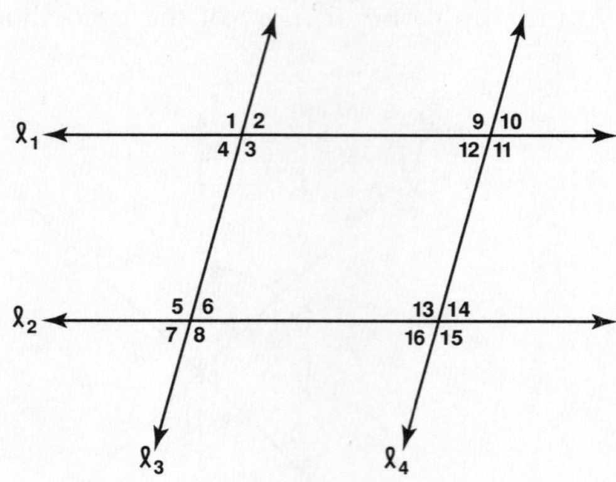

X-REF **You'll get to try a relatively difficult transversal question during this lesson's Brain Teaser.**

TRIANGLES

The *triangle* (a three-sided polygon) is the test-makers' favorite geometric figure. You'll need to understand triangles not only to solve "pure" triangle problems but also to solve some problems involving four-sided figures, three-dimensional figures, and even circles. After a very brief review of the properties of any triangle, we'll focus on three special types of triangles.

- Right triangles (which include one right, or 90°, angle)
- Isosceles triangles (in which two sides, and two angles, are congruent)
- Equilateral triangles (in which all sides, and all angles, are congruent)

PROPERTIES OF ALL TRIANGLES

There are four properties that all triangles share:

1. *Length of the sides*

   Each side is shorter than the sum of the lengths of the other two sides.

2. *Angle measures*

   The sum of the measures of the three angles = 180°.

3. *Angles and opposite sides*

   Comparative angle measures correspond to the comparative lengths of the sides opposite those angles. For example, a triangle's largest angle is opposite its longest side. (The sides opposite two congruent angles are also congruent.)

Don't take this rule too far! The ratio among angle sizes need not be identical to the ratio among lengths of sides! For example, if a certain triangle has angle measures of 30°, 60°, and 90°, the ratio of the angles is 1:2:3. But does this mean that the ratio of the opposite sides is also 1:2:3? No, and you'll soon learn why.

4. *Area.*

   The area of any triangle is equal to one-half the product of its base and its height (or "altitude"): Area $= \frac{1}{2} \times$ base $\times$ height. You can use any side as the base to calculate area.

Do not equate altitude (height) with any particular side. Instead, imagine the base on flat ground, and drop a plumb line straight down from the top peak of the triangle to define height or altitude. The only type of triangle in which the altitude equals the length of one side is the *right* triangle, as you'll see next.

RIGHT TRIANGLES AND THE PYTHAGOREAN THEOREM

In a right triangle, one angle measures 90° (and, of course, each of the other two angles measures less than 90°). The Pythagorean theorem expresses the relationship among the sides of any right triangle. In the following expression of the theorem, a and b are the two legs that form the right angle, and c is the *hypotenuse*—the longest side, opposite the right angle:

$$a^2 + b^2 = c^2$$

For any right triangle, if you know the length of two sides, you can determine the length of the third side with the theorem.

Easier right-triangle questions will provide two of the sides and ask for the third. A difficult right-triangle question might involve one or more of the following:

- Multiple applications of the theorem (to more than one triangle)
- The theorem as well as the formula for a triangle's area
- The use of variables to represent lengths of sides (instead of, or in addition to, numbers)

Here's a complex right-triangle problem that incorporates the first two features:

Q

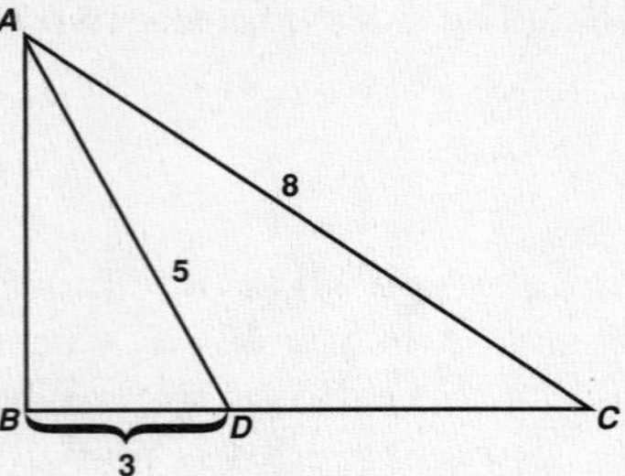

In the figure above, what is the area of ΔABC?

(A) $4\sqrt{3}$

(B) $\frac{15\sqrt{2}}{2}$

(C) $8\sqrt{3}$

(D) 14

(E) 16

A

The correct answer is (C). Don't be intimidated by complex problems such as this one. You already have the tools to solve the problem. First, determine what values you need to know to answer the question, and then perform the steps to find each of those values. To calculate the area of ΔABC, you need to know its base (BC) and its height (AB). Determine AB by applying the Pythagorean theorem to ΔABD:

$$3^2 + (AB)^2 = 5^2$$
$$(AB)^2 = 25 - 9$$
$$(AB)^2 = 16$$
$$AB = 4$$

Now find BC by applying the theorem again, this time to ΔABC:

$$4^2 + (BC)^2 = 8^2$$
$$(BC)^2 = 64 - 16$$
$$(BC)^2 = 48$$
$$BC = \sqrt{48}, \text{ or } 4\sqrt{3}$$

Now you can find the area of ΔABC:

$$\text{Area of } \Delta ABC = \frac{1}{2}(4)(4\sqrt{3}) = 8\sqrt{3}$$

Pythagorean Side Triplets

A *Pythagorean side triplet* is a specific ratio among the sides of a triangle that satisfies the Pythagorean theorem. In each of the following triplets, the first two numbers represent the comparative lengths of the two legs, whereas the third—and greatest—number represents the comparative length of the hypotenuse (on the ACT, the first four appear far more frequently than the last two):

$1{:}1{:}\sqrt{2}$ $\quad 1^2 + 1^2 = (\sqrt{2})^2$

$1{:}\sqrt{3}{:}2$ $\quad 1^2 + (\sqrt{3})^2 = 2^2$

$3{:}4{:}5$ $\quad 3^2 + 4^2 = 5^2$

$5{:}12{:}13$ $\quad 5^2 + 12^2 = 13^2$

$8{:}15{:}17$ $\quad 8^2 + 15^2 = 17^2$

$7{:}24{:}25$ $\quad 7^2 + 24^2 = 25^2$

Each triplet above is expressed as a *ratio* because it represents a proportion among the triangle's sides. All right triangles with sides having the same proportion, or ratio, have the same shape. For example, a right triangle with sides of 5, 12, and 13 is smaller but exactly the same shape (proportion) as a triangle with sides of 15, 36, and 39.

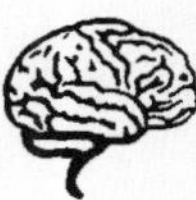

To save valuable time on right-triangle problems, learn to recognize given numbers (lengths of triangle sides) as multiples of Pythagorean triplets. In the previous Problem Solving question, for instance, you could have saved time by recognizing that ΔABD is a 3:4:5 triangle.

Pythagorean Angle Triplets

In two (and only two) of the unique triangles identified in the preceding section as Pythagorean side triplets, all degree measures are integers:

1. The corresponding angles opposite the sides of a $1{:}1{:}\sqrt{2}$ triangle are 45°, 45°, and 90°.
2. The corresponding angles opposite the sides of a $1{:}\sqrt{3}{:}2$ triangle are 30°, 60°, and 90°.

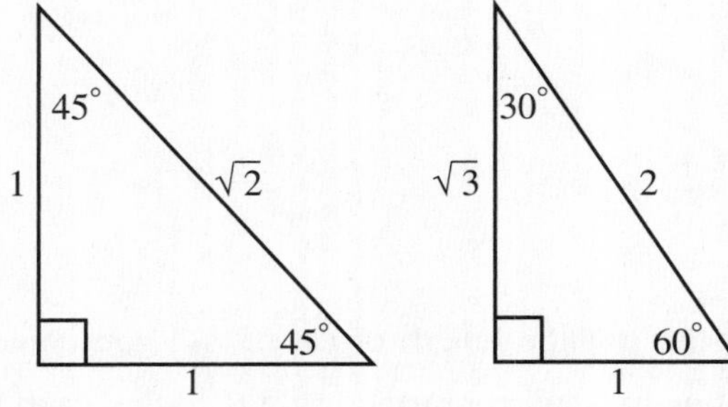

Therefore, if you know that the triangle is a right triangle (one angle measures 90°) and that one of the other angles is either 30°, 45°, or 60°, then given the length of any side you can determine the unknown lengths and angle measures.

Two identical 45°-45°-90° triangles pieced together at the hypotenuse form a square, and two identical 30°-60°-90° triangles pieced together at the longer leg form an equilateral triangle. (Go ahead and draw them.) This phenomenon fascinates the test-makers, so it should interest you as well.

ISOSCELES TRIANGLES

An *isosceles* triangle has the following special properties:

1. Two of the sides are congruent (equal in length).
2. The two angles opposite the two congruent sides are congruent, called base angles (equal degree measure). The other angle is the vertex angle.
3. A line bisecting the triangle's vertex angle bisects its opposite side.

The left-hand triangle in the following figure indicates the first two properties.

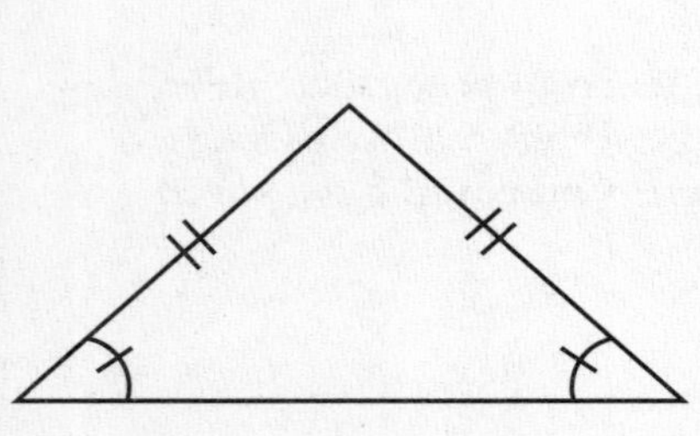

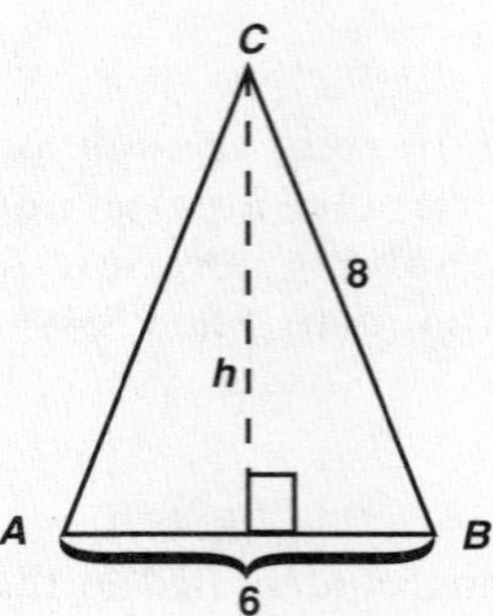

If you know the length of each of the two congruent sides, you can easily determine the triangle's area by applying the Pythagorean theorem. In the right-hand triangle above, for instance, you can determine the triangle's height (h) by applying the Theorem:

$$3^2 + h^2 = 8^2$$
$$h^2 = 64 - 9$$
$$h^2 = 55$$
$$h = \sqrt{55}$$

Thus, the area of $\Delta ABC = \frac{1}{2}(6)\sqrt{55}$. If you knew h but not the length of $\overline{CB}$ or $\overline{AC}$, you could determine these lengths. The altitude line (h) bisects the base $\overline{AB}$, creating two "mirror-image" right triangles, each with legs of length 3 and $\sqrt{55}$. Apply the Pythagorean theorem:

$$x^2 = 3^2 + (\sqrt{55})^2$$
$$x^2 = 9 + 55$$
$$x^2 = 64$$
$$x = 8$$

EQUILATERAL TRIANGLES

An equilateral triangle has the following three properties:

1. All three sides are congruent (equal in length).
2. Each angle measures 60°.
3. Area $= \frac{s^2\sqrt{3}}{4}$ (s = any side).

Any line bisecting one of the 60° angles divides an equilateral triangle into two right triangles with angle measures of 30°, 60°, and 90°; in other words, into two $1{:}\sqrt{3}{:}2$ triangles, as shown in the right-hand triangle in the next figure. (Remember that Pythagorean angle triplet?)

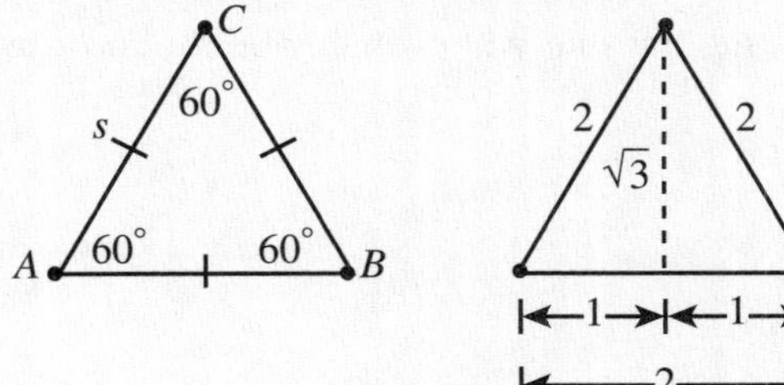

In the left-hand triangle, if $s = 6$, the area of the triangle $= 9\sqrt{3}$. To confirm this formula, bisect the triangle into two 30°-60°-90° ($1{:}\sqrt{3}{:}2$) triangles (as in the right-hand triangle in the preceding figure). The area of this equilateral triangle is $\frac{1}{2}(2)\sqrt{3}$, or $\sqrt{3}$. The area of each smaller right triangle is $\frac{\sqrt{3}}{2}$.

X-REF **On the ACT, equilateral triangles usually appear in problems involving *circles*. (You'll see how during the next lesson.)**

RIGHT TRIANGLE TRIGONOMETRY

Right triangle trigonometry involves the ratios between sides of right triangles and the angle measures that correspond to these ratios. Refer to the following right triangle, in which the sides opposite angles A, B, and C are labeled a, b, and c, respectively (A and B are the two acute angles):

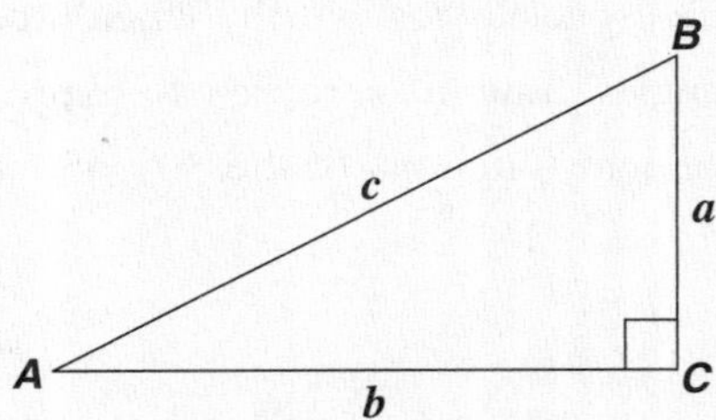

Referring to ΔABC, here's how you would express and define the six trigonometric functions sine, cosine, tangent, cotangent, secant, and cosecant for angle A (notice that the functions in the right column are reciprocals of the functions in the left column):

$\sin A = \frac{a}{c}$ $\quad \cot A = \frac{b}{a}$

$\cos A = \frac{b}{c}$ $\quad \sec A = \frac{c}{b}$

$\tan A = \frac{a}{b}$ $\quad \csc A = \frac{c}{a}$

The six functions for angle B would be expressed and defined similarly. The sine, cosine, and tangent functions are by far the most important, so be sure to memorize the following three general definitions (for the test, these three functions should be second-nature to you):

$$\text{sine} = \frac{\text{opposite}}{\text{hypotenuse}}$$

$$\text{cosine} = \frac{\text{adjacent}}{\text{hypotenuse}}$$

$$\text{tangent} = \frac{\text{opposite}}{\text{adjacent}}$$

You should also keep in mind the following identities (of the four, the first one will probably be the most useful for the ACT):

$$\text{tangent} = \frac{\text{sine}}{\text{cosine}}$$

$$\text{cotangent} = \frac{1}{\text{tangent}}$$

$$\text{cosecant} = \frac{1}{\text{sine}}$$

$$\text{secant} = \frac{1}{\text{cosine}}$$

The relationships among the sine, cosine, and tangent functions result in the following additional observations for a triangle with acute angles A and B:

- By definition, $\tan A \times \tan B = 1$.
- For all right triangles, $\sin A = \cos B$ (and $\sin B = \cos A$). For all other triangles, $\sin A \neq \cos B$ (and $\sin B \neq \cos A$).
- In a right isosceles triangle (in which A and B each measure 45°), $\sin A = \sin B = \cos A = \cos B = \frac{\sqrt{2}}{2}$.

The acute angles of the Pythagorean triplets 45°-45°-90° and 30°-60°-90° are especially test-worthy when it comes to right-triangle trigonometry questions. That's because the values of these angles' functions are easy to express using the theorem. For the ACT, you should memorize the sine, cosine, and tangent functions of the 30°, 45°, and 60° angles of a right triangle:

$$\sin 30° = \frac{1}{2} \qquad \sin 45° = \frac{\sqrt{2}}{2} \qquad \sin 60° = \frac{\sqrt{3}}{2}$$

$$\cos 30° = \frac{\sqrt{3}}{2} \qquad \cos 45° = \frac{\sqrt{2}}{2} \qquad \cos 60° = \frac{1}{2}$$

$$\tan 30° = \frac{\sqrt{3}}{3} \qquad \tan 45° = 1 \qquad \tan 60° = \sqrt{3}$$

X-REF **The trigonometric functions of 0° and 90° are also commonly tested on the ACT, but these two angles aren't relevant to right-angle trigonometry, which involves only the two acute angles (each of which must be greater than 0° but less than 90°). Where the angles 0° and 90° become significant is in *graphing* trigonometric functions—a topic for lesson 14.**

Easy ACT questions on the topic of right-angle trigonometry test you simply on the definitions of sine, cosine, and tangent. For instance, referring to the next figure, a question might provide the lengths of a right triangle's two legs and ask you for the sine, cosine, or tangent of angle x.

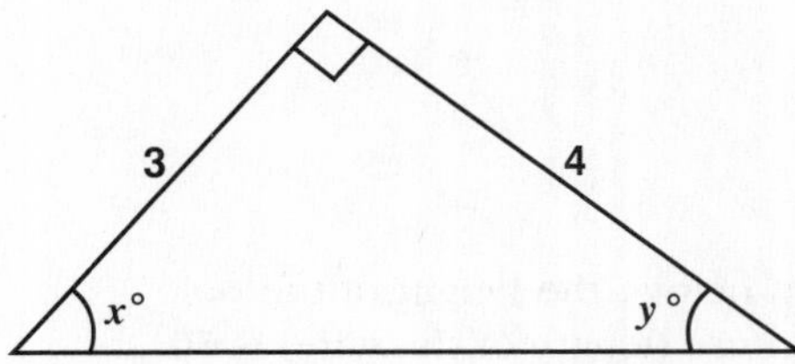

The value of $\tan x$ is clearly $\frac{4}{3}$. As for $\sin x$ and $\cos x$, you should recognize the Pythagorean side triplet 3:4:5 and, accordingly, that the length of the hypotenuse is 5. Hence, $\sin x = \frac{4}{5}$, $\cos x = \frac{3}{5}$.

To spice up "no-brainer" questions like these, the test-makers might use numbers that don't correspond neatly to a Pythagorean triplet, or they might ask you to combine two different functions by one of the four basic operations. For instance, referring again to the preceding figure:

$$(\tan x)(\tan y) = \left(\frac{3}{4}\right)\left(\frac{4}{3}\right) = 1$$

$$\sin x - \sin y = \frac{4}{5} - \frac{3}{5} = \frac{1}{5}$$

$$\cos x \div \cos y = \frac{3}{5} \div \frac{4}{5} = \frac{3}{4}$$

Many other combinations are possible, but they all involve a similar drill: determine two functions, and then combine them.

A slightly tougher question might test you on the tangent identity, which serves as a shortcut to the solution that otherwise might elude you:

Q If $\sin A = x$, which of the following expressions is equal to x at all points for which it is defined?

(A) $1 - \cos A$
(B) $(\cot A)(\cos A)$
(C) $(\tan A)(\cos A)$
(D) $\cos A - 1$
(E) $\sec A \div \tan A$

A **The correct answer is (C).** Applying the tangent identity $\tan A = \frac{\sin A}{\cos A}$ to choice (D):

$$(\tan A)(\cos A) = \left(\frac{\sin A}{\cos A}\right) = \sin A$$

A more complex question involving right-triangle trigonometry might provide one angle measure and one side length, then ask for another side length *in terms of* one of the trigonometry functions. These questions are often cast as word problems, as in this example:

Q A 50-foot wire is attached to the top of a vertical electric pole and is anchored on the ground. If the wire rises in a straight line at a 70°-angle from the ground, what is the height of the pole, in linear feet?

(A) $50\sin 70°$
(B) $50\cos 70°$
(C) $50\tan 70°$
(D) $\frac{\cos 70°}{50}$
(E) $\frac{50}{\cos 70°}$

A **The correct answer is (A).** As shown in the diagram below, the height of the pole (x) is opposite the 70° angle, and the triangle's hypotenuse (length of the wire) is 50. Since sine = opposite divided by hypotenuse:

$$\frac{x}{50} = \sin 70°$$
$$x = 50\sin 70°$$

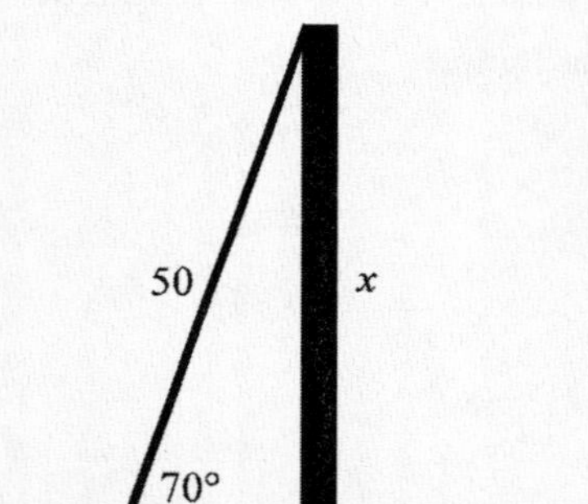

To further complicate this type of question and to reward ACT Brainiacs, the test-makers might require you to construct a right triangle from a *non*-right triangle, or they might require you to work with two separate triangles that share one common vertex. (Either scenario makes for the most complex type of right-triangle trigonometry question.) Here's an example that incorporates the first complication (during this lesson's Brain Teaser, you'll tackle one involving the second complication):

Q In the figure below, if m$\angle ABC$ = 130°, then what is the unit area of ΔABC?

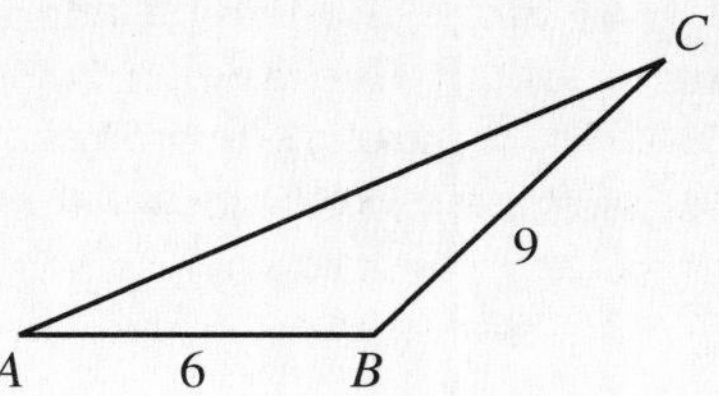

(A) 27sin50°
(B) 27cos50°
(C) $\frac{27}{\sin 50°}$
(D) 54cos50°
(E) 54sin50°

A **The correct answer is (A).** Dropping a perpendicular from C down to the extension of $\overline{AB}$ (see the diagram below), you can see that m$\angle CBD$ = 50°, and hence, that $\sin 50° = \frac{h}{9}$ (the triangle's altitude h divided by its hypotenuse). Thus, $h = 9\sin 50°$. Now that you know the base and height of ΔABC, you can determine its area: $\frac{1}{2}(6)(9\sin 50°) = 27\sin 50°$.

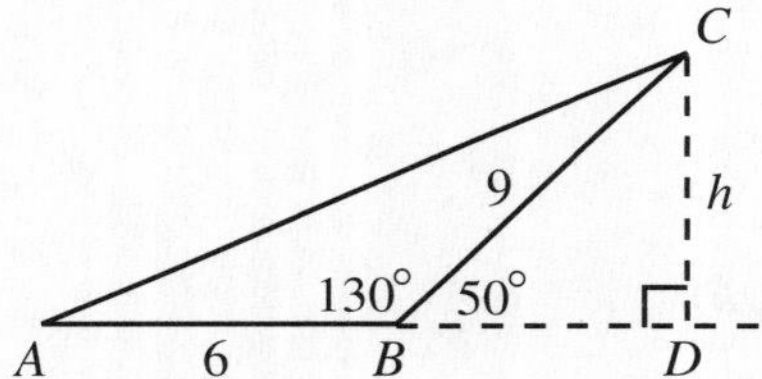

On the ACT, you won't find any trigonometric tables, which list angle measures and their corresponding trigonometry function values. Instead, you'll express solutions to problems like the two preceding ones *in terms of* trigonometric functions.

QUADRILATERALS (4-SIDED FIGURES)

For the ACT, you should be familiar with the following types of quadrilaterals:

- Squares
- Rectangles
- Trapezoids
- Parallelograms
- Rhombuses

The first two shapes—squares and rectangles—are easier to understand, so you'll review these briefly. The other three shapes make for trickier ACT questions, so you'll examine those in greater detail.

X-REF ***All* quadrilaterals share one important property: the sum of the measures of the four interior angles is 360°, exactly 180° more than for a triangle. And in a pentagon, the sum of the measures of all five angles is 540°, exactly 180° more than for a quadrilateral. Is there a pattern here? Yes, and you'll learn more about it in the next lesson when we cover general rules for polygons.**

RECTANGLES AND SQUARES

The following are the properties of rectangles and squares:

Characteristics of all rectangles (including squares):

1. Opposite sides are equal in length.
2. All four angles are right angles (90°).
3. The sum of the measures of all four angles is 360°.
4. Perimeter = $2l + 2w$
5. Area = $l \times w$

Characteristics of squares:

1. All four sides are equal in length.
2. All four angles are right angles (90°).
3. The sum of the measures of all four angles is 360°.
4. Perimeter = $4s$ [s = side]
5. Area = s^2

Most ACT test-takers will know these basic properties. But what many don't know is what happens when you add diagonals to a rectangle (and to a square). Referring to the next figure, diagonals create a whole slew of rules and relationships, any of which is fair game on the ACT:

1. Diagonals are equal in length ($AC = BD$).
2. Diagonals bisect each other ($AE = BE = CE = DE$).
3. Diagonals are perpendicular if (and only if) the rectangle is a square.
4. Diagonals bisect each 90° angle of the rectangle if (and only if) the rectangle is a square.
5. Diagonals create four distinct congruent triangles, each having an area one-half the area of the rectangle: ΔABD, ΔACD, ΔABC, and ΔBCD
6. $\Delta ABE \cong \Delta CDE$; both triangles are isosceles (but they are right triangles *only* if the rectangle is a square).
7. $\Delta BEC \cong \Delta AED$; both triangles are isosceles (but they are right triangles *only* if the rectangle is a square).

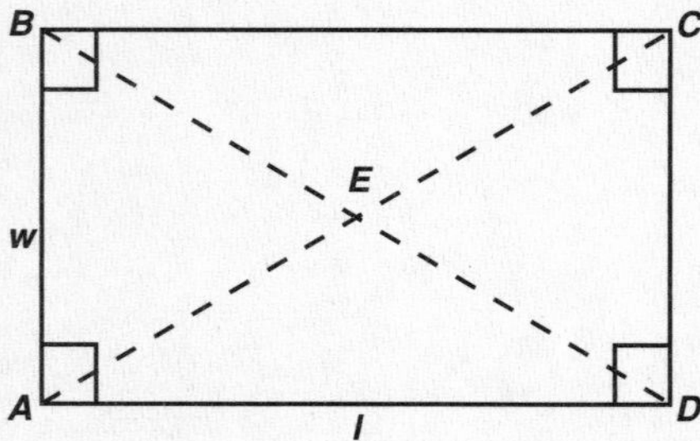

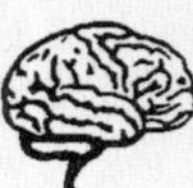

Hey Brainiacs, here are two lesser-known facts about rectangles and squares (both facts make for prime ACT fodder):

- **If, and only if, a rectangle is a square, you can divide the square of either diagonal by 2 to obtain the area of the square. (This quirk is the Pythagorean side triplet 1:1:$\sqrt{2}$ at work!)**
- **Adding diagonals to a rectangle (or any other quadrilateral) creates a total of 8 distinct triangles. (Go ahead and count them.)**

TRAPEZOIDS

This next figure shows a trapezoid. All trapezoids share these properties:

1. Only one pair of opposite sides is parallel ($\overline{BC} \parallel \overline{AD}$).
2. The sum of the measures of all four interior angles is 360°.
3. Perimeter = $AB + BC + CD + AD$.
4. Area = $\frac{BC + AD}{2} \times$ altitude (that is, one-half the sum of the two parallel sides multiplied by the altitude).

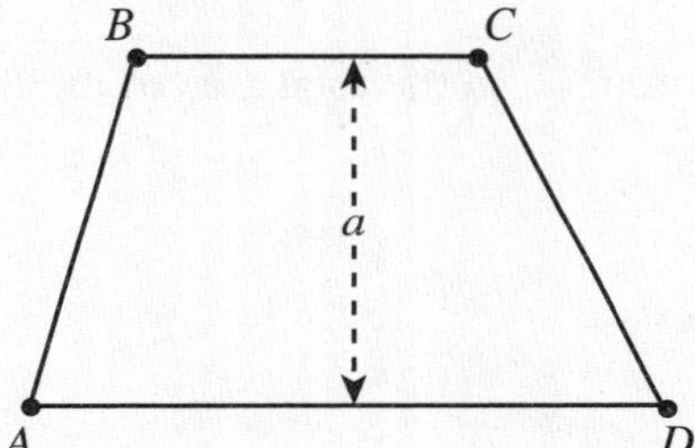

No predictable patterns emerge from the addition of two diagonals to a trapezoid.

On the ACT, a tough trapezoid problem might do either of the following:

- Require that you calculate the altitude using the Pythagorean theorem
- Cast the problem as a story

Here's an example that incorporates the latter feature (during this lesson's Brain Teaser, you'll try a trapezoid question that includes the first feature):

Q

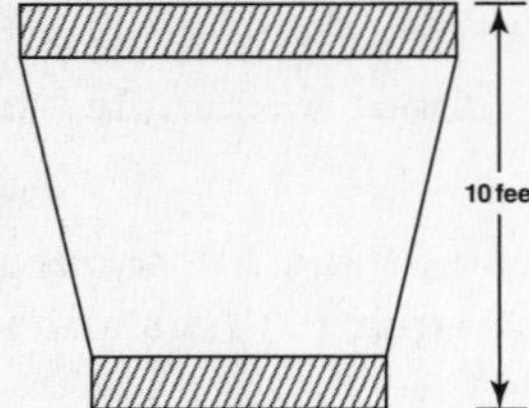

To cover the floor of an entry hall, a 1′ × 12′ strip of carpet is cut into two pieces, shown as the shaded strips in the figure above, and each piece is connected to a third carpet piece as shown. If the 1′ strips run parallel to each other, what is the total area of the carpeted floor, in square feet?

(A) 46
(B) 48
(C) 52.5
(D) 56
(E) 60

A

The correct answer is (E). The altitude of the trapezoidal piece is 8. The sum of the two parallel sides of this piece is 12' (the length of the 1′ × 12′ strip before it was cut). You can apply the trapezoid formula to determine the area of this piece:

$$A = 8 \times \frac{12}{2} = 48$$

The total area of the two shaded strips is 12 square feet, so the total area of the floor is 60 square feet.

PARALLELOGRAMS AND RHOMBUSES

All *parallelograms* (including rhombuses) share these properties:

1. Opposite sides are parallel.
2. Opposite sides are equal in length.
3. Opposite angles are congruent (equal in degree measure).
4. The sum of the measures of all four angles is 360°.
6. Perimeter = $2l + 2w$.
7. Area = base (b) × altitude (a).

A *rhombus* is a special type of parallelogram with these characteristics:

1. All four sides are equal in length.
2. Perimeter = $4s$.
3. Area = side (s) × altitude (a).
4. No angles are right angles (this is what distinguishes a rhombus from a square).

Technically, rhombuses and rectangles are special types of parallelograms. For the ACT, however, you don't need to know the definition of either one.

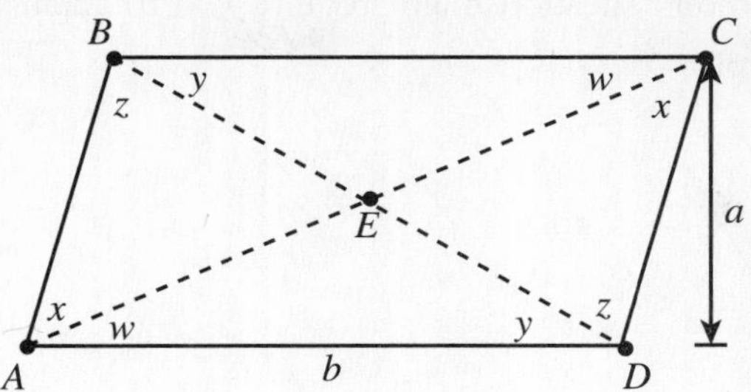

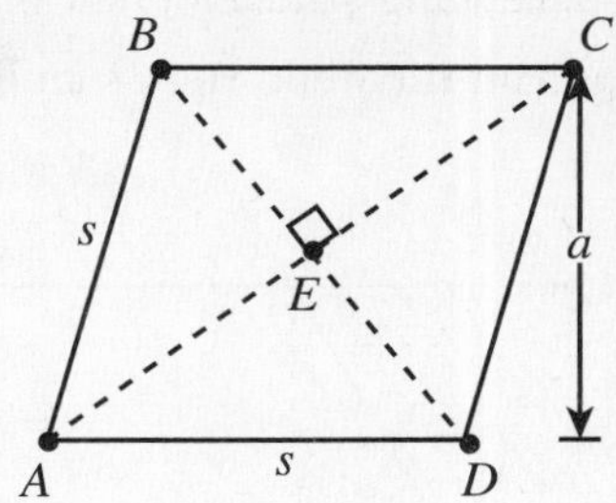

Referring to the preceding diagram, here's what happens when you add diagonals to a parallelogram (try to visualize the characteristics that apply only to certain types of parallelograms):

1. Diagonals bisect each other ($BE = ED$, $CE = AE$).
2. Diagonals ($\overline{AC}$ and $\overline{BD}$) are *not* equal in length (unless the parallelogram is a rectangle).
3. Diagonals are *not* perpendicular (unless the figure is a square or rhombus, in which case they are).
4. Diagonals do *not* bisect each angle of the parallelogram (unless it is a square or rhombus, in which case they do).
5. Diagonals create two pairs of congruent triangles, each having an area one-half the area of the parallelogram: ΔABD is congruent to ΔDBC, and ΔACD is congruent to ΔCAB.
6. ΔABE is congruent to ΔDCE (they are mirror-imaged horizontally *and* vertically); the triangles are isosceles only if the figure is a rectangle.
7. ΔBEC is congruent to ΔDEA (they are mirror-imaged horizontally *and* vertically); the triangles are isosceles only if the figure is a rectangle.

Adding diagonals to a rhombus creates these additional features (again, refer to the preceding diagram):

1. Area of the rhombus $= \frac{1}{2}(AC)(BD)$ (one-half the product of the diagonals).
2. Diagonals are perpendicular (their intersection creates four right angles).
3. Diagonals create two pairs of *congruent* (the same shape and size) *isosceles* triangles, each triangle having an area one-half the area of the rhombus (ΔABD is congruent to ΔBCD, and triangle ΔACD is congruent to ΔABC). None of these four triangles are right triangles (otherwise, the figure would be a square).
4. Triangle ΔABE is congruent to ΔCDE; both are right triangles (but not isosceles; otherwise, the figure would be a square).
5. Triangle ΔBEC is congruent to ΔDEA; both are right triangles (but not isosceles; otherwise, the figure would be a square).

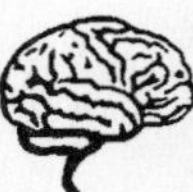

Feature 1 applies to squares as well as rhombuses (but not to any other type of quadrilateral). So, if you know the length of a square's diagonal, you can find the square's area using the rhombus-area formula. Since the diagonals of a square are congruent: the area of a square = $\left(\frac{1}{2}\right)$(diagonal)^2.

On the test, a challenging parallelogram or rhombus question might require you to calculate the figure's altitude using the Pythagorean theorem. Here's an example:

Q

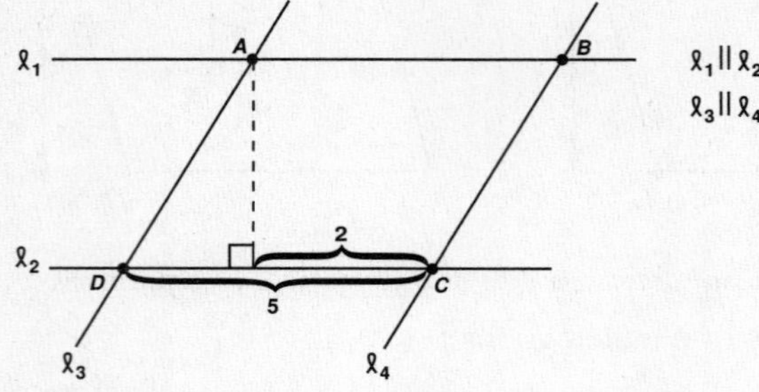

In the figure above, if the length of $\overline{AB}$ equals the length of $\overline{AD}$, what is the area of *ABCD*?

(A) 30
(B) 26
(C) 22.5
(D) 20
(E) 18

A **The correct answer is (D).** Given that opposite sides of *ABCD* are parallel, and that *AB* = *AD*, *ABCD* must be a rhombus in which each side = 5. The right triangle formed by the dotted line is the altitude of the rhombus. Its base is 3, and its hypotenuse (*AD*) is 5. Thus, it is a 3:4:5 triangle, and the altitude is 4. The area of rhombus *ABCD* = base × altitude = 4 × 5 = 20.

BRAIN TEASER

In this quiz, you'll attempt 10 tough ACT-style questions covering the topics from this lesson. Focus on applying the concepts and techniques you learned in this lesson, *not* on answering the questions as quickly as possible. Then read the explanations that follow the quiz, even for the questions you answered correctly.

QUIZ

1. In triangle ABC, $AB = BC$. If the degree measure of $\angle B$ is b, which of the following represents the degree measure of $\angle A$?

(A) b
(B) $180 - b$
(C) $180 - \frac{b}{2}$
(D) $90 - b$
(E) $90 - \frac{b}{2}$

2. A rancher uses 64 feet of fencing to create a rectangular horse corral. If the ratio of the corral's length to width is 3:1, which of the following most closely approximates the minimum length of additional fencing needed to divide the rectangular corral into three triangular corrals, one of which is exactly twice the area of the other two?

(F) 24 feet
(G) 29 feet
(H) 36 feet
(J) 41 feet
(K) 48 feet

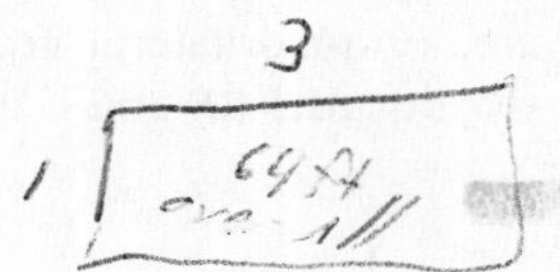

3. 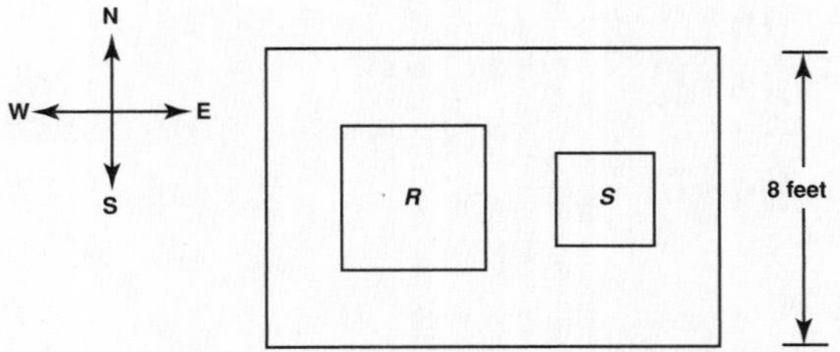

Two square rugs R and S of integral sidelength are placed on a floor whose area is 112 square feet, as shown above. Measured east to west, each rug is placed the same distance from the other rug as from the nearest east or west edge of the floor. If the area of rug R is four times the area of rug S, which of the following choices would be a possible distance for the rugs to be apart?

(A) 1 foot, 6 inches
(B) 2 feet
(C) 2 feet, 8 inches
(D) 3 feet
(E) 3 feet, 4 inches

4. A surveyor standing at a point 50 meters from the base of a vertical cliff measures the angle of elevation to the top as 40°. The surveyor then walks another M meters directly away from the cliff until the angle of elevation to the top is 20°. M is equal to?

(F) $50\tan 40° - 50\tan 20°$
(G) $\frac{50\tan 40° - 50\tan 20°}{\tan 40°}$
(H) $\frac{50\tan 20°}{\tan 40° - \tan 20°}$
(J) $\frac{50\tan 40° - 50\tan 20°}{\tan 20°}$
(K) $\frac{50\tan 40°}{\tan 40° - \tan 20°}$

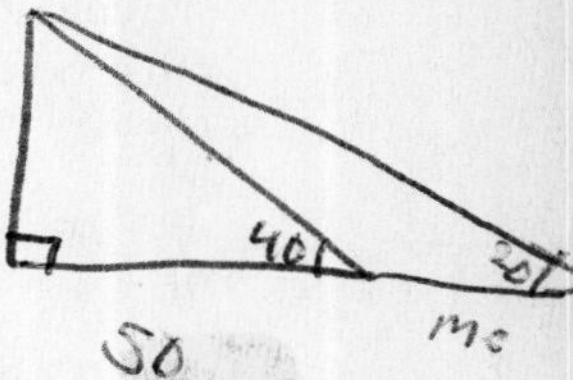

5. 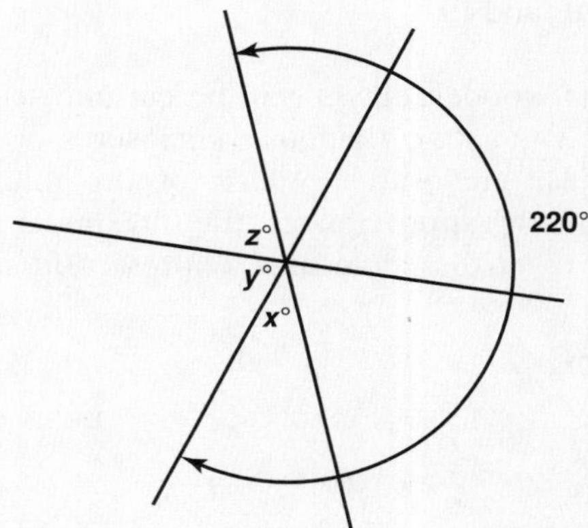

In the figure above, $x = ?$

(A) 50°
(B) 45°
(C) 40°
(D) 35°
(E) 30°

6. 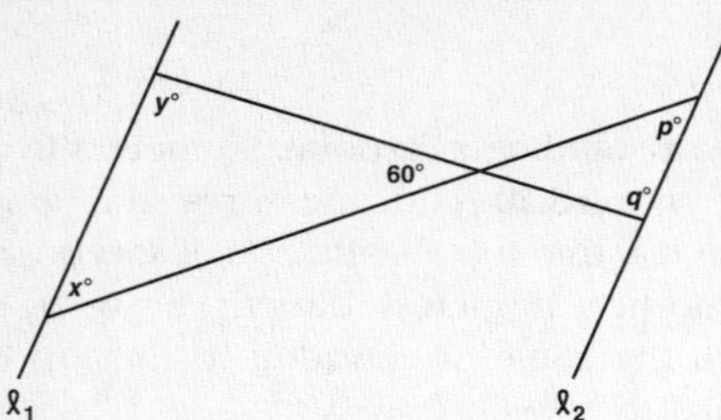

In the figure above, $l_1 \parallel l_2$. Which of the following statements about the degree measures in the figure must be true?

I. $x - y = p - q$
II. $x - y = q - p$
III. $x - q = y - p$

(F) I only
(G) II only
(H) I and II only
(J) II and III only
(K) I, II, and III

7. A 12-foot wooden dowel is to be cut into sections to form either two triangular enclosures or three rectangular enclosures. Which of the following most closely approximates the maximum combined area of the enclosures, expressed in square feet?

(A) 2.7
(B) 3
(C) 3.2
(D) 3.4
(E) 4.6

8. A parallelogram with adjacent sides measuring P and Q contains a 45° angle. Which of the following represents the area of the parallelogram?

(F) PQ
(G) $\frac{2PQ}{3}$
(H) $\frac{\sqrt{2}PQ}{2}$ 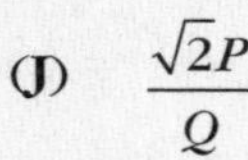
(J) $\frac{\sqrt{2}P}{Q}$
(K) $\frac{\sqrt{2}Q}{P}$

9. 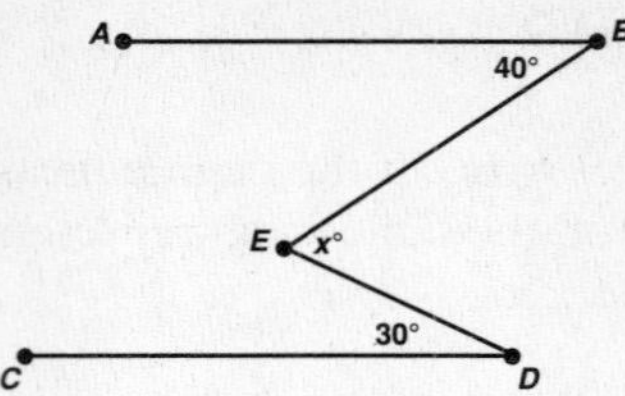

In the figure above, if $\overline{AB}$ is parallel to $\overline{CD}$, then x =?

(A) 80
(B) 75
(C) 70
(D) 65
(E) 60

10. 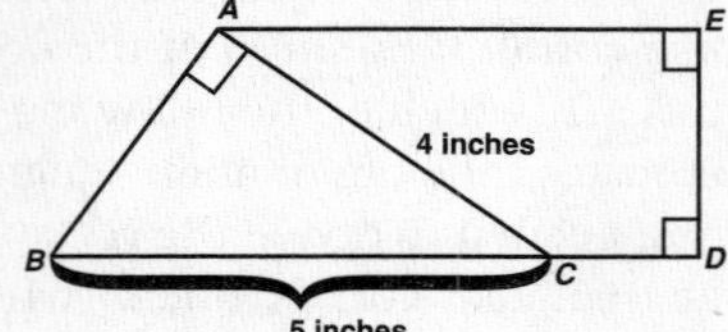

In the figure above, the area of ΔABC equals the area of quadrilateral $ACDE$. What is the sum of the two lengths AE and CD, in inches?

(F) 5
(G) $\frac{11}{2}$
(H) 6
(J) $\frac{13}{2}$
(K) 7

ANSWERS AND EXPLANATIONS

1. **The correct answer is (E).** The triangle is isosceles, so m∠*A* = m∠*C*. Letting *a*, *b*, and *c* represent the degree measures of ∠*A*, ∠*B*, and ∠*C*, respectively, solve for *a*:

$$a + b + c = 180$$
$$2a + b = 180 \; [a = c]$$
$$2a = \frac{180}{2} - \frac{b}{2}$$
$$a = 90 - \frac{b}{2}$$

2. **The correct answer is (G).** Your first step is to determine the dimensions of the rectangular corral. Given a 3:1 length-to-width ratio, you can solve for the width (*w*) of the field using the perimeter formula:

$$2(3w) + 2(w) = 64$$
$$8w = 64$$
$$w = 8$$

Accordingly, the length of the rectangular corral is 24 feet. Next, determine how the rancher must configure the additional fencing to meet the stated criteria. This requires a bit of visualization and logical reasoning. Only two possible configurations create three triangular corrals with the desired ratios:

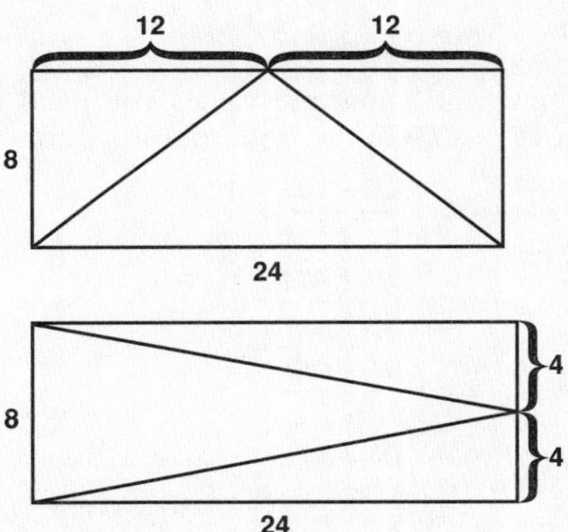

The top figure requires less fencing. You can determine this fact by calculating each length (using the Pythagorean theorem). Or you can also use logic and visualization: As a rectangle becomes flatter ("less square"), the shorter length approaches zero (0), at which point the minimum amount of fencing needed in the top configuration would decrease, approaching the length of the longer side. However, in the bottom design, the amount of fencing needed would increase, approaching twice the length of the longer side.

Your final step is to calculate the amount of fencing required by the top design, applying the theorem (let x = either length of cross-fencing):

$$8^2 + 12^2 = x^2$$
$$64 + 144 = x^2$$
$$208 = x^2$$
$$x = \sqrt{208} \approx 14.4$$

Thus, a minimum of approximately 28.8 feet of fencing is needed. Choice (G) approximates this solution.

You can use a calculator to find $\sqrt{208}$. However, since the question asks for an approximation, it's a safe bet that estimating $\sqrt{208}$ to the nearest integer will suffice. If you learned your "times tables," you know that 14 × 14 = 196, and 15 × 15 = 225. So $\sqrt{208}$ must be between 14 and 15. That's close enough to focus in on (G), which provides twice that estimate, as the best answer choice.

3. **The correct answer is (C).** Rug R must be 4′ × 4′, and rug S must be 2′ × 2′. Though the rugs could be different sizes, this is the only possible size given as an answer choice. Also, since the floor's area is 112 and its length is 8, the floor's width = 14, which in turn equals the sum of the following five lengths (let x = the distance between the two rugs, as well as from each rug to the nearest east or west edge):

$$x + 4 + x + 2 + x = 14$$
$$3x = 8$$
$$x = \frac{8}{3}$$
$$= 2\frac{2}{3} \text{ feet, or 2 feet, 8 inches}$$

4. **The correct answer is (J).** Calling the height of the cliff h and illustrating the scenario with the diagram below, you can see that $\Delta BCD \; \frac{h}{50} = \tan 40°$; that is, $h = 50\tan 40°$. Then, in ΔACD, you can see that $\frac{h}{50 + M} = \tan 20°$; that is, $h = 50\tan 20° + M\tan 20°$.

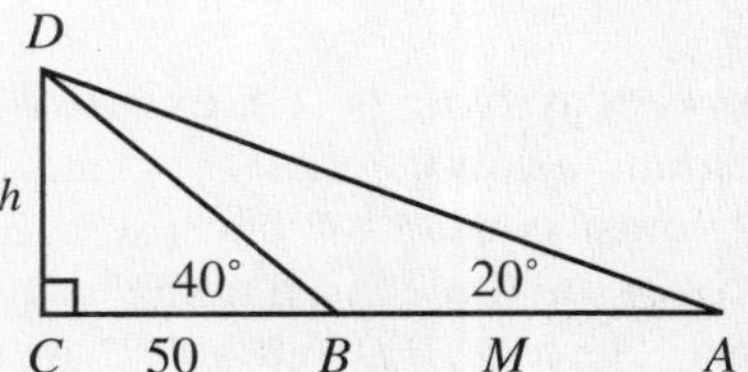

Equating the two expressions, since both are equal to h: 50tan40° = 50tan20° + Mtan20°. Solving for M results in the expression given by choice (J).

5. **The correct answer is (C).** The sum of the measures of all six angles formed by the intersecting lines in the figure is 360°. Given that the sum of all angles other than y and z is 220°, $y + z$ must equal 140 (360 − 220). Since angles x, y, and z form a straight line (180°), x must equal 40°.

6. **The correct answer is (F).** Because the two lines are parallel, the two triangles are the same shape, and their corresponding angles are congruent ($x = p$ and $y = q$), and therefore $x - y = p - q$. However, the quantity $x - y$ is being compared here to $q - p$, not $p - q$. The two quantities are equal in size only if all four angles are equal (60°). It is not possible to determine whether all four angles are the same size, regardless of the fact that the third angle of each triangle is 60°. Hence, neither statement (II) nor (III), which are different forms of the same equation, need be true.

7. **The correct answer is (D).** A triangle with a fixed perimeter has maximum area if the triangle is equilateral. Similarly, a rectangle with fixed perimeter has maximum area if the rectangle is a square. In either case, the sections must all be equal in length. Each side of each of the two triangles would have a length of 2 inches. Applying the area formula for equilateral triangles, the area of each triangle is $\frac{2^2\sqrt{3}}{4} = \sqrt{3}$, and the total area for both triangles is $2\sqrt{3}$, or about 3.4 inches (using 1.7 as an approximate value for $\sqrt{3}$). Given a dowel length of 12 and 12 sides for three squares, the length of each side of each square $= \frac{12}{12} = 1$. Accordingly, the area of each square would be 1 square inch, and the total area of all three squares would be 3 square inches. (Hence, the combined area of the enclosures is maximized with three equilateral triangles.)

8. **The correct answer is (H).** Drawing an altitude from any side forms a 45°-45°-90° right triangle in which the altitude is $\frac{\sqrt{2}P}{2}$ or $\frac{\sqrt{2}Q}{2}$, depending on which length (P or Q) is the hypotenuse. To find the parallelogram's area, multiply the altitude by the other length (either Q or P). In either case, the product is $\frac{\sqrt{2}PQ}{2}$.

9. **The correct answer is (C).** Extend BE to F (as in the diagram below). $m\angle EFD = m\angle ABE = 40°$. $m\angle FED$ must equal 110° because the sum of the measures of the three interior angles of ΔDEF must total 180°. Since $\angle BED$ and $\angle FED$ are supplementary (the sum of their measures is 180°), $m\angle BED = 70°$ ($x = 70$).

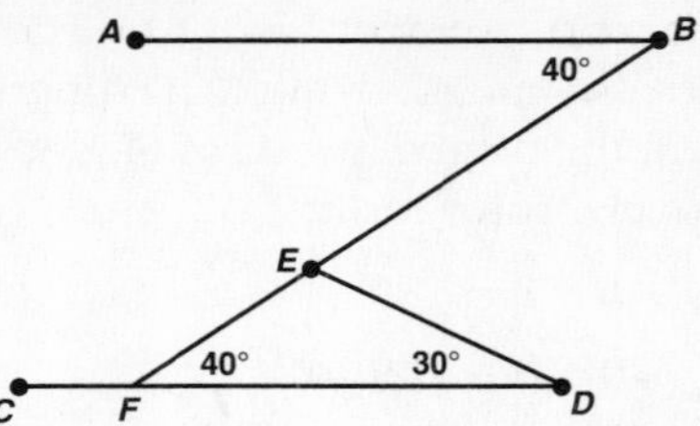

10. **The correct answer is (F).** $ACDE$ is a trapezoid. The question asks for one of the terms in the area formula for a trapezoid:

$$\text{Area} = \frac{AE + CD}{2} \times ED$$

To solve for ($AE + CD$), you need to know the area of $ACDE$ and the length of ED. Since the area of $ACDE$ equals that of ΔABC, first find the area of ΔABC. The 3:4:5 Pythagorean side triplet makes the calculation easy ($AB = 3$): $A = \frac{1}{2}(3)(4) = 6$. Thus, the area of trapezoid $ACDE = 6$.

Next, find ED by calculating the altitude (a) of ΔABC, using BC as the triangle's base (b):

$$A = \frac{1}{2}(b)(a)$$

$$6 = \frac{1}{2}(5)(a)$$

$$a = \frac{12}{5}$$

Now you know the values you need to solve for ($AE + CD$) in the trapezoid-area formula:

$$6 = \frac{AE + CD}{2} \times \frac{12}{5}$$

$$6 = \frac{AE + CD}{1} \times \frac{6}{5}$$

$$1 = \frac{AE + CD}{5}$$

$$5 = AE + CD$$

What if the question had asked for the length of either $\overline{AE}$ or $\overline{CD}$ (rather than the sum)? Could you find either of those two values? A true Brainiac could! Draw an altitude $\overline{AF}$ up from point C to $\overline{AE}$ $\left(\frac{12}{5}\right)$, creating right triangle ACF and rectangle $CDEF$. Solve for length AF using the Pythagorean theorem, and then subtract length AF from ($AE + CD$)—which you already know equals 5—to find the length of $\overline{CD}$ (or EF).

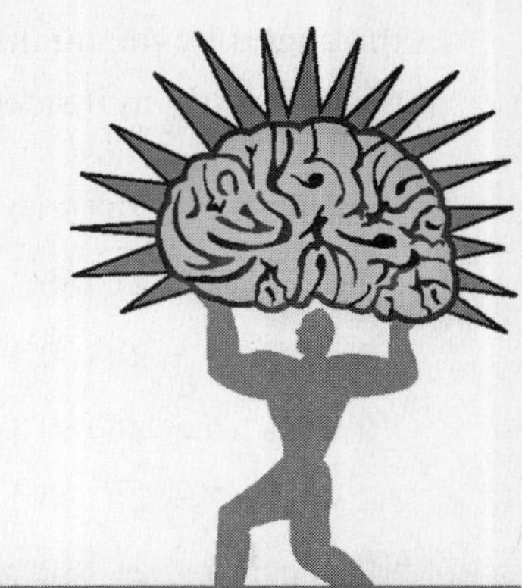

LESSON 13

Advanced Plane Geometry

In this geometry lesson, you'll learn how the test-makers design tough questions covering:

- The properties of polygons (including those with more than four sides)
- The properties of a circle
- Relationships created by combining a circle with another geometry figure (such as a triangle, square, or another circle)
- Properties of certain three-dimensional figures (rectangular solids and right cylinders)

Most of what you'll encounter in this lesson builds on concepts covered in the previous one and, therefore, is inherently more advanced. Even if you're an ultra-Brainiac, expect to be challenged by this lesson's examples and Brain Teaser questions.

POLYGONS

Polygons include all plane figures formed only by straight lines. During the previous lesson, you focused on only two types of polygons: three-sided (triangles) and four-sided (quadrilaterals). Now, take a quick look at the key characteristics of all polygons.

A polygon in which all sides are congruent and all angles are congruent is called a *regular* polygon. But for the ACT, you don't need to know the terminology—just the principle.

You can use the following formula to determine the sum of the measures of all the interior angles of *any* polygon whose angles each measure less than 180° (n = number of sides):

$(n - 2)(180°)$ = sum of the measures of the interior angles

For *regular* polygons, the average angle measure is also the measure of every angle. But for *any* polygon (except for those with an angle exceeding 180°), you can find the average angle measure by dividing the sum of the measures of the angles by the number of sides. One way to shortcut the math is to memorize the angle sums and averages for polygons with 3 to 8 sides:

3 sides: $(3 - 2)(180°) = 180° \div 3 = 60°$

4 sides: $(4 - 2)(180°) = 360° \div 4 = 90°$

5 sides: $(5 - 2)(180°) = 540° \div 5 = 108°$

6 sides: $(6 - 2)(180°) = 720° \div 6 = 120°$

7 sides: $(7 - 2)(180°) = 900° \div 7 \approx 129°$

8 sides: $(8 - 2)(180°) = 1{,}080° \div 8 = 135°$

X-REF **On the ACT, if you encounter a polygon with five or more sides, it'll probably either circumscribe or be circumscribed by a circle. You'll see example questions of this type during this lesson's Brain Teaser.**

CIRCLES

For the ACT, you'll need to know the following basic terminology involving circles:

Circumference
the distance around the circle (its *perimeter*)

Radius
the distance from a circle's center to any point on the circle's circumference

Diameter
the greatest distance from one point to another on the circle's circumference (twice the length of the radius)

Chord
a line segment connecting two points on the circle's circumference (a circle's longest possible chord is its diameter, passing through the circle's center)

Arc
a segment of a circle's circumference (an arc can be defined as either a length or a degree measure)

Minor arc
the shortest arc connecting two points on a circle's circumference

You'll also need to apply the two basic formulas involving circles:

Circumference $= 2\pi r$, or πd

Area $= \pi r^2$

With the two formulas, all you need is one value—area, circumference, diameter, or radius— and you can determine all the others.

The value of π is approximately 3.14, or $\frac{22}{7}$. For the test, you won't need to work with a value for π any more precise than that. In fact, in most circle problems, the solution is expressed in terms of π rather than numerically.

ACT circle problems almost always involve other geometric figures as well, so they're inherently more difficult than average. The most common such "hybrids" involve triangles, squares, and other circles. In the following sections, you'll learn all you need to know to handle any hybrid problem.

TRIANGLES INSIDE CIRCLES

On the ACT, look for any of the following three "special" varieties of triangles inside circles:

1. A *right* triangle with the 90°-angle at the circle's center and the other two vertices on the circle's circumference. (ΔABO in the figure below). Given either that $m\angle AOB = 90°$ or that $AB = r\sqrt{2}$, here's what else you know about ΔABO (r = radius):

   $AO = r$, and $OB = r$ ($\overline{OA}$ and $\overline{OB}$ are each congruent to the circle's radius)

   $AO = OB$ (ΔABO is a right isosceles triangle)

   $\angle OAB = m\angle OBA = 45°$

   $AB = r\sqrt{2}$ (the ratio of the triangle's sides is $1:1:\sqrt{2}$)

   Area of $\Delta ABO = \frac{r^2}{2}$

2. An *equilateral* triangle with one vertex at the circle's center and the other two on the circumference (ΔODC in the figure below). Given either that $m\angle DOC = 60°$ or that $DC = r$, you know that ΔODC is equilateral ($OD = OC = DC = r$, all angles measure 60°).

3. A triangle *inscribed* inside a circle (all three vertices lie on the circle's circumference), where one of the triangle's sides is the circle's diameter (ΔFGH in the figure below). ΔFGH must be a right triangle (it must include one 90°-angle)—regardless of where point G lies on the circle's circumference. (If you don't believe it, go ahead and draw some more triangles, moving G around the circumference.)

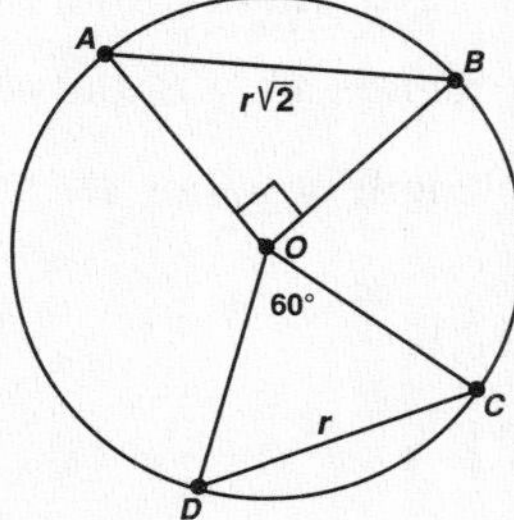

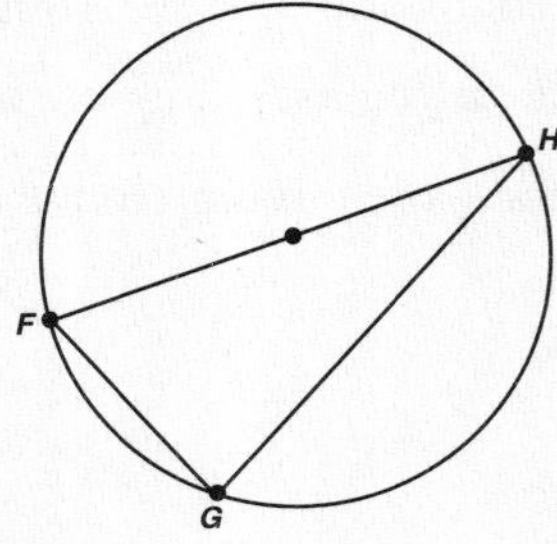

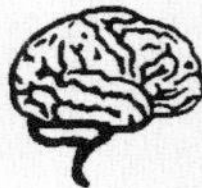

The length of an arc relative to the circle's circumference is directly proportionate to the arc's degree measure as a fraction of the circle's total degree measure of 360°. This makes sense, since an arc and its opposite angle each establish how big a "slice" of the circle you're dealing with. For example, in the preceding figure, minor arcs *AB* and *CD* measure $\frac{90}{360}$ and $\frac{60}{360}$ (or $\frac{1}{4}$ and $\frac{1}{6}$) the circle's circumference, respectively.

On the ACT, a challenging circle-triangle question might require you to do either of the following:

- Measure or compare arcs created by one or more triangles inside a circle
- Visualize a triangle as it changes shape inside the circle

Here's a difficult question involving the first complication (you'll get to try an example of the second one in this lesson's Brain Teaser):

Q

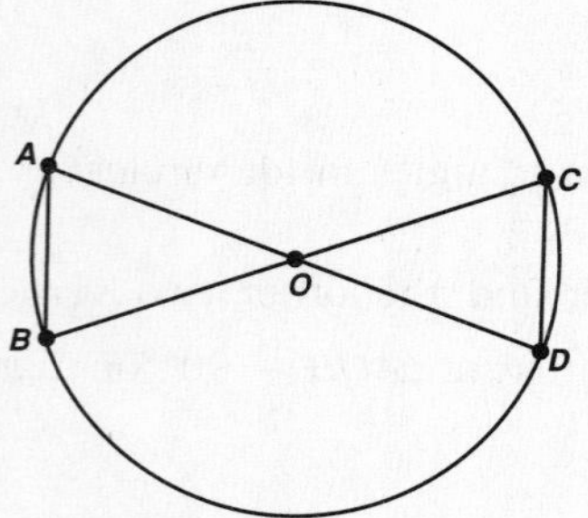

In the circle above, whose center is point O, $m\angle AOB = 40°$. If the circle's circumference is 9, what is the length of minor arc $\overset{\frown}{BD}$?

(A) 4

(B) $\frac{11}{3}$

(C) $\frac{7}{2}$

(D) $\frac{13}{4}$

(E) 3

A

The correct answer is (C). $\angle AOB$ (which measures 40°) accounts for $\frac{1}{9}$ of the circle's entire 360°. Accordingly, minor arc $\overset{\frown}{AB}$ accounts for $\frac{1}{9}$ of the circle's circumference of 9. Hence, the length of minor arc $\overset{\frown}{AB}$ is 1. (Remember: Angles from a circle's center are proportional to the arcs they create.) Since minor arc $\overset{\frown}{AB}$ and minor arc BD together account for $\frac{1}{2}$ the circumference of 9, the length of minor arc $\overset{\frown}{BD}$ is $\frac{9}{2} - 1 = \frac{7}{2}$.

SQUARES INSIDE CIRCLES (AND VICE VERSA)

On the ACT, watch out for either of two circle-square scenarios:

- A circle with an *inscribed* square, in which each vertex of the square lies along the circle's circumference (as in the left-hand figure below)
- A circle with a *circumscribed* square, in which the circle is tangent to all sides of the square (as in the right-hand figure below)

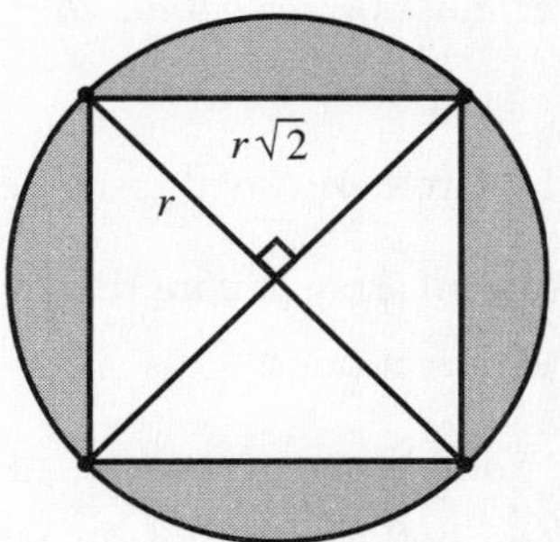

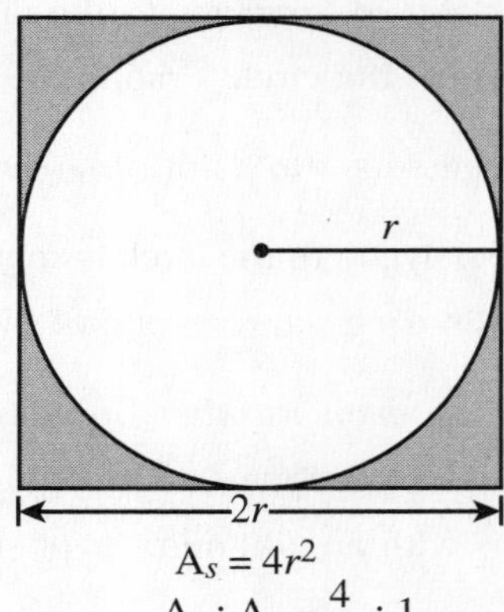

$A_s = 2r^2$
$A_s : A_c = 2 : \pi$

$A_s = 4r^2$
$A_s : A_c = \frac{4}{\pi} : 1$

In either case, the square touches the circle at four and only four points. Here are the characteristics you should recognize in these two figures:

In the left-hand figure:

- The four smallest triangles formed by the diagonals are each a 1:1: $\sqrt{2}$ triangle.
- In each of the four smallest triangles, the ratio of the hypotenuse (same as the side of the square) to the legs (same as circle's radius) is $\sqrt{2}$: 1.
- The area of the square inscribed in the circle is $\left(r\sqrt{2}\right)^2$, or $2r^2$.
- The ratio of the inscribed square's area to the circle's area is 2:π.
- The *difference* between the two areas—the total shaded area—is $\pi r^2 - 2r^2$.
- The area of each crescent-shaped shaded area is $\frac{1}{4}(\pi r^2 - 2r^2)$.

In the right-hand figure:

- Each side of the square is $2r$ in length.
- The square's area is $(2r)^2$, or $4r^2$.
- The ratio of the square's area to that of the inscribed circle is $\frac{4}{\pi}$:1.
- The *difference* between the two areas—the total shaded area—is $4r^2 - \pi r^2$, or $r^2(4 - \pi)$.
- The area of each separate (smaller) shaded area is $\frac{1}{4}r^2(4-\pi)$.

X-REF **In this lesson's Brain Teaser, you'll tackle a question involving a circle circumscribed by a square.**

CIRCLES CIRCUMSCRIBED BY REGULAR POLYGONS

A circle circumscribed by *any regular* polygon (a polygon in which all sides are congruent) creates certain relationships (the next two figures will help you visualize them):

- A line segment connecting any *point of tangency* to the circle's center must be *perpendicular* to the line. (The line segment's length will equal the circle's radius, of course.)
- For each of the polygon's line segments, the point of tangency with the circle *bisects* the segment.
- If you *connect each vertex* of the polygon to the circle's center, you create an array of congruent angles, arcs, and triangles. The shaded region in each figure is one of five (or six) identical ones.
- For triangles and polygons with an *even number of sides*, any line running perpendicular to a point of tangency bisects the opposite angle, as shown in the right-hand diagram below. (Except for triangles, this rule does NOT apply to polygons with an odd number of sides.)

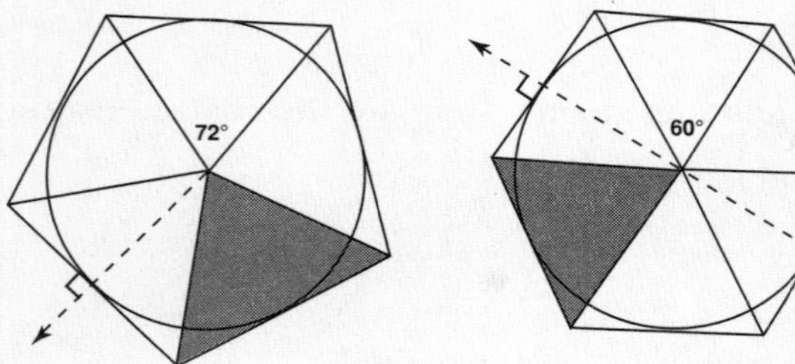

(In this lesson's Brain Teaser, you'll tackle a question involving a circle circumscribed by a hexagon.)

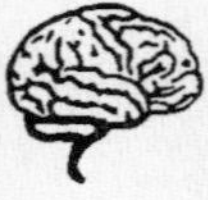

If a circle is circumscribed by a triangle (all sides are tangent to the circumference), the triangle must be isosceles, but not necessarily equilateral. But no quirky fact like this one applies to any polygon with four or more sides. (If you don't believe it, try drawing some figures of your own.)

CONCENTRIC CIRCLES

When you talk about *concentric* circles, you're talking about a "bulls-eye"—a circle inside another circle, both with the same center. On the ACT, most bulls-eye questions come in two varieties. You must do either of the following:

- Calculate the *differences* between radii, circumferences, or areas
- Determine *ratios* involving the two circles and their radii, circumferences, and areas

To calculate a *difference* between the radii, circumferences, or areas, just calculate each area or circumference, and then subtract. And if the question asks you for a difference between proportionate *segments* of the two circles, first find the difference between the circular areas, then calculate the fractional portion. No sweat, right?

A more complex ACT bulls-eye question might ask you to determine the ratio of the smaller circle's radius (or circumference or area) to the larger circle's radius (or circumference or area). To handle the question, you need to understand that the relationship between a circle's radius or circumference and its area is *exponential*, not linear (because $A = \pi r^2$). For example, if one circle's radius is *twice* that of another, the ratio of the circles' areas is 1:4 ($\pi r^2 : \pi(2r)^2$). If the larger circle's radius is *three* times that of the smaller circle (as in the bulls-eye below), the ratio is 1:9 [$\pi r^2 : \pi(3r)^2$]. A 1:4 ratio between radii results in a 1:16 area ratio (and so forth).

The same proportions apply if you compare circumferences and areas. If the circumference ratio is 2:1, then the area ratio is 4:1. If the circumference ratio is 4:1, then the area ratio is 16:1.

Here's how a tough ACT question might test you on these concepts:

Q

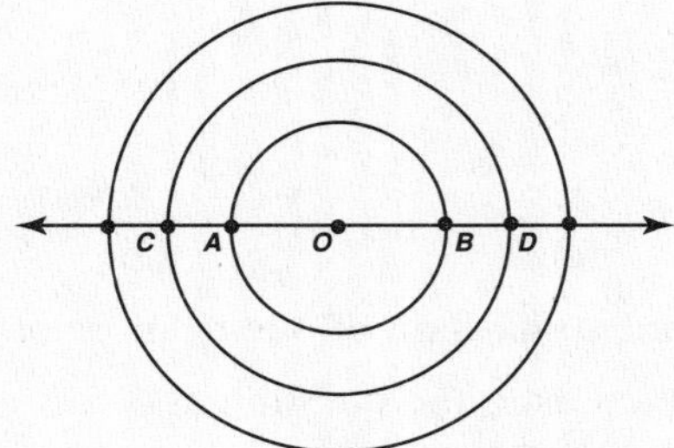

In the figure above, which contains three circles having the same center (*O*), $AB = \frac{CD}{3}$. If the largest circle's area is 16 times greater than the smallest circle's area, what is the middle-sized circle's area as a portion of the largest circle's area?

(A) $\frac{3}{8}$

(B) $\frac{7}{16}$

(C) $\frac{1}{2}$

(D) $\frac{9}{16}$

(E) $\frac{5}{8}$

A

The correct answer is (B). Since the ratio between the area of the largest and smallest circles is 16:1, the ratio between their radii is 4:1. (Remember, the relationship is exponential.) The ratio between the radii of the two smaller circles is 3:1, so the ratio between their areas is 9:1. You now know the ratios among all three circles:

Radii: 1:3:4
Areas: 1:9:16

Since the area of the middle-sized circle is $\frac{9}{16}$ that of the largest circle, to answer the question, subtract $\frac{9}{16}$ from 1.

CUBES AND OTHER RECTANGULAR SOLIDS

ACT questions involving *rectangular solids* always involve one or both of two basic formulas (l = length, w = width, h = height):

Volume = lwh

Surface Area = $2lw + 2wh + 2lw = 2(lw + wh + lh)$

For *cubes*, the volume and surface-area formulas are even simpler than for other rectangular solids (let s = any edge):

Volume = s^3, or $s = \sqrt[3]{\text{Volume}}$

Surface Area = $6s^2$

But the corollaries of these cube formulas are a bit trickier (pay close attention to them):

$$\text{Volume} = \left(\sqrt{\frac{\text{Surface Area}}{6}}\right)^3$$

$$\text{Surface Area} = \left(\sqrt[3]{\text{Volume}}\right)^2$$

An easier rectangular-solid question will involve a straightforward application of one or more of the formulas. Plug what you know into the formula, then solve for whatever characteristic the question asks for. And if the question requires you to deal with both formulas (surface area and volume), set up a system of two equations in two variables using the formulas, then solve for the unknown variable. No big deal.

A more complex rectangular-solid question might fall into one of these two categories:

- *Ratio* questions, which involve the ratios among the linear, square, and cubic measurements of one or more rectangular solids
- *"Packing"* questions, in which you determine how many smaller "boxes" fit into a large container and/or how to arrange the boxes (these questions usually require calculations as well as visualization)

Here's an example of the first type (you'll find a "packing" question in this lesson's Brain Teaser):

Q If the volume of one cube is 8 times greater than that of another, what is the ratio of the area of one square face of the larger cube to that of the smaller cube?

(A) 16 : 1
(B) 12 : 1
(C) 8 : 1
(D) 4 : 1
(E) 2 : 1

A **The correct answer is (D).** The ratio of the two volumes is 8:1. Thus, the linear ratio of the cubes' edges is the cube root of this ratio, or 2:1. The area ratio is the square of the linear ratio, or 4:1.

CYLINDERS

The only kind of cylinder covered on the ACT is a *right* circular cylinder (a tube sliced at 90° angles). The *surface area* of a right cylinder is the sum of the areas of:

1. The circular base
2. The circular top
3. The rectangular surface around the cylinder's vertical face (visualize a rectangular label wrapped around a soup can)

The area of the vertical face is the product of the circular base's circumference (i.e., the rectangle's width) and the cylinder's height. Thus, given a radius r and height h of a cylinder:

Surface Area (SA) $= 2\pi r^2 + (2\pi r)(h)$

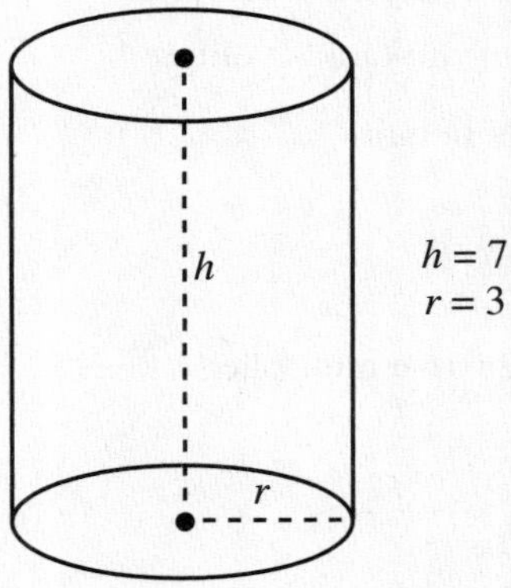

$h = 7$
$r = 3$

Given a cylinder's radius and height, you can determine its *volume* by multiplying the area of its circular base by its height:

Volume $= \pi r^2 h$

On the ACT, an easy cylinder question will require little more than the straightforward application of the formula for either surface area or volume. As with rectangular-solid questions, just plug what you know into the formula, then solve for what the question asks for. A tougher cylinder problem might involve one or more of the following:

- Both formulas (surface area and volume)
- Unit conversions
- Additional math skills and concepts

Here's a challenging cylinder problem that involves not only a unit conversion, but also the concept of proportion:

Q One hose dispenses water at the rate of one gallon per minute, and a second hose dispenses water at the rate of $1\frac{1}{2}$ gallons per minute. At the same time, the two hoses begin filling a cylindrical tank which is 14 inches in diameter and has a height of 10 inches. Which of the following most closely approximates the water level, measured in inches up from the tank's circular base, after $1\frac{1}{2}$ minutes? [231 cubic inches = 1 gallon]

(A) 3.5
(B) 4.2
(C) 4.8
(D) 5.6
(E) 6.7

A **The correct answer is (D).** After $1\frac{1}{2}$ minutes, the two hoses have dispensed a total of 3.75 gallons. Set up a proportion in which 3.75, as a portion of the tank's volume equals the water level after $1\frac{1}{2}$ minutes, as a portion of the tank's height:

$$\frac{3.75}{V} = \frac{x}{10}$$

The *volume* of the cylindrical pail is equal to the area of its circular base multiplied by its height:

$$V = \pi r^2 h = \frac{22}{7}(49)(10) = 1{,}540 \text{ cubic inches}$$

The *gallon* capacity of the pail = 1,540 ÷ 231, or about 6.7. Plug this value into the proportion. Then, solve for x:

$$\frac{3.75}{6.7} = \frac{x}{10}$$

$$6.7x = 37.5$$

$$x = 5.6$$

BRAIN TEASER

In this quiz, you'll attempt ten tough ACT-style questions covering the topics from this lesson. Focus on applying the concepts and techniques you learned in this lesson, *not* on answering the questions as quickly as possible. Then, read the explanations that follow the quiz, even for the questions you answered correctly.

QUIZ

1. 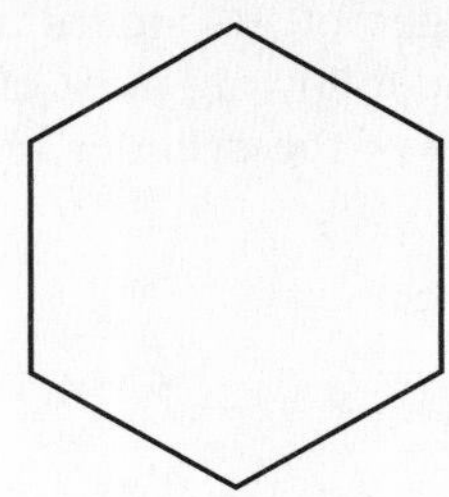

If each side of the hexagon shown above is one meter in length, what is the area of the hexagon?

(A) $\frac{2\sqrt{3}}{3}$
(B) $\sqrt{3}$
(C) $\frac{3\sqrt{3}}{2}$
(D) $2\sqrt{2} + 1$
(E) 4

2. 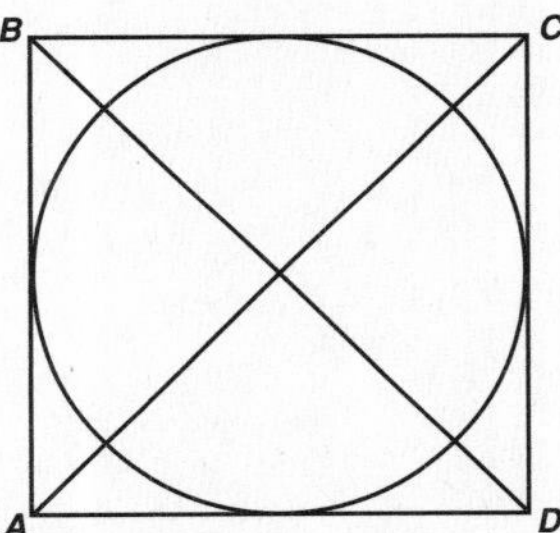

If the circumference of the circle shown above is 16π, and if AC equals BD in length, what is the length of AC?

(F) 12
(G) $8\sqrt{2}$
(H) 16
(J) $12\sqrt{3}$
(K) $16\sqrt{2}$

3. If all three vertices of a triangle lie along a circle's circumference, and if one of the triangle's sides is equal in length to the circle's diameter, what is the largest possible perimeter of the triangle, in terms of the circle's diameter (d)?

(A) $\frac{4}{3}d$
(B) $\frac{\pi d}{2}$
(C) $d\sqrt{2} + d$
(D) $d + \frac{2\sqrt{3}}{d}$
(E) $d(d + \sqrt{3})$

4. If the diameter of a circle increases by 50%, which of the following statements is true?

I. The circle's circumference increases by 50%.
II. The circle's radius increases by 100%.
III. The circle's area increases by 150%.

(F) I only
(G) II only
(H) I and II only
(J) I and III only
(K) I, II, and III

5. 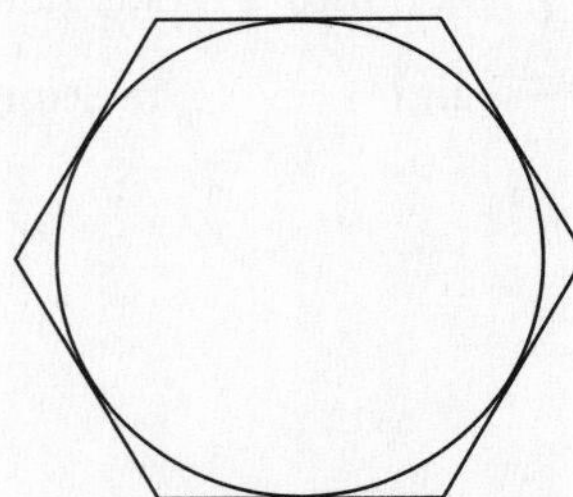

A circle is circumscribed by a hexagon whose sides are all equal in length, as shown above. If the area of the circle is 3π, what is the area of the hexagon?

(A) $2\pi\sqrt{2}$
(B) $6\sqrt{3}$
(C) $\frac{11}{3}\pi$
(D) $9\sqrt{2}$
(E) $\frac{9}{2}\pi$

6.

In the figure above, the centers of all three circles lie on the same line. The radius of the middle-sized circle is twice that of the smallest circle. If the radius of the smallest circle is 1, what is the length of the boundary of the shaded region?

(F) 9
(G) 3π
(H) 12
(J) 6π
(K) 12π

7. If a circle with a radius of x has an area of 4, what is the area of a circle with a radius of $3x$?

(A) 40
(B) 36
(C) 28
(D) 24
(E) 20

8. If s is an integer greater than 1, how many entire 1-inch cubes can be packed into a rectangular box having sides s, $s + \frac{3}{2}$, and $s - 1$, measured in inches?

(F) $s^3 - s$
(G) $s^3 + \frac{s^2}{2} + \frac{s}{2}$
(H) $s^3 - 2s + s$
(J) $s^3 + s^2 - s$
(K) None of the above

9. The volume of a cube, each face of which has an area of 16 square inches, equals the volume of a right cylinder with a height of 16 inches and a circular base. Which of the following most closely approximates the diameter of the cylinder's base?

(A) $1\frac{1}{5}$ inches
(B) $2\frac{1}{4}$ inches
(C) 4 inches
(D) $6\frac{1}{2}$ inches
(E) 8 inches

10. The volumes of two rectangular solids having the same proportions are 250 and 128. If one edge of the larger solid is 25 centimeters in length, what is the centimeter length of the corresponding edge of the smaller solid?

(F) 34
(G) 30
(H) 27.5
(J) 20
(K) 14.4

ANSWERS AND EXPLANATIONS

1. **The correct answer is (C).** The sum of the measures of the six interior angles must total 720°. Since the hexagon's sides are all the same length, the six angles are all equal in mesure: 120°. You can divide up the figure as indicated here:

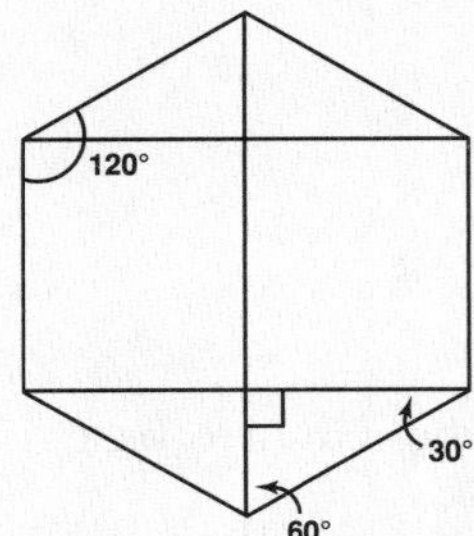

Each of the four triangles is a 30°-60°-90° triangle, so the ratio of the sides of each is $1:\sqrt{3}:2$. The hypotenuse is 1, so the other two sides are $\frac{1}{2}$ and $\frac{\sqrt{3}}{2}$. The area of each triangle $= \frac{1}{2} \times \frac{1}{2} \times \frac{\sqrt{3}}{2} = \frac{\sqrt{3}}{8}$. The hexagon includes four such triangles, so their total area is $\frac{\sqrt{2}}{2}$. The area of each of the two rectangles is $1 \times \frac{\sqrt{3}}{2}$, so the area of both rectangles combined is $\sqrt{3}$. The total area of all triangles and both rectangles is $\sqrt{3} + \frac{\sqrt{3}}{2}$, or $\frac{3\sqrt{3}}{2}$.

2. **The correct answer is (K).** First find the circle's diameter. Given the circle's circumference of 16π, its diameter = 16. Thus, each of the square's sides = 16. The ratio of the square's side to its diagonal is $1:\sqrt{2}$. (Remember the Pythagorean triplet $1:1:\sqrt{2}$ from the previous lesson?) Thus, diagonal $AC = 16\sqrt{2}$.

3. **The correct answer is (C).** The largest possible triangle meeting the stated criteria is an isosceles triangle, in which the triangle's third point lies midway between the other two along the circle's circumference. You can determine this by visualization and a bit of logic. As you move the third vertex away from that midway point, the triangle's perimeter and area decrease (the perimeter approaching the circle's diameter while the area approaches zero). To determine the length of each of these triangle's legs, divide the triangle into two right triangles, each conforming to the Pythagorean triplet $1:1:\sqrt{2}$ (the two legs each equal the circle's radius, or $\frac{d}{2}$):

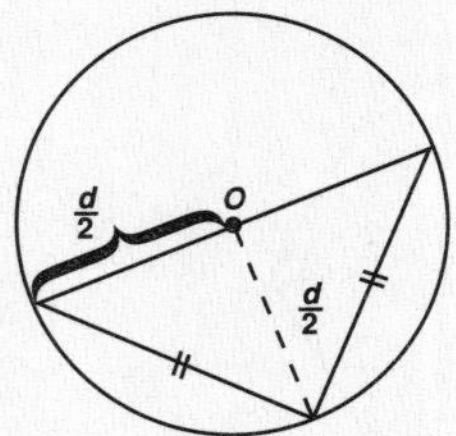

Applying the same triplet to the large triangle, in terms of d each leg of the *large* triangle $= \frac{d\sqrt{2}}{2}$. Thus, you can express the triangle's perimeter (the sum of all the sides) as:

$$\frac{d\sqrt{2}}{2} + \frac{d\sqrt{2}}{2} + d = \frac{2d\sqrt{2}}{2} + d = d\sqrt{2} + d$$

What about working backward from the answer choices by plugging in a simple value for *d*? This strategy would not help much, would it? You'd still need to analyze the problem as shown above. (Remember: Working backward helps for some problem solving questions but not for others.)

4. **The correct answer is (F).** If you forgot the ratios you learned in this lesson, try plugging in a simple number, such as 2, for *d*. Here's the analysis of each statement (let $d = 2$, or $r = 1$):

(I) is true. $C = \pi d = 2\pi$. The new circumference $= (1.5)(2\pi) = 3\pi$. The new circumference is $\frac{3}{2}$ the circumference of (or 50% greater than) the original one.

(II) is false. $r = \frac{d}{2} = 1$. The new diameter $= 2(1.5) = 3$. (The new diameter is 1.5 times the original one (or 50% greater than) the original one. The new radius is $\frac{d}{2}$=1.5, 1.5 times (or 50% greater than, not 100% greater than) the original one.

(III) is false. $A = \pi r^2 = \pi 1^2 = \pi$. The new area $= \pi\left(\frac{3r}{2}\right)^2 = \frac{9}{4}\pi$. The new area is $\frac{9}{4}$ the area of (or 125% greater than) the original one.

5. **The correct answer is (B).** Construct two right triangles as shown in the next figure. In each right triangle, the angles measure 30°, 60°, and 90° (one of the Pythagorean angle triplets). Accordingly, the triangle's sides conform to the Pythagorean side triplet $1:\sqrt{3}:2$.

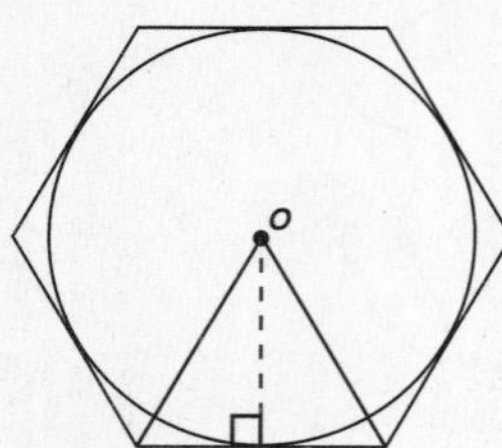

Given that the circle's area is 3π, its radius (which is also the longer leg of the right triangle) equals $\sqrt{3}(3\pi = \pi r^2)$. Accordingly, the area of each right triangle $= \frac{1}{2}bh = \frac{1}{2}(1)\left(\sqrt{3}\right) = \frac{\sqrt{3}}{2}$. The hexagon is comprised of 12 of these right triangles, all having the same area. Thus, the hexagon's area $= \frac{12\sqrt{3}}{2} = 6\sqrt{3}$.

6. **The correct answer is (J).** Since the smallest circle has a radius of 1, the medium circle has a radius of 2, and, therefore, the diameter of the large circle must be 6, which makes its radius 3. The arc of a semi-circle is half the circle's circumference—that is, πr. So, the length of the boundary of the shaded region is the sum of the arcs of the three semi-circles: $\pi + 2\pi + 3\pi = 6\pi$.

7. **The correct answer is (B).** The area of a circle is πr^2. The area of a circle with a radius of x is πx^2, which is given as 4. The area of a circle with radius $3x$ is $\pi(3x)^2 = 9\pi x^2$. Therefore, the area of the larger circle is 9 times the area of the smaller circle.

8. **The correct answer is (F).** The edge $\left(s + \frac{3}{2}\right)$ only accommodates $(s + 1)$ 1-inch cubes along its edge. The additional half-inch is unused space. Thus, the number of 1-inch cubes that can be packed into the box is the product of the three edges: $(s)(s + 1)(s - 1) = s(s^2 - 1) = s^3 - s$.

9. **The correct answer is (B).** Since the area of each square face of the box is 16 inches, each edge is $\sqrt{16}$, or 4, inches in length. Accordingly, the volume of the box is 4^3, or 64, cubic inches. Apply the formula for a cylinder's volume ($V = \pi r^2 h$), solving for radius (r):

$$64 = (\pi r^2)(16)$$
$$4 = \pi r^2$$
$$\frac{4}{\pi} = r^2$$
$$\frac{2}{\sqrt{\pi}} = r$$

The diameter of the circular base is twice its radius, or $\frac{4}{\sqrt{\pi}}$. Using 1.8 as the approximate value of $\sqrt{\pi}$ yields a diameter of approximately $2\frac{1}{4}$ inches.

10. **The correct answer is (J).** Since the two solids are proportionately identical, the ratio of the volumes is equal to the cube of the linear ratio of each pair of corresponding edges. The ratio of the two volumes can be expressed and simplified in this way: $\frac{250}{128} = \frac{125}{64}$. From here, you can determine that the linear ratio of the two edges is 5 to 4:

$$\frac{\sqrt[3]{125}}{\sqrt[3]{64}} = \frac{5}{4} \text{ (or 5:4)}$$

Using the proportion method, set up an algebraic equation to solve for the length of the smaller edge (x):

$$\frac{5}{4} = \frac{25}{x}$$
$$5x = 100$$
$$x = 20$$

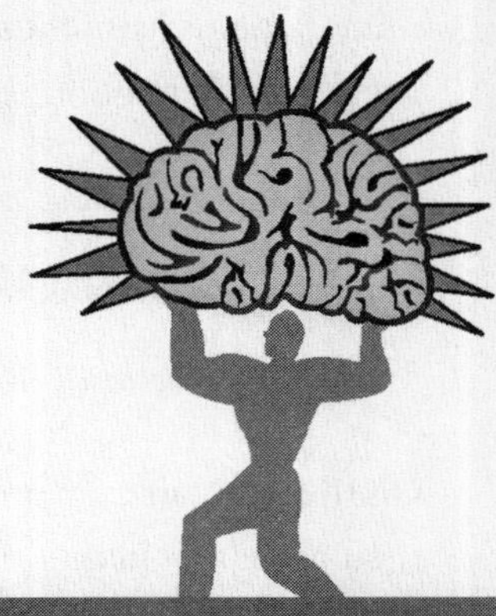

LESSON 14

Coordinate Geometry and Trigonometric Graphs

In this lesson, you'll learn how the test-makers design brain-taxing questions involving the standard (x,y) coordinate plane. Here are the specific topics you'll cover:

- Defining and plotting lines on the (x,y) plane
- Applying the midpoint and distance formulas to problems involving simple 2-dimensional figures
- Understanding the equations of conic sections (circles and ellipses) and of parabolas and hyperbolas—and their corresponding graphs on the (x,y) plane
- Graphing trigonometric functions on the (x,y) plane

All of these topics build on concepts covered in earlier lessons, making the material you'll encounter in the pages ahead more advanced.

Equations and graphs of ellipses, parabolas, and hyperbolas, as well as trigonometric graphs, are key areas that distinguish the ACT from the "whimpier" SAT, which doesn't cover any of these topics.

DEFINING A LINE ON THE COORDINATE PLANE

You can define any line on the coordinate plane by the equation $y = mx + b$. In this equation:

- m is the slope of the line
- b is the y-intercept (where the line crosses the y-axis)
- x and y are the coordinates of any point on the line
- Any (x,y) pair defining a point on the line can substitute for the variables x and y

Determining the *slope* of a line is usually crucial to solving ACT problems of this type. Think of the slope as a fraction whose numerator indicates the vertical change from one point to another on the line (moving left to right). The

numerator corresponds to a given horizontal change indicated by the fraction's denominator. The common term used for this fraction is "rise-over-run." Thus:

- A line sloping *upward* from left to right has a positive slope (m).
- A line sloping *downward* from left to right has a negative slope (m).
- A *horizontal* line has a slope of zero ($m = 0$, and $mx = 0$).

On the ACT, an easy problem involving this equation might provide coordinates for two points (which define a line), then ask you whether certain other points lie on the same line. To handle the problem, formulate the line's equation using the two original points, and then plug the coordinates for the other points into the equation to see if they work. Easy, right?

More complex problems of this type typically involve *two intersecting lines*. You might need to determine their point of intersection or where they cross either the x- or y-axis. Or, if the two lines help form a certain geometric figure (usually a triangle), you might need to determine certain characteristics of the figure (as in the next example). These problems can be challenging. Here's one that only true Brainiacs can handle:

Q In the standard xy-coordinate plane, the xy-pairs $(-6,2)$ and $(-14, -4)$ define a line, and the xy-pairs $(12,1)$ and $(-3, -11)$ define another line. What is the unit length of the longest side of a triangle formed by these two lines along with the y-axis?

(A) 23
(B) 21.5
(C) 19
(D) 17.5
(E) 15

A **The correct answer is (B).** For each line, formulate its equation by determining slope (m), then y-intercept (b):

For the pairs (−6,2) and (−14, −4):

$$y = \frac{6}{8}x + b \text{ (slope } = \frac{3}{4})$$

$$2 = \frac{3}{4}(-6) + b$$

$$2 = -4\frac{1}{2} + b$$

$$2 + 4\frac{1}{2} = b$$

$$6\frac{1}{2} = b$$

For the pairs (12,1) and (−3, −11):

$$y = -\frac{12}{9}x + b \text{ (slope } = -\frac{4}{3})$$

$$1 = -\frac{4}{3}(-12) + b$$

$$1 = \frac{48}{3} + b$$

$$1 - 16 = b$$

$$-15 = b$$

The two y-intercepts are $6\frac{1}{2}$ and -15. Thus, the length of the triangle's side along the y-axis is 21.5. But is this the longest side? Yes. Notice that the slopes of the other two lines (l_1 and l_2) are negative reciprocals of each other: $\left(\frac{3}{4}\right)\left(-\frac{4}{3}\right) = -1$. This means that they're perpendicular, forming the two legs of a right triangle in which the y-axis is the hypotenuse (the longest side).

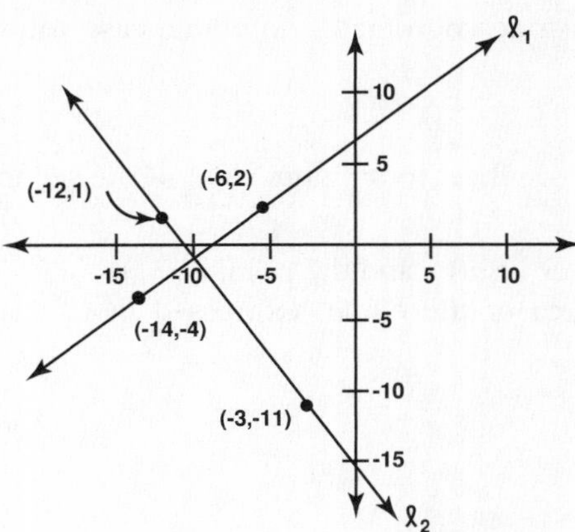

If the preceding question had instead asked for the point at which the two lines intersect, to answer the question you would formulate the equations for both lines, then solve for x and y with this system of two equations in two variables.

THE MIDPOINT AND DISTANCE FORMULAS

To be ready for ACT coordinate geometry, you should know these two formulas like the back of your hand. Both are basic and easy to apply, so this review will be brief. To find the coordinates of the midpoint of a line segment, simply average the two endpoints' x-values and y-values:

$$x_M = \frac{x_1 + x_2}{2} \text{ and } y_M = \frac{y_1 + y_2}{2}$$

For example, the midpoint between $(-3,1)$ and $(2,4) = \left(\frac{-3+2}{2}, \frac{1+4}{2}\right)$, or $\left(-\frac{1}{2}, \frac{5}{2}\right)$.

To find the *distance* between two points that have the same x-coordinate (or y-coordinate), simply compute the difference between the two y-values (or x-values). Otherwise, the line segment is neither vertical nor horizontal, and you'll need to apply the *distance formula*, which is actually the Pythagorean theorem in disguise (it measures the length of a right triangle's hypotenuse):

$$d = \sqrt{(x_1 - x_2)^2 + (y_1 - y_2)^2}$$

For example, the distance between $(-3,1)$ and $(2,4) = \sqrt{(-3-2)^2 + (1-4)^2} = \sqrt{25+9} = \sqrt{34}$.

In the distance formula, it doesn't matter which of the two points (x_1, y_1) signifies, or which point (x_2, y_2) signifies. But whichever pair you choose as (x_1, y_1), be sure not to inadvertently switch x_1 with x_2, or y_1 with y_2. Among Brainiacs, this is the most common error in applying the formula.

An easy ACT question might simply ask you to find the midpoint or distance between two given points (a no-brainer). A more challenging question might do either of the following:

- Use a line segment's midpoint or length as the basis for you to construct or analyze a geometric figure such as a triangle, quadrilateral, or circle.
- Provide the midpoint or distance and ask for the value of a missing coordinate—in which case you solve for the missing x-value or y-value in the formula.

Here's an example of the first type (during this lesson's Brain Teaser, you'll get to try a question of the second type):

Q In the standard (xy) coordinate plane, a circle has center $(2,-1)$, and the point $(-3,3)$ lies along the circle's circumference. What is the area of the circle, expressed in square coordinate units?

(A) 36π
(B) $\frac{81\pi}{2}$
(C) 41π
(D) 48π
(E) 57π

A **The correct answer is (C).** The circle's radius is the distance between its center $(2, -1)$ and any point along its circumference, including $(-3,3)$. Hence, you can find r by applying the distance formula: $\sqrt{(-3-2)^2+(-1-3)^2} = \sqrt{25+16} = \sqrt{41}$. The area of the circle $= \pi(\sqrt{41})^2 = 41\pi$.

In any geometry problem involving right triangles, look out for the Pythagorean triplet "fake-out," in which you'll see the correct ratio—but between the wrong two sides. For instance, in the preceding problem, the lengths of the two legs of a triangle whose hypotenuse is the circle's radius are 4 and 5. But the triangle does *not* conform to the 3:4:5 Pythagorean side triplet! Instead, the ratio is $4:5:\sqrt{41}$.

EQUATIONS AND GRAPHS OF CIRCLES

In the standard (x,y) coordinate plane, the equation for a circle whose radius is r and whose center is at the origin is $x^2 + y^2 = r^2$. Similarly, the equation for a circle whose radius is r and whose center is at (h,k) is $(x - h)^2 + (y - k)^2 = r^2$. To handle easier ACT questions involving these formulas, all you need to know is what the terms x, y, h, k, and r signify—a no-brainer for any test-taker who knows the formula. To complicate things, the test-makers might require you to calculate r, given either the circle's area or circumference (or vice versa), as in this example:

Q In the standard (x,y) coordinate plane, which of the following equations represents the circle that has center $(4,-2)$ and whose enclosed area, expressed in square coordinate units, is 9π?

(A) $(x - 4)^2 + (y + 2)^2 = 9$
(B) $(x - 4)^2 + (y + 2)^2 = 3$
(C) $(x - 4)^2 + (y - 2)^2 = 9$
(D) $(x + 4)^2 + (y + 2)^2 = 9$
(E) $(x - 4)^2 + (y - 2)^2 = 3$

A **The correct answer is (A).** In the standard form $(x - h)^2 + (y - k)^2 = r^2$, $h = 4$ and $k = -2$. Eliminate choices (C), (D), and (E). Find r^2 by applying the area formula: $A = \pi r^2$; $9\pi = \pi r^2$; $9 = r^2$, as choice (A) provides.

In questions like the preceding one, pay close attention to plus and minus signs in the answer choices. When either *h* or *k* (or both) are negative numbers, it's especially easy to overlook that subtracting a negative number is the same as adding a positive one.

In a tougher circle-graph question, you might need to supply the equation. You might also need to solve for either x or y, in which case two solutions, or roots, are possible. Here's an example that incorporates both complications:

Q In the standard (x,y) coordinate plane, the point $(t,-1)$ lies on the circumference of a circle that has center (4,2) and radius 5. Possible values of t include

I. 0
II. 2
III. 8

(A) II only
(B) III only
(C) I and III only
(D) I and II only
(E) II and III only

A **The correct answer is (C).** In the equation for a graph of a circle, let $x = t$, $y = -1$ and $r = 5$. Solve for x:

$$(t - 4)^2 + (-1 - 2)^2 = 5^2$$
$$(t^2 - 8t + 16) + 9 = 25$$
$$t^2 - 8t = 0$$
$$t(t - 8) = 0$$
$$t = 0, 8$$

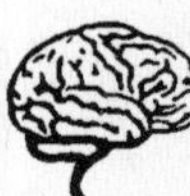

Unless a line that passes through a circle is tangent to the circle, the line will cross the circle's circumference at exactly *two* points. That's why, in the equation for the graph of a circle on the (x,y) plane, for every value of x, two values for y are possible (and vice versa).

EQUATIONS AND GRAPHS OF ELLIPSES

The general equation for the graph of an ellipse is $\frac{(x-h)^2}{a^2}+\frac{(y-k)^2}{b^2}=1$ or $\frac{(x-h)^2}{b^2}+\frac{(y-k)^2}{a^2}=1$, where h and k are the (x,y) coordinates of the ellipse's center, and where the ellipse's major (longer) axis equals $2a$ and its minor (shorter) axis equals $2b$. If the greater denominator is under the variable x, then the ellipse is horizontally oriented (and the first equation applies), whereas if it is under the variable y, then the ellipse is vertically oriented (and the second equation applies instead).

In the next figure, the left-hand ellipse, which is horizontally oriented, has center (0,0), so you can easily see the lengths of the major axis ($2a$) and minor axis ($2b$). In the right-hand ellipse, which is vertically oriented, the center is in Quadrant I at point (h,k). The value of $2a$ is 4, which is the distance from (2,2) to (6,2). The value of $2b$ is 6, which is the distance from (4,5) to (4, −1). Accordingly, $a^2 = 4$ and $b^2 = 9$.

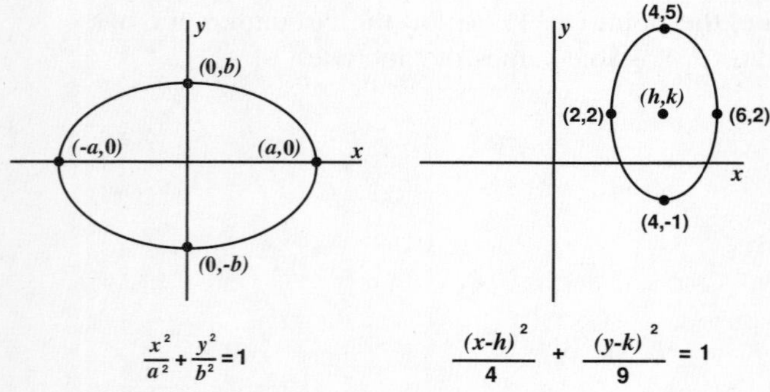

The easiest-level ellipse question might provide an equation for an ellipse in standard form, then ask you to identify one of the ellipse's features—its center or the length of its major or minor axis. Or, the question might provide an ellipse's graph and ask you to match the graph with its equation. Any average test-taker who knows the standard form of the equation for an ellipse can handle questions like these.

To complicate these easy questions, the test-makers might require you to manipulate the equation for an ellipse in order to put it in standard form. For instance, although it's easy to see that the center of the ellipse defined by the equation $3(x + 3)^2 + 5(y - 4)^2 = 15$ is $(-3,4)$, the values of a and b—and therefore what the ellipse's graph looks like—aren't so obvious. You need to divide both sides of the equation by 15, so that the right side equals 1:

$$\frac{3(x+3)^2}{15}+\frac{5(y-4)^2}{15}=\frac{15}{15}$$

$$\frac{(x+3)^2}{5}+\frac{(y-4)^2}{3}=1$$

Now you can see that $a = \sqrt{5}$ and $b = \sqrt{3}$, and that, accordingly, the length of the ellipse's horizontal and vertical axes are $2\sqrt{5}$ and $2\sqrt{3}$, respectively.

At Brainiac-level of difficulty, an ellipse question might call for you to do one or both of the following:

- Rewrite an equation in standard form
- Recognize the relationship between a circle and an ellipse (and between their equations)

Here's a tough question that requires both tasks (you'll encounter an even tougher one during this lesson's Brain Teaser):

Q An ellipse with equation $4(x+2)^2 + 4(y-2)^2 = 36$ is inscribed in a circle. Which of the following is the equation of the circle?

(A) $x^2 + y^2 = 4$
(B) $x^2 + y^2 = 36$
(C) $(x+2)^2 + (y-2)^2 = 6$
(D) $(x+2)^2 + (y-2)^2 = 9$
(E) $(x-4)^2 + (y-9)^2 = 6$

A **The correct answer is (D).** First, rewrite the ellipse's equation in standard form: $\frac{4(x+2)^2}{36} + \frac{4(y-2)^2}{36} = 1$. One way of defining a circle is as an ellipse in which the two axes are equal in length—that is, in the equation for an ellipse, $a = b$. In other words, a circle is simply an ellipse with equal axes. Hence, the equation of the circle that inscribes the ellipse is $\frac{(x+2)^2}{9} + \frac{(y-2)^2}{9} = 1$, or $(x+2)^2 + (y-2)^2 = 9$.

EQUATIONS AND GRAPHS OF PARABOLAS

In the standard (x,y) coordinate plane, the general equation for a *parabola* is one of the following two (depending on the parabola's orientation, either vertical or horizontal):

$y - k = a(x - h)^2$ The parabola extends either up or down, depending on whether the function (the relation between the equation's two sides) is positive or negative.

$x - h = a(y - k)^2$ The parabola extends either right or left, depending on whether the function (the relation between the equation's two sides) is positive or negative.

In these equations, point (h,k) is the parabola's vertex and the constant a determines the parabola's shape (the greater the value of a, the "steeper" and "narrower" the curve). To understand the relationship between a parabola's equation and its graph, examine the following two graphs and their corresponding equations:

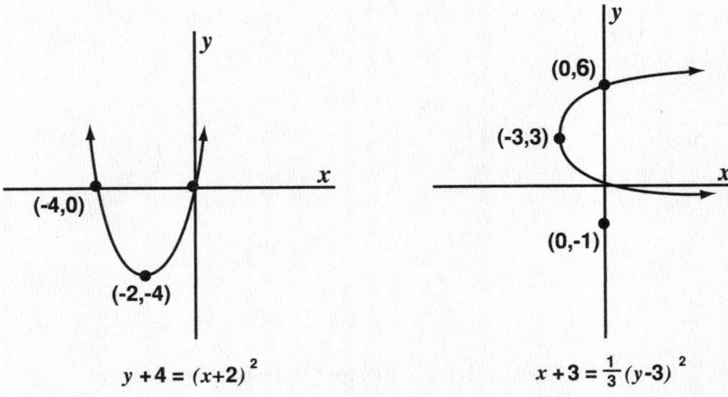

$y + 4 = (x+2)^2$ $x + 3 = \frac{1}{3}(y-3)^2$

Notice that the right-hand parabola, for which $a = \frac{1}{3}$, is "wider" than the left-hand parabola, for which $a = 1$.

To confirm the two y-intercepts (0,0) and (−4,0) shown in the left-hand parabola, let $y = 0$ and find the two roots of the equation $0 = (x+2)^2 - 4$. Similarly, to confirm the two x-intercepts (0,6) and (0,0) shown in the right-hand parabola, let $x = 0$ and find the two roots of the equation $0 = \frac{1}{3}(y-3)^2 - 3$.

To answer an easier ACT parabola question, you might need to match the graph of a parabola to its equation by identifying the parabola's vertex and/or its direction (up, down, left, or right). To complicate this type of question just a bit, the test-makers may give an equation in nonstandard form. For instance, the equations of the two parabolas in the preceding graph might be expressed instead as $y = (x + 2)^2 - 4$ and $x = \frac{1}{3}(y - 3)^2 - 3$. Rewriting the equation in standard form will help you identify the parabola's vertex and direction. (You'll check out an ACT-style example during this lesson's Brain Teaser.)

To answer a more difficult parabola question, you might need to do one of the following:

- Draw the graph of a parabola's equation (in order to analyze the question)
- Recognize a relationship between two parabolas, or between a parabola and another shape, such as a circle

Here's a tough question that incorporates both complications:

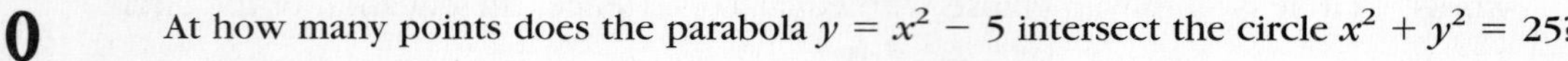

Q At how many points does the parabola $y = x^2 - 5$ intersect the circle $x^2 + y^2 = 25$?

(A) 0
(B) 1
(C) 2
(D) 3
(E) 4

A **The correct answer is (D).** One way to approach this question is by drawing both shapes on the same coordinate plane. The circle has radius 5 and center (0,0). Rewriting the parabola's equation as $y + 5 = (x - 0)^2$ tells you that the parabola is vertically oriented opening upward and has vertex $(0,-5)$. Plot the two x-intercepts by letting $y = 0$ and solving for x in the parabola's equation: $x^2 = 5$; $x = \pm\sqrt{5}$. You now have all the data you need to draw both graphs accurately enough to answer the question (as you can see, the two shapes intersect at three points):

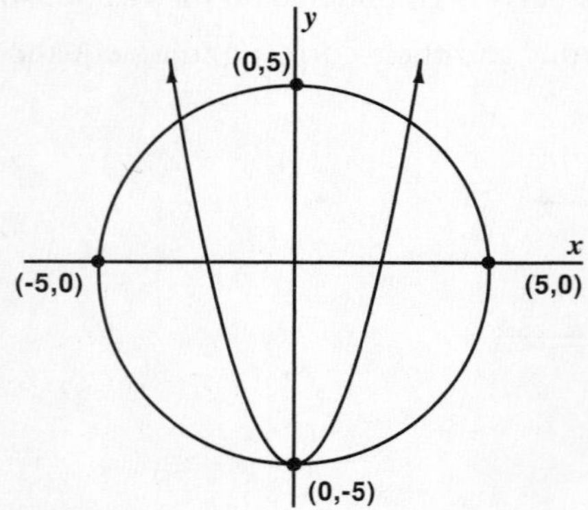

Another, less efficient, way to approach this question is by algebraic substitution. For instance, you can substitute $(y + 5)$ for x^2 (based on the parabola's equation) in the circle's equation, then solve for y:

$$x^2 + y^2 = 25$$
$$(y + 5) + y^2 = 25$$
$$y^2 + y - 20 = 0$$
$$(y + 5)(y - 4) = 20$$
$$y = -5,\ 4$$

Then, plug in each value for y in both equations. On either curve, $y = -5$ at, and *only* at, point (0,−5). In either equation, letting $y = 4$ yields $x^2 = 9$, or $x = \pm 3$ (two solutions); that is, on either curve, $y = 4$ at points (3,4) and (−3,4). Hence, there are three points of intersection altogether: (0,−5), (3,4), and (−3,4).

EQUATIONS AND GRAPHS OF HYPERBOLAS

A *hyperbola* actually consists of two parabolas that "open up" in opposite directions and are symmetrical about the same line—called the *transverse axis* (the y-axis in the left-hand graph below and the x-axis in the right-hand graph below). They are *asymptotic* about the same two lines, which means that they approach but never meet the two lines (the dotted lines, called the *asymptotes*, in the following two graphs).

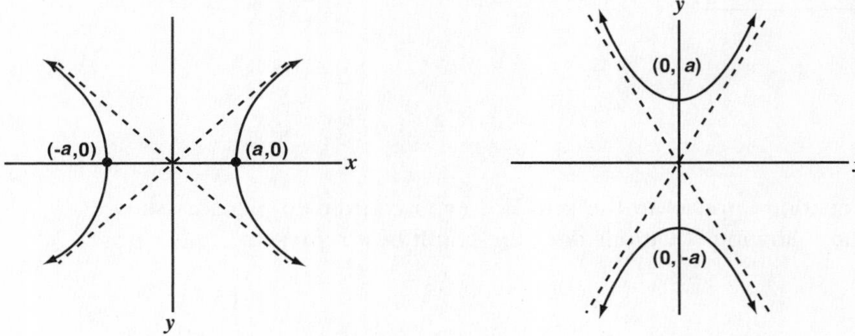

The general equation for the graph of a hyperbola can be either of the following two, depending on the hyperbole's orientation (horizontal or vertical). In these equations, h and k are the (x,y) coordinates of the hyperbola's center, which is the midpoint between the two vertices, along the transverse axis:

$$\frac{(x-h)^2}{a^2} - \frac{(y-k)^2}{b^2} = 1$$

The transverse axis is horizontal, and the hyperbola "opens up" to the left as well as to the right.

$$\frac{(y-k)^2}{a^2} - \frac{(x-h)^2}{b^2} = 1$$

The transverse axis is vertical, and the hyperbola "opens up" in upward and downward directions.

The distance between the two vertices (along the transverse axis) equals $2a$.

The axis perpendicular to the transverse axis is called the *conjugate axis*. The value of b is calculated as a segment length along this axis. But for the ACT, you won't need to determine b.

The equations for the asymptotes of a hyperbola whose center is at (0,0) and whose axes are the x-axis and y-axis, as in the two preceding graphs, are as follows:

$$\frac{x}{a} - \frac{y}{b} = 0 \quad \text{and} \quad \frac{x}{a} + \frac{y}{b} = 0$$

If you find all these equations a bit confusing, you're not alone. Adding to the confusion is the fact that a hyperbola can be oriented at any angle—that is, the transverse axis need not be either vertical or horizontal. The test-makers realize that hyperbolas are more complex than the other curves that the ACT covers and that you've learned about in this lesson. Therefore, they tend to keep their hyperbola questions simple.

To handle a typical hyperbola question, which will probably ask you to match an equation to its graph, just tabulate and plot a few sample (x,y) pairs. Or, if the asymptotes happen to be vertical and horizontal, you might also be able to handle the question by determining the unique values for x and y that lead to undefined solutions, which the two asymptotes represent graphically. Here's a good illustrative example:

Q

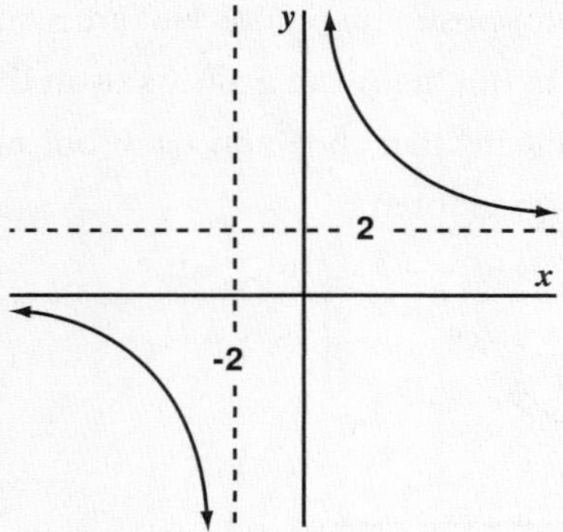

The graph of an equation appears in the standard (x,y) coordinate plane as shown above. Which of the following equations does the graph best represent?

(A) $y = \frac{1}{x} + 2$

(B) $x = \frac{1}{y} + 2$

(C) $y = \frac{1}{x + 2} + 2$

(D) $x = \frac{1}{y + 2} + 2$

(E) $y = \frac{1}{x + 2} - 2$

A

The correct answer is (C). The graph shows the hyperbola asymptotic at $x = -2$ and at $y = 2$. Hence, in the graph's equation, if $x = -2$, then y is not a real number and, conversely, if $y = 2$, then x is not a real number. Of the five answer choices, only in choices (C) and (E) is y undefined for $x = -2$. Of these two choices, only choice (C) is x undefined for $y = 2$ as well. By elimination, then, (C) must be the correct answer.

Another way to approach this question is to plot sample points for each of the five equations in turn, which is less efficient than the more intuitive approach described above. Nevertheless, you should plot a few points of the equation provided in choice (C), just to confirm that (C) is indeed the correct answer.

In all likelihood, any ACT hyperbola question you run across won't be any trickier than the preceding one, and you won't need to resort to the standard equation forms you saw a bit earlier. But you should keep these equations in your "pocket," anyway, just in case the ACT deals you a question like the one on the following page (don't worry: this one is as tough and tricky as the test-makers might design a hyperbola question):

Q

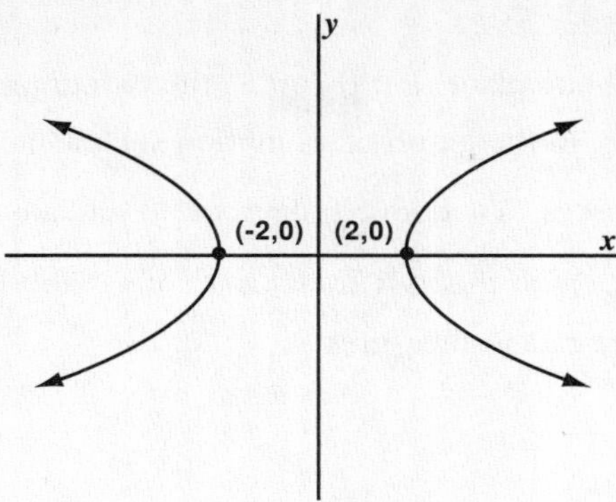

The graph of an equation is shown in the standard (x,y) coordinate plane above. Which of the following equations does the graph best represent?

(A) $4y^2 - 9x^2 = 36$
(B) $4y^2 - 9x^2 = -36$
(C) $4x^2 - 9y^2 = -36$
(D) $9y^2 - 4x^2 = 36$
(E) $9x^2 - 4y^2 = -36$

A

The correct answer is (B). The graph shows a horizontally oriented hyperbola with center (0,0). Thus, the general form for the hyperbola's equation is:

$$\frac{(x-h)^2}{a^2} - \frac{(y-k)^2}{b^2} = 1$$

The graph shows that the center (h,k) is at (0,0) and that $a = 2$. Accordingly, the hyperbola's equation is:

$$\frac{x^2}{2^2} - \frac{y^2}{b^2} = 1$$

To rewrite the equation in a form that matches the form of the answer choices, multiply both sides of the equation by 36:

$$\frac{36x^2}{4} - \frac{36y^2}{b^2} = 36$$

$$9x^2 - \left(\frac{36}{b^2}\right)y^2 = 36$$

Although none of the answer choices match this precise form, multiplying both sides of the equation by -1 yields $4y^2 - 9x^2 = -36$. Of the five equations, the one provided by choice (B) is the only possible match for the graph.

Notice that you didn't need to know the value of *b* to answer the preceding question. Nor did you need to know the equations for the asymptotes or even their slopes. In these respects, the question is typical of ACT hyperbola questions, which tend to focus on the overall "shape" of hyperbolas rather than on their precise specifications.

TRIGONOMETRIC GRAPHS

You can graph any trigonometric function on the *xy*-coordinate plane. For the ACT, the two graphs, or "curves," you should be most familiar with are the *sine* and *cosine* curves. In the graph of a function such as $y = \sin x$ or $y = \cos x$, the variable x is expressed in *radians* rather than degrees. To convert degrees to radians, multiply by $\frac{\pi}{180}$. (Conversely, to convert radians to degrees, multiply by $\frac{180}{\pi}$.) On the ACT, radians are invariably expressed in terms of π and usually involve one of the following seven degree radian measures:

$30° = \frac{\pi}{6}$ $\quad 180° = \pi$

$45° = \frac{\pi}{4}$ $\quad 270° = \frac{3\pi}{2}$

$60° = \frac{\pi}{3}$ $\quad 360° = 2\pi$

$90° = \frac{\pi}{2}$

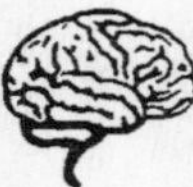

Radians are a measure of the distance along a circle's circumference. By definition, 1 radian = the circle's radius. Since a circle's circumference = $2\pi r$, 360° = 2π radians. The degree/radian conversion formula is derived from this equation.

Here's a graph of the trigonometric functions $y = \sin x$ and $y = \cos x$ for all values of x from 0 to 2π. Notice that the graph completes one cycle, or "period," over the "interval" $[0,2\pi]$:

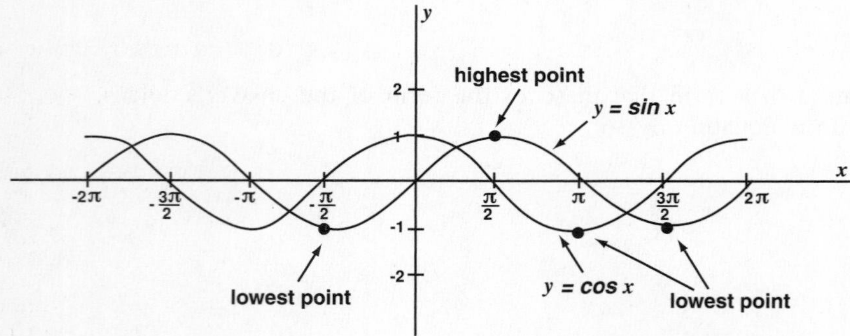

Note the following test-worthy characteristics of these two curves:

- The maximum value of either a sine or cosine is 1, and the minimum value of either function is -1.
- When one function, either sine or cosine, is at either its maximum or minimum value (1 or -1), the value of the other function is 0.
- $\sin x = \cos x$ exactly twice over one period—at $\frac{\pi}{4}$ and $\frac{5\pi}{4}$, or in terms of degree measure, when $x = 45°$ and 225°.

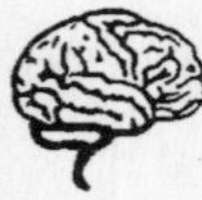

At this point, it may be helpful to review the sines and cosines of 30°, 45°, and 60° from the earlier lesson on right-triangle trigonometry. If you convert those three degree measures into radians, you'll see that the two curves above confirm the values of each one's sine and cosine.

In a function of the form $y = A\sin kx$ or $y = A\cos kx$, the letter A represents the curve's *amplitude*—the maximum value (and the minimum value's absolute value) of either function—and the letter k represents the curve's *frequency*, which is the number of full cycles completed over one period, the interval $[0,2\pi]$. As the preceding graphs show, for $y = \sin x$ and $y = \cos x$, the values of A as well as k are 1. Compare those two graphs with the following two, which illustrate just a few other possibilities for amplitude (A) and frequency (k):

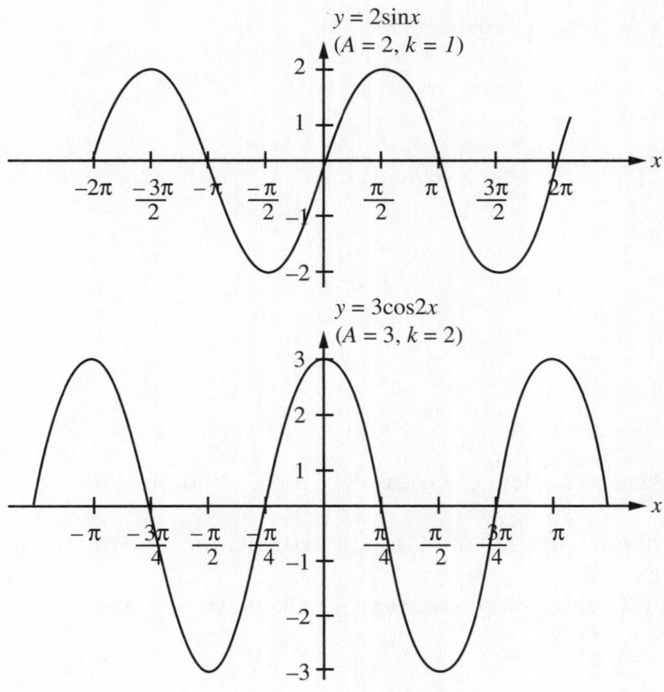

How might the test-makers cover what you just reviewed? An easier question will call for you to recognize one of the characteristics of a sine or cosine curve. This first example focuses on the minimum value of a cosine (answer choices are omitted):

Q Over all real numbers x, what is the minimum value of $3\cos 5x$?

A **The correct answer is -3.** The minimum value of a cosine is -1. Substituting -1 for $\cos 5x$, the minimum value of $3\cos 5x = (3)(-1) = -3$.

This second example focuses on the definition of *frequency* (again, answer choices are omitted):

Q What is the period of the graph of $y = 3\sin\frac{x}{2}$?

A **The correct answer is 4π.** The function's frequency $= \frac{1}{2}$. Since the curve completes one-half cycle over a 2π period, it would complete one cycle over a 4π period.

A tougher question might require you to plot a point along a function's curve somewhere between an x-intercept and the nearest point of amplitude; that is, between the function's minimum and maximum value, but not at 0. The ACT doesn't provide trigonometric tables for this purpose. Instead, questions like these will involve angle measures for which you can easily determine the sine and cosine by using the Pythagorean theorem or by referring to a familiar Pythagorean triplet. Here's an example:

Q What is the least possible value of x for which $4\cos 2x = 2$?

(A) $\frac{\pi}{12}$

(B) $\frac{\pi}{6}$

(C) $\frac{\pi}{4}$

(D) $\frac{\pi}{3}$

(E) $\frac{\pi}{2}$

A **The correct answer is (B).** $4\cos 2x = 2$. Hence, $\cos 2x = \frac{2}{4}$, or $\frac{1}{2}$. You should recognize the value $\frac{1}{2}$ as the cosine of 60°. (In a 30°-60°-90° right triangle, the ratio of the shorter leg to the hypotenuse is 1:2.) Since 60° converts to $\frac{\pi}{3}$ radians, $2x = \frac{\pi}{3}$, and $x = \frac{\pi}{6}$.

BRAIN TEASER

In this quiz, you'll attempt 10 tough ACT-style questions covering the topics from this lesson. Focus on applying the concepts and techniques you learned in this lesson, *not* on answering the questions as quickly as possible. Then read the explanations that follow the quiz, even for the questions you answered correctly.

QUIZ

1. 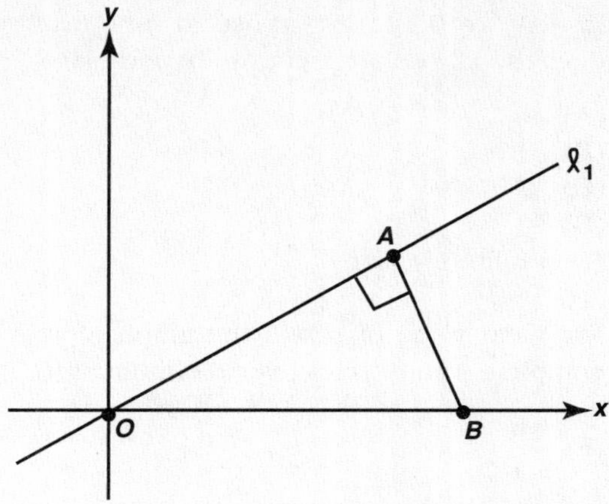

In the standard (x,y) coordinate plane shown above, if the equation of l_1 is $y = \frac{x}{2}$, and if point B is at (5,0), what is the area of ΔOAB?

(A) 4

(B) $3\sqrt{2}$

(C) $2\sqrt{5}$

(D) 5

(E) 7

2. What is the equation of the line that is the perpendicular bisector of the line segment connecting points $(-1,1)$ and $(3,5)$ in the standard (x,y) coordinate plane?

(F) $y = 2x + 1$
(G) $y = x - 2$
(H) $y = -x + 4$
(J) $y = -3x + 2$
(K) $y = x + 3$

3. In the standard (x,y) coordinate plane, if the point $(4,t)$ is equidistant from the points (1,1) and (5,3), then $t = ?$

(A) $\frac{3}{2}$

(B) 1

(C) 0

(D) $-\frac{1}{4}$

(E) -4

4. In the standard (x,y) coordinate plane, two points P and Q, defined by the (x,y) coordinates $(-1,0)$ and (3,3), respectively, are connected to form a chord of a circle that also lies on the plane. If the area of the circle is $\frac{25}{4}\pi$, what are the coordinates of the center of the circle?

(F) $\left(\frac{1}{2}, \frac{1}{2}\right)$

(G) $\left(1, 1\frac{1}{2}\right)$

(H) (0, 1)

(J) $\left(\frac{1}{2}, 1\right)$

(K) $\left(-1\frac{1}{2}, \frac{1}{2}\right)$

5. In the standard (x,y) coordinate plane are four points: $(-1,-1)$, $(-4,3)$, $(2,-1)$, and (3,3). What is the unit area of the quadrilateral formed by connecting the four points?

(A) $12\sqrt{2}$
(B) $11\sqrt{3}$
(C) 18
(D) 20
(E) 25

6. In the standard (x,y) coordinate plane, the graph of $(x - 6)^2 + (y + 8)^2 = 49$ is a circle. Which of the following indicates all possible values of y ?

(F) $15 \geq y \geq 1$
(G) $14 \geq y \geq -1$
(H) $1 \geq y \geq -13$
(J) $8 \geq y \geq -8$
(K) $-1 \geq y \geq -15$

7. In the standard (x,y) coordinate plane, a certain circle is defined by the equation $(x + 3)^2 + (y - 4)^2 = 10$. Which of the following could be the equation of an ellipse that is inscribed in the circle?

I. $5(x + 3)^2 + 15(y - 4)^2 = 100$
II. $10(x + 3)^2 + 6(y - 4)^2 = 100$
III. $20(x + 3)^2 + 10(y - 4)^2 = 100$

(A) II only
(B) III only
(C) I and II only
(D) II and III only
(E) I, II, and III

8.

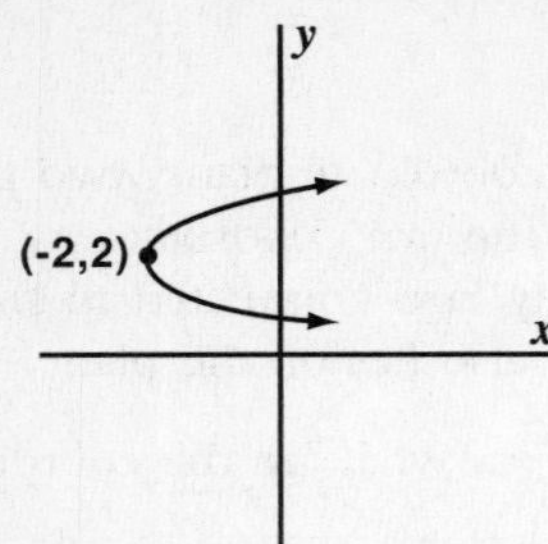

The figure above shows a parabola in the standard (x,y) coordinate plane. Which of the following equations does the graph best represent?

(F) $x = y^2 - 4y + 2$
(G) $x = y^2 - 2y + 2$
(H) $x = y^2 + 4y - 4$
(J) $x = y^2 - 4y - 2$
(K) $x = y^2 + 2y + 4$

9. The graph of the equation $\frac{1}{4}x^2 + (y + 1)^2 = 1$ is an ellipse, and the graph of the equation $(y + 1)^2 - (x + 1)^2 = 1$ is a hyperbola. At how many points does the ellipse intersect the hyperbola?

(A) 0
(B) 1
(C) 2
(D) 3
(E) Infinitely many

10. For what value of b will the graph of $y = \sin 4x$ complete 3 full cycles over the interval $[0,b]$?

(F) $\frac{\pi}{4}$
(G) $\frac{\pi}{2}$
(H) $\frac{3\pi}{4}$
(J) π
(K) $\frac{3\pi}{2}$

ANSWERS AND EXPLANATIONS

1. **The correct answer is (D).** The key to this problem involves perpendicular lines and the concept of *slope*. The slope of l_1 is $\frac{1}{2}$, which means that every 2 units from left to right (the line's "run") corresponds to 1 unit upward (vertically) on the plane (the line's "rise"). Since the angle at point A is a right angle, the slope of AB must be -2 (a "drop" or "negative rise" of 2 units for every 1 unit from left to right). Drawing a plumb line down from point A reveals that, in order to attain these slopes, the height (altitude) of ΔOAB must be 2:

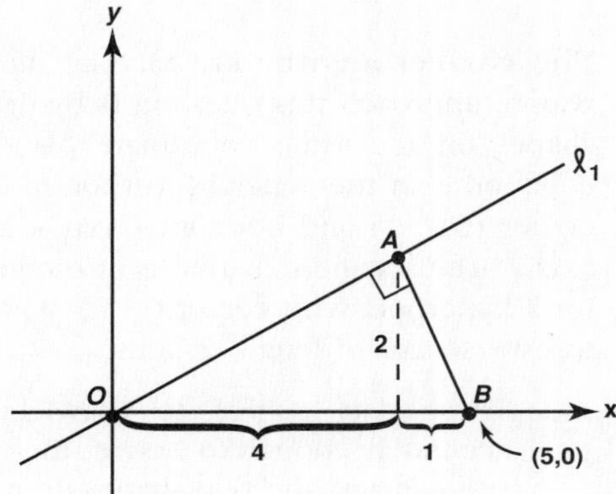

The area of any triangle is defined as one-half the product of its base and height (altitude). Given a base (OB) of 5 and an altitude of 2, the area of ΔOAB must equal 5.

2. **The correct answer is (H).** The segment connecting points $(-1,1)$ and $(3,5)$ has a slope of $m = \frac{5-1}{3-(-1)} = \frac{4}{4} = 1$. Hence, the slope of the segment's perpendicular bisector must be the negative reciprocal of 1, which is -1. Thus, the bisector's equation must be $y = -x + b$. Since the line bisects the segment, it must pass through its midpoint. Find this midpoint by averaging the coordinates of the endpoints: $\left(\frac{-1+3}{2}, \frac{1+5}{2}\right)$, or $(1,3)$. To determine the value of b, substitute $(1,3)$ for (x,y) in the line's equation: $3 = -1 + b$; $b = 4$. Hence, the line's equation is $y = -x + 4$.

3. **The correct answer is (C).** Since the distance from the two given points are the same, apply the distance formula twice, then equate the results and solve for t:

$$\sqrt{(4-1)^2 + (t-1)^2} = \sqrt{(5-4)^2 + (3-t)^2}$$
$$\sqrt{9 + (t^2 - 2t + 1)} = \sqrt{1 + (9 - 6t + t^2)}$$
$$\sqrt{10 + t^2 - 2t} = \sqrt{10 - 6t + t^2}$$
$$10 + t^2 - 2t = 10 - 6t + t^2$$
$$-2t = -6t$$
$$4t = 0$$
$$t = 0$$

4. **The correct answer is (G).** Given that the area of the circle is $\frac{25}{4}\pi$, you can determine the circle's radius and diameter:

$$A = \pi r^2$$
$$\frac{25\pi}{4} = \pi r^2$$
$$\frac{25}{4} = r^2$$
$$r = \frac{5}{2}$$
$$\therefore d = 5$$

On the coordinate plane, the distance between the points whose coordinates are $(-1,0)$ and $(3,3)$ is 5 (the chord forms the hypotenuse of a 3:4:5 right triangle, as illustrated in the figure below). Because these two points are five units apart, chord PQ must be the circle's diameter. The circle's center lies on chord PQ midway between P and Q. The x-coordinate of the center is midway between the x-coordinates of P and Q (-1 and 3), whereas the y-coordinate is midway between the y-coordinates of P and Q (0 and 3). Thus, the center of the circle is the point $\left(1, 1\frac{1}{2}\right)$.

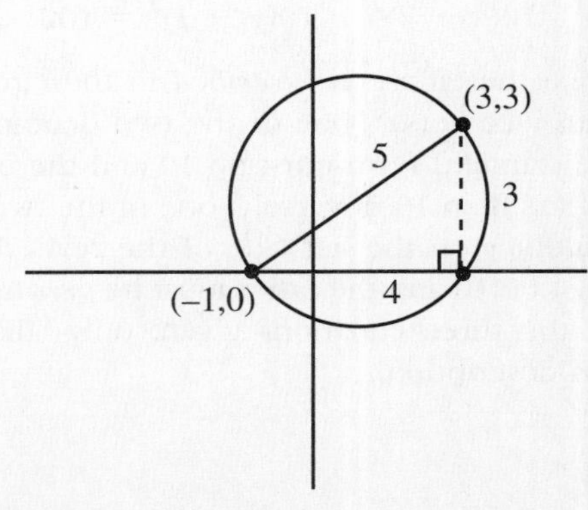

5. **The correct answer is (D).** Points $(-1,-1)$ and $(2,-1)$ connect to form a horizontal line segment of length 3. Similarly, points (3,3) and $(-4,3)$ connect to form a horizontal line segment of length 7. Since the two segments are parallel, the resulting quadrilateral is a trapezoid. The vertical distance between the two parallel segments is 4. Apply the formula for a trapezoid's area (*AB* and *CD* represent the two parallel segments, and *h* is the quadrilateral's height):

$$A = \frac{AB + CD}{2} \times h$$

$$A = \frac{3+7}{2} \times 4$$

$$A = 20$$

You can also plot the quadrilateral on the grid, divide it into two right triangles and one rectangle, and then calculate the area of each one. (Combine the three areas to determine the large quadrilateral's area.) But applying the trapezoid formula is easier.

6. **The correct answer choice is (K).** In the general equation $(x - h)^2 + (y - k)^2 = r^2$, in which k is the y-coordinate of the circle's center and r is the circle's radius, $k = -8$ and $r = 7$. A vertical line through the circle's center passes through both the highest and lowest possible points on the circle's circumference—each point 7 units ($r = 7$) from the circle's center. Hence, the greatest possible value for y is $-8 + 7 = -1$, and the least possible value for y is $-8 - 7 = -15$.

7. **The correct answer is (B).** You can rewrite the circle's equation $(x + 3)^2 + (y - 4)^2 = 10$ in the standard form for an ellipse by dividing both sides by 10:

$$\frac{(x+3)^2}{10} + \frac{(y-4)^2}{10} = 1$$

To rewrite the equation so that it matches the form in which the answer choices are written, multiply both sides by 100:

$$10(x + 2)^2 + 10(y - 2)^2 = 100$$

Since the ellipse is *inscribed* in the circle (rather than vice versa), one of the two denominators in the standard form must be 10 and the other must be less than 10. Inversely, one of the two constant multiples on the left side of the revised equation must be 10 and the other must be *greater* than 10. Of the three equations given, only (III) matches this description.

8. **The correct answer is (F).** The graph shows a horizontally oriented parabola. Thus, the general form for parabola's equation is $x - h = a(y - k)^2$. Since the vertex is at $(-2,2)$, $h = -2$ and $k = 2$, and the parabola's equation is:

$$(x + 2) = a(y - 2)^2$$

Each answer choice expresses an equation in terms of x and in unfactored form. Accordingly, rewrite the equation above in the same manner:

$$x + 2 = (y - 2)^2$$
$$x = (y - 2)(y - 2) - 2$$
$$x = y^2 - 4y + 4 - 2$$
$$x = y^2 - 4y + 2$$

9. **The correct answer is (A).** The most efficient way to approach this question is by drawing both shapes on the same coordinate plane. The first equation is in the general form for an ellipse with center $(0, -1)$ and horizontal axis 4 and vertical axis 2. The second equation is in the general form for a hyperbola with center $(-1, -1)$ and vertical transverse axis of length 2 units:

These data suffice to draw both graphs accurately enough to answer the question (as you can see, the two shapes do not intersect at any point):

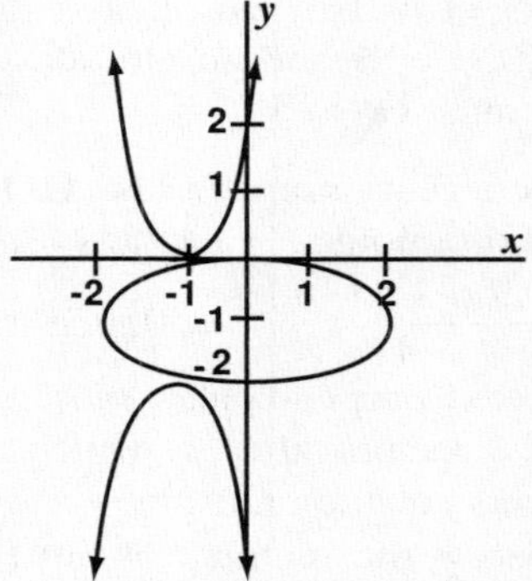

10. **The correct answer is (K).** Since the function has a frequency of 4, it will complete four full cycles over the interval $[0,2\pi]$. Hence, it will complete three full cycles over $\frac{3}{4}$ of that interval: $\frac{3}{4}(2\pi) = \frac{3\pi}{2}$.

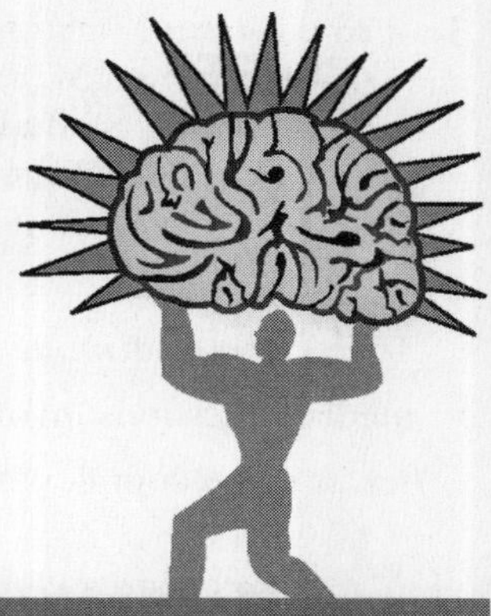

LESSON 15

Statistics, Sets, Series, and Sequence

In this lesson, we'll explore the following topics, all of which involve sets (defined groups) of quantitative terms or other objects:

- Mean, median, and mode (how a set of numbers can be described quantitatively, as a whole)
- Permutations (the possibilities for arranging a set of objects)
- Combinations (the possibilities for selecting groups of objects from a set)
- Probability (the statistical chances of a certain event, permutation, or combination occurring)
- Progressions (the arithmetic or geometric pattern from one number to the next in a series, or sequence, of numbers)
- Matrices (operations on rectangular arrays of numbers)

Applying the concepts of permutation, combination, and probability requires a larger dose of logical reasoning than math. Be forewarned: Even if you're an ultra-Brainiac, expect to be challenged as you apply these concepts to ACT-style questions. So, slow down, and pay close attention.

STATISTICAL MEAN, MEDIAN, AND MODE

Statistical *mean* (also called *arithmetic mean* and *simple average*), *median*, and *mode* are different ways of measuring (or describing) a set of numbers or other quantitative terms as a whole. For the ACT, these are the only concepts from the field of math called *descriptive statistics* that you need to know, and all three are easy enough to understand. Just for the record, for any set of terms:

- The *arithmetic mean* (*AM*) is the sum of the terms ($a + b + c + \ldots$) divided by the number of terms (n) in the set. $AM = \dfrac{(a + b + c + \ldots)}{n}$
- The *median* is the middle term in value, when arranged in increasing or decreasing order, if the set contains an odd number of terms, or the arithmetic mean (average) of the two middle terms if the set contains an even number of terms.
- The *mode* is the term that appears most often in the set.

X-REF **When the terms in a set are assigned varying weights, you need to apply the concept of *weighted average* using a variation of the arithmetic-mean formula. You learned about weighted averages and how the concept can make for tough ACT questions in Lesson 11. Remember?**

The concept of *mode* is a no-brainer, so you'll focus here on the other two: *mean* and *median*. Easier mean and median questions involve simply adding numbers together and dividing sums, or identifying the middle term(s) of a set. A more complex mean or median question might ask you to perform one or more of the following tasks:

- Calculate a *change* (increase or decrease) in the mean or median
- Deal with *variables* instead of (or in addition to) numbers
- Solve for *one of the set's terms* (from a given mean or median)
- Here's a challenging question that incorporates the second and third ploys (during this lesson's Brain Teaser, you'll tackle a question that incorporates the first and second ploys):

Q Which of following expressions represents the fifth term of a set that also includes the four terms p, q, $(p + q)$, and $(p - 1)$, if $\frac{3}{5}(p + q)$ represents the arithmetic mean (average) of all five terms?

(A) $q - p$
(B) $q + 1$
(C) $p + q$
(D) $p - q$
(E) $p + 1$

A **The correct answer is (B).** The starting point in solving this problem is the same formula for solving easier arithmetic-mean problems:

$$AM = \frac{(a + b + c + \ldots)}{n}$$

However, in this problem we need to add a fifth term (let's call it x) to the list of four known terms in the set, then isolate x on one side of our equation—requiring more algebraic steps than if we were solving for AM:

$$AM = \frac{p + q + (p + q) + (p - 1) + x}{5}$$

$$\frac{3}{5}(p + q) = \frac{p + q + (p + q) + (p - 1) + x}{5}$$

$$\frac{3}{5}(p + q) = \frac{3p + 2q - 1 + x}{5}$$

$$3(p + q) = 3p + 2q - 1 + x$$

$$3p + 3q = 3p + 2q - 1 + x$$

$$q + 1 = x$$

To really crank up the difficulty level of a mean or median question, the test-makers might make it even more complex by requiring you to perform one or both of these tasks:

1. Determine either mean or median, then use that value and whatever clues the question provides to determine the other
2. Apply some other arithmetic or algebraic concept (or skill)

This next question (a variation on the previous one) incorporates both additional complications, boosting it to the exam's highest difficulty level. As you tackle the question, notice that it adds *median* to its "mean" mix, as well as tests your facility with *number theory* and *algebraic substitution*.

Q If $0 < q < p$, and if the median of the four terms p, q, $(p + q)$, and $(q - p)$ is 2, which of the following expresses the arithmetic mean (average) of the four terms?

(A) $2(p + q) - 1$

(B) $4 - p - q$

(C) $2 + \frac{q - p}{4}$

(D) $8 + p - q$

(E) $\frac{p + q}{2}$

A **The correct answer is (C).** This problem is difficult, and the steps to solving it are anything but obvious to most test-takers. Ultimately, you'll need to solve for *AM* in the following equation:

$$AM = \frac{q + p + (p + q) + (q - p)}{4}$$

But combining the p-terms and q-terms terms on the equation's right side fails to yield anything resembling one of the five answer choices. The additional information supplied must be the key. Perhaps the median (given as 2) can substitute for one the set's terms (expressed in variables). To test this theory, determine the median in terms of p and q by ranking the set's four terms from least to greatest in value:

Given $q < p$ and that p and q are both positive, $(q - p)$ must be negative and thus, least in value among the four terms, while $(q + p)$ must be greatest in value among the four terms. Here are the four terms, then, ranked from least to greatest in value:

$$(q - p) \ldots q \ldots p \ldots (p + q)$$

The median value, given as 2, is the average (arithmetic mean) of the two middle terms p and q:

$$2 = \frac{p + q}{2}$$

$$4 = p + q$$

Now perhaps you have the information you need to answer the question (that is, to express the arithmetic mean as a match for one of the answer choices). Substitute the number 4 for $(p + q)$ in the arithmetic-mean formula, then solve for AM:

$$AM = \frac{q + p + (p + q) + (q - p)}{4}$$

$$= \frac{(p + q) + (p + q) + (q - p)}{4}$$

$$= \frac{4 + 4 + (q - p)}{4}$$

$$= \frac{8 + (q - p)}{4}$$

$$= 2 + \frac{q - p}{4}$$

Voila! This solution matches (C).

There's no shortcut to doing the calculations for this problem. Since the problem gives you a number value for the median, you can't just plug in your own "easy" numbers for p and q, then test each answer choice. And scanning the answer choices tells you only that the solution must contain p and q—which you probably already knew.

PERMUTATIONS

A *permutation* is an arrangement of objects whose order (sequence) is important. Each arrangement of the letters A, B, C, and D, for example, is a different permutation of the four letters. There are two different ways to determine the number of permutations for a group of objects.

1. List all the permutations methodically to make sure you don't overlook any. For the letters A, B, C, and D, start with A in the first position, then list all possibilities for the second position, along with all possibilities for the third and fourth positions (you'll discover six permutations):

   A *B* C D   A *C* B D   A *D* B C

   A *B* D C   A *C* D B   A *D* C B

   Placing B in the first position would also result in six permutations. The same applies to either C or D in the first position. Therefore, the total number of permutations is $6 \times 4 = 24$.

2. Use the following formula (let n = the number of objects), and limit the number of terms to the counting numbers, or positive integers:

   Number of permutations $= n(n - 1)(n - 2)(n - 3) \ldots$

   The number of permutations can be expressed as $n!$ (*n factorial*). Using the factorial formula is much easier than compiling a list of permutations. For example, try applying the formula to the letters A, B, C, and D:

   $4! = 4(4 - 1)(4 - 2)(4 - 3) = 4 \times 3 \times 2 \times 1 = 24$

A tougher permutation question might place constraints on the possibilities. In this type of question, you'll need to calculate multiple permutations, then add them together—applying a dose of logic along the way. Here's an example:

Q Five children, two boys and three girls, are standing in a single-file line. If the first in line is a girl, how many different arrangements of the five children are possible?

(A) 16
(B) 20
(C) 36
(D) 45
(E) 72

A **The correct answer is (E).** Label the five children B1, B2, G1, G2, and G3. If G1 is first in line, with the other four children in any order, the number of permutations is 4!, or 24. The same applies to either G2 or G3 in the first position. Therefore, the total number of permutations is 4! + 4! + 4! = 72.

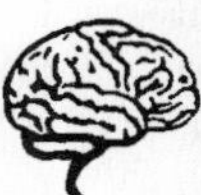

True Brainiacs can shortcut common factorial calculations by memorizing them: 3! = 6, 4! = 24, 5! = 120, and 6! = 720.

COMBINATIONS

A *combination* is a group of certain objects selected from a larger set. The order of objects in the group is not important. You can determine the total number of possible combinations by listing the possible groups in a methodical manner. For instance, to determine the number of possible three-letter groups among the letters A, B, C, D, and E, work methodically, starting with A as a group member paired with B, C, D, and then E. Be sure not to repeat combinations (repetitions are indicated in parentheses here):

A, B, C	(A, C, B)	(A, D, B)	(A, E, B)
A, B, D	A, C, D	(A, D, C)	(A, E, C)
A, B, E	A, C, E	A, D, E	(A, E, D)

Notice that each parenthesized combination backtracks to an earlier letter. To be sure you don't repeat any combination, don't backtrack to an earlier object.

Perform the same task assuming B is in the group, then assuming C is in the group (all combinations not listed here repeat what's already listed):

B, C, D	C, D, E
B, C, E	
B, D, E	

The total number of combinations is ten.

On the ACT, a challenging combination question might require you to do one or both of the following:

- Determine the number of combinations involving two or more sets of objects
- Combine permutations and combinations

Here's a question requiring both of these tasks:

Q From a group of three violinists and four pianists, a judge must select two violinists and two pianists to perform one at a time at a music recital. How many different arrangements for the recital are possible?

(A) 72
(B) 108
(C) 216
(D) 356
(E) 432

A **The correct answer is (E).** The judge must select two of three violinists, for a total of three possible combinations. The judge must select two of four pianists, for a total of six possible combinations. For each pair of violinists, there are six possible pairs of pianists; therefore, the total number of four-musician combinations is $6 \times 3 = 18$. Each of the 18 four-musician combinations involves 24 permutations. Thus, the total number of permutations is $24 \times 18 = 432$.

X-REF **You can approach combination problems as *probability* problems as well. How? Think of the "probability" of any single combination as "one divided by" the total number of combinations (a fraction between zero and 1). Use the quickest method for the question at hand. The topic of probability is next.**

PROBABLILITY

Probability refers to the statistical chances, or "odds," of an event occurring (or not occurring). By definition, probability ranges from 0 to 1. (Probability is never negative, and it's never greater than 1.) Here's the basic formula for determining probability:

Probability = (number of ways the event can occur) ÷ (total number of possible occurrences)

To calculate the probability of an event NOT occurring, just *subtract* the probability of the event occurring *from 1*.

Here's a simple illustration to help you understand how the formula works:

If you randomly select one candy from a jar containing two cherry candies, two licorice candies, and one peppermint candy:

- The probability of selecting a cherry candy is $\frac{2}{5}$, or 20%. (There are 2 ways the event can occur among 5 possible occurrences.)
- The probability of not selecting a cherry candy is $\frac{3}{5}$, or 60%. (Subtract $\frac{2}{5}$ from 1.)

A more difficult probability question will involve this basic formula, but it will also add a complication. It might require you to determine any of the following:

- Certain missing facts needed for a given probability
- Probabilities involving two (or more) *independent* events
- Probabilities involving an event that is *dependent* on another event

Think twice before you try to "intuit" the answer for these three types of probability questions. Probabilities involving complex scenarios such as these are often greater or lesser than even a Brainiac might expect.

MISSING FACTS NEEDED FOR A GIVEN PROBABILITY

In this question type, instead of calculating probability, determine the missing number needed for a given probability. Don't panic; just plug what you know into the basic formula, and solve for the missing number. Here's a grid-in example:

Q A piggy-bank contains a certain number of coins, of which 53 are dimes and 19 are nickels. The remainder of the coins in the bank are quarters. If the probability of selecting a quarter from this bank is $\frac{1}{4}$, how many quarters does the bank contain?

(A) 30
(B) 27
(C) 24
(D) 21
(E) 16

A **The correct answer is (C).** This question looks complicated, but it's really not. Just plug what you know into the probability formula. Let x = the number of quarters in the bank (the numerator of the formula's fraction), and let $x + 72$ = the total number of coins (the fraction's denominator). Then, solve for x (using the cross-product method to clear fractions):

$$\frac{1}{4} = \frac{x}{x + 72}$$
$$x + 72 = 4x$$
$$72 = 3x$$
$$24 = x$$

PROBABILITY INVOLVING TWO (OR MORE) INDEPENDENT EVENTS

Two events are *independent* if neither event affects the probability that the other will occur. (You'll look at *dependent* events a few pages ahead.) On the ACT, look for either of these scenarios involving independent events:

- Randomly selecting one object from *each of two or more groups*
- Randomly selecting one object from a group, then *replacing* it and selecting again (as in a "second round" or "another turn" of a game)

In either scenario, the simplest calculation involves finding the probability of two events *both* occurring. All you need to do is *multiply* together their individual probabilities:

(probability of event 1 occurring) × (probability of event 2 occurring) = (probability of both events occurring)

For example, assume that you randomly select one letter from each of two sets: {A,B} and {C,D,E}. The probability of selecting A and C $= \frac{1}{2} \times \frac{1}{3}$, or $\frac{1}{6}$.

To determine the probability that *three* events will all occur is no big deal; just multiply the third event's probability by the other two.

To make this type of question a little more mind-bending, the test-makers might turn it on its head or side. Here are four variations, any of which would leave average test-takers in the ACT dust:

1. To calculate the probability that two events will *not both* occur, *subtract from 1* the probability of both events occurring:

   (1 − probability of both events occurring) = (probability that the events will not both occur)

2. To calculate the probability that *neither* of two events will occur, *multiply* together individual probabilities as follows:

   (probability of event 1 *not* occurring) × (probability of event 2 *not* occurring) = (probability of neither event occurring)

3. To calculate the probability that *either or both* (at least one) of two events will occur, *subtract from 1* the probability of neither event occurring:

   (1 − probability of neither event occurring) = (probability of at least one event occurring)

4. To calculate the probability that *either*, *but not both*, of two events will occur, *add* together the two sets of probabilities, or *subtract from 1* the probability of each event *not* occurring:

   (probability of event 1 occurring) × (probability of event 2 *not* occurring) + (probability of event 2 occurring) × (probability of event 1 *not* occurring) = (probability of one, but not both, occurring)

   1 − (probability of both events occurring) − (probability of neither event occurring) = (probability of one, but not both, occurring)

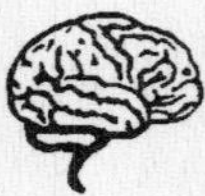

In variation 4, why subtract two probabilities from 1 as indicated? Think about it. Considered together, the three probabilities in the equation cover all possibilities, so their sum must be 1.

To get a handle on these four variations (and how they differ), assume again that you randomly select one letter from each of two sets: {A,B} and {C,D,E}. Here's how to calculate each probability (the two "events" are the selection of A and the selection of C):

1. Probability of not selecting both A and C:

   (1 − probability of selecting A and C)

   $$1-\left(\frac{1}{2}\right)\left(\frac{1}{3}\right)=1-\frac{1}{6}=\frac{5}{6}$$

2. Probability of selecting neither A nor C:

   (probability of not selecting A) × (probability of not selecting C)

   $$\left(1-\frac{1}{2}\right)\left(1-\frac{1}{3}\right)=\frac{1}{2}\times\frac{2}{3}=\frac{2}{6},\text{ or }\frac{1}{3}$$

3. Probability of selecting either A or C, or both:

   1 − (probability of selecting neither A nor C)

   $$1-\left(\frac{1}{2}\right)\left(\frac{2}{3}\right)=1-\frac{1}{3}=\frac{2}{3}$$

4. Probability of selecting either A or C, but not both:

   (probability of selecting A) × (probability of not selecting C) + (probability of selecting C) × (probability of not selecting A)

   $$\left(\frac{1}{2}\right)\left(\frac{2}{3}\right)+\left(\frac{1}{3}\right)\left(\frac{1}{2}\right)=\frac{2}{6}+\frac{1}{6}=\frac{1}{2}$$

   OR

   1 − (probability of selecting neither A nor C) − (probability of selecting A and C)

   $$1-\frac{1}{3}-\frac{1}{6}=\frac{1}{2}$$

Now, try applying the formula for the first of these variations to an ACT-style Problem Solving question:

Q If one student is chosen randomly out of a group of seven students, then one student is again chosen randomly from the same group of seven, what is the probability that two different students will be chosen?

(A) $\frac{36}{49}$

(B) $\frac{6}{7}$

(C) $\frac{19}{21}$

(D) $\frac{13}{14}$

(E) $\frac{48}{49}$

A **The correct answer is (E).** You must first calculate the chances of picking *the same student twice,* by multiplying together the two individual probabilities for the student: $\frac{1}{7} \times \frac{1}{7} = \frac{1}{49}$. The probability of picking the same student twice, added to the probability of not picking the same student twice, equals 1. To answer the question, then, subtract $\frac{1}{49}$ from 1.

In one selection, the probability of *not* selecting a certain student from the group of seven is $\frac{6}{7}$ (the probability of selecting the student, subtracted from 1). But does this mean that the probability of not selecting the same student twice = $\frac{6}{7} \times \frac{6}{7} = \frac{36}{49}$? No! Make sure you understand the difference, or you'll have to stop calling yourself Brainiac.

PROBABILITY INVOLVING A DEPENDENT EVENT

Two distinct events might be related in that one event affects the probability of the other one occurring—for example, randomly selecting one object from a group, then selecting a second object from the same group *without replacing* the first selection. Removing one object from the group *increases the odds* of selecting any particular object from those that remain.

Handle this type of problem as you would any other probability problem: calculate individual probabilities, then combine them. Here's a typical example:

Q In a random selection of two people from a group of five—A, B, C, D, and E—what is the probability of selecting A and B, without replacement?

(A) $\frac{2}{5}$

(B) $\frac{1}{5}$

(C) $\frac{1}{10}$

(D) $\frac{1}{15}$

(E) $\frac{1}{20}$

A **The correct answer is (C).** Consider each of the two selections separately. In the first selection, the probability of selecting either A or B is $\frac{2}{5}$. But the probability of selecting the second of the two is $\frac{1}{4}$, because after the first selection, only four people remain from whom to select. Since the question asks for the odds of selecting both A and B (as opposed to either one), multiply the two individual probabilities:

$$\frac{2}{5} \times \frac{1}{4} = \frac{2}{20} = \frac{1}{10}$$

You can also approach a question such as this one as a *combination* problem. For this question, here are all the possibilities:

A and either B, C, D, or E (4 combinations)

B and either C, D, or E (3 combinations)

C and either D or E (2 combinations)

D and E (1 combination)

There are ten possible combinations, so the probability of selecting A and B is 1 in 10.

Because probability questions can be among the very toughest on the ACT, strategies such as plugging-in test numbers, working backward, and even sizing up the answer choices don't work for most questions of this kind (including this one).

PROGRESSIONS (SEQUENCES OR SERIES)

An ACT question involving a *progression* (or *sequence* or *series*) of numbers or other terms might come in either one of two flavors:

- An *arithmetic series*, in which there is a constant (unchanging) difference between successive terms (e.g., 4, 7, 10, 13, . . .)
- A *geometric series*, in which each term is a constant multiple of the preceding one (e.g., 2, 4, 8, 16, . . .)—in other words, the ratio between any term and the preceding one is constant (e.g., the ratio 2:1 in the series 2, 4, 8, 16, . . .)

The question might ask for the sum of some or all of the terms in the series, or it might ask for a simple average (arithmetic mean).

Handling an *arithmetic-series* question is a no-brainer. The sum of the terms is simply the average of the first and last terms multiplied by the number of terms. In other words, arithmetic-series questions are actually simple-average questions, in which you apply the arithmetic mean formula to the problem at hand.

Questions involving *geometric series* are much trickier—Brainiac territory, indeed. Unless the progression is obvious from the information the question provides (e.g., "What is the eighth term of the series: 2, 4, 8, 16, . . .?"), you'll need to memorize and apply certain formulas to solve the problem. In the following formula, r = the constant multiple (or the ratio between each term and the preceding one), a = the first term in the series, n = the position number for any particular term in the series, and T = the particular term itself:

$$ar^{(n-1)} = T$$

You can solve for any of the formula's variables, as long as you know the values for the other three. Look at the two following examples:

If $a = 3$ and $r = 2$, then the third term $= (3)(2)^2 = 12$, and the sixth term $= (3)(2)^5 = (3)(32) = 96$.

If the sixth term is $-\frac{1}{16}$ and the constant ratio is $\frac{1}{2}$, then the first term (a) = −2:

$$a\left(\frac{1}{2}\right)^5 = -\frac{1}{16}$$

$$a\left(\frac{1}{32}\right) = -\frac{1}{16}$$

$$a = \left(-\frac{1}{16}\right)(32) = -2$$

The algebra is simple enough—but you need to know the formula, of course. An even more difficult geometric-series question might involve the sum of the terms in the series, or perhaps even the difference between two partial sums. To handle these questions, you need to memorize and apply the following additional formula, which builds on the previous one (S = the sum of the terms in the series):

$$S = a\left(\frac{1 - r^n}{1 - r}\right)$$

Here's a very tough question for which you'll need to apply both formulas you just learned. (If you can handle this one, you're ready for any ACT geometric-series question):

Q In a geometric series, each term is a constant multiple of the preceding one. If the fourth and seventh terms of a geometric series are 5 and −40, respectively, then the sum of the first five terms = ?

(A) $-\frac{55}{8}$

(B) $\frac{55}{8}$

(C) 3

(D) $\frac{33}{8}$

(E) $\frac{55}{8}$

A **The correct answer is (A).** Given the fourth and seventh terms, you can write two equations: $ar^3 = 5$ and $ar^6 = -40$. You can solve for r by dividing the second equation by the first:

$$\frac{ar^6}{ar^3} = \frac{-4}{5}$$

$$r^3 = -8$$

$$r = -2$$

Since $ar^3 = 5$ and $r^3 = -8$, $a = \frac{5}{8}$. Now you can determine the sum of the first five terms:

$$S = -\frac{5}{8}\left[\frac{1 - (-2)^5}{1 - (-2)}\right] = -\frac{5}{8}\left(\frac{33}{3}\right) = -\frac{55}{8}$$

MATRICES

A *matrix* is a rectangular array of numbers. Matrices with the same "shape" (the same number of rows and columns) can be added or subtracted simply by adding or subtracting entries in their positions. Look at the following example:

If $a = \begin{pmatrix} 2 & 6 \\ 3 & -1 \end{pmatrix}$ and $B = \begin{pmatrix} 4 & 0 \\ 2 & 1 \end{pmatrix}$, then $A + B = \begin{pmatrix} 6 & 6 \\ 5 & 0 \end{pmatrix}$

To multiply a matrix *A* by a *scalar* (number) *k*, multiply every entry in *A* by *k*. For example:

$$3\begin{pmatrix} 2 & 6 \\ 3 & -1 \end{pmatrix} = \begin{pmatrix} 6 & 18 \\ 9 & -3 \end{pmatrix}$$

As you can see, each of the three operations just described is *nearly* a no-brainer. Combining matrices by multiplication is much trickier, however. To form the product of two matrices, you first need to know how to form the product of a single-row matrix and a single-column matrix. The product, *RC*, of row-matrix *R* and column-matrix *C* can be defined only if the number of entries in each is the same. When this occurs, product *RC* is the sum of the products of each corresponding pair of entries. For example:

If $R = (1\ 2\ 3)$ and $C = \begin{pmatrix} 4 \\ 5 \\ 6 \end{pmatrix}$, then $RC = (1)(4) + (2)(5) + (3)(6) = 32$

Only if the number of rows in one matrix equals either the number of rows *or* the number of columns in another matrix can you define the product of the two matrices. To form a product matrix, determine the product of each row in one matrix and each column in the other matrix. Enter each product in the position in the product matrix that corresponds to the row and column you combined for the entry. For instance, the product of row 2 of matrix *A* and column 1 of matrix *B* will be the entry for row 2, column 1 of matrix *AB*. A moderately difficult ACT matrix question might test you on this very procedure. Here's a typical example:

Q If $A = \begin{pmatrix} 2 & 6 \\ 3 & -1 \end{pmatrix}$ and $B = \begin{pmatrix} 4 & 3 & -2 \\ 2 & 1 & 5 \end{pmatrix}$, then the entry in the second row, third column of *AB* will be

(A) 20
(B) 11
(C) 1
(D) −1
(E) −11

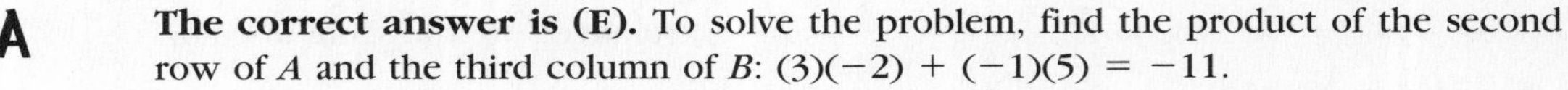

A **The correct answer is (E).** To solve the problem, find the product of the second row of *A* and the third column of *B*: $(3)(-2) + (-1)(5) = -11$.

To complicate a product matrix question, the test-makers might ask you to form an entire product matrix, rather than just a single entry, as in the preceding question. (You'll get to try one such question during this lesson's Brain Teaser.)

To combine matrices by addition (or subtraction), you add (or subtract) corresponding entries. But to multiply one matrix by another, you do *not* simply multiply together corresponding entries, even if the two matrices have the same "shape" (the same number of rows and columns).

BRAIN TEASER

In this quiz, you'll attempt 10 tough ACT-style questions covering the topics from this lesson. Focus on applying the concepts and techniques you learned in this lesson, *not* on answering the questions as quickly as possible. Then, read the explanations that follow the quiz, even for the questions you answered correctly.

QUIZ

1. The arithmetic mean (average) of two numbers, one of which is q, is pq. If a third number is added, the arithmetic mean of all three numbers is $\frac{p + 2pq}{3}$. Which of the following represents the third number?

(A) $2p - q$
(B) $q - p$
(C) $3(q + p)$
(D) pq
(E) p

2. In a room, five chairs are placed to accommodate three people, one person to a chair. How many seating arrangements are possible?

(F) 45
(G) 60
(H) 72
(J) 90
(K) 120

3. A bouquet of flowers contains four times as many carnations as roses and twice as many white roses as red roses. If these are the only flowers in the bouquet, what is the probability of picking a red rose from the bouquet?

(A) $\frac{2}{15}$
(B) $\frac{1}{10}$
(C) $\frac{1}{15}$
(D) $\frac{1}{16}$
(E) $\frac{1}{30}$

4. The median of four distinct numbers is 0 (zero), and the difference between the least and greatest of the four numbers is 4. Which of the following statements must be true?

I. The arithmetic mean (simple average) of the four numbers is 0.
II. The least number's absolute value is less than 4.
III. The greatest number is less than 4.

(F) I only
(G) II only
(H) I and III only
(J) II and III only
(K) I, II, and III

5. Three letters are selected randomly from a set containing only two letters, A and B, as follows: {A,A,A,B,B}. What is the probability of selecting exactly one letter "A" from the set?

(A) $\frac{2}{5}$
(B) $\frac{3}{10}$
(C) $\frac{4}{15}$
(D) $\frac{1}{5}$
(E) $\frac{2}{15}$

6. Three socks are randomly removed from a drawer containing socks: two black, two blue, and one white. What is the probability that no two socks removed are the same in color?

(F) $\frac{1}{5}$
(G) $\frac{2}{5}$
(H) $\frac{3}{5}$
(J) $\frac{1}{15}$
(K) $\frac{2}{15}$

7. If the average (arithmetic mean) of the first sixteen positive integers is subtracted from the average (arithmetic mean) of the next sixteen positive integers, what is the result?

(A) 128
(B) 64
(C) 32
(D) 16
(E) 0

8. A bag of cards contains 185 cards: 160 "Try Again" cards and 25 "Winner" cards. How many "Try Again" cards must be removed for the probability of selecting a "Winner" card among 25 such cards to be $\frac{1}{6}$?

(F) 35
(G) 40
(H) 42
(J) 48
(K) 64

9. In a geometric series, each term is a constant multiple of the preceding one. If the first three terms in a geometric series are -2, x, and -32, which of the following could be the sixth term in the series?

(A) $-4{,}096$
(B) $-1{,}024$
(C) 512
(D) 1,024
(E) 2,048

10. If $A = \begin{pmatrix} 4 & -3 \\ 1 & 2 \end{pmatrix}$ and $B = \begin{pmatrix} 3 & 0 \\ 1 & 5 \\ -2 & 4 \end{pmatrix}$, then $AB =$?

(F) $\begin{pmatrix} 12 & 0 \\ 1 & 10 \\ -2 & 4 \end{pmatrix}$

(G) $\begin{pmatrix} -12 & 0 \\ 2 & 5 \\ 4 & -8 \end{pmatrix}$

(H) $\begin{pmatrix} 12 & -9 \\ 9 & 7 \\ -4 & 14 \end{pmatrix}$

(J) $\begin{pmatrix} 4 & -12 \\ 5 & 10 \\ -2 & 9 \end{pmatrix}$

(K) $\begin{pmatrix} 12 & 0 \\ 9 & 0 \\ -4 & 0 \end{pmatrix}$

ANSWERS AND EXPLANATIONS

1. **The correct answer is (E).** To answer the question, solve for the third number using the arithmetic-mean formula. You'll need the second of the original two numbers to do this. To find that number, plug the given information into the arithmetic mean formula, then solve for it (let x represent the second number):

$$AM = \frac{q + x}{2}$$

$$pq = \frac{q + x}{2}$$

$$2pq = q + x$$

$$2pq - q = x$$

Now, you can plug this value into the same formula, this time for all three terms (let y represent the third number):

$$\frac{p+2pq}{3} = \frac{q+(2pq-q)+y}{3}$$

$$p + 2pq = q + (2pq - q) + y$$

$$p = y$$

Can you use the plug-in strategy to solve this problem, testing each answer choice by substituting simple numbers for p and q? No; it's too complex. You'll need to be flexible, using shortcuts whenever you can but recognizing their limitations.

2. **The correct answer is (G).** To solve this problem without resorting to listing possibilities, you need to apply the factorial formula as well as a bit of logic. If you think of each of the two empty chairs (C1 and C2) as a distinct object along with each of the three people (X, Y, and Z), the number of permutations is $5! = 5 \times 4 \times 3 \times 2 \times 1 = 120$. However, each permutation is coupled with another in which the two empty chairs are reversed—for example:

X, Y, Z, C1, C2
X, Y, Z, C2, C1

Since the question makes no distinction between the chairs, reduce the number of permutations by 50%, to 60.

3. **The correct answer is (C).** You can solve this problem algebraically with the probability formula:

Let x = the number of red roses
Let $2x$ = the number of white roses
Let $12x$ = the number of carnations

Let $3x + 12x$, or $15x$ = the total number of flowers in the bouquet.

$$\frac{\text{\# of roses}}{\text{total \# of flowers}} = \frac{x}{15x} = \frac{1}{15}$$

What about using the plug-in strategy to solve this problem? Well, you can, but picking "test" numbers that work is a bit tricky. For instance, if you try using 10 roses and 40 carnations, you end up with $3\frac{1}{3}$ red roses ($\frac{1}{3}$ the number of white roses), so you need to try numbers that yield only "whole flowers." The simplest numbers to use are the least ones: 1 red rose, 2 white roses, and 12 carnations.

4. **The correct answer is (J).** The median is the arithmetic mean of the two middle numbers. Since that mean is 0 (zero), the two numbers must have the same absolute value, although one must be negative while the other is positive (for example, -1 and 1). Accordingly, the least of the four numbers must be negative, while the greatest must be positive. Given that the difference between these two numbers on the number line is 4, the least number must be greater than -4 but less than 0; otherwise, the greatest number would not be positive. Therefore, the least number's absolute value must be less than 4. Similarly, the greatest number must be less than 4 (but greater than 0); otherwise, the least number would not be negative. Hence, statements (II) and (III) must both be true. However, the absolute values of the least and greatest numbers do not need to be equal. For instance, the four numbers might be -3, $-\frac{1}{2}$, $\frac{1}{2}$, and 1. Hence, statement (I) is not necessarily true.

5. **The correct answer is (B).** Instead of using the probability formula, it's quicker to think of each A and each B as distinct (A1, A2, A3, B1, B2), then tally up the number of three-letter combinations (you'll find ten of them):

   A1 and A2, plus either A3, B1 or B2
   A1 and A3, plus either B1 or B2
   A1, B1, and B2
   A2 and A3, plus either B1 or B2
   A2, B1, and B2
   A3, B1, and B2

   Of these ten combinations, three include one A and two Bs. Thus, the probability of selecting exactly one A is $\frac{3}{10}$.

6. **The correct answer is (G).** The probability of removing the white sock is $\frac{1}{5}$. Four socks remain. The probability of removing a black sock from among the remaining four is $\frac{2}{4}$. Three socks remain, so the probability of removing a blue sock is $\frac{2}{3}$. Combine the three probabilities by multiplying: $\frac{1}{5} \times \frac{1}{2} \times \frac{2}{3} = \frac{2}{30}$, or $\frac{1}{15}$.

   We must then multiply this value by 3! (the number of ways to arrange 3 items into 3 positions). So, $\frac{1}{5} \bullet 3! = \frac{1}{15} \bullet 6 = \frac{6}{15} = \frac{2}{5}$.

7. **The correct answer is (D).** Do you really need to add all of the digits together, then divide by 16 twice— once for each series? Of course not. Since neither series skips any integers, your intuition should tell you that for each one, the mean is the same as the median: exactly midway between the least and greatest numbers.

   Mean of first series: $\frac{1 + 16}{2} = \frac{17}{2}$

   Mean of second series: $\frac{17 + 32}{2} = \frac{49}{2}$

   Now, do the subtraction: $\frac{49}{2} - \frac{17}{2} = \frac{32}{2}$, or 16.

Before performing time-consuming calculations, such as combining a long string of numbers, look for a shortcut. Chances are, you'll find one. The test-makers build shortcuts into the questions to reward Brainiacs.

8. **The correct answer is (F).** Solve this problem using the basic probability formula:

   $$\frac{\text{winner card}}{\text{total cards}} = \frac{1}{6}$$

   In this case, total cards (the fraction's denominator) equal 25 + 160, less the number of "Try Again" cards to be removed (let x equal this number):

   $$\frac{\text{winner card}}{\text{total cards}} = \frac{25}{25 + (160 - x)} = \frac{1}{6}$$

   Solve for x (use the cross-product method to clear fractions):

   $$\frac{25}{25+(160-x)} = \frac{1}{6}$$

   $$25 + 160 - x = 150$$
   $$-x = -35$$
   $$x = 35$$

9. **The correct answer is (E).** Since all pairs of successive terms must have the same ratio, $\frac{-2}{x} = \frac{x}{-8}$. Cross-multiplying, $x^2 = 64$, and, thus, $x = \pm 8$. So, the ration between the terms (r) is ± 4. For $+4$, the sixth term would be $(-2)(4)^5 = -2{,}048$, while for -4 it would be 2,048.

10. **The correct answer is (H).** The number of rows in *A* equals the number of columns in B. Accordingly, to form product matrix *AB*, multiply each row of *B* by each column of *A*, arranging the six resulting entries in a 3-row, 2-column matrix as follows:

    Column 1
    Row 1: (*B* row 1)(*A* col. 1) = (3)(4) + (0)(1) = 12

    Row 2: (*B* row 2)(*A* col. 1) = (1)(4) + (5)(1) = 9

    Row 3: (*B* row 3)(*A* col. 1) = (-2)(4) + (4)(1) = −4

    Column 2
    Row 1: (*B* row 1)(*A* col. 2) = (3)(-3) + (0)(2) = −9
    Row 2: (*B* row 2)(*A* col. 2) = (1)(−3) + (5)(2) = 7
    Row 3: (B row 3)(*A* col. 2) = (-2)(−3) + (4)(2) = 14

    $$\text{Matrix } AB = \begin{pmatrix} 12 & -9 \\ 9 & 7 \\ -4 & 14 \end{pmatrix}$$

PART IV

THE ACT READING TEST

LESSON 16
Reading Strategies

This lesson is the first of two covering Brainiac strategies for the ACT Reading Test. In this lesson, you'll:

- Review some key facts about the Reading Test
- Learn how Brainiacs figure out the most common reading questions by using special insights and other tools at their cognitive disposal (Six sample questions will serve as illustrations.)
- Apply Brainiac insights to fifteen brain-teasing questions based on three reading passages.

KEY FACTS ABOUT THE READING TEST

You should keep the following facts in mind:

- Each passage is labeled according to its broad category—Natural Science, Social Studies, Humanities, or Prose Fiction. (Remember: You'll encounter one of each type on the test.)
- Every fifth line of each passage is numbered. Some questions refer to line numbers, so you can quickly locate the specific part of the passage to which the question refers.
- You don't need to know anything about a passage's topic to handle the questions. This portion of the ACT measures your verbal reasoning abilities, not your knowledge of certain subjects.
- The test-makers carefully select and edit excerpts and design questions so that test-takers who happen to be familiar with the topic hold no advantage over other test-takers when it comes to answering the questions.

WHAT MAKES FOR A MIND-BENDING READING PASSAGE OR QUESTION?

All ACT reading passages are not created equal—equally difficult, that is. Comparatively tough passages are typically written in a drier, more *academic* style than easier ones. The syntax of these passages is more complex, and the vocabulary is more advanced. The topic might deal with ideas and concepts that are more difficult to grasp, or it might be organized in a way that makes it more difficult to follow. A challenging passage can involve a topic from any academic field within the natural sciences, social sciences, or humanities. What makes a passage mind-bending is not the specific topic itself, but rather how the passage is written, organized, and edited.

All ACT reading questions are not created equal either. Questions that require you to simply recall or look up passage information are almost always easier than ones that require you to understand, interpret, or apply what's in the passage. To boost the difficulty level of any reading question, the test-makers often employ complex syntax and advanced vocabulary, just as they do to create tougher passages. A difficult question might also require a close judgment call between the best answer choice and a "runner-up" choice.

Prose fiction passages (excerpts from novels and short stories) are the exception to the preceding observations. Unlike the three other types, these passages don't focus on "concepts," they aren't analytical in nature, and their organization is irrelevant. In short, they're a different animal. Accordingly, the questions based on prose fiction passages are a bit different in focus than the ones based on the other types. You'll notice this for yourself during this lesson's Brain Teaser.

The reading passages and questions in this lesson and the next (as well is in Part V) are, for the most part, tougher-than-average in the ways just described. If you can handle the passages and questions in this book, you're ready for any hand the test-makers might deal.

SAMPLE READING QUESTIONS (1-6)

Before we get to Brainiac strategies for handling ACT reading questions, read the following two passages and answer the three questions based on each one. (While some of the questions are average in difficulty level, some are tougher than average; there are no easy questions in the bunch.) In the next section, you'll examine the test-makers' favorite question types and analyze each of these types.

These two passages are about one third the average length of the ones on the ACT. In this lesson's Brain Teaser, as well as in the next lesson and in Part V, you'll deal with passages similar in length to the ones on the test.

PASSAGE I—Natural Science

(Questions 1–3)

Line The arrival of a non-indigenous plant or animal species in a new location may be either intentional or unintentional. Rates of species movement driven by human transformations of natural environments as well as by human mobility—through commerce, tourism, and travel—dwarf natural rates by comparison. While geographic distributions of species naturally expand or contract over historical time intervals (tens to hundreds of years), species' ranges rarely expand thousands of miles or across physical barriers such as oceans or mountains.

A number of factors confound quantitative evaluation of the relative importance of various entry pathways. Time lags often occur between establishment of non-indigenous species and their detection, and tracing the pathway for a long-established species is difficult. Experts estimate that non-indigenous weeds are usually detected only after having been in the country for thirty years or having spread to at least ten thousand acres. In addition, federal port inspection, although a major source of information on non-indigenous species pathways, especially for agricultural pests, provides data only when such species enter via scrutinized routes. Finally, some comparisons between pathways defy quantitative analysis—for example, which is more "important": the entry pathway of one very harmful species or one by which many but less harmful species enter the country?

1. Which of the following statements about species movement is best supported by the passage?

(A) Species movement is affected more by habitat modifications than by human mobility.
(B) Human-driven factors affect the rate at which species move more than they affect the long-term amount of such movements.
(C) Natural environments created by commerce, tourism, and travel contribute significantly to species movement.
(D) Movement of a species within a continent depends largely upon the geographic extent of human mobility within the continent.

2. The second paragraph as a whole is concerned with

(F) identifying the problems in assessing the relative significance of various entry pathways for non-indigenous species.
(G) discussing the role that time lags and geographic expansion of non-indigenous species play in species detection.
(H) pointing out the inadequacy of the federal port inspection system in detecting the entry of non-indigenous species.
(J) explaining why it is difficult to trace the entry pathways for long-established non-indigenous species.

3. Whether the entry pathway for a particular non-indigenous species can be determined is LEAST likely to depend upon which of the following?

(A) Whether the species is considered to be a pest
(B) Whether the species gains entry through a scrutinized route
(C) How long the species has been established
(D) The size of the average member of the species

PASSAGE II—Humanities

(Questions 4–6)

The encounter a portrait records is most tangibly the sitting itself. The sitting may be brief or extended, collegial or confrontational. Cartier-Bresson has expressed his passion for portrait photography, for instance, by characterizing it as "a duel without rules . . ." Such a metaphor contrasts quite sharply with Richard Avedon's conception of a sitting. While Cartier-Bresson reveals himself as an interloper and opportunist, Avedon confesses—perhaps uncomfortably—to a role as diagnostician and (by implication) psychic healer: not as someone who necessarily transforms his subjects, but as someone who reveals their essential nature. Both photographers appear to agree on one premise, however, which is that the fundamental dynamic in this process lies squarely in the hands of the artist.

A quite-different paradigm has its roots not in confrontation or consultation but in active collaboration between the artist and sitter. This very different kind of relationship was formulated most vividly by William Hazlitt in his essay entitled "On Sitting for One's Picture" (1823). To Hazlitt, the "bond of connection" between painter and sitter is most like the relationship between two people in love: "they are always thinking and talking of the same thing, in which their self love finds an equal counterpart."

Hazlitt fleshes out his thesis by recounting particular episodes from the career of Sir Joshua Reynolds. According to Hazlitt, Reynolds' sitters, accompanied by their friends, were meant to enjoy an atmosphere that was both comfortable for them and conducive to the enterprise of the portrait painter, who was simultaneously their host and their contractual employee. In the case of artists like Reynolds—who I take to be a paradigmatic case—no fundamental difference exists between the artist's studio and all those other rooms in which the sitters spin out the days of their lives. The act of entering Reynolds' studio—this social and aesthetic encounter—did not necessarily transform those who sat for him. Collaboration in portraiture such as Reynolds' is based on the sitter's comfort and security as well as on his desire to experiment with something new; and it is in this "creation of another self," as Hazlitt put it, that the painter's subjects may properly see themselves for the first time.

4. A portrait artist operating under the Reynolds paradigm would probably disagree that

(F) a portraiture sitting often changes the way the sitter views himself or herself.
(G) the portraiture encounter provides a means for both artist and subject to display their vanity.
(H) a successful portrait depends more upon the artist's initiative than upon the subject.
(J) the success of a portrait depends largely upon whether the artist and sitter are socially compatible.

5. Which of the following best characterizes the portraiture experience as viewed by Avedon?

(A) A collaboration
(B) A mutual accommodation
(C) A consultation
(D) An uncomfortable encounter

6. Which of the following best expresses the main idea of the passage?

(F) The success of a portrait depends largely upon the relationship between artist and subject.
(G) The social aspect of portraiture sitting plays an important part in the sitting's outcome.
(H) Portraits, more than most other art forms, provide insight into the artist's social relationships.
(J) The paintings of Reynolds provide a record of his success in achieving a social bond with his subjects.

THE TEST-MAKERS' FOUR FAVORITE QUESTION TYPES

The test-makers are very predictable when it comes to how they design reading questions. The following four distinct types of questions appear most frequently on the test (you'll examine each type in the sections that follow):

- Simple Recall/Detail (the easiest and most common type)
- Recap
- Restatement
- Inference

The following four additional question types are inherently more complex than the preceding four and appear less frequently on the test (you'll examine each of these during the next lesson):

- Application (or Extrapolation)
- Assumption (or Inference)
- Additional Information
- Method

X-REF

You must "think outside the box" (the box being the passage's text) when you encounter one of the four more difficult question types—a high-level skill that distinguishes Brainiacs from the rest. That's why you'll be devoting most of the next lesson to these four types.

SIMPLE RECALL QUESTIONS

For these questions, you must identify the answer choice that provides the information from the passage that the question asks about. The question stem might look something like one of the following:

"Which of the following does the author mention as an example of . . .?"

"According to the passage, . . . is caused by . . .?"

Simple Recall questions are the most common question type and are the easiest because all you need to do is rely on your memory or go back and locate the appropriate information in the passage.

To "trick up" a Simple Recall question, the test-makers might turn the question around by asking you to identify an exception to the information provided in the passage (with a word such as "except" or "least" in upper-case letters):

"The author mentions all of the following as examples of . . . EXCEPT:"

"According to the passage, . . . could be caused by any of the following EXCEPT:"

Of course, no Brainiac worth his or her gray matter would be tricked by this variation. Just eliminate all choices that the passage covers and that are relevant to the question, and you'll be left with one choice—the correct one. It's not exactly rocket science. In fact, you probably found the Question 3 from Passage I) pretty easy, although it's about as tough a Simple Recall question as you'll find on the ACT. Here it is again, along with an explanatory answer:

Q 3. Whether the entry pathway for a particular non-indigenous species can be determined is LEAST likely to depend upon which of the following?

(A) Whether the species is considered to be a pest
(B) Whether the species gains entry through a scrutinized route
(C) How long the species has been established
(D) The size of the average member of the species

A **The correct answer is (D).** Nowhere in the passage does the author state or imply that the physical size of a species' members affects whether the entry pathway for the species can be determined.

You can easily eliminate choices (B) and (C) because both are mentioned explicitly in the second paragraph as factors affecting how precisely the entry pathway(s) of a species can be determined. Choice (A) is a bit trickier, and it's the "runner-up" choice. Unlike the other incorrect choices, (A) is not explicitly supported by the passage. However, the author mentions in the final paragraph that federal port inspection is "a major source of information on non-indigenous species pathways, especially for agricultural pests." Accordingly, whether a species is an agricultural pest might have some bearing upon whether or not its entry is detected (by port inspectors). Hence, choice (A) is not as good as choice (D), which finds no support in the passage whatsoever.

In a tougher Simple Recall question, one wrong-answer choice will be more tempting than the others because the passage will implicitly support it. Don't be fooled; you will find a better choice among the four.

RECAP QUESTIONS

For *Recap* questions, you must recognize either the main idea, or thesis, of the passage (or a particular paragraph) as a whole or the author's primary purpose or concern in the passage (or in a particular paragraph) as a whole. In other words, you recap what the passage or paragraph is generally about. The question stem will look a lot like one of the following:

"Which of the following best expresses the main idea of the passage?"

"Among the following characterizations, the passage is best viewed as"

"Which of the following would be the most appropriate title of the passage?"

"The author's primary purpose in the passage [or "in the third paragraph"] is to"

"The passage [or "in the first paragraph"] is primarily concerned with"

You need to recognize the passage's (or paragraph's) overall scope and its main emphasis. Most of the wrong-answer choices will fall into these categories:

- Too broad (embracing ideas outside the scope of the passage or paragraph)
- Too narrow (focusing on only a certain portion or aspect of the discussion)
- Distorted (an inaccurate reflection of the passage's ideas or the author's perspective on the topic)

The test-makers might include a "runner-up" answer choice that's just a bit off the mark to try to throw you off. Question 6 from Passage II is a good example of this tactic. Here it is again, along with an explanatory answer:

Q 6. Which of the following best expresses the main idea of the passage?

(F) The success of a portrait depends largely upon the relationship between artist and subject.
(G) The social aspect of portraiture sitting plays an important part in the sitting's outcome.
(H) Portraits, more than most other art forms, provide insight into the artist's social relationships.
(J) The paintings of Reynolds provide a record of his success in achieving a social bond with his subjects.

A **The correct answer is (G).** Although it is difficult to articulate a single main idea or thesis of this passage, the author seems to be most concerned with emphasizing that a portrait sitting is a social encounter, not just an artistic exercise, and that artists consider their relationships with their sitters to be significant in some way. Thus, choice (G) is a good statement of the author's primary point.

Choice (F) is the "runner-up". Without choice (G), choice (F) would be the best choice—it embraces the passage as a whole and properly focuses on the author's primary concern with exploring the relationship between artist and sitter. However, the passage does not discuss how or whether this relationship results in a "successful" portrait; thus, choice (F) distorts the information in the passage.

Choice (H) distorts the information in the passage and departs from the topic at hand. Although the passage does support the notion that a portrait might reveal something about the relationship between artist and sitter, the author neither states nor implies that a portrait reveals anything about the artist's other relationships. Moreover, nowhere in the passage does the author compare portraiture with other art forms.

Choice (J) is too narrow and refers to information not mentioned in the passage. The passage is not just about Reynolds, but also about the portraiture encounter in general. Also, the author does not comment on Reynolds' "success" or about how his relationship with his sitters may have contributed to his success.

Question 2 from Passage I is another good example of a moderately difficult Recap question—this one focusing on just one paragraph, the second one. An easier question would provide wrong-answer choices that refer to information in the first paragraph. But it's not as easy to rule out answer choices in Question 2. Here's the question again along with an explanatory answer:

Q 2. The second paragraph as a whole is concerned with

(F) identifying the problems in assessing the relative significance of various entry pathways for non-indigenous species.
(G) discussing the role that time lags and geographic expansion of non-indigenous species play in species detection.
(H) pointing out the inadequacy of the federal port inspection system in detecting the entry of non-indigenous species.
(J) explaining why it is difficult to trace the entry pathways for long-established non-indigenous species.

A **The correct answer is (F).** In the first sentence of the second paragraph, the author claims that "[a] number of factors confound quantitative evaluation of the relative importance of various entry pathways." In the remainder of the paragraph, the author identifies three such problems: (1) the difficulty of early detection, (2) the inadequacy of port inspection, and (3) the inherent subjectivity in determining the "importance" of a pathway. Choice (F) provides a good "recap" of what the second paragraph accomplishes.

Choice (G) is a distortion. Although the author mentions these factors, they are not "discussed" in any detail, as choice (G) suggests. Also, the primary concern of the second paragraph is not with identifying the factors affecting species detection, but rather with identifying the problems in quantifying the relative importance of various entry pathways.

Choice (H) is too narrow. The author is concerned with identifying other problems as well as determining the relative importance of various entry pathways.

Choice (J) is a distortion. Although the author asserts that it is difficult to trace an entry pathway once a species is well established, the author does not explain why this is so.

On the ACT, expect the Social Studies, Natural Science, and Humanities passages to each be accompanied by one or two Recap questions. However, you probably won't find any Recap questions that are based on the prose fiction passage.

RESTATEMENT QUESTIONS

For *Restatement* questions, you must understand a specific idea the author is trying to convey in the passage. What makes Restatement questions different from—and more difficult than—Simple Recall questions is that the answer won't be explicitly stated in the text. A Restatement question stem looks something like one of the following:

"Which of the following statements about . . . is most strongly supported by the passage's information?"

"With which of the following statements about . . . would the author most likely agree?"

"Which of the following best characterizes . . . as viewed by . . .?"

Question 1 from Passage I is a good example of a moderately difficult Restatement question. This question is more difficult because the wrong answer choices are designed to confuse you by combining details from the passage that relate to the question—but don't add up. Here's the question again, along with an explanatory answer:

Q

1. Which of the following statements about species movement is best supported by the passage?
   (A) Species movement is affected more by habitat modifications than by human mobility.
   (B) Human-driven factors affect the rate at which species move more than they affect the long-term amount of such movements.
   (C) Natural environments created by commerce, tourism, and travel contribute significantly to species movement.
   (D) Movement of a species within a continent depends largely upon the geographic extent of human mobility within the continent.

A

The correct answer is (D). This choice restates the point made by the author in the first paragraph that rates of species movement driven by human transformation of the natural environment and by human mobility dwarf natural rates by comparison.

Choice (A) is the most tempting wrong-answer choice. Based on the passage, habitat modifications and human mobility can both affect species movement, as choice (A) implies. Also, the passage does make a comparison involving human-driven species movement. Therefore, choice (A) looks appealing. However, the comparison made in the passage is between natural species movement and human-driven movement, not between human modification of habitats and human mobility; therefore, choice (A) confuses the details of the passage.

Choice (B) is easier to eliminate because it is completely unsupported by the passage. The author makes no attempt to compare rate (interpreted either as frequency or speed) of species movement to total amounts of movement (distance).

Choice (C) is the easiest one to eliminate. You don't even need to read the passage to recognize that choice (C) is a nonsensical statement. Human mobility (commerce, tourism, and travel) does not create "natural" environments. It is human mobility itself, not the "natural environment" created by it, that contributes significantly to species movement.

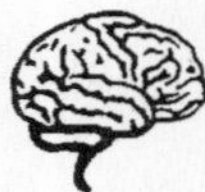

Brainiacs know that many answer choices simply won't make much sense and aren't fooled into second-guessing themselves when they don't understand what a choice means.

Question 4 based on Passage II is a good example of how the test-makers might further boost the difficulty level of a Restatement question. As you read it again here, along with the explanatory answer, notice that the incorrect answer choices are each reasonable interpretations (restatements) of how the passage describes the portraiture experience with Reynolds. This feature, along with the use of sophisticated language ("paradigm"), boosts the difficulty rating of this question to challenging:

Q 4. A portrait artist operating under the Reynolds paradigm would probably disagree that

(F) a portraiture sitting often changes the way the sitter views himself or herself.
(G) the portraiture encounter provides a means for both artist and subject to display their vanity.
(H) a successful portrait depends more upon the artist's initiative than upon the subject.
(J) the success of a portrait depends largely upon whether the artist and sitter are socially compatible.

A **The correct answer is (H).** The author describes a sitting under the Reynolds paradigm as a "collaboration" (line 20), which is based in part on the sitter's "desire to experiment with something new" (line 21) suggesting that the sitter and artist both play active roles in the process. Choice (H) runs contrary to this suggestion.

Choice (G) is the "runner-up" choice. It is not as explicitly supported by the passage as the other incorrect responses. However, choice (G) is supported (albeit implicitly) by Hazlitt's analogy between the collaboration of artist and subject and the relationship between two lovers. Hazlitt describes both relationships as a sharing of each person's self-love (i.e., mutual displaying of each person's vanity).

Choice (F) is supported by the last sentence of the passage, which suggests that the portraiture experience provides the sitter with a new (and more accurate) view of himself or herself.

Choice (J) is implicitly supported. Hazlitt, as well as the author, seems to emphasize the importance of putting the sitter at ease socially—the artist is host, as well as contractual employee, and collaboration (under the Reynolds paradigm) depends ("is based") upon the sitter's comfort. Hence, choice (J) is a reasonable interpretation of the Reynolds paradigm.

The word paradigm means "example or pattern." But you wouldn't need to know its precise definition to handle the preceding question.

INFERENCE QUESTIONS

Inference questions test your ability to recognize what the passage implies or infers but does not state explicitly—in other words, your ability to "read between the lines." You'll need to see a logical connection between two bits of information in the passage (usually in two consecutive sentences) and draw a reasonable conclusion.

In a typical Inference question, the stem will include a word such as "infer" or "probably," as in each of these examples:

"It can be inferred from the passage that the reason for . . . is that . . ."

"The discussion about . . . most reasonably infers which of the following?"

"The author mentions . . . (lines X–X) most probably in order to"

"The example discussed in (lines X–X) is probably intended to illustrate"

Inference questions based on Prose Fiction passages often look a bit different from the preceding ones. A Prose Fiction question might ask what the story's narration "suggests," or what a particular dialogue "suggests" or "implies" about the story's characters—their thoughts, motives, and so forth. You'll see some examples during this lesson's Brain Teaser.

To increase the difficulty level of an Inference question, the test-makers will probably resort to one or both of two ploys:

- Include a "runner-up" answer choice in which the inference is a bit more speculative than the inference in the best choice.
- Require you to combine information from different parts of the passage in order to make the logical inference needed to answer the question.

During this lesson's Brain Teaser, you'll see an example of the first ploy. Right now, look again at Question 5 from the second passage, which incorporates the second ploy. Here it is again, along with an explanatory answer:

Q **5.** Which of the following best characterizes the portraiture experience as viewed by Avedon?

(A) A collaboration
(B) A mutual accommodation
(C) A consultation
(D) An uncomfortable encounter

A **The correct answer is (C).** In the first sentence of the second paragraph, the author distinguishes a "quite-different paradigm" (i.e., the case of Reynolds) from the conceptions of Cartier-Bresson and Avedon, in that the Reynolds paradigm "has its roots not in confrontation or consultation, but in active collaboration between artist and sitter" (lines 9–10). The earlier Cartier-Bresson quotation, in which he characterized portrait photography as "a duel," strongly suggests that Cartier-Bresson conceives the encounter as "confrontational." Hence, by piecing together these two parts of the passage, you can logically infer that the author is characterizing an Avedon sitting as a "consultation."

Each of the incorrect answer choices confuses information in the passage. Choice (A) is wrong because it is the Reynolds paradigm discussed in the third paragraph, not Avedon's view that the author characterizes as a "collaboration" (line 20). Choice (B) confuses what the passage infers about Avedon with what it infers about Hazlitt. Although the term "mutual accommodation" does not appear in the passage, this term suggests a relationship in which both artist and painter allow for the other's needs or desires. Such a description aligns more closely with Hazlitt's analogy of two people in love than with Avedon's view of the artist as diagnostician and psychic healer. Choice (D) confuses Avedon's portraiture encounters with his "uncomfortabl[e]" confession. According to the passage, Avedon confesses "uncomfortably" to his role as diagnostician and psychic healer (lines 4–5). It does not necessarily follow, however, that Avedon finds his encounters with his sitters to be uncomfortable.

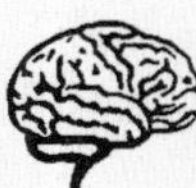

Brainiacs know the difference between a reasonable inference, which no rational person could dispute based on the passage's information, and mere speculation, which requires additional information to hold water.

TOP 10 BRAiNiAC STRATEGIES FOR ANSWERING READING QUESTIONS

If you read the explanations for the preceding six questions, then you've already picked up some strategies that Brainiacs know how to use in answering reading questions. Here, you'll review them and learn about some others.

X-REF

These tips are for answering the questions. In the next lesson, you'll examine strategies for reading the passages.

1. BRAiNiACS READ EVERY WORD OF EVERY ANSWER CHOICE.

Never forget that you're looking for the best response. Often, more than one answer choice will have some merit. (You saw several examples of "runner-up" choices in the preceding section.) Don't hastily select or eliminate answer choices without reading them all. ACT test-takers miss more questions for this reason than for any other!

2. BRAiNiACS DON'T OVER-ANALYZE QUESTIONS OR SECOND-GUESS THEMSELVES.

If you believe you understand a passage fairly well but a particular answer choice seems confusing or a bit nonsensical, don't assume that it's your fault. Many wrong answer choices simply don't make much sense! If a choice strikes you this way, don't examine it further; eliminate it! And if you've read and considered all four choices, and one response strikes you as the best one, more often than not, your initial response will be correct!

3. BRAiNiACS DON'T MAKE THE QUESTIONS TOUGHER THAN THEY REALLY ARE.

Any question in a set could potentially be the easiest (or toughest) one. Any question that strikes you as a "no-brainer" might be just that, regardless of its type. In short: Don't fight a question by assuming it's trickier or more difficult than it might really be.

Don't panic when you come across lengthy questions or answer choices. Although longer questions are usually more challenging than questions that are less wordy, lengthiness doesn't necessarily indicate difficulty level. If you shy away from a question based on its length, you might skip what could actually be an easier question!

4. BRAiNiACS CROSS-REFERENCE QUESTIONS IN THE SAME SET.

Although each question is distinct, it might be possible to check your response to one question by examining your response to another question in the same set. Check to see if you've contradicted yourself in your responses. If so, go back and change one of your answers. For example, your response to a thesis or "main idea" question should be consistent with your response to a question that asks about the author's primary purpose, attitude toward the subject, or position on the issue at hand.

5. BRAiNiACS ELIMINATE ANSWER CHOICES THAT RUN CONTRARY TO THE THESIS.

Regardless of the type of question you're dealing with, keep in mind the overall thesis, main idea, or point that the author is making in the passage. Any answer choice to any question that runs contrary to or is inconsistent with that thesis can be eliminated.

6. BRAiNiACS NEVER ASSUME THAT ACCURATE INFORMATION ALONE MAKES FOR A BEST ANSWER CHOICE.

Be on the lookout for answer choices that provide information supported by the passage but are not responsive to the question. This is probably the test-makers' favorite wrong-answer ploy, and you saw many examples of it in the previous section.

7. BRAiNiACS KEEP A MENTAL CHECKLIST OF WRONG-ANSWER PLOYS TO HELP NARROW ANSWER CHOICES.

In the previous section, you encountered numerous examples of wrong-answer ploys. The following checklist of the test-makers' favorites includes ploys you've already seen, as well as a few new ones. Keep this list in mind during the test to help you narrow down the choices and improve your odds of choosing a correct answer.

- Mentioned in the passage, but does not respond to the question: includes accurate information based on the passage but does not respond appropriately to the question at hand
- Distorts the information in the passage: understates, overstates, or twists the information in the passage or the author's point in presenting that information
- Speculation or unsupported inference: calls for some measure of speculation in that the statement is not readily (reliably) inferable from the information in the passage
- Contrary to the passage or stated backwards: contradicts passage information or gets information backward
- Too narrow (specific): focuses on particular information in the passage that is too specific or narrowly-focused in terms of the question posed
- Too broad (general): embraces information or ideas that are too general or widely-focused in terms of the question posed
- Unsupported (not mentioned) in the passage: brings forth information not found anywhere in the passage

The first ploy in this list is by far the most popular among the test-makers. That's why it merits its very own tip (number 6 above).

8. BRAiNiACS DON'T GET HUNG UP ON FIGURING OUT WHY WRONG ANSWER CHOICES ARE WRONG.

Sure, it helps to keep in mind the preceding checklist of wrong-answer ploys. But you won't score any points for knowing exactly why three answer choices are wrong if, out of the remaining two, you make the wrong choice. Don't go overboard when it comes to recognizing wrong-answer ploys at work. If you're certain but not sure why an answer choice is wrong, don't worry about it. Cross it out and move on.

9. BRAiNiACS TENTATIVELY ANSWER THE QUESTIONS AS THEY GO . . . PARAGRAPH BY PARAGRAPH.

The order of the questions in a set generally corresponds to the order in which information needed to answer them appears in the passage. (This is a general rule only—so you will encounter some exceptions.) After reading the first paragraph, check the first two question stems to see if you can respond to them, at least tentatively. Then, go back and read the second paragraph and check the next two or three question stems. Continue working back and forth in this manner until you've finished the passage and answered all the questions.

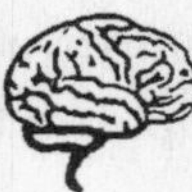

The first paragraph might also provide enough information for an educated guess at a Recap question involving the whole passage. After reading the first paragraph, scan for this question type and take a stab at it. Then, go back to it again after you've read the entire passage.

10. BRAiNiACS WAIT UNTIL THEY'VE COMPLETED AN ENTIRE QUESTION SET BEFORE FILLING IN THEIR ANSWER SHEET.

Wait to fill in your answers on the answer sheet until you've completed every question in a reading set; otherwise, you'll interrupt your train of thought. What's more, cross-referencing questions might reveal an earlier, incorrect answer choice. If you wait to bubble in your answers, you won't need to correct the answer sheet. (Don't underestimate how annoying and unnerving it can be to erase and re-bubble on the answer sheet.)

BRAIN TEASER

In this quiz, you'll read three ACT-length passages and answer five questions based on each one. Passage I is a longer version of one of the passages you encountered earlier in this lesson. Passages II and III are new. For each of the fifteen questions, we'll give you a hint to help you handle it.

On the ACT, you'll answer ten questions based on each reading passage, ranging from "no-brainers" to true brain teasers. In this quiz, however, we've filtered out the no-brainers, leaving only the toughest five questions per passage. So, even if you're an ultra-Brainiac, don't expect this quiz to be a cakewalk!

Attempt all fifteen questions, but don't put yourself under a time limit. Focus instead on applying the strategies for handling the four question types you learned about in this lesson. Then, be sure to read the explanations that follow the quiz. They're just as important as the questions, because they explain how to apply the strategies to the questions.

QUIZ

PASSAGE I—Natural Science

(Questions 1–5)

Non-indigenous species of plants and animals arrive by way of two general types of pathways. First, species having origins outside of the United States may enter the country and become established either as free-living populations or under human cultivation—for example, in agriculture, horticulture, aquaculture, or as pets. Some cultivated species subsequently escape or are released and also become established as free-living populations. Second, species of either U.S. or foreign origin and already within the United States may spread to new locales. Pathways of both types include intentional as well as unintentional species transfers. Rates of species movement driven by human transformations of natural environments as well as by human mobility—through commerce, tourism, and travel—dwarf natural rates by comparison. While geographic distributions of species naturally expand or contract over historical time intervals (tens to hundreds of years), species' ranges rarely expand thousands of miles or across physical barriers such as oceans or mountains.

Habitat modification can create conditions favorable to the establishment of non-indigenous species. Soil disturbed in construction and agriculture is open for colonization by non-indigenous weeds, which in turn may provide habitats for the non-indigenous insects that evolved with them. For example, the European viper's bugloss, a weed common along roads and railroad tracks, provides a habitat for the Eurasian lace bug. Human-generated changes in fire frequency, grazing intensity, as well as soil stability and nutrient levels similarly facilitate the spread and establishment of non-indigenous plants. When human changes to natural environments span large geographical areas, they effectively create conduits for species movement between previously isolated locales. The rapid spread of the Russian wheat aphid to fifteen states in just two years following its 1986 arrival has been attributed in part to the prevalence of alternative host plants that are available when wheat is not. Many of these are non-indigenous grasses recommended for planting on the forty million or more acres enrolled in the U.S. Department of Agriculture Conservation Reserve Program.

A number of factors confound quantitative evaluation of the relative importance of various entry pathways. Time lags often occur between establishment of non-indigenous species and their detection, and tracing the pathway for a long-established species is difficult. Experts estimate that non-indigenous weeds are usually detected only after having been in the country for thirty years or having spread to at least ten thousand acres. In addition, federal port inspection, although a major source of information on non-indigenous species pathways, especially for agricultural pests, provides data only when such species enter via scrutinized routes. Finally, some comparisons between pathways defy quantitative analysis—for example, which is more "important": the entry pathway of one very harmful species or one by which many but less harmful species enter the country?

1. Which of the following statements about the European viper's bugloss is best supported by the passage?

- **(A)** They serve as host plants for the Russian wheat aphid.
- **(B)** Their natural rate of movement is comparable to that of the Eurasian lace bug.
- **(C)** They find certain human pathways to be habitable.
- **(D)** Their entry into the United States went undetected for more than thirty years.

Hint: The best answer choice won't match the passage's information precisely. Instead, it will restate the information in the passage in similar terms.

2. It can be inferred from the passage that the U.S. Department of Agriculture

- **(F)** contributed to the spread of the Russian wheat aphid.
- **(G)** provides data about non-indigenous species entering the United States through scrutinized routes.
- **(H)** has attempted unsuccessfully to isolate the Russian wheat aphid.
- **(J)** favors the planting of non-indigenous grasses for the purpose of protecting certain species of insects.

Hint: The best answer choice must provide a nearly certain conclusion based on the passage's information. You can rule out any choice that requires additional information or calls for speculation.

3. It can be inferred from the passage that all of the following influence the movement of non-indigenous species EXCEPT

(A) soil nutrient levels.
(B) import restrictions.
(C) the popularity of aquaculture.
(D) geographic terrain.

Hint: To answer this question, you'll need information from various parts of the passage. Look out for a "runner-up" response that the passage supports implicitly.

4. The question that the author poses in the last sentence of the passage is intended to

(F) criticize the policies and practices of federal port inspectors.
(G) point out one of the difficult choices federal port inspectors often face.
(H) illustrate the problems in trying to quantify harm done by non-indigenous species.
(J) emphasize that time lags between entry and detection add to the difficulty of determining the extent of harm done by a non-indigenous species.

Hint: Look at the whole paragraph for clues to the answer, but beware of answer choices that provide details from other parts of the paragraph.

5. Which of the following is the most appropriate title for the passage?

(A) "Determining Entry Pathways for Non-Indigenous Species"
(B) "The Impact of Human Activity on Species Movement"
(C) "Non-Indigenous Plants: Pathways for Entry"
(D) "Problems in Halting the Spread of Harmful Non-Indigenous Species"

Hint: Essentially, this Recap question asks about the passage's primary concern. Don't look for an ideal title; instead, compare the answer choices to zero in on the best among them.

PASSAGE II—Social Studies

(Questions 6–10)

Line Scientists have long made two claims about their discipline: that it requires freedom to flourish and progress, and that it is inherently international, transcending the divisions of national and political boundaries. These are related claims, since the internationalism of science lies partly in the freedom to communicate openly with all of one's scientific colleagues, wherever they may live. Though these ideals have not always been attained, especially in the area of international scientific relations, they have served as normative assumptions for most scientists.

Before the twentieth century, challenges to these assumptions came primarily from religious quarters—for example, Galileo's trial by the Catholic Church and the controversy surrounding Darwin's Descent of Man. But in the twentieth century, they have come largely from political and ideological pressures, growing out of the increasing importance of science to social and national life. The close link between science and national governments, largely spurred by scientific contributions to warfare and defense in World War I, and even more decisively in World War II, facilitated large and expensive projects, such as the particle-accelerator and space programs, that would have been difficult to fund through private sources. But the connection also channeled the direction of scientific research increasingly toward military defense; scientific knowledge had become closely linked with national security and could no longer be so freely communicated to all scientific colleagues without any restrictions.

One of the most interesting and complex challenges to science's normative assumptions involves the diverse developments related to science that have arisen in Russia since the Bolshevik Revolution of 1917. The new Soviet state based itself on science in a way no previous government ever had. Yet Soviet scientists occupied an ambiguous position from the beginning, for while the government encouraged and generally supported scientific research, it simultaneously imposed significant restrictions on science and scientists.

The Soviets strongly emphasized planned science, sparking criticism from many Western scientists, who charged that planned science could not be free since the choice of investigation had been taken from the researcher, and that without such freedom science could not progress. A strong nationalistic emphasis on science led at times to the dismissal of all non-Russian scientific work as irrelevant to Soviet science. One leading Soviet philosopher wrote, in 1940, that "it is impossible to speak of a world science as something single, whole and continuous." A 1973 article in *Literatunaya Gazeta*, a Soviet publication, insisted that: "World science is based upon national schools, so the weakening of one or another national school inevitably leads to stagnation in the development of world science." Scientific internationalism was further challenged in a more profound way by the assertion that there are two kinds of science—a socialist science and a capitalistic, or bourgeois, science—each developing out of the particular economic organization of the society in which it arises. According to the Soviet regime, socialist science is one that must be consistent with, and in fact grows out of, the Marxism-Leninism political ideology. Soviet scientists were frequently exhorted to build a genuinely socialist science rather than conduct an impartial search for nature's truths.

Toward these ends, the Soviet regime curtailed many of the freedoms considered essential for the advancement of science. Where scientific work conflicted with political criteria, the work was often disrupted. During the Stalinist purges of the 1930s, many Soviet scientists simply disappeared. In the 1970s, Soviet scientists who were part of the refusenik movement lost their jobs, were barred from access to scientific resources, were shunned by colleagues, and even imprisoned. The government even sought to erase their previous contributions by removing their books and articles from libraries and by excising citations to their work from the scientific literature. Some scientific theories or fields, such as relativity, genetics, and cybernetics, were criticized, or even abolished, because they deviated from Marxism-Leninism.

Of course, hindrances to scientific freedom and scientific internationalism in this century are not limited to the Soviet Union. In the 1930s a nationalistic science promoted in Nazi Germany proclaimed the existence of a Deutsche Physik, which the Nazis distinguished from "Jewish physics." More recently, scientists in South American countries, especially Argentina, were fired from their positions or arrested for political reasons. But the Soviet Union constitutes the longest-lived instance of a seemingly contradictory situation, which couples a strong dependence on, and support for, science with stringent restrictions on that very scientific activity.

6. Which of the following is NOT mentioned as a Soviet attempt to impinge upon scientific freedom?

(F) Governmental interference with scientific research
(G) Charges respecting the relevance of scientific research performed in other countries
(H) Criticism of scientific inquiry relating to theories that conflicted with the Soviet regime's political ideology
(J) Dissemination of the notion of two types of science: socialist and naturalist

Hint: Don't make Simple Recall questions tougher than they really are. Look for an answer choice that contains information that finds no support whatsoever in the passage.

7. In stating that scientific knowledge had become closely linked with national security and could no longer be freely communicated, the author implies that

(A) expensive research projects such as the particle accelerator and space programs apply technology that can also be applied toward projects relating to national security.
(B) governments have subordinated the ideal of scientific freedom to national security interests.
(C) without free access to new scientific knowledge, scientists in different countries are less able to communicate with one another.
(D) government funding of scientific research undermines the ideal of scientific freedom to a greater extent than private funding.

Hint: The word "implies" means "infers" here. Look out for a "runner-up" choice that calls for speculation.

8. Among the following statements, which one finds the LEAST support in the passage?

(F) Intervention by the Soviet government in scientific research reached its zenith during the Stalinist era of the 1930s.
(G) Soviet attempts to suppress scientific freedom during the 1970s resembled those made by the Argentinean government.
(H) Like the Soviet regime, the Nazi regime promoted the notion of a national science and attempted to distinguish it from other science.
(J) The notion of "world science" runs contrary to the Nazi's Deutsche Physik.

Hint: Compare "runner-up" answer choices that the passage supports only implicitly with the correct choice, which the passage fails to support in any way.

9. Which of the following does the author identify as a fundamental cause of twentieth-century challenges to scientific freedom?

(A) The increasing role that science has played in national life
(B) Religious intolerance, particularly in the Soviet Union and in Nazi Germany
(C) The Bolshevik Revolution of 1917 and the Marxist-Leninist political ideology
(D) Increasing disloyalty on the part of scientists to their governments

Hint: Look out for the "runner-up" choice that answers a question that's more specific than the one here.

10. In the passage, the author seeks to

(F) criticize a certain point of view.
(G) expose a widespread misconception.
(H) elucidate a specific phenomenon.
(J) defend a particular ideal.

Hint: To answer this question, ask yourself whether the author has a point of view or an opinion about the ideals of science or about the various historical attempts to suppress those ideals. Then, focus on the first word of each answer choice.

PASSAGE III—Prose Fiction

(Questions 11–15)

This passage is adapted from "The Open Boat" by Stephen Crane.

Line Shipwrecks are apropos of nothing. If men could only train for them and have them occur when they had reached peak condition, there would be less drowning at sea.

Of the four in the dinghy, none had slept any time worth mentioning for two days and two nights previous to embarking in the dinghy, and in the excitement of clambering about the deck of a floundering ship they had also forgotten to eat heartily.

For these reasons, and for others, neither the oiler nor the correspondent was fond of rowing at this time. The correspondent wondered how, in the name of all that was sane, there could be people who thought it amusing to row a boat. It was not an amusement; it was a diabolical punishment, and even a genius of mental aberrations could never conclude that it was anything but a horror to the muscles and a crime against the back. He mentioned to the boat in general how the amusement of rowing struck him, and the weary-faced oiler smiled in full sympathy. Previously to the floundering, by the way, the oiler had worked double-watch in the engine room of the ship.

"Take her easy, now, boys," said the captain. "Don't spend yourselves. If we have to run a surf you'll need all your strength, because we'll sure have to swim for it. Take your time."

Slowly the land arose from the sea. From a black line it became a line of black and a line of white, trees and sand. Finally, the captain said that he could make out a house on the shore.

"That's the house of refuge, sure," said the cook. "They'll see us before long, and come out after us."

The distant lighthouse reared high. "The keeper ought to be able to make us out now, if he's looking through a spyglass," said the captain. "He'll notify the life-saving people."

"None of those other boats could have got ashore to give word of the wreck," said the oiler, in a low voice. "Else the life-boat would be out hunting us."

Slowly and beautifully the land loomed out of the sea. The wind came again. It had veered from the northeast to the southeast. Finally, a new sound struck the ears of the men in the boat. It was the low thunder of the surf on the shore. All but the oarsman watched the shore grow. Under the influence of this expansion, doubt and direful apprehension was leaving the minds of the men. The management of the boat was still most absorbing, but it could not prevent a quiet cheerfulness. In an hour, perhaps, they would be ashore.

Their backbones had become thoroughly used to balancing in the boat, and they now rode this wild colt of a dinghy like circus men. The correspondent thought that he had been drenched to the skin, but happening to feel in the top pocket of his coat, he found therein eight cigars. Four of them were soaked with seawater; four were perfectly dry. After a search, somebody produced three dry matches, and thereupon, the four waifs rode impudently in their little boat, and with an assurance of an impending rescue shining in their eyes, puffed at the big cigars and judged well and ill of all men. Everybody took a drink of water.

But then: "Cook," remarked the captain, "there don't seem to be any signs of life about your house of refuge."

"No," replied the cook. "Funny they don't see us!"

The surf's roar was dulled, but its tone was, nevertheless, thunderous and mighty. As the boat swam over the great rollers, the men sat listening to this roar. "We'll swamp sure," said everybody.

It is fair to say here that there was not a life-saving station within twenty miles in either direction, but the men did not know this fact, and, in consequence, they made dark and opprobrious remarks concerning the eyesight of the nation's life-savers. Four scowling men sat in the dinghy and surpassed records in the invention of epithets.

"Funny they don't see us."

The lightheartedness of a former time had completely faded. To their sharpened minds it was easy to conjure pictures of all kinds of incompetency and blindness and, indeed, cowardice. There was the shore of the populous land, and it was bitter and bitter to them that from it came no sign.

"Well," said the captain, ultimately. "I suppose we'll have to make a try for ourselves. If we stay out here too long, we'll none of us have strength left to swim after the boat swamps."

And so the oiler, who was at the oars, turned the boat straight for the shore. There was a sudden tightening of muscle. There was some thinking.

"If we don't all get ashore-" said the captain. "If we don't all get ashore, I suppose you fellows know where to send news of my finish?" They briefly exchanged some addresses and admonitions. The shore was still afar.

11. It can be inferred from the passage that the men in the dinghy are weary partly because they

(A) have been rowing the dinghy for the past two days.
(B) have not eaten heartily since abandoning the ship.
(C) had spent the previous two days on a sinking ship.
(D) have not slept since embarking in the dinghy.

Hint: Don't look for an explicit answer to the question; you'll need to consider several sentences that, as a whole, infer it.

Hint: Look out for answer choices that confuse the information in the passage.

12. The men in the dinghy experience a sense of "quiet cheerfulness" (line 55) because they

(F) know that the storm that sank their ship is past.
(G) see the shore getting closer and closer.
(H) believe that the lifeboat is out searching for them.
(J) think their dinghy will be able to land safely on shore.

Hint: Just because an answer choice refers to narration near the cited line doesn't necessarily mean it's the correct one.

13. In stating that "the four waifs rode impudently in their little boat" (lines 66–67), the narrator is suggesting that the men

(A) are momentarily distracted from their peril by enjoying a good cigar.
(B) are celebrating their good fortune at having survived the shipwreck.
(C) believe that their skill at seamanship will save them from disaster.
(D) feel certain they will soon be rescued.

Hint: You don't need to know what "impudently" means to answer the question; the rhetorical context of the quoted line will provide the clues you need.

14. The passage implies that the greatest danger to the men in the dinghy arises from the fact that

(F) their boat is too small to safely navigate the great waves breaking on the shore.
(G) the shoreline is uninhabited for many miles in both directions.
(H) they are unable to steer their boat in the direction of the shore.
(J) they are too exhausted to row their boat toward the land.

Hint: Beware of answer choices that are true but don't respond to the question.

15. As it is used in the passage, the word "dark" (line 84) means most nearly

(A) obscure.
(B) harsh.
(C) pessimistic.
(D) gloomy.

Hint: This question tests you on a common word that has more than one meaning; to answer, examine the context in which it is used.

ANSWERS AND EXPLANATIONS

1. **The correct answer is (C).** According to the passage, the bugloss is common "along roads and railroad tracks," that is, along human pathways. Choice (D) is the "runner-up" response; it might very well provide an accurate statement. The European viper's bugloss is a type of weed, and the passage does indeed indicate that non-indigenous weeds usually go undetected for at least thirty years. But it's unfair to infer that the European viper's bugloss was, in fact, one such weed. Choice (A) confuses the information in the passage, as the bugloss serves as a host plant for the Eurasian lace bug, not for the Russian wheat aphid. Choice (B) calls for an unwarranted inference because, although you might infer that human-driven movement—for example, movement associated with road construction—of the bugloss and lace bug are comparable, you can't reasonably make a similar inference about their natural movement.

2. **The correct answer is (F).** According to the information in the second paragraph, the rapid spread of the Russian wheat aphid resulted partly from the availability of alternative host plants (non-indigenous grasses), which were recommended for planting on lands controlled by the U.S. Department of Agriculture. Thus, the Department was partly responsible for the rapid spread of the Russian wheat aphid. Choice (J) is the "runner-up" response; it is only partly supported by the information in the passage. Although it appears that the Department intentionally planted various non-indigenous grasses, as choice (J) suggests, the author makes no mention of the reason for this. Choice (G) confuses the information in the passage. Federal port inspection (not the U.S. Department of Agriculture) provides data about species entering through scrutinized routes. Choice (H) is unsupported by the information in the passage. The author neither states nor implies that the Department made any attempts to isolate the Russian wheat aphid either before or since the rapid spread of the species.

3. **The correct answer is (B).** The only discussion in the passage related to importing is the discussion in the final paragraph about the limitations of federal port inspection in detecting the entry of non-indigenous species. While common sense might suggest that import restrictions would probably affect the movement of non-indigenous plants and animals, the subject of import restrictions is not mentioned in the final paragraph or anywhere else in the passage. Choice (C) is the "runner-up" response. Although not supported implicitly by the passage, "aquaculture" is mentioned in line 7 as a form of human cultivation that helps to establish non-indigenous species. Thus, it can be reasonably inferred that the popularity of this activity would affect the movement of certain non-indigenous species. Choice (A) is supported explicitly by the passage. According to the passage, human-generated changes in soil nutrient levels "facilitate the spread and establishment of non-indigenous species" (lines 37–38). Choice (D) is supported explicitly by the passage. According to the passage, physical barriers such as mountains (i.e., natural terrain) limit species movement (lines 19–24).

4. **The correct answer is (H).** The first sentence of the final paragraph tells you that the author will be listing various respects in which harm done by non-indigenous species can defy quantitative analysis. The paragraph's final sentence, a rhetorical question, indicates one of those respects. Choice (F) distorts the author's message. Although the author does point out what you might call a "failure" of port inspectors to completely prevent entry of harmful non-indigenous species, the author does not go as far as to explicitly criticize their policies or practices. Choice (G) is the "runner-up" choice because, based on the passage's last sentence, it might very well be true that inspectors face difficult choices about where to focus their efforts in preventing entry of harmful species. But choice (G) misses the immediate point of the final sentence, which is that quantifying harm done by non-indigenous species is problematic, not that inspectors face difficult choices as a result of the problem. Choice (J) confuses the point of the final sentence with that of an earlier sentence in the paragraph.

5. **The correct answer is (A).** Although choice (A) may not provide an ideal title for the passage, it is the best among the five responses. It expresses the ideas presented in the passage as a whole—the various types of entry pathways (first paragraph), the effects of habitat modification by humans on the establishment of non-indigenous species (second paragraph), and the problems in determining the relative significance of entry pathways (final paragraph). Choice (B) is too narrow. Although the title suggested in choice (B) fairly characterizes the author's concern in the second paragraph, it fails to encompass the author's chief concern with identifying the problems in determining the relative importance of various entry pathways. Choice (C) is too broad in one sense and too narrow in another sense. The author's specific

concern is with unintentional entry pathways (not with both intentional and unintentional pathways); in this sense, then, choice (C) is too broad. At the same time, the passage is concerned not just with plant species, but also with animal species; thus, in this sense, choice (C) is too narrow. Choice (D) distorts the passage. Although the final paragraph does identify some of the problems in obtaining information needed to prevent the establishment of non-indigenous species, the author does not focus on (or even suggest) the need to halt the spread of harmful, non-indigenous species.

6. **The correct answer is (J).** The two types of science that the Soviet regime identified included socialist and capitalist (or bourgeois) science, not naturalist science; the term "naturalist" is not used anywhere in the passage. Each of the other responses is either mentioned explicitly or is described in either the fourth or fifth paragraph.

7. **The correct answer is (B).** Scientific knowledge related to military defense is kept secret presumably in order to prevent that knowledge from leaking to enemy countries, which might use it to threaten national security. Thus, it is reasonable to infer that in keeping this knowledge secret, a government is placing a higher value on national security than on scientific freedom. Choice (D) is the "runner-up" response. From the information in the second paragraph, you could make the argument that government-funded research is more likely than privately funded research to relate to matters affecting national security (i.e., military defense). However, if this inference is to be based upon the excerpt mentioned in the question stem, the inference is far more speculative than the one in choice (B). Choice (A) is unsupported. No connection is implied between the particle-accelerator and space programs and national security. Choice (C) is not responsive to the question and is a bit nonsensical. Even if choice (C) were turned around to make some logical sense (e.g., "Without the ability to communicate with scientists from other countries, scientists do not have free access to new scientific knowledge"), the statement would still not respond to the question.

8. **The correct answer is (F).** Choice (F) provides the best response because it calls for an unwarranted inference that is unsupported by the passage. Although the author does refer in the fifth paragraph to the Stalinist purges of the 1930s, nowhere does the author state or suggest that the events of this particular time period marked the peak (zenith) of government interference with scientific research. Choice (G) is strongly supported; lines 103–106 mention scientists losing their jobs and being arrested in Argentina, while lines 85–89 mention similar acts of suppression against Soviet refuseniks (scientists were fired and/or imprisoned). Choice (H) is less explicit in the passage than choice (G); nevertheless, choice (H) is supported by the passage; while the Soviets distinguished socialist science from capitalistic science, the Nazis distinguished their Deutsche Physik from Jewish physics. Choice (J) is less explicit in the passage than choice (G); nevertheless, choice (J) can be inferred from the fourth and sixth paragraphs considered together. According to lines 99–103, a nationalistic science in Germany proclaimed the existence of a Deutsche Physik and distinguished it from other science. It can be reasonably inferred from this statement that Deutsche Physik would run contrary to the idea of a "world science" (the notion of "world science" was mentioned in the fourth paragraph in the context of Soviet attempts to dismiss or redefine the concept).

9. **The correct answer is (A).** The passage states explicitly in the second paragraph that twentieth-century challenges to science's normative assumptions (i.e., scientific freedom) have grown "out of the increasing importance of science to social and national life." Choice (C) is the "runner-up" response. The question asks for the fundamental cause of a general phenomenon, not of the specific challenges of the Soviet regime. Thus, choice (C) is too narrow. Choice (B) is unsupported. The passage makes no mention of religious intolerance in the twentieth-century Soviet Union and alludes only briefly in the last paragraph to Jewish physics, a reference that suggests more of a racial bias than a religious one on the part of the Nazis. Choice (D) is unsupported; nowhere in the passage does the author state or suggest that disloyalty of scientists prompted restrictions upon their freedom.

10. **The correct answer is (H).** The "phenomenon" with which the passage is concerned is the recurring challenge, in various forms and from various sources, to certain ideals held by the scientific community. The author elucidates (explains) this phenomenon by providing various examples of this challenge. Choices (F) and (J) each distort the author's message in the passage. Nothing in the passage suggests that the author has a point of view or opinion about the subject. Choice (G) finds no support whatsoever in the passage, which neither mentions nor suggests a "misconception" of any sort.

11. **The correct answer is (C).** The second paragraph and the last sentence of the third paragraph

combine to answer this question. They make it clear that the weariness of the men in the dinghy is a result of the fact that they have spent the last two days prior to embarking in the dinghy "clambering about the deck of a floundering [that is, sinking] ship." Choice (A) confuses the passage information, which indicates that the men had spent two days on the sinking ship, not in the dinghy. Choice (B) also confuses the passage information, which indicates that the men had not eaten heartily while on the sinking ship—not while in the dinghy. Choice (D) is unsupported by the passage.

12. **The correct answer is (G).** The (temporary) good mood of the men is attributed, in the same paragraph, to "the influence of this expansion"—namely, the growing visibility of the shore as their little boat gets closer and closer to it. Of the incorrect choices, choice (J) is the most tempting, especially considering the last sentence in the same paragraph: "In an hour, perhaps, they would be ashore." Presently, however, the men believe that a lifeboat will come to their rescue, not that their dinghy will reach the shore safely.

13. **The correct answer is (D).** The description of the men smoking their cigars includes the explanatory phrase, "with an assurance of an impending rescue shining in their eyes." Hence, choice (D) is a reasonable explanation for the imagery contained in the quote. Choice (B) is the "runner-up" choice. Cigar smoking is often associated with rejoicing or celebrating. However, the paragraph does not explicitly support choice (B), whereas it does explicitly support choice (D). Thus, choice (D) is a better choice. Choice (A) is also tempting, especially since it immediately precedes the quoted statement. However, the paragraph neither states nor suggests that the cigars provided a distraction from their peril; furthermore, at this point, the men believe that they will soon be rescued—that is, that they are no longer in peril. Choice (C) finds no support in the passage, in which the narrator neither states nor suggests that their skill at seamanship might be responsible for saving them.

14. **The correct answer is (F).** The growing fear of the men is attributed to their belief that "We'll swamp sure" in the mighty surf whose noise they hear. In other words, the waves breaking on the shore are so large and powerful that it will be impossible for them to land their boat safely. Choice (J) is the "runner-up" choice. The men are exhausted, as choice (J) asserts, but the problem is not that they cannot row toward shore—they can. The problem is that they can't land safely once they get there. Choices (G) and (H) both run contrary to the narration, which indicates that the oiler spotted a lighthouse on shore and, later, that the oiler "turned the boat straight for the shore."

15. **The correct answer is (B).** The word "dark" is used in the phrase "dark and opprobrious remarks," describing the angry comments made by the men in the dinghy toward the lifesavers, by whom they feel they are being ignored. The context makes it clear that the remarks are harshly negative ones—"dark" in that sense only.

Question 15 is typical of ACT "vocabulary-in-context" questions. It focuses on a commonly used word that carries more than one possible meaning.

LESSON 17

Mind-Bending Reading Questions

In this second lesson covering the ACT Reading Test, you'll:

- Explore the most mind-bending (and least common) reading question types (and learn how to handle these questions like a true Brainiac)
- Review reading techniques that Brainiacs use to master any reading passage
- Tackle each of the advanced question types covered in this lesson, plus additional question sets covered in the previous lesson

ADVANCED READING QUESTION TYPES

In the previous lesson, you learned about the most common types of ACT reading questions. Now it's time to focus on the more difficult question types you may encounter on the test—questions that further separate Brainiacs from all the rest. You'll learn how to identify each question type when you see it—with true Brainiac flair:

- Assumption Questions
- Additional Information Questions
- Application Questions
- Method Questions

A question based on any of these four types might accompany an ACT Natural Science, Social Studies, or Humanities passage—but *not* a Prose Fiction passage. What you'll learn here applies to three of the four categories of ACT Reading passages.

In the pages ahead, you'll look at examples of all four question types relating each to the following passage. Read the passage carefully before looking at the questions that follow. As ACT reading passages go, this one is not especially difficult. The focus here is on tough *questions* rather than tough *passages*.

Passage I—Social Studies

Francis Bacon contributed to the scientific enterprise a prophetic understanding of how science would one day be put to use in the service of technology, and how such a symbiosis between the two would radically impact both man and his surroundings. As inseparable as they are today, it is hard to imagine science and technology as inhabiting separate domains. But in Bacon's world of the sixteenth century, science was not generally viewed as a practical instrument for improving the physical conditions of life. Anticipating the two notable nineteenth-century science fiction writers Jules Verne and H. G. Wells by three hundred years, Bacon foresaw not only the extent to which science would contribute to the enlargement of technology, but also how technology would come to be seen as the ultimate justification of science.

There is little doubt that others before Bacon understood that discovering the mysteries of air, water, fire, and earth could lead toward useful applications. But Bacon's systematic elaboration of the promise of joining science with technology was a major leap forward in closing the gap between the two endeavors. He, more than any before him, stressed the need for collective organizations for scientific inquiry and application—the forerunners of our vast government, academic, and corporate-sponsored research and development departments. Bacon did not ignore the necessity for creative and dedicated individuals to spur science onwards. Rather, he declared that such individuals would need the help of state aid, corporate organization, official conferences and publications, and regulated social and pecuniary incentives in order for their experiments and insights to have the widest possible application.

The danger that Bacon did not foresee was that corporate influences could restrict the opportunities of the individual scientist, and that a time could come when no scientific work would be possible without corporate support. The most important ramification of these new conditions is that the judgment and moral grounding possible of individual scientists must now compete with the concerns of industrial collectives. Entangled within the scientific/technological system, the modern scientist has jeopardized the qualities once exalted as the very hallmarks of science: the detachment from worldly gains and the disinterested pursuit of truth. Influenced by political and economic pressures, scientists have less and less power to enact any controls over the scientific establishment that pursues the Baconian ideals of riches and power over another of his stated uses for science, "the relief of man's estate." Scientists are losing the power to say "No."

No one questions the immense benefits already conferred by science's efficient methodology. However, since individual scientists must now choose between improving standards of living and obtaining financial support for their research, there is cause for concern. In light of current circumstances, we must ask certain questions about science that Bacon, from a sixteenth-century perspective, could not possibly have put to himself.

ASSUMPTION QUESTIONS

Assumption questions ask you to fill in gaps in the author's argument or in a position put forth by some other character in the passage. An assumption is an unstated yet necessary part of an argument. These questions can be difficult because, in order to recognize the assumption required to hold the argument together, you must understand both the conclusion that's drawn and the evidence offered in support of it.

An ACT Assumption question usually contains some form of the word "assumption." Here are a few typical examples:

"The author's discussion about . . . assumes that . . ."

"The author's argument is based on the assumption that . . ."

An assumption in a passage will not necessarily be an assumption by the *author*. It might instead be an assumption made by a character or other person discussed in the passage.

When you see an Assumption question, you should follow these three steps:

1. Focus on the point established (the conclusion) and the evidence used to support it.
2. Look for a link between the evidence and the conclusion that is necessary to the logic yet not explicitly stated in the passage.
3. Eliminate choices that are outside the scope of the argument. In order for something to be necessary to an argument, it must first be relevant.

Now, apply these steps to a question that relates to the passage about Francis Bacon. Use the line reference to find the phrase in question, and read the entire sentence carefully. As you read it, try to figure out what the author is *not* saying that nevertheless must be true for the argument in that sentence to make sense. That unstated premise is the assumption.

In stating the case for his "cause for concern" (line 29), the author assumes that

(A) individual scientists have sacrificed all power of choice with regard to the direction of their research.
(B) it is not in the financial interest of the scientific establishment to improve standards of living.
(C) science's efficient methodology has led to the solution of most of society's problems.
(D) no scientists will choose to devote their time to improving standards of living.

A

The correct answer is (B). The author is concerned that scientists will have to choose between improving standards of living and getting money from the scientific establishment for their research. But this concern is not so well founded if scientists receive money from the establishment for projects that will improve the standards of living. In making his argument, the author must *assume* that the scientific establishment does not have an interest in improving standards of living. If it *did*, then the author's concern would make less sense. Now let's examine the other three choices to see why none can compete with choice (B).

Choice (A): The author need not assume that scientists have sacrificed all control over their work. In fact, the argument in question indicates that scientists still have a choice regarding what they do. The author is concerned because it is a choice that may not bode well for society, but his concern does not rely on the notion in choice (A).

Choice (C): The reference to "science's efficient methodology" comes from the previous sentence and is just there to acknowledge science's achievements before the author states his concern. This concern does not rely on the notion that science has solved most of society's problems, so choice (C) is not the assumption we're looking for here.

Choice (D): The argument in question indicates that scientists still have a choice regarding what they do. The author's concern does not rely on the idea that not one single scientist will choose to improve standards of living. A handful may, and the author would still be concerned because the nature of the choice that has arisen in the modern scientific community does not bode well for society overall. Choice (D) is not the necessary assumption we seek.

ADDITIONAL INFORMATION QUESTIONS

Additional Information questions ask you to recognize an additional fact that would make an argument within the passage more or less convincing—that is, stronger or weaker. These two question types are more taxing than average because they require you to challenge the text and to be an active reader as opposed to a passive reader who assimilates what's on the page.

A Strengthen question typically contains a word such as "support" or "strengthen," as in these two question stems:

> "Which of the following, if true, would provide the most direct support for the author's assertion that *[a specific claim made by the author]*?"
>
> "Which of the following statements, if true, would best strengthen the contention that *[a specific point mentioned in the passage]*?"

To identify a Weaken question, look for a word such as "weaken," "undermine," contradict," or "refute," as in these two question stems:

> "Which of the following statements, if true, would contradict most directly the author's claim that *[a specific claim made by the author]*?"
>
> "Which of the following, if true, would most seriously weaken the author's argument that *[a specific conclusion made by the author]*?"

To handle a Strengthen or Weaken question, follow these steps:

1. Make sure you have a clear understanding of the argument in question. You won't have much luck strengthening or weakening an argument that you don't understand.
2. Look for assumptions in the argument. Often, the key to strengthening or weakening an argument lies in building up or breaking down an author's central assumption.
3. Beware of choices that are true but don't have the desired effect. A choice may reflect perfectly what's in the passage; however, if it doesn't strengthen or weaken the argument (based on what you're asked to do), then it cannot be correct. Don't select a choice simply because it seems "true"—that may not be good enough.

Apply these steps to the following Weaken question about the Francis Bacon passage. To handle the questions, find the relevant text, and then reread what the author says about what Bacon didn't foresee—that is, what Bacon missed in his analysis. Keep in mind that you're asked to weaken the *author's* point, not the arguments that Bacon himself makes. Get into the mindset of challenging the author as you go back to read this part of the passage.

Q The author's assertion regarding what "Bacon did not foresee" (line 18) would be most seriously weakened if it were determined that Bacon

(F) outlined the mechanisms of corporate support necessary to adequately fund scientific research.
(G) stated in his writings that the economic and political requirements for a stable society were intertwined with the efficient functioning of the scientific establishment.
(H) suggested that passionate and creative people were indispensable to the advancement of the scientific enterprise.
(J) warned of the dangers to scientific inquiry that would result if collective organization became an integral part of scientific research.

A **The correct answer is (J).** Paraphrasing the text, the author says that Bacon didn't realize that corporate/institutional support would become so essential to science that no science would be possible without it. If, however, we find that Bacon *did* in fact warn of the dangers to science of such corporate control ("collective organization"), then the author's argument here would carry much less weight. Choice (J) is the best "weakener" of the bunch.

Now, let's examine the other three choices to see why none can compete with choice (J):

Choice (F): The author credits Bacon with the idea that corporate support would be necessary for science to flourish. If it were determined that somewhere Bacon spelled out what that support would consist of, that would still do nothing to damage the author's claim that Bacon missed the point that such corporate control of science could have negative consequences.

Choice (G): It wouldn't be surprising to find such a claim in Bacon's writings, considering what we know about his ideas from the passage. However, this wouldn't in any way damage the author's claim that Bacon missed the point that corporate control of science could have negative consequences.

Choice (H): The author states that "Bacon did not ignore the necessity for creative and dedicated individuals to spur science onwards," so it wouldn't be surprising to find the suggestion described in choice (H) in Bacon's writings. However, this wouldn't in any way damage the author's claim that Bacon missed the point that corporate control of science could have negative consequences.

APPLICATION QUESTIONS

Application questions ask you to relate ideas and situations described in the passage to outside scenarios. They test whether you can understand how examples represented in the passage might be applied in a different context. Application questions are inherently difficult because the choices involve situations foreign to the topic of the passage, and a leap is required on your part to connect the correct choice to the relevant idea or example in the passage.

Here is what Application questions typically look like:

"As described in the passage, *[something the author describes]* is most nearly analogous to which of the following"

"Which of the following best exemplifies *[something mentioned in the passage]*?"

"Which of the following would the author consider to be most similar to *[something mentioned in the passage]*?"

When you see an Application question, you should follow these four steps:

1. Go back to the example or idea in question and reread it to make sure you have a firm grasp of it.

2. Put the example or idea into general terms. This will help you because it is the general logic of the example that will somehow relate to the correct answer choice.

3. Rigorously test the choices to see whether each one matches the example or idea in question. Beware of choices that distort the meaning of the example.

4. Do not eliminate a choice simply because you think it's beyond the scope of the passage! All the choices should appear that way since they are usually about a different subject altogether. But exactly one of the choices relates to the underlying meaning of the example in question.

Now try answering an Application question about the Francis Bacon passage. For this question, remember that the key to an Application question is to *generalize a situation and recognize its essence embodied in another situation.* Think about the plight of the modern scientist and try to put it into general terms. Then, check the choices and determine which one best corresponds to such a scenario.

Q The situation of the modern scientist as described in the passage is most nearly analogous to that of

(A) a painter who participates in an artistic community in order to gain exposure for his works.
(B) a doctor who is required to attend a yearly conference in order to keep up with developments in her field.
(C) a musician who needs to alter her vision for a recording project in order to maintain the support of her record company.
(D) an executive who is fired for disobeying company policy.

A **The correct answer is (C).** According to the author, the modern scientist depends for support on a large organization that forces him to conduct his work according to the demands of the organization. Similarly, the musician in choice (C) depends on a record company that forces her to change what she wants to create in order to make the company happy. Choice (C) offers the best analogy to the author's description of the modern scientist's plight.

Now, let's examine the other three choices to see why none can compete with choice (C):

Choice (A): According to the author, the modern scientist depends on a large organization for support, forcing him to conduct his work according to the demands of the organization. This results in a problem for the scientist, whereas the painter in choice (A) benefits from his attachment to the artistic community.

Choice (B): According to the author, the modern scientist depends for support on a large organization that forces him to conduct his work according to the demands of the organization. A doctor required to attend a conference is not in the same situation, since nothing implies that the doctor must alter, against her will, the way she goes about practicing medicine.

Choice (D): According to the author, the modern scientist depends for support on a large organization that forces him to conduct his work according to the demands of that organization. A fired executive need not fit into the same general category. Maybe he deserved to be fired, maybe he didn't, but either way, a company has a right to determine how its employees should behave. However, the scientist, according to the author, was once independent and needs to be independent for society to benefit. The predicament of the scientist, as the author describes it, is therefore not similar to the situation of a fired executive.

METHOD QUESTIONS

Method questions ask you to recognize what the author is doing in the passage; that is, how the author goes about making her points. Some Method questions ask for the author's overall approach in the passage, while others ask about how a specific point is made or about the structure of a particular paragraph. Method questions can be difficult because the answer choices are usually stated very generally, and it's up to you to connect the general wording of the choices with what's going on in the passage.

A Method question can appear in many forms. Here are just some examples of what the question stem might look like:

"Which of the following best describes the approach of the passage?"

"In the last paragraph, the author proceeds by"

"How does the fourth paragraph function in relation to the third paragraph?"

"Which of the following most accurately describes the organization of the second paragraph?"

"Which of the following techniques is used in the last sentence of paragraph 3?"

When you see a Method question, you should follow these steps:

1. Let the question guide you to the appropriate area of the passage and then reread that section carefully.
2. Focus on what the author is doing and don't get bogged down in details. Method questions concern how the author makes her points, not what those points are. The latter is the subject of Detail and Inference questions as discussed in lesson 16.
3. Test the choices rigorously. Every word in the correct choice must be consistent with what's going on in the passage. Incorrect choices will contain elements that go against the author's approach, or that are simply not represented in the passage.

Now apply these steps to a Method question about the Francis Bacon passage. The final paragraph is short enough to skim quickly before checking out the choices. But read it with a very specific goal in mind: to determine what the author is doing in these few lines. (Details really won't help you here, so don't get caught up in them.) Then, test the choices rigorously, making sure every word of the choice you select matches what's going on in this part of the passage.

Which of the following most accurately describes the organization of the last paragraph of the passage?

(F) An assertion is made and is backed up by evidence.
(G) A viewpoint is expressed and an opposing viewpoint is stated and countered.
(H) An admission is offered and is followed by a warning and recommendation.
(J) Contradictory claims are presented and then reconciled.

The correct answer is (H). The notion that no one questions the benefits of science does qualify as an admission in the context of the paragraph; that is, the author admits that science has given mankind enormous benefits, but then goes on to voice his concern regarding the current state of the scientific enterprise. Note how the contrast signal word "however" screams at us that some kind of change must come after the author admits that science has conferred immense benefits. Indeed, what comes next is, as choice (H) puts it, a warning: there is cause for concern. The recommendation that rounds out choice (H) appears in the final sentence, highlighted by the words "we must ask certain questions . . ." Every element in choice (H) is present and accounted for, so this choice correctly describes the organization of the paragraph.

Now, let's examine the other three choices to see why none can compete with choice (H):

Choice (F): This choice says that the paragraph begins with an assertion, and we can surely accept that: the assertion that no one questions the benefits of science. Is this then backed up by evidence? No. The contrast signal word "however" alerts us that a shift is coming, not evidence for the statement in the first sentence. And indeed, the rest does go off in a different direction.

Choice (G): This choice doesn't reflect what's going on here. It says that the final paragraph begins with a viewpoint, and we can surely accept the view that no one questions the benefits of science. But does an opposing viewpoint—an argument against the benefits of science—follow? No. The author is instead concerned about the way science is now conducted. He doesn't mention or counter the position that tries to downplay what science has already accomplished.

The contrast signal word "however" offers a promising start for the organization described in choice (G): It alerts us of an upcoming change, so it would certainly be reasonable for an opposing viewpoint to enter the story at this point. But it doesn't; instead, the author goes in a different direction than what's described at the end of this choice.

Choice (J): This choice is incorrect because there are no contradictory claims here. The author admits that science has given mankind enormous benefits, but then goes on to voice his concern regarding the current state of the scientific enterprise. Because these claims aren't contradictory, and nothing in the paragraph contradicts either claim, choice (J) can't be correct.

8 AWESOME TECHNIQUES FOR EFFECTIVE READING

If you're like most verbal Brainiacs, you're a voracious reader who's already developed the kinds of good reading habits that will serve you well on the ACT Reading Test. So there's certainly no need here for an *ad nauseum* discourse on how to read effectively. But it can't hurt to review the basic reading techniques that apply most directly to the ACT. Besides, even verbal Brainiacs are likely to pick up a few useful techniques here.

If you're an aspiring Brainiac, don't expect to just walk into the ACT testing room and apply these techniques without practicing them first. Try them first, during your ACT practice testing until you become comfortable with them.

1. MARK UP THE PASSAGE (THAT'S WHAT YOUR PENCIL IS FOR!)

Selective annotating (e.g., circling and underlining key words and phrases) serves three important purposes:

1. It helps you maintain an active frame of mind since it prompts you to shop for important ideas and information.
2. It provides a pre-written outline. After you read (and annotate) the entire passage, reviewing the annotated words and phrases can be an effective way to recap the passage for yourself.
3. If you need to refer to the passage as you answer the questions, effective annotating will help you quickly locate the needed information.

What sort of information should you annotate? If you under-annotate, you will not be able to effectively recap the passage by reviewing your annotations. If you over-annotate, your annotations will lose their meaning, and you might as well not have annotated at all. Here are some suggestions for finding just the right balance:

- Mark areas of discussion that you may need to locate again to answer one or more of the questions.
- Instead of underlining complete sentences, select key words or phrases that trigger main ideas or points of sentences and paragraphs.
- Mark structural connectors—key words that connect the logical building blocks of the passage.
- In chronological passages, mark historical benchmarks and divisions (centuries, years, decades, or historical periods) that help to form the structure of the author's discussion.
- Use arrows to connect words on the page that signify related ideas, for example:
  - To clarify cause and effect in the natural sciences or in the context of historical events
  - To indicate who influenced whom in literature, music, psychology, etc.
  - To connect names (philosophers, scientists, authors, etc.) with dates, events, other names, theories, or schools of thought, works, etc.
  - To indicate the chronological order in which historical events occurred
- Create your own visual cues to earmark possible thesis statements, major supporting points, and points of author disagreement.

2. MAKE MARGIN NOTES AND (FOR SELECT PASSAGES) OUTLINES

In the left-hand margin, make shorthand notes to summarize paragraphs, earmark areas of discussion, locate details more quickly, and recap the passage more effectively. Keep your notes as brief as possible; two or three words should provide a sufficient cue.

Don't bother constructing a formal outline of the passage; it takes more time than it's worth. Instead, rely on your margin notes and annotations to indicate the flow of the discussion. For certain high-density passages, however, some organized notes (a "mini-outline") may be necessary. A few shorthand notes at the bottom of the page may help to keep certain details straight in your mind. Here are some scenarios that typically call for the mini-outline:

- If the passage categorizes or classifies various phenomena, notes may help clarify which phenomena belong in which categories.

- If the passage mentions numerous individual names (e.g., authors, artists, political figures, etc.), use notes to link them according to influence, agreement or disagreement, and so forth.

3. PAUSE AFTER EACH PARAGRAPH TO SUM UP AND ANTICIPATE

After you read each paragraph, pause for a moment to evaluate the paragraph as a whole. Try to recapitulate or summarize the paragraph as two or three basic ideas. After each paragraph, ask yourself the following questions:

- How would I sum up the discussion to this point?
- At what point is the discussion now?
- What basic points is the author trying to get across in this paragraph? Do these ideas continue a line of thought, or do they begin a new one?
- Where is the discussion likely to go from here?
- Pause after each logical "block" (perhaps after each paragraph) to think briefly about what basic points the author makes in the block, how these points are connected to earlier ones, and in which direction the discussion is likely to head. Jot down a brief outline as you go.

4. PAY ATTENTION TO THE PASSAGE'S OVERALL STRUCTURE

Different types of reading passages are organized in different ways. For example:

- A passage that traces historical causes or consequences will probably be organized chronologically.
- A passage that critiques a theory will probably describe the theory first, and then explain its problems, one at a time.
- A passage that draws a comparison (pointing out similarities and differences) between two things might first list similarities, then differences.
- A passage that describes a classification system will probably begin by defining the main class, then branch out to each sub-class level.

If you understand how the passage is organized (structured), you can articulate the main idea and purpose of the passage, understand the author's reasons for mentioning particular details, and distinguish between main points and minor details, all of which will help you answer the questions.

5. LOOK FOR STRUCTURAL CLUES OR "TRIGGERS"

"Triggers" are key words and phrases that provide clues as to the structure and organization of the passage and the direction in which the discussion is flowing. The lists below contain many common trigger words and phrases. Underline or circle trigger words as you read the passage. Review your annotations to help you recap the passage and to see its structure and organization.

Words that precede an item in a list (e.g., examples, classes, reasons, or characteristics):

first, second (etc.) in addition, also, another

Words that signal that the author is contrasting two phenomena:

alternatively, by contrast, however, on the other hand, rather than, while, yet

Words that signal a logical conclusion based upon preceding material:

consequently, in conclusion, then, thus, therefore, as a result, accordingly

Words that signal that the author is comparing (identifying similarities between) two phenomena:

similarly, in the same way, analogous, parallel, likewise, just as, also, as

Words that signal evidence (factual information) used to support the author's argument:

because, since, in light of

Words that signal an example of a phenomenon:

for instance, e.g., such as, . . . is an illustration of

6. DON'T GET BOGGED DOWN IN DETAILS

ACT reading passages are packed with details: lists, statistics and other numbers, dates, titles, and so forth. If you try to absorb all of the details as you read, you'll not only lose sight of the main points, but you'll also lose reading speed. In the left-hand margin, note where particular examples, lists, and other details are located. If a particular question involving those details is included, you can quickly and easily locate them and read them more carefully.

7. DON'T BOTHER PREVIEWING, UNLESS YOU'RE SHORT ON TIME

Many ACT prep books recommend performing one or both of the following "pre-reading" steps before reading a passage straight through:

- *Read all question "stems"* (the questions but not the answer choices) for hints about the subject of the passage and possible thesis.
- *Preview the passage* by reading the first (and perhaps last) sentence of each paragraph.

The first technique supposedly helps you anticipate the information in the passage you should focus on. The second technique supposedly provides clues about the scope of the passage, the author's thesis or major conclusions, and the structure and flow of the discussion. Although these techniques make sense *in theory,* there are several reasons why *in practice* they are rarely helpful on the ACT:

- You'll quickly forget most, if not all, of what you've learned from previewing once you're immersed in the passage itself.
- These techniques call for you to read the same material twice. Does that sound efficient to you?
- Previewing takes time that you might not be able to afford under timed testing conditions.
- While reading the beginning and end of each paragraph may be helpful for some passages, for others this technique will be of little or no help—and there's no way to know whether you're wasting your time until you've already wasted it.

The only situation in which you should preview is if you're running out of time. Certain questions, especially ones that refer to particular line numbers, can be answered quickly by reading just one paragraph or perhaps a few sentences. A quick scan of the first and last few sentences of the passage *could* provide clues about the passage's main idea or primary purpose, so that you can at least take an educated guess.

8. SUM UP THE PASSAGE AFTER YOU READ IT

After reading the entire passage, take a few seconds to recap it. What was the author's main point, and what were the major supporting points? Remind yourself about the flow of the discussion, without thinking about all the details. Chances are, you'll be able to answer at least one or two of the questions based solely on your recap.

BRAIN TEASER

In this quiz, you'll first answer four additional Reading questions (one of each type we examined in this lesson) based on the Francis Bacon passage. Then, to reinforce what you've learned in this lesson and the previous one, you'll tackle *two* entirely new passages and question sets. A hint follows each quiz question to help you analyze the question.

Like the Brain Teaser in Lesson 16, we've removed the no-brainer questions and left you with only the toughies. Remember: You'll see more questions per passage (a total of 10) on the actual test than you'll see here, because the real test includes easier questions as well.

Attempt all 15 questions, but don't put yourself under a time limit. Focus instead on applying the strategies you learned in this lesson and the previous one. Then be sure to read the explanations that follow the quiz. They're just as important as the questions themselves, because they explain how to apply the strategies to the questions.

QUIZ

PASSAGE I—Social Studies

Questions 1–4

Francis Bacon contributed to the scientific enterprise a prophetic understanding of how science would one day be put to use in the service of technology, and how such a symbiosis between the two would radically impact both man and his surroundings. As inseparable as they are today, it is hard to imagine science and technology as inhabiting separate domains. But in Bacon's world of the sixteenth century, science was not generally viewed as a practical instrument for improving the physical conditions of life. Anticipating the two notable nineteenth-century science fiction writers Jules Verne and H. G. Wells by three hundred years, Bacon foresaw not only the extent to which science would contribute to the enlargement of technology, but also how technology would come to be seen as the ultimate justification of science.

There is little doubt that others before Bacon understood that discovering the mysteries of air, water, fire, and earth could lead toward useful applications. But Bacon's systematic elaboration of the promise of joining science with technology was a major leap forward in closing the gap between the two endeavors. He, more than any before him, stressed the need for collective organizations for scientific inquiry and application—the forerunners of our vast government, academic, and corporate-sponsored research and development departments. Bacon did not ignore the necessity for creative and dedicated individuals to spur science onwards. Rather, he declared that such individuals would need the help of state aid, corporate organization, official conferences and publications, and regulated social and pecuniary incentives in order for their experiments and insights to have the widest possible application.

The danger that Bacon did not foresee was that corporate influences could restrict the opportunities of the individual scientist, and that a time could come when no scientific work would be possible without corporate support. The most important ramification of these new conditions is that the judgment and moral grounding possible of individual scientists must now compete with the concerns of industrial collectives. Entangled within the scientific/technological system, the modern scientist has jeopardized the qualities once exalted as the very hallmarks of science: the detachment from worldly gains and the disinterested pursuit of truth. Influenced by political and economic pressures, scientists have less and less power to enact any controls over the scientific establishment that pursues the Baconian ideals of riches and power over another of his stated uses for science, "the relief of man's estate." Scientists are losing the power to say "No."

No one questions the immense benefits already conferred by science's efficient methodology. However, since individual scientists must now choose between improving standards of living and obtaining financial support for their research, there is cause for concern. In light of current circumstances, we must ask certain questions about science that Bacon, from a sixteenth-century perspective, could not possibly have put to himself.

1. The author assumes that the pressures placed on individual scientists by the scientific establishment

(A) discourages the faithful enactment of every Baconian ideal.
(B) leads to the enrichment of scientists.
(C) aids in the discovery of truth.
(D) outweighs the personal influence scientists may have on scientific policy decisions.

Hint: Try to paraphrase the author's conclusion and evidence for that conclusion. Then, think about the missing link between the two, which is the assumption that the correct choice will provide.

2. Which of the following, if true, would best serve to validate the author's primary concern in the passage?

(F) Science and technology associations generally establish strict requirements for the individuals to which they grant membership.
(G) Scientific journals publish the research of many individual scientists unaffiliated with major scientific institutions.
(H) Individual scientists often do not share the views of industrial scientific collectives.
(J) Corporate support for non-scientific endeavors places many restrictions on the individuals involved.

Hint: Review the main concern of the author. (If you need to consult the passage, the main concern is summarized nicely at the end.) Then select the choice that best supports the validity of that concern.

3. As discussed in the passage, the "symbiosis" between science and technology (lines 4–5) is best illustrated by which of the following scenarios?

(A) A biologist writes an article documenting a new strain of influenza that is subsequently published and taught in medical schools around the world

(B) A breakthrough in the field of psychology enables psychoanalysts to diagnose patients with greater accuracy

(C) An engineering firm hires a public relations agency to advertise the benefits of a labor-saving mechanical device

(D) A physics discovery leads to the development of a machine that helps researchers view previously uncharted areas of the ocean floor

Hint: Simplify the concept of "symbiosis" using your own words. You'll need to understand the idea behind this "symbiosis" in order to apply the concept to the choices. If you don't know what "symbiosis" means, use the context of the passage to figure it out.

4. How does the passage's third paragraph function in relation to the second paragraph?

(F) It resolves a paradoxical situation presented in the second paragraph.

(G) It proposes a recommendation to deal with a problem discussed in the second paragraph.

(H) It details the results of an oversight described in the second paragraph.

(J) It introduces a consequence of an achievement described in the second paragraph.

Hint: Consult you annotations or notes to help you remember the gist of the second and third paragraphs. When you can summarize what each one is about, you'll be better able to see how what happens in the third paragraph relates to what happens in the second one.

PASSAGE II—Natural Science

Questions 5–10

Line The Andean *cordillera* is made up of many interwoven mountain ranges, which include high intermontane plateaus, basins, and valleys. The Northern Andes contain several broad ecosystems falling into four altitudinal belts. Its northern subregion is distinguished from the rest of the region by higher relative humidity and greater climatic symmetry between the eastern and western flanks of the range. The Central Andes are characterized by a succession of agricultural zones with varied climatic conditions along the mountains' flanks and by large, high-altitude plateaus, variously called *puna* or *altiplano*, which do not occur in the Northern Andes. The soil fertility of the northern *altiplano* is generally good. The western Central Andean ranges are relatively arid with desert-like soils, whereas the eastern ranges are more humid and have more diverse soils. The eastern slopes of the Central Andes in many ways are similar to the wet forests of the Northern Andes. Unlike the Northern Andes, however, these slopes have a dry season.

In regions of gentle topography (such as the central United States or Amazon basin), regional climatic variation can be determined from a few widely spaced measurements. By contrast, in the Andean *cordillera*, with its extreme topographic and climatic features, regional projections are difficult. For example, while air temperature generally decreases with increasing altitude, variability of mountain topography can produce much lower than expected air temperatures. Nevertheless, some general climatic patterns are discernible. For example, with increasing distance south of the equator, the seasonality of precipitation increases, whereas the total annual amount generally decreases. Humidity commonly increases with increasing altitude, but only to some intermediate altitude, above which it declines. The variability of mountain terrain also affects precipitation, such that conditions of extreme wetness and aridity may exist in close proximity. Related to this temperature gradient is a pattern of greater rainfall at the valley heads, and less rain at lower altitudes, resulting in part from mountain rainshadow effect.

The weather patterns of the Andean *cordillera* and Amazon basin in general reflect movements of high- and low-pressure cells associated with the Intertropical Convergence Zone, a low-pressure trough that moves further north and south on a seasonal basis. Precipitation is high throughout the year in the highlands and on the coast in the Northern Andes. South of central Ecuador, at about the latitude of Guayaquil, coastal aridity increases, culminating in the Atacama Desert of northern Chile. In the Central Andes, highland precipitation is seasonal, and amounts are approximately one half those measured in the northern Andes. The aridity of the Central Andean coastal zone is the result of the drying effect of the cold Pacific Humboldt current and the southern Pacific high-pressure cell. Much of the southern portion of the Central Andes in Bolivia is also arid. The dry season causes soil moisture deficits and diminished stream flow for a part of each year.

At the regional or macroscale level, vegetation patterns in the Northern and Central Andes tend to reflect climatic zones determined by latitude and altitude. At the local or mesoscale level, however, this correspondence becomes less precise, as local variations in soil type, slope, drainage, climate, and human intervention come into play.

5. In this passage, the author's primary concern is to

(A) describe the climate and topography of various regions of the Andean *cordillera.*
(B) discuss the factors affecting the climate of the Andean *cordillera.*
(C) suggest alternative explanations for the diversity of climate among the various regions of the Andean *cordillera.*
(D) examine the effects of topography on the climate and vegetation of the Andean *cordillera.*

Hint: The correct answer to a Recap question embraces the whole passage; it is neither too narrow nor too broad in its focus.

6. The air temperatures in the Andean *cordillera* are often "lower than expected" (line 33–34) probably because

(F) the Intertropical Convergence Zone creates unexpected high pressure cells.
(G) the elevation varies dramatically in the mountain regions.
(H) prior measurements were based upon inaccurate topographical maps.
(J) the humidity varies dramatically in the mountain regions.

Hint: Wrong answers to Inference questions often supply information that the passage strongly supports.

7. Which of the following statements finds LEAST support from the passage?

(A) The northern subregion of the Northern Andes is more humid than the western subregion of the Central Andes.
(B) The soil in the northern subregion of the Central Andes is more fertile than the soil in the western subregion of the Central Andes.
(C) The eastern subregion of the Central Andes is more humid than the western subregion of the Central Andes.
(D) The coastal subregion of the Central Andes is less arid than the southern subregion of the Central Andes.

Hint: Beware of the "runner-up" choice. Although the passage does not *explicitly* support this choice, it nevertheless provides some *implicit* support for it.

8. According to the passage, all of the following affect the climate of the Central Andes *cordillera* EXCEPT

(F) the Intertropical Convergence Zone.
(G) the rainshadow effect.
(H) the southern Pacific high-pressure cell.
(J) the symmetry of the mountain ranges.

Hint: The correct answer to this type of Simple Recall question typically confuses the information in the passage.

9. Which of the following statements about vegetation patterns in the Andean *cordillera* does the passage most strongly support?

(A) Local vegetation patterns are determined by the same factors as regional vegetation patterns.
(B) Vegetation patterns are affected by more factors at the mesoscale level than at the local level.
(C) Human intervention has a greater effect than either altitude or latitude upon vegetation patterns.
(D) Some factors affecting vegetation patterns have only a local impact, whereas others have a broader impact.

Hint: The correct answer to a Restatement question often combines different pieces of information from the passage.

10. Among the following, the passage would most logically continue by

(F) describing the climate and topography of portions of the Andean *cordillera* other than the Northern and Central regions.
(G) exploring how proximity to the equator affects vegetation in the Andes *cordillera.*
(H) identifying problems in determining the relationship between soil type and vegetation in the Andean *cordillera.*
(J) examining the effects of vegetation patterns on the topography of the Andean *cordillera.*

Hint: Narrow your choices by eliminating those that are inconsistent with the information in the final paragraph.

PASSAGE III—Humanities

Questions 11–15

In 1930, the centenary of Christina Rossetti's birth, Virginia Woolf reviewed a new biography of hers, in which she identified the Victorian poetess as one of Shakespeare's more recent sisters whose life had been reclusively Victorian but whose achievement as an artist was enduring. Rossetti's potent sensual imagery—the richest since Keats—compelled Edmond Gosse, perhaps the most influential critic and bibliophile in late Victorian England, to observe that Christina Rossetti "does not shrink from strong delineation of the pleasures of life even when denouncing them." In the face of Rossetti's virtual canonization by critics at the end of the nineteenth century, Woolf ignores her apparent conservatism, instead seeing in her something of curiosity value and a model of artistic purity and integrity for women writers. What Woolf remembers Rossetti for are her four volumes of explosively original poems loaded with vivid images and dense emotional energy.

"A Birthday," for instance, is no typical Victorian poem and is certainly unlike predictable works of the era's best-known women poets. Rossetti's most famous poem, "Goblin Market," bridges the generic space between simplistic fairy tale and complex adult allegory (at once Christian, psychological, and profeminist). Like many of Rossetti's works, it is extraordinary in its originality and unorthodox in its form. Its subject matter is radical and therefore risky for a Victorian poetess because it implies castigations of an economic (and even marital) marketplace dominated by men, whose motives are, at best, suspect. Its Christian allusions are obvious but grounded in opulent images whose lushness borders on the erotic. From Rossetti's work emerges not only emotional force, artistic polish, frequently ironic playfulness, and intellectual vigor but also an intriguing, enigmatic quality. "Winter: My Secret," for example, combines these traits along with a very high (and un-Victorian) level of poetic self-consciousness.

"How does one reconcile the aesthetic sensuality of Rossetti's poetry with her repressed, ascetic lifestyle?" Woolf wondered (as have many critics after her). That Rossetti did indeed withhold a "secret" both from those intimate with her and from posterity is an argument found at the center of Lona Packer's 1963 biography of Rossetti. While Packer believed Rossetti's to be a secret of the heart, her thesis has been disproved through the discovery of approximately seventeen hundred letters by Rossetti which reinforce the conventional image of her as pious, scrupulously abstinent, and semi-reclusive. The passions expressed in her love poems, if not entirely the products of fantasy or literary tradition, seem to have been largely repressed in real life.

Yet those poems, read properly, do expose the "secret" at the heart of both Rossetti's life and art: a willingness to forego worldly pleasures in favor of an aestheticized Christian version of transcendent fulfillment in the heavenly afterlife. Her sonnet "The World," therefore, becomes pivotal in understanding Rossetti's literary project as a whole—including her rhymes for children, her fairy tale narratives, her love poems, her bleak verses of spiritual desolation and death-longing, as well as her books of devotional commentary. The world, for Rossetti, is a fallen place. Her work is pervasively designed to force upon readers an acute sensitivity to this inescapable Christian truth. The beauty of her poetry must be seen therefore as an artistic strategy, a means toward a moral end.

11. Based upon the information in the passage, Virginia Woolf would most likely agree that Rossetti's work

(A) exposes a secret about Rossetti's life.
(B) describes yet at the same time denounces life's pleasures.
(C) affirms that Rossetti was pious and reclusive.
(D) serves as a model of artistic integrity.

Hint: Be sure not to confuse the opinions of Woolf with those of the passage's author or of Edmund Goose.

12. Which of the following statements is most reasonably inferable from the passage?

(F) "Winter: My Secret" is Rossetti's best-known poem.
(G) Rossetti was not among the best-known poets during her era.
(H) The accounts of Rossetti's life contained in Packer's biography of Rossetti differ from those included in Woolf's biography of Rossetti.
(J) Rossetti's display of poetic self-consciousness drew criticism from her contemporaries.

Hint: The correct answer choice must provide an almost unavoidable conclusion—*a very tight logical inference.*

13. The author discusses Packer's thesis and its flaws in order to

(A) contrast the sensuality of Rossetti's poetry with the relative starkness of her devotional commentary.
(B) reveal the secret to which Rossetti alludes in "Winter: My Secret."
(C) call into question the authenticity of recently discovered letters written by Rossetti.
(D) provide a foundation for the author's own theory about Rossetti's life and work.

Hint: To answer the question, you'll need to combine information from more than one of the passage's paragraphs.

14. The author implies that Rossetti's "The World"

(F) was Rossetti's last major work.
(G) is the most helpful expression of Rossetti's motives.
(H) was Rossetti's longest work.
(J) reflects Rossetti's shift away from her earlier feminist viewpoint.

Hint: You'll need to consider the last paragraph as a whole to answer the question.

Hint: As with any Inference question, look out for answer choices that call for speculation.

15. Which of the following best expresses the main idea of the passage?

(A) Newly discovered evidence suggests that Rossetti's works were misinterpreted by earlier critics and scholars.
(B) Rossetti can be compared to Shakespeare both in her private life and in the enduring quality of her work.
(C) Victorian poetry can be properly interpreted only by considering the personal life of the particular poet.
(D) The apparent inconsistency between Rossetti's personal life and literary work are explained by Rossetti's poems themselves.

Hint: The best answer choice must embrace the author's perspective on Rossetti, not just the viewpoints of others mentioned in the passage.

ANSWERS AND EXPLANATIONS

1. **The correct answer is (D).** The phrase "influenced by political and economic pressures" brings you to the heart of the matter. Scientists, the author argues, have less and less power to control the establishment that's more interested in money and power than making things better for people. The evidence is that all scientific work requires corporate support—that is, that scientists can't go against the system when it comes to carrying out their work. But if scientists could still personally influence decision-making, then it wouldn't be fair to say they have little influence over the scientific direction. In making his case, the author *assumes* that the pressure the scientific establishment exerts on scientists outweighs any personal influence scientists may have. Choice (A) can't be the author's assumption, because the author argues that the pressure on scientists actually favors certain Baconian ideals—namely, the pursuit of riches and power. As for choice (B), the pressure, you're told, *does* damage the scientist's traditional "detachment from worldly gains," which means that scientists do have to consider "worldly gains"—that is, money—as a key element in what they do. But it is not necessary for scientists *themselves* to get rich in order for the author's argument to hold up—the "worldly gains" in question may all go to the corporations of the scientific establishment. So, choice (B) need not be assumed here. Choice (C) is nearly opposite to the assumption you're looking for. The pressure from the scientific establishment actually *jeopardizes* the pursuit of truth that once characterized science. So, the author certainly doesn't assume that such pressure will help in the discovery of truth.

2. **The correct answer is (H).** The author's main concern is that scientists are forced by the scientific establishment that supports them to conduct research in line with the objectives of that establishment. He is worried that the individual voices of scientists will be drowned out by restrictions placed on what they're allowed to say. That is, however, only a concern if what scientists have to say is significantly different from the views of the establishment. Choice (H) supports the author's argument by making it more likely that independent views *are* being drowned out by the system that he describes. Choice (F) is too vague to lend any validity to the author's concern. You don't know what role such associations play in the grand scheme of things, nor do you know what the strict requirements entail. In short, choice (F) accomplishes little to make the author's concern even more justified. Choice (G) provides just the opposite of what a correct choice should provide. If choice (G) were true, then we'd have to think that the author's concern is *less* valid, since the existence of many independent journal articles would suggest that non-establishment views *are* being expressed. The author is worried that such views are being stifled by the system. As for choice (J), the passage concerns corporate control of the scientific enterprise. *Non*-scientific endeavors are outside the scope of the passage.

3. **The correct answer is (D).** The phrase "and how *such* a symbiosis between the two . . ." tells us that what comes before this phrase is an example of what the author means by the tough word "symbiosis." There we're told that science is used to help develop technology. The sentence that follows calls them "inseparable." The end of the paragraph further clarifies this: science contributes to technology, but technology also contributes to science. So we need to find the choice that illustrates this linkage between the two. Choice (D) does the trick: A science discovery in one area (physics) leads to the invention of a technology (a machine) that helps scientists make discoveries in another field (oceanography). The interplay between science and technology in this example is a valid application of the author's description of "symbiosis" in paragraph 1. Choice (A) fails on the technology count, basically because there's no technology side of this story. It's all about science, so it doesn't illustrate the symbiosis the author describes. Choice (B) tells of a scientific breakthrough. But there's nothing about the interplay between science and technology, so this choice doesn't illustrate the symbiosis the author describes. If there's an interplay at work at all in choice (C), it's between technology (a new mechanical device) and marketing. There's nothing about science here, so this choice doesn't illustrate the symbiosis that the author describes.

4. **The correct answer is (J).** Paragraph 2 is about Bacon's achievements and correct predictions. He came up with and communicated the idea that science and technology would be joined and that an organizational infrastructure would be necessary for science to flourish. His elaboration of the promise of joining science and technology was a "major leap forward" in bringing the two together—and that certainly counts as an achievement. The major theme of paragraph 3 is captured by its first two words: "The danger. . ."—and a glance through the paragraph confirms that it is about the dangers to science of the scientific establishment

that Bacon's insights bring about. So, it's fair to say that the third paragraph shows a consequence of an achievement described in the second. You can easily eliminate choice (F) by recognizing that there is no paradoxical situation described in paragraph 2. A paradox is a situation in which two conflicting things seem to exist at the same time. There's nothing like that in paragraph 2. You can quickly eliminate choice (G) once you see that there is nothing resembling a recommendation in paragraph 3. You must wait until the very end of paragraph 4 for a recommendation from the author. As for choice (H), the oversight—what "Bacon did not foresee"—is discussed in paragraph 3, not paragraph 2. There is no oversight discussed in paragraph 2, which is solely about Bacon's achievements and correct predictions—that is, what Bacon did see.

5. **The correct answer is (B).** The bulk of the passage—the entire second and third paragraphs—is concerned with examining the factors affecting the climate of various portions of the Andean *cordillera*. The first paragraph provides a framework for this discussion by describing the climate and topography of the various regions. Choice (A) is too narrow; it indicates the author's purpose in the first paragraph only, omitting the discussion of the factors influencing climate. Choice (C) distorts the passage. Nowhere does the passage state or imply that competing explanations or theories exist to account for climatic differences among the different regions of the Andean *cordillera*. Also, the author is just as concerned with identifying the similarities among the regions as with discussing their differences. Choice (D) is off focus in two respects. First, although the author is concerned with the effects of topography on climate, topography is only one of several such factors discussed in the passage. Second, the effect of topography on vegetation is only briefly suggested in the final paragraph; since this topic is not explored in any detail, it is not fair to say that it is of primary concern to the author.

6. **The correct answer is (G).** The passage points out that while air temperature generally decreases as altitude increases, "variability of mountain topography" (i.e., dramatic changes in elevation) makes it difficult to determine temperature in any given spot from widely spaced measurements. It can be reasonably inferred from this information that an unexpected temperature would probably be the result of unexpected altitude. Choice (H) is a "runner-up" choice and is supported (at least in part) by the passage insofar as the author implies that in measuring altitude in mountainous regions, "widely spaced measurements" do not provide an accurate report for areas between the measured points. However, nowhere in the passage is the reliability of older maps compared with that of newer maps. Choice (J) is a "runner-up" choice and is supported by the passage insofar as the author indicates a correlation between humidity and altitude (lines 39–41). However, the passage makes no correlation between humidity and air temperature. Thus, choice (J) calls for an unwarranted inference (read: speculation). What's more, choice (J) does not respond to the question. Choice (F) confuses the information in the passage. The topic of air pressure (discussed in the third paragraph) is unrelated to the question, which deals with information in the second paragraph.

7. **The correct answer is (D).** The author refers in line 64 to the "aridity of the Central Andean coastal zone" as well as indicating (in lines 67–69) that "[m]uch of the southern portion of the Central Andes in Bolivia is also arid." However, nowhere does the author compare the two regions in this respect. Choice (B) is the "runner-up" choice. The author describes the soil fertility in the northern *altiplano* as "generally good" (line 16). Although the author does not specify in which subregion(s) the *altiplano* lie, the description in the passage suggests that they run in a north-south direction through the different regions. Thus, the "northern" *altiplano* are probably located in the northern subregion. By contrast, the passage describes the soil in the western subregion as "desert-like." Choice (A) is well supported. The northern portion of the Northern Andes is characterized by "higher relative humidity" than other subregions (line 7), and the author mentions its "wet forests" in line 21. By contrast, the western portion of the Central Andes is described as "relatively arid with desert-like soils" (lines 17–18). Choice (C) is explicitly supported in the passage: The author describes the western portion of the Central Andes as "relatively arid" compared to the humidity of the eastern subregion (lines 17–18).

8. **The correct answer is (J).** The only discussion of mountain symmetry is in the first paragraph, which mentions the symmetry in climate between the east and west flanks of the Northern Andes mountains. No mention is made anywhere in the passage of any symmetry with respect to the Central Andes mountains. Choices (F), (G), and (H) are all mentioned in the passage as factors affecting the climate of the Central Andes *cordillera*.

9. **The correct answer is (D).** This question focuses on the information in the last paragraph. The author first notes that vegetation patterns correspond generally with climate (as determined

primarily by latitude and altitude). Accordingly, altitude and latitude affect vegetation patterns throughout the region. Then, in the final sentence the author points out that, in spite of the general correspondence between climate and vegetation, local patterns may not correspond so precisely with climate, due to a number of local factors. Choice (D) accurately reflects the information in the final paragraph. Choice (A) runs contrary to the information in the last paragraph. Regional patterns do not depend upon local variations; thus, fewer factors come into play in identifying these broader patterns. Choice (B) confuses the terms used by the author. The author equates "mesoscale" with "local." Accordingly, choice (B) makes no sense. Choice (C) is an exaggeration. Although the author identifies human intervention as one factor that might distort the effect of climate (altitude and latitude) upon vegetation patterns, the author neither states nor implies that the impact of human intervention is greater than that of climate (altitude and latitude).

10. **The correct answer is (G).** In the final paragraph, the author asserts that altitude as well as latitude (proximity to the equator) determine climatic zones as reflected by vegetation patterns. Accordingly, a more detailed discussion about why different forms of vegetation appear at different latitudes is a logical continuation. Choice (H) is the runner-up choice and is consistent with the content of the final paragraph. What's more, the author does suggest a relationship between soil type and vegetation (presumably, soil type determines what forms of vegetation will thrive). However, the final paragraph neither indicates nor suggests any potential "problems" in determining such a relationship. Choice (F) ignores the direction of the final paragraph. In addition, nowhere in the passage does the author suggest that regions other than the Northern and Central regions will be or should be examined. Choice (J) appears at first glance to be a reasonable response since it includes the same subject matter (i.e., vegetation) as the final paragraph. However, choice (J) is a bit nonsensical—it is unlikely that vegetation would have much of an effect upon topography; even if it did, nothing in the final paragraph indicates that this is the direction in which the discussion is likely to turn.

11. **The correct answer is (D).** In lines 17–18, the author states that Woolf saw in Rossetti "a model of artistic purity and integrity for women writers." Choice (A) confuses the opinion of Woolf with that of the author. The author does indeed discuss, in the third and fourth paragraphs, how some of Rossetti's works revealed a secret about her life and art. However, this is the author's opinion, not Woolf's. Choice (B) confuses the opinion of Woolf with that of Edmond Gosse. It was Gosse, not Woolf, who commented that Rossetti "does not shrink from a strong delineation of the pleasures in life even when denouncing them" (lines 11–13). Choice (C) confuses the information in the passage. In the third paragraph, the author discusses how Rossetti's recently discovered letters confirm that she was pious, scrupulously abstinent, and semi-reclusive. These are not Woolf's impressions of Rossetti's work but rather the author's analysis of Rossetti's personal letters.

12. **The correct answer is (G).** In the first sentence of the second paragraph, the author states that " 'A Birthday' is no typical Victorian poem and is certainly unlike predictable works of the era's best-known women poets." It is reasonably inferable that Rossetti was not among the era's best-known women poets, at least during her time. Choice (F) is contradicted by the passage. The author states that "Goblin Market" is Rossetti's most famous poem (lines 26–27). Choice (H) confuses the information in the passage. Woolf reviewed but did not write a biography of Rossetti. Choice (J) distorts the information in the passage. The author does indicate that in "Winter: My Secret," Rossetti displayed a high level of poetic self-consciousness (lines 42–45). However, the author neither states nor implies that Rossetti drew criticism during her lifetime as a result. To the contrary, the fact that she was virtually canonized by critics at the end of the nineteenth century (lines 13–15) suggests her work was the object of very little negative criticism from her contemporaries.

13. **The correct answer is (D).** The author's threshold purpose in discussing Packer's biography is to affirm that Rossetti's style of writing was not a reflection of her personal lifestyle. Having dismissed the theory that Rossetti was keeping secrets about her life, the author goes on (in the final paragraph) to offer a better explanation for the apparent contradiction between Rossetti's lifestyle and the emotional, sensual style of her poetry. Choice (A) distorts the information in the passage. First, the passage does not indicate that Rossetti's devotional commentary was in the form of prose rather than poetry. Second, nowhere in the passage does the author compare or contrast Rossetti's devotional commentary with her other works. Choice (B) distorts and actually runs contrary to the author's purpose. The author discusses Packer's biography to affirm that Rossetti's style of writing was not a reflection of her personal lifestyle—in other words, that she was not keeping

secrets about her life. In this sense, choice (B) actually runs contrary to the author's purpose. Choice (C) distorts the information in the third paragraph. The author does not raise the issue of whether these letters were actually written by Rossetti. In fact, insofar as the author mentions these letters to disprove Packer's thesis, the author seems to affirm that the letters are indeed authentic.

14. **The correct answer is (G).** In the final paragraph, the author states that "The World" is "pivotal in understanding Rossetti's literary project as a whole." Based upon the remainder of the final paragraph, the author seems to understand Rossetti's "literary project as a whole" as an attempt to convey an inescapable Christian truth to her readers (see lines 75–78). It is reasonably inferable, then, that "The World" provides significant insight into Rossetti's motives. Choice (F) calls for speculation. Although "The World" is the last of Rossetti's works discussed in the passage, it does not necessarily follow that it was Rossetti's last major work. Choice (H) calls for speculation. The author neither states nor implies that "The World" is Rossetti's longest work; indeed, nowhere in the passage does the author mention the length of any of Rossetti's works. Choice (J) distorts the information in the passage. The author suggests that "The World" is pivotal in understanding Rossetti's general literary agenda: to convey an inescapable Christian truth to her readers. However, the author neither states nor implies that Rossetti's motives in writing "The World" or her viewpoint at the time she wrote it departed from earlier motives or viewpoints.

15. **The correct answer is (D).** The author's primary concern in the first two paragraphs is to point out that Rossetti's work conflicts with her apparently conservative personal life. The author's own impressions of Rossetti's work are corroborated by those of Woolf and Gosse. The third paragraph begins by asking how to reconcile this apparent conflict (the newly discovered letters discussed in the third paragraph only reinforce the inconsistency between her personal life and literary work). In the last paragraph, the author attempts to explain the inconsistency by examining Rossetti's love poems (particularly, her sonnet "The World"). Choice (A) is the "runner-up" choice. The newly discovered personal letters disprove Packer's thesis that Rossetti may have had personal affairs of the heart that she kept secret. Thus, Packer (and possibly Woolf) may have misinterpreted Rossetti's works by assuming that Rossetti wrote from personal experience. However, the author does not make this point explicit in the passage. Moreover, this point is far too narrow. It ignores the author's own explanation (in the final paragraph) for the apparent inconsistency between Rossetti's personal life and her work. Choice (B) is off focus. Admittedly, in the first paragraph the author does point out that Woolf compared Rossetti to Shakespeare in both of these respects. However, the author makes no further attempt to explain or describe these similarities. Moreover, the point made in choice (B) is Woolf's point, not the author's. Choice (C) distorts the author's argument and is too broad. In the last paragraph the author seems to claim that, through a proper reading of Rossetti's love poems, one can understand the ironic, enigmatic, contradictory nature of her work (in turn explaining the inconsistency between Rossetti's personal life and work). In this sense, choice (C) distorts and actually runs contrary to the author's argument. Second, the passage concerns only Rossetti, not Victorian poetry or poetry in general, as choice (C) suggests; in this sense, then, choice (C) is too broad.

PART V

THE ACT SCIENCE REASONING TEST

LESSON 18
Science Reasoning Strategies

This lesson covers Brainiac strategies for the ACT Science Reasoning Test. In this lesson, you'll:

- Review the format and test directions for the Science Reasoning Test
- Learn how Brainiacs figure out the most common Science Reasoning questions by applying special insights and other tools at their cognitive disposal (Nine sample questions will serve as illustrations.)
- Apply Brainiac insights to 10 tough questions based on two ACT-style Science Reasoning passages

THE SCIENCE REASONING TEST—DIRECTIONS REVISITED

You took a first glance at the features of the ACT Science Reasoning Test in Lesson 2. To refresh your memory, here is the test format.

Data Representation (15 questions)

This format presents scientific information in textual as well as visual forms such as graphs, scatter plots, and tables. Data Representation questions gauge your ability to read, interpret, and draw conclusions from the graphical data.

Research Summaries (18 questions)

This format provides an account of one or more scientific experiments. Research Summary questions test your ability to understand or critique the design of the experiment(s) and to interpret the their results.

Conflicting Viewpoints (7 questions)

This format presents two or more conflicting hypotheses or viewpoints, each based on the same premises or data. Conflicting Viewpoints questions measure your ability to understand, compare, and evaluate the hypotheses or viewpoints.

No format or question type is inherently easier than another. Whatever the skill, the test-makers can devise no-brainers as well as mind-benders.

THE ACT SCIENCE REASONING TEST IS *NOT* A SCIENCE TEST

The Science Reasoning Test includes passages drawn from four broad disciplines:

- *Biology*—including cell biology, botany, zoology, microbiology, ecology, genetics, and evolution
- *Earth/Space Sciences*—including geology, meteorology, oceanography, astronomy, and environmental sciences
- *Chemistry*—including atomic theory, inorganic chemical reactions, chemical bonding, reaction rates, solutions, equilibriums, gas laws, electrochemistry, organic chemistry, biochemistry, and properties and states of matter
- *Physics*—including mechanics, energy, thermodynamics, electromagnetism, fluids, solids, and light waves

For the ACT, it's helpful to know at least the very basics covered in introductory high-school coursework in the four broad areas listed above. However, information beyond the basics will be provided. For example, in a passage dealing with the life cycle of bacteria (biology), the test-makers would assume that you know that the cell is the basic building block of life, but they *won't* assume that you know specifically how bacteria reproduce. That's because the ACT Science Reasoning Test is not really a "science" test. It doesn't test you on your *knowledge* of science; rather, it tests your ability to understand the scientific *approach* to a problem, which involves certain ways of *reasoning*. Luckily, this approach (or way of reasoning) is just a special form of common sense.

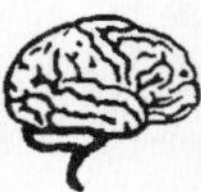

This doesn't mean that science nerds don't have an advantage over other test-takers when it comes to ACT Science Reasoning. To the contrary, if your science background is strong, you'll feel more comfortable and score higher on the Science Reasoning Test—just as you will on the Mathematicals Test if you have a strong math background.

THREE SAMPLE QUESTION SETS

Before learning the strategies that Brainiacs use for handling ACT Science Reasoning questions, read the following three passages and answer the three questions based on each one. (The difficulty level of the questions ranges from easier to tougher than average.) In the next section, you'll analyze each of the 9 questions.

The number of questions based on each of the following three passages is less than what you'll encounter on the ACT—where each passage is accompanied by 5–7 questions. During this lesson's questions and in Part VI, you'll tackle sets that include 5 questions each.

Passage I (Format: Data Representation)

Phytoplankton are tiny aquatic plants that are an important food source for larger animals and may be an important source of carbon (the element that is a building block of all living organisms). Phytoplankton abundance is dependent on the presence of warm surface waters. Consequently, changes in phytoplankton abundance can be used as an indicator of changes in surface water temperature.

A system for documenting phytoplankton abundance has been developed using filtering silk towed by merchant ships. The organisms color the silk green, and the intensity of the color is correlated with their abundance. The first figure shows data on the average monthly phytoplankton abundance for four decades, as determined by the color index system. Data is given for two ocean areas in the Northern Atlantic just below the arctic circle. The boundaries of these areas are depicted in the second figure.

Figure 1

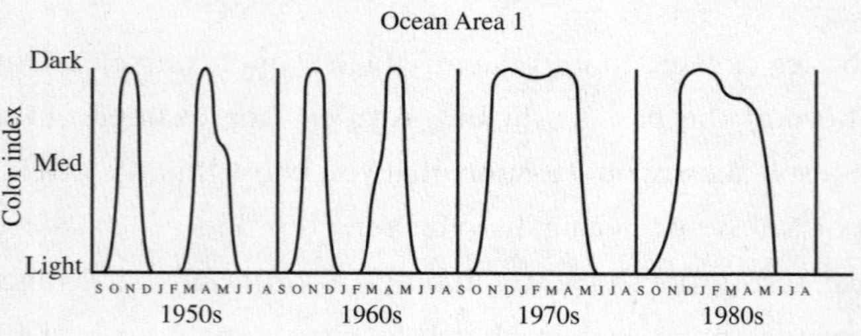

Figure 2

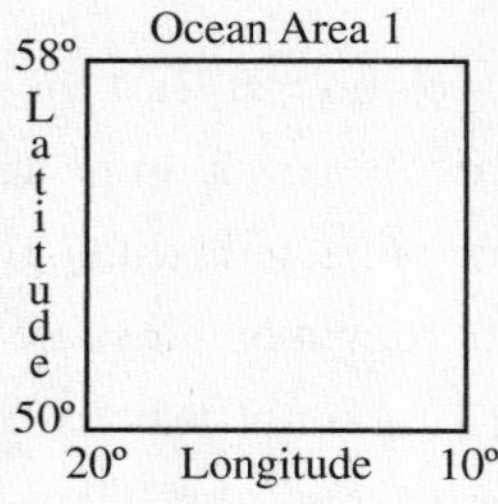

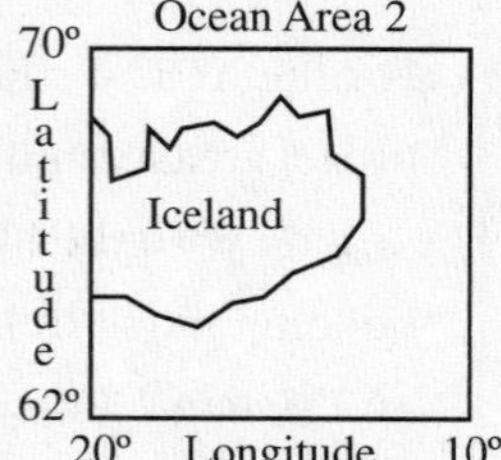

Q **1.** Based on the information in the first figure, which of the following statements concerning phytoplankton abundance in the four decades of the study is correct?

(A) There was no discernible change in patterns of phytoplankton abundance in Ocean Area 1.
(B) Annual phytoplankton abundance increased in Ocean Area 2.
(C) Annual phytoplankton abundance increased in ocean area 1 and decreased in Ocean Area 2.
(D) The season of high phytoplankton abundance increased in length in both Ocean Areas.

A **The correct answer is (C).** This question is the easiest of the three in this set, for two reasons. First, it involves only one of the two figures. Second, you can literally "see" the answer to this question by glancing at the graphs in the figure. In Ocean Area 1, the two annual periods of phytoplankton abundance grew much longer as the decades passed, until they merged into a single long period of abundance lasting half the year. By contrast, in Ocean Area 2, the two peaks got "thinner" as time passed, indicating a marked decrease in the phytoplankton population over the four-decade period.

Q 2. Assuming that the changes in phytoplankton abundance seen in the study occurred solely because of surface water temperature variations, the information in the figures indicates that which of the following statements is true?

(A) Surface ocean waters above latitude 62° North in the map areas cooled during the study.
(B) Surface ocean waters above latitude 50° North in the map areas cooled during the study.
(C) Surface ocean waters east of longitude 10° in the map areas warmed during the study.
(D) Surface ocean waters west of longitude 10° in the map areas cooled during the study.

A **The correct answer is (A).** This is a more challenging question than question 1, for two reasons. First, it involves information in both figures as well as a key portion of the textual information. Second, to handle it, you need to not only "read" and interpret the graphical and textual information but also apply it to a given scenario (the hypothetical situation that the question poses). Only choice (A) provides information consistent with the data in the graphs. Ocean Area 2 is north of latitude 62°; if the waters there got cooler, it would make sense that phytoplankton abundance would decrease. (See the second sentence of the passage.)

Q 3. Some researchers hypothesize that the changes in phytoplankton abundance reflect an increase in global temperature over the last century (global warming). Which of the following findings would support this hypothesis and fit the data seen in the first figure?

(A) A greater abundance of fresh water from melted ice and permafrost has begun flowing south to north from the Antarctic during the last century.
(B) A greater abundance of fresh water from melted ice and permafrost has begun flowing north to south from the Arctic during the last century.
(C) Warmer temperatures have been recorded in and around Iceland during the last century.
(D) Barring a few exceptions, phytoplankton numbers have begun to decrease dramatically in ocean areas around the globe during the last century.

A **The correct answer is (B).** This question is the toughest and trickiest of the three in this set. As with question 2, you need to understand both figures in order to handle it. What's more, the passage's textual and graphical information says nothing about ice or melted ice, and so it's tempting to dismiss the correct choice (B) out of hand as irrelevant. But choice (B) would fit both the global warming hypothesis and the data shown in the graphs in several ways. First, the graphs for Ocean Area 1, showing an increase in phytoplankton, certainly fit the notion of global warming. Second, the idea that Arctic ice is melting would fit that idea as well. Finally, the abundance of fresh water newly melted from ice appearing in the northern reaches of the Atlantic could help explain why phytoplankton has actually declined around Iceland: the water temperature there has decreased slightly as a result of the melting ice.

Passage II (Format: Research Summary)

Airplane wings must be designed *aerodynamically* (with consideration to the airflow over the body of the plane) to ensure efficient flight. Aerodynamic design considers *lift* and *drag*.

Lift is the force acting upward on the plane. It is generated because the top of a wing is curved, while the bottom is flat. The air moving over the top of the wings must move faster than the air moving over the bottom. This results in a lower pressure area above the wing.

Drag is the air resistance generated by the plane. This is a force acting in opposition to the planes forward movement. The most efficient planes are those with the highest lift to drag ratio.

Researchers testing new wing designs conducted a series of experiments to measure their efficiency.

Experiment 1

Researchers tested aircraft with four wing designs (see the following figure) in a *wind tunnel* (a tunnel in which air is blown over a craft to simulate flight conditions). This test simulated flight at 400 mph. The lift and drag measured for each wing shape are recorded in Table 1.

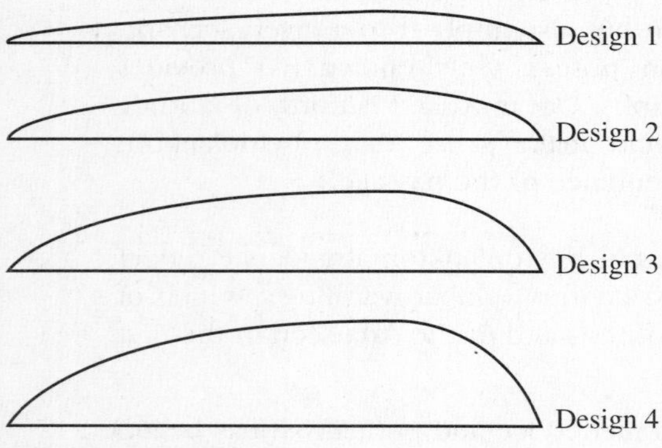

Table 1

Wing Design	Lift (neutrons)	Drag (neutrons)	Efficiency
1	3	.15	20:1
2	8	.2	40:1
3	10	1	10:1
4	18	2	9:1

Experiment 2

Aircraft with the four wing types depicted in the figure were tested under similar flight conditions to gauge fuel consumption. After reaching cruising altitude, the planes maintained a speed of 400 mph. The results appear in Table 2.

Table 2

Wing	Fuel consumption (gallons/hr)
1	40
2	20
3	80
4	88

Experiment 3

Lift, drag, and efficiency are dependent on airspeed. The researchers tested wing designs 1 and 2 at different speeds. Efficiency (lift to drag ratio) was recorded (Table 3).

Table 3

Airspeed (mph)	Design 1 (Efficiency)	Design 2 (Efficiency)
200	22:1	43:1
300	21:1	42:1
400	20:1	40:1
500	18:1	12:1
600	10:1	8:1

Q **4.** A passenger plane is able to carry a fixed weight, including passengers and fuel. Which wing design would be best for such a plane?

(A) Design 1
(B) Design 2
(C) Design 3
(D) Design 4

A **The correct answer is (B).** This is a fairly easy question, but it's not a "no-brainer." To handle the question, you need to *infer* that the "best" design would be one that is most efficient in terms of its lift-to-drag ratio as well as in terms of fuel consumption. Fortunately, Tables 1 and 2 each show that design 2 is most efficient.

Q **5.** In cold, damp weather, the buildup of ice on airplane wings can pose significant aerodynamic problems. Which of the following effects would you expect?

(A) As ice builds up on the top of the wing, drag increases.
(B) As ice builds up on the top of the wing, lift increases.
(C) As ice builds up on the bottom of the wing, lift decreases.
(D) All of the above

A **The correct answer is (D).** To answer this question, you need to understand the concepts of lift and drag. You also need to recognize that Table 1 provides the data relevant to the question. These features make this a moderately difficult question. Ice building up on top of the wing would increase lift, since the higher the curved upper surface of the wing, the greater the difference between the speed of air moving under the wing and above it. It would also increase drag, as suggested by the third column of Table 1: Notice how the wings with the higher upper surface also have greater drag. Finally, ice building up under the wing would decrease the speed of air moving under the wing and so reduce lift. Thus, all three effects would occur.

Q **6.** New fighter jets are being designed so that the wing is modifiable, depending on the speed at which the plane is going. Which of the following would be a logical adjustment of the wing for such jets?

(A) At speeds above 500 mph, the top of the wing would become flatter.
(B) At speeds above 500 mph, the top of the wing would become more curved.
(C) At speeds above 500 mph, the bottom of the wing would become curved.
(D) None of the above

A **The correct answer is (A).** Even though you need only consult one table (Table 3) to analyze this question, the question would be considered a toughie—chiefly because it's very easy to overlook the trend reversal that is key to the question. Since the question deals with speed, it's a good bet that experiment 3 (Table 3) is the one that's most relevant. In Table 3, notice that wing design 2 is more efficient than design 1 at lower speeds, but once a speed of 500 mph is reached, design 1 outperforms design 2. Thus, it appears that at high speeds a "flatter" wing design is more beneficial.

Passage III (Format: Conflicting Viewpoints)

A greenish, potato-sized meteorite discovered in Antarctica is believed to have originated on Mars. Investigations of the meteorite have revealed a number of unusual features. Some scientists believe that these features are evidence of primitive life on Mars, while other scientists believe that they are more probably the result of non-biological (nonliving) processes, such as hydrothermal synthesis.

Hydrothermal Synthesis Hypothesis

The meteorite crystallized slowly from *magma* (molten rock) on Mars 4.5 million years ago. About half a million years later, the rock became fractured. This was a time when Mars was much warmer and had abundant water. Deep inside the planet, in a process called *hydrothermal synthesis*, hot water and carbon seeped into the fractured rock and formed new complex *organic* compounds called polycyclic aromatic hydrocarbons (PAHs). (Organic compounds, or those that contain carbon, are formed from life processes, such as bacterial decay, as well as processes that are not associated with life, including hydrothermal synthesis and star formation.)

As the chemical environment of the planet changed over time, crystals of magnetite, iron sulfides, and carbonate formed in the rock. The crystallization of the carbonate resulted in the formation of unusual elongated and egg-shaped structures within the crystals.

Primitive Life Hypothesis

The meteorite crystallized slowly from *magma* (molten rock) on Mars 4.5 million years ago. About half a million years later, the rock became fractured. This was a time when Mars was much warmer and had abundant water. The rock was immersed in water rich in carbon dioxide, which allowed carbon to collect inside the fractured rock, along with primitive bacteria.

The bacteria began to manufacture magnetite and iron sulfide crystals, just as bacteria on Earth do. As generations of bacteria died and began to decay, they created PAHs inside of the meteorite's carbon molecules. Finally, some of the bacteria themselves were preserved as elongated egg-shaped fossils inside of the rock.

Q 7. About which of the following points do the two hypotheses differ?

(A) The meteorite's age
(B) The origin of the meteorite's organic molecules
(C) The conditions on Mars when the meteorite formed
(D) The origin of the fractures in the meteorite

A **The correct answer is (B).** This question, which is easier than average, calls for you to recognize the essence of the conflict between the two viewpoints; therefore, it's a main-idea question. The Hydrothermal Synthesis Hypothesis states that the PAHs (the organic molecules in the meteorite) were formed by hydrothermal synthesis, while the Primitive Life Hypothesis says that they were formed by the decay of bacteria. This difference between the two theories is what the passage is all about: Are the egg-shaped structures within the crystals evidence of an organic process (and therefore of life on Mars) or an inorganic one?

Q 8. Which of the following represents a difference in opinion between proponents of the two theories?

(A) Proponents of the Primitive Life Hypothesis maintain that Mars has changed substantially since the meteorite was formed.
(B) Proponents of the Primitive Life Hypothesis dispute the notion that PAHs can occur from processes other than bacterial decay.
(C) Proponents of the Hydrothermal Synthesis Hypothesis believe that hot water and carbon formed organic compounds in the rock.
(D) Proponents of the Hydrothermal Synthesis Hypothesis believe that the fossils found inside the meteorite were probably the remains of an organism other than a bacteria.

A **The correct answer is (C).** This question is average in difficulty. It's a bit tougher than question 1 because of how the wrong answer choices are written. Notice that choice (A) is actually a true statement, based on the passage. It would be a tempting choice for many test-takers. However, choice (A) describes a belief that is actually *shared* by proponents of both theories. Hence, it doesn't respond to the specific question. Choice (B) is particularly tricky because, according to the passage, proponents of the Primitive Life Hypothesis do believe that PAHs in the meteor occurred as a result of bacterial decay. However, the passage does not go so far as to make the assertion provided in choice (B). Choice (D) is tricky because it is *partly true*—the proponents of Hydrothermal Synthesis Hypothesis do believe that the fossils were not the remains of bacteria. But choice (C), the correct one, provides the only true statement that also names a difference between the proponents of the two theories.

Q 9. Which of the following additional findings would help the case of proponents of the Primitive Life Hypothesis?

(A) Researchers analyzing glacial ice found very low concentrations of PAHs.
(B) Organic molecules were also discovered in meteorites known to have originated in the **asteroid belt** (an area that is rich in asteroids and that orbits the sun).
(C) Some of the carbonates in which the PAHs were found had element ratios that are similar to those found on Earth.
(D) Experiments with the weathering of rocks have shown that under certain conditions, molecules in the environment can make their way deep within a rock.

A **The correct answer is (A).** This question is tougher than average. It requires you not only to understand what PAHs are, but also to determine the effect of additional evidence on both hypotheses. To handle the question, you also need to know that Antarctica consists primarily of glacial ice—a fact that the passage does not supply but one that the test-makers assume you know. The fact that low concentrations of PAHs were found in glacial ice, choice (A), mildly strengthens the Primitive Life Hypothesis by tending to *disprove* the notion that the PAHs in the meteorite seeped in after the rock landed in Antarctica. Choices (B) and (C) are wrong because, according to the passage, PAHs can be formed not just from life processes but also from processes that are not associated with life. Therefore, neither additional finding makes one hypothesis more compelling than the other. Choice (D) would actually hurt the case of proponents of the Primitive Life Hypothesis. How? By accomplishing just the opposite of choice (A): tending to prove the notion that the PAHs in the meteorite seeped in from the environment after the rock landed in Antarctica.

TOP 10 BRAiNiAC STRATEGIES FOR ANSWERING SCIENCE REASONING TEST QUESTIONS

If you read the explanations for the preceding 9 questions, you already picked up a few strategies that Brainiacs use in answering Science Reasoning questions. You'll review them here, and learn about some others.

X-REF

Most of the strategies here apply to all three Science Reasoning formats: Data Representation, Research Summary, and Conflicting Viewpoints. During the next two lessons, you'll focus on strategies that are specific to each format.

1. BRAINIACS START BY SKIMMING THE PASSAGE FOR THE BIG PICTURE.

Your first step with each of the seven Science Reasoning passages should be to spend 20–30 seconds glancing through all of the information provided. Of course, the first task is to determine the format of the passage: Data Representation, Research Summary, or Conflicting Viewpoints. (This task should only take you a few seconds.) Then, skim the page, letting your eye move down the columns of type and data, getting a feel for what it's all about.

Because previewing is a brief process, don't try to absorb a lot of information. You're about to read the passage in more detail, which will draw you much deeper into its contents.

2. BRAINIACS FOCUS ON *TRENDS* AND *PATTERNS* WHEN ANALYZING GRAPHICAL DATA.

The key to understanding ACT tables and graphs is to look primarily for *trends* and *patterns* in the graphical data. Why? Because it's the proverbial "forest" (trends and patterns) rather than the "trees" (all the specific numbers) that most questions will focus on.

Passage I:

In the first figure, the annual period of phytoplankton abundance increased markedly from the 1960s to the 1970s. This fact is the key to answering questions 1 and 3.

Passage II:

All three tables show a certain consistency, or pattern—namely, that design 2 is comparatively efficient. Tables 1 and 2 also show a clear trend. Any "thinner" than the wing in design 2, and a wing is less efficient. And, as a wing is designed "fatter" than the one in design 2, efficiency decreases dramatically. If you recognized these features, you had no trouble handling questions 1 and 2.

3. BRAINIACS FOCUS ON *CONTROLS* AND *VARIABLES* WHEN READING RESEARCH SUMMARIES.

When it comes to Research Summary passages, *controls* and *variables* are what it's all about. A *control* is a factor that is kept unchanged, or constant, during an experiment, while a *variable* is a factor that is changed. In performing a scientific experiment, unless you keep all factors constant (that is, controlled) but one, it's impossible to know for certain what factor caused the particular outcome of your experiment.

Passage II:

Notice that in all three experiments, only one factor changes, while other flight conditions are kept constant. Also, as you examined the four wing designs, you might have noticed that the only difference was the curved height of the wing tops. All other factors—wing length, shape of the bottoms, wing weight, and so forth, were the same and would be considered controls. Look again at the three questions for this passage. Notice how various controls are built into each question.

X-REF

The ACT will assume that you know the two terms control and variable. (The test won't define them or explain them.) In Lesson 19, you'll examine the use of controls and variables, and how the ACT Research Summary questions test you on these concepts, in greater detail.

4. BRAINIACS FOCUS MORE ON DIFFERENCES THAN ON SIMILARITIES BETWEEN CONFLICTING VIEWPOINTS.

The word "Conflicting" in "Conflicting Viewpoints" is a huge clue that the hypotheses that the passage describes will differ in various ways. And it's those differences, more than any other feature, that the questions will cover. (Expect about half of the questions in a Conflicting Viewpoints set to focus on *differences* between hypotheses.) Of course, the passage won't indicate the differences explicitly. (For example, don't expect to read: "The main difference between theory X and theory Y is that . . .") Instead, it'll be up to you to compare and contrast the two hypotheses—specifically, what facts they rely on and what they assume to be true.

Passage III:

Questions 7 and 8 focus on *differences* between the Hydrothermal Synthesis Hypothesis and the Primitive Life Hypothesis. But also notice that, in question 9, choices (B) and (C) focus on a *similarity* between the two hypotheses. Therefore, you will be tested on similarities as well, but not as heavily as you will be tested on differences.

5. BRAINIACS AREN'T RELUCTANT TO TAKE A PENCIL TO THE PASSAGE.

The average test-taker won't annotate Science Reasoning passages—probably because he or she won't consider them "reading" passages. But they are! In fact, annotating, and especially note-taking, are even more useful for the ACT Science Reasoning Test than for the ACT Reading Test. That's because the science passages, by their nature, generally involve classifications, categories, causes-and-effects, and other logical relationships that good note-taking can help organize.

Here are some suggestions for annotating and note-taking that Brainiacs put into practice as they gear up for the test:

- In passages that contain graphical data, circle key features of graphs and tables. If a graph or table shows a trend or pattern, make a brief note of it beside the data, in the margin.
- In Research Summary passages, make a note that identifies the *controls* and the *variables* in each experiment and as the passage progresses from one experiment to the next.
- In Conflicting Viewpoint passages, underline or make a note of the key differences between hypotheses. That way, the differences are easily distinguishable from the similarities (or points of agreement).
- In Conflicting Viewpoint passages, don't trust your memory to keep straight what hypothesis is associated with what details. Set up two columns on your scratch paper—one for each theory—and jot down the key points that are unique to each hypothesis.
- Make simple flow charts of key cause-and-effect relationships.

6. BRAINIACS DON'T GET BOGGED DOWN IN DETAILS—ESPECIALLY NOT NUMBERS.

You learned in Part IV that every passage on the ACT Reading Test is made up of two kinds of elements: main ideas and details. The same division between main ideas and details applies to Science Reasoning passages, most of which include *dozens* of details: the individual data points on each graph; the specific numbers that fill the grid of a table or chart; the readings or values obtained in each experiment described. There's no way you can master or memorize them all. And you don't need to. Remember, of the 5–7 questions for each passage, only a few will focus on specific details—and you can always look those details up as needed.

Passage I:

In Figure 1, the specific points on the curves, which correspond to particular months, didn't matter at all in handling the questions. And, in each of the passage's two paragraphs, notice that the first sentence is irrelevant to answering any of the questions. These sentences merely provide background information.

Passage II:

In the three tables, the specific ratios and other numbers didn't matter. Instead, it was the overall patterns and trends that were important. Also, specific units of measurement (neutrons, gallons per hour, and miles per hour) are provided but are irrelevant to answering the questions.

Passage III:

Many of the details in the two hypothesis under discussion don't matter—for example, precisely how long ago the meteorite crystallized, how much later the rock fractured, how the chemical environment of Mars changed over time, and what the shape of the structures were within the crystals. Also, the passage's first two sentences merely provide background information; they don't come into play in the questions.

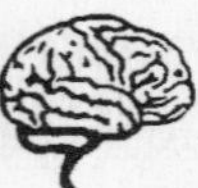

Brainiacs know that each passage will include some irrelevant information—unrelated to any of the questions. It may appear in the introductory paragraphs or in the body of the passage, including in graphs, tables, or charts. Don't let this confuse you. Focus on the main ideas of the passage, skim the details, and then tackle the questions. If some—perhaps most!—of the details turn out to be unnecessary, so be it.

7. BRAINIACS DON'T GET BOGGED DOWN IN SCIENTIFIC JARGON.

No matter how big a science nerd you are, some of the passages *will* deal with topics that are unfamiliar to you, and many will use terms, abbreviations, symbols, and phrases you haven't seen before. Don't worry about this. All the information you need to answer the questions is included in the passage, and you can safely ignore the unfamiliar terms.

Passage I:

Notice that you don't really need to know what *phytoplankton* are to understand the passage and answer the questions.

Passage III:

This passage is especially laden with scientific terminology. But how many of these terms do you really need to know? Only the acronym *PAH*. And you don't need to know what this acronym stands for or what it really is. All you need to know is that whenever the passage or question mentions PAHs, it's referring to "that organic *stuff* formed when hot water and rock seeped into fractured rock."

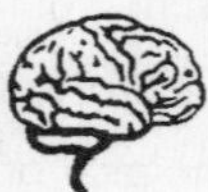

Brainiacs know better than to be intimidated by scary-looking scientific jargon and verbiage. In almost every case, it's irrelevant to answering the questions correctly.

8. BRAINIACS RECAP THE PASSAGE AFTER READING IT.

This should sound like more advice for the ACT Reading Test because the same principle applies to Science Reasoning passages—with a slight slant. After reading the passage, spend a final 30 seconds solidifying your understanding of how the pieces of information fit together. For example, for a Research Summary passage, remind yourself of the objective with which the experiments were originally designed. When reviewing a Conflicting Viewpoints passage, refresh your memory about the scientific phenomenon that the differing theories explain. Reviewing will also help you recall where various details appear within a passage, in the event you must retrieve a particular detail.

9. BRAINIACS KNOW THE TEST-MAKERS' FAVORITE ANSWER-CHOICE PLOYS.

You already know that the ACT Science Reasoning Test is a lot like the ACT Reading Test. Another similarity between the two tests is the appearance of certain wrong-answer ploys. For example:

- *Contrary to the passage or stated backward:* contradicts passage information or gets information backward.
- *Mentioned in the passage, but does not respond to the question:* includes accurate information based on the passage but does not respond appropriately to the question at hand.
- *Speculation or unsupported inference:* calls for some measure of speculation in that the statement is not readily (reliably) inferable from the information in the passage.
- *Partly supported, but partly unsupported:* true and responsive to the question only in part.

Question 8:

This question actually uses three of the ploys listed above. Choice (A) gets the question backward (it describes a similarity, not a difference, between the two hypotheses). Choice (B) calls for an unwarranted speculation (a leap in reasoning that the passage information does not justify). Choice (D) is only partly accurate.

In addition to looking out for the *wrong*-answer ploys listed above, you should also stay alert to a certain *right*-answer ploy that's unique to the Science Reasoning Test. In all three question formats, you're likely to see at least one or two application or extrapolation questions, which require you to reason beyond the information in the passage. You might be asked to apply a theory to a certain situation, assess the effect of new evidence on the strength of a hypothesis, and so forth. In handling these questions, keep an open mind! The test-makers love to play the reverse psychology game with you, by providing wrong answer choices that involve passage information and a correct answer choice that does not. Don't fall for this ploy.

Question 3:

The passage's textual and graphical information says nothing about ice or melted ice, and so it's tempting to dismiss the correct choice (B) out of hand as irrelevant. By the same token, choices (C) and (D) don't appear to stray as far from the passage's content—yet both are wrong.

Question 9:

The passage says nothing about glacial ice, so it's tempting to dismiss the correct choice (A) out of hand as irrelevant. By the same token, choices (B), (C), and (D) appear to stick closer to the topic—yet all are wrong.

Don't take this advice too far. Just because an answer choice goes furthest outside the scope of the passage, it doesn't necessary mean that it is the correct choice.

10. BRAINIACS DON'T MAKE ACT SCIENCE REASONING TOUGHER THAN IT REALLY IS.

You already know that there were no "gimmees" among the 9 questions from earlier in this lesson. Keep in mind: You will encounter many questions on the test that are easier than the "easy" ones you saw here—almost insultingly easy to someone of your cerebral stature. The science Brainiac's tendency is to invent complications where none exist. Resist this tendency!

Question 4:

This was an easy question, but it could have been even easier. Here's one realistic possibility:

The most efficient wing tested in Experiment 1 was

(A) design 1.

(B) design 2.

(C) design 3.

(D) design 4.

To answer this question, all you'd need to do is consult Table 1 as to which design corresponds to the largest efficiency number. (The only way to miss the question would be to incorrectly think that a *lower* lift-to-drag ratio corresponds to a *higher* efficiency.) Believe it or not, you will see questions on the ACT that are as easy as this one. By the way, the correct answer is (B)—but hopefully, you already knew that.

BRAIN TEASER

In this quiz, you'll tackle two Science Reasoning sets, each one containing 5 questions. (Remember: On the ACT, each set contains 5-7 questions.) For each of the 10 questions, you'll see a hint to help you handle it. Just as with the other quizzes in this book, you won't find any no-brainers or "gimmees" here. Each question is at least average in level of difficulty, and most are tougher than average.

X-REF

Some of the hints that follow the questions recall the general strategies you learned in this lesson. But other tips are new and are more specific—pertaining to a certain format, question type, or wrong-answer type. We'll revisit these specific tips in the following two lessons; therefore, this quiz serves not only as a *review*, but also as a *preview* of what's to come in Part V.

Attempt all ten questions, but don't put yourself under a time limit. Focus instead on applying the strategies you learned in this lesson. Then be sure to read the explanations that follow the quiz. They're just as important as the questions themselves, because they explain how to apply the strategies to the questions.

QUIZ

Passage I

Researchers are interested in optimizing methods for cooling electronic components such as *semiconductors* (a type of computer chip). Semiconductors generate heat as they operate, but excess levels of heat cause such components to malfunction or may shorten their life-span. However, cold objects cannot be applied directly to these components, because they are too sensitive.

One cooling method that has been used is the placement of foam material between the semiconductors and a cooling plate. Foam acts as a *heat conductor*. Heat from the computer chip flows through the foam, towards the cooling plate. As heat is conducted through the foam in this manner, the semiconductor is cooled, and the temperature difference between the cooling plate and the semiconductor becomes smaller. Various experiments were performed to determine more about the heat conduction properties of foam.

Experiment 1

Foam pads that all had a surface area of 1 inch^2 but were of various thicknesses were inserted between a semiconductor and a cooling plate. The temperature of the cooling plate was kept constant. The semiconductor was generating 1 watt of heat. The researchers measured the difference in temperature between the semiconductor and the cooling plate. Results appear in Table 1.

Table 1

Trial #	Thickness of Foam (mm)	Measured Temperature Difference Between Computer Chip and Plate (°C)
1	1	2.2
2	2	3.9
3	4	7.2
4	6	11.0
5	8	14.2
6	10	16.3

Experiment 2

Researchers placed a foam pad between a semiconductor and a cooling plate, but in this experiment the thickness of the pad was 6 mm in all cases, while the surface area of the pad varied. The heat generated by the semiconductor remained at 1 watt. Results appear in Table 2.

Table 2

Trial #	Foam Surface Area (inches^2)	Measured Temperature Difference Between Computer Chip and Plate (°C)
1	0.2	17.4
2	0.4	13.3
3	0.6	11.0
4	0.8	8.3
5	1.0	7.1
6	1.5	5.3

Experiment 3

The researchers were interested in seeing the performance of the foam cooling system when the heat dissipated (released) by the semiconductor was varied. To vary the heat dissipation, they varied the wattage generated by the semiconductors. A foam pad that had a surface area of 1 inch^2 and a thickness of 6 mm was used in all of the tests. The results appear in Table 3.

Table 3

Trial #	Heat Dissipation (watts)	Measured Temperature Difference Between Computer Chip and Plate (°C)
1	.25	4.2
2	.5	6.3
3	1.0	11.3
4	2.0	17.6
5	3.0	22.5
6	5.0	24.0

1. Under which of the following conditions would you predict the lowest temperature difference between the semiconductor and the cooling plate?

(A) A foam pad 1 mm thick and 1.5 $inches^2$ is used to cool a conductor producing 0.25 watts.
(B) A foam pad 1 mm thick and 1.0 $inch^2$ surface area is used to cool a semiconductor producing 1 watt.
(C) A foam pad 10 mm thick and 0.2 $inch^2$ surface area is used to cool a semiconductor producing 5 watts.
(D) A foam pad 1 mm thick and 1.5 $inch^2$ surface area is used to cool a semiconductor producing 1 watt.

Hint: For each table, think about the trend that the data shows, then try to predict the essential features of the correct answer choice.

2. If a foam pad with a surface area of 1 $inch^2$ and an unknown thickness were used with a semiconductor generating 1 watt of heat, and the measured temperature difference between the semiconductor and the cooling plate was found to be 15.0°C, which of the following is probably closest to the thickness of the pad?

(F) 3 mm
(G) 5 mm
(H) 9 mm
(J) 12 mm

Hint: Some Science Reasoning questions require you to either interpolate or extrapolate from given data. These questions never require precise calculations.

3. A foam pad 6 mm thick with a surface area of 1 $inch^2$ is used to cool a semiconductor generating 1 watt of heat. Which of the following steps, by itself, would result in the greatest measured temperature difference between the chip and the cooling plate?

(A) Reducing the wattage generated by 50%
(B) Decreasing the thickness of the foam by one third
(C) Increasing the surface area of the foam by 50%
(D) It cannot be determined from the information provided.

Hint: Sometimes you can eliminate an answer choice based on common sense.

4. Which of the following graphs best represents the relationships between foam thickness, foam surface area, and heat conduction seen in experiments 1 and 2? (In the following graphs, Td = Temperature difference between semiconductor and cooling plate.)

Figure 1

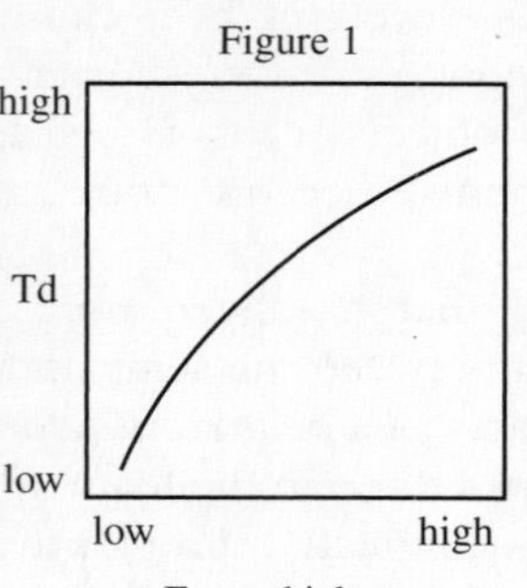

Figure 2

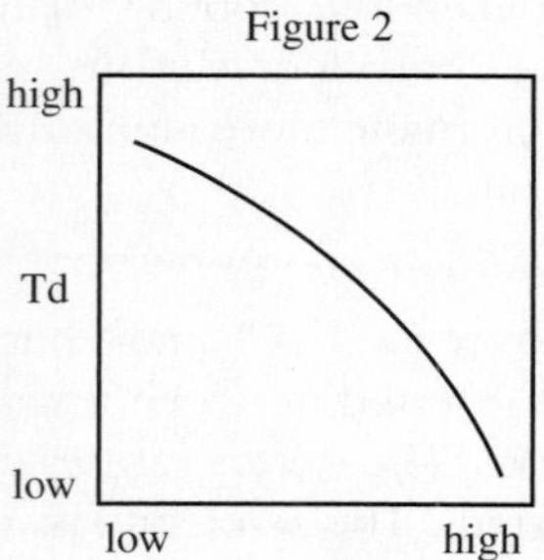

Figure 3

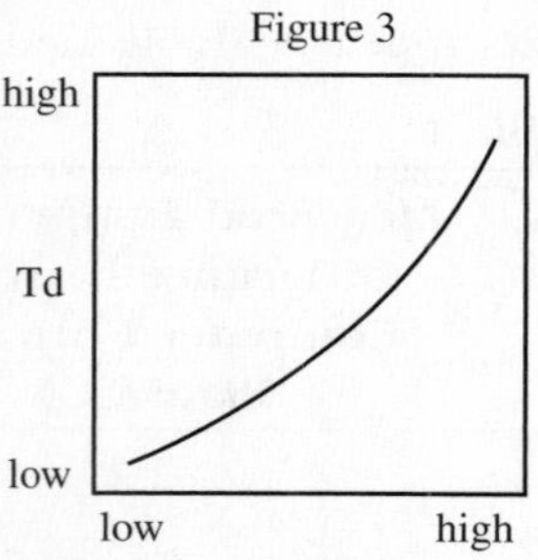

Figure 4

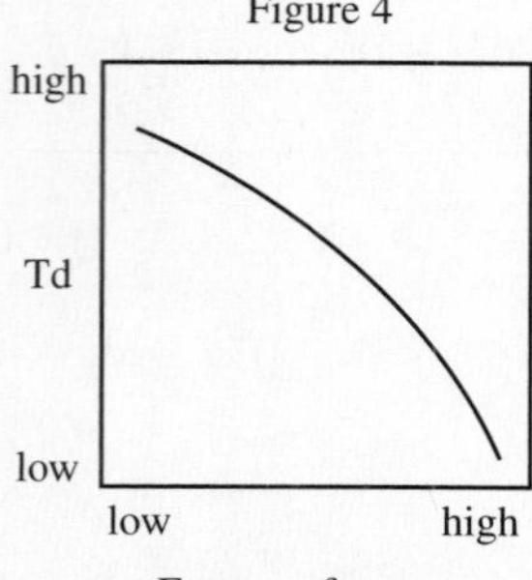

(F) Figures 1 and 4
(G) Figures 1 and 3
(H) Figures 2 and 4
(J) Figures 2 and 3

Hint: Focus on the trends shown by the data in Tables 1 and 2.

5. Experiment 3 indicates that the foam seems to be a better conductor at higher temperatures (the difference in temperature between the semiconductor and the cooling plate rises more slowly as the semiconductor wattage goes higher). Which of the following statements could be a practical explanation for this observation?

I. At higher temperatures, the foam expands, which gives it a larger surface area for conduction.
II. At higher temperatures, more of the heat is conducted through the air, giving the appearance that the foam is a better conductor.
III. At higher temperatures, the molecular structure of the foam may be altered slightly to allow greater conduction.

(A) I and II only
(B) I and III only
(C) II and III only
(D) I, II, and III

Hint: When handling Application questions, keep an open mind about information that might appear at first to be irrelevant.

Hint: As long as a practical explanation is not inconsistent with the scientific data, it should not be ruled out.

Passage II

Schizophrenia is a mental illness that involves the dissociation of reason and emotion, resulting in symptoms including hallucinations, hearing voices, intense withdrawal, delusions, and paranoia. The average age at which schizophrenia is diagnosed is 18 years for men and 23 years for women. It has been observed to run in families.

The cause remains a mystery, but there are several competing theories. These theories are based in part on findings from twin studies, which look at identical twins in which one or both have the disease. (Identical twins share 100 percent of their genetic material, while nonidentical twins share about 50 percent.) In 50 percent of the cases, when one identical twin is affected, the other will also suffer from schizophrenia. Identical twin pairs in which one individual is ill and the other is well are referred to as *discordant twins*.

Genetic Theory

One school of thought is that schizophrenia is a *genetic disorder* (one passed through the genes from parents to children). This theory gained support from the fact that schizophrenia runs in families. While it was originally believed that it was the family environment that caused this, a study has shown that children of schizophrenics adopted by families without the disease have the same risk of developing the illness as those raised by their birth parents. A final piece of evidence is the fact that the children of discordant identical twins all have the same chance of developing the illness: 17 percent. This indicates that even the healthy twin is somehow carrying the agent of the disease, presumably in the genes.

Infection Theory

Another school of thought is that schizophrenia arises because of a viral infection of the brain. Studies have shown that a class of viruses called "slow viruses" can linger in the brain for 20 years or longer before the infected person shows symptoms. Brain infections with viruses such as the common cold-sore virus and herpes simplex type 1 can cause symptoms that resemble schizophrenia. Schizophrenia is also more common in children born in the winter, the season when viral infections are more common. Also, one study looking at families with a history of schizophrenia showed a 70 percent increase in the rate of schizophrenia among children whose mothers had the flu during the second trimester of pregnancy.

6. Which of the following findings best supports the Genetic Theory?

(F) Parents of discordant twins report that the behavior of the twins begins to diverge at about five years of age, on average.
(G) In discordant identical twin pairs, a brain structure called the basal ganglia is activated more often in the ill twin than in the healthy twin.
(H) An identical twin of a schizophrenia sufferer is four times as likely to have the illness as a nonidentical twin of a schizophrenia sufferer.
(J) Studies have shown that viral infections sometimes infect one identical twin in the uterus and not the other.

Hint: Just because certain evidence supports a particular theory doesn't necessarily mean that this evidence also weakens an opposing theory.

7. The infection theory is most effective at explaining the fact that

   I. schizophrenic patients do poorly on some memory tests.
   II. among identical twins discordant for schizophrenia, the healthy twin may have some borderline schizophrenic traits.
   III. ill twins in discordant pairs have higher rates of finger abnormalities, which can be an indication of a viral infection that occurred in the womb.

   (A) I only
   (B) II only
   (C) III only
   (D) II and III only

   Hint: Never rule out an answer choice just because it brings forth information that the passage never mentions.

8. With which of the following hypotheses might supporters of both theories agree?

   I. Individuals with schizophrenia have certain genes that predispose them to the disease, but require a trigger to turn the disease on.
   II. Individuals with schizophrenia have certain genes that predispose them to viral infections of the brain.
   III. Schizophrenia is not one disease but a collection of diseases.

   (F) I and II only
   (G) I and III only
   (H) II and III only
   (J) I, II, and III

   Hint: Proponents of a certain theory "might" agree with any hypothesis that is not inconsistent with the theory.)

   Hint: If you can rule *in* one option, then you might be able to rule *out* one or more answer choices.

9. Assume that an identical pair of twins is found, one of which was adopted at birth. As teenagers, both are diagnosed as having schizophrenia. Supporters of the Infection Theory might offer which of following as an explanation?

   (A) Children are most prone to viral infections when they are of school age, long after the infant in this case was adopted.
   (B) The stress of being an adopted child may have triggered schizophrenia in the predisposed twin.
   (C) Since 50 percent of identical twin pairs with schizophrenia are discordant for the disease, this case does not shed light on its origin.
   (D) The brains of both twins may have been infected with a slow-acting virus when they were still in the womb.

   Hint: Try to prephrase, or predict, the "ideal" correct answer. Ask yourself: What kinds of additional facts would explain the case and best support the Infection Theory?

10. Which of the following studies would be most logical for supporters of the Genetic Theory to conduct next?

    (F) A study that looks for finger abnormalities in the parents and grandparents of schizophrenic children
    (G) A study that looks for differences in the chromosomes (which hold the genes) of schizophrenic individuals and healthy individuals
    (H) A study that looks for scarring in the brains of schizophrenic individuals, which might be a sign of an early injury or infection
    (J) A study that looks at the home environments of discordant twins, one of which is schizophenic

    Hint: Proponents of a certain theory would naturally, and logically, seek additional evidence that directly supports that theory—as opposed to evidence that weakens a competing theory.

ANSWERS AND EXPLANATIONS

Passage I

Understanding the Passage

Here are the key ideas you should have gleaned from Passage I during your preview, reading, and recap—and *before* attempting the five questions:

- A heat conductor such as foam serves to cool whatever it draws heat from (in this case, a semiconductor).
- The data from Experiment 1 show that thicker foam is less effective as a heat conductor. (This is the key trend in the Table 1 data.)
- The data from Experiment 2 show that foam with a larger surface area is more effective as a heat conductor. (This is the key trend in the Table 2 data.)
- The data from Experiment 3 show that the more heat released from the semiconductor, the greater the temperature difference between the semiconductor and the plate. What this means is that the foam is effective as a conductor only to some extent—it will only conduct a certain amount of the released heat. Nevertheless, it appears from Table 3 that at high heat dissipation levels, the foam becomes more effective as a conductor. From trial 5 to trial 6, notice the small increase in temperature difference (from 22.5° to 24.0°) compared to the large increase in heat dissipation (from 3.0 to 5.0 watts).

You should have also noticed that each experiment involved one variable: foam thickness (Experiment 1), foam surface area (Experiment 2), and semiconductor temperature (Experiment 3). All other factors were controls. Recognizing the variables and distinguishing them from the controls is crucial to recognizing the three trends indicated above.

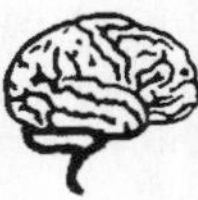

None of the three tables showed any reversal in trend beyond a certain point (thickness, surface area, or temperature). But you should always be on the lookout for this phenomenon. It makes for the kind of tricky test questions that average test-takers typically overlook.

1. **The correct answer is (A).** Of the four alternatives, this choice gives you the thinnest foam pad, the largest surface area, and the lowest-wattage semiconductor—all conditions chosen to maximize heat conduction and minimize the temperature difference.

2. **The correct answer is (H).** Refer to Table 1, which shows the results of trials involving pads one square inch in area with a 1-watt semiconductor. You can see in the third column that a temperature difference of 15.0° would fall right between trials 5 and 6; in other words, between a pad 8 mm thick and one 10 mm thick. Therefore, it seems reasonable to conclude that the pad in the trial described would probably be midway between those two in thickness—9 mm

3. **The correct answer is (C).** The conditions described in the question match Experiment 1, trial 4 and Experiment 2, trial 3: in both, the temperature difference was measured at 11.0°. From Experiment 3, trial 2, we can see that reducing the wattage by 50 percent (to .5 watts) would reduce the temperature difference to 6.3°, choice (A). From Experiment 1, trial 4, decreasing the thickness of the foam by one third would make the difference 7.2°, choice (B). From Experiment 2, trial 6, increasing the surface area by 50 percent would make it 5.3°, choice (C)—the greatest difference.

Once your realize that you can compute the differences that answer choices (A), (B), and (C) call for, common sense tells you that you can rule out choice (D).

4. **The correct answer is (F).** The graphs in Figures 1 and 4 match the data given. Figure 1 shows a low temperature difference when the foam thickness is low and a high temperature difference when the thickness is high. Figure 2 shows a high temperature difference when the area is low and a low temperature difference when the area is high.

5. **The correct answer is (D).** This is the toughest question in the set because it requires you to consider possible cause-and-effect relationships. None of the three explanations suggested is inconsistent with the observation made in the question. Thus, any one *could* serve as a practical explanation for the observation.

Passage II

Understanding the Passage

Here's an outline of the key ideas you should have gleened from Passage II during your preview, reading, and recap—*before* you tackled the questions (if you took notes while reading the passage, perhaps your notes resemble this outline):

- Evidence for genetic theory
  - —runs in families
  - —adoption makes no difference
  - —discordant twins each have same chance
- Evidence for infection theory
  - —slow viruses linger 20 years before showing (so onset at age 18–23 makes sense)
  - —symptoms similar to disorders known to be viral
  - —winter births (flu season) → schiz. more likely
  - —virus during pregnancy → schiz. more likely

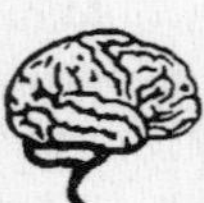

In handling Conflicting Viewpoint sets, Brainiacs don't rely completely on memory. Brief, but organized, notes that list supporting points for each hypothesis help keep the details straight and save time otherwise spend rereading the passage.

6. **The correct answer is (H).** The fact that the shared incidence of schizophrenia is four times as great between identical twins as between nonidentical twins supports the idea that shared genetic material is a major factor in the development of the disorder. Choice (F) provides further evidence against the claim that family environment is the cause of the disorder. In doing so, choice (F) actually lends equal support to both the Genetic Theory and the Infection Theory. Thus, choice (F) is not as good a choice as (H). Choice (G), lacking information about why this structure is activated more often in one twin, provides no particular support for either theory. Choice (J) weakens the Genetic Theory (and strengthens the Infection Theory) by providing evidence that a virus might explain the discordant-twin phenomenon.

In Conflicting Viewpoint questions like the preceding one, look out for the wrong-answer choice that supports the viewpoint the question asks about but also supports the conflicting viewpoint—for example, choice (A) in the preceding question. Such choices will merely be "runners-up." The *best* choice will favor one viewpoint *over the conflicting one.*

7. **The correct answer is (C).** The phenomenon described in option III, although never mentioned in the passage, would be consistent with the idea that an infection occurred during prenatal development, thus supporting the Infection Theory. The phenomenon described in option I, like the one in option III, is never mentioned in the passage. But unlike option III, option I suggests no cause-and-effect connection between the phenomenon (memory loss) and viral infection. The phenomenon described in option II might be explained by either theory—the trace of schizophenia in the healthier twin could just as likely be attributed to genetics as to a virus.

8. **The correct answer is (J).** The key to analyzing this question is to realize that neither theory claims that no other factor can possibly contribute to causing the disorder. According to hypothesis I, genetic factors and another "triggering" factor (such as a viral infection) must combine in order to cause the disorder. Hypothesis I essentially validates both theories—it's just that each one provides only part of the equation. Hence, proponents of both theories might agree with it. Hypothesis II also asserts that genetic and viral factors combine to cause the disorder. Hypothesis III is a bit trickier. Most test-takers would eliminate hypothesis III and select choice (A) as the correct answer. Hypothesis II is more vague than either hypothesis I or II, isn't it? But ask yourself why a proponent of either theory wouldn't agree with hypothesis III. Vague as it is, it's not inconsistent with either theory. Besides, the "collection" of diseases might very well include gentically as well as virally caused ones.

9. **The correct answer is (D).** Since the twins were separated at birth but both have the same disorder, a proponent of the Infection Theory must point to a shared viral infection occurring before birth—while the twins were still in the womb. That's exactly what choice (D) provides. Choice (A) is probably the most tempting wrong-answer choice because it talks about viruses. But to explain this case as the result of two *completely unrelated* viral incidents occuring when the twins were teenagers is to make an unconvincing case, especially compared with choice (D). Choice (B) would support a family-environment theory but not the Infection Theory. Choice (C) accomplishes nothing in support of any theory—including the Infection Theory.

10. **The correct answer is (G).** It would be natural for supporters of the Genetic Theory to want to study the genes themselves in the hope of substantiating their theory by pinpointing the actual genetic differences that cause (or help to cause) the illness. Choice (F) might be tempting, simply because it involves a physical characteristic that you assume might have a genetic cause. But it assumes a strong correlation between finger abnormalities and a gene that causes schizophrenia, whereas the passage provides absolutely no information that suggests any connection between the two. Hence, this study would be essentially irrelevant. Choice (H) indicates a study that proponents of the Infection Theory would be more interested in conducting next—because evidence of early infection would relate *directly* to that theory. Choice (J) marks the third time in this set of questions that "family environment" is mentioned. Again, the passage explicitly ruled this out as a viable theory for the cause of schizophrenia. And, even if the evidence helps rule out home environment as a cause of the disorder, this fact would not help proponents of the Genetic Theory nearly as much as affirmative evidence of a link between genes and schizophrenia.

LESSON 19
Research Summaries

Most likely, three of the seven question sets on the ACT Science Reasoning Test will involve Research Summaries. In this lesson, you'll focus exclusively on this format. More specifically, you'll:

- Learn how those principles come to bear on ACT Research Summaries
- Learn how to predict the kinds of questions (and answers) that may accompany a typical ACT Research Summary
- Prepare for the toughest and most complex kinds of Research Summary questions that the test-makers might pose
- Apply what you've reviewed to 10 tough ACT-style questions based on two Research Summaries

THE SCIENTIFIC METHOD—FROM HYPOTHESIS TO EXPERIMENT

To begin this lesson, you will briefly review the key principles of scientific experimentation. You learned these concepts in your high school science coursework, but since they form the basis of ACT Research Summary passages and questions, they're worth reviewing.

> **X-REF** **A few pages ahead, you'll apply these concepts to a sample Research Summary passage.**

INDUCTIVE AND DEDUCTIVE REASONING

Scientists employ two types of logic to explain the natural and physical world: *inductive* and *deductive* reasoning. Inductive reasoning moves from the specific to the general. Scientists do this when they use data from experiments or observations as the basis for a more general theory. Deductive reasoning, on the other hand, involves applying general laws to specific cases. Scientists do this when they use existing theories to explain experimental results or observations.

Induction and deduction, in combination, form the underpinnings of the scientific method. Both processes are involved in the development of a scientific theory. Although ACT Research Summaries involve both kinds of reasoning, the emphasis here will be on *inductive* reasoning.

STARTING WITH A HYPOTHESIS

The scientific method involves first forming a *hypothesis,* and then testing that hypothesis through observation, experimentation, and/or prediction. A hypothesis is a tentative explanation for some natural phenomenon, one that has not been tested or verified in any way. Think of a hypothesis as an educated guess about why something happens or about the nature of the relationship between two or more variables. Nearly all scientific research, and *most* ACT Research Summary experiments, starts with a hypothesis.

THE DESIGN OF A SCIENTIFIC EXPERIMENT

The crucial objectives in the design of all scientific experimentation are *objectivity* and *reproducibility*. Objectivity refers to the need to design an experiment so as to eliminate the effects of personal bias, either intentional or unintentional, on the part of any experimenter or of anyone who participates in analyzing the resulting data. Reproducibility means that it must be possible to duplicate the procedures in the experiment so as to test the validity of the results. Since these objectives are both aspects of experimental design, they're fair game for the ACT. However, the ACT does not commonly test on these two objectives.

INDEPENDENT AND DEPENDENT VARIABLES

Nearly all experiments are designed with certain elements in common. Two of these basic elements are the *independent* and *dependent variables*. The independent variable is so named because it is adjusted independently of other factors. Independent variables are usually controlled by the experimenter (as part of the experiment's design), while dependent variables (i.e., what the experimenter observes) hinge upon the independent variables. For instance, in a simple experiment designed to determine how time of day affects temperature, the independent variable would be the time of day, while the dependent variable would be the temperature.

It's desirable to have only one independent variable in a given experiment. Experiments with two or more variables are harder to reproduce and more difficult to draw reliable conclusions from. This is because it's usually impossible to determine the relative importance of each variable—or the unpredictable ways that two or more variables may affect each other. Ideally, scientists need to be able to account for all the phenomena they observe, or else they cannot say for sure why changes occur.

X-REF

If the relationship between independent and dependent variables sounds like something you've encountered earlier in this book, you're right. Here's a hint: A dependent variable is, by definition, a *function* of an independent variable. Remember logarithmic or trigonometric functions, from Lesson 14?

THE CONTROL

Another element used in nearly all experiments is the *control*. The control is an experimental subject for which all the relevant variables, including the independent variable, are held constant. Because the independent variable is held constant, any changes observed in the control must be caused by other factors. These changes can then be accounted for throughout the rest of the experiment.

For example, in testing a new experimental therapy for AIDS, researchers might study two groups of patients: a group receiving the new treatment and a control group that is not receiving the new treatment. It would be important to match the two groups as closely as possible in every other way: the average age, the severity of AIDS symptoms, the nature of any other health problems suffered, and so on. If this is done, and if the experimental group shows a markedly better rate of recovery than the control group, it would be reasonable to determine that the improvement is due to the new therapy rather than any other factor.

ULTRA-BRAiNiAC INSIGHTS INTO RESEARCH SUMMARIES

In the previous lesson, you learned to "recap" each Science Reasoning passage after reading it and *before* answering the questions. In essence, you learned to ask (and answer) certain questions about a passage that are likely to show up as test questions.

The questions you should ask and answer for yourself vary, depending on the type of passage you're dealing with. For Research Summary passages, here are the kind of questions that you should be asking (and answering) as you read and recap the passage (notice that many of these questions focus on the principles you have just reviewed):

- What relationships are described in the background information preceding the description of the experiments?
- In each experiment, what is the *hypothesis* that is being tested, if any?
- In each experiment, what are the *independent* and *dependent variables*?
- In each experiment, what are the *controls* (factors that are kept stable, or constant during an experiment, and possibly from one experiment to another as well)?
- In each table or graph, what relationship (general pattern or trend) is shown between the variables?
- What relationship, if any, is there between the data resulting from the experiments? Do the data from one experiment support the data from the other, or is there a conflict?

Now see how a Brainiac might apply this "Q&A" approach to a specific Research Summary passage. The purpose of this exercise is to show how Brainiacs can actually predict many of the test questions and answers! Read the following passage, and then recap by asking and answering questions similar to the preceding ones.

Passage I

Enzymes are special proteins that act as catalysts to speed up chemical reactions in cells. Enzymes catalyze reactions by first having their active site bind to its substrate—usually the molecule that is undergoing reaction. The ability of an enzyme to bind substrate is called its activity. Thus, activity is also a measure of how well an enzyme catalyzes a reaction. The active site of an enzyme is very specific for its substrate. This specificity is created by the three-dimensional shape of the enzyme. However, this three-dimensional shape is dependent upon environmental factors, such as temperature and pH, a measure of acidity.

If the shape of the enzyme is changed, the enzyme may no longer be able to bind to its substrate. In this case, the enzyme is said to be denatured. Extremes of either temperature or pH can cause enzymes to denature.

A scientist isolated three enzymes from a mammalian cell. These enzymes will be denoted Enzyme A, Enzyme B, and Enzyme C.

Experiment 1

A scientist placed samples of Enzyme A into twelve different tubes. Each tube contained a buffer solution at a different pH such that the first tube was at pH = 1, the second tube at pH = 2, the third tube at pH = 3, and so on up to the twelfth tube, which was at pH = 12. The scientist then added an indicator, which would turn the solution yellow if bound by the enzyme. Thus, the solution would turn more yellow when more indicator was bound. The temperature for all the tubes was 25 °C. This procedure was repeated for Enzyme B and Enzyme C. The scientist was then able to create the graph shown in the following figure.

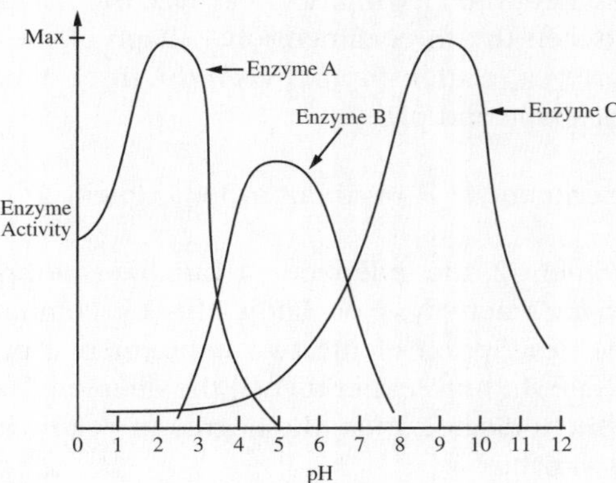

Experiment 2

A sample of Enzyme A was placed into a single tube containing a buffer solution at the pH that gave the greatest activity in Experiment 1. The tube was then brought to near freezing, and a sample was taken and tested for activity by addition of the same indicator above. The tube was then gradually warmed, with samples taken every five degrees and tested for activity. The process was repeated for Enzyme B and Enzyme C. The scientist was then able to make the graph shown in the following figure.

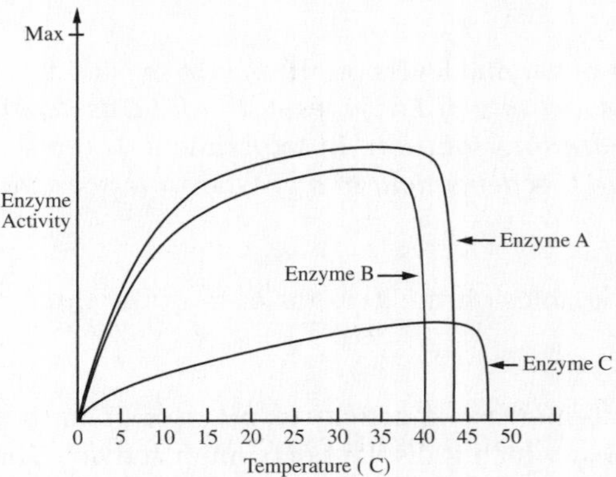

READING AND RECAPPING THE PASSAGE

As you read and recapped the passage and analyzed the graphs, did you ask and answer questions like the ones on the previous page? Because Research Summary questions vary, it's okay if your questions weren't exactly the same as the ones given. For example, in some passages, the different tables or graphs are closely related to one other, while in others they're not. Also, in some passages you'll find a different hypothesis for each experiment, while in others you won't. (You might find one hypothesis for all experiments, or you might not find any stated hypothesis.)

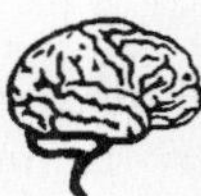

Brainiacs know that Research Summary passages do not all follow in the same cookie-cutter pattern. Accordingly, Brainiacs tailor their "Q&A" (dialogue with the passage) to the specific passage at hand.

Here is an example of a Brainiac's Q&A, or dialogue, for Passage I. Perhaps your dialogue was similar?

Q: What relationships are described in the background information (preceding the description of the experiments)?

A: Certain relationships among all the terms defined in the first paragraph of the passage are described there. If the three-dimensional shape of the enzyme is changed, then the ability of the enzyme to bind the substrate is lessened. If the enzyme's ability to bind the substrate is lessened, then its ability to catalyze the reaction (i.e., activity) is lessened. Therefore, there is a relationship between the three-dimensional shape of the enzyme and its activity. Furthermore, in certain circumstances, there is a relationship between the three-dimensional shape and temperature and between the three-dimensional shape and pH.

Q: What are the independent and dependent variables in Experiment 1? How about in Experiment 2?

A: In Experiment 1, the independent variable is pH. In Experiment 2, the independent variable is temperature. For both experiments, the scientist is observing the enzyme's activity. You know this by combining the information in the first paragraph of the passage with the description of the two experimental protocols. Activity, you've seen, is defined as the ability to bind substrate. In both experiments, the degree of yellow in the solution is used to measure how much enzyme binds the indicator; thus, the degree of yellow indicates the enzyme's activity. The activity, then, is the dependent variable.

Q: What factor(s) are kept stable in Experiment 1? In Experiment 2? In both experiments?

A: In Experiment 1, temperature is kept stable (to highlight the effects of varying pH levels in the twelve tubes). In Experiment 2, pH is kept stable (to highlight the effects of varying temperatures). In both experiments, the same solution and cell types were used, and the same three enzymes were used.

Q: In each experiment, what is the hypothesis being tested?

A: In Experiment 1, since the scientist is measuring the effect of varying levels of pH on enzyme activity, you can infer that the hypothesis being tested is the following: *The activity of Enzymes A, B, and C is dependent to a greater or lesser extent upon the pH level of the surrounding solution.* In Experiment 2, the scientist is hypothesizing as follows: *The activity of Enzymes A, B, and C is dependent to a greater or lesser extent upon the temperature of the surrounding solution.*

Q: In each graph, what relationship is shown between the variables on the axes for each of the three enzymes (A, B, and C)?

A: In the first figure, each enzyme shows the tendency first to increase in activity as pH rises, then to decrease in activity as pH rises further. Thus, each enzyme has a pH at which it displays maximum activity. This differs for each enzyme. For Enzyme A, the pH at which maximum activity occurs is around 2; for Enzyme B, it is around 6; for Enzyme C, it is around 10.

In the second figure, each enzyme shows the tendency to slowly increase in activity as temperature rises. This increase eventually levels out, and the enzyme activity is stable over a range of temperatures. Then, it suddenly drops off to no activity. The temperatures at which the enzyme activity rises and (suddenly) falls differ from enzyme to enzyme. In addition, Enzymes A and B attain a markedly higher level of activity than Enzyme C.

Q: How are the two graphs similar, and how are they different? What relationship, if any, is there between the data in the two graphs?

A: The graphs are similar in that they both present data regarding the activity levels of the same three enzymes (A, B, and C). However, the independent variable is different in each. Therefore, there is no direct relationship between the two graphs; each shows the effect on enzyme activity of a different key variable.

Let's take a look at a set of ACT-style questions that could accompany Passage I. We'll focus here just on the question stems, so that you can see how the right Q&A helps the Brainiac anticipate questions and predict correct answers. (The questions generally get tougher as you go along.)

As you read each question, try to draft your own "correct' answer choice, based on what you know from the preceding Q&A. Then read the analysis of each question. You'll notice that asking and answering the right questions as you read and recap can give you all the information you need to handle the questions!

Q: At which of the following pH levels would you expect the greatest chemical reaction in Enzyme A [or B or C]?

A: The greatest chemical reaction is also the one that exhibits the most activity (the dependent variable, measured along the vertical axes). Check the appropriate curve in Figure 1 (Enzyme A, B, or C), then match each answer choice (the pH level along the horizontal axis) to the highest point on that curve.

Q: Which of the following statements about enzyme activity is best supported by the data?

A: The key to answering this question probably lies in recognizing the trends shown in one, or both graphs. The correct answer might read something like this: *With all three enzymes, activity increased with temperature to a point, then declined precipitously above a certain temperature.* Or it might read something like this: *Among the three enzymes, Enzyme C exhibits a chemical reaction to the highest temperature.*

Q: Which of the following was a control in both experiments?

A: The correct answer might be either the buffer solution or the type of cell (mammalian) used in the experiments. The incorrect answers would include the independent variables—pH level, temperature, and the enzyme—as well as the dependent variable: the color of the solution, chemical reaction, or activity (all three are essentially the same variable).

Q: At pH levels where Enzyme C is exhibiting high activity, which of the following observations about enzymes A and B is best supported by the data?

A: In the two graphs, look at the points (pH and temperatures) where Enzyme C activity is highest. At those points, check to see whether enzymes A and B share a common characteristic. Here's one possible correct answer: *Both enzymes exhibit lower levels of activity than enzyme C.* Here's another possible correct answer: *Enzyme A is unable to bind to its substrate.* Of course, any answer choice that involves temperature must be incorrect, because the two graphs do not relate directly to one another.

Q: Which of the following hypotheses do the experimenters appear to be testing?

A: Experiment 1 appears to test the hypothesis that the activity of Enzymes A, B, and C is dependent on pH levels. Experiment 2 appears to test the hypothesis that the activity of Enzymes A, B, and C is dependent on temperature. (Either hypothesis would be a correct answer.) An incorrect answer might confuse independent variables with dependant variables—for example: *pH levels (or temperature) of an enzyme is dependent on the enzyme's level of activity.* Another incorrect answer might provide a hypothesis that is too general—for example: *Chemical reactions in mammalian cells increase in speed when an enzyme is used as a catalyst for the reaction.*

Q: Based on the experimental data, at which of the following combination of pH and temperature could you expect the highest activity for Enzyme A [or B or C]?

A: The vertical axes of both graphs indicate activity. However, no units of activity are indicated in either graph. Thus, you cannot necessarily make a direct comparison of levels between the two graphs. So, a correct answer to this question would probably be that it is impossible to determine based on the information given.

MASTERING THE TOUGHEST RESEARCH-SUMMARY QUESTIONS

According to the ACT test-makers, a test question about a Research Summary might involve the design of an experiment or the interpretation of experimental results. How much help is that information? Not much! Here's a more detailed breakdown of the reasoning skills you'll need to apply to Research Summary questions. These skills are very similar to the ones you'll need to apply to questions in the Data Interpretation and Conflicting Viewpoints format. To answer Research Summary questions, you'll need to:

- *Understand* the basic purpose, design, and method of the experiments and *"read"* the experimental data, which is usually presented in the form of tables
- *Analyze* the experimental results (especially, recognize trends, patterns, and anomalies)
- *Evaluate* a stated hypothesis in light of the experimental data
- *Draw inferences and conclusions* from the experimental data (especially, formulate a hypotheses or theories) and recognize what conclusions *cannot* be drawn from the data
- *Extrapolate* from the data to predict what additional data are likely or what additional experiments might produce

The first two skills listed above are the most basic, and test questions that involve these particular skills are typically the easiest. (About half the questions in each set will cover these skills.) So as not to insult your intelligence, the rest of this lesson will focus strictly on the tougher stuff. In the pages ahead, you'll gain a true Brainiac's insight into the following four types of Research Summary questions:

- Analyzing, then hypothesizing, from the data
- Evaluating a hypothesis
- Drawing general conclusions from the data
- Assessing the effect of additional information

Before we look at these question types, read the following Research Summary passage on which the questions that follow it are based.

X-REF **Use this passage to practice the type of Q&A process you learned about earlier in this lesson.**

PASSAGE II

Industrial melanism, the spread of darkly colored moths and butterflies near polluted, industrial centers, was observed in the late 1840s in England. Before the 1840s, tree trunks throughout Britain were a whitish color due to the growth of lichens in trees. These lichens are sensitive to airborne pollutants and are unable to survive near major industrial centers. In the polluted areas, the lack of lichens results in the trees being darker than the trees in the unpolluted areas.

The peppered moth (*Biston betularia*) began to appear more and more in its melanic form in the polluted areas. In certain areas, the darker moths constituted 98 percent of the population. Scientists hypothesized that the comparative decline in the light-colored moths may be due to predation by birds and may not be a result of the pollution itself.

Scientists performed an experiment to determine the selective force that caused the predominance of the darker moths. They distributed light and melanic moths in polluted and non-polluted areas and recorded the results shown in the table below.

	Light	Melanic
Dorset, England		
Woodland (light background)		
Released	496	473
Recaptured	62	30
Percent Recaptured	12.5	6.3
Birmingham, England		
Woodland (dark background)		
Released	137	447
Recaptured	18	123
Percent Recaptured	13.1	27.5

Before you look at the kinds of tough questions the test-makers might design for this passage, here are some ideas for the easier questions:

Certain easier questions would focus on the design of the experiments:

- An easy question might ask about the purpose of the experiments, or ask you to characterize (describe) the experiments.
- A slightly "less easy" question might ask you to distinguish between a control (in this case, the background) and a variable (for example, the type of moth).

Other easy questions would focus on the experimental data:

- A very easy question might ask *how many* melanic (or light) moths were recaptured from the polluted (or unpolluted) region?
- A slightly "less easy" question might ask for a numerical or percent difference between the polluted and unpolluted regions. Or the question might ask whether the percent (or number) of light (or melanic) moths had increased, decreased, or was equal.

Now, on to more challenging question types.

ANALYZING, THEN HYPOTHESIZING FROM, THE DATA

In this more challenging question type, your job is to decide which hypothesis (among four answer choices) is best supported by the experimental data. This question type is more difficult because it requires you to recognize key trends or patterns in the various data and also to recognize reasonable (and unreasonable) conclusions based on the data.

Here's the key to handling these questions: The correct answer choice need not provide a completely convincing, bulletproof hypothesis—one that is proven with 100 percent certainty by the data. In fact, the correct answer need only provide a plausible hypothesis—one that is *not inconsistent* with the experimental data. Each of the wrong answer choices will either be *inconsistent* with the data (or with the passage's textual information) or will call for an unwarranted inference, or *speculation*—a conclusion beyond what a reasonable person (read: a good scientist) would infer from the data.

To make these questions even tougher, the test-makers might incorporate one or more of the following features, requiring you to:

- Analyze a table in both directions—across different rows as well as down different columns
- Analyze data from more than one experiment
- Analyze key information from the text

Here's a question about the moth experiments that incorporates all three features—as well as a few of the wrong-answer ploys you encountered during the previous lesson.

Q The passage and experimental data best support which of the following hypotheses?

(A) The presence of pollution negatively affects the survival of melanic moths.
(B) The existence of lichens on trees generally increases the chances of a moth's survival.
(C) Birds eat more moths that differ in color from their background trees than moths that do not.
(D) The existence of lichens on trees generally decreases the chances of a moth's survival.

A **The correct answer is (C).** To analyze this question, you need to analyze the table two ways—across rows and down columns. In other words, you need to look at the background (light/dark) as well as moth color (light/melanic). The table shows that where trees provide a light background, a greater percentage of dark moths disappear (that is, are *not* recaptured) than light moths. And, conversely, where the tree color is dark, a greater percentage of light moths disappear. One plausible explanation for this phenomenon is that birds tend to eat moths that differ in color from their background. Hence, choice (C) is consistent with the tabular data. Now let's look at the wrong answer choices:

Choice (A) contradicts the passage information, which indicates that darker (melanic) moths became more predominant in polluted areas. Therefore, to eliminate choice (A), you need to recall specific passage information. The data does not support choice (B), which makes no distinction between light and melanic moths. The table shows that, where lichens grow on trees, light-colored moths have about an *equal* (not greater) chance of survival, and that dark-colored moths actually have a *smaller* chance of survival (a 6.3 percent versus 27.5 percent recapture rate). Just like choice (B), choice (D) makes no distinction between light and melanic moths. Although the table does suggest that, where lichens grow on trees, dark-colored moths have a greater chance of survival (a 27.5 percent versus 6.3 percent recapture rate), light-colored moths appear to have about an *equal* (not greater) chance of survival against either a light or dark background.

Notice the wrong-answer ploys in the preceding question. Choices (B) and (D) are opposites, but they both over-generalize (they call for speculation about *all* moths). Also, choice (D) is only partly accurate.

Now try an even tougher question of this type. Remember: Any explanation (hypothesis) that is *not inconsistent* with the data would be considered plausible and hence a possible hypothesis.

Q Which of the following might possibly explain the data observed?

I. The pollution itself causes the light moth's difficulty with survival as compared to the dark moth.
II. A selective force selects against the melanic moths in the unpolluted area and light moths in the polluted area.
III. Too few light moths were released in the polluted areas to make a valid comparison.

(A) I only
(B) II only
(C) I and II only
(D) I, II, and III

A **The correct answer is (D).** Here's an analysis of each statement:

Statement I: The whole purpose of the experiment is to determine the reason for the predominance of dark-colored over light-colored moths in polluted areas. One possible explanation (and probably the most obvious one) is that the pollution *directly*, and adversely, affects the light moth's ability to thrive.

Statement II: The passage does not define *selective force*. However, common sense should tell you that this term refers to an external factor that discriminates between light and dark moths. If there is such a force at work here, the passage information and tabular data clearly suggest that the force discriminates against *melanic* moths in unpolluted areas but against *light* moths in polluted areas. In other words, statement II is consistent with the passage information and tabular data.

Statement III: This statement is testing you on a basic assumption upon which all scientific experiments depend—namely, that the number of samples (or amount of data gathered) is sufficiently large to draw reliable conclusions based on those samples (or data). For example, if only *one* light moth had been released in Birmingham (dark background), whether that moth had been recaptured wouldn't provide convincing support for any hypothesis, simply because the sample size of 1 is so small. In the table, notice the small number of light moths released in Birmingham (137) compared to the other three numbers of moths released (496, 473, and 447). Statement III essentially points out that this low number renders any conclusions based on it somewhat unreliable.

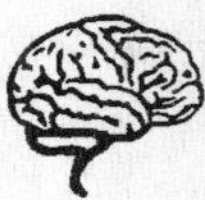

You can draw reliable conclusions from experimental data only if the sample group from which the data is drawn is *representative* of the overall population about which the conclusion is drawn. The larger the sample group, the more likely it represents the overall population—and the more reliable the conclusion based on data about the sample group.

EVALUATING A HYPOTHESIS

As a Brainiac, you should be able to anticipate this type of question (and the correct answer) before you even see it. How? When you read and recap the passage, you should notice if certain data (results of the experiment) conflict with the hypothesis being tested—in other words, take note if the data tend to disprove the hypothesis. If you discover this feature (read: problem) as you read and recap the passage, make a note of it. It's a sure bet that you'll encounter a question that focuses on it.

In an easier question of this type, the data might blatantly contradict the hypothesis. In a tougher question, the conflict will be less obvious. You might see mixed results among the data—some supporting the hypothesis, some not. Here's a good example based on the moth passage:

Look out for wrong answer choices that provide accurate but irrelevant information, as well as choices that confuse percentages with raw numbers.

Q A critic of the experiment would point out that the scientists have NOT adequately accounted for which of the following?

(A) Over both trials, the percentage of melanic moths that survived was about twice the percentage of light moths that survived.
(B) With a light background, the percentage of melanic moths recaptured was only about one fourth the percentage of melanic moths recaptured where there was a dark background.
(C) Light moths were recaptured in approximately the same percentage regardless of background color.
(D) With a light background, the number of melanic moths recaptured was nearly twice the number of light moths recaptured where the background was dark.

A **The correct answer is (C).** Choice (C) makes an accurate observation: In both trials, light moths were recaptured in almost equal percentages. Hence, you could conclude that the light moths survive at the same levels regardless of pollution and presence of lichen. This conclusion runs contrary to the rest of the passage information, which suggests that light moths are less likely to survive against a dark background than a light background. Now, let's look at the wrong answer choices:

Choice (A) is accurate with respect to a dark background, but when it comes to a light background, it gets it backward. (The percentage of melanic moths recaptured is *half* that of light moths.) Choice (B) provides an accurate observation. However, this observation serves as additional evidence that melanic moths survive better against a dark background than a light one—a basic premise of the scientists' hypothesis and reason for the experiment in the first place. Hence, choice (B) is hardly one that a critic of the experiment would be quick to point out. Choice (D) provides an accurate statement, but so what? The number of moths recaptured, in itself, is not important. What's key is a comparison of percentages.

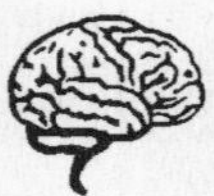

Not every ACT Research Summary passage will provide a stated hypothesis. If you notice one, however, pay close attention and distinguish between data that support the hypothesis and data that weaken it. (Chances are you'll find both kinds of data—just as in the moth experiment.)

DRAWING GENERAL CONCLUSIONS FROM THE DATA

Questions of this type essentially ask: "What general statements do the experimental data best support?" These questions can be tough because the data will typically provide some support for more than one listed statement. What's more, like other question types you've encountered in this lesson, any general statement that is *not inconsistent* with the data could be a correct answer choice.

To handle these questions, you need to be comfortable with going outside the passage information and with statements that are not proven beyond any doubt. To complicate these questions, the test-makers might turn the question around, asking you to identify the weakest among four generalizations. Here's a good example:

Q The increase in the percentage of melanic moths recaptured in polluted areas is LEAST consistent with which of the following?

(A) A selective force can be strong enough to nearly complete a color change in a species over a short time period.
(B) Melanic moths do not depend on lichen for survival to as great an extent as light moths do.
(C) Pollution is a force that affects the survival rate of light moths but not of melanic moths.
(D) Bird prey can escape detection by predator birds if they blend in with their immediate environment.

A **The correct answer is (C).** The increase in the number of melanic moths in polluted areas appears to go hand-in-hand with the decrease of light moths. Based on the information in the passage, pollution seems to be the indirect cause of both. Hence, choice (C) is the correct choice. Now, let's look at the wrong answer choices (remember: you can eliminate any choice that is *not inconsistent* with the data):

First, choice (A): The passage points out a phenomenon that occurred "in the late 1840s"; hence, it's reasonable to characterize the increase of dark moths to 98 percent of the moth population as a "nearly complete" color change in the species "over a short time period." Choice (B) provides one plausible explanation for the predominance of melanic moths in polluted areas. (It might not be the most convincing explanation, but it is nevertheless plausible, and it's not inconsistent with the passage.) Choice (D) provides a plausible explanation for the increase cited in the question. Specifically, given a dark background, it's easier for birds to detect lighter moths than darker, melanic moths.

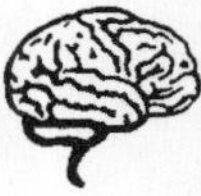

When generalizing based on experimental data, Brainiacs are comfortable with uncertainty. They recognize that broad generalizations based on a few experiments are never bulletproof and don't need to be. In other words, a fair generalization need only be plausible—not certain.

ASSESSING THE EFFECT OF NEW INFORMATION

A question of this type will provide a new finding or other fact, then ask about its impact on either the stated hypothesis (if any) or on a previously unstated argument based on the original data. Potentially, any additional piece of information might support, weaken, or have no effect on an argument.

A "less-tough" question of this type might provide new evidence that blatantly conflicts with a stated hypothesis. A more complicated question will incorporate other, previously unstated arguments, or possible explanations for the original data. The use of the Roman-numeral format, as in the next example, can also complicate the question by rendering the process-of-elimination strategy less useful.

Q Assume that the change in color of the *Biston betularia* is due to a genetic mutation and that, once the mutation occurs, the new coloration is dominant and can therefore more successfully be passed to a greater percentage of offspring. This finding in itself would

I. support the argument that pollution was responsible for the increase in melanic moths in polluted areas.
II. have no effect on the scientists' hypothesis that bird predation was the cause of the comparative decline in light colored moths.
III. help explain why darker moths constituted as much as 98 percent of the moth population in polluted areas.

(A) I only
(B) II only
(C) I and II only
(D) II and III only

A **The correct answer is (D).** Let's look at an analysis of the three statements:

Statement I: The new finding would support the argument in statement I if pollution were the cause of the genetic mutation. But you can't assume that this is the case. Hence, the new finding, in itself, would not support the argument.

Statement II: The finding would tend to explain the predominance of dark-colored moths over light colored ones.

Statement III: Based on the finding, it is logical to infer that the dominant coloration becomes more and more dominant with each successive generation of moths. This trend would help explain how the dark-colored moths could virtually take over the moth population in polluted areas.

In real life, and on the ACT, people often draw conclusions based on assumptions rather than strictly on facts. If an argument relies on a hidden assumption that is not substantiated by evidence, then the argument's conclusion is weak. Statement I in the previous question is a perfect example.

BRAIN TEASER

In this quiz, you'll tackle two Research Summary sets, each one containing 5 questions. (Remember: On the ACT, each set contains 5–7 questions.) In each set, only the first question is easier than average; most are tougher than average.

Attempt all 10 questions, but don't put yourself under a time limit. Focus instead on applying what you have learned in this lesson. Then be sure to read the explanations that follow the quiz.

QUIZ

Passage I

Seychelles warblers are insect-eating birds that usually lay one egg per year. Young warblers, particularly females, often remain with their parents for several years helping them prepare and care for the next *hatchlings* (newly hatched birds), rather than mating themselves. A *breeding pair* (mating male and female) stays in the same territory from year to year.

Two experiments regarding the breeding behavior of the Seychelles warblers were performed.

Experiment 1

Biologists rated the territories of Seychelles warblers based on the density of insects available. They followed 100 breeding pairs in high- and low-quality territories over one breeding season, recording the breeding success (determined by the survival of a hatchling to the point of leaving the nest) for pairs with various numbers of helpers (previous offspring remaining with the mating pair). The results are seen in Table 1.

Table 1

Helper #	Reproductive Success (%)
High-Quality Territory	
0	86%
1	94%
2	95%
3	79%
Low-Quality Territory	
0	75%
1	65%
2	66%
3	64%

Experiment 2

The researchers hypothesized that Seychelles warblers might be able to adjust the sex ratio (number of males versus number of females) of their hatchlings depending on territory quality or number of helpers present. They again looked at 100 breeding pairs with various numbers of helpers in high- and low-quality territories and recorded the sex of their offspring for one breeding season. The results appear in Table 2.

Table 2

Helper #	Male Hatchlings (%)	Female Hatchlings (%)
High-Quality Territory		
0	15%	85%
1	13%	87%
2	78%	22%
3	76%	24%
Low-Quality Territory		
0	75%	25%
1	80%	20%
2	79%	21%
3	74%	26%

1. Which of the following was a control in both experiments?

(A) The number of helpers
(B) The number of eggs laid by a breeding pair
(C) The number of breeding pairs studied
(D) The density of insects

2. Based on the information in the passage, which of the following statements about reproductive success in Seychelles warblers is most accurate?

(F) Reproductive success in low-quality territories decreases with helper number.
(G) Reproductive success in high-quality territories decreases with helper number.
(H) Reproductive success is dependent on helper number, but not on territory quality.
(J) Reproductive success in high-quality territories increases if there are one or two helpers and decreases if there are more than two.

3. Which of the following statements about helper number is correct?

(A) Helper number has no effect on the sex ratios of hatchlings.
(B) Helper number has no effect on the sex ratio of hatchlings in low-quality territories.
(C) Warblers with zero or one helper have a greater proportion of female hatchlings.
(D) Warblers with zero or one helper have a greater proportion of male hatchlings.

4. Which of the following theories fits the data collected in Experiments 1 and 2?

(F) In high-quality areas, one or two helpers are useful, but more than two will put a drain on resources. Therefore, breeding pairs with several helpers will adjust the sex ratios of their hatchlings to favor males.
(G) Breeding pairs in low-quality territories need the most help in raising their hatchling and will adjust the sex ratios of their hatchlings in an attempt to gain more males.
(H) All breeding pairs benefit from at least one helper and will adjust the sex ratios of their hatchlings to favor females if they have no helpers.
(J) Male hatchlings require more resources than female hatchlings, so only birds in high-quality territories with several helpers will adjust the sex ratios of their hatchlings to favor males.

5. Assuming that the hypothesis of the researchers conducting Experiment 2 is correct, which of the following results would you expect from experiments in which breeding pairs and their helpers were moved to different territories?

(A) Breeding pairs with several helpers moved from high-quality territories to low-quality territories switched to having more male hatchlings.
(B) Breeding pairs with one helper moved from high-quality territories to low-quality territories attempted to increase their helper number.
(C) Breeding pairs with one or two helpers moved from low-quality territories to high-quality territories switched to having mainly female hatchlings.
(D) Breeding pairs with two or more helpers moved from low-quality territories to high-quality territories did not change the sex ratios of their hatchlings.

Passage II

The state forestry commission engaged a group of ecologists to study the nutrient flow in a forest on federal lands that was being considered for lease to a logging company. They were also asked to study the effects of clear-cutting in selected areas to predict what the long-term effects on the nutrient budget might be. The scientists selected several small sections of the forest for observation and experiment.

The first task was to estimate the average nutrient flow within the entire forest area. Table 1 shows their estimate based on six experimental areas chosen within the forest. Nutrients enter the forest ecosystem via precipitation, so rain gauges were set up in various locations in the study areas. Nutrients exit the ecosystem through runoff from streams and rivers, so the ecologists measured stream flows in the designated areas.

Table 1
Average Concentrations of Dissolved Substances in Bulk Precipitation and Stream Water in 6 Undisturbed Experimental Watersheds.

Substance	Precipitation	Stream Water	Percent Change
Calcium	0.21	1.5	−619%
Magnesium	0.05	0.37	−640%
Potassium	0.10	0.23	−130%
Sodium	0.12	0.94	−683%
Aluminum	0.01	0.24	−2,300%
Ammonium	0.22	0.05	340%
Sulfate	3.10	6.20	−100%
Nitrate	1.30	1.14	12%
Chloride	0.42	0.64	−52%
Dissolved Silica	0.03	4.59	−15,300%

Notes: Data is given in kilograms per dry weight materials per hectare of the watershed. Basin-caught materials are coarse, net-caught materials are fine and filter-caught materials are super-fine.

After estimating the overall nutrient flow in this forest, the ecologists had one 15-hectare* area cleared of trees in order to determine the amount of increase that would occur in runoff. The trees were removed from the area, but nothing else was disturbed. For the first two years after the logging, an herbicide was applied so that no vegetation would grow back. The ecologists then compared this cleared watershed with one of the intact watersheds under study. They measured the stream flow for the first three years after the logging took place. Table 2 summarizes the amounts of organic and inorganic matter found at the watershed basin. A net and filter system was utilized to catch finer matter as the runoff exited the watershed area.

* *A hectare is a metric unit of measure equal to 2.471 acres.*

Table 2
Annual Losses of Particulate Matter

		Watershed 1 Undisturbed Area		Watershed 2 Deforested Area	
Source of Output	**Year**	**Organic**	**Inorganic**	**Organic**	**Inorganic**
Ponding Basin	1	4.62	8.30	35.41	158.32
Net	1	0.43	0.02	0.26	0.01
Filter	1	2.64	2.80	4.23	4.80
Ponding Basin	2	11.39	31.00	45.13	321.88
Net	2	0.43	0.02	0.25	0.03
Filter	2	3.32	3.70	6.24	7.10
Ponding Basin	3	3.83	5.78	53.72	540.32
Net	3	0.42	0.01	0.27	0.04
Filter	3	2.61	2.97	8.73	12.98

Notes: Data is given in kilograms per dry weight materials per hectare of the watershed. Basin-caught materials are coarse, net-caught materials are fine and filter-caught materials are super-fine.

6. Based on the figures reported in Table 1, which of the following is apparently true of the nutrient budget as estimated using the six experimental areas?

(F) There is a net loss for all measured nutrients entering the ecosystem.
(G) There is a net gain for all measured nutrients entering the ecosystem.
(H) There is a net loss for all measured nutrients except for ammonium and nitrate.
(J) There is a net gain for all measured nutrients except for ammonium and nitrate.

7. Which of the following best explains why the scientists chose to use three different collection methods?

(A) It enabled them to collect particulate matter at different watersheds.
(B) It enabled them to collect particulate matter of different sizes.
(C) All of the collected particulate matter was quite coarse.
(D) The collected particulate matter was dissolved in water.

8. Which of the following hypotheses concerning the effects of logging on the forest ecosystem is supported by the data?

(F) Logging decreases the loss of organic and inorganic matter from the forest ecosystem.
(G) Logging increases the loss of organic matter but has no effect on inorganic matter in the forest ecosystem.
(H) Logging increases the loss of inorganic matter but has no effect on organic matter in the forest ecosystem.
(J) Logging increases the loss of organic and inorganic matter from the forest ecosystem.

9. Based on the trend in the numbers over the first three years of observing the undisturbed and logged watershed areas reported in Table 2, it would be reasonable to predict that the runoff

(A) would vary from year to year within narrow limits in the undisturbed area but steadily increase in the logged area.
(B) in both experimental areas would steadily increase over the years.
(C) in both experimental areas would vary from year to year.
(D) in the undistributed area would remain constant, but the runoff in the logged area would vary from year to year.

10. The ecologists inform the state officials that the bark in trees contains a significant proportion of nutrients. If the state officials are committed to leasing a set amount of this federal land to a logging company, they might reduce the nutrient loss in that region by

(F) removing all remains from the trees after they are cut down so that the area is clear for new growth.
(G) applying herbicide immediately after any logging operation.
(H) allowing the logging companies to use the cleared areas for roads.
(J) stripping the bark from all logged trees and leaving it behind in the cleared area.

ANSWERS AND EXPLANATIONS

Passage I

1. **The correct answer is (C).** In both experiments, the number of breeding pairs studied was kept constant at 100 in high-quality territory and 100 in a low-quality territory. The number of helpers, choice (A), and density of insects, choice (D), were independent variables. As for choice (B), although the passage's first sentence indicates that warblers usually lay one egg per year, the number of eggs laid was not accounted for at all in the design of either the experiment—either as a control or as a variable.

2. **The correct answer is (J).** As you can see in Table 1, the highest level of reproductive success in high-quality territories is found when one or two helpers are present (94 and 95 percent success); the rate falls off when a third helper appears (79 percent).

3. **The correct answer is (B).** Look at the lower half of Table 2. In low-quality territories, the percentage of male hatchlings varies in a narrow, seemingly random range (between 74 and 80 percent) as the number of helpers varies, suggesting that the number of helpers has no real effect on the sex ratio among hatchlings there.

4. **The correct answer is (F).** This is the only theory that even begins to explain the curious data in Table 2, in which all warbler pairs except low-helper pairs in high-quality territories produce more male offspring than female. If we assume that a shortage of resources favors male hatchlings (who perhaps have some different behavior from females; greater aggressiveness in pursuit of food, for example), then the pattern in Table 2 becomes at least understandable and consistent.

5. **The correct answer is (D).** Since all warbler pairs with two or more helpers have high male-to-female hatchling ratios—regardless of whether they are in high-quality or low-quality territories—one would expect no change in the ratio even with a change from one territory to another.

Passage II

6. **The correct answer is (H).** Choice (H) is correct because although most nutrients are decreasing, the table shows a net gain for these two.

7. **The correct answer is (B).** The purpose of using the different techniques was to insure that the scientists could capture the different sizes of material exiting the ecosystem.

8. **The correct answer is (J).** The experiment was designed to track the effects of logging on watersheds that were already losing nutrients. The design of the experiment and the design/display of the results in Table 2 show that ecologists' concern about loss of nutrients to be of crucial importance. Choice (J) is the only option that reflects this concern.

9. **The correct answer is (A).** Close examination of the results displayed in Table 2 show that there is no pattern to the loss of substances in the undisturbed watershed and that the loss is relatively small. The logged area is losing nutrients and this phenomenon is increasing year to year. The only answer that reflects this comparison is choice (A).

10. **The correct answer is (J).** Nutrients are more dramatically depleted in the logged areas, so discovering a way to retain some of the nutrients would be useful. If tree bark contains many nutrients, keeping it in the system would help toward this end.

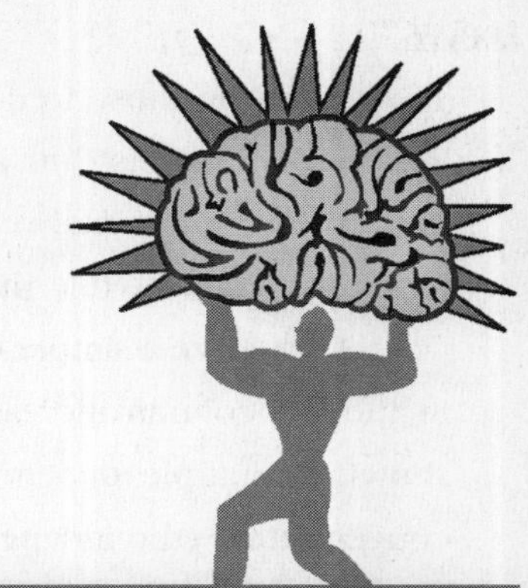

LESSON 20

Data Representation and Conflicting Viewpoints

On the ACT Science Reasoning Test, expect to encounter *three* question sets (15–17 questions total) in the data representation format, and *one* set (5–7 questions) in the conflicting viewpoints format. In this lesson, you will focus on these two formats. Specifically, you will:

- Review the various ways of presenting data in tabular or graphical form, and how to "read" and interpret data in each form
- Learn how to predict the kinds of questions (and answers) that will accompany passages in the two formats
- Prepare for the toughest and most complex kinds of data representation and conflicting viewpoints questions
- Apply what you have learned to 10 tough ACT-style questions based on two passages—one in each format

WAYS OF PRESENTING DATA

First, you'll briefly review the following four forms for presenting data:

- Tables
- Line graphs
- Bar graphs
- Scatter plots

You've already seen most of these forms in this book, but let's take a more detailed look at them here.

The four types of displays listed above may not be the only ones you'll encounter during the ACT Science Reasoning Test—but they're the ones you will most likely run across.

TABLES

Tables appear most frequently on the ACT Science Reasoning Test. You'll encounter tables not just in Data Representation sets, but also in Research Summary sets, as you saw in the previous lesson. Tables are generally divided into horizontal rows and vertical columns. The values for the *independent* variable usually appear in the leftmost column, while the values for the *dependent* variable(s) appear in columnar form to the right.

To analyze a simple two-column table, you might fill in the blank for yourself in this sentence: "As the number in the left column increases, the number in the right column __________." You would do the same for a table showing multiple dependent variables. For instance, in analyzing Table 1, you might say to yourself: "As Jolt concentration (the independent variable) increases, plant growth, in inches, and the number of observed buds (the two dependent variables) both decrease."

Table 1
The Effect on Plant Growth of Watering with Varying Concentrations of Jolt Cola Solution

Jolt Concentration (%)	Growth in Inches
0.0	10
0.5	8
1.0	6
1.5	4
2.0	2
2.5	0

The test-makers' favorite way of "tricking up" a table is to subdivide dependent variables. In Table 2, for instance, each of two dependent variables—industrial environment and rural environment—is divided by sub-environment, either indoor or outdoor. Therefore, the table shows a total of four dependent variables.

Table 2

Volatile Chemical	NJ Industrial ($\mu g/m^3$)		Maine Rural Township ($\mu g/m^3$)	
	Indoor	Outdoor	Indoor	Outdoor
Trichloro ethane	21	4	14	3
Tetrachloro ethylene	9	3	8	1
Chloroform	5	0.2	2	0.1
O-oxylene	5	3	3	2
Styrene	5	0.5	1	0.2

Table 2 is different than Table 1 in another respect. In Table 2, notice that the independent variable (leftmost column) is not a number, but rather a chemical type. So, to analyze the table, you wouldn't look for increases or decreases in the values for each dependent variable. Instead, you'd compare numbers *horizontally*—that is, across the four columns. In doing so, you should notice that in each row (for each chemical) the outdoor values are lower than the indoor values.

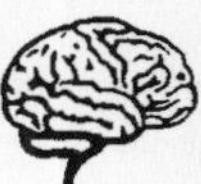

Brainiacs know that different tables call for different analytic approaches. To analyze certain tables, the key is to compare *numerical trends* (increases and decreases) as you scan *down* the different columns. For other tables, the key is to compare the *sizes of numbers* in the different columns as you scan *across* columns.

LINE GRAPHS

A *line graph* plots value pairs on an *xy*-coordinate plane rather than in a table. By convention, a line graph's horizontal axis (*x*-axis) tracks the independent variable, and its vertical axis (*y*-axis) tracks the dependent variable. To analyze a line graph that contains a single line, you might fill in the blank for yourself in the following sentence: "As the value of x increases, the value of y __________." Or, to simply "look up" information in the graph, fill in the blanks in this sentence: "When x equals __________, y equals __________."

Not exactly rocket science—especially compared to Lesson 14's coordinate geometry problems. ACT line graphs can get a bit more complex. For instance, look at the graph in Figure 1, which shows the effect of temperature (the independent variable) on a substance's solubility (the dependent variable). As you can see, the graph includes four lines, representing four different solutes.

Figure 1

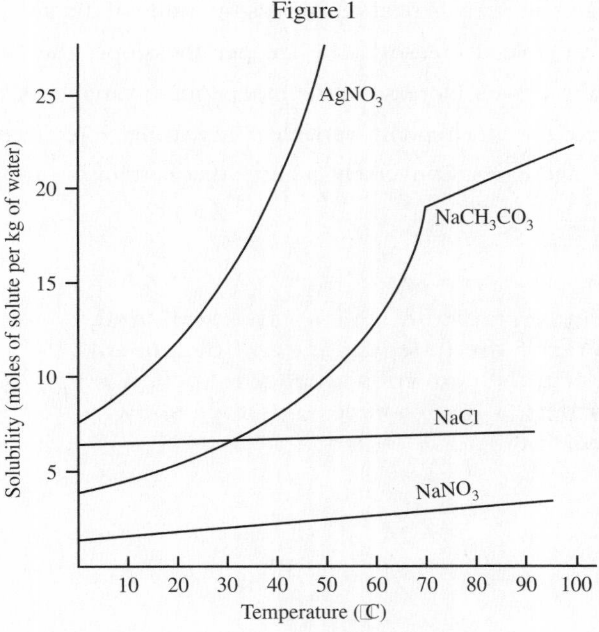

To analyze the relationship between temperature and solubility for $NaNO_3$ in this graph, for instance, you'd fill in the blank in the earlier sentence as follows: "As temperature (the value of x) increases, the solubility of $NaNO_3$ (the value of y) *increases gradually but steadily*." Or, to simply "look up" information for $NaNO_3$: "When temperature (x) equals 60, y equals *approximately 3*."

Notice the italicized word *approximately* in the preceding sentence. In reading ACT line graphs, you won't need to determine precise values, for the obvious reason that it's difficult to determine the precise coordinates of a point along an angled line on a line graph. The test-makers aren't interested in testing your visual acuity; therefore, in defining points on ACT line graphs, rest assured that approximations will suffice.

The trickier aspects of line graphs—aspects that Brainiacs understand but other test-takers might not—have to do with the *shapes* and *slopes* of lines. Keep in mind the following Brainiac insights:

- A line moving *upward* from left to right (for example, $NaNO_3$ in Figure 1) indicates a *direct* relationship (as the value of the independent variable increases, so does the value of the dependent variable). The steeper the slope, the larger the increase in the value of the dependent variable for a given increase in the independent variable. (If the line is straight, as in the line for $NaNO_3$ in Figure 1, those increases remain in the same proportion. A line that curves upward (for example, the lines for $AgNO_3$ and $NaCH_3CO_3$ in Figure 1) indicates the independent variable's increasing "effectiveness" on the dependent variable as the value of the former increases. Conversely, a curve that flattens out from left to right indicates decreasing effectiveness.
- A line moving *downward* from left to right indicates an *inverse* relationship (as the value of the independent variable increases, the value of the dependent variable decreases). The steeper the slope, the larger the decrease in the value of the dependent variable for a given increase in the independent variable. A line that curves downward from left to right would indicate the independent variable's increasing "effectiveness" on the dependent variable as the value of the former decreases. Conversely, a curve that flattens out from left to right indicates decreasing effectiveness.

Direct and inverse relationships can be shown in table form as well. And, if the proportion between the value of the independent and dependent variables changes in a decided pattern, the pattern is tougher to recognize in a table than in a line graph—where a line's shape and slope show a visual representation of the pattern.

BAR GRAPHS

Like line graphs, *bar graphs* almost always track the independent variable along the *x*-axis and the dependent variable along the *y*-axis. But unlike line graphs, which can show continuous changes, bar graphs can show only quantum (step-like) changes. This doesn't mean that you can't plot a line graph and bar graph on the same display. You can, as illustrated in Figure 2.

Figure 2

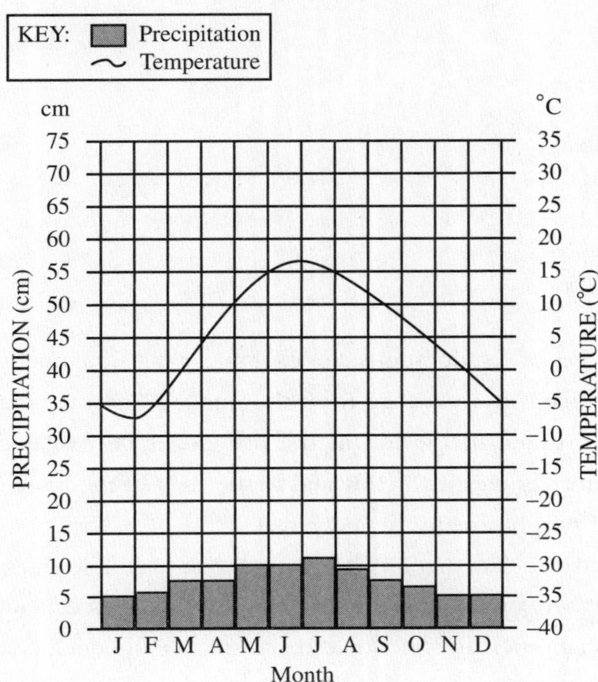

In Figure 2, notice that the bar graph and line graph track the same independent variable (month) but different dependent variables. (The bar graph tracks monthly precipitation totals while the line graph tracks temperature.)

To track temperature, a bar graph could have been used instead of a line graph. But the bar graph could only show average monthly temperature, not continuous changes. Can you picture what that bar graph might look like? For each month, you would see a second bar overlapping and extending higher than the precipitation bar. From January to June, the temperature bars would rise in height (peaking in June and July), and then decrease in height.

SCATTER PLOTS

A *scatter plot* is useful when the points on an *xy*-graph cannot be connected to form a smooth line, perhaps because the relationship between the independent and dependent variables is complex or influenced by other, secondary factors. For example, a person's height and weight tend to influence each other (their relationship is direct). But other factors, such as diet, play a role as well, and there are certainly exceptions to the general relationship. Thus, a graph depicting the height and weight of 20 randomly selected people would probably not yield dots that could be connected to form a neat, smooth line. Instead, it would probably yield a scattering of points only *roughly* reflecting the general relationship between the two variables. In Figure 3, notice that the 20 discrete points imply a smooth line, suggesting the general relationship between the two variables, but not attempting to "connect the dots."

Figure 3

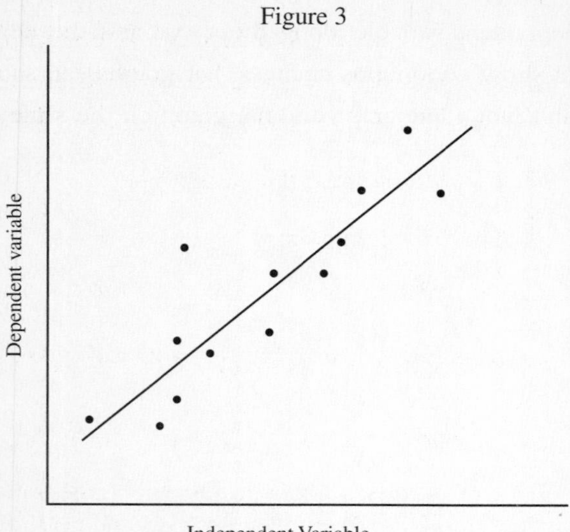

By their nature, scatter plots lend themselves to unique types of test questions. For example, a question might ask for a reasonable explanation for an anomalous point—one that's at a distance from the implied line that shows the general pattern. In Figure 3, any point significantly above and to the left of the line might be explained by a secondary factor, such as overeating. Conversely, any point significantly below and to the right of the line might be explained by a health problem that resulted in abnormal weight loss in the individual.

Or, a scatter-plot question might provide additional data—data that diverges from the implied line and suggests that the line needs revising—then ask for a hypothesis or theory to explain the divergence. For instance, if additional data points imply a curved line that becomes flatter as height increases, it would be reasonable to conclude that tall people tend to be proportionately thinner than shorter people.

READING AND RECAPPING DATA REPRESENTATION PASSAGES

Because you learned in Lesson 19 what questions to ask (and answer) when reading and recapping a Research Summary passage, you are better able to predict the questions (and answers) that follow the Data Representation passage. Since Research Summary passages often contain graphical data, the questions you ask about those passages will be similar to the ones listed below for Data Representation (notice that all but the first question focuses on the principles of Data Representation you just reviewed):

- What relationships are described in the background information preceding the graphical data?
- In each table or graph, what are the *independent* and *dependent variables*?
- In each table or graph, what relationship (general pattern or trend) is shown between the variables?
- What relationship, if any, is there between the data in the different tables or graphs? Do the data in one support the data in the other?
- What general *conclusions* or *hypotheses*, if any, can you draw from the trends, patterns, or relationships among the data?

MASTERING THE TOUGHEST DATA REPRESENTATION QUESTIONS

In a typical Data Representation set, about half the questions will ask you to "look up" information in a table, graph, or other display, or to recognize an obvious trend or pattern in the data. As you might expect, questions that call for these basic skills tend to be easier than average. So you will focus strictly on the following three more challenging question types:

- Questions requiring you to piece together separate graphs or tables, logically speaking
- Questions requiring you to distinguish meaningful patterns from random data
- Questions requiring you to theorize from the data

Before you look at these question types, read the following Data Representation passage and the questions that follow it.

Passage I

By studying rock samples, geologists can reconstruct much of an area's geologic history. Table 1 lists rock samplings taken along the shoreline, in 20-mile intervals. The sampled rock found at each distance is shown, and crystallization temperature and ages typical of each type of rock are listed. Figure 1 shows the cross-sectional area of measurement and the altitude corresponding to each rock sampling indicated in Table 1.

Table 1

Distance East (miles	Type of Rock in Sample	Crystalization Temp* (°C)	Estimated Age (millions of years)
0 (shoreline)	Rhyolite	750°	10.0
20	Diorite	860°	250.0
40	Periodtitec	1,200°	200.0
60	Shale	750°	0.1
80	Limestone	800°	6.0
100	Breccia	750°	0.5
120	Andesite	950°	3.6
140	Andesite	900°	4.0
160	Gabbro	1,100°	300.0
180	Granite	700°	400.0

* (Crystallization temperature is based on the interal composition of the rock)

Figure 1

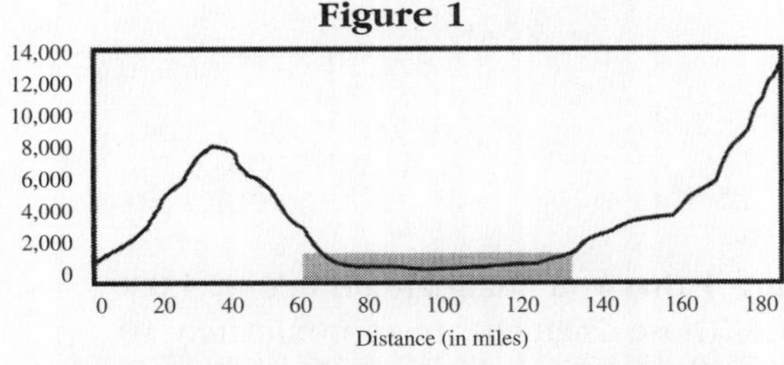

Before you look at the kinds of tough questions that the test-makers might design for this passage, here is an overview of the easier questions. An easy question about Table 1 may ask you to:

- Determine the value of one variable—for instance, distance, rock type, crystallization temperature, or age—given the value of another one of those variables. In other words, you may be asked to "look up" information in the table.
- Recognize an obvious pattern in the data; for instance, you may notice that the ages of the samples decrease as you move inland from the shoreline, and then begin to increase as you move even further inland.

An easy question about Figure 1 might ask you:

- What type of measurement is shown on the vertical (or horizontal) axis?
- What was the altitude where the sample was collected, given the distance from shore where it was collected?

Now, on to more challenging question types that are worthy of your Brainiac attention.

"PIECING TOGETHER" SEPARATE GRAPHS OR TABLES

If a Data Representation passage includes more than one data display (table, graph, or chart), chances are that at least one question will require you to connect the two displays, logically speaking. To handle this question type, you'll need to recognize where they connect. In Passage I, you should have noticed that distance from shore is shown on both displays. This connection allows you to match either the rock type, crystallization temperature, or rock age to the corresponding altitude where the sample was collected.

An even more challenging question of this type, based on Passage I, might also require one or more of the following tasks:

- Recognize a *pattern* or *trend* in the relationship between altitude (the dependent variable in Figure 1) and one of the three dependent variables (rock type, temperature, or age) in Table
- Recognize *more than one possible value pair* when matching a given altitude to one of the dependent variables in Table 1
- *Interpolate* from known data points to estimate a value between them

Here's a question that incorporates all three requirements—as well as a few of the wrong-answer ploys you encountered so far:

Q Based on the data, you might expect a sample collected at an altitude of 4,000 feet to have an estimated age of about

I. 125 million years.
II. 200 million years.
III. 300 million years.

(A) I only
(B) Either I or II only
(C) Either II or III only
(D) Either I, II, or III

A **The correct answer is (D).** Notice in Figure 1 that you attain an altitude of 4,000 feet at *three* different distances from the shore. Those distances are approximately 10, 40, and 160 miles. (Approximations suffice for determining these three corresponding distances in Figure 1, since the question doesn't require precisely measured values.) Accordingly, you need to "look up" the estimated age corresponding to all three distances in Table 1. The ages corresponding to 40 and 160 miles are 200 million and 300 million years, respectively. However, Table 1 does not provide data for a distance of 10 miles from the shore. But, you can *interpolate* from the data provided for the nearest distances less and greater than 10 miles. Since a distance of 10 miles is midway between the shore (0 miles) and 20 miles, it's reasonable to expect an age midway between 10 million and 250 million years. Option I provides a close enough number. Hence, all three options (I, II, and III) provide ages that you might reasonably expect of a rock at an altitude of 4,000 feet.

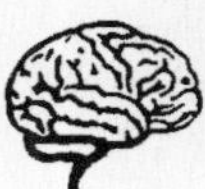

In the preceding question, true Brainiacs would have asked themselves whether it's okay to interpolate from known values. The answer is *yes*—because Table 1 and Figure 1, considered together, show a definite correlation (a pattern) between altitude and rock age. Generally, the higher the altitude at which a sample was collected, the older the sample. Had the table shown no such pattern, then you could not interpolate as described above, and the correct answer choice would have been (C) instead of (D).

DISTINGUISHING MEANINGFUL PATTERNS FROM RANDOM DATA

As a Brainiac, you should be able to anticipate this type of question (and the correct answer) as you read, and especially recap, the passage. During these steps, you should be on the lookout for strong patterns or trends in the data—for example, the tendency for the value of a certain dependent variable to increase (or decrease) with any increase (or decrease) in the value of a certain independent variable.

Your ability to recognize such patterns and trends is a big part of what you're being tested on in Data Representation questions. But you'll also be tested on distinguishing significant, meaningful patterns from mere coincidences—random data that, by mere happenstance, appear to form a pattern. In a tougher question, you might encounter a "quasi-trend" or "mini-trend"—one that only *some* of the data support. Such trends make great fodder for wrong answer choices. Here's a good example that tests your ability to make this kind of distinction:

Q The data best support which of the following statements?

(A) Rocks more than 100 miles inland generally have higher crystallization temperatures than those closer to shore.
(B) Rocks found at high altitudes generally have higher crystallization temperatures than those found at lower altitudes.
(C) Rocks having high crystallization temperatures are generally older than those having lower crystallization temperatures.
(D) Rocks found at high altitudes are generally older than those found at lower altitudes.

A **The correct answer is (D).** Table 1 and Figure 1, considered together, show a definite correlation (a pattern) between altitude and rock age. Generally, the higher the altitude at which a sample was collected, the older the sample. Choice (A) is not supported by the data. The relationship between the two variables appears to be random. Choice (B) finds support from only part of the data—specifically, up to 160 miles from shore. Notice that further inland, the altitude at which samples were collected increases sharply, while the crystallization temperature *decreases* markedly (from 1,100° at about 3,500 feet to 700° at about 13,000 feet). Since choice (B) is not supported by the totality of the data, it is not as good an answer as choice (D). Choice (C), like (B), finds support from some of the data, but conflicts with other data. If you focus on the two highest recorded temperatures—1,200° and 1,100°—you'll see that the estimated ages of those samples were high in comparison to most. But the oldest sample, the one collected 180 miles inland, has a relatively low temperature—lower than the youngest sample among the group! Hence, choice (C) is wrong for essentially the same reason as choice (B).

There's a tendency among ACT test-takers (and among scientists as well) to want to find patterns and trends in scientific data, because it is patterns and trends that allow you to formulate and prove scientific theories. But keep in mind: In science and on the ACT, sometimes data won't show any pattern or trend. So be careful not to invent a pattern where none exists!

THEORIZING FROM THE DATA

Questions of this type essentially ask: "What theory (among the ones listed) does the experimental data best support?" These questions can be tough because the data will typically provide *some* support for more than one listed theory. What's more, like other question types you encountered in the previous lesson, any general statement that is *not inconsistent* with the data, and is relevant to it, could be a potentially correct answer. So, you might need to make a close judgment call between two or more answer choices. To make things even trickier, the question might incorporate one or more of the following:

- Additional information, which you need to assimilate and combine with what's already provided
- Tempting theories (wrong answers) that make perfect real-world sense, but aren't supported by the specific data provided
- A theory (wrong answer) that gets the data backward (if you're not paying close attention, you might not catch the reversal)

Here's a question based on Passage I that incorporates all three features:

Q Limestone is sedimentary rock that develops from the accumulated deposits of sea organisms with shells. Andesite is igneous rock deposited by lava flows from volcanoes. Which of the following is the best hypothesis about the geologic record of the shaded area?

(A) Lava flows from volcanoes isolated the shaded area from the body of water west of the shoreline.
(B) Volcanic activity created a valley west of the volcanoes, then a sea formed in the valley.
(C) Volcanoes erupted to the east of an existing sea, located in the shaded area.
(D) Lava flows from volcanoes flowed westward into a sea, resulting in the sea's eventual disappearance.

A **The correct answer is (C).** Limestone is found 80 miles inland, and andesite is found 120 and 140 miles inland. The andesite is further east than the limestone. The limestone is 6.0 million years old. The andesite is 3.6 to 4.0 million years old. Andesite from volcanoes would have had to erupt *after* the deposit of the limestone—that is, after the sea existed. The theory in choice (C) is consistent with this chronology and with the location of limestone and andesite. You can easily eliminate choice (B) because it gets the chronology backward. Choice (A) is consistent with the chronology, but not with the location of the andesite. The theory in (A) would be viable only if andesite were found *west* (rather than east) of the shaded area. Choice (D) is consistent with the chronology and with the location of andesite to the west of the limestone. However, if lava had flowed into the sea, you would expect to find limestone and andesite together in the shaded area. Since the data does not show both types in the same sample, the assertion that lava actually flowed *into the sea* amounts to mere speculation.

When evaluating theories based on graphical data, look out for theories that the data only partially support. Also be wary of theories that make real-world sense but that do not jive with the data.

CONFLICTING VIEWPOINTS—QUESTION TYPES

On the ACT, you'll encounter *one* Conflicting Viewpoints set, which will contain 5 to 7 questions. Expect about half the questions to test you on the following fundamental skills:

- Identifying the basic scientific issue that the different viewpoints seek to address
- Understanding the essence of each viewpoint on the issue
- Recognizing similarities (explicit points of agreement) between viewpoints
- Recognizing key dissimilarities (explicit points of disagreement) between viewpoints

Questions that call for these basic skills tend to be easier than average. Tougher question types—the ones you'll focus on just ahead—include the following:

- Questions requiring you to *critique* a theory by identifying its hidden assumptions
- Questions requiring you to assess the effect of *additional evidence* on one or more of the theories presented
- Questions requiring you to recognize *implicit* points of agreement between the theories presented

READING AND RECAPPING CONFLICTING VIEWPOINT PASSAGES

Just as with Research Summary and Data Representation passages, you can essentially predict the questions (and their answers) that will follow a Conflicting Viewpoint passage by engaging in the right Q&A as you read and recap the passage. Since Conflicting Viewpoint passages generally don't contain graphical data, your Q&A will be quite different than for the other two formats. Here are five questions you should ask and answer for any Conflicting Viewpoint passage:

- What is the scientific issue that the different viewpoints seek to address?
- What is the essence of each viewpoint on the issue?
- What are the similarities (explicit points of agreement) between the viewpoints?
- What are the key dissimilarities (explicit points of disagreement) between the viewpoints?
- On what crucial, but unsubstantiated, assumptions do each of the viewpoints depend?

MASTERING THE TOUGHEST CONFLICTING VIEWPOINT QUESTIONS

Your final task in this lesson is to learn how to handle the three toughest Conflicting Viewpoints question types. Before you do that, however, read the following Conflicting Viewpoints passage and the questions that follow it. (As you read this passage, be sure to apply the Q&A method you just learned.)

X-REF **Conflicting Viewpoints sets that present more than two viewpoints are inherently tougher than ones that present only two. The passage here contains two viewpoints. During this lesson's Brain Teaser, you'll tackle a slightly tougher passage involving three distinct viewpoints.**

Passage II

The apparent bird-dinosaur evolutionary connection has been a source of considerable debate among paleontologists since early in the second half of the twentieth century. This connection was proposed on the basis of numerous anatomical similarities, and has been supported by the discovery of fossils of a small number of seeming transitional forma uncovered in Europe and Asia. Yet scientists differ in their interpretation of the significance of these similarities and the nature of the fossil evidence as well.

Paleontologist A

The discovery of fossil reptiles equipped with feathers, wings, and beak-like snouts may be significant, but more likely provides only limited support for the dinosaur-into-birds hypothesis. Convergent evolution often provides animals very distant in lineage with similar appendages—witness, for example, the similarities in the body shape and presence of fins in fish and cetaceans such as whales and dolphins. We would never put forth the idea that orcas evolved from sharks based on the morphological similarities of these creatures; it would be immediately deemed absurd.

It is more likely the case that birds and dinosaurs share a very different common ancestor, perhaps from among the thecodonts. These prototypical reptiles of the late Permian Age survived the largest mass extinction recorded in the planet's history to bring forth many more recent lines; crocodiles, dinosaurs, pterosaurs, and birds are the most notable among these.

Paleontologist B

In our studies of numerous dinosaur fossils, it has become obvious that the lifestyles of dinosaurs were amazingly varied. No longer is it acceptable to view dinosaurs only as lumbering, cold-blooded monsters; indeed, the most frightening dinosaurs did not lumber at all. They were agile, swift, and some even possessed limited flying capabilities. Lightweight muscular body structure would be crucial to the success of this type of predator.

Based upon this observation, along with a number of obvious physical similarities and evidence from the fossil record, we are convinced that birds evolved from small, carnivorous dinosaurs called theropods. A mere examination of the forelimb, hindlimb, and feet of a theropod fossil, and a comparison to one of the five available specimens of *Archaeopteryx** will bear this out. In addition, more recent discoveries of fossil dinosaurs with birdlike traits and habits, particularly the finds uncovered in the Liaoning province of China, lend further credible support for our position that birds are for all intents and purposes actual members of the lineage Dinosauria living and thriving in our midst.

IDENTIFYING A THEORY'S HIDDEN ASSUMPTIONS

Any theory presented in a Conflicting Viewpoints passage will rely on one or more unstated, or "hidden," assumptions. What this means is that certain facts that aren't provided must in fact be true in order for the theory to be convincing. Don't expect a theory's proponent to come right out and list the various assumptions on which the theory relies. You'll need to figure out for yourself what crucial assumptions underlie the theory—which is what makes these questions more difficult than others.

The key to handling these questions is to understand that ACT Conflicting Viewpoints provide, in essence, alternative explanations for what *causes* certain observed scientific phenomenon. And, in almost every case, each theory will ignore or overlook other possible causes. Accordingly, a key assumption underlying a typical ACT viewpoint is that there are no other plausible explanations for the observed phenomenon. Here's a question based on Passage II that tests you on this kind of assumption:

* Archaeopteryx was a feathered reptile of the late Jurassic Era thought to represent an intermediate form between dinosaurs and birds.

Q Which of the following is a criticism that Paleontologist A would make of the evolutionary hypothesis of Paleontologist B?

(A) It ignores the possibility of the existence of transitional forms.
(B) It ignores the impact of a very large mass extinction.
(C) It assumes that morphological similarities are a result of direct lineage.
(D) It proposes that the lineage from which dinosaurs arose is quite distinct from the one from which birds arose.

A **The correct answer is (C).** The hypothesis of Paleontologist B relies on the crucial assumption that there's no possible explanation for the body similarities between dinosaurs and early birds other than that birds descended directly from dinosaurs. Choice (A) contradicts the position of Paleontologist B, whose argument not only acknowledges, but also relies upon, the possible existence of transitional forms. Choice (B) provides an accurate statement, but so what? The large mass extinction that Paleontologist A mentions is irrelevant to Paleontologist B's argument. Choice (D) provides the essential hypothesis of Paleontologist A, not Paleontologist B.

ASSESSING THE EFFECT OF ADDITIONAL EVIDENCE

A question of this type will provide a new finding or other fact, then ask about its impact on one or more of the conflicting theories. Potentially, any additional piece of information might do one of the following:

- Support one viewpoint, but weaken another
- Weaken both viewpoints
- Support one viewpoint, but have no effect on the other viewpoint
- Weaken one viewpoint, but have no effect on the other viewpoint
- Have no effect on either viewpoint

What makes these questions more complex is that they require you to assimilate the whole passage—to understand all the viewpoints, as well as to recognize their similarities and differences. A less complex question of this type might provide new evidence that blatantly conflicts with one viewpoint and, just as blatantly, supports another.

Q If genetic evidence were established to date the lineage of birds 85 million years prior to the rise of *Archaeopteryx*, this finding would tend to

(A) support the theory of Paleontologist A.
(B) support the theory of Paleontologist B.
(C) support the theories of both paleontologists.
(D) refute the theories of both paleontologists.

A **The correct answer is (A).** Choice (A) contradicts the theory of Paleontologist B because Paleontologist B suggests that birds arose from dinosaurs. Paleontologist A suggests that the two arose from an extremely distant ancestor, and the theory of convergent evolution is not inconsistent with birds appearing before dinosaurs.

A tougher question of this sort might provide evidence that either strengthens or weakens one theory but has no effect on the other. The use of the Roman-numeral format, as in the next example, can also complicate the question by rendering the process-of-elimination strategy less useful.

Q Which of the following types of evidence, if found, would lend support to the position of Paleontologist A?

I. Discovery of thecodont fossils with characteristics of modern birds and existing dinosaur fossils
II. Discovery of another possible intermediate form between dinosaurs and birds from the Jurassic era
III. Discovery of a bird prototype dating back to before the beginning of the era of dinosaur dominance

(A) I only
(B) II only
(C) I and III only
(D) II and III only

A **The correct answer is (A).** Paleontologist A believes that dinosaurs and birds share a common ancestor. A fossil find with common features dating from before the age of the dinosaurs would support this view. The evidence cited in option II would actually support the position of Paleontologist B by providing further evidence of an evolutionary link between birds and dinosaurs. The evidence cited in option III would tend to weaken the position of Paleontologist A, who believes that dinosaurs and birds share a common ancestor. A fossil find with features like those of modern birds, but unlike those of dinosaurs, would tend to show that the lineage of birds is distinct from that of dinosaurs.

Just because evidence weakens one theory does not mean that the same evidence supports an opposing theory. For example, in the preceding question, the evidence provided in option III would tend to weaken the positions of *both* paleontologists.

The most difficult type of question involving additional facts or findings will *appear* (at least to most test-takers) to make a theory airtight. But, if you're paying close attention, you'll realize that whether or not the additional evidence proves the theory depends on whether certain *assumptions* can be substantiated.

Q If Paleontologist B could confirm that birds appeared much later in evolutionary history than any dinosaurs, which of the following statements would reconcile this fact with the theory of Paleontologist A?

(A) The ancestors of birds and the ancestors of dinosaurs were simultaneously exposed to specific environmental conditions, and this caused the development of similar characteristics.
(B) The ancestors of birds and the ancestors of dinosaurs were exposed to specific environmental conditions that caused the development of similar characteristics, but the dinosaur ancestors were exposed to these environmental conditions later than the bird ancestors were.
(C) The rate of evolutionary change from the thecodont ancestor was much slower for the lineage that resulted in birds than for the lineage that resulted in dinosaurs.
(D) The rate of evolutionary change from the thecodont ancestor was much faster for the lineage that resulted in birds than for the lineage that resulted in dinosaurs.

A **The correct answer is (C).** Paleontologist A postulates the existence of a very distant common ancestor for birds and dinosaurs. The development of birds much later than that of dinosaurs might seem to refute this argument. However, the rate of evolutionary change is not constant across different lineages. Dinosaurs may have developed relatively rapidly from thecodonts, for example, whereas birds did not evolve until much later.

RECOGNIZING IMPLICIT POINTS OF AGREEMENT

In handling Conflicting Viewpoints sets, one of your basic tasks is to understand the similarities between the viewpoints presented. Think of these similarities as points of agreement between the proponents of the different theories. Some points of agreement will be explicit in the passage. You'll find them in the background information as well as in the opening sentences of each viewpoint. But other points of agreement might be implied rather than expressed. These points make for tougher test questions because you need to do more than just "look up" the information in the passage.

Questions of this type are not likely to ask about "agreement" or "similarities." Instead, look for a question stem that asks what is "consistent" with more than one of the viewpoints presented. Here is the key point in handling these questions: Whatever is *not inconsistent* with a theory or viewpoint is something that the theory's proponent might agree with. For example, something that is *not* consistent with Paleontologist A's theory might be something Paleontologist B agrees with.

Here's an ACT-style example, based on Passage II that illustrates this key point:

Q Which of the following perspectives would be consistent with the views of both paleontologists?

(A) Convergent evolution produces similar forms in diverse lineages.
(B) Dinosaurs and birds may have evolved from the same ancestor.
(C) Birds and dinosaurs arose out of completely separate lineages.
(D) Birds arose out of a lineage of dinosaurs.

A **The correct answer is (B).** Neither Paleontologist B's belief that birds arose out of a lineage of dinosaurs, nor Paleontologist A's belief that they did not, is inconsistent with the view expressed in choice (B). Choices (A) and (C) are consistent with Paleontologist A's hypothesis but inconsistent with Paleontologist B's. Choice (D) provides the essence of Paleontologist B's hypothesis but is antithetical to Paleontologist A's.

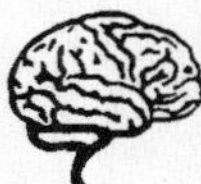

Brainiacs understand that a statement can be consistent with each of two conflicting viewpoints, even though the statement is not an *explicit* point of agreement between proponents of the conflicting viewpoints.

BRAIN TEASER

In this quiz, you'll tackle one Data Representation set and one Conflicting Viewpoints set, each containing 5 questions. (Remember: On the ACT, each set will contain 5 to 7 questions.) In each set, only the first question is easier than average, and most are tougher than average.

Attempt all ten questions, but don't put yourself under a time limit. Focus instead on applying what you learned in this lesson. Then be sure to read the explanations that follow the quiz.

QUIZ

Passage I

A chemist, a biologist, and a doctor spent several years studying and measuring their respective populations in an Alaskan fishing community. Some of their observations are recorded below.

Chemist: Seawater Salinity*/Temperature (°C) (Seasonal Average)

	Winter	Spring	Summer	Fall
Surface	0/−1°	25/1°	32/12°	15/2°
5 meters deep	0/−1°	29/5°	32/7°	26/7°
20 meters deep (ocean floor)	39/4°	32/5°	32/6°	34/5°

* Seawater salinity is measured in parts/thousand.

Biologist: Population Counts (Seasonal Average)

	Winter	Spring	Summer	Fall
Bay (free-swimming)				
Fur seals (number successfully hunted)	6.3	3.0	5.4	2.2
Salmon (tonnage caught)	0	122.5	1,152.6	4,259.5
Gray whales (number observed)	0	29.8	32.4	1.4
Bay (bottom-dwelling amphipods)				
Gammarus duebeni (sample count in one gallon of seawater)	50	25	15	60
Gammarus locusta (sample count in one gallon of seawater)	340	5	5	260
Land species				
Kodiak Bears (number observed)	0	4	11	21
Humans (number counted)	63	66	85	117

Doctor: Number of Medical Complaints (Seasonal Average)

	Winter	Spring	Summer	Fall
Dehydration-related illnesses	0.0	0.0	3.4	0.9
Bear attacks	0.0	0.2	1.1	2.2
Protein deficiency-related illnesses	10.4	4.1	1.0	0.0

1. The temperature and salinity readings at the ocean floor support which of the following conclusions?
   (A) *Gammarus duebeni* is sensitive to temperature changes.
   (B) *Gammarus locusta* is sensitive to temperature changes.
   (C) *Gammarus locusta* is sensitive to salinity changes.
   (D) Both species of *gammarus* are equally sensitive to salinity changes.

2. Which graph best expresses the relationship between the seasonal salmon catch and the incidence of protein deficiency-related illnesses in the doctor's data?

(F)

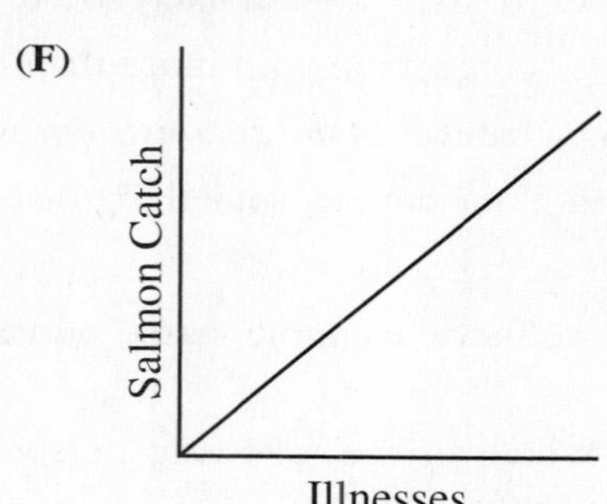

(G)

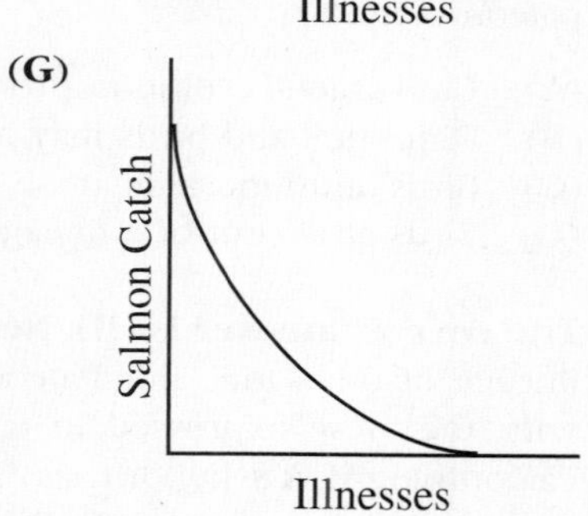

(H)

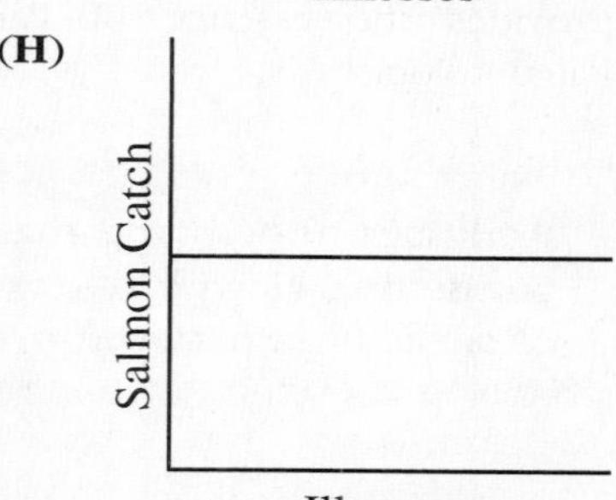

(J)

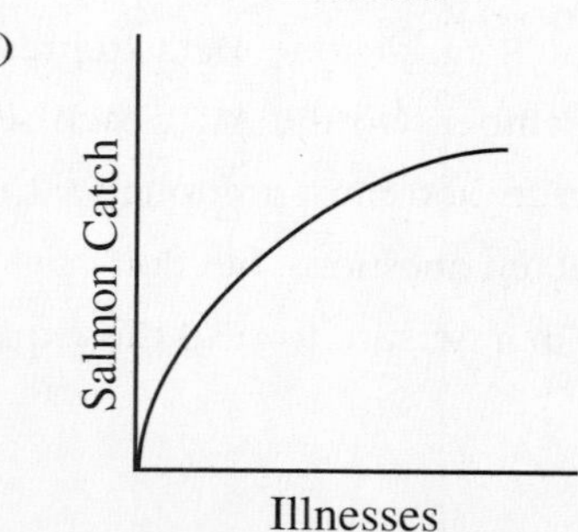

3. Which of the following supports the trend observed with respect to dehydration-related illnesses?

(A) In the fall, there is ample freshwater due to frequent rainy periods.
(B) In the winter, all freshwater reserves are frozen and cannot be accessed as drinking water.
(C) In the spring, not enough ice has melted to provide enough freshwater.
(D) In the summer, all of the ice that stores freshwater reserves melts, and the freshwater is lost to the ocean.

4. Which of the following statements is NOT supported by the evidence?

(F) Whales are most commonly seen in the area in the spring and summer.
(G) Summer and fall are the primary salmon fishing seasons.
(H) Spring and summer are the primary fur seal hunting seasons.
(J) Bear attacks are uncommon in the winter.

5. A biologist wants to isolate the effect on the bear population due to salmon levels from the effect due to human influences—in particular, the availability of an alternative food source in the village. What could the biologist do to help obtain the most accurate measure of the bear population when they have access only to their natural salmon food supply?

(A) Feed the bears salmon to replace their intake of village garbage and food
(B) Ensure that the village's garbage containers and food storage containers are kept locked
(C) Remove the salmon from the area and measure the effect on the bears
(D) Increase the frequency of the bear population survey from weekly to daily

Passage II

Although astronomers have a general outline for the steps that lead up to the formation of the wide-ranging interplanetary bodies called *comets*, there remain many questions as to where and exactly how comets were formed. The major points of dispute involve the location of their formation and the processes by which the comets were drawn into the Oort Cloud, becoming permanent members of our Solar System. Three astronomers describe their views on this process.

Astronomer 1

The flattened, rotating disk of the nebula* out of which our Sun and its companion planets were formed is the ideal place for comets to have been born. The long, slow collapse of a nebula that evolved into a planetary system included the type of compression that would facilitate the accretion of the key specks of matter into comet pellets. At a certain concentration level, these pellets began to clump into cometesimals and later aggregated into larger bodies. When our Solar System was formed, the bodies that formed in the outskirts became the population of comets known as the Oort Cloud. Those comets that formed among the planets likely collided with the giant members of the Sun's family, coalescing into them. There is sufficient evidence of significant disturbance among the outer giant planets and their companion satellites in the early solar system to support this theory.

Astronomer 2

We may reasonably suspect that the nebula out of which our Sun formed was at least twice the mass of the Sun at its current stage. We believe that the processes that formed the inner Solar System worked rapidly and were completed within 100,000 years. The remaining, less thoroughly coalesced matter was blown into the outer regions of the infant Solar System. The larger masses eventually became the four outer gas giants: Jupiter, Saturn, Uranus, and Neptune. The smaller masses were thrown much farther, forming the Oort Cloud. There, so distant from the gravitational influence of their parent sun, they were much more subject to the random forces of other nearby stars. Some of them are pushed in towards us, making their periodic and sometimes spectacular visits; others are pushed out to wander unseen in the vast galaxy.

Astronomer 3

The interstellar clouds out of which stars are formed are more vast, cold, and formless than can easily be imagined. In the absence of evidence that all the members of the Solar System arose out of the same nebula, it is difficult to explain the birth of the wandering comets. The most likely scenario based on the actual evidence available is that icy grains of matter in these vast gas-molecular clouds slowly grew by aggregation as they wandered in cold, dark space. Eventually, the masses would grow large enough to be deemed cometary. When the Sun compressed and ignited, it possessed enough gravity to capture a large number of these cometary masses, forming a captive population of comets now orbiting far beyond the realm of the other solar companions.

* A nebula is a vast cloud of interstellar gas and dust.

6. Which of the following statements about the formation of comets would be most consistent with the views of Astronomer 1, but not with the views of Astronomer 2?

(F) Gravity from other stars is a crucial factor in the birth of comets.
(G) Comets were not originally members of our Solar System.
(H) The Sun, planets, and comets formed out of the same nebula.
(J) Comets previously existed in the same region as planets.

7. Astronomer 2 would most likely criticize the theory of Astronomer 3 by saying that

(A) evidence shows that the formation of comets occurred outside our Solar System.
(B) Astronomer 3 ignores the influence of forces from other stars.
(C) the formation of the Sun occurred too rapidly to account for the formation of comets.
(D) there is no evidence that comets formed out of a different nebula than the Sun and planets did.

8. Which of the following is the most reasonable conclusion based on the theory of Astronomer 2?

(F) The combined gravitational force of our Solar System's planets is at least as strong as that of our Sun.
(G) The outer planets and their companions experienced violent collisions during their formative stages.
(H) The comets were not originally members of our Solar System.
(J) The time needed to complete the formation of the outer regions of the Solar System was greater than for the inner Solar System.

9. The fact that sometimes comets nearly collide with Earth

(A) lends greater support to the theory of Astronomer 1 than to the theories of Astronomers 2 or 3.
(B) lends greater support to the theory of Astronomer 3 than to the theories of Astronomers 1 or 2.
(C) lends equal support to the theories of all three astronomers.
(D) lends equal support to the theories of Astronomers 1and 2, but less support to the theory of Astronomer 3.

10. The theory of Astronomer 1 does not conflict with the theories of either Astronomer 2 or Astronomer 3 regarding

(F) the formation of comets outside our Solar System.
(G) the role of the Sun or other stars influencing the orbit of comets.
(H) the quickness with which the nebula would have collapsed to form comets.
(J) the evidence of the origin of comets within our Solar System.

ANSWERS AND EXPLANATIONS

Passage I

1. **The correct answer is (C).** The number of *gammarus locusta* changes most drastically as salinity changes at the ocean floor.

2. **The correct answer is (G).** When the salmon catch is high, the number of protein deficiency-related illnesses is low, and when the salmon catch is low, the number of protein deficiency-related illnesses is high.

3. **The correct answer is (D).** This is the only answer that is consistent with the number of illnesses recorded.

4. **The correct answer is (H).** There is no primary season for fur seal hunting, since they seem to be caught at fluctuating levels throughout the year.

5. **The correct answer is (B).** This would force the bears to depend upon their natural food supply and not rely on the food from the village.

Passage II

6. **The correct answer is (J).** Astronomer 1's theory calls for the existence of comets in the region occupied by planets, whereas Astronomer 2's theory allows for comets *beyond* the region of the planets as well. Choice (F) is consistent with Astronomer 2's theory and not with Astronomer 1's theory. Choice (G) is inconsistent with both theories, while choice (H) is consistent with both theories.

7. **The correct answer is (B).** This is an Assumption question, even though the word *assumption* does not appear in the question stem. Astronomer 3 assumes that our star is the only one whose gravitational force influences the motion of the comets in the Oort Cloud—whereas Astronomer 2 acknowledges that other stars might very well influence this motion as well. Choice (A) indicates a belief that Astronomer 3 holds and therefore makes no sense as a criticism of it. Choice (C), if true, would undermine Astronomer 2's own theory, which holds that the rapid formation of the Sun was part of the process that led to the formation of comets. Choice (D) points out a weakness in the theories of both Astronomers 2 and 3—namely, that there is no firm evidence proving either theory.

8. **The correct answer is (J).** Astronomer 2 describes how the inner solar system formed rapidly and the ignition of the Sun blew lighter elements out to form the outer Solar System. If this description is accurate, then there must have been a difference in the time of formation for these two regions. Choice (F) is an overstatement: Although Astronomer 2's theory depends on gravitational influences of celestial bodies other than our Sun, it does *not* depend on those influences being at least as strong as that of the Sun—only on their being *some* influence. Choice (G) describes an aspect of the theory of Astronomer 1 (not Astronomer 2). Choice (H) describes an aspect of the theory of Astronomer 3 (not Astronomer 2).

9. **The correct answer is (C).** This fact is merely evidence that comets exist in our Solar System and sometimes travel toward the inner part of the system. The three theories have to do with their origins.

10. **The correct answer is (G).** Astronomer 1 does not comment on the effect that the Sun or other stars have on comets; hence, Astronomer 1 would have no conflict with either Astronomer 2 or Astronomer 3 on this point. Choice (F) is wrong because Astronomer 3's theory describes the formation of comets outside our Solar System, whereas the theories of the other two astronomers describe their formation only within our Solar System. Choice (H) is wrong because Astronomer 1 believes the collapse to have been slow, while Astronomer 2 believes it to have been rapid. Choice (J) is wrong because Astronomer 1 claims that planetary disturbances are evidence that comets formed in our Solar System, while Astronomer 3 seems to deny the existence of any evidence that comets formed from the same nebula as did the planets of our Solar System.

PART VI

THE BRAINIAC CHALLENGE

CHALLENGE 1

English Questions

Directions: This challenge consists of two passages in which particular words or phrases are underlined and numbered. Alongside the passage, you will see alternative words and phrases that could be substituted for the underlined portions. Select the alternative that expresses the idea most clearly and correctly or that best fits the style and tone of the entire passage. If the original version is best, select "No Change."

The challenge also includes questions about entire paragraphs and the passage as a whole. These questions are identified by a number in a box.

After you select the correct answer for each question, mark your answer in the book or on a separate sheet of paper.

Questions 1–30

Passage I

The Poetry of Economics

"The poetry of economics?" a reader might ask. "How can 'the dismal science' be associated with the subtlety and creativity of poetry?" You're (1) skepticism is understandable, and (2) perhaps a story from an economist's life can sketch the poetry of economics at work.

Shortly after the Second World War, the agricultural economist Theodore Schultz, later to win a Nobel Prize, spent a term based at Auburn University in Alabama, during which he (3) interviewed farmers in the neighborhood. One day he interviewed an old and poor farm couple and he was struck (4) by how contented they seemed. He asked them why they were so contented, even though they were very poor. Their response was that he was wrong—that they were rich, not poor. They explained to the professor that they had used their farm to educate four children through college, remaking (5) fertile land and well-stocked pens into knowledge of law and Latin.

The parents told Schultz that this sort of physical capital, that economists would think they understand, (6) is in some sense just like the human capital of education. The children now owned it, and so the parents did, too. (7)

Once it had been rail fences and hog pens and mules. Now it was in the children's brains, this human capital. The farm couple was indeed rich. The average economist (8) was willing to accept the discovery of human capital as soon as he understood it, which is in fact how many scientific and scholarly discoveries get received. It was an argument in a metaphor (or, if you like, an analogy, a simile, a model). A hog pen, Schultz would say to another economist, is "just like" Latin 101.

The other economist would have to admit that there was something to it. (9) The hog pen, as well as the Latin instruction, are (10) paid for by saving. As economists put it, (11) both are valuable assets for earning income, understanding income to mean "a stream of satisfaction." Year after year, the hog pen and the Latin cause (12) satisfaction to stream out just as (13) water from a dam. Both last a long time, but finally wear out—when the pen falls down and the Latin-learned brain dies.

And the one piece of "capital" can be made into the other. An educated farmer, because of his agricultural degree (14) from Auburn, can get a bank loan to build a hog pen; and when his children grow up he can sell off the part of the farm with the hog pen to pay for another term for Junior and Sis up at Auburn, too. [15]

1. (A) NO CHANGE
   (B) Your
   (C) A reader's
   (D) OMIT the underlined portion (begin the sentence with *Skepticism*)

2. (F) NO CHANGE
   (G) but
   (H) therefore
   (J) and so

3. (A) NO CHANGE
   (B) Alabama, during the time when he
   (C) Alabama, near where he
   (D) Alabama, having

4. (F) NO CHANGE
   (G) couple who struck him
   (H) couple, and he was struck
   (J) couple about whom he was struck

5. (A) NO CHANGE
   (B) making
   (C) as well as to make
   (D) in order to make

6. (F) NO CHANGE
   (G) understood by economists, or so they think
   (H) which economists only think they understand
   (J) OMIT the underlined portion

7. (A) NO CHANGE
   (B) as did the parents.
   (C) as well as the parents.
   (D) and the parents also did.

8. (F) NO CHANGE
   (G) (Begin new paragraph) The
   (H) (Begin new paragraph) Yet the
   (J) (Do NOT begin new paragraph) Yet the

9. (A) NO CHANGE
   (B) what he would say
   (C) this argument
   (D) think about

10. (F) NO CHANGE
    (G) are both
    (H) are each
    (J) is

11. Which of the following is the best suggestion for the underlined portion, disregarding punctuation and case?

(A) NO CHANGE
(B) Move the underlined portion to the end of the sentence
(C) Reposition the underlined portion between *income* and *understanding*
(D) OMIT the underlined portion

12. (F) NO CHANGE
(G) result in
(H) will cause
(J) are responsible for

13. (A) NO CHANGE
(B) just as does
(C) similar to
(D) like

14. (F) NO CHANGE
(G) due to his obtaining a degree in agriculture
(H) having obtained a degree in agriculture
(J) by getting a degree in agriculture

15. The writer wants to link the passage's opening and conclusion. If inserted at the end of the passage, which of the following sentences best achieves this effect?

(A) The wisdom of the farmer is greater, in the end, than the wisdom of the economics professor.
(B) Human capital is a concept based on a metaphor—and metaphor is the essential tool of poetry.
(C) Thus, education is the most valuable form of human capital, even for the farmer.
(D) Physical capital and human capital are ultimately not so different after all.

Passage II

The Devastation of El Niño

[1]

Throughout 1998, it seemed that, whenever anything went wrong, someone could be heard exclaiming, "Blame it on El Niño!" This unusually powerful weather system received so much attention in the news media around the world that El Niño came to seem like a good (16) scapegoat for almost any mishap. [17]

[2]

Every year, in late December, oceanic winds from the West tend to shift, causing warm water from the western Pacific to move towards South America, which heats (18) the waters along its coast. The term *El Niño* refers to these hot currents and the weather disturbances they cause. Usually, the temperature of the water increases for six months and then returns to normal. But in 1998, the wind shifts began around April and didn't actually peak until nine months later in (19) January. Because the wind shifts lasted substantially longer than usual, (20) the resulting storms and other climatic changes produced widespread flooding and erosion. And, among other problems, these changes devastated Peru's wildlife populations, especially sea life.

[3]

When El Niño hit, vast schools of small fish, such as anchovies and sardines, sought cooler temperatures down in further depths of the Pacific than the levels where they are usually found. While this protected the fish from the unseasonable weather conditions, their predators were unable to reach them at these new, greater depths. [22]

21

[4]

Aquatic mammals were hit especially hard. Along one Peruvian beach, the Punta San Juan, where a whole season's pup production of fur seals and sea lions died, as well as thousands of juveniles and breeding adults. By May 13, 1998, only 15 fur seals were counted, when there are usually hundreds. Yet, only 1,500 sea lions were found in an area that usually houses 8,000.

23 24 25

[5]

The Humboldt penguins also faced population losses due to El Niño. These penguins had normally bred twice a year; but in 1998, their second breeding ground was flooded by 52 consecutive hours of rain. Only 50 of the 3,500 to 5,000 penguins that usually lay eggs were able to do so.

26 27

[6]

Because Peru is so close in distance to the Pacific regions where the wind shifts and water warming of El Niño originate, it experiences the harshest effects of this unpredictable weather phenomenon. [29] 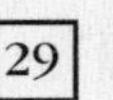

28

16. (F) NO CHANGE
(G) to be a
(H) as if it were a
(J) as a

17. Which of the following provides the most appropriate transition between the first and second paragraphs?

(A) Yet the underlying meteorological causes of El Niño are readily explainable.
(B) Unfortunately, the problems it really caused, especially for creatures living on the Pacific coast of Peru, were all too real.
(C) People all along the coast of North and South America knew all too well, however, that El Niño was responsible only for certain natural disturbances.
(D) But the real effects of El Niño occurred only around Christmas time.

18. (F) NO CHANGE
(G) then heating
(H) the warm water then heating
(J) heating

19. (A) NO CHANGE
(B) had passed—during
(C) later, in
(D) later; during the month of

20. Which of the following is the best proposal for the underlined portion?

(F) NO CHANGE
(G) Move the underlined portion to the end of the previous sentence (following *January*)
(H) Move the underlined portion to the end of the sentence (following *erosion*)
(J) OMIT the underlined portion

21. (A) NO CHANGE
(B) further down, in the
(C) further down in the
(D) in the furthest

22. The writer is considering adding the following sentence at this point in the passage:

"Thus, the predators suddenly lost their regular food supply."

Would this sentence be a relevant and appropriate addition to the passage, and why?

(F) Yes, because it explains why the small fish that were prey survived El Niño while their predators did not.
(G) Yes, because it helps provide support for a key point that the writer makes in the previous paragraph.
(H) No, because the paragraph is concerned primarily with El Niño's impact on small fish such as anchovies and sardines, not on their predators.
(J) No, because the sentence provides an awkward transition to the subject of the next paragraph.

23. (A) NO CHANGE
(B) hard along
(C) hard, especially along
(D) hard—for instance, along

24. (F) NO CHANGE
(G) both juveniles and
(H) juvenile and
(J) juveniles, along with

25. (A) NO CHANGE
(B) Besides
(C) Furthermore
(D) Similarly

26. (F) NO CHANGE
(G) normally breed
(H) breed, normally
(J) used to breed

27. (A) NO CHANGE
(B) capable of this
(C) able to lay them
(D) to

28. (F) NO CHANGE
(G) very close in distance
(H) not distant
(J) so close

29. Which of the following sentences, if added here, would provide the most effective concluding sentence for the passage?

(A) Two or three more such years may spell an end to many species of wildlife that once thrived on Peruvian shores.
(B) Fortunately, other countries in South America do not suffer the ill effects of El Niño to the same extent as does Peru.
(C) Government officials in Peru are currently at work to develop plans for dealing with the problems caused by El Niño the next time it strikes.
(D) However, aid from foreign countries has helped Peru save certain endangered species that El Niño decimated.

30. Suppose the writer is considering eliminating one of the passage's six paragraphs. Which of the following responses would be the best advice?

(F) Eliminate Paragraph 1, because it is merely introductory in nature.
(G) Eliminate Paragraph 3, because the passage already provides sufficient examples of the destructive power of El Niño.
(H) Eliminate Paragraph 4, because Paragraph 5 makes clear enough that the wildlife of Peru are especially hard hit by El Niño.
(J) Do not eliminate any paragraph; all six are essential for a cohesive, unified passage.

ANSWERS AND EXPLANATIONS

Passage I

1. **The correct answer is (B).** In the original version, "you're," a contraction of "you are," makes no sense in context. The writer should have used the possessive pronoun "your" instead. Choice (C) is not the best choice because the paragraph's first sentence already refers to "a reader." From that point forward, it would be more appropriate to refer specifically to "the reader." Similarly, choice (D) provides an option that is too general in its use of "skepticism." The more specific phrase "such skepticism" would work better here.

2. **The correct answer is (J).** The second part of the sentence (following the comma) provides a conclusion based on the first part. The underlined portion fails to provide this logical connection between them. Choices (H) and (J) each provide an appropriate transition from a premise to a conclusion. Choice (H), however, results in a run-on sentence. Hence, (J) is the better option.

3. **The correct answer is (A).** The noun "term" is the intended antecedent of the phrase "during which." (Schultz interviewed farmers *during a term* at Auburn.) Despite two intervening nouns, "Auburn University" and "Alabama," the reference is clear enough. Choice (B) clarifies a modifier-antecedent relationship that doesn't require clarification; the result is unnecessarily wordy. Choice (C) is wordy and confusing; what's more, it distorts the sentence's meaning. As for choice (D), the use of the past perfect tense (*having interviewed*) inappropriately implies that the interviews took place *before* Schultz's term.

4. **The correct answer is (H).** The original version connects two independent clauses (each of which can stand alone as a complete sentence) with "and," but omits a punctuation mark, which is needed in this situation. Choice (H) corrects the error. Choice (G) attempts to correct the error by creating a subordinate clause, but the result is the improper idiom "struck him by how." (In the active voice, the word "by" should be omitted.) Choice (J) is wordy and awkward.

5. **The correct answer is (A).** It's idiomatic to say that you are *remaking* (which means "transforming") one thing *into* another, rather than *making* one thing *into* another. Hence, the original version is correct, and all three alternatives (each of which use "making") are incorrect.

6. **The correct answer is (H).** The original version uses the word "that" where "which" should be used. Also, "would" is unnecessary and should be omitted. Choice (H) fixes both problems. What's more, the addition of the word "only" enhances the sentence's rhetorical effectiveness. (It helps make the writer's implicit point that economists don't actually understand the concept—they *only* think they do.) Choice (G) is very awkward. As for choice (J), it would be wrong to delete the phrase altogether, since it ties into one of the passage's main ideas: how Schultz used a poetic metaphor to explain a new economic idea through analogy with an old, familiar idea.

7. **The correct answer is (B).** The original version is redundant; the words "too" and "so" convey the same idea. Either one or the other should be omitted, or the underlined portion should be reworked in some other way. Choice (B) solves the redundancy problem by replacing the underlined portion with a clear, idiomatic phrase. Choice (C) provides a phrase that nonsensically suggests that the children owned their parents. Choice (D) is wordy and awkward; choice (B) is more concise and clear.

8. **The correct answer is (G).** It makes sense to begin a new paragraph here, since the specific topic has shifted. The previous paragraph summarizes the old farm couple's concept of "human capital"; the new paragraph, which would begin at this point, discusses how metaphors can help to explain new theoretical concepts. Choice (H) is wrong because the word "yet," like the words "but" and "however," signals that the idea following it is in opposition to the one preceding it. In this case, however, the two ideas are similar.

9. **The correct answer is (C).** It would make sense for the pronoun "it" to refer to either "an argument" or "a metaphor." However, the intervening sentence ("A hog pen, . . .") obscures the reference. Choice (C) solves the problem by replacing the pronoun with one of the possible nouns to which it might appropriately refer. Choice (B) is awkward, and choice (D) makes no sense in context.

10. **The correct answer is (J).** Notice the modifying clause ("as well as . . .") set off by commas. The sentence should be grammatically correct even if that clause is omitted. But it isn't—the singular subject "hog pen" does not agree with the plural verb "are." Only (J) corrects this grammatical error.

11. **The correct answer is (B).** The idiomatic phrase "As . . . puts it" should be used to refer to a precise quote. In this sentence, the quote is "stream of satisfaction." Moving the underlined portion to the

end of the sentence makes this reference clearer. Moving the portion as suggested in choice (C) would only further confuse the reference. Omitting the underlined portion, as choice (D) suggests, renders the source of the quote unclear.

12. **The correct answer is (F).** It is idiomatic to say that one thing *causes* another *to do something*. And, the word "cause" makes sense in this context, since it is the hog pen and the Latin instruction that are responsible for satisfaction streaming out. The phrase in (H) employs the future tense, which inappropriately limits the idea to the future. In order for "result in," choice (G), to be correct, the infinitive "to stream" must be replaced with the gerund "streaming." (It is idiomatic to say "result in . . . streaming"—not "result in . . . to stream."). Choice (J) is wrong for the same reason as (H).

13. **The correct answer is (D).** The economist (through the writer's essay) is attempting to draw an analogy between two similar things: a stream of satisfaction and a stream of water. The word "like" is appropriate for an analogy. You can eliminate choice (A) because the word "as," used alone here, is appropriate for a simile, not an analogy. Choice (B) is wordy and awkward. Although choice (C) fixes the word-choice problem, the phrase "stream out similar to water . . ." is awkward. Choice (D) makes the point more concisely and clearly.

14. **The correct answer is (H).** In the original version, "agricultural degree" is idiomatically improper. The phrase suggests nonsensically that the degree *itself* was agricultural rather than *in the academic field of* agriculture. (Had the writer used "agriculture" instead, the original version would have been the best of the four options.) Choices (G) and (J) are both idiomatic and grammatically correct. However, (G) is a bit wordy and awkward compared with (H). As for (J), the word "getting" is a bit too colloquial and informal for this passage. What's more, choice (J) creates ambiguity as to whether the farmer is considered "educated" because of the degree *or*, once already educated, the farmer can get the degree and, in turn, the bank loan.

15. **The correct answer is (B).** This sentence serves the stated purpose best because it summarizes the main point of the passage by linking its opening and closing paragraphs, using the concept of "the poetry of economics" as the connecting theme.

Passage II

16. **The correct answer is (F).** It's idiomatic to say that something "seems like" something else, rather than "seems as" something else. Hence, the original version is correct, and (J) is incorrect. Choices (G) and (H) are both wordy and awkward.

17. **The correct answer is (B).** The first paragraph speaks in a somewhat light-hearted way about how people blamed all kinds of problems on El Niño, while the second paragraph begins to describe the very serious problems El Niño really caused, particularly for Peruvian sea life. A transitional sentence is needed to help the reader anticipate the shift in tone and treatment. Choice (B) provides just such a sentence.

18. **The correct answer is (J).** In the original version, the relative pronoun "which" seems to refer to South America. Of course, it is warm water from the western Pacific, *not* South America that heats the waters along South America's coast. Choice (J) fixes this confusing pronoun reference by omitting the pronoun. The phrase in choice (G) incorrectly suggests that oceanic winds, rather than water, heat the waters along South America's coast. Choice (H) is the "runner-up", but (J) is more concise and clear.

19. **The correct answer is (C).** The modifying phrase "in January" is intended to specify what month is "nine months later." To make this intention clear, the phrase should be set off by either a dash or a comma, as in choice (C). The "runner-up," choice (B), also provides appropriate punctuation, and "during January" is idiomatically proper. However, (C) is clearer and more concise than (B). Choice (D) is wrong for two reasons. First, the use of a semicolon is inappropriate here because what follows cannot stand alone as a sentence. Second, "the month of" makes for an unnecessarily wordy phrase and can simply be omitted.

20. **The correct answer is (J).** The previous sentence already makes clear that the wind shifts lasted substantially longer than usual. The rhetorical use of the word "actually" helps to make that point. Hence, the underlined portion is unnecessary. The word "resulting" (in the next sentence) suffices to make the logical connection between the two sentences.

21. **The correct answer is (C).** It is idiomatic to say "further down . . . than," as in choice (C). By inserting a comma, choice (B) confuses the meaning of the sentence. Choice (D) is wrong because it uses the superlative "furthest" (instead of the comparative "further") in a sentence that seeks to compare *only two* things.

22. **The correct answer is (G).** At the end of Paragraph 2, the writer asserts that El Niño's impact on sea life was especially devastating. The next paragraph, and, in fact, the rest of the passage, is devoted to supporting this assertion. The proposed sentence is not only relevant to the writer's main purpose but also completes the line of reasoning in the previous two sentences. Choice (F) is wrong because the reason that these small fish survived is not relevant to the writer's primary concern, as just described. Choice (H) gets the paragraph's primary concern backwards. As for (J), the next paragraph shifts the focus to aquatic animals. The sentence that precedes the proposed one provides no information that anticipates, or transitions to, that new topic. Thus, adding the proposed sentence doesn't effect the transition in any way.

23. **The correct answer is (D).** The original version results in a sentence fragment (beginning with "Along"). Choice (D) solves the problem by replacing the period with a dash. (D) also adds "for instance," which is an effective way to introduce material that supports the point just made. Choice (B) creates a complete sentence by omitting the period between "hard" and "Along"—but by doing so, implies that a previous portion of the passage already discussed the impact of El Niño on aquatic mammals (which is not the case). Choice (C) results in the awkward "especially hard, especially along."

24. **The correct answer is (F).** The original version is clear, concise, and grammatically correct. Choice (G) results in the confusing and ambiguous phrase "thousands of both juveniles . . . ." Choice (H) transforms the noun "juveniles" into the adjective "juvenile"; in the grammatical context of the sentence, the result is a nonsensical, oxymoronic reference to "juvenile adults." Choice (J) unjustifiably alters the intended meaning of the sentence, in which "thousands" should refer to the aggregate number of juveniles and breeding adults, not to the number of juveniles only.

25. **The correct answer is (D).** The word "Yet"—like *but* and *however*—should be used to signal opposing ideas. But the preceding sentence describes a situation *similar to* the one described in the paragraph's final sentence. Hence, "yet" is entirely inappropriate in context. The word "similarly," choice (D), is the most rhetorically appropriate of the four options.

26. **The correct answer is (G).** The original version uses the past perfect tense, which is appropriate to describe a condition that might not apply presently or in the future. But the writer is discussing only one year, 1998, and as an exception to what's normal. Hence, choice (G) provides a more appropriate phrase, using the present tense. Choice (H) provides a *very* awkward, stilted way of asserting that the Humboldt penguins normally breed twice a year. Choice (J) uses the past tense and is therefore wrong for essentially the same reason as the original version.

27. **The correct answer is (A).** The original wording is a proper idiom. Choice (B) is vague, what does "this" refer to? Choice (C) is wordy and repetitive. Choice (D) is the most concise one, but therein lies the problem: it leaves the reader wondering, "to *what*?"

28. **The correct answer is (J).** The phrase "in distance" is redundant, since "close" obviously refers to distance; thus, "in distance" should be eliminated. Choice (G) fails to eliminate the redundancy. Choice (H) eliminates the redundancy, but does not make the writer's point as effectively as (J).

29. **The correct answer is (A).** This sentence neatly ties together the various destructive effects of El Niño on wildlife living on the shores of Peru. None of the other options accomplish what (A) does. What's more, each one introduces new information—hardly an apt final sentence for the passage.

30. **The correct answer is (F).** The passage talks about how El Niño affects the climate and wildlife, especially of Peru. Paragraph 1 contains no information that is needed to understand the passage's concepts or its purpose. Paragraph 3 is necessary for the reader to understand how El Niño affects the Peruvian mammals by reducing the availability of their food. Paragraph 4 is necessary if the reader is to understand how El Niño affected the seals and sea lions in Peru.

CHALLENGE 2

Mathematics Questions

Directions: Solve each problem, then mark the letter corresponding to the correct answer either in your book or on a separate sheet of scrap paper.

Be careful not to spend too much time on any one question. Instead, solve as many problems as possible, and then use the remaining time to return to the questions you were unable to answer at first.

You may use a calculator for any problem on this challenge. However, some problems can best be solved without the use of a calculator.

Note: Unless otherwise stated, you can assume that

- Diagrams that accompany problems are not necessarily drawn to scale
- All figures lie in the same plane
- The word "line" refers to a straight line (and lines that appear straight are straight)
- The word "average" refers to arithmetic mean

Questions 1–30

1. P percent of $20\sqrt{3}$ is 3. $P = ?$

(A) $\sqrt{3}$

(B) 3

(C) $5\sqrt{3}$

(D) $10\sqrt{3}$

(E) 20

2. A field can be plowed by 8 machines in 6 hours. If 3 of the machines are broken and cannot be used, how many hours will it take to plow the field?

(F) $12\frac{4}{5}$

(G) $11\frac{1}{2}$

(H) $10\frac{3}{4}$

(J) $9\frac{3}{5}$

(K) $8\frac{2}{3}$

3. 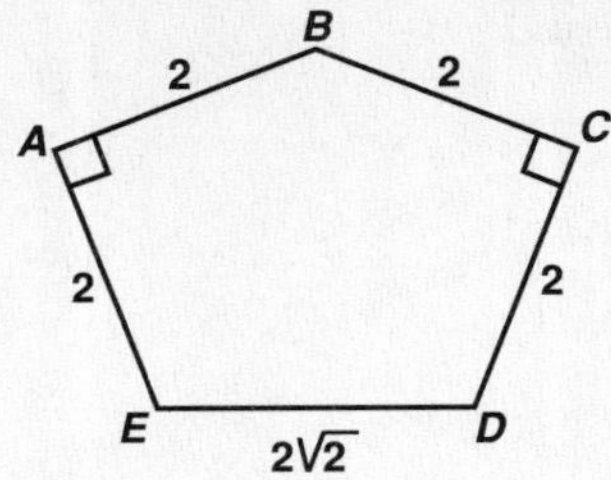

What is the area of polygon *ABCDE* shown above?

(A) $4 + 2\sqrt{3}$
(B) $3 + 3\sqrt{2}$
(C) $6\sqrt{3}$
(D) $2 + 6\sqrt{2}$
(E) $8\sqrt{2}$

4. If x and y are negative integers, and if $x - y = 1$, what is the least possible value of xy?

(F) -2
(G) -1
(H) 0
(J) 1
(K) 2

5. 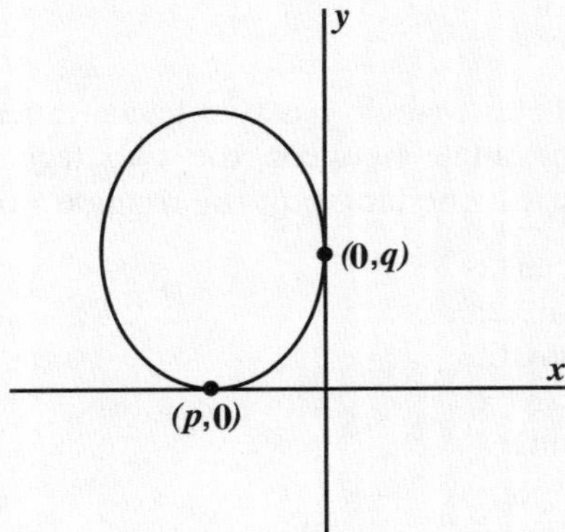

In the standard (x,y) coordinate plane, an ellipse is tangent to the x-axis and the y-axis, as shown in the graph. If $|p| < q$, then which of the following is the equation of the ellipse?

(A) $\frac{(x-q)^2}{4q^2} + \frac{(y-p)^2}{4p^2} = 1$

(B) $\frac{(x+p)^2}{p^2} + \frac{(y-q)^2}{q^2} = 1$

(C) $\frac{(x-p)^2}{p^2} + \frac{(y-q)^2}{q^2} = 1$

(D) $\frac{(x-p)^2}{2p^2} + \frac{(y-q)^2}{2q^2} = 1$

(D) $\frac{(x-p)^2}{q^2} + \frac{(y-q)^2}{p^2} = 1$

6. If $m = 121 - 5k$, and m is divisible by 3, which of the following could be true?

I. m is odd
II. m is even
III. k is divisible by 3

(F) I only
(G) II only
(H) I and II only
(J) II and III only
(K) I, II, and III

7. What is the perimeter of a rectangle that is three times as long as it is wide and has the same area as a circle of circumference 6?

(A) $\frac{8\sqrt{3\pi}}{\pi}$

(B) $\frac{8\sqrt{\pi}}{3}$

(C) $4\sqrt{3\pi}$
(D) $8\sqrt{\pi}$
(E) $8\sqrt{3\pi}$

8. A bag contains six numbered slips of paper. Four of the slips are numbered zero (0), and the other two are not. If two slips are drawn at random from the bag, what is the probability that the product of the two numbers is NOT zero?

(F) $\frac{1}{15}$

(G) $\frac{1}{12}$

(H) $\frac{2}{15}$

(J) $\frac{1}{6}$

(K) $\frac{1}{3}$

9. If a fleet of m buses uses g gallons of gasoline every two days, how many gallons of gasoline will be used by four buses every five days?

(A) $\frac{10g}{m}$

(B) $10gm$

(C) $\frac{10m}{g}$

(D) $\frac{20g}{m}$

(E) $\frac{5g}{4m}$

10.

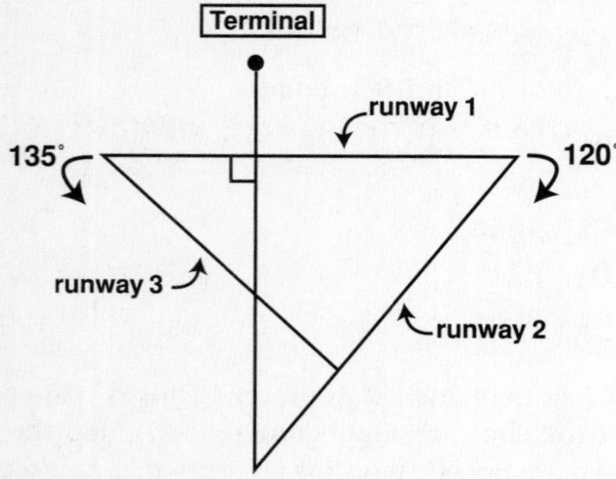

As shown in the figure above, from runway 1, airplanes must turn either 120° to the right onto runway 2 or 135° to the left onto runway 3. Which of the following does NOT indicate a complete turn from one runway to another?

(F) 105°
(G) 75°
(H) 60°
(J) 55°
(K) 30°

11. If $A = \begin{pmatrix} 2 & -1 \\ 3 & -2 \end{pmatrix}$ and $B = \begin{pmatrix} 0 & 3 & 2 \\ 1 & -2 & -1 \end{pmatrix}$, then $2AB = ?$

(A) $\begin{pmatrix} 0 & 6 & -10 \\ 2 & -12 & 4 \end{pmatrix}$

(B) $\begin{pmatrix} -2 & 6 & 12 \\ -4 & 26 & 16 \end{pmatrix}$

(C) $\begin{pmatrix} -2 & 16 & 10 \\ -4 & 10 & 0 \end{pmatrix}$

(D) $\begin{pmatrix} -2 & 16 & 10 \\ -4 & 26 & 16 \end{pmatrix}$

(E) $\begin{pmatrix} -2 & 8 & 14 \\ 2 & 16 & -8 \end{pmatrix}$

12. If $f(x) = 6^x$ and $g(x) = \log_6 x$, which of the following expressions is equal to $f(2g(M))$?

(F) $2M$
(G) 6^M
(H) M^6
(J) M^2
(K) 6^{2M}

13. An isosceles triangle has two legs at a length of 3 feet. The angle between the two legs measures 32°. What is the length of the triangle's third side?

(A) 3cos32°
(B) 3sin32°
(C) 3sin16°
(D) 6tan16°
(E) 6sin16°

14. If $r = \frac{3p + q}{2}$ and $s = p - q$, for which of the following values of p would $r^2 = s^2$?

(F) $\frac{1}{5}q$

(G) $10 - \frac{3}{2}q$

(H) $q - 1$

(J) $3q$

(K) $\frac{9}{2}q - 9$

15. The ratio of Elaine's weekly salary to Carl's weekly salary is 3:2. If Elaine receives a 20% raise and Carl receives a $200 raise, the ratio will change to 6:5. Elaine's current salary is

(A) $720
(B) $600
(C) $480
(D) $400
(E) $200

16.

In the figure above, the centers of all three circles lie on the same line. The radius of the middle-sized circle is twice that of the smallest circle. If the radius of the smallest circle is 1, what is the length of the boundary of the shaded region?

(F) 9
(G) 3π
(H) 12
(J) 6π
(K) 12π

17. In the standard (x,y) coordinate plane, point $(a,5)$ lies along a line of slope $\frac{1}{3}$ that passes through point $(2,-3)$. What is the value of a?

(A) 35
(B) 26
(C) 3
(D) -3
(E) -26

18. How many distinct triple-scoop ice cream cones, scoops stacked one atop another, can be created using at least one but not more than three ice-cream flavors, if each scoop contains only one flavor?

(F) 9
(G) 12
(H) 15
(J) 21
(K) 27

19. If $\frac{x}{y}$ is a negative integer, which of the following terms must also be a negative integer?

(A) $\frac{x^2}{y}$

(B) $-\frac{x^2}{y^2}$

(C) $\frac{x}{y^2}$

(D) $x + y$

(E) xy

20. If A and B are positive integers, and if the square root of $24AB$ is an integer, then which of the following CANNOT be true?

I. Both A and B are odd.
II. The square root of AB is an integer.
III. Both A and B are divisible by 6.

(F) I only
(G) II only
(H) III only
(J) I and II only
(K) I, II, and III

21. If the arithmetic mean (simple average) of four numbers is 4, and if the number 6 is added to these four numbers, by what percent has the arithmetic mean changed?

(A) 10%
(B) 20%
(C) 40%
(D) 50%
(E) 60%

22. How many gallons of milk that is 2% butterfat must be mixed with milk that is 3.5% butterfat to get 10 gallons that is 3% butterfat?

(F) 4

(G) $\frac{11}{3}$

(H) $\frac{7}{2}$

(J) $\frac{10}{3}$

(K) 3

23. 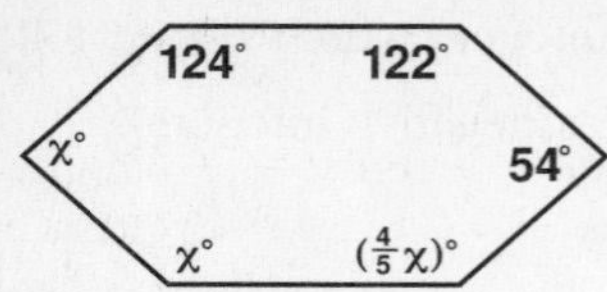

If two of the angles of the polygon shown above are congruent, what is the least possible sum of two of the polygon's angle measures?

(A) 162°
(B) 174°
(C) 176°
(D) 204°
(E) 216°

24. In a geometric series, each term is a constant multiple of the preceding one. If 4, x, and y are the first three terms in a geometric series, which of the following represents the fifth term in the series?

(F) $\frac{y^2}{4}$
(G) $\frac{64}{y^2}$
(H) $8y^2$
(J) $\frac{y^2}{16}$
(K) $\frac{2}{y^2}$

25. Which of the following is one root of the equation $x^2 + 13 = 4x$?

(A) $4 + i$
(B) $3 - 2i$
(C) $4 + 3i$
(D) $2 - 6i$
(E) $2 + 3i$

26. In the standard (x,y) coordinate plane, the graph of $y = 3\sin 3x$ contains all of the following (x,y) pairs EXCEPT

(F) $\left(\frac{4}{3}\pi, 0\right)$
(G) $\left(\frac{5}{6}\pi, 3\right)$
(H) $\left(\frac{1}{2}\pi, -3\right)$
(J) $\left(\frac{1}{4}\pi, \frac{3}{2}\right)$
(K) $\left(\frac{11}{6}\pi, -\frac{3}{2}\right)$

27. One marble is picked randomly from a bag containing one red marble and two green marbles. One marble is also picked randomly from another bag, which contains three red marbles and four blue marbles. What is the probability that neither marble picked is red?

(A) $\frac{10}{21}$
(B) $\frac{3}{7}$
(C) $\frac{8}{21}$
(D) $\frac{5}{14}$
(E) $\frac{1}{3}$

28. If $x = \log 2$, $y = \log 3$, and $z = \log 5$, then $\log\frac{5}{12} = ?$

(F) $z - x - 2y$
(G) $z + x - 2y$
(H) $z - x + 2y$
(J) $z + 2x - y$
(K) $z - 2x - y$

29. The sum of three consecutive even integers is added to the sum of three consecutive odd integers. If the sum of all six integers, each integer a positive number, is less than 30, the six integers must include each of the following EXCEPT

(A) 2
(B) 3
(C) 4
(D) 5
(E) 6

30. A closed rectangular box contains 384 cubic feet. If the box's height is two-thirds its length, and if the box's height is twice its width, what is the box's total surface area (which includes all six faces) in square feet?

(F) 176
(G) 192
(H) 248
(J) 264
(K) 352

ANSWERS AND EXPLANATIONS

1. **The correct answer is (C).** P percent means $\frac{P}{100}$. Hence, $\frac{P}{100} \times 20\sqrt{3} = 3$. To answer the question, solve for P:

$$\frac{P}{100} \times 20\sqrt{3} = 3$$

$$\frac{P\sqrt{3}}{5} = 3$$

$$P\sqrt{3} = 15$$

$$P = \frac{15}{\sqrt{3}} = \frac{15\sqrt{3}}{\sqrt{3}\sqrt{3}} = \frac{15\sqrt{3}}{3} = 5\sqrt{3}$$

2. **The correct answer is (J).** In this inverse-variation problem, the number of machines multiplied by the number of hours remains constant:

$$(8)(6) = (5)(x)$$

$$5x = 48$$

$$x = 9\frac{3}{5}$$

3. **The correct answer is (A).** Divide the polygon into three triangles as shown below. The area of each of the two outer triangles $= \frac{1}{2}bh = \frac{1}{2}(2)(2) = 2$. (Their combined area is 4.) Since the two outer triangles are both $1:1:\sqrt{2}$ right triangles, $BE = BD = 2\sqrt{2}$. Hence, the central triangle is equilateral. To calculate its area: $\frac{s^2\sqrt{3}}{4} = \frac{(2\sqrt{2})^2\sqrt{3}}{4} = \frac{8\sqrt{3}}{4} = 2\sqrt{3}$. Hence, the area of the polygon is $4 + 2\sqrt{3}$.

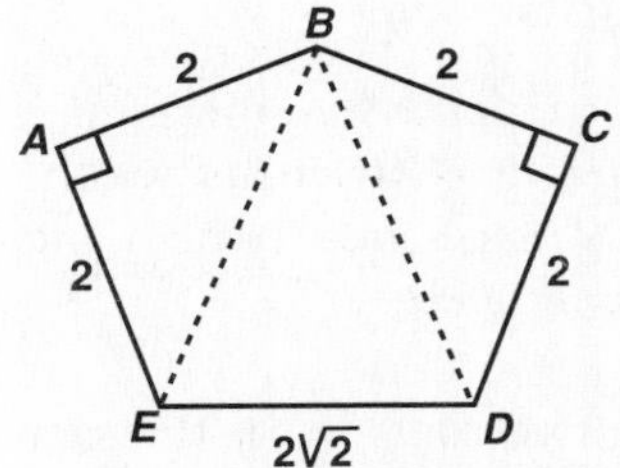

4. **The correct answer is (K).** Solve this problem using the rules for signs and with a bit of logical reasoning. Using negative integers approaching zero (0) will yield the least product. Start with -1, then decrease the values of x and y if necessary. The first two values that satisfy the equation are: $y = -2$, $x = -1$ $[-1 - (-2) = 1]$. Accordingly, $xy = 2$.

5. **The correct answer is (C).** The ellipse's center is at (p,q); hence, applying the standard form of the equation for an ellipse, in which the ellipse's center is at (h,k), $h = p$ and $k = q$. The length of the ellipse's x-axis is $-2p$, and the length of its y-axis is $2q$. Since $|p| < q$, the ellipse is vertically oriented. Accordingly, in the standard form of the equation for an ellipse, the larger denominator, in this case q^2, is under the variable y:

$$\frac{(x-p)^2}{p^2} + \frac{(y-q)^2}{q^2} = 1$$

6. **The correct answer is (H).** A number that is divisible by 3 could be either odd or even. For example, m could be 18 (even) or 21 (odd). Therefore, either statement I or statement II could be true. However, k cannot be divisible by 3, because 121 is not. (A number divisible by 3 subtracted from a number that is not yields a number that is not—for example, $14 - 6 = 8$.)

7. **The correct answer is (A).** A circle's circumference $= 2\pi r$. Given a circumference of 6, $r = \frac{3}{\pi}$. The area of a circle with this radius is $\pi\left(\frac{3}{\pi}\right)^2 = \frac{9}{\pi}$. Letting w equal the rectangle's width, its length is $3w$ and its area is $(w)(3w) = 3w^2$. Given the area of the circle equals that of the rectangle, $3w^2 = \frac{9}{\pi}$. In order to find the rectangle's perimeter, first solve for w:

$$3w^2 = \frac{9}{\pi}$$

$$w^2 = \frac{3}{\pi}$$

$$w = \sqrt{\frac{3}{\pi}} = \frac{\sqrt{3}}{\sqrt{\pi}}$$

The perimeter is $2l + 2w = 6w + 2w = 8w = \frac{8\sqrt{3}}{\sqrt{\pi}} = \frac{8\sqrt{3\pi}}{\pi}$.

8. **The correct answer is (F).** The probability of drawing a non-zero number on the first draw is 2 in 6, or $\frac{1}{3}$. In this event, 1 of the remaining 5 slips is non-zero, and hence the probability of drawing that slip is 1 in 5, or $\frac{1}{5}$. To calculate the probability of a non-zero product, multiply together the two individual probabilities you just calculated: $\frac{1}{3} \times \frac{1}{5} = \frac{1}{15}$.

9. **The correct answer is (A).** The surest way of handling this problem is to substitute simple numbers for g and m. If $g = 2$ and $m = 1$, then each bus uses 1 gallon of gasoline each day and, accordingly, 4 buses would use a total of 20 gallons every 5 days. Substituting the number 2 for g and 1 for m in choice (A) yields the result you're looking for: $\frac{10g}{m} = \frac{(10)(2)}{4} = 20$.

10. **The correct answer is (J).** The key to this problem is in determining the interior angles of the various triangles formed by the runways. The interior angle formed by the 120°-turn from runway 1 to 2 is 60° (a 180°-turn would reverse the airplane's direction). Similarly, the interior angle formed by the 135°-turn from runway 1 to 3 is 45° (180° − 135°). Two triangle "angle triplets" emerge: a 45°-45°-90° triplet and a 30°-60°-90° triplet, as shown in the figure below. Since the sum of any triangle's interior angles is 180°, the remaining angles can also be determined:

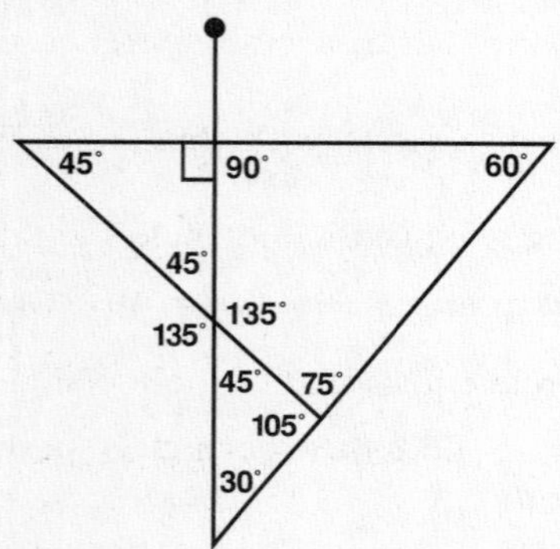

The only answer choice not appearing in the figure above is 55°.

11. **The correct answer is (D).** The number of columns in A equals the number of rows in B. Accordingly, to form product matrix AB, multiply each row of A by each column of B, arranging the six resulting entries in a 2-row, 3-column matrix as follows:

Column 1:

Row 1: (A row 1)(B col. 1) = (2)(0) + (−1)(1) = −1

Row 2: (A row 2)(B col. 1) = (3)(0) + (−2)(1) = −2

Column 2:

Row 1: (A row 1)(B col. 2) = (2)(3) + (−1)(−2) = 8

Row 2: (A row 2)(B col. 2) = (3)(3) + (−2)(−2) = 13

Column 3:

Row 1: (A row 1)(B col. 3) = (2)(2) + (−1)(−1) = 5

Row 2: (A row 2)(B col. 3) = (3)(2) + (−2)(−1) = 8

Matrix $AB = \begin{pmatrix} -1 & 8 & 5 \\ -2 & 13 & 8 \end{pmatrix}$. Accordingly, $2AB = \begin{pmatrix} -2 & 16 & 10 \\ -4 & 26 & 16 \end{pmatrix}$

12. **The correct answer is (J).** $2g(M) = 2\log_6 M = \log_6 M^2$. Hence, $f(2g(M)) = M^2$.

13. **The correct answer is (E).** As you can see from the figure below, letting x = half the length of the base, $\sin 16° = \frac{x}{3}$; $x = 3\sin 16°$; and the length of the entire base = $6\sin 16°$.

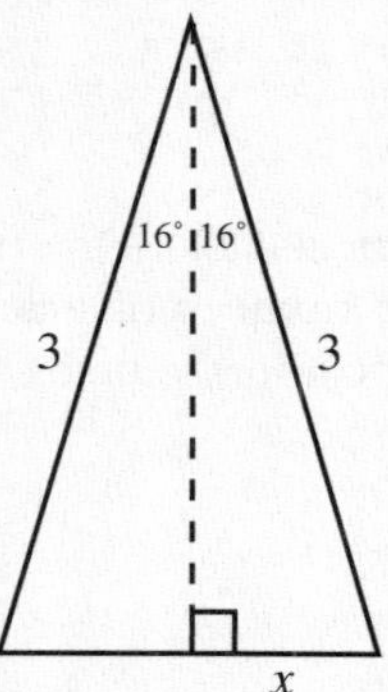

14. **The correct answer is (F).** Assuming that $r^2 = s^2$, $\left(\frac{3p+q}{2}\right)^2 = (p+q)^2$. Square both quantities in this equation, isolate zero (0) on one side of the equation, then factor the quadratic expression into two binomials. Find the two roots of p by setting each binomial equal to 0:

$$\frac{9p^2 + 6pq + q^2}{4} = p^2 - 2pq + q^2$$
$$9p^2 + 6pq + q^2 = 4p^2 - 8pq + 4q^2$$
$$5p^2 + 14pq - 3q^2 = 0$$
$$(5p - q)(p + 3q) = 0$$
$$5p - q = 0,\ p + 3q = 0$$
$$5p = q,\ p = -3q$$
$$p = \frac{q}{5},\ -3q$$

One of these two roots, $\frac{q}{5}$, is the same as $\frac{1}{5}q$.

15. The correct answer is (B). Let Elaine's salary be $3k$, and Carl's salary be $2k$. A 20% raise for Elaine will bring her salary to $(1.2)(3k) = 3.6k$, while a $200 raise for Carl will bring his salary to $2k + 200$. Thus,

$(3.6k) : (2k + 200) = 6:5$. Express the proportion as a fraction, then solve for k:

$$\frac{3.6k}{2k+200} = \frac{6}{5}$$
$$18k = 12k + 1,200$$
$$6k = 1,200$$
$$k = 200$$

Elaine's salary is $3k$, or $600.

16. The correct answer is (J). Since the smallest circle has a radius of 1, the medium circle has a radius of 2, and hence the diameter of the large circle must be 6, which makes its radius 3. The arc of a semi-circle is half the circle's circumference—that is, πr. So the length of the boundary of the shaded region is the sum of the arcs of the three semi-circles: $\pi + 2\pi + 3\pi = 6\pi$.

17. The correct answer is (B). Given any two xy-coordinate points, a line's slope $m = \frac{y_1 - y_2}{x_1 - x_2}$. Accordingly, $\frac{1}{3} = \frac{5-(-3)}{a-2}$. Simplify, then cross-multiply to solve for a:

$$\frac{1}{3} = \frac{8}{a-2}$$
$$a - 2 = (3)(8)$$
$$a - 2 = 24$$
$$a = 26$$

18. The correct answer is (K). List the possibilities methodically. Letting A, B, and C signify the three flavors, here's one way to do it:

All three scoops same flavor: 3 possibilities (AAA, BBB, CCC)

Each scoop a different flavor: 6 permutations (ABC, ACB, BAC, BCA, CAB, CBA)

Two of the scoops same flavor: 18 possibilities, 6 permutations for each flavor. (For example, if flavor A is used for two scoops, here are the six permutations: AAB, AAC, ABA, ACA, BAA, CAA.)

19. The correct answer is (B). $-\frac{x^2}{y^2}$ must be a negative integer, even if x and y are not themselves integers. Because the overall fraction is an integer, $\frac{x^2}{y^2}$ must be an integer. Any number squared is positive, so $\frac{x^2}{y^2}$ must be positive. Accordingly, $-\frac{x^2}{y^2}$ must be negative. Choice (A) can be either a positive or negative integer, depending on whether y is positive or negative. Choice (C) can be a non-integer, since the denominator of the original expression is squared. Also, (C) can be either positive or negative, depending on the sign of x. Choice (D) might be either an integer or a non-integer, and can be either positive or negative, depending on whether x is negative or y is negative. Choice (E) must be negative, but it is not necessarily an integer—for example:

$$-\frac{\frac{2}{3}}{\frac{2}{3}} = -1, \text{ but } -\frac{2}{3} \times \frac{2}{3} = -\frac{4}{9} \text{ (a non-integer)}$$

20. The correct answer is (J). The prime factorization of 24 is $2 \times 2 \times 2 \times 3$. Given that $24AB$ is a perfect square (that is, its square root is an integer), B must have a factor of 2 as well as a factor of 3. Since 2 is a factor of AB, A and B cannot both be odd. (The product of two odd integers is always an odd integer, which is not divisible by 2.) So statement I cannot be true. As for statement II, if AB and $24AB$ were both perfect squares, then 24 would be a perfect square. But it's not; so statement II cannot be true. As for statement III, if A were 6 and B were 36, for example, $24B$ would be a perfect square with both A and B divisible by 6:

$$\sqrt{(24)(6)(36)} = \sqrt{(144)(36)} = (12)(6)$$

A single example such as this one shows that statement III could be true. Hence, only statements I and II cannot be true.

21. The correct answer is (A). Since the average of the four original numbers is 4, their sum must be 16. To calculate the average of all five numbers, divide the new sum (22) by the number of terms (5). The new average is $\frac{22}{5}$, which is 10%, or $\frac{2}{20}$, greater than the original average $\left(\frac{20}{5}\right)$.

22. The correct answer is (J). Letting g represent the number of gallons that is 2% butterfat, $10 - g$ is the amount that is 3.5% butterfat. Solve for g in the following equation:

$$.02g + .035(10 - g) = .03(10)$$
$$.02g + .35 - .035g = .3$$
$$20g + 350 - 35g = 300$$
$$-15g = -50$$
$$g = \frac{10}{3}$$

23. The correct answer is (B). The figure shows a hexagon. The sum of the measures of the six angles = 720°. Subtracting the three known angles from 720 leaves 420°, which is the sum of the measures of the three unknown angles. Set up an equation, then solve for x:

$$x + x + \frac{4}{5}x = 420$$
$$\frac{14}{5}x = 420$$
$$x = (420)\frac{5}{14} = (30)(5) = 150$$

Of the three unknown angles, two measure 150° each. The third unknown angle measures 120°. The polygon's two least possible angles are 54° and 120°. Their sum is 174°.

24. The correct answer is (F). Since the ratio between each term and the one that precedes it is constant, you can set up an equal proportion, then cross-multiply to solve for x:

$$\frac{x}{4} = \frac{y}{x}$$
$$x^2 = 4y$$
$$x = \pm 2\sqrt{y}$$

(The fifth term $T_5 = ar^{(5-1)}$, where a = the first term and r = the constant ratio). To solve the problem, express r in terms of y, then simplify:

$$T_5 = 4\left(\frac{y}{x}\right)^4 = 4\left(\frac{y}{2\sqrt{y}}\right)^4 = \frac{4y^4}{16y^2} = \frac{y^2}{4}$$

25. The correct answer is (E). First, express the equation in standard form: $x^2 - 4x + 13 = 0$ [$a = 1$, $b = -4$, $c = 13$]. Then, apply the quadratic formula:

$$x = \frac{-(-4) \pm \sqrt{(-4)^2 - 4(1)(13)}}{2(1)}$$
$$= \frac{4 \pm \sqrt{16 - 52}}{2}$$
$$= \frac{4 \pm \sqrt{-36}}{2}$$
$$= \frac{4 \pm 6i}{2}$$
$$= 2 \pm 3i$$

The two roots are $2 + 3i$, choice (E), and $2 - 3i$.

26. The correct answer is (K). The curve's amplitude and its frequency over period 2π are each 3. Here's the curve's graph:

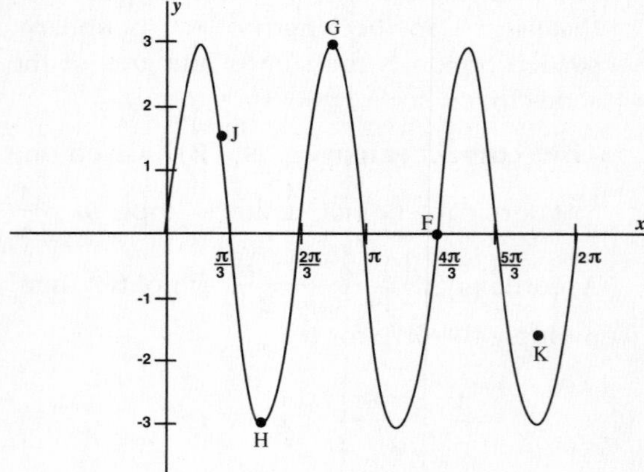

Observation reveals that the graph intercepts the x-axis in regular $\frac{1}{3}\pi$ intervals beginning at $x = \frac{1}{3}\pi$, and that it attains its positive as well as negative amplitude at regular $\frac{1}{3}\pi$ intervals as well. Choices (J) and (K) are the only two that provide points between an amplitude point and x-intercept. The point $\left(\frac{1}{4}\pi, \frac{3}{2}\right)$ which is choice (J), is the precise midpoint between $\left(\frac{1}{6}\pi, 3\right)$ and $\left(\frac{1}{3}\pi, 0\right)$, and therefore is a point on the curve. However, at $x = x = \frac{11}{6}\pi$, the curve is at negative amplitude -3. Hence, $\left(\frac{11}{6}\pi, -\frac{3}{2}\right)$, which is choice (K), cannot be a point on the curve.

27. **The correct answer is (C).** The probability of selecting two red marbles is $\frac{1}{3} \times \frac{3}{7}$, or $\frac{3}{21}$. To find the probability of selecting *no* red marbles, subtract from 1 each individual probability you just calculated, then combine by multiplying: $\left(1 - \frac{1}{3}\right) \times \left(1 - \frac{3}{7}\right) = \frac{2}{3} \times \frac{4}{7} = \frac{8}{21}$.

28. **The correct answer is (K).** Applying the laws of algorithms, $\log\frac{5}{12} = \log\frac{5}{(2^2)(3)} = \log 5 - (\log 2^2 + \log 3) = \log 5 - 2\log 2 - \log 3 = z - 2x - y$.

29. **The correct answer is (A).** To solve this problem, apply a dose of logic and some methodical trial and error. The sum of all six numbers must be an odd integer because *three* of the terms are *odd*. The least possible sum is 21 [(1 + 3 + 5) + (2 + 4 + 6)]. Thus the only other sums to consider are 23, 25, 27, and 29. A bit of trial and error reveals that, among these four sums, only 27 meets the criteria for the six integers, and only with one combination: [(1 + 3 + 5) + (4 + 6 + 8)]. The two possible groups of six integers share in common the integers 1, 3, 4, 5, and 6. Thus among the five answer choices, (A) is the only one that does *not* appear in each set.

30. **The correct answer is (K).** The ratio of the box's three linear dimensions (length : height : width) is 3:2:1. You can find the box's width w as follows:

$$(w)(2w)(3w) = 384$$
$$6w^3 = 384$$
$$w = 64$$

Since $w = 4$, $h = 8$ and $l = 12$. Determine the box's surface area as follows:

$$2lw + 2wh + 2lh = 2(48) + 2(32) + 2(96)$$
$$= 96 + 64 + 192$$
$$= 352$$

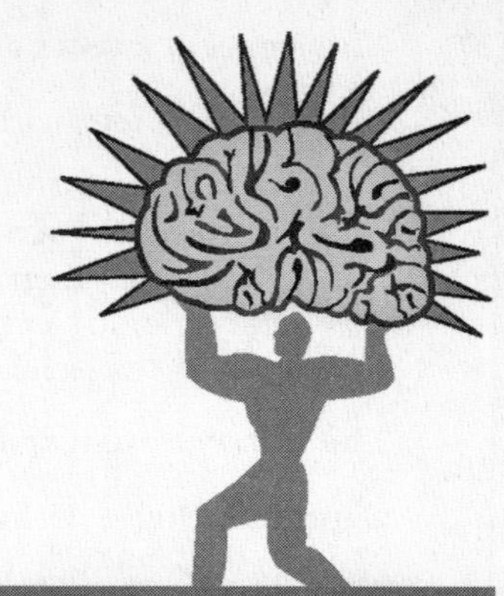

CHALLENGE 3

Reading Questions

Directions: Each of the following five passages is accompanied by several questions. Read each passage and select the best answer for each question. Mark your answer in the book or on a separate sheet of scrap paper.

Questions 1–30

Passage—Natural Science

If you've ever cupped your hand around a blinking firefly or noticed an eerie glow in the ocean at night, you are familiar with the phenomenon of bioluminescence. The ability of certain plants and animals to emit light has long been a source of fascination to humans. Why do certain species of mushrooms glow? Why are midwater squids designed with ornate light-emitting organs underneath their eyes and ink glands? Why do certain particles and biological detritus floating in the depths of the ocean sparkle after a physical disturbance? Are these light displays simply an example of nature in its most flamboyant mode—a case of "if you've got it, flaunt it"—or do they serve any practical purposes?

As it turns out, the manifestations of bioluminescence are as diverse as they are elegant. Yet virtually all of the known or proposed ways in which bioluminescence functions may be classed under three major rubrics: assisting predation, helping escape from predators, and communicating.

Many examples of the first two uses can be observed in the ocean's midwaters, a zone that extends from about 100 meters deep to a few kilometers below the surface. Almost all of the animals that inhabit the murky depths where sunlight barely penetrates are capable of producing light in one way or another. Certain animals, when feeding, are attracted to a spot of light as a possible food source. Hence, other animals use their own luminescence to attract them. Just in front of the angler fish's mouth is a dangling luminescent ball suspended from a structure attached to its head. What unwitting marine creatures see as food is really a bait to lure them into the angler fish's gaping maw.

The uses of luminescence to elude predators are just as sophisticated and various. Some creatures take advantage of the scant sunlight in their realm by using bioluminescence as a form of camouflage. The glow generated by photophores, light-producing organs on the undersides of some fishes and squids, acts to hide them through a phenomenon known as countershading: the weak downward lighting created by the photophores effectively erases the animals' shadows when viewed from below against the (relatively) lighted waters above.

Some marine animals use bioluminescence more actively in their own defense, turning their predators into prey. For instance, there is the so-called "burglar alarm effect," in which an animal coats an advancing predator with sticky glowing tissue that makes the would-be attacker vulnerable to visually-cued hunters—like bank robbers marked by exploding dye packets hidden in stolen currency.

Bioluminescence is used not only in such interspecific feeding frays between predators and prey, but also as an intraspecific communication facilitator. The fireflies that seem to blink on and off randomly in the summer woods are actually male and female members signaling each other during courtship. Certain fish use their luminescence as a kind of Morse code: a male fish sends out a flash, which is answered by the female with her own flash exactly two seconds later, which the male in turn recognizes by its timing.

Bioluminescence clearly functions to help certain species ensure their survival, whether it helps them to trick predators or to mate and produce offspring. Yet, when we look at the larger evolutionary picture, bioluminescence as such is generally considered a "nonessential" characteristic. After all, closely related species and even strains of the same species may have both luminous and nonluminous members, and the nonluminous ones appear just as viable and vigorous as their glowing counterparts. For instance, while numerous small marine organisms known as dinoflagellates are luminous, many are not. Yet, on closer inspection, we find that the nonluminous dinoflagellates may benefit from the diversionary flashing tactics of the luminous ones. When the sea is disturbed and light flashes create phosphorescence, the species that flash may provide enough light to serve the entire population. Thus, selection pressure for the development or maintenance of luminescence in additional species is not great if light generated by a part of the population serves the entire community.

There are instances in which bioluminescence seems truly purposeless. What does one make of a creature, such as a newly discovered species of a tomopterid worm, that emits light for no apparent purpose? This agile swimmer with a multitude of paired legs spews a bright yellow bioluminescent fluid from each of its leg pores. While other types of spewers use this strategy to create a visual distraction, this worm's display remains enigmatic, particularly since the light produced is yellow, while most midwater animals have eyes that are sensitive only to blue-green light. Perhaps some animal species are simply exploiting their capacity for flamboyance, in the same way that some humans bring a distinctively colorful flair to whatever they do.

1. From the author's description of the angler fish in lines 34-38, we can infer that this fish

(A) is attracted to light as a possible food source.
(B) uses its light-producing organ to deter predators.
(C) dwells primarily in the ocean's midwaters.
(D) uses countershading to elude predators below.

2. Which of the following statements about the use of bioluminescence in countershading finds the LEAST support in the passage?

(F) The light given off by photophores underneath certain fish and squid makes the animals appear to blend in with the sunlit waters above them.
(G) Bioluminescence allows the parts of an animal normally in shadow to appear lighter.
(H) Countershading is used most effectively in regions of relatively weak sunlight.
(J) Animals who dwell near the water's surface are unlikely to use countershading to elude predators, even if they have the capability to do so.

3. If bioluminescence were NOT a nonessential characteristic, which of the following would be true, according to the passage's implication?

(A) Luminous species would be seen to thrive more successfully than closely related nonluminous ones.
(B) Nonluminous species would enjoy a reproductive advantage by comparison to luminous ones.
(C) Luminous species would gradually die out and be replaced by closely related nonluminous ones.
(D) Luminous and nonluminous species would not be observed living in close proximity to one another.

4. The phrase "selection pressure" in lines 91-92 refers to

(F) the potential extinction of an animal species due to the depletion of essential resources.
(G) environmental factors that favor development of a particular biological characteristic.
(H) competition among predators for a finite population of prey.
(J) selective winnowing of an animal population based on the attractiveness of specific individuals.

5. Which of the following discoveries would most seriously call into question the author's comments about the tomopterid worm?

(A) Other species of midwater animals that produce bioluminescent yellow fluids
(B) Another species of tomopterid worm that produces bioluminescent blue-green fluid
(C) A prey of the tomopterid worm that does not exhibit bioluminescence
(D) A predator of the tomopterid worm that is sensitive to yellow light

6. The passage focuses on all of the following aspects of bioluminescence EXCEPT
   (F) how it can actually reverse the relationship between predator and prey.
   (G) its role in helping animals to communicate with others of the same species.
   (H) whether bioluminescence is a purely functional feature.
   (J) how the biolumniescence of one species may serve nonluminous members of the same species.

Passage II—Humanities

The half-decade of 1850–1855 saw the appearance of an unusually rich cluster of literary works in America. This period, known as the American Renaissance, represented the first flowering of a national literature with characteristically American settings and themes. Not a rebirth in the sense of a recovery of the lost arts of the past, it was rather a confluence of two streams of thought that emerged in early nineteenth-century America: a determination to cut loose from European literary forms and a desire to explore the millennial belief that an ideal world was forming in America.

When Ralph Waldo Emerson pronounced America's declaration of cultural independence from Europe in his "American Scholar" address of 1837, he was actually articulating the transcendental assumptions of Jefferson's declaration of political independence. In the ideal new world envisioned by Emerson and his transcendental associates, America was to become a perfect democracy of free and self-reliant individuals. Because the transcendentalists considered the potentialities of the individual to be infinite, the possibility of achieving the democratic ideal seemed, for them, within reach. Bringing Emerson's metaphysics down to earth, Thoreau, in his *Walden* (1854), asserted that in America, one can live entirely without encumbrances and thus can realize the transcendental doctrine of self-reliance. Emerson wanted to visualize Thoreau as the ideal scholar in action that he had called for in the "American Scholar," but in the end Emerson regretted Thoreau's too-private individualism which failed to signal the vibrant revolution in national consciousness that Emerson had prophesied.

For Emerson, what Thoreau lacked, Whitman embodied in full. On reading *Leaves of Grass* (1855), Emerson saw in Whitman the "prophet of democracy" whom he had sought—the poet-seer with the charisma to propel transcendentalist ideas into the national consciousness and to awaken Americans to a sense of the sublime social perfection that lay within their grasp. The other writers of the American Renaissance were less sanguine about the fulfillment of the democratic ideal. In *The Scarlet Letter* (1850), while portraying Hester Prynne's assertion of transcendental freedom as heroic, Hawthorne concluded that such antinomianism leads to moral anarchy. And Melville, who saw in his story of *Pierre* (1852) a metaphor for the misguided assumptions of democratic idealism, declared the transcendentalist dream unrealizable. Ironically, the literary vigor with which both Hawthorne and Melville explored the ideal showed their deep sympathy with it even as they dramatized its delusions.

Thus, the writers of the American Renaissance waged a kind of imaginary debate over the American democratic ideal, with Emerson, Thoreau, and Whitman affirming it as vibrantly emergent and Hawthorne and Melville warning that it was sadly specious. Although the Civil War seemed to corroborate the ideals of freedom and democracy, the rise of realism in literature and of pragmatism in philosophy during the latter half of the century revealed that the debate was not over.

7. The author of the passage seeks primarily to
   (A) explore the impact of the American Renaissance writers on the literature of the late eighteenth century.
   (B) illustrate how American literature of the mid-eighteenth century differed in form from European literature of the same time period.
   (C) identify two schools of thought among American Renaissance writers regarding the democratic ideal.
   (D) point out how Emerson's democratic idealism was mirrored by the works of the American Renaissance writers.

8. Based on the information in the passage, Emerson might be characterized as any of the following EXCEPT
   (F) a literary critic.
   (G) an American Renaissance writer.
   (H) a would-be prophet.
   (J) a political pragmatist.

9. The passage mentions works of the American Renaissance period by all of the following EXCEPT

(A) Emerson.
(B) Hawthorne.
(C) Thoreau.
(D) Whitman.

10. With which of the following statements about Melville and Hawthorne would the author most likely agree?

(F) Both men were disillusioned transcendentalists.
(G) They agreed as to what the transcendentalist dream would ultimately lead to.
(H) Both men believed the idealists to be misguided.
(J) Hawthorne politicized the transcendental ideal, while Melville personalized it.

11. Which of the following statements about *Leaves of Grass* is best supported by the information in the passage?

(A) It dramatized the delusions of the democratic ideal.
(B) It marked the beginning rise of realism in literature.
(C) Emerson read it after he read Thoreau's *Walden*.
(D) Its form was a departure from established European literary forms.

12. The author would most likely agree that the Civil War

(F) led to the rise of realism in American literature.
(G) affirmed that the democratic ideal was unrealistic.
(H) demonstrated that the transcendental dream in America was alive.
(J) effectively terminated the American Renaissance.

Passage III—Social Studies

The following passage was written in 1993.

In recent years, the People's Republic of China has been one of the fastest growing economies of the world. Its gross national product has increased at an average annual rate of 12.8 percent over the last three years and is projected to increase at an average annual rate of 8 to 9 percent during the next decade. Foreign trade as a percentage of China's gross national product rose from about 10 percent in the late 1970s to 38 percent in 1992.

This dynamic growth can be attributed to several factors. Trade between the United States and China resumed in 1972, after a twenty-year hiatus, following the signing of the Shanghai Communique at the conclusion of Nixon's historic trip to China. Trade has developed rapidly since normalization of diplomatic relations in 1979; two-way trade increased from 2.3 billion dollars in 1979 to 33.1 billion dollars in 1992. Economic growth is also attributable largely to China's policies of economic reform. The pace of reform quickened in the wake of senior leader Deng Xiaoping's call in early 1992 for more growth, greater openness, and stepped-up reform. Deng's policies were endorsed that year by the Fourteenth Congress of the Chinese Communist Party, by the Eighth National People's Congress in 1993, and also in 1993 by the Third Plenum of the Chinese Communists Party's Fourteenth Central Committee. The Third Plenum adopted several new reform initiatives aimed at transforming the Chinese economy into a market system; priority areas for reform included state-owned enterprises, banking and taxation, foreign trade, social security, and economic structure.

These bold reform measures will no doubt result in many promising business opportunities, especially in the areas of energy, telecommunications, and transportation. The United States is likely to be a primary beneficiary of Chinese economic reform. The Chinese have a high regard for American products and are encouraging American companies to enter the Chinese market. Potential for United States exports to China was enhanced by two particular agreements between these countries in 1992. The first regards the protection of intellectual-property rights by which the Chinese government pledged to significantly upgrade its intellectual-property regime. The second is a market-access agreement that calls for the Chinese government to substantially reduce nontariff import barriers, especially in product categories of great interest to United States firms. Notwithstanding these developments, the issue of annual renewal of China's current Most Favored Nation status is and will continue to be of primary significance to United States firms.

Chinese leadership continues to stress economic development as the country's primary objective, paying little attention officially to political reform. What are the possible intra-national political consequences of the government's current agenda? Certain regions are experiencing a greater economic boom than others. Guangdong province, for example, has benefited from neighboring Hong Kong's freewheeling capitalistic economy, and the movement of Hong Kong's manufacturing sector into the province has created what is probably the most dynamic economy in the world. Such anomalies in economic development are likely to create unrest in the less prosperous areas. Political instability might also result if current inflationary trends become uncontrollable. Further, the question of leadership succession remains unresolved, a situation that might generate political unrest. On the whole, however, as long as economic expansion continues and spreads to the internal regions, political unrest should remain relatively dormant.

13. According to the passage, foreign trade as a percentage of China's gross national product

(A) is projected to increase at an average annual rate of 8 to 9 percent during the next decade.
(B) increased from 2.3 percent in 1979 to 33.1 percent in 1992.
(C) increased by more than 25 percent in less than twenty years.
(D) increased in the wake of Xiaoping's call for greater openness with other countries.

14. It can be reasonably inferred from the passage that the amount of trade between the United States and China

(F) was greater during the period immediately preceding 1952 than during the years immediately following 1952.
(G) decreased from 1972 to 1979, then increased from 1979 to 1992.
(H) decreased during the years immediately preceding the Shanghai Communique.
(J) increased after the Eighth National People's Congress.

15. The passage mentions all of the following as factors contributing to China's economic growth EXCEPT

(A) renewed political relations between China and the United States.
(B) the policies of Deng Xiaoping.
(C) particular initiatives of the Third Plenum.
(D) a decrease in the number of state-owned enterprises.

16. The author discusses Guangdong province primarily in order to

(F) illustrate a political phenomenon.
(G) discount an economic theory.
(H) support a prediction.
(J) help define an historical trend.

17. Which of the following best expresses the main idea of the last paragraph in the passage?

(A) Unless accompanied by political reforms, economic growth and reform in China may result in political instability.
(B) In order to ensure future economic growth, China must continue to trade with the United States.
(C) China's recent economic growth is the result of both improving political relations with the United States and reforms in economic policy.
(D) While positive political developments have been largely responsible for China's recent economic growth, continued unfettered growth may ironically have adverse political consequences in the future.

18. All of the following factors positively affecting business opportunities for the United States in China are mentioned in the passage EXCEPT

(F) consumer sentiment in China toward American products.
(G) China's laws regarding intellectual property.
(H) China's current policies regarding tariffs on imported products.
(J) China's Most Favored Nation Status.

19. Which of the following would be the most appropriate title for the passage?

(A) "Is Political Unrest Inevitable in Light of China's Current Economic Agenda?"
(B) "A Prescription for Economic Reform in China"
(C) "Trade Relations Between the United States and China: Historical Perspective and Future Outlook"
(D) "The Booming Economy of China: Economic and Political Implications"

Passage IV—Prose Fiction

Newland Archer was speaking with his fiancée, May Welland. He had failed to stop at his club on the way up from the office where he exercised the profession of the law in the leisurely manner common to well-to-do New Yorkers of his class in the middle of the nineteenth century. He was out of spirits and slightly out of temper, and a haunting horror of doing the same thing every day at the same hour besieged his brain.

"Sameness—sameness!" he muttered, the word running through his head like a persecuting tune as he saw the familiar tall-hatted figures lounging behind the plate glass; and because he usually dropped in at the club at that hour, he had passed by instead. And now he began to talk to May of their own plans, their future, and Ms. Welland's insistence on a long engagement.

"If you call it long!" May cried. "Isabel Chivers and Reggie were engaged for two years, Grace and Thorley for nearly a year and a half. Why aren't we very well off as we are?"

It was the traditional maidenly interrogation, and Archer felt ashamed of himself for finding it childish. No doubt she simply echoed what was said for her, but she was nearing her twenty-second birthday, and he wondered at what age "nice" women like May began to speak for themselves.

"Never, if we won't let them, I suppose," he mused, and recalled his mad outburst to his friend Jackson: "Women ought to be as free as we are—!"

It would soon be his task to take the bandage from this young woman's eyes, and bid her look forth on the world. But how many generations of women before her had descended bandaged to the family vault? He shivered a little, remembering some of the new ideas in his scientific books, and the much-cited instance of the Kentucky cave-fish, which had ceased to develop eyes because they had no use for them. What if, when he had bidden May Welland to open hers, they could only look out blankly at blankness?

"We might be much better off. We might be truly together—we might travel."

Her face lit up. "That would be lovely," she admitted; she would love to travel. But her mother would not understand their wanting to do things so differently.

"As if the fact that it is different doesn't account for it!" Archer insisted.

"Newland! You're so original!" she exulted.

His heart sank. He saw that he was saying all the things that young men in the same situation were expected to say, and that she was making the answers that instinct and tradition taught her to make—even to the point of calling him original.

"Original! We're all as like each other as those dolls cut out of the same folded paper. We're like patterns stenciled on a wall. Can't you and I strike out for ourselves, May?"

"Goodness—shall we elope?" she laughed.

"If you would—"

"You do love me, Newland! I'm so happy."

"But then—why not be happier?"

"We can't behave like people in novels, though, can we?"

"Why not—why not—why not?"

She looked a little bored by his insistence. She knew very well why they couldn't, but it was troublesome to have to produce a reason. "I'm not clever enough to argue with you. But that kind of thing is rather—vulgar, isn't it?" she suggested, relieved to have hit on a word that would certainly extinguish the whole subject.

"Are you so much afraid, then, of being vulgar?"

She was evidently staggered by this. "Of course I should hate it—and so would you," she rejoined, a trifle irritably.

He stood silent, beating his walking-stick nervously against his shoe-top. Feeling that she had indeed found the right way of closing the discussion, she went on lightheartedly, "Oh, did I tell you that I showed cousin Ellen my engagement ring? She thinks it the most beautiful setting she ever saw. There's nothing like it in Paris, she said. I do love you, Newland, for being so artistic!"

20. The reference to "the Kentucky cave-fish" (line 42) underscores Archer's concern about May Welland's

(F) conventionality.
(G) timidity.
(H) naivete.
(J) bossiness.

21. It can be inferred from the passage that Archer's engagement is expected to last

(A) two or three months.
(B) somewhat less than a year and a half.
(C) about two years.
(D) over two years.

22. The fifth paragraph suggests that Archer considers most women in the society of his time

(F) unduly powerful.
(G) indecisive and irresponsible.
(H) unfairly dominated by men.
(J) excessively demanding.

23. Which of the following conclusions about the relationship between Archer and May Welland is best supported by the details in the passage?

(A) Archer's eagerness to accelerate their wedding is motivated by his passion for his fiancée.
(B) Archer and May Welland both feel trapped in an unhappy relationship by social restrictions.
(C) Archer feels stultified by his fiancée's conventionality, but feels unable to alter the situation.
(D) May Welland is eager to do whatever she can to satisfy the emotional needs of her fiancé.

24. Archer regards May Welland's attitudes as having been excessively influenced by which of the following?

I. The traditions of her sex and class
II. Her mother
III. The novels she has read
IV. Her friends Isabel and Grace

(F) I and II only
(G) II and III only
(H) I and IV only
(J) II and IV only

Passage V—Social Studies

Line Although accounts differ as to which of two men—Hiawatha or Degandawida—played a more significant role in founding the Iroquois League of Indian nations, it is generally agreed among anthropologists and historians that the principles on which the League was founded were formulated by Degandawida, while Hiawatha served as his advocate. Because the League proposed by Degandawida was a radical step in an unfamiliar direction for the warring and fiercely autonomous Iroquois nations, acceptance required that the League be tied to familiar Iroquois customs and institutions.

Degandawida's philosophy that warring nations could lay down their arms and become partners was embraced by the Iroquois only by his associating this notion with the Iroquois custom by which the families of slain warriors adopted war prisoners into the tribe to prevent the tribe's male population from dwindling. Degandawida also used unquestioned social institutions as symbols. He compared the League to the traditional Iroquois clan in which several families share a "Longhouse," likening the Great Council, comprised of representatives from each member nation, to the ever-burning Council Fire of the Longhouse. To ease the Iroquois' fear of losing national identity, Degandawida assigned a meaningful League title as well as specific duties to each nation. The powerful Mohawks, for example, were given the title "Keepers of the Eastern Door" and given a council veto, while the Onondagas, who were centrally-positioned geographically, were made "Fire Keepers" or perpetual hosts. Degandawida also replicated the power structure of the traditional Iroquois clan. Each of the five Iroquois nations were comprised of matriarchal totemic clans in which, although the clan's chiefs were men, the heads of the clan were women. A chief's children were considered members of his wife's clan. Degandawida determined that the heads of each nation should select their League representatives, thereby effectively precluding the possibility of League representatives passing their power on to their sons, as well as decreasing the likelihood that a pro-war representative would be appointed.

Unification of the Iroquois nations lasted for over two hundred years, until the American Revolution of 1776, when disagreement as to whether they should become involved in the war divided the Iroquois. Due to the success of the revolutionaries and the encroachment upon Iroquois lands that followed, many Iroquois resettled in Canada, while those who remained behind lost the respect they had enjoyed among other Indian nations. The introduction of distilled spirits resulted in widespread alcoholism, leading in turn to the rapid decline of both the culture and population. The influence of the Quakers impeded, yet in another sense contributed, to this decline. By establishing schools for the Iroquois and by introducing them to modern technology for agriculture and husbandry, the Quakers instilled in the Iroquois some hope for the future, yet undermined the Iroquois' sense of national identity.

Ironically, it was the half-brother of Seneca Cornplanter, perhaps the most outspoken proponent among the Iroquois for assimilation of white customs and institutions, who can be credited with reviving the Iroquois culture. Inspired by a near-death vision in 1799, Handsome Lake, a former member of the Great

Council, established a new religion among the Iroquois that tied the more useful aspects of Christianity to traditional Indian beliefs and customs. Within a year, Handsome Lake had converted most of the Iroquois to his religion and had assumed an unprecedented position of power in the tribe. His teachings became firmly entrenched among the Iroquois and sparked reunification and renewed confidence, while also helping to end rampant alcoholism. The influence of Handsome Lake is still evident today; many modern-day Iroquois belong to both the religion of Handsome Lake and to one or another Christian religion. However, due in part to this dualism and in part to an absence of hierarchy, organization, or even a name, the extent of his influence upon modern-day Iroquois culture is not readily determinable.

25. The passage refers to all of the following ways by which Degandawida persuaded the Iroquois to join his League of Indian Nations EXCEPT

(A) assigning each member nation its own specific duties.
(B) devising a system of representation that avoided family dynasties.
(C) likening the notion that enemies could become allies to the adoption of war prisoners.
(D) allowing each nation a council veto in matters affecting all nations.

26. In stating that the heads of the nations should select council representatives, thereby "decreasing the likelihood that a pro-war representative would be appointed" (lines 47–49), the author infers that

(F) women were more likely than men to select peace-loving representatives.
(G) war was more likely where power was passed down by a chief to his children.
(H) a chief's children were more likely to favor war than other members of the totemic clan.
(J) children of clan heads were less likely to favor war than the chief's children.

27. Which of the following best characterizes the structure of the passage as a whole?

(A) A theory is presented and then applied to two related historical phenomena.
(B) Two historical figures are introduced, then the nature and extent of their influence is compared.
(C) The inception of an historical phenomenon is examined, then the subsequent life of the phenomenon is traced.
(D) Competing views respecting an historical phenomenon are presented and then evaluated based upon empirical evidence.

28. The passage mentions all of the following events as contributing to the decline of the Iroquois culture EXCEPT

(F) new educational opportunities for the Iroquois people.
(G) divisive power struggles among the leaders of the Iroquois nations.
(H) introduction of new farming technologies.
(J) territorial threats against the Iroquois nations.

29. Among the following reasons, it is most likely that the author considers Handsome Lake's leading a revival of the Iroquois culture to be "ironic" (line 71) because

(A) he was a former member of the Great Council.
(B) he was not a full-blooded relative of Seneca Cornplanter.
(C) he was related by blood to a chief proponent of assimilation.
(D) his religious beliefs conflicted with traditional Iroquois beliefs.

30. Based upon the information in the passage, the author would agree that Degandawida and Handsome Lake most resembled each other in which of the following respects?

(F) They combined traditional Iroquois religious beliefs and the most useful aspects of Christianity.
(G) They drew upon their knowledge of Iroquois customs and traditions to persuade the Iroquois people.
(H) Their policies were aimed at uniting the Iroquois people against the white settlers.
(J) Their efforts resulted in peace among the formerly feuding Iroquois factions.

ANSWERS AND EXPLANATIONS

Passage I

1. **The correct answer is (C).** The first sentence of the third paragraph of the passage, which is where the angler fish is discussed, makes it clear that the paragraph is entirely devoted to examples of bioluminescence found in the midwaters of the ocean.

2. **The correct answer is (J).** Choices (F), (G), and (H) are accurate statements about countershading, as described in the fourth paragraph. Support for choice (J) is not nearly as strong. Admittedly, the passage's reference to the sunlit waters "above" a countershading animal does suggest that animals do not use countershading *at* the water's surface. However, choice (J) goes beyond what is reasonably inferable from the passage, to assert unfairly that these animals are "unlikely" to use countershading "near" the water's surface.

3. **The correct answer is (A).** According to the passage's seventh paragraph, bioluminescence is considered nonessential because nonluminous species seem to thrive as well as luminous ones. Based on this statement, it is reasonable to infer that, if bioluminescence were essential, the opposite would be true: luminous species would fair better than nonluminous ones.

4. **The correct answer is (G).** In the eighth paragraph, "selection pressure" is discussed specifically as an environmental force that helps promote "the development or maintenance of luminescence" among animal species. Choice (G) paraphrases this concept.

5. **The correct answer is (D).** This discovery would suggest that the tomopterid worm's bioluminescence is, in fact, useful, since it would mean that the yellow fluid it spews could help to distract dangerous predators.

6. **The correct answer is (F).** The fifth paragraph discusses how certain animals can coat a would-be predator with sticky glowing tissue, which makes these predators easier prey for their own predators. But the author neither states nor suggests that the would-be prey using this defense mechanism turns the tables to become predator. The aspects referred to in choices (G), (H), and (J) are the focus of the sixth, eighth, and seventh paragraphs, respectively.

Passage II

7. **The correct answer is (C).** The passage describes an imaginary debate over the American democratic ideal among the writers of the American Renaissance, in which Emerson, Thoreau, and Whitman are grouped together in one school of thought while Hawthorne and Melville are paired in another.

8. **The correct answer is (J).** The author makes clear throughout the passage that Emerson is an idealist, which is just the opposite of a pragmatist. Choice (F) is the "runner-up" choice because it is not supported as explicitly by the passage as either choice (G) or choice (H). Nevertheless, in regretting Thoreau's "too-private individualism" (line 35), Emerson is criticizing Thoreau for the ideas presented in *Walden*, thereby playing the role of literary critic. Choice (G) is implied by the first sentence of the final paragraph: "Thus the writers of the American Renaissance waged a kind of imaginary debate over the American democratic ideal, with Emerson, Thoreau, and Whitman affirming it as vibrantly emergent . . . ." It can be reasonably inferred from this statement that Emerson was one of the American Renaissance writers. Choice (H) is supported by the passage, which asserts that Thoreau "failed to signal the vibrant revolution in national consciousness that Emerson had prophesied" (lines 35–37). Also, the passage supports the idea that Emerson anticipated and predicted that America would become "a perfect democracy of free and self-reliant individuals" (lines 22–23).

9. **The correct answer is (A).** The only "work" by Emerson mentioned in the passage is his "American Scholar" address. Even if a public address can be considered a "work," since Emerson gave the address in 1837 and not during the American Renaissance period (1850–1855), the address would not be considered an American Renaissance work. The passage mentions specific works by Hawthorne (*The Scarlet Letter*), Thoreau (*Walden*), and Whitman (*Leaves of Grass*), all created during the period from 1850–1855.

10. **The correct answer is (H).** According to the passage, Melville, through his story of *Pierre*, conveyed the notion that democratic idealism was based upon "misguided assumptions." Although the author is not so explicit that Hawthorne also believed idealists to be misguided, Hawthorne's conclusion that transcendental freedom leads to moral anarchy can reasonably be interpreted as such.

11. **The correct answer is (D).** In lines 10–11, the author states that the literature of the American Renaissance period reflected "a determination to cut loose from the European literary forms." It is reasonable to infer, then, that *Leaves of Grass* (an example of American Renaissance literature) differed in form from European literature.

12. **The correct answer is (H)**. According to the passage, the Civil War "seemed to corroborate the ideals of freedom and democracy." Choice (H) restates this idea.

Passage III

13. **The correct answer is (C)**. In the first paragraph, the author states explicitly that foreign trade as a percentage of China's gross national product rose from about 10 percent in the late 1970s to 38 percent in 1992. Choice (A) refers to China's gross national product as a whole rather than to foreign trade as a percentage of the gross national product. Choice (B) refers to the increase in trade between China and the United States from 1979 to 1992, not to foreign trade as a percentage of China's gross national product, and confuses percentage figures with dollar amounts. Choice (D) is neither explicitly stated in the passage nor well supported by the passage. Although Xiaoping's call for greater openness (line 24) may have resulted in increased foreign trade, the passage does not suggest that such an increase exceeded the percentage increase in China's gross national product as a whole.

14. **The correct answer is (F)**. In mentioning a twenty-year hiatus (break) in trade between the United States and China (lines 13–14), the author implies that the two countries were engaged in trade just prior to the beginning of that twenty-year period. Since the twenty-year period ended in 1972, it began in 1952. Choice (G) is partly accurate, but not fully supported by the passage. Although the passage is explicit that trade between the two countries increased between 1979 and 1992 (lines 18–20), the passage does not address whether trade increased or decreased between 1972 and 1979; the passage merely indicates that trade "resumed" in 1972; in fact, an increase, rather than a decrease, in trade would seem far more likely during the years immediately following the hiatus. Thus, choice (G) is neither fully supported by nor inferable from the passage.

15. **The correct answer is (D)**. Although, according to the passage, The Third Plenum adopted initiatives aimed in part at reforming state-owned enterprises (lines 31–36), the passage does not support the assertion that any such reforms occurred or that such reforms actually included a reduction in the number of such enterprises. Choices (A), (B), and (C) are all mentioned explicitly in the second paragraph following the author's assertion at the beginning of that paragraph that the Chinese economy's "dynamic growth can be attributed to several factors." Accordingly, choices (A), (B), and (C) are all clearly such factors and are thus incorrect responses.

16. **The correct answer is (H)**. In pointing out the prosperity of Guangdong province, the author seeks to point out the disparity in economic development among various regions within China and asserts that such disparity may result in political unrest in the less prosperous areas (lines 68–76). Thus, the prosperity of Guangdong is evidence in support of the author's prediction of political unrest.

17. **The correct answer is (A)**. In the last paragraph, the author deals exclusively with the possible political consequences of economic reform without political reform, presenting three possible scenarios that may result in political instability.

18. **The correct answer is (H)**. Although the passage mentions the reduction of nontariff import barriers, tariffs are not mentioned. Choices (F), (G), and (J) are all mentioned explicitly in the third paragraph as reasons why the United States is likely to be a primary beneficiary of Chinese economic reform.

19. **The correct answer is (D)**. The first part of the title encompasses the first and second paragraphs insofar as these paragraphs describe and explain the current economic boom in China. The second part of the title embraces the third and fourth paragraphs—the third paragraph addresses how the boom will impact the economies of other countries (the United States, in particular), while the fourth paragraph considers the internal political implications of the boom.

Passage IV

20. **The correct answer is (H)**. Archer fears that Welland is becoming figuratively "blind," that is, unable to perceive reality because of the conventionality of her upbringing and her social surroundings. The cave-fish symbolizes his fear that Welland will never be grown-up enough to see and think for herself. The word "naivete," which means ignorance due to inexperience, aptly expresses Archer's view of Welland here. Choice (F) is a tempting choice, because Archer does comment on their conventionality ("We're all like each other...."). However, this dialogue has nothing to do with Archer's reference to the Kentucky cave-fish.

21. **The correct answer is (B)**. Paragraph 3 makes it clear that the Archer-Welland engagement will be somewhat shorter than that of Welland's friends "Grace and Thorley," which engagement was "nearly a year and a half." However, it can't be much shorter than theirs; otherwise Archer would hardly be complaining about its length. Hence, the best choice is (B).

22. **The correct answer is (H).** Archer recalls saying to his friend Jackson, "Women ought to be as free as we are—!" And earlier in the paragraph, he muses that "nice" women may begin "to speak for themselves" "[N]ever, if we won't let them." The two statements in combination show that Archer feels that men ("we") are largely responsible for constraining women and taking away their freedom. Choice (F) runs contrary to Archer's comments indicated above. Choices (G) and (J) are unsupported by the passage.

23. **The correct answer is (C).** Throughout the passage, Archer feels trapped by the "sameness" and conventionality of his relationship with Welland. Yet when she rejects his ideas about breaking out of this conventionality, he apparently is helpless to respond and reduced to standing silently, "beating his walking-stick nervously against his shoe-top."

24. **The correct answer is (F).** The third, fifth, and tenth paragraphs refer to family, class, and gender traditions as the constraining forces that control Welland's attitudes. The second and eighth paragraphs refer to Welland's mother as the source of the idea that a long engagement is necessary. Welland mentions "novels" only as the kind of guide to behavior she would never follow, and her friends are mentioned merely for comparison's sake, not as sources of her beliefs.

Passage V

25. **The correct answer is (D).** The last sentence in the first paragraph suggests that the second paragraph will discuss ways in which Degandawida tied the League to familiar Iroquois customs and institutions to gain acceptance of his League. Choice (D) is the only choice that is not supported explicitly by the information in the second paragraph. Although the Mohawks were given a council veto in order to acknowledge their power, the passage does not indicate that any other nations were given veto power.

26. **The correct answer is (F).** The passage states that the heads of each nation (i.e., the clan heads) were women, while the chiefs were men; the passage goes on to state that, according to Degandawida, the clan heads (women) rather than the chiefs (men) should select League representatives because the likelihood that a pro-war representative would be appointed would be decreased thereby. Among the five choices, choice (F) the only choice that infers from this information that Degandawida believed the men to be more pro-war than the women.

27. **The correct answer is (C).** The first and second paragraphs are concerned with the inception of the Iroquois League, while the third and fourth paragraphs outline the subsequent history of the League from its decline through its subsequent resurgence under Handsome Lake. Choice (C) recaps this overall structure. Choice (A) is the "runner-up" choice. It could be argued that the author is presenting a "theory" as to how the Iroquois were swayed by Degandawida and later by Handsome Lake, and that the "two related historical phenomena" mentioned in choice (A) refer to the inception of the League (under Degandawida) and its revival (under Handsome Lake). However, the author presents the information as historical facts rather than as theories—that is, the passage merely recounts historical events rather than seeking to explain them by way of a more fundamental theory. What's more, choice (A) omits the discussion in the third paragraph concerning the decline of the Iroquois culture. So in this sense, choice (A) is too narrow.

28. **The correct answer is (G).** Nowhere in this paragraph does the author mention any power struggles among the leaders of the Iroquois nations. Although the third paragraph does refer to a dispute among the Iroquois leaders, the dispute regarded the role that the Iroquois should play in the American Revolution. Choices (F), (H), and (J) are all explicitly mentioned in the third paragraph as factors contributing to the decline of the Iroquois culture.

29. **The correct answer is (C).** The passage states that Cornplanter was an outspoken proponent of assimilation and that Handsome Lake was related to Cornplanter as a half-brother. The fact that Lake was responsible for the Iroquois reasserting their national identity is ironic, then, in light of Lake's blood relationship to Cornplanter. Choices (A) and (B) are accurate statements, based upon the information in the passage. However, they do not respond to the question. Choice (D) runs contrary to the information in the passage and fails to respond to the question. Lake emphasized the similarities between Christianity and his brand of Iroquois religion; the passage does not deal with the differences between Christianity and the Iroquois' traditional beliefs. Moreover, even if choice (D) were supported by the passage, it is not the irony to which the author refers.

30. **The correct answer is (G).** Both men had a thorough understanding of Iroquois traditions. Degandawida used Iroquois traditions as symbols to convey concepts and as models for the structure of his League, all with the goal of persuading the nations to join his League. Similarly, Handsome Lake's use of traditional religious beliefs helped convert the Iroquois people to his new religion.

CHALLENGE 4

Science Reasoning Questions

Directions: This challenge consists of six passages, each followed by several questions. Read each passage and then select the best answer for each of the questions that follow it. Mark your answers either in the book or on a separate sheet of scrap paper. You may NOT use a calculator on this test.

Questions 1–30

Passage I

Electrical circuits that allow electrical signals with some *frequencies* (number of waves per second) to pass while suppressing others are called *filters*. They are used in nearly every electronic device, from computers to VCRs. They may contain *resistors*, which resist the flow of current through a wire, *inductors*, which resist change in the current, and *capacitors*, which store electric charge. The following figure shows the design of three types of filters.

Filter Type 1

Sine wave in — Sine wave out

Filter Type 2

Sine wave in — Sine wave out

Filter Type 3

Sine wave in — Sine wave out

Key:

= capacitor

= resistor

= inductor

= ground

The effects of a filter can be demonstrated with a *frequency response curve*. Such a curve depicts the *amplitude* (wave height) of the output (vertical axis) as one varies the input frequency (horizontal axis), while keeping the input amplitude constant. Several experiments were conducted to test the effects of some filters.

Experiment 1

Researchers fed *sine waves* (oscillating voltage) into an electrical circuit containing the three filters depicted in the figure. The input amplitude was fixed at 2.0 volts. The amplitude of the resulting waves was measured, and the frequency response curves in the following figure were obtained.

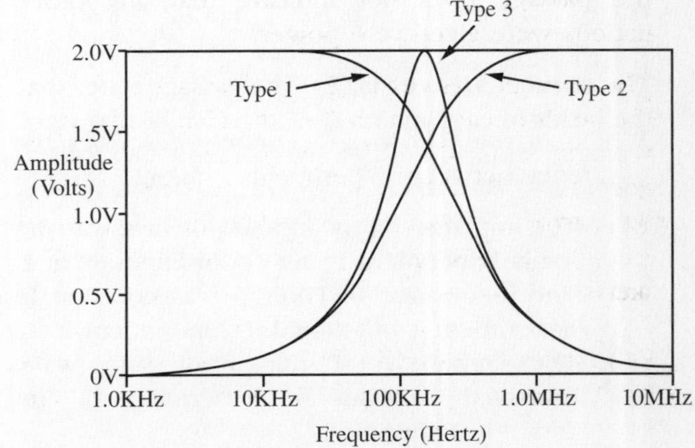

K=1000

M=1 Million

Experiment 2

A sine wave with an amplitude fixed at 2.0 volts was fed into a circuit with a Type 3 filter, but in this experiment the researchers used four different values for the inductance (L). The resulting frequency response curves are shown in the following figure.

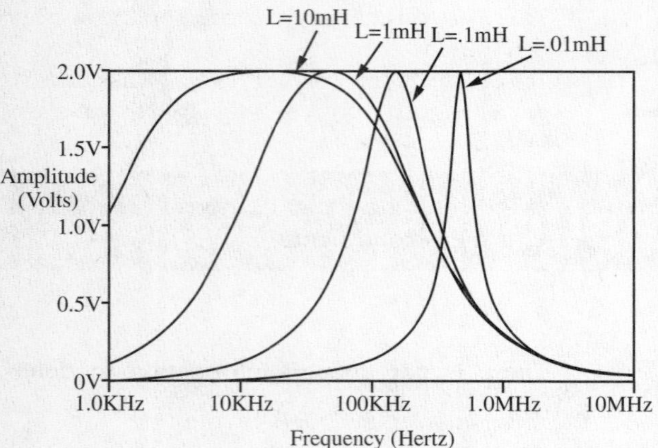

Experiment 3

Again, the researchers fed a sine wave with an amplitude fixed at 2.0 volts into a circuit with a Type 3 filter. The inductance was held at 0.1 MHz, while four different values of capacitance C were used. The resulting frequency response curves are shown in the following figure.

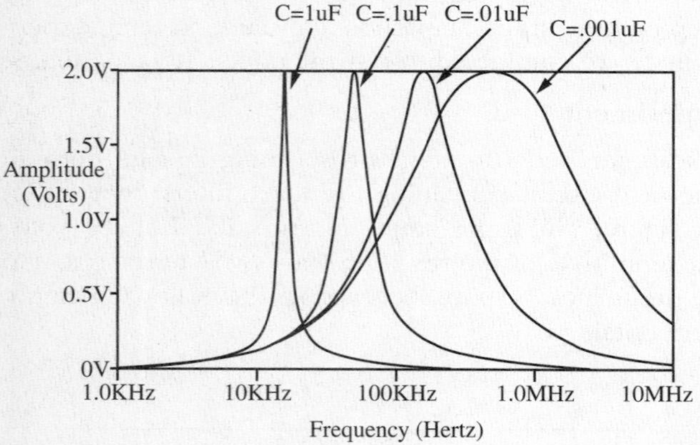

1. Which of the following accurately describes the difference between Experiments 1 and 2?

   (A) The frequency of the input sign wave was varied in Experiment 1, but not in Experiment 2.
   (B) The inductance of Filter 3 was constant in Experiment 1 but varied in Experiment 2.
   (C) The amplitude of the input sign wave remained constant in Experiment 1 but varied in Experiment 2.
   (D) The amplitude of the output sign wave remained constant in Experiment 1 but varied in Experiment 2.

2. When capacitance is increased for Filter 3, which of the following effect occurs?

   (F) The output amplitude is increased.
   (G) The range of frequencies that the filter does not suppress increases.
   (H) A smaller range of frequencies is accepted.
   (J) The accepted frequencies are in a higher range.

3. In Experiment 2, the capacitance was most likely set at

   (A) 1μF
   (B) 0.1μF
   (C) 0.01μF
   (D) 0.001μF

4. The frequency response curves suggest possible applications for the three filters. Which of the following applications would be most logical?

   (F) Filter Type 1 used by a radio receiver to screen out radio signals, which are at a lower frequency than that of the desired station.
   (G) Filter Type 2 used in an audio circuit to eliminate high-frequency audio hum.
   (H) Filter Type 2 used in a radio receiver to tune in a particular radio station at a fixed frequency.
   (J) Filter Type 3 used in a radio receiver to tune in a particular radio station at a fixed frequency.

5. It is often very important to design filters with *high Q* (a very narrow peak in the frequency response curve). An engineer discovers that the *tuned frequency* (the frequency at which the frequency response curve peaks) of a circuit with a Type 3 filter is too low. Which of the following should he do in order to raise the tuned frequency and keep a high Q filter circuit?

   (A) Lower the capacitance
   (B) Lower the inductance
   (C) Raise the capacitance and the inductance
   (D) Raise the resistance

Passage II

Individuals usually have two copies of each gene (the basic unit of genetic material, found on the *chromosomes*), one from their mother and one from their father. Genetic or inherited diseases are those that can be passed down to the next generation through the genes. These diseases follow a number of patterns. Two of the basic ones are *dominant* and *recessive* inheritance.

In a genetic disease with a recessive inheritance pattern, an individual will not be affected by the disease unless he or she is passed two copies of the disease gene, one from each parent. An individual who is passed one copy of the disease gene is called a *healthy carrier*. He or she will not have the disease, but can still pass the gene on to an offspring. The first of the following figures shows a family with this type of genetic disease.

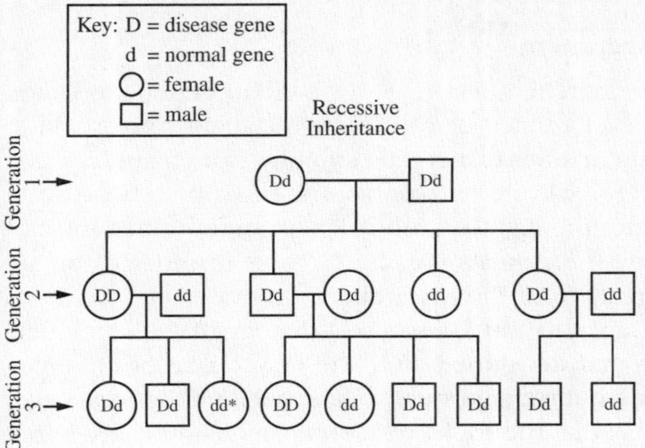

In a disease with a dominant inheritance pattern, any individual with a copy of the disease gene will have the disease. (Depending on the disease, individuals with two copies may have an accelerated or more severe disease course, or may be unable to survive). There is no such thing as a healthy carrier with this type of disease. The second figure shows a family with this type of genetic disease.

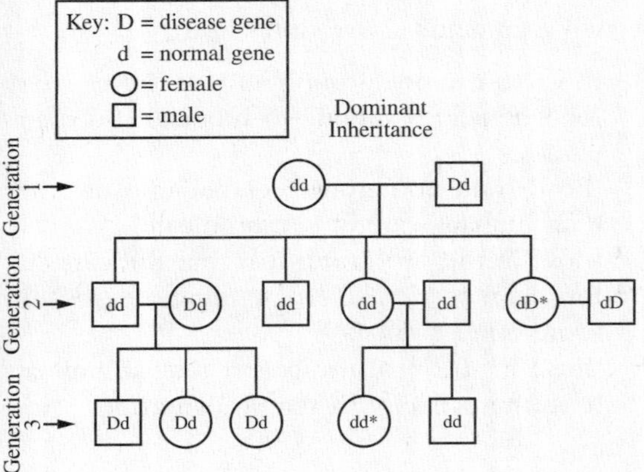

6. Which of the following statements about the first figure is true?
   (F) The mother in the first generation had to have at least one parent with the disease.
   (G) The father in the first generation had to have at least one parent who had one or more of the disease genes.
   (H) The children of the healthy carriers in the family could end up with the disease even if the other parent is not a carrier.
   (J) The daughter marked with an asterisk in the third generation could pass the disease on to her children.

7. Which of the following statements about the family in the second figure is true?
   (A) Either the mother or father of the first generation father must have had the disease.
   (B) Either the mother or father of the first generation mother must have been a carrier of the disease gene.
   (C) There are three healthy carriers in the second generation.
   (D) The couple marked with an asterisk in the second generation will be unable to have any healthy children.

8. What is the correct number of individuals with the disease in the second figure?
   (F) 5
   (G) 6
   (H) 7
   (J) There is not enough information to determine this.

9. If the generation 3 daughter marked with an asterisk in the family in the second figure was planning on having children, which of the following would be accurate advice for her regarding genetic testing?
   (A) She should be tested to rule out the possibility that one or more of her children would be carriers of the disease gene, but she could be sure that none of them would develop the disease.
   (B) Both she and her husband need to be tested to rule out the possibility that they are healthy carriers of the disease gene.
   (C) Testing is unnecessary for the daughter; she is not carrying the disease gene.
   (D) Testing one of the parents is sufficient to rule out the disease in the children.

10. The family in the following figure has a genetic disease that follows either the dominant or recessive pattern. Which of the following statements concerning this family is true?

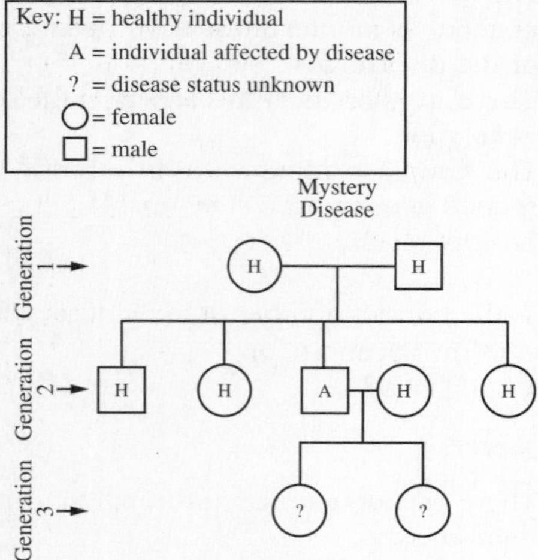

(F) Either the father or the mother in the first generation is not carrying the disease gene.
(G) The family is definitely not suffering from a dominantly inherited genetic disorder.
(H) The healthy son in the second generation would have no reason to undergo genetic testing before having children.
(J) We can be sure that both of the affected son's daughters will have the disease.

Passage III

Scientists disagree over whether language is unique to humans. Part of the argument is what constitutes language as opposed to simple communication skills, which many animals are known to possess. However, most would agree that language is a system of words or symbols used in organized combinations and patterns to express thoughts and feelings.

In recent studies, Bonobo chimps have been taught to use a keyboard with symbols representing various words. The argument now is over whether the feats of these chimpanzees represent language.

Pro Argument

Researchers working with the chimpanzees argue that there is not an unbridgeable language divide between humans and the rest of the animals, but rather a gradation of linguistic skills in humans and some other animals. They point out that their chimpanzees have vocabularies of up to 200 words, and that some have learned to understand and respond to complex sentences. 70 percent of the time the animals can follow a command that they have not heard before, as long as they are familiar with the words being used.

Some chimpanzees have learned to string together two to three words, including noun and verb combinations. While the ability of the chimpanzees to string words together in complex ways does not compare to the same ability in human children, researchers argue that comprehension, the area in which the chimpanzees have performed more impressively, is more difficult.

Con Argument

Some researchers feel that the Bonobo chimpanzees are simply well-trained or *conditioned* (taught to respond in a certain manner to a certain stimulus, for example, a dog taught to salivate at the sound of a bell because it associates the bell with food). They point out that most of the time the animals use the symbols in order to obtain food treats from the researchers.

Generally, opponents feel that language is uniquely human and developed after the family tree of chimpanzees and human ancestors split, several million years ago. They feel that the ability to acquire language is hard-wired into human brains. As proof, they point out the ease with which humans learn this task. Children move rapidly from two-word phrases to complex sentences with phrases embedded within phrases. Furthermore, there is evidence for universal rules of grammar that unite all human languages. Finally, they argue that the real test of language is not in understanding strings of symbols, but in using such strings in complex ways.

11. The two arguments above differ in that

(A) those in the pro group feel that the capacity for language is unique to humans and chimpanzees.
(B) those in the con group feel that animals other than humans cannot communicate.

(C) those in the pro group feel that the capacity for language exists in varying degrees in some other animals.
(D) those in the pro group feel that all animals have the capacity to acquire language.

12. In early studies of chimpanzee language, claims were made that a type of chimp known as the common chimpanzee was taught to communicate with sign language. These studies were discredited when it was shown that the animals were simply moving their hands in complicated configurations to please their trainers, and the trainers were wishfully seeing words. How would proponents of the present studies defend themselves against similar attacks?

(F) By pointing out that the keyboard symbol system eliminates the ambiguity of hand signals
(G) By pointing out that different chimps were used in their experiments
(H) By pointing out the controversy over whether sign language is a true language or not
(J) None of the above

13. Most opponents of the chimpanzee language studies would agree that

(A) the ability to acquire language developed in humans in the last few thousand years.
(B) the ability to acquire language developed in human ancestors in the last few million years.
(C) the ability to acquire language developed in human ancestors at least 5 million years ago.
(D) human ancestors split from chimpanzees earlier than is currently estimated.

14. In one experiment, a Bonobo chimp had access to a key that could be used to obtain a banana. Another chimp was shown where the key was hidden. This second chimp then used a keyboard to successfully communicate the whereabouts of the key to the first chimp. What objection might researchers in the con group raise against this experiment?

(F) The chimp retrieving the key was acting in a conditioned manner.
(G) The chimp retrieving the key was simply following a command, which is not as difficult as generating language.
(H) The chimp that knew where the key was hidden had simply been trained to use the keyboard to indicate its whereabouts in order to obtain a food reward.
(J) The first chimp may have been hitting the keyboard in a random manner in order to please its trainers.

15. Scientists in both the pro and the con group would agree that the Bonobo chimps described in the passage

(A) are unable to produce complex combinations of symbols.
(B) understand the meaning of a long sentence.
(C) represent a middle point between animals and humans in linguistic ability.
(D) are behaving in ways conditioned by food rewards.

Passage IV

Environmental levels of the organic volatile chemical benzene are of concern to public health officials because studies have shown that continual exposure to high concentrations of this compound can cause leukemia. Organic volatile chemicals are carbon-containing compounds that are easily vaporized and therefore present in the air. Experiments to test for the presence of such chemicals were devised.

Experiment 1

Researchers outfitted individuals in urban, suburban, and rural areas with monitoring instruments that they could wear throughout the day. These instruments recorded the concentrations of benzene they were exposed to as they went about their normal activities. Other monitoring devices were used to record the benzene output of various known sources in the participants' environment. Both the average percentage of total benzene that participants were exposed to from various sources and the average percentage of total output from these sources are given in Table 1.

Table 1

Sources	% of Total Benzene Emissions	% of Total Benzene Exposure
Automobiles	80%	20%
Industry	15%	4%
Household sources (e.g., stored paints and gasoline)	4.5%	35%
Cigarettes	0.5%	41%

Experiment 2

The researchers decided to look at whether other volatile organic compounds were found in greater concentrations indoors or outdoors. Residents from two areas wore monitoring devices that recorded the levels of a number of volatile organic compounds they were exposed to during outdoor and indoor activities for several days. The first area was a highly industrial New Jersey city and the other was a rural township in Maine. The average exposure levels of residents in these areas are listed in Table 2.

Table 2

Volatile Chemical	NJ Industrial (μg/m^3)		Maine Rural Township (μg/m^3)	
	Indoor	Outdoor	Indoor	Outdoor
Trichloroethane	21	4	14	3
Tetrachloroethylene	9	3	8	1
Chloroform	5	0.2	2	0.1
O-oxylene	5	3	3	2
Styrene	5	0.5	1	0.2

Experiment 3

Fine particles in the air, particularly breathable particles (those that are 10 microns or smaller and are able to penetrate into the lungs), are another environmental concern. Large population studies have suggested that elevated outdoor concentrations of fine particles are associated with premature death. Most fine particles form through processes of combustion, such as cooking, burning candles, smoking, or burning firewood.

Table 3

	Day			Night		
	Personal Exposure μg/m^3	Indoor Levels μg/m^3	Outdoor Levels μg/m^3	Personal Exposure μg/m^3	Indoor Exposure μg/m^3	Outdoor Exposure μg/m^3
NJ Industrial City	152	98	100	75	65	95
Maine Rural Township	149	95	93	73	72	90

Researchers wanted to see what the total levels of such particles were indoors and outdoors and how these levels compared with an individual's exposure levels. Monitors that recorded levels of breathable particles were put inside and outside the homes of one individual from both of the communities in Experiment 2. These individuals were also asked to wear monitoring devices for one day and one night. The results from this experiment are shown in Table 3 above.

16. One of the differences between Experiment 1 and Experiment 2 is that

(F) Experiment 1 did not investigate a volatile compound.
(G) Experiment 2 showed that people are exposed to higher levels of volatile organic compounds indoors, a finding that was contradicted by Experiment 1.
(H) Experiment 1 looked at compound emission levels, while Experiment 2 looked only at compound exposure levels.
(J) Experiment 2 looked at the average compound exposure levels from a pool of data, while Experiment 1 looked at individuals' compound exposure levels.

17. Which of the following hypotheses would best explain the results seen in Experiment 3?

(A) Moving about stirs up a personal cloud of breathable particles.
(B) Industrial sites tend to perform most combustion activities in the night hours, thus raising particle levels at night.
(C) Particles formed during cooking and smoking tend to remain suspended for at least 24 hours, so that daytime levels generally do not drop off at night.
(D) Exposure to breathable particles is largely attributable to automobile exhaust.

18. If the researchers conducting Experiment 3 added another study subject and found that he had a daytime indoor exposure level of 75 micrograms/meter^3, which of the following would be the most likely daytime personal exposure level for this individual?

(F) 65 micrograms/meter^3
(G) 75 micrograms/meter^3
(H) 85 micrograms/meter^3

(J) 125 micrograms/meter^3

19. Researchers hypothesized that volatile organic compounds follow the same pattern of personal exposure versus indoor exposure levels as that seen with breathable particles in Experiment 3. If this hypothesis is correct, which of the following is probably closest to the actual indoor level of trichloroethane in the rural Maine township?

(A) 1 micrograms/meter^3
(B) 9 micrograms/meter^3
(C) 15 micrograms/meter^3
(D) 19 micrograms/meter^3

20. To prove the hypothesis in question 19, researchers would need to do which of the following?

(F) Conduct Experiment 2 again, but ask the subjects to wear monitoring devices only during the day.
(G) Conduct Experiment 3 again, this time asking all of the subjects from Experiment 2 to participate.
(H) Conduct Experiment 2 again, but this time place monitors in the indoor settings in addition to those worn by individuals.
(J) Conduct Experiment 2 again, but break down the individual exposure levels into those encountered during the day and during the night.

Passage V

Recently, flywheels with magnetic bearings have been designed (see figure below). These flywheels produce none of the friction associated with mechanical bearings, making them efficient energy storage devices. One application they may have is in alternative energy cars. In experimental designs, a flywheel is "spun-up" while the car is at rest with the electrical power supplied from a standard electrical outlet. After the flywheel has reached a high rate of rotation, the car can be disconnected from the socket, and the energy can be extracted from the high-speed rotating flywheel.

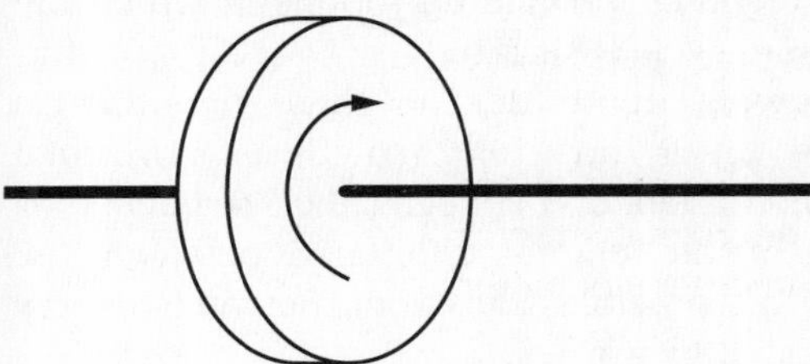

Experiment 1

Researchers looked at flywheels with different radii to gauge the effect of size on the total energy they could store. The wheels were all started at an initial frequency of 50 revolutions per second (rev/sec). All of the flywheels were *disk-type* (they had a uniform thickness along their entire radius), all were made of the same material, and all had the same thickness. After reaching the initial speed, a uniform resisting force was applied to determine how much energy it took to stop the wheel. The results of this experiment appear in Table 4.

Table 4

Radius (cm)	Energy Stored (joules)
10	100
20	1600
30	8100
40	25600

Experiment 2

Next, a disk-type flywheel with a radius of 30 cm was brought up to various initial speeds by an electric motor. The energy stored at each speed was measured. Results appear in Table 5.

Table 5

Frequency (rev/sec)	Energy Stored
40	5184
60	11664
80	20736
100	32400

Experiment 3

One of the limiting factors in the use of flywheels is the *centrifugal force* (the force pulling outward from the rim) that is generated as the wheel is turning. When this force becomes too great, it causes the wheel to fly apart or explode. The centrifugal force is determined by the frequency and the radius of the wheel. A doubling of the radius results in a doubling of the centrifugal force; a doubling of the frequency results in a quadrupling of the centrifugal force.

Researchers tested four wheel designs (see figure below). All of the wheels had a radius of 30 cm and the same mass; wheel thickness was changed to keep the mass constant. The frequency of each wheel was increased slowly until it exploded. The frequency at which this occurred, as well as the energy stored in the wheel at the time, was recorded. Results appear in Table 6.

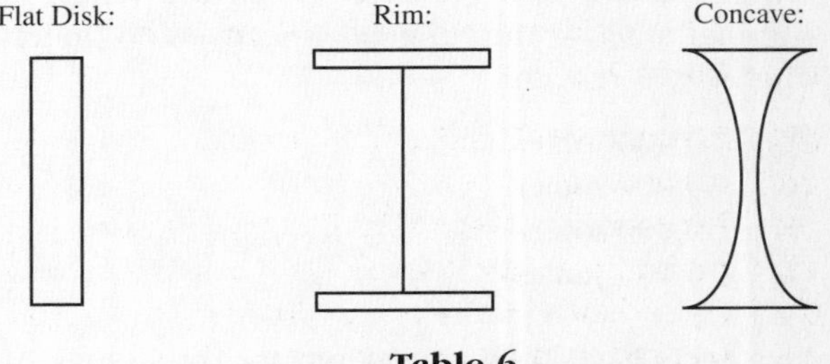

Table 6

Flywheel Type	Energy Stored (Joules)	Strength (Maximum Frequency) (rev/sec)
Flat Disk	17266	73
Rimmed	16231	42
Concave Disk	19627	72

21. Assuming that the researchers considered energy storage and wheel strength to be of equal importance, which of the wheel designs in Experiment 3 would they conclude was optimal?

    (A) Flat disk
    (B) Rimmed wheel
    (C) Concave disk
    (D) The best design would depend on the wheel radius.

22. The experimental data indicate that for optimal energy storage, the flywheel should be a

    (F) concave wheel with a large radius.
    (G) rimmed wheel a small radius.
    (H) flat disk wheel with a large radius.
    (J) concave wheel with a small radius.

23. Which of the following statements about the centrifugal force on a flywheel is best supported by the data presented?

(A) A graph of the force versus wheel radius would look similar to a graph of frequency versus energy stored.
(B) A graph of the force versus wheel radius would look similar to a graph of energy stored versus wheel strength.
(C) A graph of the force versus frequency would look similar to a graph of frequency versus energy stored.
(D) A graph of the force versus frequency would look similar to a graph of energy stored versus wheel strength.

24. A car has a disk-type flywheel with a radius of 30 cm. The disk is initially storing 120,000 joules while rotating at 64 rev/sec. When the wheel is turning at half the original speed, how much energy will remain?

(F) 10,000 joules
(G) 30,000 joules
(H) 50,000 joules
(J) 70,000 joules

25. Flywheels have been considered for the storage of energy that is collected using solar panels during the day. This stored energy could be used as a city power source at night. Such a flywheel would need to handle vast amounts of energy, perhaps 5 million Megajoules. In consideration of these energy storage needs and safety, which of the following would be the best design for such a system?

I. One very large flywheel that would turn at a relatively slow frequency
II. Collections of small flywheels each turning at high frequencies
III. One large flywheel that would transfer its energy to many smaller flywheels as it slowed down

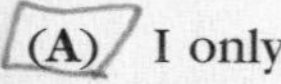

(A) I only
(B) II only
(C) III only
(D) I or III only

Passage VI

Interstellar objects (objects among the stars) in outer galaxies are often investigated using a method known as spectroscopy. *Spectroscopy* is a method of determining the atomic or molecular makeup of something by observing the object's *spectral lines*. Atoms and molecules have fixed energy levels. When an electron in an atom moves from one of its possible energy states to another, the atom releases light. This light has energy equal to the difference in the two energy levels through which the electron moved. These energy transitions are observed as a sequence of spectral lines. Spectral lines that are close together indicate transitions in which the change in energy levels is similar.

The following figure depicts three hypothetical atoms. Energy levels are represented as horizontal segments. The distance between the segments is representative of the energy difference between the various levels. All possible transitions between energy levels are indicated by arrows.

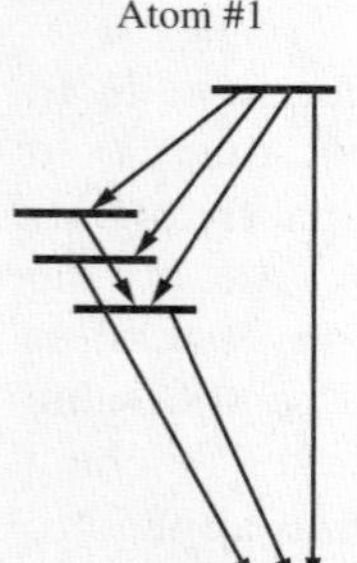

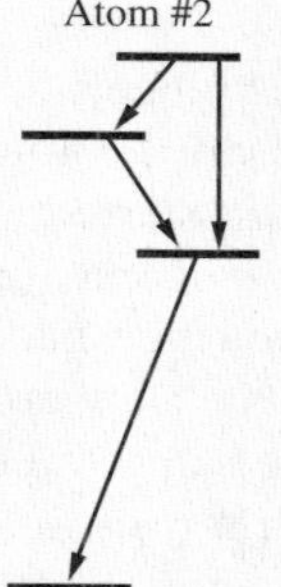

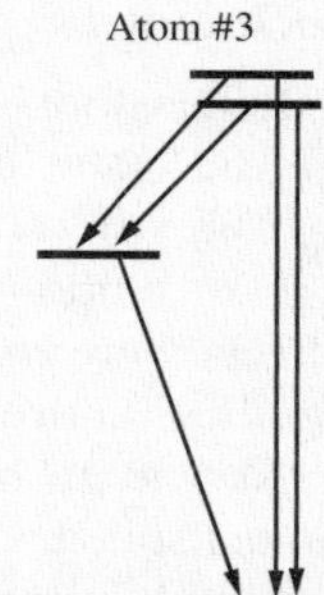

Scientists can observe the spectral lines of atoms that are dominant in far-away galaxies. Due to the speed at which these galaxies are traveling, these lines are shifted, but their pattern remains the same. This allows researchers to use the spectral pattern to determine which atoms they are seeing. Table 7 shows spectroscopic measurements made by researchers trying to determine the atomic makeup of a particular far-away galaxy. Light energy is not measured directly, but rather is determined from measuring the frequency of light, which is proportional to the energy.

Table 7

Frequencies Measured
2096400
2092790
2021140
1940200
1946260

26. Which of the following statements is most likely to be incorrect, based on the information in the figure?

(F) Atom 1 would emit six spectral lines.
(G) Atom 2 would emit four spectral lines.
(H) Atom 3 would emit five spectral lines.
(J) The number of spectral lines emitted by an atom does not necessarily match the number of energy levels.

27. Physicists using spectroscopy to investigate the atoms depicted in the figure would observe which of the following?

(A) Atom 2 would have three spectral lines that are very close together.
(B) Atom 3 would have two spectral lines that are very close together and three more spectral lines that are relatively far from each other.
(C) Atom 3 would have three spectral lines that are very close together.
(D) Atom 1 would have three spectral lines that are close together, as well as another pair of spectral lines that are very close together.

28. The researchers making the measurements for Table 7 might reach which of the following conclusions?

I. The atoms appear to have five energy levels, indicating that they could be the same as atom 1.
II. The atoms appear to be emitting two sets of two closely spaced frequencies, indicating that they could be the same as atom 3.
III. The observed atoms do not appear to be going through any transitions in energy levels.

(F) I only
(G) II only
(H) III only
(J) II and III only

29. Atoms have "forbidden" transitions. These are transitions between energy levels that are not allowed by the laws of conservation in atomic physics. Which of the following statements concerning the atoms in the figure are true?

(A) Atom 1 has no forbidden transitions.
(B) Atom 2 has no forbidden transition.
(C) Atom 3 has no forbidden transitions.
(D) Atom 3 has more than one forbidden transition.

30. The difference in the information represented in the figure and in Table 7 is that

(F) the figure was arrived at with spectroscopic measurements, while the information in Table 7 was arrived at using only a mathematical formula.
(G) the figure indicates the pattern of frequencies emitted by an atom, while Table 7 indicates the exact frequencies emitted by an atom.
(H) the figure indicates the number of energy levels that an atom has, while in Table 7 this number can be determined only by identifying the atom being observed.
(J) the figure gives an idea of the proximity of spectral lines associated with the atoms, while Table 7 indicates only the energy levels associated with the atoms observed.

ANSWERS AND EXPLANATIONS

Passage I

1. **The correct answer is (B).** In both experiments, the input amplitude was fixed at 2.0 volts, and the frequency was varied (along the horizontal scale of each graph). However, the inductance was varied in Experiment 2 only.

2. **The correct answer is (H).** Look at the figure. As you go from right to left in the graph, the capacitance figures increase. And as you do so, the graphed lines form "steeper," "sharper," more "pointy" curves. This indicates that a narrower range of frequencies is permitted through by the filter.

3. **The correct answer is (C).** To answer this question, you need to compare Experiments 2 and 3, along with the graphs showing the results. You're told that the inductance in Experiment 3 was held at 0.1 MHz. This corresponds to the third line from the left in the figure. Since that line most closely resembles the third line from the left in the figure—and since you're told that, for that line, the capacitance was set at 0.01μF—it makes sense to assume that the same capacitance must have been used to produce the matching line in Experiment 2.

4. **The correct answer is (J).** Look at the figure. Since filter Type 3 "zeroes in" on waves of a very specific frequency, allowing only those waves to pass through, it makes sense that one might use this type of filter to tune in the fixed frequency of a particular radio station (while eliminating all other competing signals).

5. **The correct answer is (B).** As you can see from the figure, the lower the inductance, the higher the frequency at which the response curve attains its peak.

Passage II

6. **The correct answer is (G).** Since the father (the square) in generation 1 has one disease gene D, he must have had a parent from whom he inherited that gene.

7. **The correct answer is (A).** As with the father in generation 1 in the figure, you see that the disease gene D is present in the father of this family. And since this is a dominant trait, whichever parent of that individual transmitted the disease gene to him must also have suffered from the disease.

8. **The correct answer is (H).** Anyone in the figure with even a single disease gene D will suffer from the disease. There are seven such individuals in the chart: one in generation 1, three in generation 2, and three more in generation 3.

9. **The correct answer is (C).** Since the individual in question has genes labeled dd, she has two normal genes and does not need to worry about the possibility of transmitting a disease gene to her children.

10. **The correct answer is (G).** The disease cannot be a dominant trait. You can tell this because the male in generation 2 who is affected by the disease (center of chart) has two healthy parents. If he had inherited a dominant disease trait from one of his parents, one or both of them would be affected by the disease as well.

Passage III

11. **The correct answer is (C).** The first sentence of the pro argument section of the passage summarizes this point neatly.

12. **The correct answer is (F).** As described in the question, the problem with the older studies was that the chimpanzees' trainers were interpreting hard-to-read hand movements as words out of a desire to believe that the animals were in fact using language. The best response to a similar charge against the current studies would be (F), since it would be difficult or impossible to misinterpret keyboarded messages.

13. **The correct answer is (B).** This can be inferred from the first sentence of the second paragraph of the con argument.

14. **The correct answer is (H).** The first paragraph of the con argument makes the point that animals conditioned through food rewards to use particular symbols are not really engaging in true language behavior. Choice (H) applies this argument to the example given in the question.

15. **The correct answer is (A).** Those who make the pro argument claim only that the chimps can use two- or three-word combinations; neither they nor their opponents say that chimps have learned to create complex strings of symbols.

Passage IV

16. **The correct answer is (H).** In Experiment 1, emission levels were compared to exposure levels; by contrast, in Experiment 2, only exposure levels were studied, while emission levels were ignored.

17. **The correct answer is (A).** The real anomaly in Table 3 is the high daytime "personal exposure" levels, which far exceed all the other numbers in the chart (which are all roughly comparable to one another, whether daytime or nighttime levels are considered). Of the four answer choices, (A) does the most to explain this result: If "moving about" stirs up a cloud of particles, it would explain why people have high personal exposure levels during the day. (Exposure levels subside at night when people don't move around as much as during the day.)

18. **The correct answer is (J).** Consider the second column of values in Table 3. The indoor exposure levels for the two experimental subjects shown there are quite close—98 and 95. If the third subject has an indoor exposure level of 75, that would be about 20% lower than either of the first two subjects. Now, if the personal exposure level varies by a similar amount, you'd expect the third subject to have a personal exposure level about 20% below 150—somewhere in the neighborhood of 120. Hence, (J) is the correct answer.

19. **The correct answer is (B).** You see in Table 3 that the actual indoor levels of breathable particles are about the personal exposure levels as recorded by monitoring devices. If the same relationship holds true for trichloroethane, then the level of 14 would be reduced by the same amount to about 9.

20. **The correct answer is (H).** Experiment 2 measured only personal exposure levels, while Experiment 3 monitored the indoor and outdoor environments as well. To test whether the results of Experiment 3 would be duplicated with the compounds tested in Experiment 2, indoor environmental monitors would have to be added to the experiment.

Passage V

21. **The correct answer is (C).** The concave disk design provides the best overall results in Experiment 3. As Table 6 shows, that design stores considerably more energy than either of the two alternatives, while its strength is almost equal to that of the flat disk, which is the strongest. If both criteria are equally important, then the concave disk design is the best.

22. **The correct answer is (F).** As the answer to question 21 indicates, the concave design is preferable to either the rimmed or flat disk. Experiment 1 shows that a flywheel with a larger radius is capable of storing more energy than a flywheel with a smaller radius. Thus, for optimal energy storage, a concave, large-radius wheel is best.

23. **The correct answer is (C).** As frequency increases, centrifugal force increases even more quickly; the same relationship exists between frequency and energy stored.

24. **The correct answer is (G).** Look at Table 5; by comparing the first and third lines of that table, you can see that when the speed of the flywheel is halved (from 80 to 40 revolutions per second), the amount of energy stored is quartered (from about 20,000 to about 5,000 joules). Applying this same relationship to the example in the question, you can estimate that the energy in the car flywheel will be quartered from 120,000 joules to about 30,000 joules.

25. **The correct answer is (A).** Since safety is mentioned in the question as a primary consideration, it seems logical to choose a system that uses size rather than frequency as the primary factor for storing a large amount of energy. As Experiment 3 shows, the flywheel's frequency has a far more powerful effect on centrifugal force than does the flywheel's radius.

Passage VI

26. **The correct answer is (F).** As explained in the passage, the spectral lines are emitted when an atom moves from one energy level to another. Thus, the number of spectral lines observed would correspond to the number of arrows seen in the figure (since each arrow represents an energy-level transition). Understanding this allows you to determine that (F) is *incorrect*; there are seven energy transitions possible for atom 1, so seven spectral lines would be observed, not six.

27. **The correct answer is (D).** The passage says that the amount of space between spectral lines indicates the relative size of the change in energy levels. If two energy transitions are quite similar in size, then the spectral lines will be close; if the transitions are very different in size, the spectral lines will be far apart. Based on this, you can see that statement (D) is correct: The three transitions shown on the upper left-hand side of the diagram would be represented by three spectral lines that are close together, while the two transitions shown on the lower left-hand side would produce two more spectral lines that are close together.

28. The correct answer is (G). In Table 7, the first and last two frequencies measured are very close. These would correspond to spectral lines that are close to one another and would reflect two pairs of similar energy transitions—the situation found in atom 3.

29. The correct answer is (B). A "forbidden" transition, as defined in the question, would be represented visually by a pair of horizontal lines not connected by an arrow. As you can see, atoms 1 and 3 both have one or more pairs of horizontal lines that are not connected by arrows, making choices (A) and (C) incorrect. Atom 3 has just one forbidden transition (between the two horizontal lines at the top), making choice (D) wrong. Choice (B) is correct because atom 2 has one forbidden transition, between the highest and lowest energy levels, represented by the horizontal lines at the top and bottom of the diagram.

30. The correct answer is (F). As the explanation for Table 7 says, the information in that table does not reflect direct measurement of energy but rather "the frequency of light, which is proportional to the energy." Thus, whereas the figure is generated directly by spectroscopy, Table 7 contains information analogous to, but not the same as, information derived from spectroscopy.